2/3/04

ALSO BY ALONZO L. HAMBY

Man of the People:
A Life of Harry S. Truman

Liberalism and Its Challengers

The Imperial Years:
The United States Since 1939

Beyond the New Deal:
Harry S. Truman and American Liberalism

FREE PRESS

New York   London   Toronto   Sydney

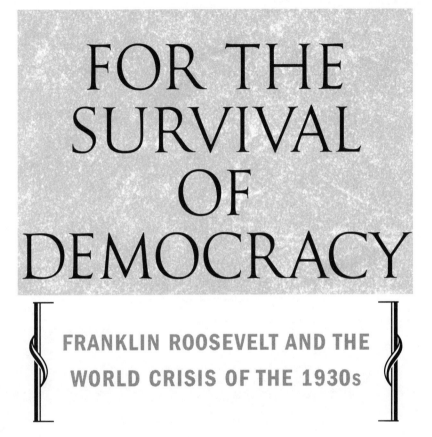

FOR THE SURVIVAL OF DEMOCRACY

FRANKLIN ROOSEVELT AND THE
WORLD CRISIS OF THE 1930s

Alonzo L. Hamby

*f*P

FREE PRESS
A Division of Simon & Schuster, Inc.
1230 Avenue of the Americas
New York, NY 10020

For information about special discounts for bulk purchases,
please contact Simon & Schuster Special Sales:
1-800-456-6798 or business@simonandschuster.com

Designed by Jeanette Olender

Manufactured in the United States of America

1   3   5   7   9   10   8   6   4   2

Library of Congress Cataloging-in-Publication Data
Hamby, Alonzo L.
For the survival of democracy: Franklin Roosevelt and the world crisis
of the 1930s / Alonzo L. Hamby.
p. cm.
Includes bibliographical references and index.
1. United States—Politics and government—1933–1945. 2. Depressions—1929—United States.
3. Roosevelt, Franklin D. (Franklin Delano), 1882–1945. 4. New Deal, 1933–1939.
5. Depressions—1929—Great Britain. 6. Depressions—1929—Germany. 7. Great Britain—
Economic conditions—1918–1945. 8. Germany—Economic conditions—1918–1945.
9. World politics—1919–1932. 10. World politics—1933–1945. I. Title.
E806.H293   2004   909.82'3—dc22   2003061807
ISBN 0-684-84340-4

To the future:

David Marion Hamby

and

Bruce and Susie Hamby,

who brought him into the world

CONTENTS

PREFACE *xi*

ACKNOWLEDGMENTS *xv*

PROLOGUE: March 1933 *2*

1. World Crisis   **6**

2. Plumbing the Depths   **42**
  Britain and Germany, Fall 1931–Winter 1933

3. Power Shift   **76**
  The United States, Fall 1931–March 1933

4. The New Deal   **114**
  The First 125 Days

5. Recovery in One Country?   **138**
  The New Deal, July 1933–May 1935

6. Triumph   **176**
  Nazi Germany, 1933–1936

7. Muddling Toward Recovery   **216**
  Britain, June 1933–June 1937

8. Challenges   **256**
  The Origins of the Second New Deal, January–May 1935

9. High Tide   **292**
  Second Hundred Days, Second New Deal, Second Term,
    June 1935–November 1936

10. Stalling Out   **326**
  The United States, 1937–1939

11. Irrepressible Conflict, 1937–1939   **370**

EPILOGUE:
Where Does the Future Lie: Flushing Meadows or Warsaw? *414*

HISTORIOGRAPHICAL NOTE *431*

NOTES *439*

INDEX *475*

PREFACE

I am barely old enough to have a dim memory of that April day in 1945 when Franklin Roosevelt died, but I grew up in the forties and fifties understanding that he had been the central political figure of a difficult time. My parents and numerous acquaintances regarded him with an awe usually reserved for deities and were convinced that he had saved the country during the Great Depression. Other people we knew hated him and were convinced he had put the United States on the road to ruin. Of course, today we can look back with confidence that America would have endured in some way without him, admire his rhetorical leadership, criticize his mistakes, and debate his policies—all with a detachment that would have been rare fifty years ago. The intense emotions Roosevelt aroused were nonetheless real in his time and testified to his impact on a nation that had never seen a president like him.

The Great Depression—capitalized throughout this book, as it would be if it had been a war—was the defining event of the twentieth century. It undermined a shaky post–World War I settlement, plunged the developed nations into varying degrees of hardship and misery, and set the stage for World War II, which in turn produced the Cold War order that lasted until just nine years before the beginning of a new century. No doubt without the Depression the world would have evolved in other ways that we cannot imagine, but it is hard to believe these would have been more malign. The Depression dealt a severe blow to democratic capitalism everywhere and relegated a traditional liberal faith in free markets to the ash heap of history. Demanding state solutions to economic catastrophe and stoking nationalistic emotions, it strengthened varieties of totalitarianism that threatened to make liberal democracy an endangered species.

I began this book perhaps a bit too jaded by the skeptical attitude that every professional historian needs to acquire. Most of the writing on Roosevelt and his New Deal has been largely celebratory, with criticism reserved for details. Work that has attempted a more frontal attack, whether from the ideological left or right, has had little impact. My own preoccupation stemmed from the fact that six years after taking office Roosevelt presided over a country still deeply mired in economic distress and that he did so while the two leading totalitarian nations, Nazi Germany and the Soviet Union, seemed to be forging ahead of the democracies. What, I wondered, would the world have been like if the United States had done as well?

This central question and others that developed along with it persuaded me that the time was right to take another look at FDR and the New Deal, but that I needed to do so in a larger international context, one that would provide necessary perspective but would not be so broad as to be utterly lacking in depth. And while statistics are necessary to measure the impact of a depression, they are no substitute for some description of the way in which it hits ordinary people, changes their political arrangements, and transforms their societies. I decided on a study that would be mostly a narrative of the American experience but also would provide a reasonably full account of events in Great Britain and Germany, the world's second and third largest economies.

An enterprise of this breadth is necessarily dependent on the work of many other scholars, whose work I have acknowledged in the endnotes and the historiographical note at the conclusion of this book. In order to avoid becoming the prisoner of other writers with widely varying agendas, I also consulted a broad range of contemporary printed sources, which helped me get a feel for the way in which participants defined the great issues of the times. I have attempted to convey a bit of that feel by reproducing contemporary "headlines" and "newsreels" in each chapter. The headlines, mostly from the *New York Times*, are genuine, but were frequently edited for length and sometimes slightly rephrased. The newsreels are descriptions of actual footage from "The Greatest Year" series, which utilizes the old Universal Newsreels, the classic "March of Time" series, and historical documentaries.

My initial questioning strikes me as essentially valid but a bit simple. There can be no doubt that the American failure to achieve a strong, durable economic recovery was a blow to the cause of democracy everywhere, but it is impossible to locate a genuine democracy that failed because of it, or collapsed at all for that matter. Democracy in 1939 was more endangered than it had been ten years earlier, but more from external aggression than internal collapse. Roosevelt, despite his ineffectiveness in addressing the American economy, had in fact become a potent symbol of the possibilities of democratic government. Moreover, captive as I was to images of hungry Englishmen signing up for a miserly dole, I initially did not realize that Britain recovered from the Depression about the same time as Nazi Germany, pursued a commendable array of social programs, and kept its middle class intact through hard times. That it had done so under the improbable leadership of Stanley Baldwin and Neville Chamberlain led me to revise my opinion of these statesmen, Baldwin especially.

On the other hand, I discovered just how miserable the recovery was for most Germans once one got beyond gross national product statistics. I also found that, much more than I previously had understood, Nazism was a socially revolutionary movement. Finally, Adolf Hitler and the people around him, I concluded, were formidable individuals possessing will, determination, and an imposing array of political talents—at least as much as Roosevelt and his crowd. Where FDR and the New Dealers demonstrated the strength and appeal of liberal democracy, Hitler and his Nazi followers displayed the terrible power of evil in a world that, much like our own today, preferred not to acknowledge its existence. In the final countdown to World War II, the "dynamic force" would be Hitler, not Roosevelt for all his forebodings, not Chamberlain with his liberal assumptions about human nature and international politics.

To some extent, this is a book about the way in which three distinct nations reacted to the modern world's greatest economic crisis. More specifically, it is about political leadership, especially Roosevelt's as seen against that of Hitler and Baldwin. It assumes that individuals, acting within the limitations of the world in which they live, make history. Neither the New Deal nor Nazism nor "Tory socialism" were foreordained in their societies. They reflected the efforts of strong and capable political leaders. This is also a book about the quest for a "Middle Way" in America and Britain at a time when totalitarianism seemed to many the wave of the future. It suggests that in this endeavor Baldwin and Chamberlain were as successful as Roosevelt.

Roosevelt nonetheless emerges secure in his long-recognized place as the premier American president of the twentieth century. I have tried to deal with his failures unsparingly but fairly. His achievements were large also. And even at this remove, one senses a presence larger than can be conveyed by any balance sheet tally of pluses and minuses. He ultimately cast a greater shadow over his time than any other Western leader.

Widespread misery, endangered democracy, strong leadership on the sides of both good and evil—all add up to a drama of great power. It is in that spirit that I have attempted to tell a compelling story.

A.L.H.
Athens, Ohio
May 2003

ACKNOWLEDGMENTS

Thanks first of all to Gerard McCauley for representing my ideas to the publishing profession. Bruce Nichols at Free Press believed in this project, was supportive when the going was tough, and provided the gentle pushes needed to help me bring it to completion. Casey Reivich challenged me often in an initial edit of the manuscript, frequently to good effect. I had the good fortune years ago to study with three historians who have made their own notable contributions to the study of Roosevelt and the world crisis of the thirties: John A. Garraty, Richard S. Kirkendall, and William E. Leuchtenburg. I learned a lot from them then and afterwards. It is natural enough that references to their work pop up throughout this book. The Ohio Gang kept my life interesting. Special thanks to Benita Blessing for reading my large chapter on Nazi Germany and commenting so helpfully on it.

Marc Selverstone and Jeff Woods helped me get started. Derek Catsam and then Shae Davidson provided vital assistance over the four-year period in which most of the book was written. Maybe I could have done it without them, but I am glad I didn't have to.

Thanks to Joyce for so much for so long.

I hope the first person named in the dedication will read this book sometime far in the future and be pleased to see his name in it.

Here in America we are waging a great and successful war. It is not alone a war against want and destitution and economic demoralization. It is more than that; it is a war for the survival of democracy.

Franklin D. Roosevelt, accepting renomination for
the presidency of the United States, June 27, 1936

PROLOGUE

March 1933

March 4, 1933. The thirty-second president of the United States, the latest in an unbroken line stretching from George Washington, took the oath of office amidst pomp and circumstance and crowds that braved a bleak, cold day to cheer him. Just four years earlier, his predecessor Herbert Hoover had told a far more optimistic and celebratory gathering: "We are steadily building a new race, a new civilization great in its own attainments."[1] Hoover had taken office in a time of unmatched prosperity and mass affluence, which seemed likely to continue into the indefinite future. He had delivered only hard times and mass unemployment. He had not been primarily to blame for a worldwide economic catastrophe, but he undeniably had failed to cope with it. As he left office a dour, bitter man, the nation seemed in a state of collapse. In many other countries, contenders for power might have been fighting in the streets.

Instead, the east front of the Capitol was clogged with 100,000 people listening hopefully to the inaugural address of Franklin D. Roosevelt. The new president repeated the oath of office in a strong, even voice, then turned to the lectern on the crowded inaugural platform and began to speak, not simply to the huge crowd in front of him but also to tens of millions of Americans at their radios. Many of these millions would see him a few days later in movie newsreels, speaking vigorously and decisively, hands firmly grasping the lectern, head bobbing from side to side: "This is a day of national consecration. . . . This great nation will endure as it has endured, will revive and will prosper. . . . The only thing we have to fear is fear itself."[2]

Roosevelt's first inaugural electrified a nation yearning for strong leadership and new directions. Crisis times produce charismatic leaders; the Depression either brought forth or gave new importance not just to Roosevelt, but to Adolf Hitler, Benito Mussolini, and Josef Stalin. Of these, Roosevelt was the premier figure. He led the most important country, made the greatest cross-national impact, and ultimately won international recognition as democracy's dynamic leader. The question for a majority of Americans was not *whether* he was great but to what extent his greatness might be qualified.

Any history in which Roosevelt looms large must consider him as more than just a Depression fighter. He also assumed roles as the magnetic leader of the people and tribune of democracy; the champion politician; the manager of a multifaceted policy initiative (the New Deal) without precedent in American history; and the chief diplomat entrusted with guarding American security in a menacing age. As leader of the people he was the all-time great communicator of American politics, capable of projecting his authority and personality across the air waves, onto newsreel screens, and into the print press. His personal presence eclipsed that of any challenger. As champion politician, he produced consecutive electoral victories that no previous president in an era of mass politics going back a century could match. Yet, given the American system of decentralized parties, even he was incapable of dominant party leadership. As manager of the New Deal, he faced a task akin to that of the conductor of a symphony orchestra filled with strong-willed performers who had their own ideas about the score and tempo, and could not be perfunctorily dismissed. Relief, recovery, various types of reform, countless egos—all contended for attention. The resulting performance was unsurprisingly dissonant. As chief diplomat, he maneuvered cautiously and indirectly in mostly futile attempts to redirect American attention to threats across the seas.

Ideologically, he affirmed the traditional Democratic party suspicion of big business and finance that could be traced back to Jefferson and Jackson. Temperamentally, he enjoyed the exercise of power, took criticism personally, and wanted to humble a Republican business-financial elite. He captured the imagination not only of a majority of Americans, but of many Europeans. Much more than a Depression fighter, he met the material and emotional needs of his supporters in numerous ways.

The paramount issue of the 1930s was the future of democracy, not in the United States, but in other parts of the world where it was less entrenched. In 1933, Great Britain and the members of the British Commonwealth, the Scandinavian states, much of Western Europe, and Czechoslovakia were all democracies. But no nation attached so expansive a meaning to the idea as did the United States. In some other countries—foremost among them Germany—democracy was a new and struggling institution on the verge of collapse. In most nations, it simply did not exist. The world economic crisis endangered the existence of free government everywhere it was not solidly imbedded. Even France displayed worrisome symptoms of instability; in 1933 the Third Republic was just sixty-two years old.

The Depression presented established democracies with a long-term test—not the prospect of a coup d'etat from within, but an enhanced threat from without made formidable by withering morale and declining economic strength. The danger was less dramatic than the left's nightmare of a fascist surge to power, but nonetheless real. Varieties of fascism spread like ugly cancers across the map; a vicious Stalinist communism consolidated its grip on the Soviet Union and sought to extend its influence by infiltrating the non-Communist "progressive forces" of the West. Democracy appeared to be in retreat. What the liberal democratic nations needed was a democratic front—a relatively united coalition facing and fighting the Depression, demonstrating the superiority of their form of government, and allied to contain the hostile powers arrayed against them. Roosevelt understood that the president of the United States was the natural leader of the world's democratic forces in times of crisis. He instinctively and articulately embraced the role, but never found practical means of implementing it. Instead, economic distress gave life and vitality to the totalitarians while weakening the forces of freedom and majority rule.

The international economic crisis of the thirties had international causes. Yet with a few notable exceptions[3] historians have generally written about it as if it were confined to the nation of their choice. This tendency possesses the dubious virtue of emulating the behavior of the time. Countries responded with distinctive national policies that were incapable of providing a general solution and frequently made things worse. The dominance of the nation-state in world politics, the instinctive turn of individuals to their governments for relief, a surge in nationalistic sentiment—these were all common responses that prevented any general international agreement and left the democratic powers divided. In some nations, notably Germany, nationalism led directly into authoritarian militarism. More often it simply mandated self-concern, tariff protectionism, competitive currency devaluations, and beggar-thy-neighbor policies.

Nationalism in policy reflected a misunderstanding of the Great

Depression, which was an international problem that begged for international solutions. Nationalism in historical writing perpetuates the misunderstanding. The decade of the 1930s was the pivot of the twentieth century. The world experienced the rise of totalitarianism, the destruction of the post–World War order, and the beginning of a second World War. Economically, and arguably politically, the three most important nations in the world were the United States, Great Britain, and Germany. A look at the way in which all three faced the Depression provides a deeper understanding of the thirties than is possible with any single national story. It also provides a much better background against which to gauge Roosevelt's achievement.

HEADLINES AND MOVIE NEWSREELS

{1929}

OCTOBER 30   Stocks Collapse in 16,410,000-Share Day

{1930}

JUNE 17   Hoover Signs Tariff Bill; Smoot Confident That Stocks Will Rise

JULY 16   Brüning Enforces Tax Bill by Decree as Reichstag Balks

{1931}

JUNE 1   Deficit Forces Treasury to Sell Largest Bond Issue Since War

JULY 7   Agreement on Hoover International Debt Moratorium Signed

JULY 14   Central Banks Agree to Help Reich; German Banks Close

AUGUST 29   Gov. Roosevelt Asks $20 Million for Jobs, 50% Income Tax Rise

SEPTEMBER 22   Britain Calm Under Gold Suspension

OCTOBER 1   London Unemployed Riot Over Cut in Dole; Police Rout Reds

OCTOBER 19   "Nazis" Battle Foes as Hitler Declares He Can Keep Order

OCTOBER 28   Tories Sweep Britain; Will Raise Tariff, Run National Govt

WORLD CRISIS

Charisma Deficit: National Leaders in Crisis Times

In good and placid times, well-regarded political leaders may become objects of amiable ridicule. Silent Cal Coolidge, a popular president during the mass prosperity of the 1920s, exemplified the risk when he let himself be memorably photographed in a ceremonial Indian war bonnet. In times of public crisis and private desperation, the people demand leaders who display forcefulness, optimism, the capacity to act, and above all the ability to inspire. After 1929, as the Western world sank into the quicksand of depression, its three major nations faced a charisma deficit that tested the durability of their political institutions.

President Hoover

Herbert Hoover in later years would be remembered primarily as Franklin Roosevelt's failed predecessor. The source of his appeal is a puzzlement to the contemporary mind. He was pudgy and moon-faced; his oratorical talent consisted of little more than an ability to speak clearly and directly into a microphone. Yet he was a vivid and commanding personality to many Americans in the 1920s for reasons that lay deep in the national psyche. His life combined themes of triumphant individualism, bureaucratic organization, and American utopianism; he encapsulated America's past, its present, and its eternal aspirations. Running for president in 1928, he promised great things, and the people believed him.

An orphan from a tiny Iowa town, he worked his way through college, became an engineer, and eventually a millionaire managing partner in a global firm. The head of Belgian relief during the World War, he emerged as a humanitarian of international renown, before returning to the United States in 1917 as the public servant who ran wartime agricultural and food conservation programs. He exemplified the rags-to-riches myth dear to most Americans: opportunity, grit, hard work, determination, inevitable success.

Yet he understood the modern world. He knew the large organization was becoming dominant in every aspect of human life and accepted the development as positive. Secretary of commerce under Presidents Harding and Coolidge, he displayed unflagging energy in his efforts to create a new America. Assuming that no area of the government was outside his sphere, he dabbled in foreign trade and farm policy, attempted to develop constructive relationships with organized labor, and above all promoted the virtues of standardization and industrial cooperation. His management of Mississippi River flood relief in 1927 reinforced his humanitarian image. His well-organized public relations operation told America that he was the Great Engineer. Swept into the presidency in 1928 on a tide of prosperity and public esteem, he asserted that America was on the verge of a new era in which poverty would disappear.

Hoover stood articulately for something resembling a democratic version of the fascist corporatism emerging from Mussolini's Italy, an organizational society in which large business, abetted by an activist government, would be the engine of progress while extending recognition to workers and farmers. In place of Mussolini's compulsion, the new system would run on a voluntarism fueled by intelligent self-interest. Organization and traditional individualism could coexist; government could be both essential and strictly limited. Businessmen, farmers, and workers would have their endeavors facilitated by Washington, act on its good advice, and prosper—all without succumbing to a dependency that would do irreversible damage to their character. Few Americans fully understood the concept, but most sensed that Hoover was an extraordinary man.

Herbert Hoover was inaugurated President of the United States on March 4, 1929, seven months and three weeks before the stock market crash.

Mr. MacDonald

In mid-1931, James Ramsay MacDonald—leader of the Labour party, well into the second year of his second term as Britain's prime minister—

was the face of socialism to most of his countrymen. In fact, like many a poor boy made good, he was more an exemplar and advocate of a style of bourgeois liberalism—one that valued the creation of opportunity equally with rights of property and identified the objective of foreign policy with peace at almost any cost. Born in 1866, the illegitimate son of a plough-man and a servant girl on a Scottish farm, he managed to obtain an edu-cation in eightpence-a-month grammar schools, barely earned a living as a young man in a variety of low-paying jobs, and was drawn to reform pol-itics. In 1886, he joined the Fabian Society and immersed himself in the gradualist socialism of an insurgent intellectual elite. In 1894, he affili-ated with the emerging Labour party and in short order established him-self as one of its leading figures. The following year, he married Margaret Gladstone, the well-to-do daughter of a noted scientist and social reformer who had helped found the Young Men's Christian Association. The marriage—which ended with his wife's premature death in 1911—made him financially independent, provided him with a devoted partner, and facilitated his progress toward a fuzzy middle ground between social-ism and liberal capitalism. In 1906, he won election to the House of Commons from Leicester, one of the beneficiaries of an emerging entente between the Liberal and Labour parties. Handsome, articulate, passion-ate in advocacy, he established himself as the dominant voice among the twenty-nine Labour members in the House. As parliamentary leader of an emerging party, he earnestly advocated justice and consideration for the industrial working class while eschewing revolutionary socialism—a stance that mirrored the attitudes of a large preponderance of the work-ers themselves. At the height of his personal and political powers over the next twenty years, he was an imposing figure with charismatic quali-ties. "What people saw was the fine figure with sad, handsome, noble face, brilliant eyes and mass of wavy, greying hair," wrote Charles Loch Mowat, "what they heard was a speaker of exalted and emotional elo-quence, using a voice of great beauty and range in a warm Scots accent."[1]

The World War was his greatest challenge. With a majority of the Labour delegation in the Commons supporting the conflict, he resigned his party leadership. Paradoxically, he denounced the decision to fight, but supported the war itself once his country was committed. His motiva-tion was more that of the liberal inclined toward pacifism than the social-ist driven by a vision of transnational class solidarity. Rejecting military service, he unsuccessfully attempted at the age of forty-eight to volunteer for the ambulance corps. Most ordinary Englishmen found his stance incomprehensible, offensive, and unpatriotic. His speaking appearances often carried a threat of violence; he became the country's most unpopular politician. At the general election of 1918, his Leicester constituency threw him out of office by a resounding majority.

MacDonald's comeback was remarkable. Without changing his principles a whit, he transformed his image from that of an unpatriotic dissenter to that of an uncompromising enemy of Bolshevism. As the Labour party split between those attracted to the Russian Revolution and the nonrevolutionary gradualists, he became the leading spokesman of moderation. Instinctively, he had chosen the right side. Many of the intellectuals and some of the left-wing union leaders might look to Lenin and Moscow. A solid majority of the working class accepted the existing order and wanted only more consideration and opportunities for advancement within it. Moreover, the rising mood of disenchantment with the war made his opposition to it less offensive. Reelected to Parliament in 1922, MacDonald won a close contest for the leadership of a Labour party that was now the second largest in Commons. The close election of 1923 made him prime minister for nine months in a Labour-Liberal coalition government. In 1929, the coalition won again, this time with what appeared to be a solid mandate.

MacDonald's second government foundered in the Great Depression. Neither he and his Liberal partners, nor in all probability a majority of his own party, were ready for an attempt at a thoroughgoing socialist remedy that would have included nationalization of major industry, strong controls on the economy, protectionism, and a managed currency. The Labour-Liberal coalition instead accepted the traditional policy options of liberal capitalism—free trade, defense of the pound, and budgetary retrenchment. But free trade was fading as other nations raised their tariffs. Budgetary retrenchment inevitably led toward cuts in social spending and unemployment compensation. Sixty-five years old in 1931, MacDonald was unable to defend his government's course with the eloquent persuasiveness that once had been natural to him. The charismatic appeal of socialism had become the tired invocation of a traditional capitalism. His story was not much different, after all, from that of President Hoover.

Amid protests about cuts in the dole from a majority of the Labour party, the government collapsed in August 1931, to be replaced by a National coalition anchored by the Conservatives. It was indicative of MacDonald's fundamental centrism that King George V suggested he might stay on as prime minister and that the Tories readily accepted. For the next four years, MacDonald would be something more than a figure-head, something less than a real head of government, influential in foreign policy where he worked tirelessly for disarmament and attempted to promote a failing League of Nations, of little consequence in the Conservative effort to reshape the British economy and the contours of British politics.

Chancellor Brüning

It was symbolic of the fate of the Weimar Republic that its last significant "democratic" leader cared little for democracy, was effective only when he could wield dictatorial powers, and was labeled by his opposition as, all too convincingly, "the hunger chancellor." Heinrich Brüning possessed neither the electoral base nor the personal qualities to guide a nation in crisis. Brüning's Center party, the de facto voice of German Catholicism, was a brave and ultimately futile effort to unite the bourgeoisie and the working class. In the tumultuous political world of Weimar Germany, it could never resolve the deep-seated conflicts among its disparate constituencies. Torn between social Christians and reactionary monarchists, it polled only about one-seventh of the total vote; its natural allies brought its constituency to little more than a third of the electorate. Brüning, the head of its right wing, could govern democratically only with the acquiescence of the Social Democrats, who were ideologically at odds with him on every question of social policy.

In such a situation, only unusual greatness of character and popular appeal could mobilize a durable majority. Brüning was devoid of such qualities. Had he been a cleric, he probably would have been the valued administrative aide to a cardinal—the man who kept the books and knew the ways of ecclesiastical politics. An unimpressive physical presence and a mediocre speaker, he possessed the skills of the parliamentary politician rather than those of the popular leader. A rationalist intellectual, he seemed to believe that intelligent and necessary policies were self-justifying. As Hajo Holborn observed, he never reached the understanding that statesmen had to win the support of the people by sentiment rather than by reason.[2] Convinced that only a policy of austerity could revive the German economy, he demanded acceptance of economic pain on an unprecedented scale. Nearly as contemptuous of democracy as the extremists of the left and right, possessing neither the talent nor the vision to rally a people to patriotic sacrifice, he privately hoped for the return of the kaiser and a reversion to Prussian autocracy. He was not responsible for the collapse of Weimar democracy, which was entering its long terminal crisis when he became chancellor, but he, more than any other leader, exemplified the dead end it had reached in less than a dozen years.

The Wall Street crash, impoverished investors, closed banks, breadlines, the spread of misery from America to the rest of the world, the rise of Nazism, the blossoming of Japanese militarism, and eventually war—these elements provide an easily comprehended sequence of development. As an explanation of the 1930s it has special appeal to liberals seeking an indictment of Republican "normalcy" and conceiving of the 1920s as a decade of greed and irresponsible isolationism. This story is, however, much too simple. To explain a phenomenon as vast as the Great Depression in all its dimensions is probably impossible, but it is essential to realize that its causes far transcended the Wall Street crash and associated American policy mistakes and that its consequences were likewise well beyond the capacity of the United States to manage.

One can understand the causes and consequences of the Great Depression only in part as an economic problem, although it surely reflected the colliding demands of industrial modernity and financial traditionalism. The Depression was also a result of the collective Western failure to establish a viable postwar political order. It grew out of a complex clash of political cultures involving irreconcilable national aspirations, deep national grievances, sharply divergent political economies, and colliding ideologies. It is to such fundamentals rather than to the mechanics of economic policy that one must look in order to understand not simply why there was a Great Depression, but also why it lasted so long.

Beginning with the first settlers at Jamestown, America was an escape from Europe—a chance for a new start in an environment uncorrupted by the history of the old world, offering rights and opportunities. The United States, the result of a colonial revolt, would be the most "liberal" of societies—liberal in the classical sense of presupposing the individual as the basic unit, affirming protection of individual liberties as the ultimate end of governance, and defining these broadly to include private property, free speech, and extensive personal liberty. Coexisting with a widely accepted majoritarian democracy, the American liberal ethic affirmed social mobility and assumed widespread opportunity while rejecting utopian ideas of equality. It recoiled from such aspects of the European experience as a rigidly structured society, inherited privilege, and bureaucratic institutions.

The United States had more diversity—ethnic, religious, economic—than any other Western nation, yet it had less class consciousness. In sharp contrast to France and Germany, somewhat less so to Great Britain, politics was conducted within two major parties, neither of them sharply class-based nor rigidly ideological. Real differences existed between American Democrats and Republicans, but they were muted by the plurality of interests and outlooks both parties had to accommodate. The two-party system was more a unifying mechanism than a divisive one. Similarly, the American acceptance of a strong presidency and celebration of charismatic leadership was yet another way of submerging differences among diverse, tightly defined groups.

The United States of the 1920s was the world's most prosperous and confident industrial nation. No other major country had so high an average level of material comfort or so great a faith that things could only get better. More than any other Western nation, the United States was the product of a national experience of victory in continental expansion and foreign war. In every imaginable way, it had been the big winner in the World War—entering late, tipping the balance without suffering the grievous human and financial losses that afflicted the other victors, profiting greatly. Yet, poised in 1920 to take world leadership, it had pulled back.

The intermittent entanglements between the United States and Europe had always ended with American reversions to separateness and affirmations of a unique destiny. The Republican return to "normalcy" after 1921 was the latest example of a long-established practice. Woodrow Wilson's idealistic evangelism and the more ambiguous proselytizing of Theodore Roosevelt had converted a substantial and articulate minority to the proposition that the future of the United States was somehow bound up with that of the Old World—but only a minority. Most Americans, as always, opted for disengagement, increasingly justifying their decision on a widespread belief that the war had achieved nothing other than to reveal once again the irredeemable depravity of European statecraft and the gullible innocence of the United States. The result was not "isolation" in any rigid sense of the word. Rather it was a policy of dealing with European powers on a wide variety of matters ranging from arms reductions to war debts while making few commitments and seeking to profit from Europe's distress.

A survey of the European scene at the beginning of the 1930s doubt-less confirmed for most Americans that such a policy, far from being immoral, was prudent. Dictatorship or chaos in nations running in a vast semicircle from the Iberian peninsula to Poland, along with unstable, tur-bulent democratic politics in France and Germany, confirmed the impres-sion that, Britain and a few small states aside, Europeans were incapable of constructive self-government. No continental leader was more admired in the United States than Benito Mussolini, who for all his dicta-torial abuses, gave the appearance (however illusory) of having brought order and progress to an otherwise ungovernable Italy. Spain, the other leading Mediterranean state, proved unable to make an effective transi-tion to democracy after the resignation of its strongman, Jose Antonio Primo de Rivera. Wracked by intense class conflict and violent civil disor-der well before the beginning of its civil war in 1936, it seemed yet another example of the European alternatives—dictatorship or anarchy.

The old Russian Empire, now the Union of Soviet Socialist Republics, headed by Josef Stalin, was a pariah state, denied diplomatic recognition by the United States. News from there was scarce and fragmentary, but those who paid attention knew that it was a communist state with an absolute ruler and a menacing determination to create both a strong new society and a new type of man. Worse, the Soviet Union was a revolu-tionary state, controlling Communist parties throughout the developed world. Typically, the Communists denied the legitimacy of any and all bourgeois institutions, playing the game of representative politics only as it suited their purposes, often purposefully engaging in rioting and street brawling as a way of undermining the authority of established institu-tions. Communist relations with moderate parties of the left and with democratic trade unions were especially venomous.

The periodic red scares that ran through American life in the twenties and thirties appear at first glance puzzling, since even at the bottom of the Depression Communism was never a mass movement. Still, the Com-munist party created a fair amount of noise and disorder and incited occasional civil wars in various segments of the labor movement. Most importantly, it challenged the monolithic American liberal belief in pri-vate property, opportunity, and individual liberty. Not surprisingly, the Communists were more hated and feared in the United States than in European countries accustomed to class warfare and ideological conflict.

With the Soviet Union a distant shadow in the American line of sight, the two European nations most visible to Americans were Great Britain and Germany, the first still seemingly a major political and economic power, the second beaten down but potentially the dominant force on the continent. Both countries had extensive economic ties to the United States. They had supplied its two dominant streams of settlement and immigration before the late nineteenth century. Like the United States they were modern industrial and financial powers, but otherwise the contrasts were great.

⟋⟍

If the United States was the most liberal of nations, Great Britain was both the runner-up and the primary source of the American political tradition, but Britain's history and political culture were far more complex. The country was the product of a thousand years of development, the largest proportion of them under medieval corporatism and authoritarian rule. Its people clung stubbornly to the artifacts of this history in the form of customs, titles, and period costumes that dominated the nation's public life and pageantry. Liberalism in the form of an assertion of individual rights and limitations on government had made an early appearance in the late seventeenth century, but had triumphed fully only in the nineteenth with the installation of authentic representative government and the adoption of free trade. By the early twentieth century political liberalism had established firm, durable political roots and the basis for a mass democracy that had abolished every significant voting restriction; its values were so deeply ingrained that the Conservative establishment could back self-governing dominion status for India in full knowledge that it was placing at risk the most precious jewel of the Empire. Economic liberalism (free trade and open markets), on the other hand, had only a weak hold on the national imagination and was under serious challenge from the Conservatives.

By European standards, Britain's social class system was relatively open, but to Americans it was unduly rigid and snobbish. The working and middle classes in Britain had a perceptibly lower standard of living than those in the United States. Britain's intense ethnic and religious homogeneity contrasted vividly with the diversity of the United States or even most of the nations of continental Europe. By and large, it remained a deferential society in which most of the population respected the social and political dominance of an entrenched well-to-do and highly educated establishment. In turn, the leadership class, whether in the Liberal or Conservative parties, generally accepted the proposition that entitlement to power carried with it a responsibility for the care of ordinary people. Once one got beyond free trade, in fact, it was hard to find deep divisions of principle between Conservatives and Liberals. In one crucial aspect, British politics resembled that of the United States far more than that of most European states—class and ideological conflict was muted. Consequently, the differences between parties tended to involve tone and emphasis rather than irreconcilable doctrine.

The primary challenge to this relative consensus came from the still young Labour party. A product of working-class suffrage and the industrial age, Labour saw itself as the political vehicle of the working class and the advocate of a watered-down socialist alternative. Although an outgrowth of the trade union movement, the party attracted numerous intellectuals who, in Britain as in the rest of the Western world, were increasingly critical of the workings of capitalism, a system in which, all the same, they flourished almost in direct ratio to the degree of their scorn and disengagement. Some of Labour's leaders saw the Soviet Union as a working model of the good society, but the party's center of gravity was democratic. Radical by American measurements, it was mushy and moderate from the perspective of the continental left. Far from achieving an electoral majority or even solid support from the working classes, it could govern only in coalition with the Liberals, a situation that put a firm brake on its left wing.

British politics differed from American in one other critical fashion. With a constitutional monarch as the symbol of the nation and the embodiment of its greatness, Britain's electoral leadership often seemed pale. If at times British parties produced overwhelming personalities, their customs and structures tended toward collective command. The prime minister was first among equals, not the equivalent of an American president or a German kaiser. His function as a parliamentary leader required skills of conciliation and consensus-building that had no natural relation to electoral charisma or popular appeal. In ordinary times, frequently even in crisis times, the head of government was likely to be a gray man. Attacking David Lloyd George in the speech that brought down the wartime coalition, Stanley Baldwin had explicitly, even scornfully, attacked charismatic leadership. As early as the mid-twenties, Winston Churchill was widely recognized as the most exciting of the Conservatives; he was also (with considerable justification) considered too erratic for the stabilizing leadership the party and the nation needed.

Britain had been one of the victorious allies during the World War, yet unlike the United States, it had neither prospered nor achieved a sense of triumph. In 1914, Britain, at the head of an empire on which the sun never set, could still envision itself as the premier world power—militarily, economically, intellectually, morally. By 1920, such pretensions were the stuff of an illusion made possible only by American default. An economic slump that began after the war and continued throughout the twenties was the material expression of a national malaise. Britain had endured four grinding years into which it had poured unimaginable wealth and resources, lost three-quarters of a million young men killed, had another million and a half wounded or gassed. The human casualties amounted to the decimation of an entire generation, with the preponderant losses among the best and the brightest. The acquisition of German colonies was insignificant compared to the cession of effective independence for most of Ireland and the prospect of the same for India. The establishment of the British Commonwealth of Nations in 1931 was a necessary concession to overseas possessions too large and restive to be treated as colonies. It also was a dramatic reminder that in the postwar era Britain would at best be a nominal sovereign. The alienation and cynicism of the intelligentsia, mainly amusing in the United States, was corrosive in England. The predominant postwar mood was less one of triumph, gain, and hope than of loss, straitened circumstances, and diminished expectations, but Britain at least had been a winner. Possessing relatively stable social and political systems rooted in a millennium of tradition, it (because of the American rejection of global leadership) could still pose as the world's preeminent power.

Germany, in contrast, was a loser, socially and economically unstable, governed by a regime with no legitimacy, and pushed to the margin of international respectability. For hundreds of years "Germany" had been little more than a geographical expression at the heart of Europe, fragmented into dozens of inconsequential states and a growing, dynamic, militaristic Prussia. Its unification under Prussian auspices in 1871 had created a dominant new power, economic as well as military, and a "German problem" for the continent. Its national and imperial ambitions conservatively managed by Otto von Bismarck, it had spent its first two decades of existence as a major player in a balance of power system. Under Kaiser Wilhelm II, it had become increasingly menacing and aggressive; if not the initial instigator in 1914, it had made the World War possible, then had provided the military resources that fueled a four-year horror. In 1918 the instincts of all the allied peoples, and of a good many Germans themselves, had been to restructure the country by forcing the kaiser into exile, dismantling in near-entirety the structures of authority associated with his regime, and establishing a liberal-democratic republic.

It was the unhappy task of the Weimar Republic to manage the consequences of the military defeat the old order had created. The job brought it few champions. Through an odd process of transference, the Republic became in the eyes of many Germans responsible for the national weakness that ensued. Its opponents contrived a sense of betrayal derived from the fact that almost none of the war had been fought on German soil; the Fatherland, they argued, had been stabbed in the back by subversives and defeatists. The accusations bore no relationship to reality, but they rang true to a people who had experienced virtually no combat damage.

It was the Republic that had to sign the Treaty of Versailles with its provisos assigning war guilt to Germany and depriving it of considerable territory. It was the Republic that had to cope with the humiliation of partial military occupation, the burden of heavy reparations, and the hyperinflation that flowed from its early efforts to deal with the reparations problem. Imperial Germany had been a strong and prosperous nation propelled by a sense of national destiny. Weimar Germany was weak and economically shaky. The mood of its intelligentsia ran the gamut from despair to nihilism. Imperial Germany had managed social conflict with a system of Bismarckian social welfarism that took the revolutionary edge away from the socialist movement. Class division in the Weimar period was sharpened by the increasing difficulty of maintaining social benefits. Imperial Germany had been an authoritarian society whose nature was scarcely concealed by a thin veil of representative and democratic institutions. Weimar attempted to breathe life into those institutions in the most unpromising circumstances.

The Weimar Republic is most widely remembered for the great inflation of the early twenties. Devastating for a large segment of the middle class and many investors, the event left in its wake moral and psychological consequences that lingered on after the currency was stabilized and revalued in 1924. Many Germans never regained confidence in Weimar currency. Savings rates plunged, and money went into consumption. The urban smart set pursued short-term pleasures and made a virtue of hedonism. It did not escape notice that those who profited from the hyperinflation were most often sharp dealers, sometimes downright crooks, almost always amoral opportunists. Stefan Zweig, writing in 1943, recalled that during the World War Germany was at least given a sense of pride by a national effort and temporary victories, but "the inflation served only to make it feel soiled, cheated, and humiliated; a whole generation never forgot or forgave the German Republic for those years."[3]

The Nazi party scored its earliest gains by appealing to the resentments of those who with varying degrees of accuracy considered themselves victims of the inflation. The country as a whole, Gerald Feldman has observed, made "a dramatic descent into the most grotesque forms of interest-group politics." Splinter parties represented narrow groups whose anger frequently expressed itself in irrational attacks against Jews and Bolshevists, boiled over into repudiation of the Republic itself or, in some instances, rejected liberal capitalism.[4] Communists on the left and populistic nationalists on the right demonstrated their contempt for liberal government by indulging in street fighting as an extension of politics and pledging themselves to the abolition of the system that tolerated them. A generous method of proportional representation encouraged extreme political fragmentation. In the 1928 Reichstag elections, ten political parties each won at least ten seats. The largest, the Social Democrats, polled under thirty percent of the vote. Such a situation required uneasy coalitions and made responsible party government nearly impossible.

If the hyperinflation influenced German political culture in many unhappy ways, so did the great, enduring, constant sense of resentment and resistance against the exactions of the World War victors. Reparations were both a genuine burden on the economy and a source of unending bitterness. In 1924, the government of Gustav Stresemann agreed to the Dawes Plan, which established an escalating schedule of reparations payments in revalued marks, but it did so only as a means of obtaining American and British support for a restored German currency. No German statesman seriously believed that his country could, or should, continue the payments as scheduled when they would reach the long-term target of RM 2.5 million in 1928. In 1929, the Young Plan, brokered by the United States, further scaled down reparations obligations but failed to end German resistance to them.

Stresemann and his successors likewise pushed constantly at the military limitations placed on Germany by the Treaty of Versailles. National bitterness over the loss of large chunks of territory, some of which had great economic value, to Poland and Czechoslovakia likely would have escalated to war or threats of war whether Hitler had come to power or not. Large numbers of Germans had become second-class citizens in foreign countries. In January 1931, the League of Nations rebuked Poland for oppressing its German population.[5] Such sentiments—and beneath them the image of Germany as an abused orphan in the international community—were part of a national consensus that extended far beyond the right-wing parties. The "German problem" remained with Europe, boiling not far beneath the surface, apt to erupt once again.

In the 1920s, Europe floundered economically while the United States prospered. Every major European nation underwent a difficult transition from war to peace, seemed to stabilize in the mid-twenties, and experienced varying degrees of economic progress in the four years before the Great Depression. At bottom, however, none fully recovered from the crushing costs of the World War—lost human resources, brutal taxation, the commitment of enormous sums of national wealth to ephemeral military production, the consequent deferment of investment in civilian pursuits, the weakening of national currencies. None had either the capital or the mass purchasing power to leap forward into the new world of mass consumption that was beginning to appear in the United States.

France, despite substantial inflation, managed to achieve apparently strong economic growth throughout the twenties, in part because a weak franc (officially devalued in 1926 from twenty U.S. cents to four) made its exports more attractive abroad. It appears also to have had the best unemployment record of the decade among the large Western European nations. The French treasury in the late twenties accumulated the greatest hoard of gold in Europe. Yet the country remained a second-rate industrial and financial power. The weak franc, heavy public spending, and French social-political culture all discouraged outside investment and domestic entrepreneurship. France's leaders and most of its citizens were well aware that the nation's economy, like the other measures of its strength, would pale beside a thoroughly revived and healthy Germany.[6]

Great Britain, like France, never effected a substantial modernization of its industry. Many of its major enterprises—shipbuilding, coal, textiles—were depressed throughout the world; new lines of business, such as automobiles, never reached the level of development they attained in the United States. The British government erred, moreover, by keeping the pound at its prewar value of $4.86. The result was to make its exports much less competitive on the world market and to set off a deflationary cycle of falling prices, stagnant wages, and large-scale unemployment. The overvalued pound left the gold reserves that backed it hostage to the next major economic crisis. The British gross national product increased steadily but slowly. For many British workers, the postwar "slump" continued throughout the twenties; national unemployment ran at nine to twelve percent for most of the decade, but was much higher in those areas dominated by the old declining industries. This dreary economic performance was but the first phase of a relentless downward trajectory relative to the other major economic powers.[7]

Germany, potentially the driving economic force of Europe, was the continent's sick man, wracked first by hyperinflation, then by the stern measures necessary to stabilize the currency. Gross domestic product, adjusted for inflation, did not surpass that of 1913 until 1927. Industrial unemployment fluctuated wildly from a low of 1.5 percent in the feverish inflationary year of 1922 to eighteen percent in the deflationary year of 1926. In the three years of relative prosperity, 1927–29, it averaged close to nine percent. More than the other important powers of Europe, Germany was dependent upon foreign loans and investment, mostly from the United States. It also had the unique position among them of being primarily responsible for producing the payments that the allies applied against their war debts to the United States. Like the others, Germany had problems with aging and declining industrial sectors, but it was richer in natural resources, applied scientific knowledge, and a trained, capable workforce. Under more benign circumstances, it could have led Western Europe in a strong economic recovery, but to many Europeans a prosperous, resurgent Germany seemed more a threat than a benefit. The international political dilemma of what to do about Germany thus spilled over into economics in ways that injured the entire continent and set the stage for the worst of all possible outcomes.[8]

American prosperity contrasted vividly with Europe's distress and stagnation. In America's cities especially, the signs of mass affluence were everywhere, setting a standard to which the rest of the world aspired. In no other country did so many blue-collar workers own automobiles and radios; in no other country was home ownership so widespread. Electrical appliances, indoor toilets, motion pictures viewed in palace-like theaters, spectator sports exciting huge crowds in enormous stadiums—all seemed to portend a new standard of living for ordinary people. No matter that perhaps forty percent of Americans lived in or close to poverty, the visions of abundance and opportunities for the less fortunate attracted the attention of the world.

The U.S. boom of the twenties was primarily a product of abundant resources, technological capabilities, and industrial power, but it also was fueled by a transfer of wealth from across the Atlantic in the form of war debt and reparations payments. The United States, before 1914 a debtor country developed by surplus capital from Europe, already had become a creditor as a result of wartime transactions with the allies. During the 1920s it received British, French, and Italian war debt payments, funded by reparations paid to these nations by Germany. Full cancellation of all these transfers would have been in the long-run interest of every nation involved. Instead, Germany, the continent's leading debtor, became the source of a substantial flow of funds to the United States, the one nation that least needed large foreign capital infusions. American investment, in turn, was essential in keeping Germany afloat.

This senseless situation was made all the worse by the U.S. protective tariff. Upon returning to power in 1921, the Republicans had quickly reversed Woodrow Wilson's policy of relatively open trade. The Fordney-McCumber Act of 1922 amounted to about a fifty percent increase in rates and led to a sharp reduction in foreign imports.[9] With access to the American market made more difficult, Germany, the former allies of the U.S., and other European nations could not raise all the dollars they needed by selling goods to the United States. Thus, they had to borrow in the private American financial markets, thereby piling future interest and repayment obligations on top of debt that already existed. The United States, possessing an abundance of capital, looked to Europe, and especially to Weimar Germany, for investment opportunities. With Herbert Hoover as secretary of commerce, President Calvin Coolidge's administration did what it could to facilitate private American loans and the sale of American products abroad, but without a healthier reciprocal trading relationship and a roughly even balance of payments, the two sides were building an inverted pyramid, certain to collapse under economic strain.

The United States had emerged most quickly and strongly from its postwar recession and readjustment. The American boom began in 1923 and surged on with barely a hiccup for the next six years, fueled by broad-based consumer demand for new housing, automobiles, and appliances, by a vast wave of highway construction that transformed the national landscape, by the rapid growth of the electrical utility industry, and by a large expansion of manufacturing in response to all these forces. Price inflation was very low, allowing a pattern of modest but steady wage increases to be translated into real gains in purchasing power throughout the decade. A growing use of consumer credit in the form of installment purchases facilitated the prosperity.

The Coolidge administration watched this process benignly and sought only to shrink the federal government back to a "normal" peacetime role after its vast expansion during the war. Coolidge acted primarily as a cheerleader for private capitalism as the engine of prosperity. Secretary of Commerce Hoover's activism, limited to advisory and support services, made no demands on the budget. Secretary of the Treasury Andrew Mellon, a strong advocate of what a later generation would call supply-side economics, pressed for and obtained large cuts in the wartime tax structure. He asserted that money left with the taxpayer would in one way or another find its way into the private economy and do more good for society than if taken and utilized for government programs. Since there was no federal tax liability for incomes below the upper-middle class figure of $5,000 and since a taxpayer had to earn ten times that amount to experience anything like a real nip, Mellon's relief went primarily to the rich. Whether this was good or bad or of no import for the economy may be endlessly debated. We do know that prosperity went on unabated for six years and that the government ran consistent budget surpluses.

Even the world's strongest economy had its flaws. As in Europe, certain industries—railroads, shipbuilding, coal, textiles—were overbuilt and in decline. The nation's biggest single economic problem was agriculture, depressed around the world in the twenties. After the end of the war farm prices had collapsed, bottoming out in 1922, then beginning a painful climb back toward "parity" (prewar purchasing power), but never quite getting there. Agricultural leaders and politicians pushed unsuccessfully for major relief in the form of the McNary-Haugen plan, a proposal that would have subsidized farm income by supporting the prices of important commodities; this expensive exercise would in theory come close to paying for itself by dumping surpluses on the world market. Unrealistic and very costly, it had no support within the Coolidge administration after the death of Secretary of Agriculture Henry C. Wallace in 1925. By the beginning of 1929, farming—a pursuit that engaged nearly one-fifth of the workforce—still lagged behind a generally prosperous economy. Many American farmers could live in relative comfort by the standards of the time. However, in the isolated countryside, only about twenty-five percent lived in easy proximity to such conveniences of urban life as up-to-date medical care, libraries, good schools, or diversified shopping; only about one in ten had electricity or running water.[10] There was a considerably higher rate of poverty among rural dwellers than among urban workers.

It was no coincidence that most of the visible political insurgency of the period was agrarian. From the late nineteenth century on, farmers had pursued political objectives through a variety of vehicles that ranged from third parties to influential interest groups. Such efforts typically had two faces, one of them affirming the fundamental virtue of rural life and asserting oppression by a variety of urban fat cats and vice mongers, the other arguing (often successfully) for a variety of federal assistance programs that delivered such concrete benefits as rural credits, protection for cooperatives, and scientific farming advice. By 1929, agriculture was the base of most "progressive" political protest in the United States.

Coping with Crisis

With hindsight, it seems odd that the Crash was unexpected everywhere. No matter what the system—American organizational conservatism, a German centrist blend of authoritarianism and proportional democracy, or British socialism—statesmen and their governments were unprepared, purposeful only in their orthodoxy, and ultimately futile in their policies. It tells us much about their ineffectiveness that the most creative among them was the American president, Herbert Hoover.

Running for President in 1928, Herbert Hoover not only capitalized on six years of Republican prosperity, he aggressively celebrated it. Who could blame him? Despite a brief economic dip in 1927 (possibly no more than a reflection of the Ford Motor Company's six-month shutdown to retool for the new Model A), the nation as a whole had never been better off. Hoover, perhaps the most esteemed individual in American politics, was a sure bet to defeat his rough-edged Irish-Catholic Democratic opponent, Governor Alfred E. Smith of New York. It seemed by no means outlandish when he asserted: "given a chance to go forward with the policies of the last eight years, we shall soon with the help of God be in sight of the day when poverty will be banished from this nation." On November 6, 1928, fifty-eight percent of the voting electorate gave Hoover an overwhelming victory.

Calvin Coolidge had been a traditional small-government conservative. Hoover was a man of action willing to explore the possibilities of social-economic guidance. He established a number of commissions to investigate and make recommendations on issues ranging from administrative efficiency to conservation to American Indian policy to child protection. His most important move, however, was a bid to address the farm problem, for which he called a special session of Congress. His program had two centerpieces: a substantial increase in tariffs for agricultural commodities, and the establishment of a Federal Farm Board with funds to buy and stockpile surpluses while giving farmers advice on market trends. By midyear, he had the Farm Board; work on the tariff bill would continue into 1930. The Farm Board suffered from obvious weaknesses of conception. It had no mechanism for mandatory control of supply and thus no guarantee that its efforts would not be swamped by the ever-growing surpluses. Its $500 million appropriation, although enormous by the standards of the twenties, would not necessarily be sufficient to deal with so great a problem. Still it was a path-breaking foray into peacetime statism, signifying Hoover's determination to make the rural population full partners in the prosperity of what he and his admirers called the New Era.

A little more than four months after Hoover had moved with characteristic energy to address the nation's biggest economic problem, the stock market crashed.

The crash was not exactly the *cause* of the Great Depression, but it was a precipitating event. A Federal Reserve low-interest-rate policy, undertaken in part to support the British pound by making American money market investments less attractive, had not simply facilitated mass consumption; it also had made stock market speculation with borrowed funds a low-cost gamble. Until early 1928, the bull market that had begun after the postwar recession had been a reasonable reflection of a strong economy. In the last year and a half or so of its life it surged ahead, perhaps not irrationally, but certainly exuberantly and too rapidly to avoid some sort of sharp pullback. By mid-1929, Wall Street was attracting "hot money" from all over the world. That September, the market hit an all-time high.

By then, however, the underlying economy was slumping. Industrial production edged downward in the summer and fall; unemployment nudged upwards, indicating a shift toward a recession. The overheated stock market trended downward in a choppy but orderly fashion until the last two weeks of October. Every decline, however, exerted more pressure on the very large number of margin accounts—those in which common stocks had been purchased on credit with as little as ten percent down. So long as stock prices were moving straight up, the "leverage" of margin buying was a good way to make easy money; when they started to move sharply down, buyers faced not simply losses but complete liquidation if they could not meet "margin calls" for money to cover those losses.

In the third week in October, the market collapsed. Thick and fast selling, the ticker tape falling farther and farther behind, order clerks overwhelmed, periods of unreasoning panic—history had numerous similar examples, all followed by waves of bankruptcies and years of hard times. But history also could also offer one encouraging moment. In 1907–08, J. P. Morgan almost single-handedly had mobilized the New York financial community to stem an earlier panic. In 1929, a group of bankers, led by Charles Mitchell of National City Bank, tried to duplicate Morgan's achievement. They ostentatiously proclaimed their confidence in the market and the economy, backed their pronouncements with huge buy orders—and got sucked below the surface. By mid-November, the market was down to almost half its September peak. Thousands of speculative investors, large and small, had been wiped out. Millions of dollars in wealth had evaporated.

Yet by the end of 1929 the country was by no means prostrate. Stock prices had recovered a bit. Unemployment was at about nine percent and the prospect of a relatively rapid recovery appeared about as likely as a prolonged slump. Through the summer and early fall of 1930, industrial production moved back up, unemployment inched down into the six percent range, the market edged up from its lows, and there seemed to be reason for optimism.

President Hoover's vigorous leadership struck many observers as decisive in turning the tide.

Many leading Republicans of the twenties had been classical laissez-faire, social-Darwinist capitalists. Secretary of the Treasury Mellon, whom Hoover inherited from Coolidge, advocated a stern policy of letting the business cycle take its course. Hoover recalled his advice as "liquidate labor, liquidate stocks, liquidate the farmers, liquidate real estate."[11] Hoover had no interest in presiding over an economic meltdown. His political career was based on a faith that the excesses of individualistic capitalism could be ameliorated by active management, animated by a humanitarian ethic and a cooperative spirit. Moving aggressively, he secured Federal Reserve cooperation in an easy credit policy, announced a speed-up of scheduled federal public works, and exhorted state and local governments to accelerate their own expenditures. Most impressively, he undertook a series of highly publicized meetings with business leaders, whom he urged to act as a countercyclical force in the crisis. His exhortations, backed by all the authority of his office, were simple and direct: Continue with expansion plans; retrenchment can only contribute to the economic slump. Avoid layoffs and maintain wage levels; the labor of working men is not a commodity to be bought at the lowest price or casually tossed aside as convenient. It is the duty of leading corporations to stand up for the public good in the understanding that the absorption of short-term losses can restore prosperity and achieve large long-term gains. The moguls of American business listened respectfully, marched out, and followed his orders.

Briefly, the plan seemed to be working, but toward the end of 1930, unemployment crossed into double digits. By late 1931, it was obvious that the industrial world in general was dealing with an economic collapse. America's gross national product, even when adjusted for deflation, was only eighty-three percent of what it had been in 1929, unemployment was approaching twenty percent, and stock prices were at a new low.

The road from crash to catastrophe was by no means straight and direct, nor did it have a single geographic beginning. Rather it is best visualized as a series of diverse paths beginning almost at random for different reasons at different places but eventually converging into a broad highway that the industrial world rode downhill toward an abyss that came to seem almost bottomless.

The crash wiped out real accumulated wealth and dealt a sharp psychological blow to the optimism that lubricates consumption-driven booms. It made some overextended banks insolvent and weakened many others, thereby putting a damper on the availability of credit. Moreover, it came at a critical time when the industries that had spurred much of the growth of the twenties were beginning to mature. By and large, Americans who could afford autos or radios had bought them, in many cases incurring substantial installment debt that discouraged big new purchases. Commercial construction was slowing down. The first middle-class suburbs had been built and occupied. A pause had been in the cards anyway; the crash made things worse.

The Wall Street debacle had serious foreign implications. A heavy flow of American money overseas in search of high returns had found its way to Europe and Latin America into what a later generation would call junk bonds. That flow quickly dried up, depriving a number of nations of the external capital that had kept them afloat in the twenties and leaving them to feed on their own economic instability. Germany was especially hard-hit.

Perhaps unwittingly, the Hoover administration contributed to the international crisis with its tariff plans. Hoover's endorsement of a few increases solely to protect hard-pressed farmers had never been a realistic prospect; the Republican party traditionally had responded to the prospect of higher tariffs in Pavlovian fashion. The president's original request had been for no more than "limited revision" of nonagricultural schedules. His congressional leaders undertook a broad, sweeping examination that continued into 1930. Economic interest groups, spurred by the October crash, lined up to press their cases in congressional hearings. Hoover looked on with some concern but made no effort to stop the juggernaut. Whatever his own feelings about excessive tariffs, he had no fundamental quarrel with some degree of protectionism. Moreover, his own recovery plan had to be reinforced with some degree of insulation from foreign competition; businesses being undersold from abroad could not hold the line on wages, production, and capital investment. In June 1930, despite a dramatic plea for a veto from more than a thousand economists, Hoover signed the Hawley-Smoot Tariff. He thereby raised rates on approximately 900 items, with the average increase for agricultural goods at twenty-eight percent and for manufactured goods at 10.6 percent.

The Democratic party, still in those days devoted to the ideal of free trade and motivated by partisan considerations, assailed Hawley-Smoot as a bonanza for big business, a callous attack on the ordinary consumer, and (as the economy worsened) an act that contributed mightily to the economic downturn. Democratic rhetoric, like most partisan talking, was overdone, but the new tariff did real damage. The largest economy and most financially sound nation in the world had put at least another row or two of bricks atop the already imposing wall that kept out much foreign competition. Other nations were starting to practice economic nationalism, but they were smaller and weaker. It was politically impossible to hew to the classical economic idea that the United States, as the world's dominant economic power, should throw open its markets to save the international economy, but to add to existing barriers was an outrage in the eyes of many other countries. Hawley-Smoot signaled nations— Britain especially—trying to preserve an open world economy that the game was up. Moreover, as an increasingly vicious deflationary cycle took hold in 1931 and 1932, its increases of specific duties (i.e., those expressed in fixed money amounts rather than percentages of declared worth) became increasingly onerous. Whatever Hoover and Congress intended, they had set off a cycle of protectionism that would hurt every nation that practiced it.[12]

Still, well into the fall of 1930, unemployment remained at mild levels of six to eight percent. President Hoover could claim at least a qualified success. Three weeks before the midterm congressional elections, he ostentatiously announced the appointment of a select committee to develop employment programs in cooperation with the states and with private industries for the difficult winter months. Not just campaign rhetoric, the announcement was yet another expression of Hoover's genuine belief that leadership and a little economic push from Washington could organize the economy for the benefit of ordinary working people. With the president pointing the way, governors, mayors, and corporate officials, all working in coordination, could refute the belief that economic forces were impersonal and unstoppable.[13]

The people were not persuaded, but neither were they ready to repudiate him, although unemployment surged perceptibly in November, probably moving into double digits for the first time since the crash. In the off-year elections, the Republicans lost control of the House of Representatives, but only by seven seats, and barely hung on to the Senate by the tie-breaking vote of Vice President Charles Curtis. The state elections were more ominous. Democrats captured eight statehouses from incumbent Republicans, while losing only one. Among the new Republican governors, two of the most notable—Gifford Pinchot of Pennsylvania and Philip La Follette of Wisconsin—were anti-Hoover progressives. The state contest that drew the most attention, however, was in New York, where Democratic governor Franklin D. Roosevelt swept to a second term by a margin twice that of any predecessor and instantly established himself as Hoover's likely opponent in 1932.[14]

Hoover could still hope that his economic recovery plan would throw the unemployment trend into reverse. Instead, the worst was yet to come.

The impact of the depression in Germany was both more immediate and more severe. The German economy was already sliding into recession; the crash dealt it a swift and severe blow. Industrial production in 1930 was approximately 12.5 percent below that of the previous year; in 1931, it was 71 percent of the 1929 level. In 1929, insured unemployment had averaged 9.3 percent; it soared to 15.3 percent in 1930 and 23.3 percent in 1931. Germany, unlike the United States, had a comprehensive social insurance system, but mass unemployment on an unprecedented scale created enormous strains. As the economy slid steadily downward, the government faced two unpalatable choices: cutting benefits or raising taxes to maintain them.

Both options were made more difficult by the continuing pressure for reparations payments. Heinrich Brüning, appointed chancellor in March 1930, pursued a policy dedicated to a stable mark and German international financial respectability. Determined to make almost any sacrifice to establish the *bona fides* that might give him the leverage to renegotiate his country's obligations, he seemed at times almost perverse in his acceptance of widespread economic misery. Yet, as dedicated as his predecessors to the overthrow of the Versailles system, he scarcely nicked a military spending program that still semi-covertly aspired to exceed treaty limitations.

On June 30, 1930, pursuant to the Young Plan agreement, allied troops withdrew from the Rhineland, setting off a jubilant national celebration that demonstrated the emotional appeal of German nationalistic assertion. But the chancellor derived little lasting benefit from such events. The foreign policy advances over which he presided could not fully compensate for the misery of a deepening depression. Nor could he satisfy the popular desire for a total end to reparations. A colorless, increasingly unpopular leader at the head of a rickety parliamentary coalition, empowered not by the people but by the autocratic President Paul von Hindenburg, Brüning cultivated a disrespect for democracy. Given presidential authority to rule by decree, he became a leading accomplice in the destruction of the Weimar order.

In July 1930, the Reichstag asserted its constitutional authority by vetoing a Cabinet decree proclaiming as law a rejected tax bill; the pathetic fifteen-vote margin of victory demonstrated the weakness of the forces of parliamentary democracy. Hindenburg and Brüning dissolved the assembly and called new elections. That September, the results— highlighted by an enormous increase in Nazi party strength and a substantial gain for the Communists—reflected declining popular faith in the Weimar order. Brüning's Center party polled a meager 11.8 percent, a couple of points below its usual tally. The most important democratic force left in the Reichstag was the Social Democratic party, with about a quarter of the seats; it decided that the authoritarianism of Hindenburg and Brüning had to be passively accepted, if not affirmatively approved. In 1931, the Reichstag would meet for only forty-two days. Power (but not necessarily authority) flowed toward the Cabinet, the president, and the bureaucracy. Brüning, thinking himself a controlling force rather than simply an instrument of Hindenburg and the conservative influentials around the elderly president, engaged in a dictatorial policy of austerity, contemplated the end of reparations, and may have plotted the restoration of the monarchy.

His policies bypassed normal political processes, did nothing to counter a sharp economic slide, and ignored serious social welfare problems. Meanwhile, more sinister forces contributed to the delegitimization of the Republic. In the 1928 Reichstag election, the Nazi party had been an insignificant player, winning only 2.6 percent of the vote for twelve of 491 seats. In 1930, it got 18.3 percent of the ballots and 107 seats, making it the second largest party. The third largest party, the Communists, polled 13.1 percent, up from 10.6 in 1928. The swiftly gathering Depression empowered angry extremists, the Nazis motivated by the lure of nationalism and populist economic policies, the Communists by revolutionary Marxism. Both had nothing but contempt for a democratic system that they saw simply as a path to power.

The Nazis regularly behaved as paramilitary thugs, attacking their political opponents in the streets, brutalizing Jews when they could, and generally employing physical intimidation as a political weapon. The Communists were probably more effective in Germany than anywhere else in their political strategy of provocative demonstration and planned riot as proto-revolutionary action. In Britain and the United States, they could from time to time precipitate riots and ugly police responses, but in both countries they remained unpopular nuisances. In Germany, Nazis and Communists were each other's favorite targets. They shared almost all the responsibility for the degeneration of Weimar politics into street brawling. On the eve of the 1930 Reichstag election, Communists situated on rooftops in Berlin fired on a Nazi motorcade attempting to flaunt the party's presence in a tightly organized working-class district. Police intervened, firing pistols and swinging clubs freely; as in most such incidents, they made little distinction between perpetrators and bystanders. Similar situations occurred in many other cities. In one case, Nazis and Communists converged to attack a parade of Social Democrats.[15]

Few deaths or truly serious injuries resulted from such incidents, but they involved more than the animal spirits of alienated young partisans. They also contributed to a common objective, that of demonstrating that the Republic could not maintain order. It is tempting to depict this organized violence as evidence of a symbiotic relationship between the extreme left and the extreme right, but given the ideologically ambiguous nature of Nazism, it is more prudent to speak of a struggle between authoritarian revolutionary parties with as many commonalities as differences. Clearly, the Communists and Nazis had different ideas about the reorganization of a capitalist economy, the emotion of nationalism, the salience of "race," and the role of "class"; but both parties sought to appeal to the workers and drew on the symbol of socialism. (Nazi was a loose acronym for National Socialist German Workers Party.) They were united in their visceral hostility toward conventional bourgeois politics and the collection of ideas that went with it—individual rights, representative government, respect for minorities, elementary civility.

A number of observers then and historians since have lamented the "division of the left" that characterized Weimar, assuming that if the Social Democrats and Communists had made common cause then the Nazis could have been blocked and a higher order of society might have prevailed. Yet surely more fundamental principles separated these two parties than united them. If the two could agree, albeit it in only a fuzzy fashion, on "socialism," they had little in common in their visions of the larger polity. The German Social Democrats, much like the British Labour party, assumed that democracy and an orderly civil society were the basis for a social transformation, not an impediment to it. The Communists dissented violently.

For the moment, the Nazis took center stage. When the new Reichstag met in Berlin on October 13, 1930, young storm troopers rampaged through the streets, smashing the show windows of Jewish-owned department stores, shouting "down with the Jews," attacking policemen, and creating an ugly, precarious crowd control situation. Inside the Reichstag, the 107 Nazi deputies, dressed in brown shirts, swastika armbands, and tan riding breeches, marched en masse into the chamber and took their seats. As political theater, the act was clumsy and greeted with widespread laughter, but as a symbolic display of the primacy of paramilitary power over civil norms, it was anything but comic.[16]

During the following year, Germany reeled from one political and economic catastrophe to another. Even as unemployment became the paramount issue, Brüning turned to foreign policy. In March 1931, his government announced an agreement to form a customs union with Austria. Superficially, the plan might be seen as a minor stimulus for the economies of both nations, but it also was widely believed to be the first step in an Anschluss (political union) of the two German-speaking nations, a development specifically prohibited by the postwar treaties.

Strenuous protests from France and several eastern European nations blocked the project, which a few months later was ruled illegal by the International Court at the Hague.

In the meantime, however, the French had exacted a terrible retaliation of their own by withdrawing all financial resources from the big, critically important Austrian bank, the Creditanstalt. After mid-May, the bank remained technically alive, because of support from the Austrian government and the Bank of England, but as a practical matter it was insolvent. The resulting crisis spread out of Austria into neighboring nations, including Germany itself. Brüning made matters worse in June by issuing a so-called "Tribute Appeal" that asked the allies to agree to a suspension of reparations payments; it emphasized the prostrate condition of the German economy in terms so graphic as to imply national bankruptcy. From the United States, President Hoover called for a one-year moratorium on all reparations and war debt payments; he quickly secured British support and grudging French agreement.

Enlightened though it was, the moratorium was not enough to prevent a financial near-meltdown in Germany. In mid-July, panicky depositors staged runs on banks, most of which closed their doors to avoid insolvency; ordinary Germans made for the nearest border to convert every mark they could accumulate into dollars or pounds; in a matter of days, foreign investors pulled an astounding half-billion dollars out of the German economy. Germany was saved by an Anglo-French-American bailout that supported the mark but maintained the German economy only at a low ebb. The Brüning government, more upset at the failure to obtain a total cancellation of reparations than elated at the nation's avoidance of total collapse, continued its deflationary policy of lower social benefits, pensions, and state salaries while increasing taxes. The result was an overvalued mark, rising unemployment, and increasing social-political chaos. Battles between Communist demonstrators and police became increasingly common. Nazi storm troopers regularly attacked political opponents and terrorized Jewish districts. By the end of 1931, approximately one of every three insured workers was out of a job; many of the rest struggled with part-time work and declining wages.

The impact of the Depression was only slightly less traumatic in Great Britain, where an already-serious industrial unemployment rate of around ten percent in 1929 degenerated to crisis proportions. By late 1930, more than fifteen percent of the insured work force was unemployed; a year later, the figure exceeded twenty percent. Even so grim a statistic understated the extent of the misery. According to official figures, in 1931, one of every two British industrial workers suffered a period of unemployment averaging 130 days, with the situation especially bad in the older industrial and mining areas of Wales, Scotland, and the northern shires of England.[17] It helped only a bit that other segments of the work force—agricultural workers, domestic servants, and public employees—generally had secure job tenure; even taking these into account, an average of one in every seven British workers was unemployed at any given time in 1931.

The Labour government of Ramsay MacDonald responded with policies that might appear ineffective in retrospect but were dictated by the generally accepted rules of the political game as it then existed. Labour ruled with the consent of the Liberals, who imposed limits on its initiatives. Most of its political leadership (as opposed to a small collection of intellectuals) had far more interest in social services for the working class than in state ownership and economic management. The Labour establishment might demand concessions in the form of higher taxes from the middle and upper classes, but it conceived of Britain as one nation and saw itself as responsible for the general welfare, not just as a single-minded advocate of the proletariat. By and large, in the absence of socialism, it accepted the orthodox rules of capitalist finance. In 1929, it had rejected proposals put forth by the old Liberal lion, David Lloyd George, and the dynamic young Labour M.P., Oswald Mosley, for a major public works program to be financed by increased national debt. When Mosley challenged the leadership on the issue in 1930, he was beaten decisively at the party convention. Soon after, he resigned to found the short-lived New Party; later, he grotesquely squandered his talents by establishing the British Union of Fascists.

Thus, while attempting to maintain a high level of relief for the unemployed, Labour never questioned the absolute necessity of defending the pound and sticking with free trade. Given Britain's position as a world financial center and trading state, the policy was arguably sound; in a less dire situation, it might have been successful. In the undertow of the Depression, it was ultimately a failure. Maintaining an overvalued currency required high interest rates and a balanced budget. The result was a deflationary spiral that wreaked substantial damage on British manufacturing. By mid-1931, British exports were in a free fall, and the "invisible" items (banking, shipping, foreign investments) that had long given

Britain a comfortable balance of payments were slipping badly. Decreased Treasury revenues threatened the continuance of social benefits. The consensus policy of the twenties had run out of time.

With substantial reserves committed to the stabilization of the German mark, with a large budget deficit in the offing, and with a serious negative balance of international payments, Britain was an obvious target for international monetary speculators. The German crisis had scarcely abated before there was a serious run on the pound, one so substantial that it threatened to drain the Bank of England's gold stockpile. Chancellor of the Exchequer Philip Snowden, backed by a blue-ribbon advisory committee, advocated a cut in unemployment compensation and numerous other budget items; in addition, although his 1930 budget had increased the income tax rate, he called for another hike. The unions rejected any decrease in benefits. The Cabinet split down the middle. MacDonald prepared to resign.

Normally, it would have been up to Conservative leader Stanley Baldwin to form a government, presumably in coalition with the Liberals, or to King George V, acting at the behest of MacDonald, to call a new election, but an election, just two years after the last and with all its uncertainties, was unpalatable. Rather quickly, the idea of a National coalition took over. Baldwin assented to it and acquiesced in the King's request for MacDonald to stay as prime minister. Taking the post of Lord President of the Council, he was actually the most important figure in the new government.

The National government moved ahead with Snowden's budget, which left the British income tax rate twenty-five percent higher than it had been when he came to office, inflicted ten percent cuts on almost every public salary or benefit, and prescribed numerous other economies. The budget raised an additional £75 million in revenues while cutting spending by £70 million despite widespread protests. The most spectacular of these was a quasi-mutiny at the Invergordon naval base. Enlisted seamen, angry at receiving deeper percentage pay cuts than did officers, undertook the equivalent of a sitdown strike. On September 15, 1931, 12,000 men refused to fall in for work, leaving three battleships and two battle cruisers effectively dead in the water of the harbor. An extreme demonstration by British standards, it was nonetheless a nonviolent affair. A few days later the Admiralty evened out the pay cuts, decided against courts-martial, and simply dismissed about three dozen of the leaders. What might have been the start of a revolution in other countries ended as an ephemeral curiosity.[18]

These budget moves did not save the pound, which continued under pressure despite large credits from Paris and New York. On September 21, 1931, with British gold reserves rapidly dwindling, the government had no choice but to take the nation off the gold standard and allow its currency to "float" at whatever price international traders were willing to pay for it. In subsequent weeks, the pound fell from $4.86 to around $3.40. This effective devaluation, like most such exercises, failed to increase British exports over the next two years. In the meantime, the Conservatives began to promote a step the party majority had long favored—tariff protection and an imperial trading bloc.

With a record that might have seemed calculated to alienate every conceivable voting bloc, the government called an election for October 27. Its candidates included all the incumbent Conservatives (now pledged to protection), most of the Liberals (half of them still pledged to free trade), and its Labour ministers, along with their few followers, all of whom had been expelled from their own party. The coalition had a dubious record of achievement and a composition that gave vivid meaning to the adjective "motley." But it had one great edge—its only opposition was a radicalized Labour party. It capitalized effectively on the wide sense of national crisis.

Advocating equality of sacrifice and proclaiming themselves instruments of national salvation, holding out to British workers the promise of protection from foreign manufactured goods, and occasionally raising the specter of Bolshevism, the Nationals won a remarkable victory—473 Conservatives, 35 National Liberals, 13 National Labourites (including MacDonald). The main opposition, the Labour party, returned with 52 seats. MacDonald would remain as prime minister, but Baldwin and the Conservatives were the controlling force in a government that now moved to put an end to free trade.

Britain, unlike a critically fragmented Germany, had reacted to crisis by embracing national unity and the center. The new government had up to five years to address the Depression. There were plenty of reasons to question its prospects, but, whatever its inadequacies, it provided a stunning affirmation of the nation's stability and its liberal political tradition.

The American voters of early November 1930 had been eerily prescient if they had voted on economic issues. The midyear economic revival had collapsed. The jobless rate remained hopelessly mired throughout 1931, averaging fifteen percent through the summer and increasing to nearly twenty percent by the end of the year. His initial plan swamped by events, Hoover struggled to recover from the setback. He would never succeed.

His fundamental error had been to emphasize recovery over relief, assuming that the latter could be handled primarily by state and local authorities. Despite the best intentions of governors, mayors, and civic leaders, most states and localities could not deal adequately with the comparatively modest rises in unemployment during the twelve months after the crash. Cincinnati, Ohio, for example, possessed one of the most efficient and esteemed municipal governments in the United States. Its business establishment, represented by the local chamber of commerce, had both a sense of social responsibility and a thoroughly modern belief that the business cycle could be managed. When hard times hit, the city and its corporate leaders were prepared with plans for relief projects and accelerated public works. The Cincinnati Plan would have been effective medicine for a mild turndown, but by the end of 1930, the Depression had swamped it. The state of Ohio, under conservative Republican governor Myers Cooper, also attempted stepped-up public works, but its program was likewise too modest.[19]

Ohio was representative of the nation in its initial optimism, its good-faith efforts, and the inadequacy of its attempt. Private charities, barely able to meet the needs of the unemployable during good times, could not handle the overload they now faced. More and more, the long-term jobless found themselves at best dependent upon working family members, at worst living a hand-to-mouth existence characterized by sporadic day labor, occasional hunger, petty thievery, and pervasive insecurity. Local relief needs varied enormously, to be sure, but few localities could handle the burden by the beginning of 1931. As Hoover neared the midpoint of his presidency, the Great Depression, measured in terms of mass distress and increasing lack of hope, was beginning to settle down hard on the United States.

Throughout the year, the president stayed with his original plan. His message to the lame-duck session of the outgoing Seventy-first Congress in December 1930 asserted that the causes of the depression were external, expressed faith in his stabilization agreements with corporate leaders, declared that his Farm Board would establish adequate support for commodity prices, and affirmed his conviction that his presidential relief committee could develop adequate aid for the unemployed without direct federal involvement. One may grant that it was still possible to hope for the best at that point; over the next twelve months, however, Hoover and his advisers moved increasingly into denial of a rushing economic catastrophe.

The outgoing Congress, many of its members fresh from meetings with constituents, was far less complacent. It provided Hoover with a preview of the conflict he could expect from its successor, which would convene in December 1931. Dissent came from Western and Midwestern progressives whose cultural and intellectual roots were in early twentieth century reform and from newer-style liberals who functioned as representatives of an urban working class composed primarily of ethnic and religious minorities. The first group had carried the burden of protest through the twenties. Among the Republican senators affiliated with it were George Norris of Nebraska, Robert La Follette, Jr., of Wisconsin, and Bronson Cutting of New Mexico; among the Democratic senators, Thomas J. Walsh and Burton K. Wheeler, both of Montana. The second group represented the future of liberal reform in America; in 1930, its two most important leaders on Capitol Hill were both New Yorkers, the colorful independent radical (if nominal Republican) congressman, Fiorello La Guardia, and the quieter but incomparably more effective Democratic senator, Robert F. Wagner. The doctrinaire progressives usually had near-unanimous support from the Democrats, waiting to take control of the House at the end of the year and scenting a big victory in the 1932 elections. From late 1930 on, Hoover faced a congressional majority that was convinced much more had to be done about the Depression and certain that the answers lay in greatly accelerated government activity.

Senator Norris managed to secure congressional passage of a plan he had pushed throughout the twenties—the federal operation of a hydroelectric facility and nitrate plant at Muscle Shoals, Alabama, as a pilot project for government-owned electrical utilities and federally subsidized fertilizer production. Hoover responded with a sharp veto, rejecting "government barter in the markets" with the declaration: "This is not liberalism, it is degeneration."[20] Wagner secured passage of bills mandating extensive federal planning for public works to be put into effect in an economic slump, increasing federal statistical gathering capabilities, and establishing a federally funded system of employment bureaus. Hoover vetoed all three; he suffered overrides on the first two, but the administration moved with glacial slowness to implement the new laws. By the time Congress adjourned at the beginning of March, a pattern of presidential-congressional stalemate was firmly established.

Convinced that Congress was far more of a hindrance than a help in fighting the depression, knowing that the new Democratic one would be more difficult, the president hoped for a spring recovery, then hung on grimly when one did not materialize. Increasingly, he drew a line in the sand against federal relief programs. "Shall we abandon the philosophy and creed of our people for 150 years?" he asked in a speech in Indianapolis that June. "Shall we establish a dole from the Federal Treasury?" Faced with an unprecedented crisis, Hoover was falling back on his bedrock values. He also was losing his old image as a Great Engineer and a man of action while acquiring a new one as a paralyzed president losing touch with reality.[21]

Hoover still had his moments. His war debt moratorium displayed him as a statesman at his best. He pushed the proposal through in intensive negotiations with the reluctant French and over the know-nothing opposition of many American politicians, including most of the progressive bloc. Still, a one-year suspension was the best he could obtain.

As the economy stagnated, so did both government finances and the banking system. Fiscal year 1931 came to an end on June 30 with a whopping $500 million deficit (in a total budget of $3.6 billion). Some states increased their relief programs but invariably had to raise taxes to do so, thus draining money from the private economy. Bank failures became more frequent, but the Federal Reserve system balked at an injection of funds to prop up the rickety American banking structure. After Britain abandoned the gold standard, defense of the dollar became an important objective, competing with depression and unemployment. The Fed actually raised interest rates, thereby administering another blow to the economy.

By December 1931, unemployment was at nineteen percent and the nation's gross national product had declined about twenty-five percent from its 1929 level. The president's earlier stabilization agreements with industrial leaders had become unsustainable. As employment declined, wages and prices fell sharply, creating a classical deflationary spiral. The collapse of world trade left no hope for an export-driven recovery. Hoover, forced at last to contend with the congress elected a year earlier, privately realized that he would have to move a step or two beyond his original anti-depression designs.

By then, the presidential campaign season was just months away. Already looming large as a possible opponent was the Democratic governor of New York, Franklin D. Roosevelt. Roosevelt had established a

Temporary Emergency Relief Administration (TERA) with a large appropriation and secured a state income tax increase to fund it. TERA could only dent the growing unemployment totals, but it was the most ambitious such state program in the country. Roosevelt had defended the program as a social necessity, not an unavoidable evil. He had staked out positions on economic and social legislation that made him acceptable to almost all progressives and liberals. Extraordinarily popular in his home state, he was sure to carry it against almost any challenger. He possessed a great name, abundant charm, and rare talent in using the new medium of radio. No one doubted he would run for the Democratic presidential nomination.[22]

By the beginning of 1932, Herbert Hoover had only several months left to achieve an economic turnaround.

The Depression had stunned a prosperous United States, bringing misery to the once-satisfactory lives of millions of people, creating unexpected crises for public policy, and threatening Hoover's ideal of ordered capitalism. In Britain and Germany, it had simply made worse already unsatisfactory situations. The British, more secure in their identity, had reacted with an impulse of national unity, rejecting politics as usual, renouncing pure market liberalism, and embracing a form of conservatism that sought to provide minimal assistance to the needy while asking for increased sacrifices from the well-off. The MacDonald-Baldwin regime affirmed the role of government, but had no recovery plan other than to hunker down while the business cycle ran its course. Its move toward tariff protection, not all that different from that of many other nations, had more than an economic purpose; it also affirmed the unique identity of Great Britain and its empire/commonwealth. A substantial majority of the people believed in its fairness.

Germany, a superficially similar economy, reacted very differently, embracing a politics of fragmentation that was a product of defeat, hyperinflation, and a gnawing reparations issue. Germany's political institutions, the product of a postwar rationalist reconstruction with few roots in the nation's history, also encouraged fragmentation. Proportional representation gave extremist groups easier access to political power than in Britain or the United States. An intense class consciousness discouraged a politics of national unity and submerged concepts of political civility and mutual equity. Most ominously, the one political force demonstrating some success in reaching beyond narrow group identities was the Nazi party. The fate of the Weimar Republic was not yet certain, but few thoughtful observers could feel a sense of optimism.

In this most severe crisis of modern capitalism, Britain had rejected "the left" in the form of the Labour party. Germany appeared to be trending in that direction also. The left, in the sense of a class-based socialist party, simply did not exist in the United States. All three nations were moving toward bigger government, but in very different and uncertain ways. The British election of 1931 gave the National government up to five years to play out its program. The German political system assured only continued instability for the foreseeable future. The United States would make its decision in the scheduled 1932 presidential election.

HEADLINES, NEWS PHOTOS, AND MOVIE NEWSREELS

{1932}

FEBRUARY 29   Permanent British Tariff; High Bar for American Imports

MAY 31   Hindenburg Ousts Brüning; Opposes Parceling Big Estates and Higher Taxes

JULY   *Adolf Hitler, dressed in Nazi paramilitary uniform, speaks to a big election campaign rally. Loud, angry, intense, he denounces Weimar democracy. "I have given myself one goal—to sweep these thirty political parties out of Germany. We have one aim, and we will follow it fanatically and ruthlessly to the grave."* (Newsreel)

AUGUST 1   Right Parties Fail to Carry Germany; Nazi Seats Doubled; Ten Slain on Eve

AUGUST 21   12 Separate Trade Pacts Signed at Ottawa; Parley Ends After All-night Dispute

NOVEMBER 6   *A long file of men march down a highway toward London. Some hold banners declaring "Down with the Means Test." Lancashire women marchers receive food from sympathizers. Central London experiences riotous disorder. Baton-wielding mounted police ride into unruly crowds. Marchers commandeer trucks to escape the police. Two bobbies restrain an unruly demonstrator.* (New York Times Rotogravure Section, "England's Hunger Marchers: First Photos of the Army of the Unemployed on its Invasion of London")

NOVEMBER 7   Hitler's Vote Cut, Communists Gain, in Reich Election

{1933}

JANUARY 31   Hitler Made Chancellor of Germany; Coalition Cabinet Limits Power

FEBRUARY 26   Chamberlain Says Britain Can't Return to Gold Until War Debts Are Settled

{ 2 }

PLUMBING THE DEPTHS

BRITAIN AND GERMANY, FALL 1931–WINTER 1933

Dynamic Forces: New Leaders, Terrible Choices

Charismatic leadership usually emerges out of a widespread sense of crisis, whether material or psychic, international or internal. The Great Depression provided crisis aplenty, magnified the appeal of some leaders—Mussolini was perhaps the prime example—and brought forth numerous midget Caesars—Salazar in Portugal, Metaxas in Greece, Gombos in Hungary among them. Several of the nations of northern and western Europe managed to get along with politicians-as-usual. The two most important were France and Britain. The French lurched from crisis to crisis under a succession of unstable premierships. Britain made do with the purposeful conservatism of Stanley Baldwin and Neville Chamberlain. The two large nations most severely impacted by the economic collapse needed more. It was the destiny of Adolf Hitler and Franklin Roosevelt to represent to the world the terrible choices that loomed out of the depression—totalitarianism v. democracy, racialist nationalism v. pluralist inclusionism, violent nihilism v. humanist optimism.

From late 1931 through the winter of 1933, the economies of the developed Western world seemed to career downwards at the speed of an out-of-control freight train on a steep, curving grade. Political leaders struggled as best they could with forces they hardly understood and for which they had only the sketchiest of guides. In general, their measures were behind the curve of a rapidly declining world economy, adequate perhaps for a situation that had existed months earlier but obsolete when put into effect. No regime—neither in Germany, nor Britain, nor the United States—could prevent sharply increasing mass unemployment and misery. The task was less recovery than endurance—either facilitated or made all but hopeless by political systems that reflected the strength and unity of the different peoples caught up in the maelstrom.

Germany: Democracy in Retreat

Hitler

Adolf Hitler became chancellor of Germany on January 30, 1933. That evening, he stood at an upper window of the *Reichschancellery* and watched thousands of torch-bearing storm troopers march below him. A vast crowd extended the fascist salute. President Hindenburg, ebbing in physical strength and mental powers, stood at an adjoining window, perhaps wondering what he had wrought.

To many Germans and alert foreigners on both sides of the Atlantic, something new, dangerous, and sinister seemed to have happened. Many others, however, assumed that Hitler and the party he headed amounted to no more than just another transient presence in the kaleidoscope of German politics. Hitler had ostentatiously rejected an armed seizure of power, been appointed to office by legitimate means, and allowed only two relatively powerless Cabinet positions for his party. The bastard offspring of an obscure Austrian civil servant, he was a parvenue; for most of his political career he was not permitted even to vote in Germany. Neither he nor his party ever came close to winning the votes of a majority of the German electorate in a free election. The men who gave him the chancellorship were aristocrats. Experienced in politics, leaders by birth, long accustomed to the exercise of power, they knew they could manage him.

The man and the movement he headed possessed will and dynamism beyond their comprehension. The window at the chancellery was at the end of a long road that had taken Hitler from impoverishment to decorated military service to politics, insurrection, imprisonment, and electoral rebirth. From the publication of the first volume of *Mein Kampf* in 1925, he had laid down his objectives and followed them tenaciously, rejecting every effort to co-opt him with offers of lesser posts. He espoused a simple-minded Darwinism that posited struggle and survival of the fittest as the means of racial and national improvement. Unlike most soldiers who had survived combat, he saw war as the ultimate human endeavor. He had never played down in any way his hatred of the Jews or non-Germanic peoples, nor had he attempted in the slightest to conceal his intention of becoming an absolute dictator. He based his movement on the savage ideals of total obedience to an all-powerful leader whose authority was based on raw force. Instinctively, he understood that extreme times welcomed extreme leadership.

His charisma was not apparent from his appearance. Speaking to huge rallies, and thence to much bigger audiences via radio, perhaps motivated by his own history of illegitimacy, powerlessness, and defeat, he passionately voiced the rage and bitterness of a huge number of Germans. The American journalist Mary Lee saw him speak at a rally in the summer of 1932. Up close, he appeared remarkably unprepossessing, by no means as imposing as Mussolini, possibly "a waiter at a restaurant, a good, reliable head porter at a hotel." When he spoke, she realized that the source of his power was his ability to connect with "the longing of the individual to lose himself in the crowd."[1] He did not sway the crowd; the crowd swayed him. He expressed its thoughts, spoke its words, appropriated its anger. He signaled his receptiveness to new approaches by using an airplane to campaign across Germany. Some of his lieutenants were street thugs, but others were organizers and propagandists of the first order. Along with his message of rage, he preached traditional values of work, order, and morality.

Above all, and like all successful political leaders, he had an instinct for power. In a matter of months, he would become the effective dictator of Germany, having suppressed all significant opposition, determined to lead his country to recovery, self-respect, and a greatness that would last a thousand years. His design for doing this was openly proclaimed—racial purification, national expansion, conquest. Those who took him seriously in 1933 foresaw a terrible future.

It was Heinrich Brüning's destiny to preside over the meltdown of Weimar liberalism. The chancellor continued his administration as, in effect, an appointed dictator into mid-1932, steadily playing out a losing hand, undisturbed by a Reichstag that seldom met. Perhaps most to his credit was his opposition, consisting primarily of the Communist party, the Nazis, and the right-wing German National People's party, politically affiliated with the ultra-conservative veterans' organization the *Stahlhelm* (Steel Helmet). Brüning remained in power solely because the Social Democrats, the only substantial democratic bloc left in the parliamentary body, saw him as the least dangerous national leader and refused to vote against him.

Brüning's attempts to deal with the deepening depression were extensive and in a sense heroic. Desperate to assure Germany's international creditors that the Reich could keep its financial house in order, mindful of the deeply ingrained middle-class fear of inflation, he ruled by decree, pursuing policies in line with the deflationary trend that was wrecking the world economy. Government workers, pensioners, and the unemployed all took stiff cuts in wages and benefits; the middle class paid higher taxes; business faced new levies on their revenues.

In December 1931, the government inflicted cuts not only on public wages but also on all private wages covered by collective bargaining agreements, increased business taxes, cut interest rates on all existing credit agreements and bank deposits, and imposed ten percent reductions on the prices of all industrial commodities. Accepting—and indeed fostering—deflation, Brüning reasoned, was the only way to narrow the national budget deficit, make German goods competitive in shrinking international markets, and save the mark from a devaluation that would poison his efforts to end reparations payments. The measures reflected an increasing belief throughout the developed world that the invisible hand of the market had failed and needed to be supplanted by state planning. The *New York Times* declared "Germany Suspends Capitalism." The real-world effect was to curtail yet further the consumer demand, corporate profitability, and investment incentives upon which economic recovery depended. Seeking to transcend market capitalism with state corporatism, Brüning succeeded only in making the depression even worse.[2]

Through it all, the chancellor pressed hard for his *sine qua non,* an end to the reparations burden. Hopeful that the Hoover moratorium could be made permanent, he periodically cited Germany's dutiful sacrifices, announced that his nation's payments could not be resumed, and asserted with only slight exaggeration that the reparations/war debts system was at the root of the Depression. Brüning could rightly argue that Germany had been financially bled to the point of exhaustion and required relief, but the end of reparations was by this time far from an economic panacea.

The German economy fell precipitously downward in the last several months of 1931. Industrial production, the most common technical measure of booms and depressions, sank to sixty percent of its 1929 peak. At its zenith in 1929, the German economy had provided 19 million jobs. By January 1932, German employment stood at about 12 million. The social insurance system was stretched to the limit. The brute misery behind such numbers encouraged a politics of extremism. The corrosive effects of idleness and loss of meaningful identity created the material for small armies of the discontented.

Years later, a former Communist and a former Nazi recalled the experience for a television interviewer. You had to sign in at the unemployment office every day. Communists, Social Democrats, Nazis were all there. The arguments started, fists flew, chairs were broken up for clubs. The melee spilled out into the streets. Young men with nothing to do could at least fight for the cause of their choice. The political parties organized them into disciplined forces.[3]

It was in this setting that Germany had to hold a presidential election.

President Hindenburg, elected for his first seven-year term in 1925, was eighty-four years old and at a glance an unlikely candidate, but no other German seemed to have a chance of holding the Weimar system together. Privately preferring a restoration of the old empire, he nevertheless had worked tirelessly on behalf of the republic. Given broad emergency powers by the constitution and accustomed to unquestioned command, he may have thought of himself as a more than satisfactory substitute for the old kaiser, who lived in exile across the Dutch border. A war hero with roots in the aristocracy, a *Junker* landowner who liked to think of himself as a yeoman farmer, benignly authoritarian, Hindenburg embodied both the strengths and the weaknesses of traditional Germany. His countrymen saw him as a final link to their nation's pre–World War greatness, prosperity, and political order. He was a Central European version of George Washington, a patriotic totem regarded so reverentially by most of his countrymen that they thought it undignified to cheer him in public. "It would be irreverent to throw up one's hat for such a heroic figure," wrote Emil Lengyel. "Religious devotion to duty is written all over this man, and therein lies his secret."[4]

Hindenburg's major opponent would be Adolf Hitler. Just eight years earlier, Hitler had been briefly imprisoned for leading a failed coup d'etat in Munich. Until the fall of 1930 his National Socialist Workers Party had languished on the fringes of German politics. Suddenly, with the economy steadily worsening, it roused crowds of alienated and displaced Germans who had suffered through the hyperinflation of the early Weimar period, been reduced to misery by the Depression, and felt a bitter resentment against the Allied treatment of Germany after the World War. A nobody by the usual standards of authority, a citizen of Austria who could not even vote in German elections, Hitler had become the major beneficiary of the collapse of the old order.

The Nazi party had become a major presence. If Hitler provided the rhetoric of revolutionary opposition, others built a party structure that collected dues, established a day-to-day presence in much of the country, and put out a constant propaganda drumbeat. By 1932, the Nazis possessed a formidable paramilitary force, the *Sturmabteilung* (SA), or Storm Troops, popularly called the Brownshirts. Numbering perhaps 400,000, the SA was a feared presence in German politics. More a collection of street brawlers than a truly disciplined military unit, it was nonetheless a potential threat to a republic whose outnumbered army would be stretched to the limit in suppressing it. Hitler's major lieutenants—SA commander Ernst Röhm, publicist Joseph Goebbels, war hero Hermann Göring, and trusted secretary Rudolf Hess—were men to be reckoned with, scarcely a notch behind their leader in their amorality, cunning, and lust for power.

Hitler's drive for German leadership was informed by one shrewd judgment. Although he made no secret of his intention to become a dictator, he renounced another *putsch*. In part, no doubt, he did so because it would be risky, but he also understood that only by coming to power through legal means could he claim full legitimacy. He expected to be the beneficiary of the suicide of Weimar liberal democracy. In a public exchange with Brüning at the end of 1931, he rejected the chancellor's contention that an anti-democratic government, even if legally chosen, could not abrogate constitutional rights and procedures: "When a constitution proves itself to be useless for its life, the nation does not die—the constitution is altered."[5]

The Nazi leader ran on a platform of rejectionism. Mincing no words in his unbridled attacks on Brüning, liberal values, and Weimar democracy, he presented himself as a leader who would destroy an existing system and save Germany by placing himself and his party at the head of a new and revived nation. Shrinking from strident criticism of Hindenburg, the Nazi movement nonetheless rejected not simply bourgeois democracy but also the imperial order of Wilhelm II. It was not coincidental that the exiled kaiser and most of the German aristocracy harbored contempt for Hitler. They knew that a Nazi Reich would be a regime of the malcontented and dispossessed in which the old leadership class would be relegated to a peripheral role.

Hitler was one of four candidates. Hindenburg was backed by the Social Democrats, the Center, and a group of small "bourgeois parties." Ernst Thälmann ran as the leader of the Communists. Count Theodor Duesterberg was the candidate of the National People's party and the Stahlhelm. All of Hitler's opponents seemingly had stronger social and institutional roots in German society, but only the old war leader Hindenburg had mass appeal. The Nazi campaign was best organized and its candidate was indisputably the most exciting. Hitler achieved German citizenship and thus made himself eligible for the presidency through an appointment made by the Nazi minister of the interior in the small state of Brunswick. He announced his candidacy only three weeks before the election, then undertook a whirlwind campaign that revealed both his personal energy and the grass roots strength of his party.

Hitler had some large contributors from the world of business and finance. Fritz Thyssen, the steel magnate, was most visible among them, but much of the political treasury came from ordinary dues-paying members, from the sale of SA uniforms, and from individual purchasers of campaign materials and party publications. Particularly notable to foreign observers was the support of the alienated university students. Goebbels, a master of communications, orchestrated large political gatherings, put imposing parades of Brownshirts into the streets, and plastered walls with posters. German state radio excluded the Nazis, but the authorities could not stop short party-produced films from being shown in theaters.

From the beginning, the Nazi campaign centered not on doctrine or program, which were vague in the extreme, but on the Führer himself. Hitler began his campaign by speaking to a rally of 20,000 followers in Berlin's Sportpalast, arriving only after Goebbels and other lieutenants had roused the crowd to a frenzy. Drawing a deafening fifteen-minute ovation, he spoke against a backdrop of uniformed bodyguards, loyal lieutenants, and German flags. Promising a new chapter in German history and a renewal of national honor, he brought the crowd to a state of near-hysteria. Journalists who interviewed Hitler in quiet one-on-one settings usually came away unimpressed. Before huge enthusiastic crowds, he displayed a ferocious charisma that was both frightening and exciting.[6]

On March 13, 1932, Germans went to the polls in an atmosphere of greater uncertainty than could have been imagined a year earlier. To many sober analysts, it seemed no more than an even bet that Germany would stay with "the old gentleman," whose war leadership and national symbolism had to be weighed against the economic catastrophe the country had experienced. Hindenburg prevailed, at first glance overwhelmingly, with 18.6 million votes (49.6 percent) to Hitler's 11.3 million (30.1 percent). Thälmann was a distant third and Duesterberg an inconsequential fourth. It was stunning that the Nazi vote had come uncomfortably close to doubling in raw numbers from the 1930 Reichstag election. It was consequential that Hitler had managed to deny Hindenburg a needed absolute majority and sobering to think of the likely result had Brüning been a presidential candidate in his stead.

The constitution mandated an April 10 runoff election in which all four candidates were free to run again with victory to the largest votegetter. Duesterberg dropped out; his supporters divided between Hindenburg and Hitler. Although Hindenburg was the sure winner, Hitler seized the opportunity to publicize himself and his cause. The government did all it could to muzzle the Nazis. Arguing the need for a holy fortnight before and after Easter Sunday (March 27), it restricted campaigning to the week before the election. Branding the Nazi paramilitary force as a national menace, it placed sharp restrictions on Hitler rallies. Hitler responded dramatically, using an airplane to campaign across Germany, appearing in twenty-one cities in seven days, occasionally not even bothering to remove his aviator's cap. The garb would look silly to a twenty-first century audience but most Germans likely would have connected it with Richthofen, the great Red Baron, rather than Snoopy. No major Western politician had ever conducted such an air campaign. "Hitler over Germany" was yet another triumph of Nazi propaganda.

The vote gave Hindenburg his absolute majority. He increased his total to 19.3 million (53 percent), but contrary to expectations Hitler's total shot up to 13.4 million (36.8 percent). Thälmann was a weaker third. Nearly two out of every three Germans had voted against the Nazis, but only a narrow majority had voted for the candidate of what had become a quasi democracy. The Nazi party had more than doubled its 1930 vote; it appeared likely to emerge with the largest representation in the next Reichstag election. The future of the Weimar Republic had been entrusted to an octogenarian field marshal who did not really believe in it and to an unpopular chancellor who seemed to possess no answers for the continuing economic crisis. Government efforts to manage the Depression had tied its economy in so many knots as to impede recovery. Even the forces of democracy ruled as a constitutional dictatorship. Germany's most dynamic political force was Adolf Hitler.

Briefly, however, the Nazi juggernaut was brought to a halt. Hitler and his lieutenants had great hopes for a breakthrough victory in state elections on April 24. Another intense and innovative campaign brought impressive gains, but the Nazis failed to win power in big, key states. Still, almost everywhere they emerged as the largest single party. In Prussia, which contained two-thirds of Germany's population, they achieved parity with the ruling Social Democratic-Centrist coalition, thereby creating a situation in which effective governance was almost impossible. In Austria, moreover, Nazism was clearly on the rise, having largely supplanted more traditional right-wing paramilitary movements.[7]

The Germany that emerged from the electoral season of early 1932 was a paradox. In many respects, it remained a nation of order and efficiency. Foreign visitors noted the way in which the trains not only ran on time but were well staffed, clean, and served good food. The products of its industry were advanced and of high quality. Its architecture led the world. Its science was at the borders of human knowledge. Even its public services, despite draconian budget cuts, continued at high standards. Yet misery was widespread. In industrial cities, unemployed families of four desperately tried to make do on little more than a dollar (4.29 marks) a day. Agricultural regions were in a state of collapse; in East Prussia, the landed estates were mostly insolvent. The middle classes, under great stress, were increasingly attracted to the Nazis. "During the Presidential campaign one was struck by the fact that there was so much personal animosity and so little discussion of programs or policies," wrote the American journalist Harold Callender. "One had the impression that flags, military music, marching battalions and vehement but vague oratory counted far more." In order to survive, the republic needed convincing signs of economic recovery and shrewd, resourceful leadership.[8]

Industrial production and employment moved upwards in the usual seasonal fashion during the spring and summer of 1932, but at its peak, the German economy regained less than a million of the three and a quarter million jobs that had been lost since mid-1931. Optimists could hope a corner had been turned; realists had to admit that prosperity was nowhere in sight. In this dreary economic setting, the fragile Weimar government self-destructed.[9]

Most of the nation's leaders, Hindenburg and Brüning included, simply did not believe in thoroughgoing liberal democracy. After his reelection, the president spent relatively little time in Berlin, preferring instead his estate in East Prussia. There access to him was difficult and he increasingly was influenced by a small entourage; its most prominent figure was the politically ambitious General Kurt von Schleicher. Schleicher represented an army officer corps and an aristocracy persuaded that the time had come to restore power to the traditional sources of authority in German history. Many of them believed that the Nazis could be used in the process. Ambitious for the chancellorship and doubtless more after Hindenburg left the scene, Schleicher became the chief conspirator in the destruction of the Brüning government.[10]

He first orchestrated the political downfall of the most powerful and respected member of Brüning's cabinet, General Wilhelm Groener, minister of defense and interior. The immediate issue was a ban on the Nazi storm troopers, the SA, which Groener backed in response to demands from many state interior ministers. At Groener's behest, Hindenburg signed an emergency decree on April 13, 1932, ordering its disbandment. Schleicher privately denounced the decree to Hindenburg and also met secretly with Hitler. The two appear to have reached an understanding that if Hitler would tolerate a new right-wing cabinet, it in turn would lift the ban on the SA and call new elections. Hitler ordered a pro forma compliance with the decree, but also demanded a ban on other paramilitary groups, including the Social Democratic Reichsbanner. The Nazis subjected Groener to vehement abuse on the floor of the Reichstag; on May 12, after Hindenburg refused a statement of backing, he resigned.

Brüning left soon afterwards. As unaware as Groener of Schleicher's intrigue, clueless as his rivals about Hitler's strength and purpose, he rejected the one stratagem that might have preserved democracy, a strong alliance with the Prussian state government, also based on a Social Democratic–Center coalition. Amazingly, he even tried to co-opt the Nazis by offering them a junior role in the government. Hitler sharply declined the overture. Obsessed with more budget cuts and looking for a safety valve for urban discontent, Brüning committed the inexplicable mistake of asking Hindenburg to approve a decree that would break up and redistribute the large, bankrupt East Prussian estates to small farmers. Few proposals could have been more obnoxious to the president. On May 30, at Hindenburg's request, Brüning resigned.

Brüning's failure marked the end of the line for what little was left of German liberalism. It was now the destiny of Kurt von Schleicher and his associate Franz von Papen to preside over the meltdown of German conservatism. Following Schleicher's suggestion, Hindenburg designated

Papen as the new chancellor. Americans remembered Papen as a German military attaché who had been expelled from the United States during the World War neutrality period for involvement in espionage and sabotage. A gentleman aristocrat, a former military officer, a monarchist, Papen was a relic of the imperial order with practically no support in the Reichstag. After he formed a "cabinet of barons" with Schleicher as minister of defense, he asked Hindenburg to dissolve the Reichstag, thereby precipitating Germany's third major electoral campaign of 1932. About a week later, the government lifted the ban on the SA.

Schleicher was clearly the primary conspirator, but Hindenburg and Papen were his close colleagues in a common plot widely understood both inside and outside of Germany. They intended to establish an authoritarian rule of the old elites, backed by the army (which would be substantially enlarged) and the right-wing anti-democratic parties, primarily the Nazis and the waning Nationalists. There were widespread rumors that they might try to reestablish the monarchy, possibly in the person of the crown prince, who had endorsed the Nazis in the Prussian election. Whatever their intentions along those lines, they intended to be the primary wielders of power; Hitler, they believed, could be managed.

Their sense of timing could not be faulted. Hindenburg had just won a strong national endorsement. Parliamentary democracy had long been a shambles. In form and operation, the Papen chancellorship would be little different from Brüning's. Moreover, the Old Right had taken power at a time when Germany was closer than ever to two goals that Brüning had worked for: an end to reparations and allied acquiescence in German rearmament. On July 9, a conference of European nations at Lausanne ended with an accord that amounted to a cancellation of war debts and reparations, pending U.S. agreement. Papen and his colleagues walked away from the gathering triumphantly displaying a victory which they had done little to earn. In the coming months, they aggressively asserted Germany's right to military parity. At the same time, they distanced themselves from Brüning's unpopular economy measures. In a move that was more symbolic than substantive, the government announced a minuscule public works program to employ young men under twenty-five even as it decreed yet another round of relief cuts.[11]

An entrenched dictatorship would require control of the Prussian government, under the Social Democrat Otto Braun. Widely considered the source of German militarism, Prussia was equally a stronghold of liberal democratic values with a tough, well-trained police force. The reinstatement of the SA, however, threatened to plunge Prussia into chaos. One lethal skirmish after another between Brownshirts and Communists or Social Democrats followed with the Papen government giving respectful attention to Nazi charges that the Prussian police was a tool of the Communists. On July 20, eleven days before the Reichstag elections, Papen issued a decree dismissing the Prussian government and effectively placing himself in control of it. Army detachments efficiently enforced the order. Displacing the Center-Left coalition in a critically important state, Papen and Schleicher had staged what amounted to a coup d'etat in pursuit of their own ambitions. They also had enormously benefited the Nazis.

The Reichstag election campaign was the first since the Nazis had emerged as a major party in September 1930. It underscored how far they had come in less than two years. Hitler once again crisscrossed Germany by airplane, speaking in two or three cities a day to large rallies of devoted followers who exchanged precious marks for admission tickets. No other candidate approached his appeal to the young and to women. The SA fought the opposition in the streets of every large city. On the eve of the balloting, at least five Germans were killed in urban brawls and scores were injured. The campaign, many observers believed, was the worst example yet of the way in which German politics had descended into violence.

Such disorder served the purposes of Schleicher and Papen. The SA's physical battering of the Center-Left weakened their main opposition. The general atmosphere of nihilistic disorder discredited party politics and parliaments. In a radio address the night before the election, Papen presented himself and his colleagues as patriots with no party attachments, interested only in the whole nation and thus uniquely qualified to govern, and as the tribunes of German liberation and equality in the world of nations. Vaguely but portentously, he proclaimed the need to "remodel" the constitution and called for a Reichstag willing to work with a strong government. The import was clear: authoritarianism had trumped democracy, nationalism had trumped liberalism.

None of the candidates advanced a comprehensive or compelling economic program beyond a common opposition to continued reparations payments. Papen talked generally, and on the whole constructively, about limited public works, pulling back from excessive government subsidies, and liberation of the economy. He had no solid blueprint. Brüning and the Center-Left offered simply more of the same austerity the government had pursued for two years. Hitler advanced no discernible plan. The Depression had made possible the chaos of German politics, but an inability to develop credible solutions had driven it to the margins of political debate. Instead, national grievances that had smoldered since 1919 eclipsed the economic crisis.[12]

There were few surprises in the vote totals and little to lift the spirits of friends of democracy. The big winners were the Nazis, who increased their representation from 107 seats to 230, their vote percentage from 18.3 to 37.3, their numerical vote from 6.4 million to 13.75 million. Their right-wing rival, the German National People's party, uninspiringly led by Alfred Hugenberg, won only 5.9% and 37 seats. The Center party and its Bavarian affiliate gained ten seats, but the Social Democrats lost an equal number. The Communists picked up twelve seats. The small bourgeois parties that had provided key backing for the Center-Left suffered losses just short of a total wipeout. The new Reichstag had 608 members. The Nazis and National People's party could muster 267 votes; the Center-Left and what remained of the bourgeois bloc, a maximum of 252; the Communists, 89. The election had returned no natural majority.[13]

Efforts to establish a government that could gain the support of both Hindenburg and a Reichstag majority of 305 centered on bringing in the Nazis. The National party would have little choice but to follow; possibly the Center, or at least a portion of it, could be brought along. Schleicher and Papen remained convinced they could control Hitler. The leading army officers with whom they were in league saw the SA as a potential military reserve of great value.

Hitler would have none of it. Overriding lieutenants who were prepared to take a gradualist path to power, he rejected appointment as vice chancellor and a deal to put the Nazis in control of several cabinet ministries. He demanded the chancellorship, declaring that he would then push through the Reichstag legislation that would give him the dictatorial emergency powers that rested with the presidency. The demand appeared irrational. Many observers rightly sensed that the Nazis had peaked with no prospect of a majority. Hindenburg was outraged. He could accept the idea of a dictatorship administered by men like himself, but not by a common agitator. In a personal meeting at the presidential palace, he rejected the Nazi leader's terms and rebuked him in the manner of a field marshal dealing with an unruly corporal.

The meeting underscored the fundamental class division within the German right. On the one side was Hitler's populistic nationalism; on the other, the traditional authoritarianism of the aristocracy, the officer corps, and those who looked to them for leadership. Hitler felt it keenly. "If God had wanted things to be the way they are, we would have come into the world wearing a monocle," he told his followers in a speech three weeks later. His obstinance upset other party leaders who saw power receding from their grasp, but no one dared cross him.[14]

The government accepted the challenge. Papen, having already effectively seized the issue of German military parity, began to develop a cautious and conservative economic recovery program in collaboration with industrial leaders. He hoped to nudge the mild economic upturn into full-fledged prosperity. Having already secured an end to reparations, he began to push for a scaling-down of foreign-held German private debt with the hope of thereby increasing the amount of capital available for productive investment. He initiated a job creation program fueled by tax credits for employers and an enlargement of the modest public works program he had already established. Emblematic of his close association with big business, however, he also instituted regulations to curb the power of unions and allowed businesses to cut wages to finance new jobs. Such policies had some merit in an environment of deflation and mass unemployment, but they demonstrated the class basis of the government and drew vehement opposition from organized labor. Papen responded that his program would create 1.75 million jobs by the end of 1933.[15]

Given the climate of German politics, the survival of the government through the first few weeks of the new Reichstag was problematic enough. Papen and Schleicher justified their rule as a rejection of parties and special interest politics. Hindenburg gave the rationale his hearty endorsement. "Always put the Fatherland high above political parties," he told students who visited him at his East Prussian estate. The Reichstag convened at the beginning of September, seething with hostility toward the cabinet. Its oldest member, the eighty-seven-year-old Communist revolutionary Clara Zetkin, opened the proceedings with a scathing denunciation of the greed and corruption of every other party. Then a coalition of Nazis, Nationalists, and Centrists elected Hermann Göring as the Reichstag's permanent president. On September 12, the Communists presented a surprise resolution of no-confidence in the government. Göring accepted it for an immediate vote, although the government had not yet formally presented its program; with dubious parliamentary rulings, he prevented Papen from speaking. To nobody's surprise, the resolution carried by an astounding 512–42.[16]

Hindenburg and his chief ministers gave serious consideration to the establishment of a presidential dictatorship. The failure of party and parliamentary politics had to be writ large in the consciousness of every sober German looking for a way out of what had become a constitutional as well as an economic crisis. In the end he, Schleicher, and Papen decided against a coup. Such a move would surely be met with some resistance, perhaps in the form of strikes from the trade unions and the Social Democrats, revolutionary activity from the Communists, and perhaps armed insurgency from the SA. The latter possibility threatened the disintegration of the right-wing bloc the government wanted to consolidate. The army could contain strikes and would destroy the Communists with gusto; it would have more difficulty mustering either the will or the power necessary to suppress the SA. Giving itself the maximum time legally allowed to continue establishing itself, promote economic recovery, and urge constitutional revision toward a presidential state, the government set November 6 as the new election date.

The contest would be primarily a test of Nazi staying power. The party presented for the first time a comprehensive economic recovery program. It called for extensive state control of the economy, national self-sufficiency (autarky), the abandonment of the gold standard, new means of credit based upon the productive power of the nation, the nationalization of the banking system, and the development of a home market in which German agriculture and industry, protected from foreign competition, would produce goods to be consumed by workers paid fair wages. It proposed returning hundreds of thousands of urban workers to small farms on reclaimed marshland. The state would control prices and manage industrial expansion, favoring it in areas that needed enlargement, prohibiting it in those that already were overbuilt. A special income tax would finance a fund for creating employment. Farmers would receive discounted credit. A generous social insurance and old-age pension system would be maintained. All young men—no exceptions for "the educated or the propertied"—would be enrolled in compulsory labor battalions, at once serving the state and dignifying manual labor.

The manifesto emphasized the "socialistic" side of National Socialism; in numerous ways it meshed well with the traditional German tolerance of a large, intrusive state managing the economy. A highly developed form of what political theorists call "corporatism," it doubtless had been suggested in large measure by Mussolini's organization of the Italian economy. Unlike the Communists or even the Social Democrats, both of whom wanted to place power in the hands of the working class, the Nazis advocated a "de-proletarianized" nation in which *all* classes would be harnessed together in mutually beneficial service to the state. Their blueprint combined the appeals of racist nationalism and socialistic organization but abandoned the concept of class revolution in favor of the idea of a unified people. This was the essential nature of twentieth-century fascism.[17]

The Nazis were nonetheless hard-pressed. The previous political campaigns had emptied their treasury. Contributions from large business interests, never very great, were harder than ever to come by. Papen's program of government support for (but not control of) industry and disdain for labor unions was much more attractive to most business leaders than the Nazi economic plan. In the beginning widely considered a lightweight, the chancellor performed well as a public orator and radio speaker. Most troubling of all for the Nazis, the economic recovery continued into the fall with industrial production moving steadily up and employment staying at its summer levels. It was possible to believe that a positive direction had been established. In large cities across Germany, German SA men found themselves working the streets with tin donation containers. The other parties were about equally broke. By mutual agreement and state decree, the campaign was limited to a week.[18]

Germany went to the polls for the last time in 1932 on November 6, just two days before the American presidential election. The results seemed to bring reassuring confirmation that the Nazi wave was receding; otherwise, however, they contained little hopeful news. The total vote declined by 1.4 million from the July election, bringing the size of the Reichstag down from 608 seats to 584. The Nazis were hit hardest, their total dropping by just over two million (14.6 percent); their Reichstag seats fell from 230 to 196. The German National People's party increased its representation from 37 to 52 seats. The Center-Left coalition also lost seats (from 230 to 211) but likewise decreased only slightly as a proportion of the whole. The Communists attracted nearly 700,000 additional votes, electing 100 deputies, up from 89. Yet, even at this—their high-water mark of the Weimar era—they controlled only a sixth of the legislative body. Many observers in and outside of Germany celebrated the Nazi setback, but Hitler's party still had more seats than any other and the Nazi-Nationalist block was the largest natural coalition. The election had changed practically nothing.[19]

A grand coalition of the Center-Right might have been put together if Hitler had been willing to play a subordinate role. Instead, he continued to rebuff the misgivings of other Nazi notables and to insist on the chancellorship with dictatorial authority. The demand was acceptable to no other party. The other alternative was to do what Hindenburg and Papen clearly preferred—dissolve the Reichstag and rule by presidential decree. Amazingly, they were stopped short by the army. Reichswehr contingency planners, reflecting the genuine caution of the high command and Schleicher's hopes of undercutting the increasingly independent Papen, predicted a worst-case but far from impossible scenario—general strikes, Communist violence, Nazi noncooperation, and a civil war that might pit the armed forces against ninety percent of the population. On December 2, Hindenburg, persuaded to continue the game of parliamentary politics, dismissed a bitter Papen and appointed Schleicher as his successor.[20]

Schleicher became chancellor just in time to bask in the glory of another triumph. On December 11, a five-power disarmament conference in Geneva capped months of negotiations by accepting Germany's long-standing demand for military equality. The Christmas season was the happiest of the past few years, with no political crisis and little turmoil in the streets. The government issued amnesties to ten thousand convicts serving time for political violence. Germans celebrated their nation's new status as an equal in the international community. The Nazi party, already fading as a result of the November elections, seemed on the brink of collapse by Christmas Day. Yet underneath all the optimism and temporary placidity, the grave problem of five to six million unemployed endured. Approximately half of them had exhausted their insurance benefits and were dependent on local poor relief programs, which were collapsing everywhere. So long as the Depression continued, it would manufacture social dynamite.[21]

Schleicher hoped to put together a broad-based Cabinet that would include the Nazis by offering the vice-chancellorship to, if not Hitler, then Gregor Strasser, deputy leader of the Nazi party. He also sought to establish good relations with every other party save the Communists by backing away from the anti-labor policies of Papen. Finally, he hoped that the upsurge in industrial production would continue and expected to augment it with a stronger jobs program.

Hitler not only rejected Schleicher's offer, but forced Strasser to resign from party office. Nor did the economy cooperate; production continued strong, but at the end of the year the usual winter increase in unemployment hit hard, adding more than a million workers to the rolls, creating understandable fears that the recovery had been aborted. Moreover,

Franz von Papen, who as chancellor had become Hindenburg's closest confidant, wanted revenge against his successor. He began talks of his own with Hitler. By late January, Schleicher, unable to construct a Reichstag majority, found himself forced to ask Hindenburg to dissolve the legislative body and establish a presidential government, in short to effect the coup d'etat that Schleicher himself had orchestrated army opposition against when Papen had advocated it.

Papen, after Byzantine negotiations with the Nazis and the Nationalists, countered with a semi-palatable alternative of a government of national concentration in which Hitler would be chancellor, Papen vice-chancellor, and only two other Nazis would be in the cabinet—Wilhelm Frick as minister of the interior and Hermann Göring as commissar for both aviation and Prussian internal affairs. Hindenburg agreed with some reluctance; both he and Papen believed that they could control the Nazi leader.[22]

Even in the depths of the Depression, the political debate in Germany (the reparations issue included) had centered around issues of national identity and international respect. These had occurred amidst unresolved constitutional debates that stemmed from the Weimar attempt to impose liberal democracy on a culture that was at its heart still authoritarian. The Depression not only created additional problems of unemployment and mass misery, it also exacerbated the earlier disputes by creating intense large-scale alienation. Structurally flawed, never possessing the allegiance of large numbers of Germans, the Weimar system gridlocked.

Still, Hitler's victory was not predetermined. The republic might have been replaced by a right-wing dictatorship under the aegis of Hindenburg if the old field marshal had been capable of dealing with the rivalries between his lieutenants. Such a regime would have been an unpleasant chapter in German history, but probably would have passed with little lasting consequence. Instead, largely because of the personal ambitions and weaknesses of the men around the president, the republic got the worst possible alternative. As Henry Turner has observed, contingency prevailed over determinacy. Chance and personality overrode rational calculation.[23]

On January 30, Hitler accepted appointment as chancellor. Hindenburg dissolved the Reichstag and issued orders for new elections on March 5. That night, Hitler stood at a window of the Reichschancellery, received the salute of his cheering followers in the great square below, and reviewed torch-bearing SA formations. Optimists still tried to convince themselves that this was just another phase in the troubled history of a young republic. Realists knew better. The depression had unleashed its most terrible and dynamic force.

Britain: Austerity and Stabilization

The United Kingdom was nominally a mass democracy, but observers who got past the formalities of mass suffrage understood that less than a thousand people really ran the country. They governed not by force, but by deference, and reflected the widespread sense that the upper crust had to provide for those at the bottom of society. Usually Oxford or Cambridge men, they were less likely to be aristocrats than wealthy men of the upper middle classes, aspiring perhaps to become titled nobility but endowed in their privilege by forebears who had made their own way in the world and had prospered as businessmen and politicians. In 1931, the two most important exemplars of the type were Stanley Baldwin and Neville Chamberlain.

Mr. Baldwin

Surely no other English statesman was so often photographed puffing reflectively on a pipe. The only son of a wealthy and paternalistic Worcestershire ironmaster, Stanley Baldwin fused the solid attributes of the successful bourgeois industrialist with the traditional sense of responsibility of his gentry forebears. Elected to his deceased father's Conservative party House of Commons seat in 1908, he served capably, if stolidly, in a series of important positions. In October 1922, he emerged as the leader of the Conservative insurgents against continuation of the wartime Conservative-Liberal coalition led by the Liberal David Lloyd George. In a balance-tipping speech to Tory members of the House of Commons, he attacked the roguish, if magnetic, Lloyd George with a declaration that epitomized his own approach to political leadership: "*a dynamic force can be a very terrible thing.*" The insurgents took control of the Conservative party, terminated the coalition, and formed a government under the ailing Andrew Bonar Law. In May 1923, Baldwin replaced him as prime minister. He lost the post to Ramsay MacDonald a few months later when a general election produced a Labour-Liberal coalition, then regained it in the 1924 election. For nearly five years he led the country, but the 1929 election brought MacDonald back to the premiership. In 1931, Baldwin returned as Lord President of the Council in the new, predominantly Conservative National coalition. From the beginning, he was the dominant figure in the new government.

Baldwin's subsequent and rather exaggerated identification with the failed policy of appeasement makes it easy to forget the depth of his popular appeal. An Englishman's Englishman, he epitomized the best virtues of the provincial upper-middle classes. Most comfortable in the role of a country squire, he evoked the rural England of an earlier and simpler era, identifying the greatness of the nation with its landscape, providing relief from the intractable problems of declining industrial strength and imperial reach. Scorning modish intellectuals and partisan ideologues, he expressed with sincerity, warmth, and articulateness sentiments of morality, domesticity, patriotism, and class reconciliation that touched the hearts of his nation's broad middle class. He understood that urban Britain had an affection for a romanticized rural past: "I speak not as the man in the street even, but as a man in a field-path, a much simpler person steeped in tradition and impervious to new ideas." A cousin of Rudyard Kipling, he wrote of rural England with a poetic flair seldom found in practical politicians. From time to time, he would talk of his desire to return to Worcestershire and tend to his pigs as if he were a simple farmer. Yet he was the first major British statesman to enhance his leadership by his radio talks. Speaking, as he put it, as if he were "addressing 2 or 3 people round a fire," he anticipated in style and effectiveness Franklin D. Roosevelt's fireside chats.[24]

His later eclipse by Churchill makes it easy to forget that for most of the interwar years, he overshadowed the erratic Churchill and every other British politician. He did so in part by making a virtue of his ordinariness. At heart a little Englander, he shrank from commitments to Europe, accepted independent dominion status for India, moved his party toward trade protectionism, and, during the abdication crisis of 1936, preserved the middle-class integrity of the crown. Although he galvanized the successful national resistance to the General Strike of 1926, he cared as deeply for the working class as his father had cared for his individual iron workers. A one-nation Conservative in the tradition of Disraeli, sometimes called a "Tory socialist," he pursued a vigorous policy of social benefits to the extent that fiscal responsibility allowed it. He prevailed because the people so thoroughly identified with him. Both his strengths and his follies were theirs. Britain's institutions of representative democracy endured unchallenged through the Depression because of the fundamental decency of leaders like him.

Mr. Chamberlain

"At no time in the past forty years have the British people been so leaderless as they are today," wrote the eminent English journalist Wickham Steed toward the end of 1933. Prime Minister MacDonald was old, tired, and clinging to office, Mr. Lloyd George likewise past his time, if still an attention-attracting gadfly in the House of Commons. Mr. Baldwin was too self-effacing and seemingly detached, Winston Churchill erratically brilliant but out of the government and totally without public confidence. The leading Liberals inside the government—Sir Herbert Samuel, Sir Archibald Sinclair, Walter Runciman, and Sir John Simon—were "first-rate, second-rate men, a trifle chilly withal and incapable of either the grand manner or the grand thoughts that stir a people to the marrow of its bones." The venerable Conservative statesman Sir Austen Chamberlain, widely respected but seventy years old and in poor health, had been relegated to the back benches. His younger half-brother, Neville, had made himself heir-apparent to the Tory leadership as a sound and tireless chancellor of the exchequer, but he ignited few emotions. "An honest, upright, plain-thinking and hard-working man, Mr. Chamberlain nevertheless commands more respect than enthusiasm, and he is a name rather than a personality to the nation at large."[25]

Sixty-two years old when the National government was formed in August 1931, Neville Chamberlain was the product of a Birmingham industrial family that assumed leadership as a matter of course and felt a keen sense of social responsibility for the welfare of the urban working classes. His family had been Unitarian in religion and entrepreneurial in business. His father, Joseph Chamberlain, had sold the family metalworking enterprise for a small fortune, gone into politics, and made himself one of the most magnetic British statesmen of the late Victorian age. As colonial secretary, he preached trade protectionism and imperial preference, established a reputation as a friend of the working man, and frequently overshadowed the prime ministers under whom he served.

As a young man, Neville left politics to his father and half-brother; in his twenties, he expended seven years of his life—and £50,000—in an arduous effort to develop the family sisal plantation in the Bahamas. The ill-conceived enterprise was a total loss. After years of psychological recovery, business success back in Birmingham, and admirable civic duty, he moved squarely into politics. His rise was rapid—the Birmingham city council in 1911 at the age of forty-two, lord mayor in 1915, minister of national service in 1917, the House of Commons in 1918, chancellor of the exchequer in Baldwin's short-lived cabinet of 1923–24, and minister of health in Baldwin's second government, 1924–29. In the latter position, he demonstrated a clear understanding that the working class, suffering from the postwar industrial decline exacerbated by the overvalued pound, required expanded social services. His ambitious agenda of legislation included housing, health insurance, pensions, and public assistance; it represented the zenith of British social reform during the three decades between 1914 and 1945.

Nonetheless, he was no charismatic man of the people. His half-brother, Austen, privately commented, "N's manner freezes people. His workers think that he does not appreciate what they do for him. Everyone respects him and he makes no friends."[26]

Fated to be remembered by later generations as a tired and weak diplomatist, he was widely perceived as the main source of energy in the National government. Yet he was an unlikely leader of an attempt to deal with a modern economic catastrophe. He had been born at the midpoint of Victoria's reign and had formed his worldview in its last and greatest years. His wing shirt collars reflected his affection for what he described as the age "before the days of motors and telephones, when new discoveries in science were thrilling the world, and the centre of Africa was still painted yellow on the map." With Baldwin content to operate as the government's chief rhetorician and behind-the-scenes manipulator, it fell to Chamberlain to develop an anti-Depression policy that would stay within the bounds of economic orthodoxy while manifesting the concern for all social classes that was implicit in the National party ideal and that he himself deeply felt. Steed notwithstanding, most observers thought him successful.[27]

The Politics of Stability and Anti-Charisma

The National government was gray and unexciting, but nevertheless commanded authority and respect. Progress was slow and austere, demanding widespread sacrifice. Occasional violent protests indicated pockets of serious dissatisfaction. Yet the National ideal, as much as the men behind it, won wide support. In operation, it most notably failed to deal with the fundamental contradiction between its hopes for international economic agreements and its protectionism. Still, by early 1933, the Depression within Britain had been stabilized, with modest signs of recovery. More, it seemed, would require transnational cooperation that had to include the active participation and leadership of the United States. As Franklin D. Roosevelt assumed the presidency at the end of the winter of 1932–33, the long wait for America to achieve its transition to a new regime was over. Whether the transfer would bring Britain the relief it needed was uncertain.

In a period of major upheaval, the National government strove somehow to combine austerity with social accomplishment. An American looking back on it from the perspective of the mid-1930s might have seen it as an effort to combine Herbert Hoover's economics with Franklin Roosevelt's social policies. Remarkably, it would be relatively successful, in large measure because it appealed to its society's sense of itself as a united people.

The government enjoyed an overwhelming parliamentary majority and a five-year mandate. Mostly Conservative, it contained a relatively small number of Liberals and renegade Labourites who provided a possibility of a broad-based coalition that might transcend the narrow party divisions of the past. Its leaders possessed immense personal authority that allowed them to wield power with wide consent. MacDonald, triumphantly reelected in his working-class district, continued as Prime Minister; not without influence, he was nevertheless effectively second to Stanley Baldwin, who was in most respects the government's chairman of the board. The Exchequer, and the de facto position of chief operating officer, went to Neville Chamberlain, already well established as Baldwin's second in command, probable successor, and the most vigorous of the senior Tories.

The government's first priority was to follow through on the major issue of the election—the establishment of a general protective tariff. Emergency legislation in November 1931 gave the Board of Trade immediate authority to levy duties of up to 100 percent on foreign manufactured goods. In February 1932, the government put through permanent general protection legislation, the Import Duties Act, which set a baseline duty of ten percent on virtually all manufactured imports, and established an Import Duties Advisory Committee, which quickly doubled the rate. The law provided free entry for a wide range of foodstuffs and raw materials. It also gave a blanket exemption to Empire and Commonwealth imports, pending the results of the Commonwealth conference scheduled for Ottawa that summer. Moderate in comparison to the trade barriers of most other industrial nations, including the United States, the British tariff was nothing less than a revolutionary development in a nation that had made free trade an article of faith for most of the preceding century. It was also yet another significant step in the death spiral of international commerce already well advanced by early 1932. Protectionism and the devalued pound gave a beleaguered nation a breathing spell, but the new policy also had unanticipated consequences and created new difficulties.[28]

Internationally, it made Britain's enormous war debt to the United States (payable in gold at the old $4.86 valuation of the pound) a larger problem than ever. The combination of devaluation and tariff also adversely affected the trade balances and finances of many other countries. Perhaps most significantly, it added to Germany's financial difficulties both by erecting barriers against German imports and by giving British goods a pricing advantage in international markets. It also brought one more contentious issue to Britain's often prickly yet strategically necessary relationship with France, which had thought nothing of raising its own trade barriers while resenting English retaliation. At home, it made foreign imports much more expensive, while subsidizing domestic products that were of lower quality or inefficiently brought to market. It also raised serious problems about the future of Britain's traditional and lucrative position as a shipping center in which goods were brought into the country only for transfer to other vessels in the stream of international commerce. In the short run, these difficulties had to be finessed.[29]

The crisis of 1931 had not only led to the enormous National election victory, it had also given birth to an outpouring of patriotic sentiment unlike anything Britain had seen since the World War. No cultural event epitomized the emotions of the time more than *Cavalcade,* a drama by Noel Coward, the most prolific of contemporary British playwrights. Evoking through the parallel stories of an upper-middle-class family and their servants the British experience from the turn of the century into the Depression, the play drew on the music and sounds of an era that began with the Boer War, pivoted on the world conflict of 1914–18, and culminated in the economic slump of the 1920s. Tragedies outnumbered triumphs. The servant couple fail in their efforts to establish a pub, but their daughter becomes a famous popular singer. The upper-crust couple lose both their sons, one honeymooning with his new wife on the *Titantic*, the other in the trenches of France. Nonetheless, in the final scene, they drink their customary toast to the new year, affirming their faith in each other and in their country's future. The central message was without appreciable nuance: there would always be an England, great and enduring, whatever the afflictions of history.

Circumstances made *Cavalcade* more than rousing soap opera. It opened at the Drury Lane Theater in London's West End during the gold standard crisis and implicitly addressed this latest national trauma with a message of national unity. Sophisticated critics trashed it as superficial and mawkishly sentimental, but it was less high drama for the ages than patriotic pageantry for the times. The public loved it. The royal family attended on October 22, 1931. After 400 performances it closed on September 10, 1932. Each and every one of the 500 players massed on stage; Coward acknowledged a wave of applause. The great theater fell silent for a moment; then the audience broke into "God Save the King." Inexorably, and with equal success, an Academy Award–winning Hollywood film followed early in the next year.[30]

Economic nationalism was equally fervent. The government overcame the consumer inconvenience of the protective tariff by instituting a "Buy British" campaign that struck to the core of English pride. A huge sign in Trafalgar Square, brightly lighted at night, made the slogan as much a part of the nation's unofficial heraldry as Nelson's lions. A *Punch* cartoon depicted John Bull buying a miniature British-made Union Jack from a pretty street vendor who stood in front of banners proclaiming "No Panic," "Investment Begins At Home," "Spend Your Pennies Wisely And The Pound Will Take Care Of Itself." Most Britons of all classes demanded British-made goods—whether they were expensive silks, automobiles, or two-shilling pieces of cookware.

Many of the well-to-do who could afford to escape the cold, damp British winter took their recreation at chilly seaside resorts instead of in the south of France. Three hundred off-season guests at such an establishment in Torquay sent a telegram to King George V describing themselves as "loyal subjects spending a British holiday." Middle-class taxpayers not only accepted the new high rates, they actually queued up days in advance to make their quarterly payments. Some citizens turned in gold sovereign coins, now worth £1.4 on the bullion market, for one-pound bills, thus giving the government a handsome profit as well as an addition to its gold reserves. Many others, attracted by the highest-ever sterling prices for precious metals, sold their gold possessions on the open market. They obtained a genuine windfall. Despite devaluation, prices for domestic goods did not rise. The average Briton accepted relatively small inconveniences as a necessary sacrifice for king and country.[31]

As early as March 1932, while both Germany and the United States were mired in economic misery and political gridlock, British officials boasted of "recovery." The Treasury was able to make early repayment of about two-thirds of the foreign loans it had taken out to stabilize the pound, which by then was experiencing a rebound from its devaluation lows. The trade balance had improved sharply. Unemployment appeared to be easing. Perhaps most significantly, Neville Chamberlain was able to present a balanced budget to the House of Commons. "I look on 1931 as England's year of danger," he declared, "and on 1932 as her year of opportunity." The talk of recovery was, of course, premature, but the National Government could take credit for having stabilized the economy and for providing steady leadership with a sense of direction.[32]

Britain had been severely impacted by the Depression, but not so badly as the United States or Germany. It suffered less from the worldwide collapse of farm prices because it had a much smaller agricultural sector. However bad the housing of the working class and the poor, no Hoovervilles blighted the fringes of British cities and, because the banking system was concentrated around five large and mutually supportive institutions, it experienced no panic. In Wales, the Midlands, and the North—areas dominated by declining industries—life was grim and bitter, but for most of the population, concentrated in the more economically diversified South, existence was simply pinched. The task of the National government was to build on its beginning and bring the country back to a semblance of prosperity. It would make progress but find that recovery was far from just around the corner.[33]

Britain's social and economic stability was real compared to the turmoil of continental Europe, but it was also relative. Unemployment peaked in 1932 at an estimated 15.6 percent of the total workforce, but in the depressed industrial provinces to the west and north of London, the jobless lived in a world of hopeless economic ruin. Their plight reflected the critical condition of a nineteenth-century economy based on cotton spinning, mining, iron works, steel mills, and shipyards. In the Bishop Auckland area of county Durham, more than seventy-five percent of the miners were on public support. In Glasgow an estimated half of the workforce was unemployed. A man with a wife and three children got a dole of approximately one and a half pounds a week, a sum that allowed a bare existence but made no allowance for the smallest emergencies.[34]

In Lancashire, the cotton textile industry, in steady decline since the end of the World War, struggled along at reduced capacity in the face of intense competition from Japanese and Indian mills. As in the United States, it had to cut costs—including wages—to the bone. The lives of the workers were little better than those of the unemployed. In August 1932, 150,000 Lancashire cotton mill operatives went out on strike in protest against wage cuts at a mill in the desolate town of Burnley, where it was common to see women wearing wooden clogs because leather shoes were unaffordable. The local council provided meals for 1,200 destitute children of the strikers. Rumors spread of Communists coming up from London to try to take charge of the strike. Union leaders made plausible predictions of calamity.

London reluctantly sent a mediator. The settlement, achieved at the end of September, changed little. Sullen operatives, putting in as much as sixty-two hours a week for a pound or so more than the dole would give them and fearing that their wages would be further depressed to Asian standards, could never be content. Smaller strikes would follow. Nearly everyone realized that the ultimate solution for the textile industry was "reorganization," a euphemistic term for consolidation, modernization, efficiency, and fewer jobs. In a liberal democracy the government could not achieve such a goal by decree. Owners and employees, offered carrot and stick incentives, would have to be brought along.[35]

From time to time, the anger and misery of the North came south in the form of organized demonstrations. Britain's Communist party was small and inconsequential, but capable of sporadic execution of the "hunger march" technique practiced by its counterparts in other countries. On the last weekend of October 1932, marchers from Scotland, Lancashire, Yorkshire, and other points north descended on London for a mass demonstration, followed by rioting that roamed across much of the central city. At some places, mounted police charged demonstrators wielding wrought-iron fence rails. Amazingly, there were no fatalities. As *New York Times* journalist Charles Selden observed, "the British police never carry revolvers, and a British mob never shoots." Such events seemed to occur less frequently in England than on the continent. The following Saturday, the marchers lined up in orderly fashion at rail stations all over London to be sent home, compliments of a private committee that paid their fares.

Most of the marchers, as Selden put it, "were unemployed but by no means starving young men who found in the march temporary respite from the monotony of a futile search for jobs in their own localities." In all societies during the Great Depression, idle and aimless young males were potential social dynamite. Germany had shown what could happen when they were organized into partisan paramilitary formations. In the United States, young drifters raised the anxiety levels of local governments almost everywhere. In October 1932, expecting to ride to power behind a force of angry men in black shirts, Sir Oswald Mosley founded the British Union of Fascists. The inbred moderation of British public life would defeat him.[36]

Despite relatively little in the way of government social programs for the unemployed young, the lethal possibilities of idle youth never led to a social explosion. Part of the explanation was the concentration of serious discontent in the provinces. But beyond that, Britain's political culture functioned almost as if it had an immune system that isolated and rendered harmless extremist viruses. Quite unlike Germany, Britain had no significant political party advocating revolutionary violence. The Labour party, reduced to less than five dozen core constituencies in the House of Commons, swung sharply to the left in its program but never deviated from its commitment to electoral politics. After the 1932 riots, its new leader George Lansbury warned that "a nation can be ruined . . . by bloody revolution," and cited "economic and moral decay," not the bourgeoisie, as Britain's greatest enemy. One of the party's leading intellectuals, C. E. M. Joad, told a gathering of party activists, "Convert the people to socialism and you may ride into power on their vote: try force and you give a sanction to every reactionary element in the country to plan a successful Fascist coup."[37]

From its inception, the National government was committed to the principle that the Depression required a multilateral agreement on trade, currency stabilization, and international debts. It was among the strongest advocates of a World Economic Conference, delayed by the American presidential election, and scheduled for London in June 1933. Yet from the beginning its policies had been unilateralist. In the course of events, nationalism would perhaps inevitably prevail over internationalism.

The tariff was the centerpiece of the government's first year in office, its benefits clearly outweighing the few disadvantages it had brought. The government turned naturally toward the development of an empire/commonwealth trading bloc in which the pound would be the standard currency. Toward this end, it arranged a conference with the commonwealth nations for Ottawa in August 1932. Still, worldwide commerce was in the island-nation's blood. Officials set a tone of reluctance to erect a closed trading system as anything more than a temporary expedient.[38] The hope was no doubt sincere. For the immediate future, however, it would be British policy to drive more nails into the already well-sealed coffin of open international trade.

An imperial trading and currency bloc was at least as much a political question as an economic one. The creation of the British Commonwealth of Nations in December 1931 had recognized as independent "dominions" Northern Ireland, the Irish Free State, Canada, Newfoundland, Australia, New Zealand, and the Union of South Africa. The National government had pledged dominion status for India, as soon as it could be negotiated. The Irish Free State was already on the verge of breaking away. The rest of the dominions were for all practical purposes independent countries with their own economic objectives and political identities. It seemed urgent to cement a political-cultural relationship with an economic union, which would account for a quarter of the world's territory and population and nearly a third of its trade. Great Britain at its head would remain a major power.[39]

Convening in Ottawa on July 21, the commonwealth conference dragged on for a month, quickly degenerating into acrimonious trench warfare as each country pressed for broad access to British markets while generally refusing to make trade concessions of its own. With the talks on the verge of disintegration by the third week in August, the various delegations mustered enough of a compromising spirit to pull a faint appearance of success from the jaws of catastrophe. Ottawa failed to achieve a single general agreement, producing instead twelve separate bilateral trade agreements, the last of which was concluded in the early morning hours of August 20. In general, Britain gave more than it got, opening its markets to commodities from the commonwealth without achieving similar terms for its manufactured goods. The commonwealth emerged more or less intact, but at a high price. The imperial preference agreements disturbed established British trade patterns with its non-commonwealth trading partners, but provided enough wiggle room to maintain most commercial relationships. At best a modest political success, Ottawa did nothing to alleviate the worldwide depression and may indeed have aggravated it.[40]

It also made the National government more Conservative than ever. Three Liberal ministers and several lesser officials resigned primarily in protest against this latest affront to the principle of free trade. They achieved only political oblivion. Hopelessly divided, the once-great Liberal party was through as a significant force in British politics. The illusion of an imperial trading bloc was attractive to the public. But it was also a step back from the sense of Britain as a nation whose commerce knew no boundaries. British trade policy and the emotions behind it were but one demonstration of the way in which the Depression everywhere broke down international ties, reawakened nationalistic passions, and all but made impossible cooperative international arrangements that probably could have turned the economic decline around.

Britain—and the United States—remained generally liberal in their outlooks, but the retreat from economic liberalism made it all the harder to deal with a disintegrating political world order. By the time Baldwin and Chamberlain returned from Ottawa, Papen was already delivering a foretaste of a resurgent and difficult Germany. In East Asia, a strident Japanese vision of expansion and national destiny had led to the seizure of Manchuria from China. The government lacked the will to put up a strong diplomatic opposition to these events. Prime Minister MacDonald's ebbing strength and lifelong quasi-pacifism discouraged any kind of international activism. Foreign Secretary Sir John Simon, leader of the National Liberals and a jurist of great distinction, was an unimpressive diplomatist. Powerful forces facilitated this weak leadership—traditional British insularity vis-à-vis continental Europe, the pressing urgency of problems at home, the need to do what seemed necessary to protect one's interests in a world without meaningful alliances.

The Depression neither created nor, by itself, unleashed international aggression, but it did encourage each major nation to seek economic salvation without regard for neighbors and erstwhile allies. From that point of departure, the imperative of national aggrandizement could easily manifest itself in military adventures on the part of countries so inclined. Britain and France both sensed a potential threat from Germany, but were too enmeshed in trade and monetary squabbles to establish effective cooperation. In early 1932, Japan having conquered Manchuria and attacked Shanghai, U.S. Secretary of State Henry L. Stimson proposed to the British Foreign Office a joint statement of nonrecognition of the Japanese conquests. Although Britain would sponsor such a resolution in the League of Nations, the National government declined a joint statement with the United States. The British understood that President Hoover would do nothing to implement it and feared it could only get in the way of other British-Japanese issues. The Stimson Doctrine would be stated unilaterally. Neither Britain nor the United States was prepared to engage in active opposition to Japanese expansionism.[41]

The war debts overshadowed everything else, keeping U.S. relations with the European democracies in a state of constant uneasiness that from time to time escalated to low-level hostility. The Europeans, having agreed to forgive German reparations, expected the United States to cancel their obligations. Instead, they ran up against the same obstinacy that had characterized American policy since 1921. Hoover, who had shown with the 1931–32 moratorium that he understood and sympathized with the logic of the European demand, thought it politically impossible. Most Republicans and Democrats, including the new president-elect Franklin D. Roosevelt, accurately reflected popular sentiment and opposed any cancellation. In December 1932, Britain, making no effort to conceal the difficulty of the action, made payment in full of its scheduled war debt installment—and stopped just short of formally declaring it the last. Of the other major European nations, only Mussolini's Italy paid up in full. France, by vote of the Chamber of Deputies, defaulted. The British and other Europeans complained of American greed, Americans decried European perfidy.[42]

By early 1933, a measure of economic stability complemented British political stability. No one thought the Depression gone, but a whole array of statistics indicated that the economy had bottomed and that a modest recovery was underway. The government could boast of having provided, however minimally, for all the jobless. By pursuing a cautious fiscal and monetary policy, it had protected the wealth and living standards of the employed classes. It also had maintained the credibility of the pound without gold backing, a substantial and necessary achievement given Britain's continuing position as a financial and shipping center.

Oppositionists argued for far more drastic action. In March 1933, Britain's most famous economist, John Maynard Keynes, wrote a series of articles (subsequently published in pamphlet form as *The Means to Prosperity*) in the London *Times*, arguing for revival of the economy through an extensive program of "loan expenditure," or deficit spending. The money devoted to such an enterprise, Keynes asserted, would have a multiplier effect, creating at least half a new job for each one funded, reducing the cost of the dole, stimulating a much-needed rise in price levels, and bringing more money into the treasury. The influx of revenues, combined with a carefully managed and intelligently coordinated treasury–central bank monetary management, could maintain the pound at its present levels. Success in Britain could lay the groundwork for a cooperative international effort overseen by a new international authority. Keynes clearly hoped to influence opinion in the United States as well as his own country. He sent an advance copy of his manifesto to President-elect Roosevelt. The pieces won him an audience with Chamberlain, but it was more a courtesy visit than a serious policy consultation.[43]

In his annual budget speech to the House of Commons on April 25, 1933, Chamberlain explicitly refuted deficit financing. Budget deficits had become the rule almost everywhere, he declared; prosperity had not followed them. However difficult its hardships, the United Kingdom had fared better than most other nations. Britain had been freed from the fear that things would get worse by following a sound financial policy that at least delivered advantageous low interest rates for its industry.[44]

Chamberlain's argument seemed sound and practical to most Britons. The chancellor still could offer little more than stabilization and a protracted struggle back toward the depressed economic normalcy of the 1920s, but he was correct in an assumption that lay behind both his thinking and that of Keynes; Britain by itself could not achieve full employment. An island nation with a chronic peacetime labor surplus, limited natural resources, and a heavy dependence on international commerce, Britain required a comprehensive international agreement on trade, currencies, and debt far more than most nations. This imperative forced the British to wait for the 1932 American elections, the formation of the new Roosevelt administration, and the convening of the long-awaited World Economic Conference in June 1933. All parties hoped that the Americans, having finally achieved a unified Democratic government, would be willing to move toward more open trade, cancellation or drastic rescheduling of debts, and a currency agreement that would allow for reestablishment of the gold standard—in short, that the United States could lead a return to the world of 1914. Such hopes, however inflated, had a basis in the traditions of the Wilsonian Democratic party from which Roosevelt had emerged.

By the time Chamberlain made his budget speech, Roosevelt had been president for approximately seven weeks, giving no definitive indication of his positions on international economic issues. Hitler was nearing the end of his third month as chancellor of Germany and clearly intent on taking Europe's most important industrial power its own way. The National government, uninspiring but steady, had brought Britain back from the brink, but also had adopted protectionist policies that got in the way of an open international order. Just about all the advanced industrial nations were in fact committed to the game of competitive devaluations and trade barriers; just about all that owed war debts to the United States were either in default or on the verge of it. It would soon become clear whether they all would have to find their own ways out of the Depression. To no country was the answer more important than Britain.

HEADLINES AND MOVIE NEWSREELS

{1931}

OCTOBER 19   Hoover Opens Drive for Aid for Nation's Idle; Stresses Individual, Duty

{1932}

FEBRUARY 3   Hoover Signs Two Billion Dollar Reconstruction Finance Corporation Bill

JUNE 8   Hoover Signs Tax Increase; Will Hit the Wealthy; Expected to Produce $1 Billion

JULY 3   Roosevelt Puts Economic Recovery First in His Acceptance Speech at Convention

JULY 10   Hoover Would Consider Capacity to Pay But Still Opposes Canceling War Debts

JULY 23   Hoover Approves Home Loans Bill; Predicts Job Rise

NOVEMBER 9   Roosevelt Winner in Landslide! Democrats Control Wet Congress

DECEMBER 25–31   *Moviegoers across America see their president-elect up close. He is a vigorous, active man. He swims, travels across the country by train, speaks with a voice that radiates authority, confidence, optimism. He has a large, attractive family. He is concerned about, but clearly believes in, America. He affirms the future.* (Newsreel, "The President-Elect")

{1933}

MARCH 4   Roosevelt Takes Office Today; Most Banks Closed; Joblessness at All-Time High

POWER SHIFT

THE UNITED STATES,

FALL 1931–MARCH 1933

Personality

FDR: Dynamic Force, American Style

Franklin Delano Roosevelt acquired by inheritance many of the characteristics that imply authority in any society. His family had a lineage that stretched back to the *Mayflower;* it possessed long-established wealth that paid for servants, tutors, horses, the best education, a country estate, foreign travel, and a listing in the social register. From the seventeenth century, Roosevelts had been leading figures in commerce and public affairs. Young Franklin grew up admiring his cousin Theodore—author, magnetic politician, war hero, governor of New York, president of the United States—and fully intending to emulate him. When he married his fifth cousin, Eleanor Roosevelt, in 1905, the first President Roosevelt, her uncle, gave the bride away.

But America, of all the advanced societies of the early twentieth century, was least amenable to an aristocracy's claim to power. All who knew Franklin as a young man agreed: he was intelligent, charming, politically ambitious, and just a bit of a lightweight. The politics of democracy required not only talent and ambition, but also hard work, a gift for self-promotion, and good luck. Emulating his great relative, young Roosevelt defined himself as a progressive reformer. Like many members of the older moneyed class, he had scant use for the *nouveau riche* corporate barons and financiers who dominated the life of the nation, or for the corrupt machine politicians who seemed to control the nation's cities. He quietly backed his wife's social and charitable work for the poor.

In 1910, he fought hard for a seat in the New York legislature, won because he had the good fortune of a split opposition, and quickly dramatized himself as an anti-boss reformer opposing the election of a Tammany hack as a U.S. senator. He took another punch at his party's establishment by supporting Woodrow Wilson for the 1912 presidential nomination. Wilson's subsequent nomination and election (also made possible by the good fortune of a divided Republican opposition) brought Roosevelt, just thirty-one in 1913, to Washington as assistant secretary of the navy, the number two person in the department. A dashing, often insubordinate, but productive tenure got him the Democratic vice-presidential nomination in 1920. He shrewdly exploited a foredoomed campaign to make hundreds of new contacts and polish an already substantial public image.

The Franklin Roosevelt who returned to New York from Washington in 1921 was already a first-rate administrator and a tough, skilled politician with an eye for the main chance, which he envisioned as the presidency itself. Suddenly, at the age of thirty-nine, stricken with polio, he was a paraplegic. It is commonly believed that Roosevelt's struggle with a paralysis he never overcame strengthened him, added depth to his character, and gave him a new sympathy with the underdogs of American life. This hypothesis almost certainly possesses a measure of truth. Any man on the brink of middle age struck by an irreversible paralysis of the legs, facing the end of his professional career, would likely plumb formerly untouched depths in his soul. There can be little doubt that Roosevelt found such reserves, but it is easy to exaggerate their importance. His hard-driving political ambition was already there; so were the broad "progressive" sympathies. His cheerful, lightweight persona had likely always been a convenient cover for a hard inner core. He had already decided in 1919 to maintain what had become a dysfunctional marriage to Eleanor rather than undergo the scandal of a divorce that would have written finis to his political life.

Through the politically inhospitable 1920s, Roosevelt divided his time between futile efforts at physical recovery and the more productive cultivation of friendships in all wings of a divided Democratic party. In 1928, he seized at the opportunity to run for governor of New York and won narrowly. His landslide reelection in 1930 made him the leading contender for his party's nomination.

Roosevelt dealt with paralysis the way most Americans of his time dealt with handicaps. He first struggled to reverse it. When he was unsuccessful, he made a virtue of denial and did his best to move on as if it did not exist. He never practiced outright concealment. Every politically conscious American knew Roosevelt had a disability. After all, as president, he started the March of Dimes Foundation to fund polio research. Still, most people did not realize just how great his handicap was. He never used a wheelchair in public. He walked haltingly and with difficulty, a cane in one hand, the other hand gripping the steadying arm of an aide. His trouser legs were cut very low to conceal the ten-pound steel braces that steadied his withered limbs. Newsreel cameramen and press photographers refrained from documenting his difficulties as much from a sense of dignity as from their conspiracy in a charade. He performed the act magnificently. Americans who in the backs of their minds knew that he had a serious physical problem focused instead on his projection of characteristics that belied infirmity—a cheerful optimism, concern for others rather than oneself, strength, decision.

To his carefully constructed and tightly controlled personality, Roosevelt added his natural patrician authority. Possessing perhaps the finest radio voice of an era in which that medium became the vehicle of political mass communication, he projected that authority to tens of millions of his countrymen at a time. Like his way of dealing with polio, his Harvard American English spoken in well-modulated tones was more impressive to his time than it might have been to a later America likely to see it as pretentious. At the beginning of 1932, his radio talks were known primarily to New Yorkers. Soon, they would become his primary means of mass political leadership. Just as Hitler seemed a lunatic to Americans, who had nothing in their experience to make central European politics understandable, Roosevelt surely would have seemed incomprehensible to most Germans; he represented no single class or interest and had no racialist basis for his politics.

In a time of crisis, Roosevelt stood for action and progressive change. This was enough to win him the Democratic nomination, but from the launch of his presidential campaign until the eve of his inauguration, perceptive and reasonably nonpartisan observers sensed a certain intellectual hollowness. His appeal was largely one of mood and personality and not being Herbert Hoover. It was not that, like all mainstream American politicians, he had no coherent ideology; he also had no coherent program. He and the people around him were products of an earlier surge of twentieth-century reform; the progressives possessed reform causes in abundance, but they never had been forced to confront a depression. That Roosevelt would be a reformer no one could doubt. Whether he could confront and vanquish an economic catastrophe was much more problematic. At noon on Saturday, March 4, 1933, the country waited for him to take the oath of office not quite knowing what he was going to do and uncertain that anyone could cope with the catastrophe that had engulfed it.

The Politics of Despair

By late 1931, the nation's economic trajectory was still downward. Economists struggling to explain it might cite the Wall Street crash, Hawley-Smoot and other tariffs around the world, the gold standard, deflationary central bank policies. But ordinary people lived in a microeconomic world. For them analysis was irrelevant, reality a continuing crisis. The Hoover administration fought to develop a grasp of the big picture, behaved as constructively as possible in dealing with international issues, and attempted to reconcile its belief in voluntary government-business cooperation with an older faith in individual self-help. What it never quite managed was an understanding of or ability to cope with the common desperation that increasingly characterized tens of thousands of localities from one end of the country to the other.

The Depression hit hardest where the economy was already in decline—in regions, whether in the United States or other countries, that produced commodities or manufactured products already in oversupply during the 1920s. These included virtually all agricultural cash crops, textiles, petroleum, and coal. One such location was Williamson County, Illinois, in the heart of one of the nation's largest coalfields.

At the beginning of 1923, Williamson County mines had employed 13,000 men. By the time of the Wall Street crash, the total was just over 5,000 men, who averaged about 180 days a year of work. By the end of 1931, employment had shrunk to about 2,900 men working about 100 days a year. Local banks were hit hard by mortgage defaults and the general malaise of the declining local economy. Of thirty-six banks doing business in Williamson and two adjoining counties, ten were already closed by the end of 1930; active deposits in those that remained had fallen from $26 million to $12 million. Building and loan associations suffered a similar fate. Most depositors got some of their money back, but in dribs and drabs over long periods of time. Tax defaults invariably accompanied mortgage defaults. In July 1931, the *Herrin Daily Journal* ran a special edition with thirty seven-column pages listing homes to be sold for unpaid taxes.[1]

By then, yearly income for those still working in the mines was about $750, about fifty-five percent of the pre-depression total. In the summer of 1932, United Mine Workers President John L. Lewis uncharacteristically capitulated to reality, endorsing an eighteen percent wage cut for his unhappy men and putting it into effect through a shamelessly rigged ballot count. He understood better than the miners that without the pay reduction, coal production in Illinois would shut down altogether.[2]

Williamson County's hardest hit town was Johnston City, a municipality of 5,900. In October 1931, a "Mulligan" soup kitchen supported by private donations fed approximately 400 children a day on a budget of forty dollars a week. By 1932, a county relief committee dispensed state assistance to nearly half the town's population. The benefits were parsimonious, the requirements stringent. Recipients were required to have exhausted their savings. By the beginning of 1933, the county relief program was supporting 4,600 families, thirty percent of the total population of 53,000. Only one bank had avoided failure, and an estimated $7 million in savings had been wiped out.[3]

Nebraska farmers fared little better. Dawson County in the central part of the state—a region of livestock, corn, alfalfa, and wheat farmers—had substantially recovered from the hard times of the twenties by 1928. The Depression ravaged its economy. By the fall of 1932, the market price for corn had fallen from its 1928 high of $0.71 a bushel to $0.13, wheat from $0.94 to $0.27 a bushel, alfalfa from $10 a ton to $4.10, cattle from $12.60 a hundredweight to $4.10, hogs from $11.50 a hundredweight to $2.30. At such prices, no farmer could avoid serious losses on his operations. There had been twelve farm foreclosure sales in 1930; in 1932, there were thirty-four. Local businesses collapsed apace in the county's three small towns. In 1932, the county seat, Lexington (population, 2,962), created a "woodpile" work project; down-and-out men sawed and split logs to stove-size lengths, taking their pay either in the wood itself, scrip negotiable at local businesses, or cash. By March 1933, the woodpile employed 121 men. The local relief committee was also giving direct payments to 137 families within the city limits.[4]

Across the country, the city of Providence, Rhode Island—the second largest city in New England (population, 253,000) and heavily peopled by foreign-born immigrants or the children of immigrants—also faced trying conditions. In November 1931, the Family Welfare Society, a private charity, reported that its assistance rolls had mushroomed from the usual five or six hundred families to four thousand. The Community Fund and other agencies also did their part, but, as in most of America, the aid levels by themselves were woefully inadequate. A Brown University study, published in December 1931, commented: "Relief has obviously been merely supplementary; families of five do not live on $16 a month."[5]

A privately financed Emergency Unemployment Committee provided jobs at a bare $15 a week. By July 1931, supporting nearly eleven thousand clients, it had reached the outer limits of its capabilities. That November, the city began its own jobs program, employing 550 men at higher prevailing wages of $0.52 an hour. They also contributed to a million-dollar budget deficit that the city council attacked the following spring with an across-the-board cut of ten percent for all municipal workers. In May 1932, the Brown University Bureau of Business Research estimated local unemployment at thirty-two percent of the workforce. With a million dollars in borrowed state funds, the city kept relief programs going. At the beginning of 1933, no end was in sight, and long-term relief capabilities, public and private, were at best problematic.[6]

Williamson County, Dawson County, and Providence were three diverse and more or less random examples of the impact of the Depression. Just how quick and how hard the blow depended on a host of variables. Much of the rural South was less affected than most areas because it was already desperately poor. A city such as Houston, tied economically to the depressed oil fields of east Texas, was harder hit than, say, Los Angeles with its connections to a more stable, if pinched, movie industry and its numerous opportunities as a rapidly growing metropolitan center. The unemployed in Kansas City, Missouri, and surrounding Jackson County, with an active and extensive bond-funded public works program, weathered hard times rather better than in Memphis, Tennessee, where local government was far more concerned about debt.[7]

⌐

But whatever the local and regional variations, the Depression hit home hard almost everywhere by 1932. Worst affected were those who lived on the margins in good times—Negroes* especially. In Chicago, for example,

---

* In the 1930s, the term "Negro" (capital "N") was demanded by American blacks as a sign of respect. It is used here in that sentiment and in an effort to write as much as possible in the language of the time.

white unemployment doubled in 1931; black unemployment tripled. Houston and many other Southern cities largely ignored black populations in distributing relief, whether public or private. Northern cities tried harder but usually ran up against budgetary realities. A New York social worker described the realities of the Depression in Harlem: "A few chanted optimistically, 'Jesus will lead me and the Welfare will feed me,' but . . . the Home Relief Bureau allowed only eight cents a meal. . . . men, women and children combed the streets and searched in garbage cans for food, foraging with dogs and cats."[8]

The unemployment statistics mostly, although not exclusively, encompassed blue-collar workers who had no unemployment insurance to sustain them and seldom much in savings. Declining prices might seem to have enhanced the standard of living of those who kept their jobs, but fortunate indeed was the man without a jobless family member or in-law to help. Moreover, wage cuts were common. In May 1932, the National Industrial Conference Board reported that on average, workers' wages had been cut 13.9 percent since 1932. It indicated, moreover, that the slashes went on up the line at somewhat higher rates to an average of some 20.3 percent for managers, directors, and executives. The super-rich no doubt survived in style, but in 1931 only seventy-five persons filed federal income tax returns reporting income of over $1 million; in 1929, there had been 513.[9]

Governments were also affected. A rapidly declining economy meant an eroding sales, property, and income tax base. If fairly reassessed, homes and farms had to be valued lower, and whether they were reassessed or not, broke farmers and unemployed home owners could not afford to pay. The bonded indebtedness undertaken by Jackson County, Missouri, to pay for road and construction projects required higher property tax rates to establish a fund for repayment. In 1931 and 1932, tax delinquencies soared. The county's chief executive officer, Judge Harry S. Truman, found himself forced to slash salaries (his own included) drastically and resort to mass layoffs—300 in 1932, another 200 in January 1933. The reactions of distressed workers ran from angry protests to tearful pleas. Thousands of state and local officials faced similar problems.[10]

The pressures intensified through 1932 with almost hydraulic force. There were no good contemporary government unemployment surveys. In October, the American Federation of Labor announced the results of an "unemployment census" that put 10.9 million people out of work—22 percent of a workforce of approximately 50 million. Retrospective scholarship suggests the estimate was significantly understated. The recession of 1930 had become the constant, aching despair of 1932.[11]

—

By December 1931, President Hoover had arrived at a cool, realistic sense that his initial efforts at a voluntaristic organization of the economy had been insufficient. He still believed that with timely government aid the system could repair itself without alteration, that a tariff-protected economy provided with sufficient government-driven credit could recover to the full-employment levels of the 1920s, that it could be based on a non-devalued gold-standard dollar secured by a sound fiscal policy, and that the repaired, smoothly functioning machine would quickly provide for ten to twelve million jobless Americans living in destitution or very close to it. This was an engineer's solution, overly mechanistic perhaps, but not unsound in its diagnosis. The problem was that its assumptions were too narrow.

Even within the American corporate establishment, Hoover's most enthusiastic constituency, murmurs of dissent were becoming vocal disagreement. In September 1931, Gerard Swope, the president of General Electric, called for a huge step beyond Hoover's philosophy of a voluntary organizational economy. Swope advocated a federally mandated, federally supervised reorganization of most businesses with over fifty employees; the plan would be carried out by existing trade associations that would stabilize prices and production, find ways to maximize employment, initiate unemployment insurance systems for workers, and establish industry-wide pension plans. He did not shrink from stating the obvious—such a solution would require repeal or suspension of the antitrust laws. Shortly afterward, Henry I. Harriman, president of the U.S. Chamber of Commerce, urged a similar plan. Both executives avoided the most obvious existing comparison to such proposals—the fascist cartelism of Mussolini's Italy.

The Swope and Harriman plans had considerable appeal in a nation that seemed to be sinking into the quicksand of economic chaos. Formulated to meet urgent problems of corporate management, they also posited a sense of responsibility to workers and a belief that class interests were compatible. Harriman also urged federal adoption of a domestic acreage allotment system to stabilize American agriculture. Both plans assumed that such endeavors could be made compatible with traditional American liberal democracy.

Hoover himself was horrified by them. His private remarks, by no means ill-conceived, revealed the way in which the classical individualistic side of his thinking had claimed dominance over the planning and organizational side. Price-fixing and production controls were the techniques of "gigantic trusts." The Swope-Harriman proposals would lead to "the decay of American industry" because they inevitably would shield "obsolete plants and inferior managements." The ultimate result, he told Attorney General William Mitchell, would be "a series of complete monopolies over the American people."[12]

Hoover was a genuine humanitarian; he also was a believer in limited government, conservative fiscal policy, individual self-help, and the virtue of private charity. He felt an instinctive revulsion at the thought of major jobs programs for the unemployed or the establishment of an American dole run and funded from Washington. He understood rightly enough that the only long-term solution for those out of work was a restored economy that could provide them with long-term, productive work. But how realistic was his belief that the system of the 1920s—one that had sputtered and stumbled outside the United States—could be restored, gold standard intact, war debts unaddressed, American protectionism unaltered? The world was changing rapidly, the shape of things to come was still indistinct, but restoration was unlikely. However good his intentions, Hoover's program would never escape the popular sense that it neglected the desperate while succoring the relatively fortunate.[13]

The conceptual inadequacies of the Hoover program were made all the larger by a political calendar that dictated a general election in eleven months. While the American system was amenable to strong executive leadership, it had no mechanism, and no appetite, for giving Hoover or any other leader the dictatorial powers still enjoyed by Brüning in Germany. Nor did it have a way for establishing the sort of National coalition that had been so quickly effected and ratified in Britain. All that it could promise was a struggle for power between a Republican president and a Democratic congress, culminating in a date-certain election in which one party or the other would likely emerge in control of both the executive and legislative branches.

Hoover—essentially a managerial executive rather than a magnetic leader—faced dim prospects for presidential achievement. The Democrats in Congress—lacking a common program, unsure just who would be their presidential standard-bearer—viewed equally daunting possibilities.

The Democratic party from its inception in the age of Jefferson and Jackson had always been in a loose sense the party of the people, disproportionately strong among the "lower orders" of society, but that did not make it necessarily "progressive." Its base since Reconstruction had been the states of the old Confederacy, the solid South, where one might detect sporadic stirrings of populist protest but would usually encounter either a managerial conservatism or an angry, reactionary, strict constructionist Jeffersonianism at war with modern progressivism. Northern Democrats possessed an organizational base centered in city machines, almost all controlled by non-ideological pols more concerned with public contracts and patronage than with ideology and programs. From 1896 to 1916, in the persons of William Jennings Bryan and then Woodrow Wilson, the Democrats had been an increasingly central force in the early twentieth-century progressive movement, but the World War and its aftermath had ended a promising chapter in the party's history.

The Democratic congressional leadership exemplified the obstacles Hoover faced. Speaker of the House John Nance Garner, a small-town banker, was in his thirtieth year as the representative of a parched rural Texas district west of San Antonio. The wiliest and best-met among the many courthouse politicians who had managed to make their way to Congress, he commanded a party delegation that for the most part respected his sense of tactics, enjoyed the good bourbon that he poured freely for his friends, and had few disagreements with his deeply Jeffersonian principles. In the days of Bryan and Wilson, when the salient issues had been trust-busting, controlling Wall Street bankers, lowering the tariff, and aiding the farmer, he had seemed a progressive. But like many other old progressives, he had no answer for the Depression. Ever distrustful of big government and committed to fiscal orthodoxy, he was a conservative. The rest of the House Democratic leadership, including his fellow Texan Sam Rayburn, was of the same mold. The party's Senate leadership—Carter Glass of Virginia, Joseph Robinson of Arkansas, and Pat Harrison of Mississippi—were similar types.

Not rigid ideologues, the congressional Democrats nonetheless leaned against extraordinary governmental measures and unbalanced budgets; a fair number found Hoover distressingly statist and fiscally unsound. What they wanted most strongly was a Democratic return to power. This yearning made them flexible and provided some running room for younger insurgents such as Senators Robert F. Wagner of New York and Edward Costigan of Colorado, but it gave them little interest in finding common ground with a Republican president. Here as elsewhere, the normal workings of democratic politics would not bode well for a solution to the Depression.

Hoover's message to the new congress featured two attention-getters: the establishment of a Reconstruction Finance Corporation (RFC), authorized to lend up to $500 million to financial institutions and to raise further capital by selling up to $1.5 billion in debentures on the open market; and a large tax increase to close a dangerously huge budget deficit expected to exceed $2 billion by the end of the fiscal year in June. Other requests included some assistance for the railroads, many of which were teetering on the brink of bankruptcy; a liberalization of the Federal Reserve authority to permit an expansion of the currency; additional farm credit funds; a Home Loan bank system to refinance home mortgages; and ratification of the war debts moratorium.[14]

Notwithstanding his blunt opposition to "any direct or indirect government dole," which he asserted was a primary cause of the continuing Depression in Europe, Hoover's requests indicated that he had moved a significant step beyond his earlier faith in voluntarist organization. He had come to the idea of a government-managed RFC late and only after cajoling leading banks to set up a National Credit Corporation, a private credit pool on which they could draw for mutual support. Established in the fall of 1931, with pledges of $500 million, the National Credit Corporation was a plausible facsimile of mutual support institutions and informal understandings that existed in numerous other developed countries, but the American banking system was spread across a vast continent, individualistic, and highly fragmented. It had no dominant leader who could impose his will on the others. The National Credit Corporation resembled a cowardly lion, large and impressive in appearance but constantly shrinking from combat. Two months of operation were enough to demonstrate its irrelevance.

The Federal Reserve system, created in 1914, was the American equivalent of a central bank; but the Fed was actually a conglomerate of twelve regional banks, among which the New York regional bank exercised the greatest influence. The Federal Reserve Board in Washington had some control over interest rates, but not the extraordinary clout that would come later. Its chairman was semi-anonymous, possessing none of the near-imperial standing of successors a half-century in the future. The board's primary mission, moreover, was protecting the dollar from devaluation, but to protect the dollar was to contribute to the deflationary spiral that was worsening the Depression and pulling weaker banks into the undertow of failure.

The RFC proposal thus was a necessary attempt to deal with structural deficiencies in the banking community. Hoover, seizing on a theme also heard in Europe, justified it by resorting to an analogy of the nation's crisis with the World War and comparing his proposal to the War Finance Corporation. Congress authorized it with greater borrowing power than Hoover requested. Up and running at the beginning of February, it faced a far more critical situation than if it had been proposed and enacted a year earlier.

Despite reflexive initial hostility from Democratic Senator Carter Glass of Virginia, a sponsor and coauthor of the original Federal Reserve Act, Congress got behind Hoover's credit expansion measure. Passed as the Glass-Steagall Act of 1932, it enlarged the varieties of commercial debt that could be rediscounted (purchased and sold) by the Fed; it also released $750 million of the federal gold supply to ease business transactions that required payment in bullion; and it facilitated an expansion of the money supply by giving previously ineligible federal securities parity with gold as backing for the dollar.

Incredibly, liberals and progressives stalled Hoover's Home Loan Bank bill. It proposed to establish a new system of support for banks holding unproductive home mortgages that would be, in effect, exchanged for cash infusions. Thereby, imperiled banks could remain open and perhaps stimulate their local economy by making new home construction loans. Prompt passage would have delivered immediate and tangible benefits to tens of thousands of home owners facing foreclosure. Instead the bill languished until July, gaining final passage only days before adjournment. Representative Fiorello La Guardia called it "a bill to bail out the mortgage bankers," and told his staff, "The bastards broke the People's back with their usury. . . . Let them die, the People will survive." His obstructionism was matched by the indifference of a Democratic leadership with no interest in giving the president a victory. Hoover finally signed the bill on July 22, issuing an overly florid statement about the hundreds of millions of dollars in home construction it would facilitate. In fact, it was about a year too late. The delay was not Hoover's fault, but he got no credit for the program when it finally became law. Many thousands of homeowners were the ultimate losers.[15]

Above all, Hoover had done little to address widespread human misery across the country. He had no effective farm program. The Federal

Farm Board, overwhelmed by surpluses, had stopped trying to support major commodity prices in mid-1931. The administration was right in its belief that further appropriations would be good money thrown after bad; but it was unwilling to contemplate production quotas or a farm dole. Instead, it simply made things worse by selling off large quantities of the commodities that it had stored. The majority of American farmers faced huge losses, foreclosure, and bankruptcy.[16]

In towns and cities, one of every five workers was unemployed, but Hoover thought he had gone as far as possible in establishing a public works agenda. He already had doubled the federal public works budget.[17] To do more would result in an enormous addition to the mountain of federal debt that already existed and would only employ a relatively small fraction of the jobless. The argument had undeniable force, but it skimmed quickly over productive and necessary work that could be developed by state and local authorities. Heavily driven by fears of an even higher federal debt, it bespoke a certain "nothing-can-be-done" attitude that had begun to creep into Hoover's rhetoric, indeed even into the weary tone of his speaking voice.

As for direct federal relief to the small army of the destitute who could now be found everywhere, Hoover and the men around him remained convinced that a federal dole was unthinkable, indeed un-American. In his December message to Congress, he had declared that "the breakdown and increased unemployment in Europe is due in part to such practices." He also had praised work of local governments and the "magnificent response" of the American people to charitable appeals. The rhetoric, not unusual among governors and mayors across the country, bespoke a certain lack of contact with reality. The *Christian Century*, the nation's leading voice of religious liberalism, commented sarcastically on a news story that celebrated the success of the city of Tulsa, Oklahoma, in feeding 10,000 charity cases on a reputedly healthy but unappetizing diet that cost six cents per day per person. The spectacle of giving unfortunates a day-after-day menu whose monotony was more suitable for livestock, it declared, was "a fit subject for some Hogarth of the wide open spaces."[18]

The final important point in Hoover's agenda was a tax increase. As late as mid-1931, he had seemed relatively unconcerned about a rapidly increasing budget deficit. The economy was in crisis, he told his cabinet, interest rates were low, and "in wartime no one dreamed of balancing budgets." By the spring of 1932, however, the time for sanguinity had passed. The budget deficit had enlarged alarmingly, and it was already possible to foresee that government revenues might cover less than half of federal outlays. A fiscal chasm of such breadth could crowd out a private recovery as the government soaked up more and more of the lending market. It might even cast doubt on the public credit and endanger the dollar.

Hoover, talking bravely of a balanced budget but actually hoping only to keep the deficit within bounds, called for a large tax increase in December. His new secretary of the treasury, Ogden Mills, prepared a plan that emphasized increases in higher income tax brackets and boosted the rate on corporations; it also raised taxes on estates and stock transfers. Americans below the median income level would have been little affected, although the proposal did call for higher excise taxes, including the one on tobacco.[19]

Surprisingly, there was little opposition to the concept of a tax increase. The economic orthodoxy of the time all but mandated one. The Democrats not only accepted the necessity for higher taxes in a collapsing economy but demonstrated more fiscal conservatism than the Republicans. They advocated a national sales tax to be levied on manufacturers (who would then pass along their higher costs to consumers). Mills, persuaded that the sales tax would produce more revenue, brought the administration along. Liberal Democrats and progressives, led by the sometimes populistic Robert "Muley" Doughton of North Carolina and La Guardia, voted it down on the floor of the House. Thereupon, Speaker Garner took the floor to make a dramatic appeal for some kind of tax bill that would balance the budget, declaring that otherwise the result would be "a financial panic such as has never been equaled in this Republic."[20]

The ultimate result, the Revenue Act of 1932, was close to Hoover's original proposal and touted to bring in an extra billion dollars. The best that could be said for it was that it did not have a regressive sales tax that would have inflicted more pain on an already desperate lower third of the population. No one of note asserted the folly of draining more money out of a critically ill economy. On July 1, Secretary Mills announced that the preliminary estimate of the budget deficit for the just-concluded fiscal year 1932 was $2.88 billion dollars, a figure well in excess of fifty percent of federal expenditures. It took the most determined optimist to believe that the new taxes would bring recovery and a balanced budget.[21]

By then Hoover faced new challenges stemming from dissatisfaction with the RFC's first months of operations and its failure to meet the national relief crisis. The RFC's big problem was that its activities had no obvious relevance to the lives of ordinary people who had felt the sting of the Depression. Perhaps its lending criteria were too conservative and loan periods (six months) too short; still, it was by any previous standards of peacetime government participation in the economy a dynamo of stimulus. In the first two months of its existence, it made loans to 160 banks, 60 railroads, and 16 building and loan associations. It had a bipartisan board of directors, a majority of whom were Democrats by mid-1932. To the extent that it kept vital components of the nation's financial and transportation systems afloat, it clearly saved many jobs, but it could not achieve a turnaround. After Congress mandated publication of its loans in July 1932, any financial institution receiving one was branded with a mark of instability that endangered its survival. Bad loans, inevitable in any credit operation, could become terrible public relations miscues. One went to a bank managed by former Republican vice president Charles Dawes, another to a bank in which Democratic senator Atlee Pomerene was a director. It was easy, if not quite fair, to see the agency as a bailout mechanism for fat cats and decry its lack of programs for the little people at the bottom of the heap—even if many of those little people were also bank depositors. As early as the spring of 1932, progressives and Democrats were pushing an amendment to its charter that would allow it to lend to state relief programs.[22]

The advocates engaged in messy quarrels among themselves over issues of scope and method. Eventually, however, the opportunity to display concern for the unemployed was too great to keep the Democrats divided. The result, sponsored in the Senate by Robert F. Wagner of New York, passed Congress on July 10. All told, it provided for nearly $2 billion dollars in loans to the states and public works. The next day, Hoover issued a stinging veto; it hinged largely on provisions that would have allowed RFC loans to states that had not exhausted all their resources and would have required a charge of $500 million against the federal budget. A week and a half later, the president signed a rejiggered bill that gave the RFC $1.5 billion for income-producing public works, $300 million in loans to the states for relief projects (to be secured by 1935 federal highway appropriations), and $200 million for the liquidation of closed banks. The legislation—officially known as the Emergency Relief and Construction Act—was precedent-setting. It also was too late to do Hoover much good in the coming presidential election. By then a majority of the RFC directors were Democrats, but they moved with the caution Hoover expected. At year's end, they had disbursed only

$30 million to the states for relief and had scarcely begun to tap the public works funds.[23]

Amazingly, prohibition and repeal of the eighteenth amendment to the Constitution were issues almost as heated and salient as the Depression in 1931 and 1932. State and local enforcement had collapsed throughout most of the country—sometimes, as in Governor Roosevelt's New York, by conscious policy decision. The federal government lacked the capability for more than random, sporadic policing of the law. In 1931, a presidential commission headed by George W. Wickersham (President William Howard Taft's attorney general) reported the obvious and suggested various "revisions" of the amendment. But the Republican base—middle-class, white, old-stock, Protestant—was preponderantly dry. Hoover himself continued to defend the status quo. Here perhaps the Quakerism of his childhood and the elitism of his adult thinking merged into a sense that the masses required a constructive social discipline.

The Democrats by 1931 were well along the path to a broadly acceptable compromise on the issue. Bitterly split on prohibition during the 1920s, they were finding wide support for repeal and, pending that, an immediate modification of its defining legislation, the Volstead Act, to allow the manufacture and sale of beer, both measures subject to the provision that states would have the option to remain dry. The prospect was made all the more enticing by the certainty that legal beer would mean new and relatively painless tax inflows at every level of government. By 1932, Hoover realized that support among Republicans was ebbing quickly. After considerable debate with his advisers, he authorized a party platform plank that, without using the word "repeal," advocated state-by-state decisions on alcohol. In his nomination-acceptance speech at a traditional notification ceremony in Washington on August 11, 1932, he tacitly admitted that prohibition had failed and declared: "It is my belief that in order to remedy present evils a change is necessary." A tepid effort at catch-up, the statement would do little to help him.[24]

Another aspect of Hoover's acceptance speech that received considerable attention was a hard and fast statement of opposition to the cancellation of war debts, tempered only by the possibility that trade preferences in debtor countries for American products and agricultural commodities might be accepted as an alternative form of payment. A non-starter in any form of negotiation, the trade proposal revealed that America, like most nations hit by the Depression, had become self-absorbed to the point of self-delusion.

The fragility of U.S. relations with its two major World War allies was potentially dangerous at a time when the democratic countries should have been searching for a common front. The fault was not solely that of the United States. France was, if anything, even more myopic in its tariff policy and redemptions of dollars for gold in huge quantities. Britain's own protectionism and efforts at imperial preference had not been helpful, although the British could rightly point out that these had occurred only after Hawley-Smoot. At bottom, war debts were the major point of contention. The American people overwhelmingly refused to recognize the manifest reality that the allies could never pay up. So, despite his enlightened one-year moratorium, did Hoover, at least in his role as a public statesmen. The Democratic contenders for the presidency displayed no more vision.

The Depression had encouraged every nation to look inward, deal with grievous social problems, and pursue narrow definitions of self-interest. No country did so more single-mindedly than the United States. Hoover, for all his international mindedness, presided over an America that by 1932 had become the most isolationist of the major world powers.

Shortly after signing the Emergency Relief and Construction Act, Hoover acted to deal with what appeared to be a minor issue of public order—the Bonus Army. Few Americans were more cohesively organized or possessed of a greater sense of entitlement than the World War veterans. Presidents might defy them; most congressmen knew better. In 1924, Congress, overriding President Coolidge's veto, had given each of them a deferred bonus in the form of a paid-up life insurance policy that would mature with full benefits in 1945. The Depression altered the timetable. What could be more natural in times of need than to want to borrow against one's life insurance policy? In 1931, under strong pressure from the veterans organizations, Congress, over Hoover's veto, allowed loans of up to one-half the 1945 value of the bonus. The president had much of the country on his side. No one believed that the loans would be repaid. Veterans were no more severely impacted by the Depression than non-veterans; moreover, they already enjoyed relatively generous federal medical and disability benefits. The New York Times estimated in June 1932 that "veterans' relief" consumed 26.1 percent of the federal budget, as compared to 5.8 and 17.5 percent in Britain and France.[25]

In 1932, the veterans representatives were back in Washington, lobbying for the other half, this time payable as a straight cash benefit. The cost to the Treasury, $2.4 billion, would nearly double an already huge deficit. In May, veterans from all over the country, some with their wives and children, descended upon Washington. Railroads let them appropriate empty boxcars. Local authorities, fearful of being stuck with more relief cases, transported them from one state line to the next. By Memorial Day, an estimated 1,200 were in the District of Columbia, billeted in an empty government building, their food provided by private subscription and congressional appropriation; thousands more were on the road. The men accepted William Waters, an ex-sergeant and unemployed cannery superintendent from Oregon, as the commander of what he called the Bonus Expeditionary Force (BEF). Living under military discipline, they vowed to stay in Washington until the government came through with their benefits. In a couple of weeks, their ragtag regiment would grow beyond division strength.[26]

On the night of June 7, they marched through the streets of Washington in loose military formation; Floyd Gibbons described them "as five thousand hungry ghosts of the heroes of 1917." Led by flag bearers, they held aloft hand-lettered placards with such slogans as "Remember 1917–18—Pay the Bonus Now" and "Here We Stay, Till the Bonus They Pay." A general sympathy for down-and-out soldiers laced with negativity about their specific cause began to give way to deeper worries. Some observed that Communist organizers were at work inside the BEF. Others saw potential brown-shirted storm troopers. Democratic Senator J. Hamilton Lewis of Illinois decried the atmosphere of "threat and coercion" the veterans were creating and warned them "as your fellow soldier and friend" that Congress would not capitulate.[27]

By mid-June, officials estimated the size of the Bonus Army at fifteen to twenty thousand. Large elements of it had spilled out of the vacant government buildings to a hot and muddy shantytown encampment on the banks of the Anacostia River. On June 15, the House of Representatives passed the Bonus Bill, 209–176, but on the same day the Senate Finance Committee reported it to the floor with an unfavorable recommendation. On the evening of June 17, ten thousand veterans massed at the Capitol as the Senate voted. The *New York Times* described the day as the tensest in Washington since the World War and observed that the closest parallel in American history had been a siege of the Continental Congress by unpaid Revolutionary War soldiers. The expected Senate defeat was by an overwhelming 3–1 margin; progressive stalwarts such as

Wagner, La Follette, and Norris voted "no." When Waters announced the tally, the men responded with a chorus of boos, then an angry buzz, but at their commander's behest, most of them sang a stanza of "America," formed ranks by state, and marched away.[28]

Much of the BEF hung on for another six weeks, despite erratic food supplies, in a state of increasing alienation. Waters talked threateningly of molding his men into a true paramilitary organization that might be called the Khaki Shirts. Communists, although generally unwelcome, continued to try to stir up disorder. A camp newspaper, the B.E.F. News, grew increasingly strident. On July 2, the Bonus Army staged another big demonstration at the Capitol. Ten days later, it started an occupation of the Capitol Plaza that went on until Congress adjourned on July 16. A few days later, a radical splinter group marched on the White House and was turned back only when police brandished tear gas bombs and arrested three leaders. Another attempt on July 25 ended in similar fashion.[29]

The BEF's lingering presence in the nation's capital was perhaps cause for some uneasiness, but despite the bravado of Waters and the machinations of the Communist fringe, no detached observer could see it as a revolutionary menace. Pathetic and poverty-stricken, it was at most a public nuisance, eliciting emotions that wavered between embarrassment, annoyance and sympathy. District of Columbia Superintendent of Police Pelham Glassford, a retired brigadier general, had been wary of the marchers at first. Soon, however, observing that some of them had served under his command in the war, he was befriending them and organizing relief aid. Perhaps in part because they were assured of something resembling shelter and nutrition, most of the marchers declined to take advantage of legislation that gave them small advances against the 1945 bonus for transportation out of town. Unhappy District commissioners ordered Glassford to conduct an evacuation by early August. The police chief stalled, hoping to achieve a peaceful resettlement in the countryside, perhaps underwritten by financing for light manufacturing and subsistence farming.

Time ran out on July 27. Hoover met with Secretary of the Treasury Mills, Attorney General Mitchell, Secretary of War Patrick J. Hurley, and Army Chief of Staff Douglas MacArthur. They decided on the immediate eviction of BEF men from vacant government buildings just a few blocks from the west front of the Capitol on Pennsylvania Avenue. Hurley and MacArthur were convinced that the BEF was the largest and most durable manifestation of a pattern of Communist demonstrations that had episodically descended upon Washington. They saw it as a revolutionary threat. Hoover, who had neither met with the BEF leaders nor sent representatives to do so, bought into the fantasy.[30]

A detachment of Washington police, personally commanded by Glassford, undertook the mission. After some tough negotiating with Waters, the process moved along in a relatively orderly fashion. Communist militants came on to the scene, threw bricks, but were arrested or dispersed without bloodshed. Early in the afternoon, however, a scuffle broke out in one of the buildings; policemen opened fire, killing two veterans. Informed of the incident, Hoover ordered Secretary of War Hurley to carry out the operation with army units. He then issued a public statement asserting that "a considerable part of those remaining are not veterans; many are Communists and persons with criminal records."

By 4:00 p.m., the army had assembled nearly 800 troops, mostly cavalry and infantry; they moved down Pennsylvania Avenue, spearheaded by five light tanks. MacArthur, wearing a full-dress uniform, personally supervised the action. Using tear gas, the soldiers sent the veterans scurrying from the vacant buildings without firing a shot or inflicting serious injuries and forced them southeast over the Eleventh Street Bridge to the shantytown on the flats. MacArthur deliberately ignored instructions from Hoover to end his movements there. Instead, he informed Glassford that he intended to clear the camp, asked the police chief to give its occupants advance notice, and held his forces for several hours, perhaps to give the veterans time to disperse, perhaps waiting for the darkness that would render newsreel cameras useless.

At 11:15 p.m., the army crossed the bridge, expecting small arms fire from handguns and rifles rumored to be in the camp. Instead the force advanced at will with no significant resistance, lobbing tear gas canisters as it systematically cleared one zone after another. Almost immediately, fires broke out, some set by the veterans, others perhaps caused by the gas projectiles. Soon the entire encampment was blazing and the air thick with gas. In the heat and confusion, a woman was run over by a horse, a fourteen-year-old boy cut by a saber, a seven-year-old bayoneted in the leg, a seven-month-old baby died, probably from gas inhalation. The fumes penetrated into nearby residential areas, forcing families to close their windows. Shortly after midnight, the New York Times reported, "a pitiful stream of refugee veterans of the World War walked out of their home of the past two months, going they knew not where."

MacArthur held a late night press conference in which he not only repeated Hoover's charges, but asserted that the BEF "was a bad-looking mob. . . . animated by the essence of revolution," that it had extorted money from Anacostia neighborhoods and imposed a reign of terror upon them, that Hoover had shown extraordinary patience but "had he let it go on another week, I believe that the institutions of our Government would have been very severely threatened." The Communist party gleefully accepted the responsibility Hoover and MacArthur assigned to it and promised new bonus marches in coming months.[31]

Most Americans seem to have perceived the BEF as pitiful refugee veterans rather than a revolutionary Red menace. As a military operation begun in city streets and culminating after dark among tents and shacks going up in flames, the eviction had been carried out with efficiency, restraint, and minimal casualties. But had a military operation against unarmed and disorganized protesters been necessary in the first place? Barricaded inside the White House, lacking the political instincts to deal with the Bonus Army in a firm but conciliatory fashion, misunderstanding popular attitudes toward it, Hoover had committed an enormous public relations blunder.

In Germany, despite considerable hardship, unemployment benefits, political party assistance programs, public housing from which the jobless could not be evicted, and workers' cooperatives made the spectacle of thousands of homeless men camped on a mud flat unthinkable. Marches on the seat of government there might be, but conducted by disciplined political militia whose members went home to their families after demonstrating. Violence aplenty there was, but conducted by political parties against each other or against favorite scapegoat groups, most notably the Jews. In Britain, the dole and charitable relief programs kept a lid on social unrest; meager as it was, relief was more comprehensively distributed in the United Kingdom than in the United States. The British middle class acceptance of punishing taxation at a time of crisis, moreover, provided something of a bridge across an enormous class gap. If occasional hunger marches in London and other big cities degenerated into riots, the disorders were quelled by unarmed police, not regular troops backed up by armor and automatic weapons.

In the United States, visceral fears aroused by "Khaki Shirts," "Communists," "Marchers," and other such words and phrases were telling. The overreaction to the Bonus Army was to some degree the result of a sense that America's history as a society apart from Europe might be coming to an end. The anxieties of MacArthur, Hurley, and ultimately Hoover about the BEF reflected a sincere sense that the country was becoming increasingly unstable, divided by class, and possibly vulnerable to a *putsch*. Having succumbed, however tentatively, to such fears, Hoover could do nothing to allay them in the coming presidential campaign.

For all the misery of the country, a strong undercurrent of optimism, faith in progress, and American triumphalism coexisted with the surface despair of the Depression. Just days after the dispersal of the Bonus Army, the Olympic Games opened in Los Angeles. Nearly a hundred thousand people jammed the Coliseum for the opening and closing ceremonies. American athletes dominated, beating the closest runners-up, the Italians, by about a 3–1 unofficial point margin and winning forty-one gold medals. Perfect weather, record performances, and astoundingly high gate receipts made the event both memorable in the annals of international sports and profitable for the organizers. Foreign participants spoke admiringly of the comparative wealth, organizational skill, everyday social discipline, and hospitality they encountered in a depression-mired America. A French yachtsman remarked of Americans: "It is not just that they are sporting in games. They are sporting in everything. Their whole life is governed by the idea of fair play."[32]

The Olympics were the ultimate feel-good event of the early years of the Depression, but other highly visible signs of American progress and achievement were equally celebrated. On May 1, 1931, the Empire State Building, the world's tallest, was completed and dedicated in a ceremony attended by Governor Franklin D. Roosevelt and his predecessor, Alfred E. Smith, now president of the company that owned it. In Washington, President Hoover pushed a button that turned on the lights in the great skyscraper. Five months later, Roosevelt and the governor of New Jersey jointly opened the George Washington Bridge, linking the New Jersey Palisades to upper Manhattan. Completed eight months ahead of schedule, stretching 3,500 feet, it was by a large margin the world's longest suspension bridge.[33]

Other indications of progress abounded. In August 1931, the C. R. Baird Company, a British-American corporation, announced with great fanfare that it shortly expected to start manufacturing and selling television receivers at a price of about $100, had arranged for broadcast production of vaudeville and drama in "a few weeks," and had perfected a "portable transmitting set" that would allow live coverage of sporting events and breaking news. That October, the DuPont Company revealed development of a new process to make synthetic rubber, touting its use-fulness for numerous commercial applications and the possibility that it could relieve fears about dependence on foreign rubber supplies in times of emergency.[34]

The symbols were magnificent, the reality less so. The George Washington Bridge was made available to traffic at a time when new auto sales were crashing to lows that doomed marginal companies. The Empire State Building corporation was able to rent only twenty percent of its space and would flounder for years. Baird's extravagant television scheme came to nothing. Synthetic rubber plans went on the shelf, rendered uneconomical by the abundant availability of cheap natural rubber. Progress had been put on hold. It seems safe to say that most Americans still had hope for the future, but it struggled against the undertow of the Depression.

Hoover could not appeal to sentiments of hope; neither his temperament nor his rhetorical talents were up to the task. His record as president could be perceived only as that of a hard-working, well-intentioned failure beaten by forces he did not understand. Could the Democrats offer a candidate capable of appealing to the positive impulses of Americans? The leading possibility was Governor Roosevelt of New York, who had long been one of the most attractive figures in American politics. Convalescing from his polio attack in the 1920s, he had established himself, in the words of Frank Freidel, as a "young elder statesman" working to unite a Democratic party bitterly divided between city and country over such issues as prohibition, immigration, and religion. His semi-recovery from polio had added a sentimental appeal to his charm. His mastery as a radio speaker was unsurpassed in the world of American politics. An upstate Protestant patrician, he long since had learned the art of appealing to immigrant urban working classes. He was by a wide margin the most popular politician in the most populous state in the union.

Roosevelt's nomination for the presidency nonetheless was a near thing. Doubts persisted among influentials about his depth and leadership qualities. In January 1932, Walter Lippmann, the nation's most renowned political journalist, published in a hundred newspapers with a total of ten million readers, wrote a scathing criticism. Lippmann, who had begun as a progressive but now wrote from the political center, had admired the Hoover of the war years and the twenties. He sympathized with the president's dogged efforts to cope with the Depression, seeing him as a man of strength and principle. In Roosevelt, whom he had observed closely for three years, he detected weakness and opportunism. Roosevelt had perfected "the art of carrying water on both shoulders," had constantly avoided political risk, and had averted his gaze from Tammany corruption. He was "a highly impressionable person, without a firm grasp of public affairs and without very strong convictions. . . . an amiable man with many philanthropic impulses, but . . . not the dangerous enemy of anything." Lippmann's blast concluded: "Franklin D. Roosevelt is no crusader. He is no tribune of the people. He is no enemy of entrenched privilege. He is a pleasant man who, without any important qualifications for the office, would very much like to be President."[35]

A shot like this from Lippmann was hard to take. It surely invigorated a stop-Roosevelt movement. A Democratic presidential nomination required two-thirds of the convention votes, a provision that made any front-runner a target for regional leaders, state favorite sons, and dark horses, all hoping to benefit from deadlock. Roosevelt's two most visible opponents were Al Smith, a hero to Northeastern Catholic Democrats who considered him a martyr to the religious bigotry that had hindered his 1928 run for the presidency, and John Nance Garner, the hard-bitten Texan who served as Speaker of the House and in a loose way represented the wing of the party that hated Smith. Long-shot aspirants abounded, most notably Newton D. Baker, a great old progressive who had been Woodrow Wilson's secretary of war. None of them had a truly national following, and none had conveyed the slightest sense that he had a significantly different agenda than Hoover for dealing with the Depression.

Roosevelt, most people sensed, would likely try something new. Those who had followed his record as governor knew of his ambitious state relief program and his progressivism. Those who had heard him on the radio were aware of his upbeat personality and often found him inspirational. But beyond displays of concern and more assistance for the down-and-out American, Roosevelt was unpredictable, and some might have said hopelessly muddled. His roots in the progressive era had given rise to a palpable instinct for change and reform, but, if only because progressivism had never faced an economic crisis, he had no ready-made Depression program. His clearest policy declaration had nothing to do with the economy and was an embarrassing display of inconsistency. Under pressure from America's most powerful press lord, William Randolph Hearst, he executed a 180-degree turn away from his long-held advocacy of American membership in the League of Nations less than three weeks after Lippmann's characterization of him as weak and feckless.

By early 1932, Roosevelt had assembled a team of policy advisers that eventually became known as the "Brains Trust" because its core consisted of three Columbia University professors—Raymond Moley, Adolf A. Berle, and Rexford G. Tugwell. All were believers in planning and regulation, a faith that implied a nationalistic approach to the Depression and a concomitant skepticism toward international solutions. All were advocates of social welfare legislation to benefit the less fortunate half or so of the population. There were significant differences between them, but in 1932 there was little internal debate between them. Political observers perceived them as a relatively united group of academic men urging an ambitious agenda of change and action upon a political leader inclined in that direction.[36]

In the spring of 1932, the Brains Trust was just taking shape. It engaged in some vigorous policy discussions at which Roosevelt was present and helped with his speeches. It was never his only source of policy advice. The governor was also in frequent communication with Felix Frankfurter of the Harvard Law School, an advocate of economic regulation and trust-busting who largely rejected the idea that the government could or should institute a planned economy. With or without Frankfurter and other policy advisers, the Brains Trust lacked the lead time needed to prepare a comprehensive anti-depression program for Roosevelt's primary campaign, and, truth to tell, he surely did not want one. He wanted to seem profoundly at odds with Hoover, intensely concerned with the plight of ordinary Americans, strongly activist by temperament, and more than any other serious candidate in tune with the populist-progressive heritage of the Democratic party.

He did so most emphatically in two notable speeches. The first of these, a radio address on April 7, called for plans "that build from the bottom up . . . that put their faith once more in the forgotten man at the bottom of the economic pyramid." The second, an address at Oglethorpe University on May 22, discussed in general terms the need for government planning: "The country needs and, unless I mistake its temper, the country demands bold, persistent experimentation. It is common sense to take a method and try it: If it fails, admit it frankly and try another. But above all, try something. The millions who are in want will not stand by silently forever. . . ."[37]

Stirring words. They served the purpose of differentiating Roosevelt from his opponents. On April 14, rising to the bait of the "forgotten man" speech, Smith emotionally declared, "This is no time for *demagogues*. . . .

When millions of men and women and children are starving throughout the land, there is always the temptation to some men to stir up class prejudice. . . . Against that effort I set myself uncompromisingly." Smith's overreaction helped Roosevelt consolidate the reformist wing of his party. Those who looked beyond mood and tone, however, found precious little substance. Roosevelt talked of the need to restore farm purchasing power but had no explicit program for doing so. He declared his sympathy for the jobless but ruled out huge public works programs as too expensive and impractical. He attacked the Hawley-Smoot Tariff as destructive of the world economy but stopped short of advocating a general lowering of rates. He expressed a determination to stem the tide of mortgage foreclosures, but had not a good word for Hoover's Home Loan Bank bill. In the spring of 1932, it was clear to everyone that Hoover was fighting a tide that threatened to overwhelm him, but at least he had a reasonably clear-cut program. Where was Roosevelt's?[38]

Credibility questions aside, the road to the nomination was bound to be difficult. Roosevelt won numerous primaries and accumulated delegates in many non-primary states, but Smith's emotional hold on Northeastern urban Democrats was hard to break. Smith won primaries in Massachusetts and New Jersey, swept the state Democratic conventions of Rhode Island and Connecticut, took nearly half the delegates at stake in the Pennsylvania primary, and laid claim to perhaps half the New York delegation. Garner had unchallenged control of the Texas delegation and considerable strength in the Southwest. Supported by the redoubtable William Gibbs McAdoo, he dealt Roosevelt a stunning defeat in the California primary. At the end of June, Roosevelt's supporters came to Chicago for the Democratic Convention with 566 publicly committed votes, a bare majority but about 200 short of two-thirds. Another 115 or so were leaning in his direction. He and his supporters understood that his candidacy now had a political life of no more than a half-dozen or so ballots.

A tentative Roosevelt foray to repeal the two-thirds rule had to be abandoned for lack of support. Rumors abounded that Smith would find an excuse to address the convention and precipitate a tidal wave of support. At the end of the first ballot on Thursday evening June 30, Roosevelt had 666 votes to Smith's 201 and Garner's 90. The voting dragged on all through the night. Second ballot: Roosevelt, 677; Smith, 194; Garner, 90. Third ballot: Roosevelt, 682; Smith, 190; Garner, 101. Adjournment at 9:15 a.m., Friday morning. Roosevelt's support was stretched to the limit and likely to break after one more indecisive ballot. Smith, or possibly Newton Baker, would be the likely beneficiary. Roosevelt, in near-constant telephone communication from Albany with his managers in Chicago, dealt frantically with Garner and McAdoo and the king-maker behind them, William Randolph Hearst. The bargain was struck before the convention reassembled on Friday afternoon. Texas and California would put Roosevelt over. Garner would get the vice-presidential nomination. McAdoo and Hearst would have the satisfaction of beating their bitter rival Smith. Roosevelt must have reflected to himself that his cave-in on the League of Nations had paid off. Garner, off in Washington, waxed philosophical to a surprised young journalist: "I'm a little older than you are, son. And politics is funny."[39]

Roosevelt had eked out a close victory in a time-honored and legitimate but uninspiring way. He immediately made himself an exciting candidate by doing something no presidential nominee before him had done. Instead of waiting several weeks for a ceremonial delegation to "inform" him of his nomination and ask his acceptance, he flew from Albany to Chicago to accept at once and in person. (Had he just possibly taken a cue from Hitler's air campaigning in Germany earlier that year?) His decision to make the flight through turbulent weather added to the drama. His jaunty presence after a day of buffeting in the air impressed the delegates, according to the journalist Arthur Krock, "as a proof of his venturesome spirit and fine physical equipment for the office of President." His speech, heard across the country, firmly established his mastery of radio and provided an ideal introduction to a people looking for an alternative to Hoover.[40]

His words reinforced the sense that he was a man of vigor, innovation, and action. They must have left many devoted Democrats thinking that he was a man of destiny. It was time, he declared, to break with foolish traditions of all sorts, to make the Democratic party a party of liberal thought and planned action, to establish an administration alive to the needs of ordinary consumers, workers, and farmers, to develop employment programs for a million men, to refinance oppressive farm and home mortgages, to reestablish international trade on a reciprocal basis. Americans wanted two things: work and a reasonable measure of security. These were his goals. "I pledge you, I pledge myself, to a new deal for the American people," he concluded. "Give me your help, not to win votes alone, but to win in this crusade to restore America to its own people."[41]

The candidate was charismatic. The words were stirring—and fairly vague. From Roosevelt's perspective, the objective of the campaign was party cohesion, not ideological coherence. He maintained his progressive identity and did not shrink from appealing to insurgent Republicans, but he was also well aware that he was standing astride regional and ideological fault lines that had divided the Democratic party since 1920. For the moment, the Depression had stilled the cultural divisions of the previous decade. The party had achieved a rough consensus in favor of repealing the Eighteenth Amendment and prohibition, but the divisions between city and country, old-stock Anglo-Saxon and new immigrant, Catholic and Protestant, metropolitan America and provincial America were not far beneath the surface. Roosevelt owed his nomination more to the South and the West—since William Jennings Bryan the traditional Democratic electoral base—than to his own Northeast, where his party was usually identified with unsavory political machines such as New York's Tammany. More than its Republican adversary, the Democratic party was an uneasy conglomerate of regional and ideological factions that had to be united by comforting generalizations, not hard and fast blueprints.

Roosevelt surely sensed that the nation wanted leadership above all else. Better to make the campaign one that featured his persona versus Hoover's than one that featured debates over half-formulated recovery plans. Better to submit to the imperatives of a two-party system that encouraged coalition, compromise, and ideological fuzziness. Better to maximize a near-certain victory than to dim its luster by alienating part of his constituency. The Democratic campaign of 1932 would emphasize its candidate's personality, promise prosperity, and establish a general sense of direction. Roosevelt campaigned energetically, traveling to the West Coast and back by train in September, then doing another circuit through the northeastern quadrant of the country in October. (The South was still safely Democratic, the West not yet populous enough to warrant a second trip.) His speeches underscored real differences on the cause and nature of the Depression with the Hoover administration and forecast many policies he actually would put into effect, but they also sent out many false signals.

The tone of the Roosevelt campaign was well in line with a Democratic platform that tore into Hoover for irresponsible spending, accused him of promoting inflation, and promised to cut federal expenditures by twenty-five percent. It also pledged "a sound currency to be preserved at all hazards" and an international monetary conference "to consider the rehabilitation of silver." Having imposed drastic financial constraints, it nonetheless promised relief for the unemployed, expanded federal public works, and "the restoration of agriculture, the nation's basic industry." It condemned the Hawley-Smoot Tariff without promising the general low-ering of rates that had been standard Democratic policy in the past. It pledged substantial new federal programs to regulate big business, public utilities, and the financial markets. Political party conventions fixated on appeals to many interests often produce internally contradictory plat-forms. All the same, it was a bit dismaying to listen to Roosevelt make a major radio speech, indicating his adherence point by point.[42]

From beginning to end, the two candidates differed sharply on the nature of the Depression. The arguments of both were political con-structs that neglected a far more complex reality and evaded the critical issues of war debts and international currency stabilization. Hoover insisted that the Depression was a foreign cataclysm that had spread to the United States. Therefore it was nearly impossible to achieve full recovery from within. Roosevelt asserted that the Depression was made in America by unsound Republican policies that neglected farmers, encouraged financial speculation, and destroyed foreign trade. The impli-cation was that he would follow a "recovery in one country" policy while leaving the rest of the world to its own devices.[43]

No one believed the Democratic candidate would be a do-nothing president. He condemned big finance and promised extensive regulation in tones reminiscent of the progressivism of Louis Brandeis. Taking a track designed to split the difference between the nationalist planners of the Brains Trust and old-fashioned low tariff progressives, he emphasized reciprocal trade agreements which would be negotiated with one nation at a time with due consideration for American interests. He called for stronger regulation of the public utilities and advocated major "yardstick" federal hydroelectric projects in each section of the country—along the Columbia River in the Northwest, at the already-begun Boulder Dam in the Southwest, on the St. Lawrence River in the Northeast, and at Sena-tor Norris's cherished Muscle Shoals in the Southeast. In a controversial, attention-getting speech at Pittsburgh, he reaffirmed the platform pledge to cut the federal budget by a quarter.[44]

In Salt Lake City, he talked of a strong federal transportation policy. In Topeka, he advocated a vague wide-ranging agricultural policy built around "the planned use of the land," but avoided the phrase "acreage allotments." His most daring address, drafted by Adolf Berle, was delivered on September 23 in San Francisco to the Commonwealth Club. Based on a sweeping interpretation of American history derived from the then-dominant "progressive" school identified with Frederick Jackson Turner and Charles A. Beard, it declared that since the turn of the century the end of the frontier, the exhaustion of free land, and the growth of large corporations had made inevitable the strong state and the planned economy. Deprived of the "safety valve" of the frontier and denied major overseas markets by tariff barriers, the American economy had achieved a state of maturity that without state interference would lead inevitably to consolidation and control by a private economic oligarchy. The necessary alternative was strong regulation and managerial guidance by a democratic state, reining in the selfish pursuit of private advantage. The generalizations would take on significance in retrospect, but here as elsewhere the speech was bereft of a specific program.[45]

Other pronouncements promised "social justice" in the form of numerous welfare programs designed to humanize an uncaring industrial system, the impersonality of which had been laid bare by the Depression. A major speech made a firm commitment to farm mortgage refinancing and promised efforts to return farms that had been foreclosed to their original owners. Roosevelt reached out in unprecedented fashion to Republican progressives, beginning a relationship that would never be without a mutual wariness but was based on a sense of reciprocal need. In McCook, Nebraska, on September 28, he eulogized Senator George Norris and received the old man's endorsement as a friend of the farmer and of public electric power. Beyond Norris, he saw a line to many other Republicans and independents.[46]

The Roosevelt of the fall of 1932 had emerged unmistakably as a man of action and an agent of change. No one could doubt that he would be a progressive president, perhaps a radical. Reform there was aplenty in his speeches. Whether there was a Depression recovery program was far less certain.

Hoover campaigned futilely against the Democratic juggernaut. He had worked himself to a point of chronic exhaustion, had gone as far in government activism as his principles would allow, and believed unequivocally that he was on the right track. Roosevelt's contradictory positions, vague generalities, and intimations of socialistic radicalism outraged him. His much more limited campaign alternated between defensive self-justification and bitter resentment. It had more than a whiff of political death about it. Writing with measured sympathy and condescension—

both emotions justified—Rexford Tugwell has observed that Hoover's public appearances revealed "a high-collared recluse who wore a weary and sourish smile. . . . so taken up with his pressing problems that he could not see the yearning for reassurance in the faces turned up to him in the crowds." Roosevelt radiated vigor, projected concern, and created audience response.[47]

Hoover believed that the economy had been recovering since the summer and would gain momentum once the uncertainty of the campaign was over. Statistically, he had a point. The AFL employment census calculated that joblessness had peaked in July and declined significantly since then. It estimated a net gain of 560,000 jobs in September but cautioned that most of the number was likely seasonal and transitory. Britain and Germany had also experienced mild upswings. Full international recovery, however, required initiatives that could come only from the United States. A more stable American government might have negotiated agreements with Britain, France, and other powers to cancel war debts, liberalize international trade, and fix currency exchange rates. Such an achievement could have transformed the world economy.

But by the end of 1932 the opportunity was gone; too much that was irreversible had happened over the past three years. In the United States, sentiment against debt cancellation was overwhelming and transcended partisan or ideological boundaries. Hoover would never have countenanced any adjustment in the gold value of the dollar. He had come to see Hawley-Smoot as a positive good in a protectionist world. The Ottawa conference had entrenched the idea of British imperial preference just about the time the campaign began. Germany, even before Hitler, was going its own way. The French, already at odds with the United States on issues ranging from war debts to raids on U.S. gold reserves, seemed to be slapping prohibitive duties on some American product every few weeks. During the campaign, the president ostentatiously ordered the Tariff Commission to reexamine with an eye to higher rates the tariff schedules on sixteen items. If protection were taken away, he declared, "the grass will grow in the streets of a hundred cities, a thousand towns; the weeds will overrun the fields of millions of farms."[48]

When Hoover came to Detroit to deliver a speech that listed ten signs of an emerging recovery, he was met at the railroad station by a crowd of angry, jeering demonstrators, and driven past blocks lined with silent, sullen spectators before he finally could speak to a crowd of partisan believers. He listed some portents of recovery—gold inflows, rising bond prices, upticks in manufacturing and construction, increased freight car loadings, higher imports and exports, declining bank failures—but these had to be weighed against the nearly eleven million unemployed still looking for work. The day after Hoover delivered his speech in Detroit, Charles C. Burlingham, the president of the New York City Welfare Council, estimated that 1,150,000 workers, approximately one-third of the city's workforce, were unemployed, a terrifying increase from the 800,000 of a year earlier. New York at least, even at the bottom of the Depression, was rich enough to provide minimal relief; much of America was not so lucky. Burlingham concluded with an admonition to those who decried the dole: "let us not be deceived—for the last three years New York has been 'doling' on a greater scale than any European city."[49]

On November 8, just two days after the German elections that had handed substantial reverses to the Nazis, the nation voted. It was quickly apparent that Roosevelt and the Democrats were the beneficiaries of an awesome landslide—forty-two states, 472 electoral votes, fifty-eight percent of the presidential vote, sixty seats in the Senate, 310 in the House. Celebrations everywhere featured the party's campaign song, "Happy Days Are Here Again."

The worst was yet to come.

In Britain and Germany, leadership shifts were quick and decisive. Roosevelt's election left him 116 days—nearly one-third of a year—from power. American presidents were still inaugurated on March 4 of the year after their election. Until then, Hoover, decisively repudiated and lacking the slightest moral authority for any new policy departures, would preside over the nation. Moreover, the old Congress would return as usual the first week in December for its customary lame-duck session, almost as devoid of authority as the president and far less responsible. During that period, numerous European nations defaulted on their war debts, Hitler became chancellor of Germany with dictatorial powers, the Reichstag building went up in flames, Japan quit the League of Nations—and the American economy seemed to slide irreversibly downward.

It is unlikely that anything approaching a full international recovery had been taking shape by mid-1932. Still, there had been some signs of upward momentum. The uncertainty of the long American election season was surely a drag on that momentum. The interregnum between Roosevelt's victory and his inauguration left the United States, and by extension the rest of the world, rudderless. An economic price was exacted by an American democracy that was turbulent in its conflicts, yet leisurely in its timetables. That price was paid not just by Americans but by the citizens of all the other countries that had to look to the American economic locomotive for forward movement.

During the four months between Roosevelt's election and his assumption of office, the U.S. economy slumped severely. Unemployment in January 1933 was about three million greater than a year earlier. Britain reported a relatively small increase of 100,000 unemployment insurance claims to 2,950,000, the peak figure of the Depression; Germany reported a slight decrease from the record high January of a year earlier. It was of course far from clear that the two European powers had hit bottom and were beginning a bounceback. It seemed certain that the American economy was sinking fast and threatened to drag the rest of the world down with it. In addition to choosing a cabinet and otherwise organizing an administration, Roosevelt as president-elect faced strong pressures to deal in some fashion with the worsening crisis; yet, whatever his moral authority, his constitutional power was nil.[50]

It was natural enough for many people to hope that he could somehow cooperate with President Hoover. The president, embittered by his defeat and highly resentful of Roosevelt, wanted cooperation and joint agreement, but only on his own terms. In addition to a prudential reluctance to undertake agreements he had no power to make, Roosevelt valued above all his freedom of action. Moreover, as the campaign had clearly indicated, his nationalist recovery agenda was at variance with Hoover's conviction that the Depression had to be attacked as an international problem. These institutional difficulties and policy differences made some sort of informal transitional regime almost impossible. Sealing the futility of the enterprise was the unhappy fact that the hostility between the two men and their aides generated a suffocating atmosphere when they met in the same room.

At the beginning of 1933, Hoover's first priority was the war debt issue, a sentiment reinforced by the urgings of numerous European foreign offices. Britain especially, having flirted with default at the end of 1932, was determined to achieve a reduction and rescheduling of payments, if not outright cancellation. The British and the rest of those who had kept payments current were, moreover, prepared to default in June if no agreement could be reached. Hoover clung to his campaign insistence that the debts could never be canceled but offered the hope of altered terms in return for trade concessions, international currency stabilization (a euphemism for a general return to the gold standard), and European arms reductions. He thus expected to link the debt question to the ongoing Geneva disarmament conference and the upcoming London World Economic Conference.

There was much to be said for an international approach—although the difficulties were enormous by early 1933—but little for Hoover's formula, which unrealistically overestimated American bargaining power. The British were determined not to be forced back to gold prematurely, but they were willing to bargain—if Roosevelt wanted to play the game. Characteristically, the president-elect declined to say "no" while never quite committing himself to the enterprise. Characteristically also, he dealt with British emissaries in a way that left them hopeful for his presidency.[51]

Within the United States in the meantime the economy was approaching a collapse that exceeded the European experience. By mid-February, the banking system appeared to be imploding. Compared to its European counterparts, it had always been rickety and decentralized. Even the Federal Reserve system as it existed then was unable to provide the regulation and support that British, French, or Germans routinely expected of a central bank. Two-thirds of the nation's banks—the weakest two-thirds—did not even belong to it. Worse yet, its board of governors in Washington was limited in power, unsophisticated in policy conceptualization, and, as a group, marginal in competence. Neither an effective mutual insurance system nor a government guarantee plan existed to provide individual banks protection against runs by frightened depositors, bad investments, or large loan defaults. The American federal system and its state-by-state regulations preempted effective national supervision of all but U.S.-chartered banks. Widespread prohibitions against branch banking meant there would be many tiny banks, a fair number of substantial ones, and only a few really large, internationally competitive institutions, most of them in New York City. During the prosperous years of the twenties, banks, mostly small and inconsequential, had failed at a rate of ten to twelve a week. But the failures were scattered, rarely affected large numbers of people, and seemed to pose no threat to the financial system.[52]

Increasingly, the Depression laid bare the weaknesses of American banking. In 1930, 1,352 banks closed their doors—a rate of twenty-six per week—with nearly half the failures coming in the last two months. In

1931, the total grew to 2,294—forty-four a week. In 1932, RFC loans and the Darwinian principle of the survival of the fittest combined to cut the number to 1433—a little less than twenty-eight a week. But by the end of 1932, bank failures had happened almost everywhere, many of them substantial. Partial restitution was increasingly rare. Millions of Americans had lost deposits—usually small but valued savings of less than $1,000—in failed banks.[53]

By then also, people were anxiety-ridden about the fate of the money they had in still-solvent banks and eager for a scapegoat. The Democratic Congress intensified the first emotion and satisfied the second. By mandating that the RFC publish a list of its loan recipients, Congress in effect established a hit list of banks. Insecure depositors lined up in city after city to withdraw their funds from RFC-supported banks, thereby nullifying the impact of the aid. The Senate Banking and Currency Committee undertook an investigation of the leaders of the financial establishment. Its chief counsel, Ferdinand Pecora, grilled them relentlessly in the manner of a prosecuting attorney about unwise loans, high salaries, bonuses, even their own income tax returns, all to demonstrate, as Kenneth Davis has put it, that they were "liars, cheats, and swindlers on a grand scale, albeit they operated generally within the letter of loosely drawn laws." The causes of the banking collapse were systemic, not personal, but the public had no taste for fine judgments. The Democrats had found a scapegoat group they would bash for years.[54]

In mid-February, banks all over the country began to close.

The collapsing economy, the attack on the banking establishment, and a fear that the new administration would devalue the dollar all combined to create a crisis of confidence that led many depositors to close out their bank accounts, in many cases with the objective of converting to gold in advance of a devaluation. Working people and huge international investors behaved alike. The only difference was that the little people put their bills or sack of gold coins in hiding places at home, while the international investors shipped their gold to safe storage in London or Paris. The effect was to create a massive drain of money and credit from the economy and to put all surviving banks in jeopardy. The resumption of large gold outflows across the Atlantic endangered the dollar. Neither the Federal Reserve nor the Treasury seemed capable of meeting the crisis.

On February 13, Henry Ford demanded the Ford Motor Company's balance of $25 million from the First National Bank of Detroit, declaring that if the government would take no action, he had no choice but to protect his interests. This much-criticized action may have displayed the mentality of a small shopkeeper, but it had an inexorable logic. It also threatened to destroy First National and possibly bring down every bank in Michigan. The governor responded by declaring a "bank holiday"—a temporary shutdown that would prevent catastrophic runs but also make it impossible to do business on an ordinary basis. There had been other such holidays, but this one set off a national trend. Over the next two weeks state authorities everywhere either ordered temporary closures or placed strict limits on withdrawals.[55]

Hoover himself would do nothing without Roosevelt's concurrence. On February 17, he dispatched an extraordinary handwritten letter to the president-elect. It demonstrated that even the steady Hoover was losing his grip. Intentionally or not, he had produced a document more likely to provoke Roosevelt than to elicit cooperation. He wrote at length of an incipient recovery that had been stalled by the actions of the Democratic Congress through the first half of 1932, had begun to gain momentum in the fall, then had been derailed by the outcome of the election and a resulting crisis of confidence. "It would steady the country greatly," he told Roosevelt, "if there could be prompt assurance that there will be no tampering or inflation of the currency; that the budget will be unquestionably balanced, even if further taxation is necessary; that the government credit will be maintained by refusal to exhaust it in the issue of securities." Roosevelt dismissed the letter as "cheeky."

Historians have been prone to portray the communication as a ploy, citing a letter Hoover wrote to Senator David Reed a few days later in which Hoover observed that if Roosevelt made the requested declaration he would in effect ratify the Republican program and abandon "90% of the so-called new deal." Read in full, however, both documents make it clear that Hoover was perfectly sincere. He was also frightened.

Roosevelt frequently seemed heedless of the urgency Hoover so deeply felt; like many progressives, he sometimes talked to aides as if only the bankers were being hurt. After another note from Hoover, he prepared a response on March 1. It contained no assurances, no program, and no hope. "I am equally concerned with you in regard to the banking situation . . . but my thought is that it is so very deep-seated that the fire is bound to spread in spite of anything that is done by way of mere statements." Fortunately, the exchange remained private. Three days before his inauguration, the new president seemed to have no solution to the banking crisis.[56]

All the same, there were reasons to believe that Roosevelt could lead a nation. In Miami on February 15, a deranged assassin named Giuseppe Zangara had fired on him, narrowly missed, and mortally wounded the mayor of Chicago, Anton Cermak. Displaying courage and composure, apparently heedless of his own near-escape, Roosevelt comforted Cermak all the way to the nearest hospital. Neither at the time nor later by all accounts did he show signs of fear or nervous aftershock. The country admired the steel he had displayed.[57]

"We are at the end of our rope," Hoover remarked to an aide late on the evening of March 3. And so it seemed might also be the country. Here and there in the midwestern farm regions, armed groups effectively prevented foreclosure sales. In Iowa, the Farmers' Holiday Association sporadically blocked shipments of products to market. In some cities, laid-off utility workers tapped electric lines to restore power to homes that had failed to pay their bills. There were scattered reports of groups invading supermarkets and appropriating supplies of food without paying. Communists staged disorderly "hunger" demonstrations across the country.[58]

Yet what was remarkable was not sporadic disorder but the prevalence of order at a time of disaster. Americans might be less deferential toward their leaders than the British, but in no country were middle-class attitudes so widely held. The nation hoped for recovery under Franklin Roosevelt, was willing to follow him if he provided leadership, and anticipated, not a revolution, but another chapter in the history of a democratic republic that was 150 years old.

HEADLINES AND MOVIE NEWSREELS

{1933}

MARCH 5   500,000 in Washington Streets Cheer Roosevelt

MARCH 26   "'Let's Try It!' Says Roosevelt" *(New York Times Magazine)*

APRIL 23   Roosevelt and MacDonald Favor World Action on Money and Trade

JUNE 18   Proposal to Peg Moneys Is Rejected by Roosevelt; Debt Defaulters Rebuked; Stabilization Opposed; President Keeps Policy of Currency Freedom to Aid Prices

JULY 2   London Conference Urged to Adjourn

JULY 9   Stocks Up in Year by $23,500,000,000; Weekly Business Index Advances to Highest Level in Three Years; Export Upturn Since First of Year

To Chicago World's Fair and Back for as little as $27.25. Once in a Lifetime a Chance Like This! (advertisement)

THE NEW DEAL

THE FIRST 125 DAYS

The Planners: Raymond Moley, Adolf A. Berle, Jr., Rexford Tugwell

The New Deal had many sources. In the end, the most fundamental were the biases and preferences of Franklin D. Roosevelt, but Roosevelt, like almost all working politicians, was a man of action, not contemplation. At most, he could provide an experimental attitude and assign the task of drawing detailed blueprints to others. On Inauguration Day, 1933, everyone assumed that foremost among the "others" were the three men who had led the Brains Trust—Raymond Moley, Adolf A. Berle, Jr., and Rexford Tugwell. All were strong advocates of national economic planning. All were professors at Columbia University. All were representatives of a new "public service intellectual" elite that had emerged at the end of the nineteenth century and laid claims to power as administrators and policy conceptualizers.[1] Although their immediate goal was the repair of the economy, Tugwell was the sole professional economist among them. Political economists in the large sense of the term, they wanted to do more than restore prosperity. They hoped to set a new course for the nation.

As a disgruntled former president, Herbert Hoover would later charge the New Deal (and by implication its early thinkers) with fascist sympathies. The Brains Trusters were of course aware of Mussolini's apparent success in bringing order and discipline to Italy. His organization of the economy into "corporations" in which both labor and management were represented doubtless struck them as attractive in theory. Tugwell also had traveled to the Soviet Union in the 1920s and had been impressed by its elaborate and seemingly effective exercise in economic planning. All the same, none of them gave the slightest indication of an affinity for anti-democratic solutions. They sought to establish not a fascist-style corporate state—all but impossible in a fluid society without a feudal past—but a progressive organizational state far different from Mussolini's political economy. In varying degrees, they did want to reduce the power and influence of the "capitalist classes" while enlarging that of the public service intellectuals like themselves.

The Brains Trusters and their blueprint for the "First New Deal" were products of the American progressive era. Pragmatists, they believed that human intelligence could organize a society in a fashion that would maximize democracy and equitably ameliorate the differences between social groups. Optimistic (perhaps excessively rationalistic) democrats, they thought that in an increasingly complex urban industrial society, the state would inevitably assume a larger mission in bringing order to economic and social relations and that the transition could be managed democratically by people like themselves.

Raymond Moley later would be remembered as the conservative renegade among the three, but in 1933 most observers saw him as the mastermind behind the most far-reaching reorganization of the American economy ever attempted. Forty-six years old when Roosevelt took the oath of office, Moley had been born near Cleveland, Ohio. He had taught school in and been elected mayor of the village of North Olmstead while still a young man. He had gone on to graduate study in state and local government at Columbia University, where he received his Ph.D. in 1918. A young progressive with Democratic party inclinations from the beginning of his political consciousness, Moley was successively devoted to William Jennings Bryan, Henry George, Tom Johnson, and Woodrow Wilson. As a graduate student, he was deeply influenced by Charles Van Hise's *Concentration and Control,* a work second in influence only to Herbert Croly's *The Promise of American Life* for its argument that it was up to the federal government to control and channel the power of big business and to develop the economy. His dissertation supervisor and lifelong influence was the radical historian-political scientist Charles A. Beard. After a few years as director of the Cleveland Foundation, he returned to Columbia as a professor of public law, combining that pursuit with public service as a member of several special commissions dealing with crime.

Organizer and informal chairman of the Brains Trust in 1932, he went to Washington with the new president, who appointed him an assistant secretary of state with the understanding that he really would be a White House aide and policy formulator. Professorial in demeanor, unremarkable in appearance, shrinking from public self-promotion, Moley nonetheless during the new regime's first six months seemed to have a hand in every initiative and was often depicted as Roosevelt's master organizer. The view was exaggerated, but Moley's thinking set the First New Deal's themes: unprecedented governmental organization of the economy, a managed currency, and a nationalist approach to recovery, accompanied by a commitment to the autonomy of corporations, labor unions, individual enterprisers, and even bankers. Following Van Hise, he and the administration accepted economic concentration; "control" meant federal guidance and coordination.

Yet after only six months Moley was out of the administration, in equal parts a casualty of his own hubris, his lack of a political base, the hostility of his nominal superior Cordell Hull, and the misconception that he could combine a career as a news magazine editor with service to the president. For the next three and a half years, he gave occasional advice and assistance to a chief executive who had no real need for him. By Roosevelt's second term, he had perceptibly moved far toward the conviction that the activist state, at least when characterized by an anti-commercial tone, was a greater threat than the unregulated market.[2]

Adolf A. Berle, Jr., would begin his political life a progressive, always remain one, and serve Roosevelt to the end. The brilliant son of a noted Boston congregational minister with social gospel inclinations, young Adolf graduated from Harvard College at the age of eighteen and Harvard Law School at twenty-one. In short order, he was an associate in the law firm of Louis Brandeis, an army intelligence officer in the World War, and a member of the American delegation at the Paris peace conference. Establishing himself in New York after the war, he began a lucrative practice in corporate law while taking *pro bono* cases on behalf of American Indian rights, doing amateur social work among the poor at the Henry Street Settlement House, and teaching at the Columbia University Law School.

In 1932, Berle, assisted by the economist Gardiner Means, published *The Modern Corporation and Private Property*. The book decried a concentration of wealth and power in approximately two hundred large corporations, controlled by a managerial class that it argued was accountable neither to stockholders (the real owners) nor the general public. Louis Brandeis had made much the same diagnosis two decades earlier to argue for breaking up big business. Berle and Means believed antitrust action was misguided. The American corporation was an unrivaled producer of wealth; it needed to be controlled, not destroyed. A vigorous government, acting in the public interest, could contain the antisocial tendencies of corporate power through institutionalized planning and regulation. This argument qualified Berle naturally for the Brains Trust, and Moley vigorously recruited him. His contribution to the campaign reached its zenith when he wrote Roosevelt's attention-getting Commonwealth Club speech.

Realizing the limits of his political clout (reinforced after 1933 by Moley's brief Washington career), Berle declined several offers of positions in the new administration. Staying in New York, he became a backer of Fiorello La Guardia and an important adviser to the independent, pro–New Deal, mayor. He corresponded fairly regularly with the president, always addressing him as "Caesar," occasionally assisted in writing speeches for him, but did not accept a Washington job until 1938. His advice, sometimes on New York politics, sometimes on wider issues, was more practical than ideological. By keeping himself away from Washington, he probably had more long-run influence with Roosevelt than his two colleagues. In 1933, however, his contribution to the emerging New Deal was primarily in his acclaimed book and its assertion that government should channel and control corporate power for the greater good.[3]

Rexford Tugwell would serve as the lightning rod for enemies of the New Deal, and fittingly so, for he stood discernibly to the left of his two associates. A native of upstate New York, he had worked as a youth on his father's prosperous orchard farm and in the family canning business. He went on to study economics at the University of Pennsylvania. There his most important teacher was Simon Patten, the progressive scholar who discerned that American capitalism was producing a "social surplus" beyond the population's requirement for a subsistence existence. Patten posited the mission of reform as the equitable allocation of the surplus through the mechanism of a planned economy with a redistributionist agenda. By 1933, Tugwell was a leader of the left wing of the "institutional school" of economists, scholars who dismissed market theory in favor of the view that the economy was an integrated whole with an identity larger than an amalgam of fleeting transactions.

From his college days, he had been powerfully affected by the intellectual ferment of progressivism in its more collectivist forms. He frequently cited Thorstein Veblen, the most flamboyant and radical of the institutionalists, to the effect that capitalist economies and their pricing mechanisms produced scarcity, that hence the economy needed to be taken away from profiteers and turned over to "engineers" who would manage it for maximum production and social abundance. He revered the utopian socialist Scott Nearing. As a college senior, Tugwell had published the sort of social poetry guaranteed to strike terror into the hearts of industrialists, bankers, and literary critics: "I am sick of a nation's stenches, / I am sick of propertied czars. . . . / I have dreamed my great dream of their passing, I have gathered my tools and my charts; / My plans are fashioned and practical; / I shall roll up my sleeves and make America over!"[4]

Appointed to the economics faculty at Columbia University in 1920, he combined research in agricultural economics with continued political activism. By the time he joined the Brains Trust, he was convinced that the agricultural problem could not be solved by the overseas dumping of surpluses. Instead, taking the idea from fellow economist and activist M. L. Wilson, he advocated subsidized acreage allotments that would reduce supply at its source.

Handsome, intellectually brilliant, confident to the point of arrogance, Tugwell attracted critics by the dozen. Not a Communist, not a Marxist, he was nevertheless a collectivist and an elitist. Effortlessly, he produced his own surplus of political enemies and ideological foes. He relished the kind of overstatement frequently made by professors trying to provoke students or colleagues. Speaking to the American Economics Association in December 1931, he criticized the proposals of business leaders Gerard Swope and Henry I. Harriman for business self-regulation and planning. Only government could do the job, he declared, and it had to be done in totality, through "the laying of rough, unholy hands upon many a sacred precedent, doubtless calling for an enlarged and national police force." He predicted a society in which "industry is government and government is industry."[5]

Roosevelt, a far more prudent man, liked him nonetheless, finding his charisma and penchant for the unorthodox appealing. In early 1933, Tugwell and the incoming secretary of agriculture, Henry A. Wallace, struck up a relationship characterized by mutual admiration. The Columbia economist was placed in the Agriculture Department, first as assistant secretary, then undersecretary, putting a new series of farm programs in place, now and again advising the president on various other topics, interesting himself in experimental cooperative relief efforts, but also doing much of the department's administrative heavy lifting. For four years, loyally supported by Wallace, he rode out one controversy after another, most of them occasioned by his sharp tongue and his gift for expressing unadorned, unhedged sentiments about social reorganization. At times, he seemed to glory in such appellations as Rex the Red. Yet when he departed in 1937, he was not dumped. He exited voluntarily, discouraged by Roosevelt's movement away from planning and by the resurgence in Washington of an old progressivism that he considered reactionary. For all its upheaval and sound and fury, the New Deal was not the revolution for which he had hoped.

In March 1933, it appeared to many observers that the leading brains trusters would play a central role in the new administration. In fact, they already had performed their mission by giving Roosevelt an overall design for recovery. After March 4, politicians would have to fill in its details. Moreover, the lack of an institutionalized presidential advisory staff meant they could not play a regular White House role. Each would suffer the fate of the dispensable appliance that had served its purpose.

They had given the president the outlines of a recovery plan that envisioned far-reaching changes in the structure of the American economy and had done so with scant regard for the conventional wisdom of economic theory. Many years later, Moley remarked that both he and Roosevelt "were bored and confused by long, learned memoranda" that analyzed an isolated economic problem. All three were essentially *reformers*, persuaded, as was Roosevelt, that their reforms would bring economic recovery. A long and difficult trial by politics lay ahead.

Saturday, March 4, 1933. Inauguration Day was cold and gray and all too reflective of the country's predicament. The nation was not on the verge of revolution; it was badly beaten down but hopeful that a new president could somehow achieve a renewal. By and large the news media—still largely the print press, supplemented a bit by movie newsreels (but not yet by serious radio news operations)—wanted to support him. He faced little vocal, reflexive partisan hostility and even less of the journalistic skepticism that would become the norm a generation later. Democrats, still usually a minority, flocked to Washington to celebrate their return to power. A half-million spectators turned out for the inaugural parade. An estimated hundred thousand people crowded into the forty acres of open space at the east front of the Capitol and endured a chill wind to witness the inaugural address. Millions of Americans waited at their radios.

Roosevelt did not disappoint. His first two minutes were sheer uplift. The nation would endure; there was nothing to fear but fear itself. Then he launched into a survey of the economic situation that demonstrated presidential awareness of an economic catastrophe. He followed with an attack on America's favorite villains, "the unscrupulous money changers" who had led the country astray. "They know only the rules of a genera-tion of self-seekers. They have no vision, and when there is no vision the people perish."

Bankers having been labeled as somehow responsible for the collapse, the new president promised "action, and action now"—putting people to work, raising agricultural prices, stemming the tide of mortgage foreclo-sures, engaging in national planning, strictly supervising "all banking and credit and investments, so that there will be an end to speculation with other people's money," and making provision for "an adequate but sound currency." He would call Congress into special session and ask for strong authority—if necessary, for "broad Executive power to wage a war against the emergency, as great as the power that would be given to me if we were in fact invaded by a foreign foe." Democracy would prevail. The people had not failed. "They have asked for discipline and direction under leadership. They have made me the present instrument of their wishes. In the spirit of the gift I take it."[6]

Parsed at a distance by disinterested scholars, some of these passages might seem a bit chilling—the blanket attack on bankers, the promise of action, the demands for strong powers, the assertion that the new chief executive represented the will of the people, the words about discipline and direction, the conviction that big majorities conferred extraordinary powers. Even Eleanor Roosevelt thought it "a little terrifying" that her husband received his greatest ovation when he talked about wielding wartime authority. But however fine it might appear, the line between leadership and dictatorship was clear to thoughtful observers. Undirected chaos was the prelude to dictatorship, Germany a paradigm of a failed, undisciplined democracy, and Hitler the barbaric outcome. In a personal meeting with Roosevelt and in his syndicated column, Walter Lippmann, clearly motivated by the example of Germany, urged the new president to assume "dictatorial powers" in order to save American freedoms. Eight days before the inauguration, he told his readers: "A democracy which fails to concentrate authority in an emergency inevitably falls into such confusion that the ground is prepared for the rise of a dictator." [7]

On the day after the inauguration, Germany was scheduled to hold a blatantly rigged election which everyone knew would ratify the Nazi dictatorship and likely would be the last for years to come. Washington, of course, was not Berlin or Rome. Roosevelt had no paramilitary units marching into the capital behind him, no intention of ruling by force and intimidation, no ambition to destroy the opposition. What he did expect to do was to mobilize popular consent to a degree rarely achieved by any American president.

Editorial comment was overwhelmingly positive, even from strongly Republican newspapers, including the *Chicago Tribune,* which hailed the inaugural address's "dominant note of courageous confidence." The Democratic *Atlanta Constitution* placed it "among the greatest of historic State papers of the nation." Some commentators believed the national spirit had been miraculously transformed. But rhetoric, however inspirational, could only pave the way for policy; a call to action had to be followed by action. Roosevelt and the men around him knew in general outline what they wanted to do. They rapidly moved to fill in the blanks. [8]

The banking crisis provided an opportunity for rapid, decisive action. On Sunday, March 5, the president issued a proclamation calling Congress into special session Thursday, March 9. At one o'clock in the morning, Monday, March 6, another proclamation ordered a "bank holiday." It was the first in a series of proclamations and executive orders, based very tenuously on provisions of the Trading with the Enemy Act of 1917; they prohibited exports of gold and silver and blocked all foreign exchange transactions for the next month. The embargo on precious metals and foreign exchange trading amounted to a de facto suspension of the gold standard and called the stability of the dollar into question. Objections were so few and scattered as to be inaudible. In the meantime, administration officials, headed by Secretary of the Treasury William Woodin, worked frantically with leading bankers (the money changers having made their way back into the temple) and Hoover Treasury holdovers to draw up an emergency banking bill.

On March 8, Roosevelt held his first press conference, genially laying down the rules to the 120 or so reporters who crowded into the Oval Office—questions no longer were required to be submitted in advance and in writing but direct quotations required authorization (in writing) from press secretary Steve Early, "background" information had to be used without attribution to the White House, "off the record" information was to remain strictly confidential. He would normally meet with reporters twice a week. For the next forty-five minutes, he sparred and joked with his questioners, displaying a style that was the antithesis of Hoover's aloof coldness, giving out very little hard news, carefully keeping some important revelations (including a statement favoring a managed currency over the gold standard) off the record.

As Kenneth Davis has observed, they probably would have gotten more substance from Hoover, but the atmospherics of a more intimate relationship and apparent confidences were overwhelming. When Early ended the session, they applauded enthusiastically. No other American chief executive, not even Cousin Theodore, had so masterfully seduced the press. Like all love affairs, this one would have its occasional spats, but it would endure for the next twelve years. Dictators told journalists what to write. Democratic leaders manipulated them, none more successfully than Franklin Roosevelt.[9]

The next day, Congress convened and found waiting for it emergency banking legislation. The president had discussed the bill with congressional leaders the previous evening and obtained their backing, but even they had not seen the final draft, which was completed only a half-hour before the special session began. Roosevelt sent a short written message with it, presenting the bill as an urgent first step and practically demanding instant ratification. The legislators complied in unprecedented fashion—no real committee consideration, no meaningful debate, passage in one day. Largely the work of former Secretary of the Treasury Ogden Mills and his staff, the bill authorized continued closure of the banks and gave the federal government blanket authority to determine which would be reopened. Other provisions allowed the Reconstruction Finance Corporation to buy newly issued preferred stock from banks that needed additional capital but were determined to be fundamentally sound. The Federal Reserve banks received authorization to provide interim loans to individuals and corporations in need of short-term credit. The message to ordinary people was simple and direct. There would be another week or two of inconvenience, but the government would protect the interests of the average depositor.[10]

The following day, as if to demonstrate his own administration's soundness, Roosevelt sent another message to Congress, requesting strong discretionary authority to slash federal expenditures. Decrying the enormous $4.1 billion increase in the national debt under Hoover and the projected $1 billion additional for the upcoming fiscal year, warning that the basic security of the nation was at stake, he demanded quick action in order to be able to present the country with a balanced budget for fiscal year 1934, which would begin on July 1. In ten days, he had his bill. The sharp cuts, especially hard with regard to veterans benefits, would follow as promised. Most commentary, probably reasonably reflective of public sentiment, was that the legislation was bitter but necessary medicine. Many observers were impressed that Roosevelt had taken on and handily vanquished the veterans lobby.[11]

In the meantime, the president delivered his first "fireside chat"* to the nation. The nature of the talk was as significant as its substance. Roosevelt could deliver long, substantial policy addresses or partisan stemwinders with a skill that the best practitioners envied. He understood, however, that from time to time another mode of speaking to the public could be even more effective—the brief, friendly, informal talk delivered as if the president were sitting next to a fireplace, visiting a typical American family in their own home. As governor of New York, he had pioneered the style. No American politician had established it before him. Among foreigners, Stanley Baldwin was perhaps the sole national leader to have used something like it effectively.

The fireside chats—as opposed to more formal radio speeches—ran for about fifteen minutes. Most were delivered Sunday night at 10:00 p.m., eastern standard time, the best day and hour to reach the maximum number of households in the country's four time zones. Roosevelt understood the dangers of overexposure; he delivered four such talks his first year in office, from one to three a year thereafter for the remainder of the decade. The firesides chats were always special events. At their most effective, they achieved a bond of sympathetic understanding and reassurance between the president and his people. None was more successful than the first.

"My friends, I want to talk for a few minutes with the people of the United States about banking," the president began. "I want to tell you what has been done in the last few days, and why it was done, and what the next steps are going to be." He explained in clear and elementary terms how the banking system worked, why even the soundest bank could not meet excessive demands for withdrawals, why it was necessary

---

* The term "fireside chat" lacks precision and was not regularly used by the White House. I have accepted the listing used by Russell Buhite and David Levy in their fine collection, *FDR's Fireside Chats* (Norman: University of Oklahoma Press, 1992).

for the country to endure the inconvenience of the bank holiday, how federal and state banking regulators would began a phased opening of only sound banks over the next week, and why it would be "safer to keep your money in a reopened bank than to keep it under the mattress." He concluded, "Let us unite in banishing fear. We have provided the machinery to restore our financial system, and it is up to you to support and make it work. . . . Together we cannot fail."[12]

The impact was enormous. The dollar surged in currency trading. On Monday, March 13, sound banks in Federal Reserve cities went back into business, the next day banks in all cities with clearinghouses. On Wednesday, March 15, the New York Stock Exchange, closed since March 3, reopened to heavy trading volume and record percentage gains. After a month, about 12,500 of the nation's 17,800 banks were back to regular operations. As the year went on, another three thousand or so would get restarted; the remainder were either liquidated, usually with considerable losses to depositors, or merged with stronger institutions. Many that needed capital infusions would be strengthened by RFC purchases of new preferred stock. Hoarded money, much of it in gold coins, flowed back into the system. Federal deposit insurance, established as part of the Glass-Steagall act of 1933, would institutionalize the confidence Roosevelt's virtuoso performance had generated.

Amid the general rejoicing that the country had been pulled back from financial disaster and the outpouring of approval for the president's strong leadership, only scattered ideologues (and some economists) observed that the New Deal had essentially restored and reinforced an inefficient, decentralized, accident-prone banking system. A fair number of socialists and progressives (as well as numerous historians since) lamented the rejection of a unique opportunity to nationalize the banks. A few Wall Streeters and kindred spirits decried a failure to consolidate financial institutions under vigorous private control and thereby create a system similar to that of Britain or France in which the banks were few in number, possessed enormous assets, and were mutually supportive during panics. In fact, the widespread sense of crisis and the time pressures generated by the emergency of March 1933 made neither course possible. Demanding quick achievement, the situation mandated restoration, not revolution.[13]

On March 22, Congress gave Roosevelt yet another victory. The Beer and Wine Revenue Act amended the Volstead Act of 1919 by legalizing 3.2 percent alcoholic beverages and establishing federal tax schedules for them. The main rationale for the measure was the need to raise federal revenues, but the political implications were much greater. The bill demonstrated how rapidly the structure of prohibition was crumbling. By the end of the year, the states would ratify the repeal of the Eighteenth Amendment, bringing the country back to the traditional sense that alcoholic beverages were to be defined and regulated by states and localities in harmony with their distinct mores. The process ended the bitter debate about national prohibition that had occurred mostly within the Democratic party and made it easier to reconcile the party's traditional rural, old-stock Southern and Western base with the emerging ethnoreligious minorities of the nation's northeastern quadrant. The end of national prohibition thereby greatly facilitated the rise of a Democratic majority in the 1930s.

In two and a half weeks, Roosevelt had accomplished far more than the most optimistic observer would have predicted on March 4. A pause might have been in order. Members of Congress, most of whom had been in Washington since December for the lame-duck session, were ready to go home. Yet the task of fighting the Depression had hardly begun, if one were to take Roosevelt and his Brains Trust at their word. The president himself realized that he was riding on enormous political momentum. Now was the time to implement a full-scale program, even if all the devilish details had to be worked out with little time for thought or informed debate. Roosevelt held an increasingly restive Congress in session until mid-June, hammering out one program after another, putting in place the First New Deal.

Many individuals were involved in the details, but the president was always the chief orchestrator. At times, he had to intervene in complex negotiations between policy wonks and interest groups. Occasionally, he commanded continuations of hopelessly stalled talks with such directives as "Lock them in a room and don't let them out until they've agreed on something." Always, he gave final approval. He knew that some consensus was necessary, that powerful congressmen had to be stroked. But he also believed his popular landslide had given him extraordinary authority. He was convinced that action and forward movement was more important than careful deliberation.

Some of the measures that emerged from this pell-mell process had the primary objective of relief; others were to be instruments of economic recovery; quite a few pointed toward reform, in the sense of a permanent change directed by the state:

MARCH 31 Civilian Conservation Corps Act, establishing a Civilian Conservation Corps (CCC) designed to enroll 250,000 young men in conservation work camps to be administered by the army.

APRIL 5 Presidential Executive Order requiring all persons possessing gold coins, gold bullion, or gold certificates with a value of over $100 to turn these items in to the government in exchange for U.S. currency. Exceptions were made only for industrial use, rare coins of numismatic interest, or gold licensed by the Treasury for commercial transactions.

APRIL 19 Prohibition of most gold shipments abroad, effectively suspending the convertibility of U.S. currency to gold. The dollar fell sharply on the foreign exchange markets.

MAY 12 Federal Emergency Relief Act, establishing a Federal Emergency Relief Administration (FERA) to supplement various state welfare programs and work relief projects on a basis of $1 for every $3 of state expenditures. Much of the agency expenditure was for "direct relief" (the dole, in British terminology), but the FERA also maintained many small-scale work projects.

MAY 12 Agricultural Adjustment Act, establishing an Agricultural Adjustment Administration (AAA), mandated to raise farm commodity prices to "parity" (fair purchasing power) levels and thereby restore farm income. It would do so primarily through an acreage "domestic allotment" system, devised in the late 1920s by Milburn L. Wilson and other agricultural economists. Much of the funding was to come from taxes on the processors of farm commodities. Reflecting traditional agrarian attraction to inflation as a way of wiping out debts, the act also gave the president authorization to devalue the gold content of the dollar, employ silver as backing for U.S. currency, or simply print up to an additional $3 billion of greenbacks.

MAY 18 Tennessee Valley Authority (TVA) Act, derived from Senator George Norris's efforts to utilize the Muscle Shoals facility, the TVA was to be a wide-ranging flood control program, generator and seller of electricity, producer of nitrogen-based fertilizers, and regional planning authority with jurisdiction in parts of seven southern states. In the short run, it provided thousands of jobs in an impoverished area. In the long run, it was a test model for other possible regional authorities and might redefine the role and scope of government in American life.

MAY 27 Federal Securities Act, initiating the first significant regulation of the stock and bond markets, requiring full disclosure of relevant information to investors and the registration of new issues with the government. In 1934, it would be augmented by the Securities Exchange Act.

JUNE 5 Gold Clause Repeal Congressional Resolution, canceling the then-standard provision made in most public and private contracts that payment must be made in gold, or its equivalent, based on the gold value of the dollar at the time the contract was agreed upon. Instead, payment could be made in nominal dollar value by legal-tender U.S. currency (paper dollars).

JUNE 6 National Employment System Act, establishing the U.S. Employment Service, which subsidized and coordinated state-run employment agencies; a useful service to some job seekers, the service would have no discernible effect on unemployment.

JUNE 13 Home Owners Refinancing Act, essentially reorganized and enlarged the Hoover Federal Home Loan Bank system by creating a new agency, the Home Owners Loan Corporation, which dealt directly with individuals in need of mortgage refinancing and home loans.

JUNE 16 Glass-Steagall Act of 1933, fundamentally changing the American Banking System by creating the Federal Deposit Insurance Corporation (FDIC) to guarantee the bank deposits of the middle class (up to $5,000), divorced investment banking from "retail" commercial banking, and strengthened the Federal Reserve Board's interest rate authority.

JUNE 16 Farm Credit Act, providing generous credit and mortgage refinancing for the farm population, administered by the Farm Credit Administration, which Roosevelt created by executive order on March 27 to run existing federal agricultural credit programs.

JUNE 16 Emergency Railroad Transportation Act, an ambitiously conceived program to promote the reorganization and consolidation of America's overbuilt and financially precarious railway system under the direction of a Federal Coordinator of Transportation. Despite the efforts of Coordinator Joseph Eastman, a widely respected rail expert, little would be accomplished during the decade. Complex conflicts of interest between rail stockholders and bondholders, management and labor, cities that faced loss of service and those that did not—all blocked significant progress. A steady stream of RFC loans would keep the major rail lines from total collapse until World War II provided them with a new lease on life.

JUNE 16 National Industrial Recovery Act, the centerpiece of the New
    Deal program for economic recovery, establishing the National Recov-
    ery Administration (NRA) to oversee industry-by-industry self-
    regulation through the adoption of "codes of fair competition" that
    would stabilize prices while providing collective bargaining, better
    wages, and improved working conditions for labor. The act also pro-
    vided for a Public Works Administration (PWA) with an appropria-
    tion of $3.3 billion to be spent on projects throughout the country
    with the objective of stimulating the economy.

Congress adjourned on June 16. The special session had lasted exactly
100 days and had produced an outpouring of legislation unprecedented
in American history. At first glance, it might seem a bewildering mélange.
Close examination displayed a coherent mosaic of programs designed to
bring relief to the unfortunate, reform dysfunctional financial institutions, and organize the nation's political economy—all under the aegis of
a greatly enlarged state functioning as a largely self-contained entity in
the wider world.

From the beginning, the New Deal's political appeal had two sources.
The first was its tangible humanitarianism in the form of relief checks,
job programs, mortgage refinancings, commodity price supports, and the
like. The second was Roosevelt, whose authority, decision, and charisma
won him nearly instant recognition as the world's outstanding leader of
liberal democracy. Americans liked his action-oriented, experimental
attitude, expressed in the title of an article by Anne O'Hare McCormick,
"'Let's Try It!' Says Roosevelt." The French journalist Jules Sauerwein
wrote, "He is a chief but, at the same time, a friend."[14]

Bankable help to desperate people, a style of leadership that combined
command with extraordinary rhetorical skills, an ability to project concern for common folk—these could carry a president and his government
a long way. The policies of national planning, government investment,
and reform would be more controversial, but they were the fundamentals
of an effort to pursue recovery in one country.

Yet the Depression was an international phenomenon; most of the world
believed it required an international solution. To any such effort, the
United States would be absolutely essential. Outside the United States,
the outlines of a multinational recovery were widely understood: cancel-

lation or drastic reduction of war debts owed the Americans, agreements to expand international trade, and (in order to make the last objective possible) a currency stabilization. By June 1933, the major Western powers and numerous lesser nations had been planning a World Economic Conference for close to two years. Hoover's reluctance, then the politics of the election, had put it off. At last, the long wait for America was over. The conference was due to begin in London on June 12.

For all his commitment to national recovery, Roosevelt had given the rest of the world some reason to hope that he would be amenable to an international approach. In one of his few assumptions of policy responsibility before becoming president, he had dispatched a group headed by the prominent investment banker James P. Warburg to assume effective control of the American delegation to the conference preparatory commission. In his inaugural address, he had stated a determination to pursue a national road to recovery but also had asserted, "I shall spare no effort to restore world trade by international economic readjustment." During his first three months in office, he held meetings to discuss economic issues with no less than eleven high foreign officials. In these conferences, he revealed one of his least fortunate characteristics, a tendency to let his visitors believe he was in general agreement with them, right down to the issuance of one joint press release after another that, to the naked eye at any rate, indicated strong support of international currency stabilization. In his second fireside chat on May 11, he told Americans that full recovery required a general international economic revival, which in turn depended upon "a cutting down of the trade barriers" and "a stabilization of currencies." He declared, "The great international conference of this summer that lies before us must succeed."[15]

Yet, as the hundred days had demonstrated, the New Deal was based upon national economic planning to a degree never approached in peacetime American history. The World Economic Conference was dedicated to reopening closed national economies through a revival of world trade, which in turn had to be based on stable currencies. But how could agricultural prices be raised if foreign-produced commodities were let into the American market? How could business and labor achieve higher prices and better wages if the elaborate regulatory system of the NRA was bypassed by a wave of foreign imports? It was no oversight that the hundred days had left the Hawley-Smoot Tariff untouched. Like Hoover, Roosevelt and his aides understood that a national planning system required trade protectionism. By cutting the dollar loose from gold and letting it float on the international currency markets, they had, in addition, engineered a devaluation that canceled out the advantages achieved by other nations that had left gold. To the dismay of Secretary of State Hull, Roosevelt had put reciprocal trade legislation (which would at best produce quasi-open trade) on the back burner to await the regular session of Congress.

To be sure, the other major nations at London had done their part to complicate an international approach to recovery. The British turn to protectionism and imperial preference might be altered by a world agreement but could not be casually tossed away. Moreover, Neville Chamberlain, the chief British economic policy maker, tended to see mutually open trade with the United States as a losing proposition. France enacted repeated tariff increases to achieve the imperative of a favorable trade balance. Possessing the second largest gold hoard in the world and fearing a reprise of the post–World War inflationary surge, it was the determined leader of the dwindling gold bloc. Germany, in its fifth month of Nazi rule when the conference began, was clearly setting out on its own path with little regard for international agreements. Italy under Mussolini had established Europe's model of the authoritarian managed economy. Japan was aggressively seeking foreign markets, displaying little inclination to open its own. Already on a path of military expansionism in China, it made no secret of its ambition for an East Asian economic empire. In both democratic and authoritarian nations, the Depression had encouraged the attitude that the international economy was a zero-sum game in which gains for one nation produced corresponding losses for others. Faith in free markets was at a low ebb everywhere; demands for state action to protect domestic economic interests were universal.

The persistent issue of war debts, officially not on the agenda, would nonetheless have to be part of any sound international stabilization agreement. German reparations to the Allies were already a thing of the past, never to be resumed. Cancellation or reduction to token amounts of Allied debts to the United States was essential for the revitalization of the international economy, but in America cancellation was still politically taboo. Roosevelt appears to have understood the problem; he decided not to talk about it.

The specter of a berserk Germany hung over the proceedings, felt but not talked about. Hitler already was overseeing myriad atrocities against Jews, ruthlessly suppressing any opposition, and engaging in inflammatory irredentist rhetoric. Not yet quite the all-powerful Führer he would later become, he nonetheless already presented the most serious threat to peace in Europe since 1918. If the United States, Britain, and France could find common ground at London, they might just lead their countries toward recovery and establish a viable alternative to Nazism. Possibly they could bring along Mussolini's Italy—at that point wary of a resurgent Germany and a far less detestable dictatorship.

The stakes, many observers realized at the time, were enormous. Nevertheless, the conference had a scent of failure from the beginning.

After months of work the preparatory commission had failed to achieve a single significant agreement that could get the conference off to a positive start. The U.S. delegation, led by Secretary of State Hull, was, to put it politely, mixed in its capabilities as well as hopelessly divided in its policy preferences. Worse yet, it had no clear instructions from the president. Roosevelt muddled the situation further by sending New York Federal Reserve Governor George Harrison and Treasury adviser Oliver Sprague to negotiate separately with British and French central bankers on currency stabilization. Apparently, he hoped unrealistically for an agreement that would preserve all the trading advantages of the unilateral dollar devaluation he already had carried out. On June 12, Harrison and Sprague managed an agreement that would have pegged the pound to the dollar within a range centered at a rate of $4.00. The current value was $4.18. Roosevelt peremptorily rejected the proposal in a fashion that scuttled the stabilization talks.

On June 17, the president left Washington for a long boating vacation on the rented yacht *Amberjack II*. With no capability for regular, direct, secure communication with Washington, Roosevelt was largely dependent upon circuitous transmissions that went to Washington in diplomatic code, then were converted, often imperfectly, to naval code, and relayed to the vessels escorting him. In London, delegation leaders made opening speeches, followed by discussions about a "tariff truce," exchange rate stabilization mechanisms and ratios, and future negotiations to open up closed economies. There was precious little leadership from any corner, especially not from the rudderless, dissension-ridden American delegation. Roosevelt, sporadically following the situation without expert advice, tired and irritable from the exhausting effort of the Hundred Days, became increasingly determined to preserve his freedom of action.[16]

Amid all the confusion, Raymond Moley (who already was scheduled to join the negotiators in London anyway) embarked from the United States on June 21 with a vague mandate from the president "to help get things straightened out." His arrival a week later only made matters worse. The press portrayed him as a carrier of specific instructions from Roosevelt and the man upon whom the fate of the conference depended. Hull openly resented the appearance that a nominal subordinate had been dispatched to give him orders. Moley nonetheless began negotiations directly with MacDonald and Chamberlain. Rather quickly, he decided that a draft resolution offered by the gold bloc nations was necessary to keep the conference going; it declared for currency stabilization based on a worldwide gold standard as an "ultimate objective." He marshaled behind him Secretary of the Treasury Woodin, seriously ill at his home in New York, and Woodin's prestigious informal advisory group— influential financier Bernard Baruch, New York Federal Reserve Governor George Harrison, and Undersecretary of the Treasury Dean Acheson. Roosevelt, unwilling to agree to even an "ultimate" surrender of his policy flexibility, responded by pulling the plug on the entire enterprise.

On July 1, Moley and Hull received a long telegram of rejection from the president, who was on his first visit in a dozen years to the old family vacation house at Campobello. All but isolated from the outside world, Roosevelt received face-to-face advice only from his long-time political counselor Louis McHenry Howe and his old friend Henry Morgenthau, Jr., a wealthy gentleman-farmer whom he had appointed to head the Farm Credit Administration. Neither of them (Morgenthau's subsequent appointment as secretary of the treasury notwithstanding) possessed the experience and judgment to advise him on critical economic issues. Howe saw nothing to be gained from the conference; Morgenthau wanted to torpedo it. After consulting only with them, the president released a public declaration on July 3. Instantly known as the "bombshell message," it harshly lectured the conference for fixating on "the specious fallacy of achieving a temporary and probably an artificial stability in foreign exchange on the part of a few large countries only." It went on to assert: "The Conference was called to better and perhaps to cure fundamental economic ills. It must not be diverted from that effort."[17]

The debacle destroyed Moley's standing within the administration. Two months later, he resigned, returning occasionally to give advice but never holding office under Roosevelt again. In time, he became a sharp critic of the New Deal. Hull, for all his joy at Moley's discomfiture, was almost equally embarrassed; but he was determined to stay on and impossible to fire. Their personal stories were insignificant compared to the larger consequences. The stunned conference managed to keep going for a few weeks but adjourned on July 27, devoid of accomplishment.

In Europe, the United States and its president were the subject of anger and derision—with one major exception. In an article for the London *Daily Mail*, John Maynard Keynes declared "President Roosevelt Is Magnificently Right." Just three months earlier, Keynes in his "Means to Prosperity" articles had advocated an elaborate system of international currency stabilization. By late June, however, he had come to feel that the conference was too divided to achieve a workable agreement. Thus, he preferred Roosevelt's monetary flexibility to the gold bloc's rigidity. He may also have come to believe from his friendships with such prominent Americans as Walter Lippmann and Felix Frankfurter that he had a better chance for policy influence in the White House than at Ten Downing Street. The best hope for Britain, he now seemed to believe, was not alignment with France and the other gold nations but with the United States. His praise of Roosevelt was more diluted than the title of his article suggests, but he thought that the American president was the dynamic force the Anglo-American world needed. Still, as he pointed out in this and subsequent writings, "There is much that Mr Roosevelt's statement has left unsaid." Keynes liked the American president's style and general direction, wanted to hitch the Commonwealth and Empire to his leadership, and hoped above all to influence him. The issue of exactly what Roosevelt wanted could ride.[18]

By July 6, the one hundred and twenty-fifth day of his presidency, Roosevelt had shown the world the full outline of the New Deal. He also had delivered the message that it would be a program for recovery in one country only, with little interest in the rest of the world. Americans generally approved. The progressives around whom the president wanted to build his support were ecstatic. Secretary of the Interior Harold Ickes wrote in his diary that Roosevelt had displayed "admirable skill and foresight" in establishing "a strictly American position."[19]

Ickes expressed a widely held American sentiment, but in fact, Roosevelt's handling of the conference contrasted starkly to the masterful leadership he had displayed from the inaugural through the hundred days. It had revealed him at his worst—impetuous and uncomprehending, taking a monumentally important decision in isolation, disregarding his most competent advisers, composing the most important diplomatic document of his short presidency in a fit of petulance. The failure of the conference was a serious setback for Western liberal democracy; the way in which Roosevelt had wrecked it was even worse. The "bombshell" verged on the insulting and seemed to demonstrate a lack of understanding of international economic mechanisms. Some foreign leaders were outraged; others simply decided that Roosevelt was less helpful than Hoover, and considerably less reliable.

The United States was not solely responsible for the breakup; every major nation was fixated on narrow interests. But the mere convening of the meeting bespoke a widespread sense of desperation and just possibly a longing for the leadership that only the United States could provide. Hard negotiating just might have yielded a meaningful first step in which at a minimum America, Britain, France, and numerous smaller countries could have joined. The significance would have been as much political as economic at a time when the liberal Western powers needed some semblance of unity and purpose. As it was, the United States had no international economic policy nor any interest in developing one. Neville Chamberlain privately called Roosevelt's message "most offensive"; the president's behavior would be vivid in his memory five years later when he dealt with Hitler at Munich. By obstinately rejecting the contention that the Depression was in some large sense an international problem, Roosevelt had defined American security in isolationist terms that had political as well as economic consequences.[20]

On May 27, 1933, the Chicago World's Fair opened to celebrate "a century of progress," achieved through the triumph of science. Postmaster General James A. Farley, substituting for President Roosevelt, delivered an altogether forgettable opening address. What was important was the generally held assumption that a presidential representative should open the event. The fair was meant to celebrate Chicago and bring money into the city. It attempted to achieve its purposes by expressing an enduring American optimism about the future, no matter the current economic distress. Rufus Dawes, the president of the corporation that organized the fair, expressed its intention clearly and tellingly: "Here are gathered the evidences of man's achievements in the realm of physical sciences— proofs of his power to prevail over all the perils that beset him. Here in the presence of such victories men may gather courage to face their unsolved problems." A year later, Roosevelt spoke from Washington to the opening of the fair's second season. He could not resist identifying his administration with its themes of "courage and confidence," faith in progress, and pragmatic science. "A plan and a definite objective existed for this exposition. . . . Likewise a definite objective is also being followed by those to whom have been entrusted the administration of national affairs. . . . we may in some respects change method while the objective remains the same. Time and experience will determine."[21]

Americans swarmed to the fair. They explored the Halls of Science, Religion, and Social Science; visited imposing buildings and exhibits developed by the largest American industrial corporations; looked at the offerings of seventeen foreign nations; and sampled the amusements of the carnival midway. On that first day in 1933 at precisely 9:15 p.m., Central Daylight Time, the grounds were illuminated by a method calculated both to evoke memories of the Chicago World's Fair of 1893 and demonstrate the march of science since those days. Telescopes at four distant observatories focused on the star Arcturus ("Job's star") forty light-years distant, captured rays of light that it had begun to send in 1893, and transmitted them to a system of photoelectric cells, from whence the amplified current sped on to Chicago and switched on the fair lights. *"Progress!"* exulted the official guidebook. "You will find that all within this great World's Fair is a definite part, a paragraph or chapter in the story of progress and advancement." The essence of the fair's vision, commented R. L. Duffus, was a scientific utopia in which mass production offered "hopes of the satisfaction without pain of almost limitless human wants."[22]

It was an ironic coincidence that the 1893 fair had begun in the gathering months of what had been the worst economic depression in American history, had equally celebrated science, progress, and a gleaming future, and had denied the reality of hunger and misery just beyond its gates. Its 1933 successor displayed scientific achievement, model homes of the future, gleaming new automobiles, all implicitly declaring that better days were ahead. The fair, Duffus observed, "must make us believe that this is the black hour before dawn and that the dawn itself will be more splendid than any we have seen." The midway (given very short shrift by the didactic official guide) also provided an opportunity for unusual fun, whether riding the roller coaster, watching alligator wrestlers, visiting freak shows, or seeing close-up "the apotheosis of America's womanly pulchritude"—in 1933 the fan dancer Sally Rand. Whether attracted by the fair's educational value or its recreational possibilities, twenty-seven million visitors came to see it in 1933, another twenty-one million during its encore season in 1934. It turned a small profit.[23]

Perhaps the most impressive foreign claim to scientific progress at the fair was the Italian pavilion, a large, imposing example of modern architecture. Referring to "the heroic deeds of Fascism," the official Italian message declared, "Progress is the keynote of modern Italy and the long and romantic history of the Italian peninsula pales before Italy's plans for the future." Such assertions reminded one that Italy seemed to have become a larger presence on the world scene under Mussolini's ten-year dictatorship. The implication that organization, discipline, and forward movement were possible only under an authoritarian regime represented a challenge to democracy—and especially to the New Deal.[24]

A week before the opening of the World's Fair, Walter Lippmann delivered a notable address in Cleveland. The hundred-day session of Congress had nearly a month to go, but the final outline of the early New Deal was discernible. Lippmann already had praised Roosevelt's strong leadership in his newspaper column. He declared to an audience of local business leaders and Harvard Club members from across the country, "We find a determination to substitute foresight and deliberate management for the play of blind, unregulated and incoherent actions." Roosevelt had used strong party leadership to subdue special interests, had asserted national authority over a dysfunctional monetary system, and was moving to establish industrial self-government that would impose order on chaotic competition. These steps could lead to an opening of the American market and a resumption of foreign trade that would be good for the entire world.

"We can do no greater service to mankind than to prove that a free people can without violence, in an orderly, cool manner, subdue the forces of disintegration and become the master of its fate," Lippmann declared. The free nations of the world, he predicted, would be stronger than the dictatorships. Had he chosen to use the language of a book he had published nearly two decades earlier, he might have said that America had rejected drift for mastery, that science and reason amplified by strong leadership would not only take the United States out of the abyss but carry it to new heights. In the euphoria of May 1933, his optimism seemed plausible.[25]

HEADLINES AND MOVIE NEWSREELS

{1933}

SEPTEMBER 14   1,500,000 Cheer Vast NRA Parade; March of 250,000 Lasts Till Midnight

OCTOBER 1   Roosevelt Decides to Buy Coal, Food and Clothing for the Needy This Winter

NOVEMBER 6   Roosevelt Sends His Aides to Quiet Striking Farmers

NOVEMBER 9   4,000,000 Idle to Be Hired; Civil Works Plan Bars 'Charity'

{1934}

FEBRUARY 1   Dollar Revalued at 59.06, Gold Put at $35 an Ounce

NOVEMBER   Democrats Gain Seats in Congressional Elections

DECEMBER   *"A year of violent labor troubles. . . ." The San Francisco general strike: idle cars and empty streets . . . "many victims" . . . "business was paralyzed" . . . "the city was threatened by hunger." The Minneapolis Teamsters strike: scenes of melees in the streets, "severe riots . . . many casualties." The Toledo Auto-Lite strike: more street rioting . . . National Guardsmen fire tear gas and "knockout gas" at labor demonstrators . . . two killed, seven wounded . . . "warfare in the streets."* (Newsreel [Year in Review], "Strikes")

{1935}

MAY 28   All NRA Enforcement Is Ended by President as Supreme Court Rules Act and Codes Void; Whole of New Deal Program in Confusion

{ 5 }

RECOVERY IN ONE COUNTRY?

THE NEW DEAL, JULY 1933–MAY 1935

The Executors

The First New Deal had been conceived by public policy intellectuals. It would be administered by men of action, attuned to the world of ideas, but mostly experienced in business or finance. All believed that the state and the private economy could enjoy a symbiotic relationship. During the first two years, the three most important of them were an imperious multi-millionaire, a shrewd but enigmatic agricultural scientist–businessman–journalist, and a retired army general.

The Money Man: Jesse H. Jones

If in early 1935 Central Casting at a Hollywood movie studio had gotten a call for an actor to play a Texas tycoon, it probably would have sent someone who looked like Jesse Holman Jones—six feet, three inches tall, head topped by an imposing shock of white hair, blunt in speech, pragmatic in behavior, possessing an aura of command that was second nature to a self-made man long accustomed to wealth and power. Born to a middling family in Tennessee, Jones had been taken into his uncle's Houston lumber company. He moved up rapidly, and inherited the enterprise upon his uncle's death. Branching out into real estate, construction, and banking, he was a leader of the Houston business community by his fortieth birthday. A civic booster who understood the ways in which government could foster economic growth, he spearheaded the drive to obtain partial federal funding for the construction of the Houston Ship Channel, a fifty-mile project that made the city a seaport and southwestern transportation hub. It opened in 1914, the same year as the Panama Canal, which it exceeded in length if not in difficulty of construction.[1]

Politics followed naturally from business prominence. A regular Democrat, Jones had voted for William Jennings Bryan three times, albeit with misgivings about Bryan's inflationist radicalism. He found Woodrow Wilson's more moderate progressivism much more congenial and campaigned earnestly for him in 1912. Wilson subsequently offered him the post of secretary of commerce, which he declined. The World War brought him to Washington to head Red Cross military relief efforts and see firsthand the way in which the War Industries Board and similar agencies organized the American economy.

During the 1920s, Jones divided his time between Houston and New York. In Texas, his power and influence, derived from his massive and steadily accumulating wealth, was statewide. He acquired the *Houston Chronicle;* an influential newspaper with a regional reach, it was both a profitable investment and a resource that enhanced his political leverage. In New York, he built the Mayfair House hotel, establishing a residence for himself in its penthouse. Over the next several years, he spent increasing amounts of time there, making himself a national figure, not just a regional baron. Finance director of the Democratic party in the mid-twenties, he was an effective fund-raiser. His personal check for $200,000 brought the Democratic convention to Houston in 1928. His wealth and imperious manner aroused resentment and envy aplenty, but few politicians dared scorn or ignore him.

Jones's enterprises weathered the first two years of the Depression well. The National Bank of Commerce, which he controlled, was Houston's strongest. He took the lead (with the help of James A. Baker, Sr.) in persuading the city's bankers to establish a credit pool against runs by depositors. The plan saved Houston's banks and added to his political clout—just in time for a return to Washington.

In 1932, President Hoover, acting on the recommendation of Speaker of the House Garner, appointed him one of the Democratic directors of the new Reconstruction Finance Corporation. Never hung up on doctrines of laissez-faire or rugged individualism when it came to practical matters, Jones enthusiastically endorsed the RFC's mission of bailing out financial institutions. He criticized the agency only for insufficient aggressiveness and a regional exclusivity that concentrated its loans in the northeastern quadrant of the country. He was even more pungent with bankers who used RFC funds for debt retirement or safe investments such as government bonds; RFC loans, he declared, were meant to be recycled into the private economy. Near-total risk aversion was incompatible with recovery. In 1933, President Roosevelt appointed him chairman of what would be a bigger and more activist RFC.

Over the next several years, Jones would have a hand in almost every New Deal program. Empowered with a large appropriation and able to credit repaid loans to the RFC's revolving fund, he controlled one of the largest piles of cash in Washington. His first master stroke was his decision to bail out problem banks by buying new issues of preferred stock from them, a move that provided them with capital to loan out rather than just another liability to be repaid sometime in the future. Acting almost as a free agent—he ran the RFC board of directors with an iron fist—Jones made large loans to many growing businesses, quite a number of them west of the Mississippi. By and the large the private loans followed a relatively conservative banker's risk principle; defaults were few, and the RFC's lendable funds grew accordingly.

The RFC also became an increasingly important financier of capital-intensive New Deal programs, financing in one way or another at least a dozen relief or credit agencies. By 1940, he had overseen $8 billion in loans, a total exceeding the entire budget of the U.S. government in the first year of the New Deal. With the lending came a position of power nearly unequaled outside the White House. Jones continued to enjoy the confidence of Garner, now vice president and enormously influential on Capitol Hill. He cultivated leading congressmen and made certain that the RFC provided money for creditworthy projects that they backed. An exception or two aside, he was successful in staving off raids on his territory and challenges to his authority from figures as well-placed as Secretary of the Treasury Morgenthau. For much of the thirties, when the South still seemed the core of the Democratic party rather than an increasingly irrelevant constituency, he was valuable to Roosevelt.

Often inadequately described as a "conservative Democrat," he was best understood as a banker who accepted the values and prospects of growth capitalism, took chances on them, and understood that government could be a capitalist tool. A Southwesterner rather than a Southerner, he possessed the outlook of a young and underdeveloped region. He had little use for labor unions and social idealism, but he was willing, presumably at White House request, to press local officials to settle the

Minneapolis Teamsters strike on terms favorable to the union. He disliked Wall Street and an eastern banking establishment that treated his part of America like a colonial possession. More a bureaucratic politician than an ideologue, he kept whatever early reservations he had about Roosevelt's direction to himself. It hardly seems fitting to call him a New Dealer, but that he was integral to the New Deal is impossible to dispute.

The Farmer's Friend: Henry A. Wallace

Roosevelt's Secretary of Agriculture, Henry Agard Wallace, would have been a most unlikely cabinet member in any previous Democratic administration. He came from a family of staunch Republicans who had been among the leaders of Iowa agriculture for a half century. His grandfather, Henry Wallace ("Uncle Henry" to two generations of Iowans), had founded a weekly farm newspaper, *Wallace's Farmer*. Combining summaries of national and world events with news of scientific farming, tips on rural homemaking, and vigorous advocacy of farm interests in politics, *Wallace's Farmer* had become by the turn of the century the most widely read such publication in the Midwest. Its editorial line reflected the mainstream position of Midwestern farming—hostile to the radicalism and inflationist panaceas of the Populist revolt of the 1890s but demanding greater consideration from a Republican party that seemed in the pockets of Northeastern industry and finance. Uncle Henry could have been secretary of agriculture had he wished. His son, Henry C., served in the position under Harding and Coolidge, until his death in 1925. Henry C., struggling to find ways to assist depressed farmers, had managed some small achievements during Harding's presidency, but Coolidge and Secretary of Commerce Herbert Hoover had rejected his reluctant advocacy of the McNary-Haugen plan. His most important legacy to farm people would be his son, Henry A.[2]

The second Secretary Wallace already had built a career that combined grand visions and great scientific achievement with practical farm advocacy. Forty-four years old when he came to Washington in March 1933, he had edited the family paper, been a leading participant in the development of hybrid corn, and founded the Pioneer Hi-Bred Company, which marketed his scientific discovery in the form of high-yielding seed to Midwestern farmers. Increasingly alienated from the Republican party after his father's death, he was in the final stages of a political pilgrimage. A near prototype of the sort of heartland progressive Roosevelt wanted

to bring into the Democratic party, he still had much of the rustic appearance and style of a provincial farm journalist with hands-on experience in
cornfields. To his admirers, he was a Lincolnian personality.

Yet alongside a life of great accomplishment was a muddled spiritual
quest, stemming from dissatisfaction with his family's mainline Presbyte-
rianism. It led him into explorations of mysticism, culminating in an ill-
advised relationship while he was a member of Roosevelt's cabinet with
the White Russian philosopher and artist Nicholas Roerich. Arguably a
genius, Roerich had a cultlike following during the 1930s. He exhibited
his paintings in his own museum on Riverside Drive in New York, advocated the laudatory objective of protecting cultural monuments from
wartime destruction, and preached a fuzzy Asian philosophy that proclaimed the essential unity of all things. Wallace addressed him in a series
of odd personal letters as "Dear Guru"; they contained references to,
among other things, "the sacred most precious casket," or "the New
Country going forth to meet the seven stars under the sign of the three
stars," or the admonition "Await the Stone." It is easy to make too much
of this strange relationship, which ended after Wallace obtained funding
for Roerich to lead a botanical expedition to Central Asia. (The guru
never returned, settling instead in India and dying there in 1947.) One
may fairly conclude that it did reveal a bifurcated mind and personality.[3]

As a practical scientist, Wallace was a genius. As a businessman, he displayed good judgment in hiring first-rate managers and marketing special-
ists to build his enterprise. As editor of the family paper, he was an
eloquent and effective advocate for farmers. Nonetheless, he possessed a
certain naïveté that too often impaired his judgment outside his areas of
expertise. He also had a shy, awkward, eccentric manner that left him ill-
adapted to the give-and-take of politics and uncomfortable with the hand-
shaking, alcoholic bonhomie that characterized so much of the social side
of the Washington scene. These were weaknesses that would attract attention much later, when he attempted a political move beyond farm politics.

In the First New Deal, he concentrated intensely and often thought-
fully on the cause for which he had been prepared since birth. He had a
shrewd understanding of his constituency, knew the major farm organizations and their leaders well, and realized the dangers of positioning
himself outside the mainstream of agricultural politics. His quixotic campaign against the Cold War a decade and a half later would cause many
observers to think he was a radical as secretary of agriculture. In fact, he
was a centrist who accurately understood that a successful agricultural

program had to meet the needs of the activist and articulate forces in farming. It was with both reluctance and realism that he decided the inarticulate and the marginal would have to wait, existing for at least the time being as relief cases. Pursuing the art of the possible and achieving considerable agrarian recovery, he was perhaps Roosevelt's most successful cabinet member in the years 1933–35.

The Industrial Organizer: Hugh S. Johnson

Roosevelt entrusted the organization of industrial recovery to Brigadier General (Ret.) Hugh S. Johnson. On paper, the choice seemed excellent. An army brat who had been born at Fort Scott, Kansas, in 1882, Johnson had surmounted an elemental, provincial background to win admission to West Point. He had graduated in 1903 in the same class as Douglas MacArthur. Over the next fourteen years, he served in various posts at home, had a tour of duty in the Philippines, studied law at the University of California (Berkeley) to qualify as a military legal officer, participated in the punitive expedition that pursued Pancho Villa through northern Mexico, helped develop the World War selective service system, and became director of the Army Purchase and Supply branch. In the latter capacity, he worked closely with the War Industries Board and won the admiration of many business executives, including WIB director Bernard Baruch. Resigning from the army in 1919, he became general counsel of the Moline Plow Company, which was headed by George Peek. Soon he and Peek, with the active encouragement of Baruch, developed what became known as the McNary-Haugen plan. Working as a team, they were the primary promoters of farm relief throughout the twenties and early thirties. Peek would become the first head of the Agricultural Adjustment Administration; Johnson seemed a natural choice to head the National Recovery Administration.

From his days with the War Industries Board up through his struggles for McNary-Haugen, Johnson had been a keen student of the relationship between government and private enterprise. Like some other New Dealers, he had been impressed by the surface achievements of Italian fascism. Secretary of Labor Frances Perkins was startled when he gave her a copy of *The Corporate State* by Raffaello Viglione, one of Mussolini's favorite economists. He was no would-be dictator, but he wanted to be a strong leader, undertaking a comprehensive ordering of the economy in which government would be the mediator between capital and labor.[4]

Johnson's impressive career profile concealed a personality ill-suited to the task of building a massive regulatory effort from the ground up. At first glance, he appeared to possess all the positive qualities of a tough senior officer from the prewar "old army." Hard-nosed, profane, bristling with energy, demanding, accomplished in the law, experienced in both business and politics—who could better manage so enormous an endeavor? But, as Raymond Moley acutely observed, despite a rough exterior, he had the sensitivity of a child. He possessed a vast bundle of anxieties that he expressed in chain-smoking and hard drinking. Skilled and practiced in the art of invective, he was nonetheless easily wounded by the barbs of his enemies. One might assume that his career had encouraged a tough-minded pragmatism; actually, he was instead a self-dramatizing romantic. Accepting the position of NRA Administrator, he remarked that he felt like a man voluntarily submitting to the guillotine on the off-chance that the blade would not fall. What was surprising was not the inevitable pull of gravity, but that it took fifteen months. He left behind a terminally wounded agency, harmed in part by his leadership but more critically damaged by the ultimate impossibility of its mission in America's liberal political culture.[5]

The Analogue of War, the Imperative of Mobilization, and "State Capitalism"

Campaigning in the British election of 1931, Ramsay MacDonald had declared the economic crisis a replay of the Great War. As the Depression relentlessly deepened, the analogy occurred to thinkers and leaders throughout the developed world. Great wars required patriotism, unity, cohesive effort, national mobilization. Britain responded with a National government, Germany with Nazism. America was receptive to neither the British nor the German solutions, but the sense of wartime emergency was also widely felt in the United States. Roosevelt himself invoked the example of the World War on numerous occasions in his presidential campaign and during the early years of his presidency.

The calls of Roosevelt and other New Dealers for unity, discipline, and organization were of course never meant as a prelude to dictatorship, but neither were they quite in the mainstream of the nation's traditions. American political culture, still highly "liberal" in the nineteenth-century individualistic sense, remained suspicious of big collectivist programs and national centralism. The New Deal efforts to manage capitalism and achieve prosperity through an organizational state and large administrative bureaucracies required either absolute power or authority resting on a high level of consensual deference. The first of these conditions could be found in Nazi Germany, the second in Great Britain. Neither were present in American life.

In his "forgotten man" speech of April 1932, Roosevelt had asserted that the United States faced "a more grave emergency than in 1917" and had called for "plans like those of 1917 that build from the bottom up and not from the top down." In his inaugural address he had declared "we must move as a trained and loyal army willing to sacrifice for the good of a common discipline." The analogue of war had several implications. It suggested the numerous temporary but immensely powerful agencies that organized the American economy during the World War. It provided cues for a wide variety of specific programs, including the Civilian Conservation Corps, many of the activities of the Tennessee Valley Authority, housing and resettlement efforts, farm subsidies, and, most noticeably, the National Recovery Administration. It implied the presidential authority that customarily accompanies wars. It enabled a major domestic propaganda drive. The New Deal had no counterpart of the World War Committee on Public Information, and it never stimulated the hysteria and coercion of the war. The public persuasion divisions of many of its agencies were nonetheless extraordinarily vocal.[6]

Assessing the New Deal in mid-June 1933, the socialist leader Norman Thomas asserted that it was "state capitalism"—a near dictatorial control of industry without the abolition of private property or the expropriation of profits. Commenting that Mussolini might applaud the president's program, he asked, "To what extent may we expect to have the economics of fascism without its politics?" Not long, he thought, however enlightened Roosevelt's own intentions might be. History had reached a turning point at which private capitalism would be left behind; the alternatives of the future were fascism or socialism. For America, fascism seemed the most likely near-term choice.[7]

Thomas was guilty of thinking like a Marxian socialist, attuned to continental European traditions of rigid class divisions and powerful state bureaucracies that had few roots in America. The real issue was not whether the First New Deal would veer sharply to the right or the left, but whether it could achieve any traction within a fundamentally unreceptive American political system. The Republican opposition would be quick to see dictatorial aspirations lurking behind every bill that made its way through Congress. Numerous conservative Democrats would quietly share the concern. While the nation was extraordinarily willing to follow Roosevelt during the first several months of his administration, dissent would become increasingly loud. New Deal programs displayed a salutary openness lacking in totalitarian alternatives. Unfortunately, openness frequently translated into conflict and inefficiency.

By early July, the outlines of the New Deal recovery strategy were clear. Banking reform along with federal loans and investments (primarily from the RFC) would stabilize the financial system. By effectively devaluing the dollar, the administration would inject a whiff of inflation into a deflated economy and counter the numerous foreign devaluations that had made American exports uncompetitive. Federal jobs programs and large-scale direct relief payments would lift employment, inject purchasing power into the economy, and create new consumer demand. By subsidizing acreage restrictions, the new farm program would instantly put money into the pockets of impoverished farmers and, some months down the line, give them higher income from rising prices. By organizing the economy under the National Recovery Administration, the industrial program hoped to bring an end to destructive cutthroat competition, restore the profitability of much of American business, and increase standards for workers. Avoiding risky foreign agreements, the New Deal would focus on recovery in the United States.

Despite its conceptual coherence, the "First New Deal" seemed to shoot off in all directions—financial props for banks and business enterprises, unprecedented relief programs for "little people," grandiose government projects, an embrace of class-conscious labor unionism, fringe collectivist endeavors that smacked of utopian socialism. Many of its initiatives mingled the objectives of relief, recovery, and reform so thoroughly as to defy classification. As a whole, it was a humanitarian success, a political triumph, and an economic failure.

The relief programs[8] were highly effective in distributing aid to millions of people, most of them in desperate straits: mortgage refinancing for farmers and homeowners facing foreclosure; jobs, often lasting only a few months, for unemployed workers of all kinds; federally financed public assistance for widows, dependent children, the indigent elderly, the disabled, and other traditional public charges. A Civilian Conservation

Corps (CCC), aimed primarily at young men leaving high school, provided money, discipline, and initiation into the world of work. A Federal
Emergency Relief Administration (FERA) combined a dole to the needy
(usually administered through state agencies) with many small-scale
work projects for the able-bodied. When economic gains stalled in the
fall of 1933, Roosevelt established a temporary Civil Works Administration (CWA) to develop hundreds of thousands of relief jobs across the
country; inevitably, many of these, which had to be developed on the
spur of the moment and with winter coming on, were contrivances. Critics decried "leaf raking" and other ephemeral enterprises as unproductive
and ultimately as demoralizing to workers as the dole. There was a lot of
such activity, but CWA also built or improved a half-million miles of secondary roads, 40,000 schools, and a thousand small airports, and did
other lasting works.

The Public Works Administration began to have its own impact, most
impressively in hundreds of huge projects that included aircraft carriers,
port facilities, and great hydroelectric dams but also thousands of much
smaller needs such as school buildings and post offices. The Tennessee
Valley Authority brought federal money and tens of thousands of jobs
into one of the most impoverished areas of the country. At the beginning
of 1935, with the economy still in depression, the president requested the
most gigantic public works appropriations in American history to finance
yet another set of work relief agencies.

It is hard to estimate just how many Americans benefited from relief
and quasi-relief programs during the first two years of the New Deal. The
FERA and CWA combined may have assisted as many as twenty million
individuals. At the end of 1934, PWA Administrator Harold Ickes
boasted of having funded three billion man-hours of work in a year and a
half; he claimed that seven million people had been helped directly or
indirectly by the agency.[9] The elderly parent whose monthly twenty dollar FERA-funded pension relieved his children of the burden of sustain-
ing him, the eighteen-year-old CCC worker who sent most of his small
salary back home to his family every month, the CWA road worker sur-
facing a dusty farm-to-market road and buying groceries for his wife and
three children with his pay—all exemplified the way in which for every
direct recipient there were usually at least a couple of others who would
be equally grateful. It is possible that a quarter or more of the population
was thus directly touched by the New Deal. The great majority of the
beneficiaries were dedicated to Roosevelt. By recognizing and dealing

with a humanitarian imperative, the New Deal created a hard core of electoral support willing to forgive almost any other shortcoming.

It was easy, if expensive, to help the truly needy. The goal of economic recovery in one country was much harder. As originally envisioned, public works would inject just enough money into the economy to, as people in that era put it, "prime the pump." The First New Deal did not anticipate the massive "loan expenditure" John Maynard Keynes had recommended for England. Federal spending was simply part of a larger formula to be administered by a benevolent federal government that would be at once larger, more experimental, and more involved in the economy than ever before. Only when one contemplates the magnitude of the ends and the novelty of the means is it possible to comprehend the odds against success.

⌐

The management of the dollar—monetary policy—was complex and difficult. Roosevelt and other key policy makers, most of whom had neither sophisticated training in economics nor practical experience in finance, faced a daunting problem of conceptualization. Throughout American history, moreover, few issues had been more persistent or more emotionally debated than that of "hard money" v. "soft money," or "stability" v. "inflation." To move in either direction likely would produce howls of fury from injured interest groups while generating only tepid approval from other parties yet to feel tangible gain. For more than a generation, the Democratic party had leaned toward the soft money/inflation side. Roosevelt moved in that direction, fully prepared to weather the anger of the Republicans and his own right wing. By the spring of 1933 prices had fallen twenty-five percent from their 1929 levels. "Reflation" was a necessity. The way in which Roosevelt went about it was problematic, unhelpful for most other national economies, and ultimately unproductive.

By suspending the convertibility of the dollar to gold, Roosevelt had already effected a competitive devaluation for international purposes, bringing for example the price of the British pound in dollar terms from about $3.40 at the beginning of March to approximately $4.60 by the time of his London conference bombshell. The result was to give a small boost to American exports but these remained too inconsequential to make a perceptible contribution to recovery. Internally, devaluation contributed to rising commodity prices and to a major rally in stock prices that drove the *New York Times* index up from 52 on March 3 to 96 by mid-July. The *Times* index of business activity also had moved up sharply from 60 to 97. Gains in employment were less robust. At best, the early months of the New Deal shaved three to five points off an unemployment rate of twenty-five percent or more; 10 to 11 million Americans remained out of work. Worse yet, by the end of July, the economy was beginning to sputter.

The flirtation with an international agreement behind him, Roosevelt pursued monetary flexibility with abandon. He and his close associate, Henry Morgenthau, had been mightily impressed by a noted Cornell University economist George Warren, who had argued for the adoption of a "commodity dollar." Focusing on price declines in major commodities as the essential element of a depression, Warren believed that increasing their prices could bring prosperity. Gold, he thought, was the key. The government could devalue the dollar through a policy of purchasing gold at higher prices. The prices of other commodities—food, fiber, minerals, petroleum, and the like—would follow apace and create a general prosperity.

Most practical financiers and academic economists thought Warren's prescription superficial; a devaluation might be merited as a response to other currency devaluations but could not in itself solve complex international problems of supply-demand imbalances and money flows. However, with Secretary of the Treasury Woodin critically ill and the Federal Reserve Board of little consequence, there was no one to block the Warren strategy. By the end of October, with business activity slipping backwards, employment stagnant, and Roosevelt afraid of "marching farmers" if agricultural prices fell, the administration was ready to try it. Meeting daily with RFC chairman Jesse Jones and with Morgenthau, whom he made acting secretary of the Treasury on November 13, the president set a price at which the RFC, acting as a proxy for the Treasury, would buy gold. In order to foil speculators, who made big bets in pursuit of marginal gains, they varied the price every day.

Roosevelt delighted in the power of his unpredictability. Unfortunately, gold buying (like his disruption of the World Economic Conference) displayed him at his least effective and least attractive—flippantly suggesting prices based on lucky numbers, operating beyond his depth, and rejecting out of hand good advice. When James Warburg argued to him that a fixed price would be necessary to allow businessmen to make long-term contractual agreements, he replied: "Poppycock! The bankers want to know everything beforehand and I've told them to go to hell."

Speaking in more measured terms in his third and last fireside chat of 1933, he declared an increase in commodity prices, especially for agricultural products, to be an overriding objective that he intended to achieve through gold buying at various prices before fixing a permanent valuation for the dollar. His aim, he said, was continuous control. "This is a policy and not an expedient. . . . We are thus continuing to move towards a managed currency."[10]

The political consequences were more spectacular than the economic results. The policy precipitated a minor purge of administration officials, including Undersecretary of the Treasury Dean Acheson, and some informal advisers, among them Warburg. Democrats such as Al Smith and Senator Carter Glass attacked the policy. Roosevelt was convinced that he was inconveniencing and perhaps extracting minimal sacrifice from the wealthy and the banking community (toward which he nourished an increasingly emotional hostility) for the sake of ninety percent of the population. In fact the impact was hardly so neat. The initial policy obligated the government to buy only newly mined U.S. gold, but it soon became apparent that this source was too small to have an impact. The offer was extended to the world market at prices so attractive that the precious metal surged into the Treasury. Still, by the end of 1933, the gold purchases had done nothing for commodity prices; the disruptive effects far outweighed any benefits. In a widely read "open letter to President Roosevelt," John Maynard Keynes bluntly criticized the policy as derived from a "crude economic doctrine" and akin to "trying to get fat by buying a larger belt." The fluctuating gold prices, he continued, had upset confidence, hindered business decisions, and decreased U.S. standing in the wider world. Economists who could gain a public hearing generally agreed.[11]

By January 1934, Roosevelt was convinced of the virtue of stabilization. He requested legislation, quickly passed as the Gold Reserve Act of 1934 on January 30, authorizing him to stabilize the dollar at fifty to sixty percent of its former gold content. The next day, he issued a proclamation pegging the dollar to gold at $35 to the ounce, a devaluation of approximately forty-one percent. The proclamation understandably infuriated large businesses and financial institutions that less than a year earlier had surrendered gold holdings at $20.67. It equally angered many middle-class Americans who cared little that the gold they had given up might have had a face value of only a few thousand dollars rather than tens of millions.

The Gold Reserve Act cut the dollar loose from gold for domestic purposes while giving it a gold value for international trade and finance. The new valuation was easily maintained; gold continued its flow into the United States from all over an increasingly turbulent world. In June 1934, moreover, Roosevelt appeased congressional inflationists by signing the Silver Purchase Act, which obligated the government to buy at above-market prices all the newly mined silver produced in the United States. A textbook example of narrow-interest legislation, the act authorized the "coinage" of this silver in the form of hard coins or dollar bills ("silver certificates"). Aside from enriching silver producers and subsidizing no more than 5,000 jobs in the industry, the only economic effect of silver buying was to raise the world price and thereby destabilize the currencies of the two major silver standard nations, Mexico and China. Over the rest of the decade most of the huge flow of gold and silver coming to the Treasury was not monetized (coined or used as a basis for paper money), but enough of it was to allow for a dramatic expansion of the money supply at a rate of about eleven percent a year from 1934 through 1937. This growth was probably a necessary condition for recovery, but not sufficient in itself. As Keynes observed, a bigger belt might be necessary to accommodate a fattening of the economy but could not generate it.[12]

Increased foreign trade could have been part of a solution, but efforts in that direction were largely nullified by the administration's determination to engage in a style of national planning that practically demanded protectionism. At the urging of Secretary of State Hull, the administration submitted a trade bill to Congress in early 1934. Signed by the president on June 12, the Reciprocal Trade Act delegated broad authority to the executive to negotiate and put into effect by executive order bilateral agreements that mutually lowered trade barriers. The act had no immediate economic effect; only one such agreement was concluded in 1934—with Cuba. The long-run impact was modest at best. Over the remainder of the 1930s the United States achieved significant reciprocity agreements with only three of its nine most important trading partners: Canada (1935), France (1935), and Great Britain (1939). Protectionist sentiment was so strong that Roosevelt and Hull justified the program in terms of promoting exports.

This was the primary excuse for extending diplomatic recognition to the Soviet Union on November 17, 1933. Actually, the decision probably had more to do with Roosevelt's apparent conviction that the time had come to recognize that the Soviet state was an enduring feature of the world scene. The action won wide acceptance. Engagement with the Soviet Union made more sense than denial of its existence, but the trade and the diplomatic benefits were minimal.

The health of the world economy would have been improved if the U.S., as the planet's greatest creditor and holder of precious metal, had been willing to run substantial trade deficits. An increased volume of global economic activity surely would have resulted in a net creation of American jobs while it also benefited foreigners, but it probably would have been beyond even Roosevelt's powers to explain such a policy to the American people. Moreover, protectionism was not just an American fallacy. Britain and many other countries clung to it stubbornly throughout the decade. Reciprocal trade delivered small benefits to the nineteen countries that signed agreements (many of them tightly limited) with the U.S. Far from an engine of prosperity, it was a cog in a sputtering machine. At best, it kept the ideal of open trade alive for a post-1945 future that would be more welcoming to it.[13]

The New Deal agricultural program was a remarkable phenomenon. Differing spectacularly from farm aid programs of the past, it achieved its objective of rescuing mainstream American farmers from ruin. It did so largely by providing government organization for a segment of the economy too fragmented to regulate itself. If it did less for the farming poor, it at least made a more extensive attempt than any federal program before it.

The Agricultural Adjustment Act, signed on May 12, 1933, authorized production quotas, export subsidies, "non-recourse loans" that were really thinly-disguised price supports, and subsidized acreage restriction. The last of these techniques, known as the domestic allotment program, was the backbone of the farm recovery program. It targeted five big staple commodities (wheat, cotton, corn, rice, and tobacco) and also sought to control the supply of hogs and dairy products. It was essentially a creation of policy intellectuals who sold it to a suspicious and reluctant farming establishment.

A large segment of farm sentiment, well-represented in Congress, advocated the historic solution of agrarian debtors to hard times—inflation whether by the free and unlimited coinage of silver or simply by the printing press. Powerful insurgent congressmen saw to it that the Agricultural Adjustment Act gave Roosevelt extensive authority to tinker with the dollar. The neopopulist National Farmers Union, dominant in the wheat-growing Great Plains states, encouraged inflation and wanted a government guarantee of "the cost of production." Veterans of the McNary-Haugen agitation of the 1920s wanted the federal government to purchase crop surpluses at a "parity" price, then dump them overseas. None of these schemes were realistic. There were no open foreign markets for surpluses; nor could anyone other than the most determined inflationists envision the mountain of money needed to support unlimited production.

Domestic allotment won out in the end because it seemed the most feasible alternative and because the American Farm Bureau Federation, the largest and most important of the farm organizations, bought into it. Strong in the cotton South and the corn-hog belt of the Midwest, closely allied to the Agriculture Department's Extension Service, the Farm Bureau had developed a center of gravity outside the historic inflationist regions. Its president, Edward O'Neal of Alabama, was an aggressive but pragmatic interest group leader. His backing made a big difference.[14]

By mid-May, the planting season had come and gone. Crops were up in fields across the country, growing toward maturity. By and large, planned acreage restriction would have to wait until next year. The immediate crisis could be solved only by crop destruction. The new agency established to administer the recovery plan, the Agricultural Adjustment Administration (AAA), started its life by paying farmers to plow under every third row of cotton and to ship six million baby pigs to designated packing plants for premature slaughter. The spectacle in a time of depression was understandably horrifying, but some of the reaction demonstrated an urban lack of acquaintance with the realities of farm life. Widespread denunciation of the slaying of the piglets led Secretary Wallace to wonder aloud if Americans thought farmers raised pigs as barnyard pets.

Fortunately, large-scale, ostentatious destruction was necessary only in these two areas. It was possible to deal with other commodities more discreetly—often through marketing agreements or government purchases. Wheat, a chronic surplus commodity, was cut back to size far more cruelly and indiscriminately by drought in the Plains States; the AAA let nature do the crop reduction. Over the next three years, productive wheat fields from Oklahoma and North Texas up into the Dakotas suffered devastating dust storms; whole counties became relief problems. By 1935, the United States was buying foreign wheat to cover a domestic shortfall.

The AAA needed time to stabilize agriculture. In the fall of 1933, farm prices fell sharply in tandem with a general economic turndown. The militant Farm Holiday Association spearheaded violent protests in Iowa, Minnesota, and Wisconsin, right down to the dynamiting of dairies and cheese plants. Regional neopopulist and radical politicians egged them on. Farm Holiday leader Milo Reno threatened a national farm strike. The spasm of rage passed after the administration created the Commodity Credit Corporation ("farm CCC") to make non-recourse loans against crops at above-market parity prices. A steady rain of AAA acreage payments, FERA relief checks, and farm CCC price-support "loans" put out the fire.[15]

The farm CCC would become increasingly important as the decade went along. The acreage allotment idea was basically sound, but precise calculations for tens of thousands of operations were impossible. Moreover, the march of agricultural science was in the direction of higher yields per acre. When Henry Wallace came to Washington, his Pioneer Hi-Bred corn seed business was still relatively small and marginally profitable. As corn farmers began to make a little money under the New Deal, they bought increasing quantities of high-yielding Pioneer seed and produced larger crops on fewer acres. Higher yields required increased subsidies and more surplus buying. Pioneer Hi-Bred's achievements in corn were being duplicated for other commodities and enhanced by newer and better fertilizers. By the end of the thirties, Wallace was on the verge of millionaire status, and control of surpluses had become an elusive target. Wallace and the men in whose hands he had put Pioneer Hi-Bred had fired the first shot in a "green revolution" that would eventually eliminate much of the world's hunger, while creating difficult and expensive agricultural policy problems for countries like the United States.[16]

However ragged its start, the agricultural program managed to achieve its immediate goals. Its allotment payments, combined with farm credit and outright relief programs, saved hundreds of thousands of farms from going under in 1933. Over the next three years, commodity prices moved upward, varying in increase from item to item, for the most part falling short of parity, but achieving profitable levels. The Commodity Credit Corporation was at least as key as the AAA in the developing recovery. The day after it was incorporated, it began to offer loans at ten cents a pound on cotton, two cents above the market, *provided that recipient producers agreed to participate in the 1934 acreage allotment program.* This disguised buying absorbed most of the surplus that remained after the earlier plowing-under, eventually raised the market price to 9.6 cents, and increased the income of cotton farmers by fifty percent over the 1932 figure. Never shy about demanding more of a good thing, cotton growers sought, and got, a twelve-cent rate in 1934. The same pattern developed for other commodities, creating huge government stockpiles of non-perishables that would not be liquidated until World War II.[17]

So vast and complex a program could be put into effect so rapidly because the Department of Agriculture already was among the largest in the government. Farmers had been demanding federal assistance of one kind or another for a half-century and had received considerable benefits in the form of credit programs and technical assistance. A substantial community of agricultural policy experts already was in place to develop and implement responses to the Depression. The Agricultural Extension Service, working through state land grant universities and informally linked in many areas to the Farm Bureau Federation, had an agent in virtually every rural county in the United States. It provided the Agricultural Adjustment Administration with an established infrastructure.[18]

Working farmers as a group might have preferred other methods of recovery, but for the most part they seem to have been satisfied enough with what they got. In Washington, however, a debate over agricultural recovery ran on within the administration. It involved two separate and critical issues: Should production be limited or encouraged? (Were acreage allotments a fair and acceptable substitute for the export of surpluses?) Was the constituency for agricultural recovery simply the middling-to-large commercial operator? (What are we going to do about the rural poor?)

Not everyone had rejected McNary-Haugenism. No agrarian spokesman was more emotionally attached to it than George Peek, who with Hugh Johnson had been the major developer of and lobbyist for the plan during the 1920s. Sixty years old in 1933, Peek had been a leading candidate for Secretary of Agriculture; he was too prominent to be left out of the administration. Roosevelt and Wallace agreed that he would have to be director of the Agricultural Adjustment Administration. Widely admired in the world of agricultural politics, promoted by the millionaire statesman Bernard Baruch, Peek was eloquent, stubborn, hardbitten, convinced that crop restriction was at best a short-term evil, and determined to fight for exports.[19]

From the beginning, he was estranged from the department's urban radicals and policy intellectuals, loosely aligned with Undersecretary Rexford Tugwell. They wanted, he believed with some accuracy, to control both farmers and the businesses that processed their production.

Unwavering in his conviction that the agricultural economy could be liberated only by opening foreign markets, Peek still thought this could be
done while maintaining tariff protection for American producers. Theoretical issues became practical policy conflicts when he demanded millions of dollars for export subsidies and Wallace denied the request. In
December, his position having become untenable, he resigned. Roosevelt,
hoping to keep him in the administration, made him a special adviser on
foreign trade. After a year and a half of conflict with Secretary of State
Hull, who thought subsidized trade deals were no substitute for an open
system, he left that post.

Peek's successor, Chester Davis, came out of the same tradition, but
was more flexible. If not his preferred way, the new regime met the pragmatic test of raising farm income. What Davis could not abide was the
continuing effort of the agricultural policy intelligentsia to convert a
price support program to a reform crusade.

The conflict that emerged within the AAA over the next year had at
least three facets. It pitted old-style agrarian progressives against younger
ideological urban liberals with a broad social vision. It revealed, indeed
spotlighted, sharp divisions that existed not just in agriculture but in
almost every cranny of the New Deal between traditional interest-group
political operatives and the new public service intellectuals, more prominent than ever before. Finally, it displayed both a handicap and a glory of
the New Deal—the sense that the "public," or the "consumer," had to be
represented in programs that targeted specific interest groups. At the
level of principle, these tendencies were high-minded; at the level of
practical operations, they led inevitably to disruptive conflict.

Within the AAA, Davis put together a team of loyalists who had sided
with him and George Peek for years to raise agricultural prices. They were
neither bad men nor reactionaries, but they were representatives of one
part of the larger farm community—those operators who produced substantial amounts of their product for the commercial market. Existing
precariously, a substantial proportion of this "farm middle class" lived on
an unpleasant edge, often without electricity, running water, or indoor
plumbing, working long hours, yet heavily in debt and haunted by fears of
bankruptcy or foreclosure. Davis and his associates were not simply the
representatives of plantation owners and agribusinesses. The farm middle
class were the agrarian equivalent of urban small businessmen—except
that they toiled much harder and accepted living standards that urban-
ites would consider impoverished.

Yet it was equally true that millions of rural Americans were even more deprived. Subsistence farmers, both black and white, who produced little for the market lived in conditions scarcely imaginable today. A considerable number owned their own marginal little farms; those at the bottom of the ladder were Southern tenant farmers and sharecroppers who eked out a living on land that belonged to the social and economic upper crust of the rural South. To the Davis group they were simply irrelevant. To the urban reformers within the Agriculture Department, they were critically important objects of social policy.

Davis's ideological adversaries possessed not just a different vision but different perspectives and backgrounds that hampered meaningful communication. Tugwell was an urban professor with a sense of mission and apparent arrogance, bent on the reordering of society. Other leading figures included Jerome Frank, general counsel of the AAA, a pioneering legal thinker and social activist, who presided over a group of young lawyers with degrees from leading law schools. Frank also established an AAA Consumers' Counsel, appointing to the post Frederic C. Howe, an iconic old progressive. Howe's much younger assistant, Gardner Jackson, was far more familiar with the travails of urban radicals and labor organizers than those of corn and hog farmers. To someone like Davis, who understood farm life from long, ingrained experience, these intellectuals had no standing to make agricultural policy. (It did not help matters when one of the young radicals, Lee Pressman, cluelessly referred to the needs of "macaroni growers.") Frank openly proclaimed the irrelevance of actual experience, asserting that brilliant young attorneys could learn what they needed to know. He believed that the AAA was but one aspect of a larger reorganization of American society for the benefit of the many rather than the few. Larger-visioned intellectuals like himself, not interest group representatives, would direct it.[20]

In October 1933, for example, he backed tobacco regulations to control not just the production and marketing of the commodity but to set limits on prices that could be charged by the tobacco-processing companies. Roosevelt, more attuned to political possibility, rejected the plan. Similar efforts to affect the pricing and marketing of meat and dairy products likewise were rebuffed. That they were even attempted indicated not only a questionable grasp of political practicality, but also the undisciplined character and overlapping jurisdictions of the New Deal. Pricing, production, and marketing issues at the processing or manufacturing level were generally the concern of the National Recovery Administration. The overreaching of the reform intellectuals attracted the wrath not simply of Davis but also of most of the important farm leaders whose views he mirrored. The audacious attempt to inflict regulations upon processors of agricultural commodities angered business leaders.

By early 1935, the reformers were concentrating on the plight of southern tenants and sharecroppers, who clearly were being hurt by the AAA. Acreage allotments made a certain percentage of them redundant on one large cotton plantation after another. Unneeded croppers were evicted to move in with relatives, look for work in the nearest city, or perhaps make for California as migrant farm laborers. In few, if any, cases did those who remained get a share of the allotment payments despite provisions that seemed to require it. Local committees that administered the program were either indifferent or hostile to complaints. Efforts to develop a Southern Tenant Farmers Union in 1934 had resulted in one episode after another of violence, openly or tacitly sanctioned by local authorities, against outside organizers. The powerful Southern Democratic bloc in Congress was solidly on the side of the status quo. In February 1935, Frank attempted a desperate gambit. He drew up an order requiring landlords to retain all existing tenants as a condition of receiving payments, waited until Davis was out of town, and talked Acting AAA Administrator Victor Cristgau into signing it. Davis returned to Washington, countermanded the order, and demanded the dismissal of Frank, Howe, and their leading staff members. He was shrewd enough to know that he occupied the center of gravity in agrarian politics, and that the liberals had chosen issues for which they could muster little support.

Wallace, however uncomfortably, agreed and gave his sanction to the firings. To its critics, the agricultural "purge" of 1935 signified that the New Deal's organizational state was reform for the benefit of the comfortable more than succor for the poor. More accurately, it indicated the limits of possibilities in a pluralistic political structure that could not be commanded from the top down. Davis won because he represented more votes than Frank; Wallace and Roosevelt understood this. Frank and other leading dissenters could be, and were, shuttled to more friendly posts in Roosevelt's growing administrative bureaucracy.[21]

By this time also, the New Deal was beginning significant attacks on rural poverty with a Subsistence Homestead Division, designed to assist and subsidize marginal farmers; under Tugwell's wing, it was about to become the more ambitious Resettlement Administration. Plans were well underway for a vast rural electrification program that would increase the quality of farm life. In the political environment of the early thirties, the politics of the organizational state could do little for the rural poor. The politics of relief could do considerably more.

The National Industrial Recovery Act was the centerpiece of the New Deal's recovery strategy. When Roosevelt signed it into law on June 16, 1933, he proclaimed it "the most important and far-reaching legislation ever enacted by the American Congress."[22] However essential the agricultural economy, the major businesses of America involved mining, manufacturing, construction, retailing, and transportation. Agricultural recovery was important as a matter of politics and equity. The revival of industry was necessary to end the Depression. The act, the most ambitious attempt in American history to establish long-run state organization of the economy, had numerous origins: the example of the European corporate state, the planning impulse dating back to the progressive era, the organization of the economy to prosecute the World War, Herbert Hoover's voluntary associationalism of the 1920s, and the responses to the Depression of such business leaders as Gerard Swope and Henry Harriman.

The progressives had assumed that a disinterested administrative class could control the economy in pursuit of the general welfare and do so in a way that advanced liberal democratic values. Looking back in 1933, many believed that the World War, with its War Industries Board and other economic management agencies, had proven them right. It was the most important single example for what became the National Recovery Administration.

In the heady first months of the New Deal, it was perhaps natural to believe that the drive for economic recovery could achieve the same moral urgency and national support as the drive for victory against Imperial Germany. But troubling questions of power and authority remained. To what extent could the New Dealers control such an organization with neither a ready-made administrative apparatus nor a solid interest group base? With labor still unorganized in most of the big industries, how could the national government achieve equity for it? How much of the economy could be effectively organized—just big business in the leading industries, or everything, everywhere? And how appropriate was the war analogy? In wartime, even liberal societies shelve many of their freedoms for the sake of survival and accept the dictates of the state. Could a peacetime government, even in a depression, even one headed by Roosevelt, muster the same grudging consent and impose its will on the economy without appearing to be a police state?

Like the agricultural program, the NRA was guided by a philosophy of managed scarcity that assumed too many goods were out in an economy with too little demand. To restore business profitability, it would establish legally enforceable industrial codes that limited production and divided up markets, thereby allowing enterprises to increase prices and sell their products at a profit. The purchasing power to buy these goods would be provided in part by labor provisions that forbade child labor, set a minimum wage rate, established maximum hours, and guaranteed collective bargaining. In addition, the other major agency established by the National Industrial Recovery Act, the Public Works Administration (PWA), would begin injecting its $3.3 billion appropriation into the economy, providing another major stimulus. The management of supply to fit demand, the provision for labor, the big fiscal stimulus—all would generate a recovery with social justice guided by the benign hand of an activist government.

Reality was messier from the beginning, and Roosevelt was a big part of the problem. One official had to run both the NRA and PWA in order to coordinate their activities. The president recoiled at the idea of appointing an industrial czar with enormous jurisdiction and a huge public works budget. The technique of dividing commands was one of the oldest in the history of human leadership, employed over the centuries by monarchs, democrats, and dictators. It made the man at the top the ultimate arbiter between insecure, squabbling subordinates. The extent to which Roosevelt consciously adopted the tactic remains unclear. There is no doubt that he delighted in playing off his aides against each other, much as a flirtatious belle might juggle anxious suitors. The trait did not bring distinction to his presidency.

The president made Secretary of the Interior Harold Ickes PWA Administrator before offering the NRA to Hugh Johnson. The stunned old general responded, "I'm ruined, I'm ruined." Finally, he yielded to persuasion, doubtless confirming the president's sense that few public men would deny themselves the visibility and ego gratification of so high profile a post. The resulting split command was made worse by the way in which Ickes and Johnson, who had never met before, took an instant personal dislike to each other. Worse yet, where Johnson was hyperactive, Ickes was ultra-cautious. Where Johnson proceeded pell-mell to organize every business and occupation in the country, Ickes moved with glacial deliberation, far more concerned with the quality of every project and honesty of every contract than with the need to jump-start the economy. By early 1935, he would have spent only a little more than half the PWA's original appropriation.[23]

Their attitudes simply exaggerated the built-in weaknesses of the entire enterprise. Even if Ickes had been more frenetic, the PWA could not have exercised a decisive impact on the American economy. Extensive public works projects required time to develop. The states were expected to provide matching grants, but many were strapped for cash. Missouri, for example, did not manage to raise the money it needed until voters approved a large bond issue in May 1934. The biggest immediate beneficiary of the PWA was the U.S. Navy, which had plans ready for new warships (and a sympathetic president). The NRA effort at organizational management of the economy ran against the grain of an American experience that feared economic concentration, celebrated individual enterprise, and had constructed a body of antitrust law without counterpart in any other developed country. The NRA design assumed that appeals for patriotism and national unity could bring all of American business together, reconcile vast differences between large corporations and small businesses, and deliver promised benefits to labor without the strife that invariably accompanied union organization.

Working largely with representatives of trade associations, the NRA produced a draft of its first code—for the cotton textile industry—in just days, but revision and presidential approval took until mid-July. As late as mid-August, codes for such basic industries as coal, oil, and steel were still works in progress. The big, visible companies and employers were obviously critical, but they were also less than the tip of an immense iceberg. The United States had an estimated 7,000 "industries," many of them represented in 2,000 national trade associations. By the end of 1933, 200 fully approved codes were in effect, covering an estimated sixty percent of American workers. By then, the nation was debating whether the agency was bane or blessing.[24]

Johnson was able to move so quickly by identifying the NRA with the spirit of American patriotism. No technique was too unsubtle, no symbol unused, no rhetoric too extravagant, no opportunity for mass demonstration passed up. The agency's symbol was a large blue eagle, wings spread, one talon clutching a cogwheel, the other holding a group of lightning bolts. Companies observing an NRA code were allowed to display the eagle on their premises, their advertising, and, when appropriate, their products. The widow of Woodrow Wilson signed a public letter comparing its efforts to those of America in the World War and calling on the nation to "enlist under the banner of the 'blue eagle.'" While disclaiming any effort at a boycott of non-compliers, Johnson and NRA spokesmen all down the line asserted that buying under the blue eagle was the only way to keep the reemployment effort going; it was not much of a jump to the conclusion that this would be an act of patriotism. In a way reminiscent of the war, the NRA had vocal and active state and local committees all over the country, asserting its virtues and working to organize the local economy.[25]

The archetypical methods of NRA mobilization were monster rallies and grand parades. On September 12, 1933, Johnson delivered a passionate stem-winding speech to a crowd of 10,000 at New York's Madison Square Garden. Extravagantly (and inaccurately) he declared that all but fifteen percent of the nation's workers were already under the blue eagle. Attacking the "rudderless drifting" that had characterized the Hoover years, he placed Roosevelt at the center of the better times that were coming. It was the president who had a grand plan, who had given the American people faith, hope, and purpose. The declaration, already a staple of New Deal rhetoric, implicitly admitted an elemental truth: the New Deal from the very beginning *was* Roosevelt. A departure so great as the NRA needed him for legitimacy. Johnson spoke in a moment of hope and triumph, seconded by numerous leaders of labor and business. The reliance on the Roosevelt persona was natural, but was this enough to make the NRA a permanent part of the American political economy?[26]

The next day, a great parade, in observance of what the city officially proclaimed "the President's NRA Day," nearly shut down New York. Governor Herbert Lehman had ordered a half-day holiday to allow workers to march. All business establishments displaying the blue eagle closed at 1:00 p.m. The parade, organized by a U.S. Army major general, formed at Washington Square in lower Manhattan, and at 1:30 began marching straight up Fifth Avenue to Seventy-second Street. At the New York Public Library on Forty-second Street, it passed a reviewing stand, occupied by the First Lady, General Johnson, Governor Lehman, Governor Moore (New Jersey), Governor Cross (Connecticut), and Mayor O'Brien of New York City. On a float at the head of the procession were "Miss NRA" and "Miss Liberty," portrayed by two fetching sisters, who appear to have been identical twins. Behind them followed marching bands and groups of workers representing the vast and diverse reach of the NRA—50,000 garment workers, 30,000 city employees, 17,000 retail employees, a brigade of uniformed policemen, 1,500 federal customs workers, city court employees, 6,000 brewery workers, a dozen artificial flower makers, and a Radio City Music Hall contingent. An estimated 250,000 in all marched from 1:30 until 11:22 p.m. past a throng estimated at one-and-a-half million. At some points the crowd, overcome by enthusiasm, spilled out into the streets, resisting police efforts to push it back. The event recalled the outpouring of emotion that had accompanied the end of the World War and the homecoming of the troops. In New York and in much of the rest of the country the mobilization seemed to be working. Momentarily, as Arthur Schlesinger, Jr., has written, Johnson—and Roosevelt—had succeeded in "transforming a government agency into a religious experience."[27]

Religious conversions are fragile things, usually requiring works as well as faith for long-term survival. The works had seemed to be coming in abundance during the first four months of the New Deal—a quick and encouraging, if modest, drop in unemployment, a sharp recovery in business activity, and an unprecedented array of federal aid programs, but even by the time of the New York NRA parade, the recovery was sputtering badly. The *New York Times* weekly business index told the story statistically. In the prosperity summer of 1929, it had peaked at 115; by early 1933, it had fallen all the way to 60. Almost from Roosevelt's inauguration, the index had embarked on a nearly straight-up trajectory, hitting 99 in July and providing hope that prosperity and full employment were only months away. By late September, however, it was down to 78, the level of late 1931. The numbers, represented on a line graph, were discouraging enough. The meaning in human terms was hopes jolted as job prospects shimmered, then disappeared like mirages in the desert. The relatively small decline in unemployment from March at least held steady, but more than 20 percent of the workforce remained jobless. The federal programs remained, providing assistance to millions. Roosevelt's voice was still an encouraging presence in the nation's homes. But the economy had stalled.

———

The first hundred and twenty-five days of the New Deal had been triumphal; the rest of 1933 was much harder. The organizational state was in crisis. By the fall, Roosevelt was flustered and angry. Meeting with his cabinet and other officials on October 17, he asserted much as had Andrew Jackson a hundred years earlier that the bankers were conspiring against him by refusing to make business loans that would fuel the recovery. The complaint, to which he would periodically return over the next several years, revealed his fervent belief in the hoariest myths of the Democratic party. As an explanation of the continuing economic malaise, however, it had little to recommend it. The bankers were afraid, he said, that a stabilized dollar in the future would put an end to the trend of increasing commodity prices. It is far more likely they thought that, until the dollar was definitively stabilized in terms of gold, lending was too risky. FDR's program of buying gold at a different price every day prolonged the uncertainty for months.[28]

At most, "the bankers" were overly pessimistic about the outlook for the economy. If there was a definable culprit it was more likely the NRA. Increasingly the agency's attempts to organize an economic recovery revealed unrealistic expectations about its capacities, built-in contradictions among the interests it attempted to harmonize, and its fundamental unsuitability to an American environment. From the beginning the NRA suffered from an identity crisis. Was it simply government-sanctioned industrial self-organization subject to a few general rules, undertaken in the belief that a resurgent business sector would pull the economy to recovery? Was it an exercise in a state-managed economy that sought to provide equally for the interest of business, labor, and the larger public, defined as consumers? Ultimately, moreover, was not either alternative an affront to a deeply ingrained American ethic that valued business fragmentation and the free market? (The framers of the National Industrial Recovery Act implicitly recognized the hold of small business and the market ideal on the country when they christened the industrial regulations "codes of fair competition," although their real purpose was to suspend competition.)

The NRA's expansiveness would be a big part of its undoing. Had it organized only twenty-five or so of the largest and most concentrated lines of enterprise in the United States, it might have been viable. Instead it defined "industry" in a fashion well beyond common perception and tried to establish rules for almost any endeavor in which people earned money. It set up codes for businesses that were typically self-run mom-and-pop endeavors in which people worked hard for long hours and lacked the resources to cope with many government regulations. Small grocery stores and dry cleaners were perhaps the two most common examples. It even established a code for the "burlesque industry." Such overreaching invited resentment, rule-breaking, and ridicule.[29]

The lack of a large federal bureaucratic infrastructure for dealing with industrial policy threw the writing and administration of codes to established trade associations almost by default. The associations themselves almost invariably represented the interests of larger, well-established businesses in their fields. The early codes seemed reassuringly brief and to the point—the one for the motor car industry was reprinted in less than a quarter of a page of the *New York Times*. But the impression was deceptive. The codes usually balanced minimum wages with minimum prices, frequently put restrictions of one sort or another on production, and often established detailed specifications for products. They squeezed marginal operators, who lacked deep pockets, legal staff, or influence. In NRA parlance, such people were "chiselers." In much of America, they were respected local enterprisers struggling to meet payrolls and keep a business going.[30]

The codes failed to bring economic recovery because they rarely achieved the balance to which they aspired. As Walter Lippmann explained it to John Maynard Keynes in April 1934: "they are a very serious check to our recovery, for the obvious reason that they have raised costs faster than production has increased."[31] They also had failed to increase wages in tandem with prices.

Section 7a of the National Industrial Recovery Act guaranteed the right of workers to organize and bargain collectively. In a mostly non-unionized economy, employers assumed that this right could be legitimately satisfied by company representation plans. The original auto code, for example, dutifully incorporated the law's labor guarantees, then declared: "In accordance with the foregoing provisions, the employers in the automobile industry propose to continue the open shop policy heretofore followed and under which unusually satisfactory and harmonious relations with employees have been maintained."

For the year and a half after passage of the National Industrial Recovery Act, strikes grew in number and vehemence. Organizers frequently used some version of the slogan "President Roosevelt wants you to join the union." Unions with an established foothold in their industries and with tough, resourceful leadership—notably the Amalgamated Clothing Workers under Sidney Hillman, the International Ladies Garment Workers under David Dubinsky, and the United Mine Workers under John L. Lewis—were successful in reversing a pre-NRA pattern of decline.

Other efforts were less successful. The existing bastion of organized labor, the American Federation of Labor (AFL) was primarily a collection of specialized craft unions. Its leaders envisioned the workforces of large and complex mass production industries as recruits for existing organizations rather than for a big, new, single union. The auto workers, for example, might be balkanized into a dozen or more unions held together only by a loose federation. The AFL chiefs, moreover, were both cautious by nature and as a group just a bit wary of the less skilled industrial workers, many of whom were of recent immigrant origin. Early AFL efforts to organize such industries as automobiles, steel, rubber, and glass flopped badly. NRA labor boards lacked the authority to be helpful. Hugh Johnson intervened episodically and erratically in several large labor stoppages, usually accomplishing nothing and alienating both sides. By early 1935, Lewis, in league with Hillman and Dubinsky, was in open revolt against the federation's ineptness.

The other source of labor drives was the radical left, which was at the center of three spectacular eruptions in 1934. A strike for recognition at the Auto-Lite sparkplug plant in Toledo, initiated by AFL organizers, became dominated by the independent Marxist American Workers Party. At about the same time, violence erupted in Minneapolis, where the Trotskyist Dunne brothers controlled the Teamsters local. In San Francisco, the International Longshoremen's Association, headed by Harry Bridges, a militant radical with open Communist ties (and secret party membership), struck for recognition, shutting down not just the port of San Francisco but the entire West Coast for two months. The Teamsters backed him. The city's Industrial Association fought back with strike breakers and the support of the city administration.

In all three cases, Marxist union leaders probably thought they were in the vanguard of a class revolution, and the business establishment feared they were right. All three job actions erupted into armed violence in which neither side had a claim to virtue. In all three states, the governors called in the National Guard to preserve order. In Minnesota, Governor Floyd B. Olson, a self-proclaimed radical, felt compelled to declare martial law. In all three cases authorities, for the sake of preserving civic peace, persuaded employers to accept settlements that on balance favored the unions.[32]

The Toledo, Minneapolis, and San Francisco strikes were local episodes in which the friction of a radical left pushing up against deeply conservative business communities generated spectacular violence. They also revealed the way in which unionized labor had never achieved the degree of acceptance in the United States that it took for granted in Britain or Weimar Germany. Union organizing, then even more than now, was a messy process that frequently involved an atmosphere of menace, outright threats, violence, and angry class-based rhetoric. All cut deeply into the consciousness of not just the well-to-do but also many far less comfortable Americans who by education and instinct were repelled by such thoughts.

The fourth cataclysmic labor upheaval of Roosevelt's second year in office was the great textile strike of 1934. Worldwide, the industry lived in a Darwinian environment in which ruthless efficiency was the key to survival. Textile workers, whether on the Japanese island of Honshu or in Britain's Lancashire or in the American South, lived at the margins of working-class existence—ragged, dirt-poor, ill-fed, medically neglected, constantly exhausted. A Communist-led strike at Gastonia, North Carolina, in 1929 had been put down brutally. On September 1, 1934, the United Textile Workers union, which claimed a quarter of a million members but enjoyed little recognition from the companies, called a strike that stretched from New England to Georgia.

The action was as doomed as it was ambitious. The union was poorly financed, had little political clout either nationally or in most of the strike localities, and was up against an industry with huge, unsold inventories. Although its leadership was non-Communist, radicals at the fringes and the memory of Gastonia left it vulnerable. The governor of Rhode Island, T. H. Green, denounced the stoppage as Communist-inspired and deployed the National Guard to break it. In the South, where any labor organizing had long been denounced as Communistic, a monolithic political establishment united against the drive. Governor Eugene Talmadge of Georgia declared martial law, arrested union organizers indiscriminately, and imprisoned more than a hundred of them in a military stockade. NRA mediation produced a settlement that, face-saving rhetoric notwithstanding, amounted to a total victory for the companies.

Although achieved more roughly, the result was little different from the defeat textile workers in Lancashire had suffered two years earlier. The economics of overextended industries possessed an inexorable force that could not be denied. The mills, mostly unprofitable, stayed afloat on part-time schedules; the mill workers and their families—malnourished, diseased (syphilis, tuberculosis, pellagra), bereft of a basic education, living in shacks—somehow endured. Reporting from Gaston County, North Carolina, to Harry Hopkins in late 1934, journalist Martha Gellhorn wrote: "We are so proud of being a new people in a free land. And we have a serf class."[33]

The strikes of 1934 demonstrated the collapse of a spirit of national mobilization and unity that the New Deal had briefly tapped. To many middle-class Americans, the increased visibility of revolutionary-minded radicals raised a profoundly disturbing specter of class conflict. Unions, having discovered that NRA labor policy was unenforceable, valued the tenacity of the radicals. Oddly, while Hugh Johnson's credibility was seriously damaged, these failures cost the president little or nothing. The Gaston County mill workers, Martha Gellhorn reported, believed in him almost as if he were God. "You heard him talk over the radio, ain't you? He's the only president who ever said anything about the forgotten man. We know he's going to stand by us."[34]

By the time the textile strike ended, the NRA was close to collapse. A classic example of bureaucratic overstretch, it had established a regulatory empire it could not manage. It had alienated organized labor, much of American business, and consumers. The agency was under widespread attack from numerous quarters as oppressively bureaucratic and monopolistic. Here the Republican opposition was the least of Roosevelt's problems. The demagogic and neopopulistic maverick Democratic senator, Huey Long, flamboyantly assailed it for unleashing an around-the-clock plague of clerks and inspectors upon ordinary working enterprisers. Father Charles Coughlin, the popular radio priest, joined in the attacks.[35]

Numerous antimonopoly progressives, Democratic and Republican, of the type that Roosevelt wanted to recruit to liberalize the Democratic party joined in. The sainted Senator George W. Norris of Nebraska, responding to complaints from constituents, told deputy NRA Administrator Donald Richberg, "the small fellow is getting the worst of the deal and the big fellow is profiteering." Senator Gerald Nye of North Dakota attacked the NRA as a breeder of monopoly. The redoubtable William Borah of Idaho seconded him. The NRA's own Consumer Advisory Board, headed by Mary Harriman Rumsey, kept up a drumbeat of criticism from within. In early 1934, General Johnson yielded to pressure and established a special National Recovery Review Board to examine the issue of monopoly. Inexplicably, he named Clarence Darrow, the great old progressive attorney, controversialist, and combatant against William Jennings Bryan in the Scopes Trial, to head it. After four months of investigation, Darrow issued the first of a series of reports that slashingly denounced the agency and virtually all of its works.[36]

It was the beginning of the end for Johnson. He had dashed from city to city, conference to conference, establishing industrial codes, trying to bring every activity in the country under the aegis of the Blue Eagle. Faced with economic stagnation and rising protest, he began a prolonged crash-and-burn, punctuated by frequent alcoholic binges. Pursuing his job to a near-total neglect of his wife, who remained at their home in New York, he engaged in a quasi-public affair with his secretary. In the wake of the Darrow investigation, the NRA was embattled from every side and hopelessly stalled. Roosevelt, who hated to fire anyone, personally requested Johnson's resignation. On October 1, 1934, the deposed administrator delivered an emotional farewell speech to NRA employees. Ending it in tears, he quoted the last words of Madame Butterfly before she committed hara-kiri. In the years that followed, he wrote a newspaper column that drifted slowly but steadily into criticism of Roosevelt and the New Deal. An executive board succeeded him; it was soon headed by his former deputy Donald Richberg, an old New Nationalist progressive. Despite efforts to trim back the number of codes and reduce the power of trade associations, the NRA was never able to pull far enough back.

Whatever the degree of overstatement, the Darrow reports made a valid point—in many industries the big guys controlled the codes and used them to force the little guys out of business. At the end of 1934, a West Virginia mine operator who had shut down entirely told a FERA investigator that his former employees had been made relief cases by the NRA regional coal code. He could, he said, pay NRA wages, if allowed to produce and price his product without restriction; but the code, written by the huge Consolidation Coal Company, required him to charge almost as much for his second-grade coal as Consolidation and other large operators charged for top-grade, which they produced in abundance. A market existed for sub-prime coal, but not at just ten cents a ton less than the best. "What Washington is doing is to force monopolization just as fast as it can go," he declared. "This is happening in all lines—the middle fellow is being forced down and out and he is the backbone of the country."[37]

Code enforcement was often a public relations disaster, not least in states that adopted the federal codes as law and established their own "little NRAs." In April 1934, a New Jersey court fined a befuddled immigrant tailor, Jacob Maged, $100 and sentenced him to thirty days in jail for the crime of charging thirty-five cents, instead of the code minimum of forty cents, to press a suit. That he served only three days and apparently never paid the fine after agreeing to adhere to the cleaners and dyers code did little to detract from the shock value of the episode.[38]

The feds fared little better. Although given broad legal powers, the agency originally had hoped to do its job through moral suasion and the pressure of public opinion, much as had the War Industries Board a decade and a half earlier. Its officials knew that the constitutionality of the whole enterprise was suspect. By the last half of 1934, however, there seemed no alternative to arrest and prosecution of the "chiselers." In the spring of 1935, moviegoers across the country watched a reenactment of one such case.

We know from the start that Fred Perkins is a regular guy. He is a for-mer Cornell fullback. He runs a small battery factory with ten employ-ees, located behind his large Victorian house. Middle-aged and balding, widely respected in his home town, he looks and talks just like his workers and gets his hands dirty. He tells his men that the big com-panies are complaining to the National Recovery Administration about his twenty-five cent an hour wage scale, fifteen cents below the NRA code minimum. It's the best he can do and stay in business. Are they willing to work for him? They understand. York is a small town. "We're with you, Fred." A few days later, he is arrested, jailed, con-victed, and fined. An impressive legal team, including John W. Davis, the 1924 Democratic candidate for President, volunteers to represent him on an appeal expected to go to the Supreme Court, which "will try, not Fred Perkins, but the NRA." Chief Justice Charles Evans Hughes speaks at the dedication of the new Supreme Court building: "The fundamental conceptions of limited governmental powers and individ-ual liberty have persisted despite crises of disruption and expansion and still remain triumphant and unyielding." (*March of Time*: "York, Pa."—Westbrook Van Voorhis, narrator)

The sympathetic portrayal was largely accurate. Small shops like Perkins' battery factory existed all over America. Their owners were generally considered legitimate businessmen who provided jobs. Perkins served as a poster boy for the embattled small entrepreneur up against arbitrary gov-ernment regulation[39]

By then, the NRA was doomed. Many Republican conservatives, motivated only partly by partisanship, opposed it as an affront to Ameri-can liberties. Progressive antitrusters from both parties assailed it as the embodiment of state-sponsored cartelism. Frustrated labor leaders sup-ported Senator Robert Wagner's effort to push a separate labor law through Congress. Due to expire in June 1935, the NRA had no chance of reauthorization on Capitol Hill. Many Democratic legislators who campaigned as devoted followers of Roosevelt were firm opponents of the agency. Perhaps its strongest support was among "progressive" big business leaders who resented the competition of the "little fellow," valued the stability that the codes brought to disorganized industries, and were willing to provide superior benefits (if not unionization) to their workers.

No one could claim that the NRA had fostered economic recovery; to the contrary, the economy had begun to stagnate just as the Blue Eagle had started to become a feature of American life. In early 1935, the NRA Research and Planning Division reported that wages had risen about six percent under the Blue Eagle but that retail price increases had risen even more; consequently, real wages were actually a bit below those of June 1933. Roosevelt, convinced that the power to organize the economy was the key to recovery, still hoped somehow to preserve the NRA, but by then he also had accepted the argument that a massive new work relief effort was an urgent necessity.[40]

The Supreme Court never heard arguments about Fred Perkins's individual case. The government had succeeded in slipping in one involving two brothers named Schechter, who dealt in live poultry. The Schechter brothers were not exactly all-American boys, but the legal issues were the same. On May 27, 1935, a unanimous Supreme Court—conservatives, liberals, centrists—ruled the NRA unconstitutional, invoking a narrow definition of interstate commerce.

What next? The grand organizational experiment was over in industry, but not in agriculture. Agricultural planning had worked because it asked little of its clients and gave much to them; moreover, a generation of agricultural politics had prepared farmers for it. American industry presented a far more complex set of issues and could draw on little in the way of political preparation. The social scientists Theda Skocpol and Kenneth Finegold have speculated that a successful NRA in tandem with the AAA might have brought the nation out of the Depression and created "a centralized system of politically managed corporatist capitalism" with the state "directly involved in planning prices and production levels and in allocating income shares to capitalists, workers, and farmers." Commercial farmers would have gained relative to industry, workers would have gotten organization but would have remained subordinate to management, and industry would have functioned under government supervision with minimal competition.[41]

Perhaps, but there was nothing in the American experience to validate so great a leap—no long history of class stratification, or top-down rule, or long-entrenched state bureaucracy, or mass ideological assaults on liberal capitalism. American history was about the competitive ethic, the reservoir of sympathy for the individual enterpriser, the tendency of business and labor to see each other as adversaries. Whatever its origins in progressive era democratic thought, the NRA in action naturally trended toward an authoritarian and European corporatist vision. It failed because it had insufficient roots in its native ground.

What then was the alternative? Was there another democratic way out of the morass? On May 28, 1934, John Maynard Keynes, on a visit to the United States, achieved a long-sought meeting with Roosevelt. Their visit lasted an hour, was amiable, and, according to legend, notably unproductive. Frances Perkins later recalled Keynes telling her that he had "supposed the President was more literate, economically speaking." Roosevelt, she remembered, said, "He left me a whole rigamarole of figures. He must be a mathematician rather than a political economist." The meeting yielded no notes, no subsequent *aide memoire.* Keynes remembered his host as charming, clever, and superficial. The president, so the impression went, remembered Keynes hardly at all. Most journalists, when they learned of the visit, attached great influence to it and have been criticized for doing so by a generation of historians.

Perkins years later recalled Keynes explaining to her in plain English the way in which "with one dollar paid out for relief or public works or anything else, you have created four dollars' worth of national income." Why, she wondered, had he not "been as concrete when he talked to Roosevelt, instead of treating him as though he belonged to the higher echelons of economic knowledge"? But why would Keynes, a man who had devoted much of his life to the art of public persuasion, have spoken to Roosevelt as an arcane academic? Is it possible Perkins took Roosevelt's breezy comment too seriously?[42]

About a week later, just before Keynes returned to Britain, he sent the president a copy of an article he was publishing in the *New York Times* and the London *Times.* It was entitled "Agenda for the President." Beginning with a statement of his "sympathy with most of the social and reforming aims" of the New Deal, Keynes as tactfully as possible suggested that the NRA had contributed little to recovery, praised the agricultural program, advised the president to devote some attention to business confidence, and devoted much of the rest of his space to his main point. Recovery rested on a high level of "emergency expenditure"—$400 million a month for at least twelve months, financed by loans, not taxation.[43]

In all likelihood, the article repeated what Keynes had told Roosevelt orally and illustrated with his "rigamarole of figures." Future decisions would demonstrate that Roosevelt may have absorbed more than either Keynes or Perkins understood.

By November 1934, the NRA, widely unpopular, was gliding toward oblivion. The economy was about where it had been two years earlier, when Americans had flocked to the polls to throw out Herbert Hoover. The Roosevelt programs had not begun to put the nation on the road to a self-sustaining, prosperous economy. The grand design for recovery in one country, managed by an organizational state unlike anything ever seen in American history, was by any clear-eyed analysis a failure. Democratic party leaders anticipated the congressional elections with apprehension, hoping that the normal midterm losses would be relatively modest.

Instead, the New Deal won a smashing endorsement. The Democrats extended their already enormous House delegation from 310 to 319 and their Senate representation from 59 to 69. If this was the price of failure, what then would be the fruits of victory?

Cynics attributed the results to an unprecedented deluge of relief checks, mortgage refinancings, work projects, and commodity price subsidies. In its first full fiscal year (July 1, 1933–June 30, 1934), the Roosevelt administration spent $6.5 billion, while taking in only $3.1 billion. Most of the beneficiaries were genuinely needy victims of an economic disaster beyond their control. Some of the work projects were unproductive, but most left behind a visible "infrastructure" improvement—a surfaced road, a bridge, a school building, a new post office. The bankruptcy of the opposition helped, too. Republican complaints about big government, deficit spending, and the demise of liberty rang hollow in a time of national emergency.

Above all, the results were an affirmation of the Roosevelt leadership. Roosevelt made the New Deal bigger than the sum of its parts. Through his radio addresses, his press conferences, his newsreel appearances, he defined a new kind of presidency that combined patrician authority with approachability, concern, and optimism. The new mass media of radio and movie newsreels—both anxious to show the president at his most appealing—allowed him to speak directly to the people like no chief executive before him. Here was a politician unlike any other who had ever occupied the White House.

Already loved by millions, the man eclipsed his program.

The election also had an ideological undertone. The non-Democrats who won big were independent progressives—including Senator Robert La Follette, Jr., and Governor Phil La Follette in Wisconsin. In California, the old socialist, Upton Sinclair, had captured the Democratic nomination for governor and nearly taken the general election on a promise to transform the state into a cooperative commonwealth. A year earlier, the city of New York had rejected Tammany Hall and elected as mayor Fiorello La Guardia, in practical terms a social democrat. The country loved Roosevelt, but if he failed it likely would look left for alternatives.

National satisfaction with the president, primarily a response to a combination of charisma and material assistance, was high at the end of 1934, but its consolidation required economic progress. After too many zigs and zags, monetary stability had been achieved on a reasonable and predictable basis, but reciprocal trade policies offered no immediate assistance. The agricultural recovery program was moving ahead steadily, but industrial recovery was stumbling badly; both were the targets of determined legal and political offensives.

As Roosevelt began his third year in office, a return to the fat years of the twenties was, if it existed out there at all, far over the horizon. The original New Deal plan for prosperity had been a failure, but FDR was still popular. As president, he controlled the agenda. The next move was up to him.

HEADLINES AND FILMS

{1933}

MARCH 5   Vote Ends One-sided Campaign; Hitler Regime Has Spared No Repression

JUNE 18   Nazis' New Slogan Shows Broad Aims; a Totalitarian State

JULY 9   Vatican and Reich Initial Concordat; Center Party Dissolution Victory for Hitler

{1934}

MARCH 22   Hitler Opens Drive for 2,000,000 Jobs; Warns Pay Must Be Low

JUNE 15   Reich Suspends Payments on All Its Foreign Debts; Berlin Blames Creditors

JULY 1   Hitler Crushes Revolt by Nazi Radicals; von Schleicher Is Slain, Röhm a Suicide

JULY 26   Austrian Nazis Kill Dolfuss, Revolt Fails; 147 Plotters Held

AUGUST 3   Hitler Takes Presidential Power; Army Swears Fealty; Ratifying Election Set

{1935}

MARCH 17   Germany Creates Army of 500,000, Orders Conscription, Scraps Treaty

AUGUST 10   Reich Shows Cuts in Idle to 1,754,000; Conscription for Labor and Army

SEPTEMBER 16   Reich Adopts Swastika as Nation's Official Flag; Anti-Jewish Laws Passed

FALL   *Hitler at Nuremberg, thronged by cheering admirers, is the incarnation of a resurgent Germany, strong, proud, and united.* ("Triumph of the Will" [documentary by Leni Riefenstahl])

{1936}

MARCH 8   Hitler Sends German Troops Into Rhineland; Versailles Curb Broken

MARCH 22   German Home Front Under Severe Economic Strain

AUGUST 17   Olympics in Berlin Close Amid Pomp; Germany Topped Rivals

TRIUMPH

NAZI GERMANY, 1933–1936

Personalities: Executors of the New Order

Perhaps the most common popular misconception about the Third Reich is to identify it with Hitler to the exclusion of other vivid and important figures. Such a view is understandable. Hitler was the leader of "the movement," its most powerful orator, and the man upon whom all attention was centered. In a very real sense, he became the totalitarian counterpart to Roosevelt, who dominated a democratic society from a comparable leadership position and utilized markedly similar skills. Just as Roosevelt quickly became not just the most important representative of an inchoate political agenda called the New Deal but its very embodiment, thus it was with Hitler and the equally opaque National Socialist movement. Both Germany and America accepted a "leader principle," albeit with vast differences in practice. Both Hitler and Roosevelt necessarily relied on top-level executors who translated their grand themes into laws, institutions, and procedures. In Hitler's case, three men were most important in the establishment of Nazi despotism.

The Hero: Hermann Göring

Hermann Göring was among the most loathsome of the Nazi high command—grossly corpulent, a drug addict, vain, greedy, unrestrained in his self-indulgence, obscenely conspicuous in his ostentatious acquisition of wealth and properties, possessed by an insatiable lust for power, indolent to the point of incompetence in his official responsibilities. Hermann Göring was a hero, a World War flying ace, handsome, dashing, well-born and well-connected; clever, articulate, charming, brave, and reliable; a fighter who stood by his friends; an unlikely Nazi who for that very reason was Hitler's greatest asset, loved by the German people more than anyone else among the leaders around the Führer.

Both statements were true.

Born in 1893 to a prominent political family (his father served as imperial governor of German Southwest Africa), Göring, unlike almost all his associates, was *of* the leadership class rather than an aspirant to it. Awarded Germany's highest military decoration for bravery, the Pour le Merite, for his wartime service, he was attracted to the intense nationalism of the Nazi party (and perhaps the opportunity to exercise power and influence in a nascent group) almost from its beginnings. Wounded in Hitler's failed Beer Hall *Putsch* of 1923, he managed to escape to Sweden, where he married into the nobility and spent the next four years polishing his connections with the cream of Northern European society. Returning to Germany in 1927 after a general amnesty, he emerged as one of Hitler's most trusted lieutenants.

After Hitler became chancellor, Göring won control of Prussia, the biggest and most important of the German states, and availed himself of the opportunities for self-aggrandizement. In an impressive display of independence, he fended off Hitler's ambitions to run Prussia directly, but tendered decisive backing in the struggle by which his leader achieved total power. The rewards were enormous—command of the Luftwaffe, authority over the rearmament program, and, by 1937, management of the entire German economy. A Nazi prince with a lust for life that he displayed uninhibitedly in his collection of castles, his accumulation of art, and his expanding girth, he retained the affection of many Germans drawn to his adolescent charm. In fact, however, he was as thoughtless in his cruelty as the worst of the leading Nazis and by a wide margin the most avaricious among them. A ninth-century man a millennium out of his element, he might have been a medieval warrior hero, a William the Conqueror or El Cid. The characteristics that made him so evil would have been considered virtues in a harder and simpler era. He embodied the Nazi effort to revive barbaric values of power and plunder as the guiding ethic of the modern world.

The Propagandist: Joseph Goebbels

Joseph Goebbels thoroughly exemplified the model of the average Nazi. Born to humble working-class origins, he developed a quick mind and a consuming ambition. Exempted from military service in the World War by a misshapen foot, he won grants and scholarships to the University of Heidelberg, where he was awarded a Ph.D. in philology. During the Weimar hyperinflation, he struggled as an unemployed writer before channeling his bitterness into the Nazi party. By 1926, he was in Hitler's inner circle. As the Nazi movement grew in strength, he was important as rabble-rouser, orator, and campaign organizer. In 1933, he became Minister of Popular Enlightenment and Propaganda.

William L. Shirer described Goebbels wickedly but accurately as "a swarthy, dwarfish, most un-Nordic looking German from the Rhineland, with a crippled foot, a nimble mind and a complicated and neurotic personality." A New York Times reporter searching for a way to make Goebbels intelligible to Americans called him "the outstanding 'go-getter' for his party." With Goebbels at least as much as with other Nazi eminences, it is necessary to look beyond the personally repulsive to a hard core of commitment, drive, and ability. A fanatical true believer, he could in tactical matters be a cynical opportunist. His appetite for power put him at odds sooner or later with just about everyone else around Hitler. Yet, however revolting his ideology, however unsearching his mind, he was perhaps the most essential man in the Nazi inner circle. Not even the Führer so thoroughly understood the requirements of modern politics. A master organizer, Goebbels brilliantly crafted the Nazi campaigns of 1930 and 1932—the staged rallies, the inspirational music, the use of the airplane. As the government's chief propagandist, he brought cheap radios to the masses as part of the total mobilization of all the media.[1]

It was characteristic of Goebbels and his party that he made little effort to disguise the purposes and methods of his cabinet ministry. His purpose was not to disseminate information but to tell Germans what to think. "There is to be created an intimate contact between the government and people," he explained in March 1933, "and such contact is indispensable if the work of reconstruction is to be carried out."[2] As the orchestrator of that contact, he took control of German radio, most newspapers and magazines, newsreels, and all the major forms of popular entertainment. There were limitations to the achievement; many Germans complained, however quietly and resignedly, about the turgidity of what they got from the media. Neither as gluttonous nor as greedy as Göring, Goebbels never displayed so insatiable a thirst for loot, but ambitious actresses discovered that as film czar, he maintained an active casting couch. He emerged from the purge of 1934 as second only to Göring among Hitler's acolytes.

The Banker: Dr. Hjalmar Schacht

"Schacht Challenges the Nazi Hotheads" read the title of a story in the *New York Times Magazine* for September 1, 1935.[3] By then, Hjalmar Schacht was the last major quasi-independent official in the Third Reich. Schacht's international prestige was comparable to that of such strong U.S. Federal Reserve chairmen of the late twentieth century as Paul Volcker and Alan Greenspan. Born in 1877 to German-Danish parents who had spent years in the United States, his full name was Hjalmar Horace Greeley Schacht. An ambitious prodigy as a student and young man, holder of a Ph.D. degree, he was at once poet, philosopher, and economist. Director of the Dresdner Bank before the age of forty, he served Germany in the World War as head of the Bank of Issue in occupied Belgium. After the war, he was a leading promoter of capitalism against the rising specter of socialism. In 1923, he was appointed president of the Reichsbank, Germany's central bank, with orders to stem the raging inflation that threatened to destroy the German economy. Already he had sufficient prestige to negotiate an enormous loan from the Bank of England to provide gold backing for a restored currency. His reputation at home and abroad thereafter was immense. He was also increasingly burdened by the weight of Germany's reparations obligation, which he saw as an impediment to a fully healthy economic revival. Persuaded that the revised payment schedules of the Young Plan, negotiated in 1929, were not sustainable, he resigned in 1930.

With an unerring sense of the future, he left the German Democratic party, a classical free-market capitalist grouping that had never been a significant force in Weimar politics, and courted the Nazis. Still a determined opponent of socialism, he abandoned economic liberalism in favor of a managed capitalism and the dream of a resurgent Germany under authoritarian rule. The Nazi party, he decided, was the only force capable of achieving the goal. Like other conservatives, he hoped to moderate it and to some extent channel it in traditional directions. He had no use for anti-Semitism and extracted a pledge from Hitler that Jewish bankers and financiers would remain unmolested. Given an unprecedented appointment as both president of the Reichsbank and minister of economics, he became one of the most powerful men in Germany. Suspending reparations and other foreign debt payments, instituting strict currency controls, and drawing on his international standing, he maintained the value of the mark while facilitating Nazi spending programs for public works and military might.

He soon found that he could not control the monster he had helped create. He found himself pushed into endorsing Nazi attacks on Jews. Like other conservatives, he ultimately discovered that Hitler no longer needed him. By late 1936, persuaded that German finances were being stretched past the breaking point, he urged Hitler with increasing vehemence to pull back on rearmament. He also faced rising resentment from business and financial circles over the command economy he had developed. His internal support eroding, he became a scapegoat for the shortcomings of Nazi prosperity. In 1937, he would be relieved as minister of economics to make way for a full-scale militarization of the economy under the leadership of Hermann Göring. At the beginning of 1939, he was dropped as president of the Reichsbank. By then, he no doubt had acquired some sense of the disaster toward which he had helped propel his country.

Totalitarianism and National Revival

The Depression made the Nazi regime possible, but alleviating it was not the first priority of the Nazi leadership. Their most urgent objective was the seizure of total power through the complete eradication of all opposition political parties. Next came the liquidation of adversaries within the Nazi party itself. Ending the Depression would be a side effect of the larger goal of establishing a resurgent Germany defined on a concept of racial unity that would push aside modern ideals of capitalism, socialism, class identity, or mass affluence. The restoration of production was more important than the restoration of prosperity. State controls would appropriate much of the wealth created by the capitalist classes, but would not destroy them. State organizations would replace independent trade unions, ruthlessly suppress any dissent, throw token benefits at workers, and dangle visions of future prosperity before them. Farmers would initially receive heavy subsidies from a regime determined to achieve as much agricultural self-sufficiency as possible, but then suffer government efforts to hold down the prices of key farm products. Germans would be fully employed but saddled with low standards of living.

Emphasizing guns instead of butter, the Nazi economic recovery imposed costs in personal freedom and relative economic deprivation that would have been unacceptable in Britain or the United States. Incessant state propaganda, the merging of the Nazi party with virtually all forms of social expression, and the widespread sense that a beaten-down people were on the road back all buoyed the regime. Merciless repression disposed of "grumblers" who attempted to throw sand in the gears of economic recovery and social revolution. Medieval values, corporatist social-economic principles, and absolute dictatorship in combination with a decade and a half of nationalist resentment made a potent formula. By mid-1936, Nazi Germany was showing the world a triumphant, unified face and apparently demonstrating that totalitarianism worked.

<hr />

The premise behind Franz von Papen's maneuverings to make Hitler chancellor was that the traditional German right could employ him and the Nazi party for his own reactionary ends, and ultimately discard both. Hitler wagered he could reverse those roles. His cabinet included Papen as deputy chancellor, German National People's party head Alfred Hugenberg as minister of economics, and General Werner von Blomberg as minister of defense. Eminent non-Nazis all, they supposedly would contain the new chancellor and control the two Nazi members, Hermann Göring, commissar for air and interior minister of Prussia, and Wilhelm Frick, minister of the interior. Papen, his allies, and a multitude of observers inside and outside of Germany saw President Hindenburg as the ultimate bulwark against Nazi power.[4]

Conceiving of politics as a chessboard of personalities, these expectations failed to take into account that the dynamic force in Germany was not the reactionary right but Nazism, a revolutionary movement that promised a new order to all Germans rather than the restoration of a widely unlamented imperial regime. Personalities were important, but the Nazis, not Papen and the conservatives, possessed greater will to power, shrewdness, and mendacity. In the end, Hitler would prove far more formidable than the feeble Hindenburg.

Hitler's dictatorial ambitions had always been open. He accepted the role of blunt instrument in an offensive against "the Marxists," both Communists and Social Democrats, because it was the essential first step in his own drive for absolute power. He had no intention of attempting to assemble a majority in the Reichstag. His plan was to hold a new election rigged to yield a right-wing majority that would pass an enabling act, allowing him to rule by decree. He proposed to use constitutional means to suppress constitutional government. The next election, Economics Minister Hugenberg declared, would be the last one. The widely understood subtext was his belief that he would displace Hitler and become the dictator he long had said Germany needed. Remarkably, this aspiration seemed credible to many observers who still saw Hitler as an upstart and Hugenberg, a press and motion picture baron with enormous banking interests, as the leader of a powerful conservative establishment.[5]

The Nazis were unstoppable. They suppressed the left and liberal forces while maintaining the facade of an alliance with Hugenberg and the National People's party. The government imposed strict restrictions upon the Communist, Socialist, and Catholic press, denied the radio to any political grouping other than the Nazi party, and authorized a wave of arrests. As interior minister of Prussia, Göring purged anti-Nazis from police command posts and ordered suppression of the Communist party in a public directive that encouraged the use of deadly force. All over Germany, SA storm troopers acted as vigilantes against the left and the center, raiding homes and offices, destroying property, beating and killing "subversives."

On the night of February 27, an unstable young Dutch Communist named Marinus van der Lubbe, probably acting on his own, set fire to the Reichstag building. Hitler used the occasion to issue a virtual declaration of war against the Communists. An "emergency decree" initiated by him and signed by Hindenburg sweepingly abolished every conceivable civil right or liberty. (It would remain in effect for the next twelve years.) By election day, almost every Communist Reichstag deputy was in custody, the party's offices and property in the hands of the government. The emergency also became an excuse to silence the Social Democratic press entirely and to intimidate the Center party with only marginally less ferocity. Hitler and Hugenberg both declared that the government would stay in power whether their coalition received a majority or not.[6]

Enjoying a near monopoly of the mass media, the Nazis succeeded in awakening widespread support for their draconian repression. Many Germans believed that the government had narrowly averted a carefully planned Communist revolution. Among the middle classes, there was little sympathy for the Social Democrats. A people with a long history of authoritarianism and social discipline accepted Nazi rule with minimal protest. With a sure grasp of modern political campaigning, the Nazis exploited the press and radio expertly. Goebbels declared the day before the election,

March 4, "The Day of National Awakening" to be marked by rallies, marches, torchlight parades, and "freedom" bonfires throughout Germany.[7]

The election, held the day after Franklin Roosevelt was inaugurated president of the United States, opened a new era in German history. According to official results, nearly eighty-nine percent of the electorate, the highest in the history of the Weimar Republic, went to the polls. Despite its commanding position, the Nazi party still fell short of an absolute majority, winning 43.9 percent of the vote. Hugenberg's National People's party, with eight percent, emerged as the minor party in the right-wing coalition. The only two parties able to campaign freely thus had won a bare majority. The non-authoritarian center had eroded perceptibly under the battering it had taken from the Depression and the first month of Hitler's chancellorship. When one allows for the Leninism of the Communists, little more than a third of the voters could be counted as advocates of democracy. As journalist Hugh Jedell accurately declared, "no government in Germany—pre-war or post-war—ever received as clear a majority mandate from the electorate."[8]

Hitler's deluded conservative allies continued to believe that they were full partners in the destruction of the Weimar Republic and the reemergence of a powerful, rearmed German state. They fantasized that the new Germany would be much like the old, controlled by the army, large landowners, and industrialists, probably with an emperor—most likely the son of Kaiser Wilhelm—as chief of state. Hitler strung them along, proclaiming only a determination to destroy Marxism, restore order, achieve justice for the workers, and bring unity to the German people. Hindenburg reinstated the old imperial flag as Germany's official banner, but with the Nazi swastika placed at its center.[9]

The SA persisted in a terror campaign against Jews and political opponents, brutalizing and arresting tens of thousands. Heinrich Himmler, the Nazi police commissioner in Munich, opened a "concentration camp" for political prisoners near the town of Dachau; several others were established around the country. The regime made no attempt to conceal their purpose, which was not simply to detain opponents (mostly Communists, it claimed), but punish them with beatings and hard labor. By the time the new Reichstag convened in Berlin on March 21, the Nazis had either won elections or simply seized power in all the German *Länder* (states). Still, Hitler was far from an absolute dictator. The army remained independent, loyal to Hindenburg, and increasingly restless over the lawlessness of the SA. The Nazi party itself, like most mass parties, was divided over numerous issues; it contained factional leaders with ambitions that were not necessarily congruent with Hitler's. The chancellor thus found it necessary both to conciliate the conservative establishment and consolidate a power base within his own party.[10]

It proved easiest to string the conservatives along. When the new Reichstag assembled in Berlin on March 21, its first state occasion was a religious service of great emotional significance to the old-line nationalists at the Garrison Church in Potsdam. Goebbels, with typical bombast, had proclaimed "The Day of the National Uprising." To the old establishment it was a day of commemoration and renewal. Frederick the Great was entombed there; no shrine was more sacred to Prussian nationalism. Sixty-two years ago to the day, Otto von Bismarck had opened the first Reichstag of a unified Imperial Germany. The empty throne of the kaiser was at the front of the church; President Hindenburg ostentatiously saluted it. Hitler, in formal morning dress, played a secondary role. Following Hindenburg deferentially, he paid respectful tribute to German nationalist heroes and traditions, affirming the ties between army, church, and nation that lay at the core of reactionary thought. No single event so lulled the right.[11]

The Reichstag session that met in Berlin's Kroll Opera House on March 23 had a far different caste. It was a blatant affirmation of Nazi power and supremacy. Armed, uniformed men, mostly from the SA, some from the SS (Hitler's personal bodyguard) and the Stahlhelm, surrounded the building, ready to put down any demonstration and arrest any Communist deputy not already imprisoned and foolish enough to show up. A huge swastika flag at the front of the chamber affirmed Nazi control. So did the large contingent of SA troops who provided "security" inside the building. A grim-visaged Hitler appeared in Nazi military uniform to demand passage of an Enabling Act, in which the Reichstag would effectively cede all its powers to him. Speaking to the outside world, he promised not to enlarge the German military—if other nations would cut their armaments. He pledged jobs, "moral renewal," and a stable currency. To those uneasy over the Nazi domination of the Länder, he said they would remain semi-sovereign components of the Reich. He declared that the rights of the Protestant and Catholic churches would in no way be curtailed.[12]

The debate that followed was brief and uneasy, marked primarily by the capitulation of the Center party, which had been reassured by the pledge to protect the Catholic Church. The Enabling Act passed 441–94, with only the Social Democrats voting against it. The Reichstag no longer existed as a legislative or policy-making body. In the future, it would serve simply as an audience for Hitler's pronouncements.

With stunning efficiency, the government moved against the tattered remnants of the political party system. The Communist party was already effectively destroyed. The Socialists soon followed. The Social Democratic militia, the Reichsbanner, formally dissolved under government pressure. In May, the government confiscated socialist trade union property and assets. Widespread arrests of union and party officials followed. Those who had evaded capture attempted to reconstitute the party in Czechoslovakia; the Nazis thereupon declared it a foreign organization and outlawed it. Just days later, the German National People's party was forced to dissolve. Alfred Hugenberg, the man who was supposed to eclipse Hitler, resigned from the cabinet and quickly achieved the status of a nonperson. The party's paramilitary organization, the Stahlhelm, also went out of existence, many of its members migrating to the Nazi SA.

This left, by the end of June 1933, only the Center. Hitler made no secret of his determination to be rid of it. State police arrested some 2,000 officials of the affiliated Bavarian People's party. Hitler also shrewdly deployed a diplomatic card, sending Franz von Papen to negotiate with the Vatican. Rome and the German Catholic bishops, apparently believing that political Catholicism could not be saved, decided to jettison the party in return for guarantees that church institutions and freedom to worship would not be infringed. On July 5, the Center party formally dissolved. Three days later, Papen and Roman Catholicism's chief diplomat, Monsignor Eugenio Pacelli, initialed a concordat; the church formally renounced political action in return for guarantees that its other functions would not be molested. It was the first formal agreement between Hitler's regime and a sovereign power.

Much criticized from the start, the concordat sacrificed little; the Center party would have been eradicated anyway. The Vatican, lacking the armored divisions that were the Nazi equivalent of appeals to reason, could only hope to save as much autonomy as possible from a rapidly developing total dictatorship. Msgr. Pacelli (later Pope Pius XII), neither a villain nor a saint, attempted a pragmatic deal in impossible circumstances. Still, exposing an inevitable gap between spiritual profession and secular interests, the concordat damaged the moral stature of the church. As usual, the Nazi government would not keep its part of the bargain. Truly devout and committed Catholics, including a significant portion of the clergy, would find it impossible to refrain from protest against the increasing horrors of life in Germany. Far from securing the church's position, the concordat was simply a prelude to years of persecution and conflict.[13]

By the standards of amoral politics, Hitler's achievement in his first six months as chancellor was astonishing. Millions of Germans idolized him. He had neutered the legislature that was supposed to be the source of his authority, annihilated the opposition political parties, and even put the swastika on the German flag. Independent trade unions had been swept away and rival paramilitary organizations disbanded. He alone seemed to command the most economically developed nation in Europe. Yet crucial obstacles still remained. Hindenburg might turn against him at any time. The army, a tenth the size of the Nazi SA but far more disciplined, was capable of mounting a coup at the old field marshal's nod. The chancellor had rivals and critics within the Nazi party itself. The dictatorship was not yet fully consolidated. Hitler would temporize for a year as Nazism went about the work of building a new state, constructing a new man, and, almost incidentally, pursuing economic recovery.

Through the rest of 1933 and the first half of 1934, the Nazi dictatorship increased its grip on Germany, instituting a reign of terror against opponents of all persuasions, bullying Jews with maniacal ferocity, proclaiming goals of racial strength and purity, pursuing an aggressive unilateralist foreign policy, boasting of a gathering economic recovery. Whatever the unrest below the surface, there seems little doubt that the government gained increased acceptance. Hitler scheduled a final Reichstag election and a plebiscite on whether German voters approved of his rule, both for November 12, 1933, one day after the fifteenth anniversary of the armistice that had ended the World War in defeat for Germany. Every other party having been outlawed, only Nazis were allowed on the ballot.

Far more important to Hitler was the plebiscite, worded as follows: "Do you, German man, and you, German woman, approve this policy of your Reich government, and are you ready to declare it to be the expression of your own view and your own will, and solemnly to give it your allegiance?" An overwhelming "yes" vote would give him a direct mandate from the people, a powerful legitimacy that could be flaunted throughout the world. It equally would be self-reinforcing inside Germany, paving the way for new plebiscites that would reaffirm his claim to represent an overwhelming popular will. The party mobilized the vote relentlessly. Posters exhorted the electorate to "stand with Hitler." Speaking to a campaign rally, the chancellor predicted the outcome: fifteen years after "the German people lost its honor . . . came a twelfth of November and then the German people restored honor to itself." Hindenburg called for one hundred percent support for the government.

On election day, there was a fair amount of ballot fraud, accompanied by open threats of retribution against those who voted in the negative. Nazi Reichstag candidates won 92.1 percent of the vote and secured all 661 seats. Hitler won a 95.1 percent endorsement in the plebiscite. Given the circumstances, some observers attached great significance to what dissent there was. Nonetheless, it was probably correct to conclude that Hitler had the willing support of a solid majority of an electorate galvanized by his defiance of the World War victors.[14]

In the wake of the election, he seemed more than ever a towering figure. Vice Chancellor Papen praised "the genius of your leadership" in an adulatory statement that revealed his own utter powerlessness.[15] Yet the underlying threats remained. Hindenburg, the army, and the conservatives had been mollified by his aggressive assertions of German sovereignty and freedom of action, but they also were concerned by the thuggish radicalism in much of the Nazi movement. An even greater problem was a fundamental quarrel within the Nazi party. Many Nazis thought "National Socialism" meant a full-fledged social revolution; others saw the term as a proxy for a form of fascist corporatism. One side wanted to destroy the conservative elites that dominated Germany, the Junkers, the big capitalists, the top-level bureaucrats. The other wanted to control the state and use its power without restraint but was not interested in fundamentally changing the distribution of wealth and property. In addition, many senior Nazis were less than unconditionally loyal to their leader. Göring, in April 1933, had deftly outmaneuvered Hitler to become premier of Prussia. (It was testament to Hitler's own shrewdness that he made no effort to unseat Göring.) Goebbels had walked a fine line between the two party factions.

Hitler's major problem was Ernst Röhm. Commander of the SA, Röhm had almost as much standing in the party as Hitler. He controlled most of the armed power the party could deploy, perhaps two million men. He was a founding father of Nazism, an effective orator, and the party's closest approximation of an open factional leader; he vocally advocated a "second revolution." Whether this would be anything more than an SA slaughter of the upper crust in a yearned-for "Night of the Long Knives" and an orgy of looting was unclear, but understandably threatening. If most of the Nazi party was obsessed by a "Hitler cult," the SA in its own publications and posters had created a "Röhm cult." Röhm pushed for the SA to become the state's main armed force, subsuming the army itself and with himself as supreme commander. Throughout the first half of 1934, he and uneasy army generals negotiated tensely on the SA's role in the new Germany. By midyear, his aspirations had become the focal point of a growing crisis, accentuated by the aged Hindenburg's increasingly precarious health.

On June 17, Vice Chancellor Papen, making his final effort to assert the power of the conservatives, delivered a sharp speech, rejecting the idea of a second revolution; it obliquely criticized Röhm and the SA. It appeared at first that the Nazi reaction would be to purge Papen. Goebbels banned publication of the address, but not before it had come out. Army commander General Werner von Blomberg underscored Papen's message. Hindenburg, critically ill at his country estate, told Hitler "to bring the revolutionary trouble-makers finally to reason."

It took no exceptional powers of analysis for Hitler to conclude that the SA was a greater long-run threat to his power than the army. If he did not act the army might do so without him, and bring him down in the resulting chaos. He soon assured himself that he could count on the support of other Nazi chiefs who saw Röhm as a threat. They included Göring, who controlled the Prussian police and could secure Berlin; Goebbels, who decided that his best interests were with Hitler; and Heinrich Himmler, the commander of the SS. By late June, there were rumors all over Germany that the Nazi party was about to suppress the SA. Here and there, storm troopers staged protest marches, but Röhm and the top SA leadership ignored the warnings.

On June 30, Hitler unleashed his own Night of the Long Knives.

In forty-eight hours, at least a hundred people were dead. Among them were Röhm (who had been personally arrested by Hitler, pistol in hand) and numerous SA leaders, also the Nazi apostate Gregor Strasser and some leftovers of the Weimar era such as General Kurt von Schleicher, assassinated along with his wife. Papen's office was raided, one of his aides killed, the rest sent to concentration camps; he himself endured several days of house arrest before being rehabilitated. Heinrich Brüning escaped death only because he was out of the country.

After two weeks of silence, Hitler appeared before the Reichstag on July 13. Surrounded by armed SS men, he spoke for two hours, asserting that he had acted in a moment of extreme emergency to avert a foreign-supported coup d'etat. The heart of the speech, delivered in an angry, emotional voice, was harsh, direct, and supremely effective:

> In this hour, I was responsible for the fate of the German nation and thereby the supreme judge of the German people . . . I gave the order to shoot those most guilty of this treason, and I further gave the order to burn out down to the raw flesh the ulcers of our internal well-poisoning and the poisoning from abroad.

The speech won acclaim throughout Germany. The arrogance and erratic violence of the SA had offended many ordinary people, the charges of a plot seemed credible, the assertion of foreign involvement elevated a power struggle into a defense of the state, and the purge of the SA promised more order in the lives of a people who valued order greatly.[16]

It remained only for Hindenburg to die.

The old man complied on August 2. He may have left with his son, Oskar, a political testament calling for restoration of the monarchy; if so, it never saw the light of day. On August 1, Hitler and the cabinet had put into effect a new law, providing that the offices of president and chancellor would be combined upon Hindenburg's death. The following day, upon announcing the old field marshal's passing, Hitler also informed the world that heretofore he would be known by the title Reichsführer. Astoundingly—and apparently at the initiative of the army—every soldier in the Reichswehr swore a new oath of loyalty, not to the new office, but to the person of Adolf Hitler. The army leadership apparently believed it would bind Hitler closer to them and pull him away from the Nazi party. Instead, it consolidated a mounting impression that he was bigger than both combined. In eighteen months, Adolf Hitler had moved from perceived puppet-chancellor to the supreme and unquestioned leader of a rapidly emerging totalitarian state.

It was soon apparent that Hitler's Germany was something more than a traditional authoritarian dictatorship. It aggressively rejected or repressed all the institutions dear to the European right. Marxists attempted to explain it in terms of a movement generated to protect the position of monopoly capitalism, but in fact most large capitalists chafed under the state controls it imposed on them. It was not a "workers' movement" in any generally understood sense; yet it seemed to have wide popular support that encompassed significant numbers from all social classes, including the workers. Calling itself the Third Reich—the successor to the empires of Frederick Barbarossa and the Hohenzollerns—it presented to the world a peculiar mixture of the medieval and the modern, combining an affirmation of technological progress with a mythology of Aryan racial purity and a mystical cult of leadership.

It was perhaps most easily understood as a species of "fascism," the movement that for a decade had ruled Italy under Mussolini. Italian fascism appealed to nationalistic sentiments, organized the economy, and proclaimed itself a "totalitarian state" that would control all aspects of the lives of its subjects. Fascism was allegedly the ultimate alternative to revolutionary Marxian socialism, but both systems were attracted to totalitarian organizational principles.[17] Nazi ideologues from the beginning openly professed the goal of totalitarianism and expected to impose it far more systematically than Mussolini had succeeded in doing. "The revolutionary forces must be directed into all channels of public life," Joseph Goebbels declared in June 1933. "This Germany is to have only one goal, one party, and one conviction; and the State organization is to be identical with the nation itself."[18] Nazism implacably sought to destroy independent institutions of civic life and repress so far as possible personal spiritual existence.

Control of the young was a prime objective and a major revolutionary tactic. Elementary and secondary education quickly became organs of Nazi propaganda, imposing the party orthodoxy on every politically sensitive subject of learning. The Hitler Youth replaced the Boy and Girl Scouts. Hitler himself warned parents who tried to keep their children at a distance from Nazi indoctrination that if necessary the state would take them from their homes and "rear them as needful for the Fatherland." A year of national service, compulsory by 1936, put eighteen-year-old males to work at manual labor and assigned young women from towns and cities to farm work. The goal was to produce healthy, robust young adults—men ready for military service, women ready for childbearing and trained for domestic service. "No one who traveled up and down Germany in those days and talked with the young in their camps and watched them work and play and sing could fail to see that, however sinister the teaching, here was an incredibly dynamic youth movement," William L. Shirer recalled years later. His mind then flashed quickly to Belgium in May 1940 and strapping, triumphant German soldiers guarding British prisoners "with their hollow chests, round shoulders, pasty complexions and bad teeth—tragic examples of the youth that England had neglected so irresponsibly in the years between the wars."[19]

The Nazis took over every university in Germany. In virtually every case they did so with the enthusiastic support of alienated students. On May 10, 1933, the party supervised book-burnings on numerous major campuses, consigning to huge bonfires the works of many leading figures in the arts and sciences. Major independent intellectuals—the philosopher and theologian Karl Barth was perhaps the most famous non-Jewish example—lost their professorial appointments if they did not toe the line. Perhaps a thousand others were also fired. Most professors, however, were pliable; perhaps the most infamous was the existential philosopher Martin Heidegger. The resultant Nazification of higher learning insisted that even in the hard sciences knowledge was validated not by empirical scientific method but by the ethnicity of its producers. It requires little imagination to visualize the impoverishment of the humanities and social sciences that ensued. Somehow, the quality of German science and engineering remained generally high, but the story of the universities under the Nazis was one of decline—in enrollments, in the advancement of knowledge, in the respect of other advanced nations.[20]

The Christian churches fared only marginally better against the Nazi drive for control. Most Protestant sects enjoyed tax support from the individual *Länder* and thus were natural targets for governmental control. Thoroughly cowed by pressure from *Land* governments and from Berlin, Protestant bishops from all over Germany agreed to a merger in July 1933, forming the German Evangelical Church, or, as the Nazis preferred to call it, the "Reich Church." The Nazis then forced the election of Rev. Ludwig Müller as its administrative head, or bishop. Müller commanded the support of only an estimated 3,000 of some 17,000 pastors. Nevertheless, he gave free rein to his most radical supporters, who advanced proposals to drop the Old Testament, rewrite the New Testament to depict the teachings of Christ as identical to those of National Socialism, and ultimately incorporate German pagan mythology into church dogma.[21]

The Nazis were successful in controlling the officialdom and plundering church property. It was much more difficult to suppress wholly the dissent of strong-minded pastors and theologians convinced both that they were the genuine German patriots and that they spoke the word of God. Their leader, Rev. Martin Niemöller, headed a few thousand clergymen who organized themselves as the "Confessing Church" and claimed to be the legitimate voice of German Protestantism. The movement, semi-tolerated as a minor nuisance, endured police harassment and suppression of demonstrations for three years. Nonetheless, it managed some significant statements of criticism. A manifesto in May 1936 daringly attacked Nazi ideology and denounced state anti-Semitism. By then, the government had sacked Müller for ineffective ham-fistedness. It also arrested hundreds of dissidents, including Niemöller, who was remanded to a concentration camp in 1938 and not released until the end of World War II.[22]

The Catholic Church, concordat with the Reich notwithstanding, fared little better. Both inside and outside of Germany, Catholic behavior was as mixed as that of Protestants, but to the Nazis, any autonomous Catholic organization was an affront. The Nazi regime undertook an offensive against the Catholic War Veterans, which it dissolved; the Catholic Youth League; and Catholic Action, whose leader was assassinated in the bloody purge of June 30, 1934. A government edict of July 1935 sharply condemned the "political activity" of Catholic priests. Dissenting priests, nuns, monks, and laymen were imprisoned, numerous publications suppressed. On September 1, 1935, the German Catholic bishops issued a pastoral letter rejecting official "paganism" and urging "obedience of God" that was read to congregations throughout the Reich. The Nazi response was to step up the repression. The secretary-general of Catholic Youth and thirty associates were imprisoned on ludicrous charges of consorting with Communists. Hundreds of Franciscan monks were hauled into court on vague charges of immorality.

The Vatican, for all its accommodationist impulses, ultimately found it impossible to avoid denunciation of Nazi atrocities. In 1937, Pope Pius XI promulgated a bitter encyclical issued in German, *Mit Brennender Sorge*, attacking almost every aspect of Nazism. The document had little impact. Mostly a long and thorough list of grievances in a church-state argument, it failed to achieve the moral force that would have come from a clear and unequivocal denunciation of the Nazi persecution of other faiths. By then most Catholics, like most Protestants, and most Germans could do little more than keep their heads down and try to stay out of trouble.[23]

This system also played itself out in the smallest localities. The historian Ian Kershaw concisely summarizes a process that proceeded with the momentum of a supercharged bulldozer: "Business and professional associations, sports clubs, choral societies, shooting clubs, patriotic associations, and most other forms of organized activity were taken under—or more frequently hastened to place themselves under—National Socialist control in the first months of the Third Reich." Independent social life, one German recalled in later years, had become impossible; even a non-Nazi bowling club was unthinkable.[24]

Newspapers, magazines, radio broadcasts, and motion picture news-reels quickly came under state control, orchestrated by Goebbels. Many liberal and independent publications, especially those with Jewish owner-ship, were simply shut down. Those that remained became organs of Nazi propaganda. The government launched a drive to make cheap radio receivers available to virtually every German, but designed them with such limited range that they could receive foreign broadcasts only in bor-der areas. Major film production enterprises, dependent upon state licenses for their product, fell into line with little complaining and no recourse. The cumulative result was a boring sameness of information that led to declining audiences for all these media, but nonetheless shaped the thoughts of even the skeptical.[25]

The control of news was routine for any dictatorship. The Nazis equally intended to mold all of German art and culture (from the refined to the lowbrow) according to their own canons of politics and taste. In November 1933, the government announced the establishment of a Reich Chamber of Culture, headed by Goebbels, to which all approved journalists, authors, performers, and artists had to belong. Those not admitted would be unable to practice their craft. The result was to make Goebbels the supreme cul-tural arbiter for the Third Reich, charged with "directing German culture in an attitude of responsibility for the nation."[26]

Music was relatively unaffected, so long as its style was relatively tradi-tional—unless the composer was a Jew. In that spirit, the works of Mendelssohn were banished from concert halls and the radio, but most great composers were safely Aryan. So were most of the star concert per-formers, who continued their careers with little interest in politics. In the realm of popular culture, the music of mobilization—of marching, of patriotic affirmation, of united effort—was especially prominent. The Nazi cinema was heavy on themes of traditional sentimentalism, at times ugly in its attacks on Jews; the same was true of radio drama.

Perhaps nowhere was the Nazification of art so pedestrian as in paint-ing and sculpture. In these areas, Hitler considered himself an authority not to be crossed. Art, he told the party's annual rally at Nuremberg in September 1933, had to be put and kept "on a Nordic basis." "Nordic art" consisted mostly of second-rate imitations of classical and neoclassical representational painting or statuary. It depicted strong, muscular males, perfectly formed women, or immaculate landscapes. Its visions of contemporary life amounted to little more than glorified images—of the Führer, party notables, soldiers, workers, and mothers. Its themes were strength, order, and discipline. Dictated by politics and bound to earlier styles, it was mediocre.

The Nazi aesthetic was a reaction against the unsettling messages of various strains of "modern art," which rejected idealized representation for abstract expressionism or unflattering realism. The themes of modern art were disintegration and decay, the incoherence of life, existential angst, uncertainty. If at times it displayed excess and confusion, it was provocative and argumentative and undeniably the product of an era in which change and chaos had overwhelmed traditional verities. It spoke to all that Nazism denied.

In July 1937, the two styles found themselves both on display in Munich. Hitler himself dedicated a new "House of German Art," which displayed 900 examples of his personal taste in a new and quickly forgettable neoclassical building he had helped design. The Führer's speech showed that he understood the subversive challenge of the modernists. "Let no one have illusions! National Socialism has set out to purge the German Reich and our people of all those influences threatening its existence and character." Across town, acting with the unwitting stupidity that from time to time surfaces when the powerful talk only to themselves, Goebbels had organized an exhibition of "degenerate art," featuring seized examples of works by, among others, Max Beckmann, Marc Chagall, Lyonel Feininger, George Grosz, Wassily Kandinsky, and Paul Klee. Shabbily housed and hard to reach, it drew three to five times as many visitors.[27]

The regime could not control all the thoughts and actions of its subjects. Arthur Schlesinger, Jr., recalls traveling through Germany as a sixteen-year-old with his parents and brother in mid-July 1934. On a train, they met an attractive German girl returning from three months abroad, telling them Hitler jokes and denouncing the regime in perfect English. Uncensored foreign newspapers and books seemed readily available. A Nuremberg cinema audience viewed a fighting speech by Nazi leader Rudolf Hess with palpable apathy. "I found Germany very pleasant," the boy wrote in his journal. "There were absolutely no traces of tension, fear, mass-hysteria or anything similar."

A more sophisticated foreigner, H. J. Haskell, the editor of the *Kansas City Star*, was in Germany a year later. "There are two Germanies," he observed. "The first is the surface Germany seen by the tourist, placid and lovely; the second the real Germany, restless and seething with the leaven of the Nazi movement." He also discovered that foreign newspapers were banned on a selective, daily basis. Many travelers no doubt met their equivalent of the girl on the train. She demonstrated only that, as a joke of the time went, the Germans had freedom of conversation (most prudently exercised in a foreign language with safe non-Germans), not freedom of speech.

As the dictatorship matured into a full-fledged approximation of totalitarian despotism, the slightest signs of dissent might result in a police investigation or the loss of employment. To vote "no" or to fail to show up at the polls to vote in a regime plebiscite could cost one his job. Hitler jokes became increasingly risky. However passive, ineffectual, or isolated these signs of resistance might be, they demonstrated that the rulers of the Third Reich could not control every thought or manipulate every emotion. Nevertheless, the regime was a constant presence in the lives of most Germans, defining the world for them far more pervasively than any other source. American and British travelers to Germany generally accepted that most European nations east of the Rhine and south of Scandinavia were destined to be dictatorships. They might be repelled by Nazi excesses but also respected an orderly, if overly organized, society moving into the future with Teutonic efficiency.[28]

The Nazis added a new dimension to the nationalistic component of fascism by asserting that race, not simply residence and emotional allegiance to the state, constituted the basis of national identity. The sense of a "Völkisch" racial identity was a long-running theme of German history, accentuated by the experience of political fragmentation before 1871. In Germany, as throughout continental Europe, anti-Semitism had a long history, largely based in the Christian tradition. Yet as a trading nation and economic power, Germany had large elements of liberal tolerance and cosmopolitanism in its culture. Historically, it had been a refuge for Jews from the east and much preferred to France or the Mediterranean countries. A large segment of its three million strong Jewish population was tightly integrated into the larger society, thought of itself as primarily German, and was widely accepted as such.

It was therefore especially shocking to most of the outside world that almost overnight Germany transformed itself into the world's most aggressive bastion of institutionalized anti-Semitism. The Nazis banned Jews from business, professions, and schools; boycotted Jewish shops; terminated Jews (defined as anyone with at least one Jewish grandparent) from the civil service and other forms of public employment; assessed collective fines against the Jewish community for this or that imagined transgression; and committed countless examples of random brutality and humiliation. Nearly universal condemnation from the other major nations of the world had no apparent effect. By mid-1935, small-scale episodic violence against Jews was epidemic throughout Germany, most of it spontaneously occurring at the local level.

In September 1935, from the party rally at Nuremberg, Hitler announced a new set of "blood laws" that deprived Jews of their status as German citizens, forbade marriage (or extramarital sexual relations) between Jews and Germans, barred Jews from employing German women under the age of forty-five as servants, and established the authority for numerous future decrees that would implement or expand the state's handling of the "Jewish problem." It is an astounding measure of the unleashed furies that the Nazi leadership saw the Nuremberg laws as a way of cooling down attacks against Jews and putting the issue on the back burner until after the Berlin Olympics.[29]

What was to be gained by persecuting a segment of the population that was disproportionately accomplished and strategically valuable? By confiscating Albert Einstein's bank account and sending him scurrying to exile in the United States? The simplest and most accurate answer is that Hitler, Goebbels, and the rest of the Nazi elite really believed what they said about the Jews. But there also was a more subtle and fundamental explanation. The ideal of a racial state, united in its Germanic pureness and implacable in a war against Jewish interlopers, was a substitute for the class-based democratic politics that had brought chaos to the Weimar Republic.[30] By making race the basis for national identity, the Nazis tapped into a consciousness common in most European nations of the 1930s. By focusing on the Jews as the antithesis of the national ideal, they drew on a ready-made body of myth and prejudice that often had erupted in sporadic violence in pre–twentieth century Europe. What stunned many Jews then and remains surprising today is that they found a large and willing audience. At least a significant minority of Germans participated in anti-Jewish activities. The rest were passive, some ambivalent, others disapproving, a few quietly supportive of Jewish acquaintances, none able to challenge a murderous regime.

The Nazis did not confine their depredations to the differently garbed, the bearded, or those with obvious "Semitic features." Anyone with one-quarter Jewish ancestry, whether professing Judaism or not, whether a decorated war veteran or a cliché money-lender, was fair game for the foulest expressions of bigotry—beatings, destruction of property, denial of medical treatment, expulsion from many towns and villages, exclusion from the normal protections of the law. Some Jews left Germany early, but as the numbers of those willing to give up everything to get out increased, the opportunities for foreign sanctuary dried up. Nations with major problems of their own, including the United States and Britain, did not want a tide of penniless immigrants. By the end of 1936, desperation and hopelessness were the prevalent moods of those who were left. Only a lucky few would make it to safety.[31]

Despite many later protests to the contrary, no German, and no outside observer who read a newspaper, could have any doubt that it was the policy of the German government to practice an institutionalized anti-Semitism of a type that had not been seen in Europe since the medieval era. Those who supported Hitler and the Nazis for other reasons nevertheless knew what they were buying into.

The purification of the race did not stop with attacks on Jews. Within six months of assuming office, the Nazi government put through legislation authorizing the involuntary sterilization of people afflicted with "hereditary" mental and physical defects and establishing special courts to administer the law. As the decade progressed, administration of the law became increasingly loose, extending to anyone who might appear to be a walking social problem. The policy rested on the dubious but widely discussed eugenics movement of the early twentieth century. Earlier eugenicists had attracted support in many areas of German society and politics, including the Social Democratic party. For the most part, they had been well-intentioned and humane. Where they saw unfortunate necessity, the Nazis saw an opportunity. By the end of the 1930s, the Nazis had sterilized at least 400,000 people. Assuming that those not fit to reproduce were less than human, they also reduced the level of care in asylums to premodern standards. By 1939, state-sanctioned euthanasia was beginning to make its appearance.[32]

Whether the Nazis fully achieved the ideal of totalitarianism may be an interesting question for debate by scholars. The realities felt by virtually all Germans speak for themselves. Building on long-accepted traditions of political authoritarianism and strong state bureaucracies, Hitler and his associates established a structure that touched the lives of virtually every citizen and terrorized not simply Jews but any dissident or nonconformist. Most voluntary associations were either destroyed or converted to organs of the Nazi party. The party itself had become synonymous with the state, a development symbolized by the adoption of its swastika flag as Germany's official banner in September 1935. The Nazi state controlled almost all the information and entertainment available to average people. It all was a close-enough approximation of total control, and a large majority of the people seemed to accept it. In the summer of 1935, a year after the Night of the Long Knives, H. J. Haskell discerned that the typical German was grateful to Hitler for restoring the nation's power and self-respect, absorbed with his job, and living placidly. "Freedom, as Americans know it, has disappeared from Germany," he wrote wistfully. "It would be a mistake, I am convinced, to suppose that most of the German people miss it."[33]

At the center of all this was Hitler himself, once a street agitator, now the Führer. For all their differences, the United States and Germany shared one characteristic—a national thirst for dynamic leadership. In the crisis world of the Great Depression, Hitler was suddenly the most charismatic of national leaders, rivaled only by Roosevelt and surpassing him in the intensity of emotions he aroused. Goebbels made it mandatory etiquette for Germans to greet and take leave of each other with a "Heil Hitler!" and a straight-arm salute. Nazi propagandists told the world, "Germany is Hitler, and Hitler is Germany." By the last half of the 1930s, a majority of Germans and foreign observers found the assertion self-evident.

In his amoral cunning, Hitler possessed no discernible equal among the leaders of Western and Central Europe. His passions were real and ferociously expressed. Withal, he remained remarkably ordinary, emanating in most settings none of the charm or presence or intensity usually associated with the word "charisma." A dark-haired man of average stature and decidedly non-athletic physique, he bore scant resemblance to the Nordic/Aryan type glorified in Nazi mythology. Probably above average in intelligence, he nonetheless was typically banal, rambling, and inclined to deliver long, self-indulgent monologues in the presence of his intimates. His intellectual tastes seem to have been as pedestrian as his artistic preferences. He was a detached administrator, his leadership marked by long periods of lassitude between speeches and public appearances. He typically made important decisions only when they no longer could be put off.

Yet the cheering throngs, the women who wept with emotion as his car passed, the hard-faced SA and SS men saluting with enthusiasm were undeniable. The frenzy of the crowds attested to his success in tapping into their darkest emotions. Hitler's frequent appearances in uniform, his often angry demeanor, his employment of the myth of a German *Volk*— all played to an audience that wanted strong leadership, had never accepted the punitive Versailles settlement, was distressed by the fragmentation and conflict in German society, and desired above all aggressive national regeneration. His appeal thus had a substantive basis.

Hitler and his lieutenants also knew that charisma could be, if not created, at least greatly enhanced by proper staging, attention-getting techniques, and effective use of the media. Here he was the beneficiary of astute advisers and talented organizers who in the early 1930s were accused of bringing American-style campaigning to Germany. In fact, they were sometimes ahead of America. What politician of any Western nation had campaigned by airplane before Hitler did it in the spring of 1932? What political gathering anywhere could compare to the grim, yet meticulously organized and disciplined, Nuremberg Nazi party rallies over which Hitler presided throughout the 1930s? Contrary to the prejudices of Western democratic popular culture, the Nazis were not buffoons. The party's organizational and administrative talent equaled that of any Western political grouping and greatly facilitated the way in which it took over the state.

Like Franklin Roosevelt and Stanley Baldwin, Hitler communicated to millions by radio, the universal instrument of charismatic leadership in the 1930s. But unlike them, he specialized in the angry harangue rather than the quiet, rational fireside talk, and he was ineffective speaking into a microphone from a studio. His oratory had to be fueled by excited audiences, and he quickly learned to limit his radio speaking to such occasions. Government-subsidized cheap radio receivers brought his voice into every village. Even in these situations, he was more effective in a mass setting. Nazi "radio wardens" set up loudspeakers in public places and encouraged community listening. His radio addresses were national occasions, regularly heard by audiences of over fifty million.[34]

Perhaps no leader of the 1930s was better presented on film. Hitler himself understood the medium brilliantly. He personally chose the brilliant, beautiful, opportunistic Leni Riefenstahl, although she was not a member of the Nazi party, to produce documentaries of the Nuremberg rallies. Her most memorable effort presented an imposing spectacle of national discipline, power, and unity, all generated by the master presence of the Führer. Hitler gave the film its title, *Triumph of the Will,* a widely understood affirmation that his own experience of defeat, recovery, and victory would parallel Germany's. He realized that carefully choreographed appearances, amplified by radio and film, could transform him into something much larger than himself.

By the time *Triumph of the Will* was released in 1935, Hitler had become Germany's Man of Destiny, a man alone, beyond normal personal relationships, embodying the nation and devoted to the people he led. He would never marry, he once remarked to Albert Speer. To do so would be to forfeit the adoration of too many women. He kept his mistress, Eva Braun, concealed from the public in order to appear single-mindedly devoted to Germany.

Hitler also stood above the fray of day-to-day power struggles. Some accounts of the Third Reich go so far as to describe him as lazy. He probably realized that charisma did not mix well with workaday details and common disputes. It is also noteworthy that for all his detachment, he generally avoided clear delegations of power, often set his subordinates to squabbling with each other, and required his assent to important final decisions, however much that might result in postponement and delay. With this not-uncommon technique of leadership, also consciously employed by Roosevelt, he enhanced his authority and protected his power.

What Hitler's own calculations and his media manipulators started, total power magnified. His charisma fed upon itself to become a cult of leadership with few precedents in the modern world. He had given the German people and the Nazi party unmistakable cues as to the directions in which they should go. As a Nazi party official put it in February 1934, "it is the duty of every single person to attempt, in the spirit of the Führer, to work toward him." In the absence of anything resembling pluralistic government or collective leadership, Nazi officials, whether in Berlin or remote rural villages, had only the pronouncements of the Führer to guide them. They worked toward Hitler without needing his active direction. "The result," Ian Kershaw has written, "was continuing radicalization of policy in a direction which brought Hitler's own ideological imperatives more plainly into view as practicable policy options."[35]

From the earliest days of the New Deal, Nazi propagandists took special pleasure in telling their American critics that Roosevelt, as much as Hitler, was a dictator. Such gibes were a crude libel, but an increasingly large number of Roosevelt's American critics, mostly frustrated Republicans, came close to adopting them. In a larger sense, it seemed natural to lump him with other apparently larger-than-life national leaders, including Hitler, Mussolini and Stalin.[36]

Some similarities between Hitler and Roosevelt are arresting. One may wonder, for example, if Roosevelt had Hitler's German presidential campaign in mind when he surprised the country by flying to the 1932 Democratic convention. Both understood the power of radio as a mode of communication with the people, however differently they utilized it. Both would launch government programs against the Depression that were sustained by campaigns of mass mobilization usually reserved for times of war. Both appear consciously to have preferred administrative disorderliness to explicit lines of authority and delegations of power.[37]

These were, of course, superficialities. The objectives of Hitler and Roosevelt were so different as to need no enumeration. The style and tone of their appeals reflected vastly different, and ultimately incompatible, political cultures. Hitler's angry, rambling speeches would have led most American voters to write him off as a crank. In the United States of the 1930s, uniformed political movements led by would-be fascist strongmen were ridiculed curiosities. Conversely, Roosevelt's democratic style would have been incomprehensible in a Germany with a long authoritarian and militarist tradition, still raging over the consequences of the World War.

Yet one clear resemblance remains. Millions of Germans worshiped Hitler; millions of Americans worshiped Roosevelt. Both nations wanted strong, dynamic leadership and responded to it. The Germans developed a word for the guiding power of the leader, the *Führerprinzip*. Americans had no equivalent term, but they, much more than the British and perhaps as much as the Germans, wanted a strong man at the top, one who could speak to their needs and fears, provide a sense of reassurance, and leave the impression that he was single-mindedly leading the nation toward better times. Roosevelt did so within the clear limits of a deeply entrenched liberal-democratic culture. Hitler faced virtually no limits in a culture sick of a failed democracy, yearning for a sense of national purpose, and receptive to an authoritarian dictatorship that with bewildering speed metamorphosed into a totalitarian society.

—✦—

Writing from Germany in the summer of 1935, H. J. Haskell described a gathering economic recovery within the framework of a tightly and comprehensively controlled economy. He found it natural to make comparisons to the American scene. As in the United States, the private economy had been subjected to a high level of state control. Businessmen privately groused about unsustainable government spending and widespread state interference. In the United States, foreign trade was a low priority. In Germany, it was likewise a small part of the economy and in addition was rigidly controlled for the benefit of the nation. Yet in Germany the Depression appeared over. Unemployment was two million, down from six million at its peak.

An interview with a distinguished economist at the University of Berlin, Haskell thought, might have been a talk with a New Deal theorist. The Berlin scholar delivered a similar message: Economics was an experimental science, not a collection of orthodox verities; a nation could survive and prosper without foreign trade so long as it marshaled its resources at home and developed its advanced industrial plant. "The country is a striking example of the extreme regimentation necessary if a nation is to live within itself," Haskell concluded. "This ultramodern, streamlined new deal requires autocratic administration and the loss of most freedom of action on the part of individuals."

Like most foreign observers, Haskell gave much of the credit for the economic advance to "Dr. Schacht," and like many he doubted that the doctor's magic act could sustain itself for much longer. Levies on business, the forced placement of short-term government bonds with large German banks, stifling foreign exchange restrictions that had made the mark effectively nonconvertible, a drive for autarkic self-sufficiency that culminated in the production of many shoddy goods, a growing diversion of national resources into armaments, the micromanagement of industry, an equally controlled and poorly paid labor force—all these could be seen as an economic house of cards certain to collapse. The government, he believed, was constructing an unsustainable system of state capitalism. A lack of foreign trade would stunt the economy; excessive government borrowing would lead to uncontrolled inflation. How long could Dr. Schacht maintain his prestidigitation? Perhaps through the end of 1936. "What will happen then, and whether an explosion will come, is anybody's guess."[38]

The Nazi and New Deal economic programs did in fact share an attraction to the idea of a managed economy, an addiction to unorthodox monetary policies, a reliance on deficit spending, a resort to public works projects, and a go-it-alone attitude toward the rest of the world. It was not altogether bizarre in the context of the mid-1930s for an observer alarmed by Franklin Roosevelt's aggressive leadership to wonder if

National Socialism was an end model toward which the American New Deal was progressing, but such apprehensions implicitly assumed that German and American political norms were roughly the same. The Nazis understood the difference. As Hermann Göring bluntly put it in May 1936, to a meeting of the Council of Ministers, "Measures that in a state with a parliamentary government would probably bring about inflation do not have the same results in a totalitarian state."[39] The crushing of almost all independent centers of interest and opinion, along with the fear of the concentration camp, suppressed the frictions of protest and dissent that animated a democratic society. The drive behind the German recovery—and its ultimate purpose—was an expansive totalitarianism that was simply not possible in the United States or Britain.

In the democracies, the purpose of economic recovery was to reinstate a primarily civilian economy that provided remunerative jobs and a relatively comfortable standard of living for most citizens. In Germany, the purpose of economic recovery was to validate the Nazi party's claim to legitimacy, establish sentiments of national resurgence, and prepare the state for war. Comfort and prosperity for the individual citizen was from the beginning a deferred promise that kept receding into the horizon. The Nazis understood that they had to make things better for the average German, that jobs and bread were the essential underpinnings of the new order, but they had little interest in establishing a society grounded in widespread consumerist affluence and self-indulgence, although they might hold out such possibilities as a future reward for present sacrifices. In the short run, they expected Germans to be satisfied with immersion in productive labor, cross-class solidarity, and the emotions of national triumphalism.

The Nazi motto *"ein Volk, ein Reich, ein Führer"* posited a sense of oneness as the basis for the Nazi regime; this was at the heart of what David Schoenbaum has called "Hitler's social revolution." From the romanticization of farm work to storm troopers parading with shovels at party rallies, the regime affirmed the dignity of manual labor. The party exhorted the middle classes to show solidarity with workers by foregoing the traditional big midday Sunday dinner and eating "one-pot" or "one-dish" meals of stew at Nazi-approved restaurants that might charge them as much as three marks for a 50 pfennig lunch; the profit went to jobless relief programs.[40]

The youth work camps best expressed the objective. They knew no class distinctions, expected the same of all, and adopted as their motto:

"Honor. Truth. Duty. Comradeship. Discipline." Even liberal-minded foreigners were invariably impressed. A Nazi official told one: "Some of
these boys may become professional men, merchants, bankers. But we
believe it will be good for them to have the experience with hard work
with their hands, and that they will look on manual workers with more
understanding and sympathy." To the observation that the camps seemed
very democratic, he replied: "We do not like the word 'democratic.' We
say we are making a united people."[41]

The economic resurgence that many observers sensed by mid-1935
was real and impressive. In that year the German Gross National Product, the classic indicator of the business cycle, exceeded the level of 1928
when measured in constant prices; during the peak summer months
unemployment eased just below ten percent. A year later, the economy
had grown by approximately ten percent and unemployment had been
cut by a third. Critics might quibble over the extent to which the employment figures were affected by the growing size of the German army, the
increased number of youths in labor camps, the temporary public works
projects, or simple statistical manipulation; but all agreed that the
Depression was over in Nazi Germany.

The Nazi recovery program organized the economy in ways that bore a
clear surface resemblance to the early New Deal. Here also, a hard-
pressed agricultural sector was a primary concern. In order to have the
ability to wage war, Germany had to be able to feed itself. In order to
grapple with the industrial crisis, a peasantry facing liquidation had to be
given the relief that would forestall migration to cities already filled with
the jobless. The government raised farm income through tax and debt
relief, divided bankrupt estates into small holdings, and instituted price
supports that raised food prices for urban consumers. It justified these
programs not simply on economic grounds but also through a widespread
sentimentalization of the tillers of the soil not unlike that encouraged by
the New Deal.

The Reichsnährstand (RNS), a sort of counterpart to the American
Agricultural Adjustment Administration, supervised marketing and
established prices for every significant commodity through regional
boards. In the short run, the peasantry prospered and workers complained about the high prices of meat and bread. By the recovery year of
1935, however, with growing demand for agricultural commodities, the
Nazi regime tried with limited success to prevent prices from rising to
natural market levels. In the United States, such a development would

have led to strong pressures for more benefits from the farm bloc in Congress and possibly to rural demonstrations reminiscent of 1933. In Germany, farmers understood there was no alternative to being grateful for what benefits they had received. As in other areas, the totalitarian state neither functioned with perfect efficiency nor achieved one hundred percent of every objective, but it effectively blocked the political frictions that made recovery so much more difficult in the major democracies.[42]

The story was much the same with business. Where the American NRA catered to trade associations and developed code authorities, the German organization of industry was built around preexisting cartels, upon which were imposed state-constructed "estates." In both cases, moreover, the program primarily benefited large enterprises. The differences in nomenclature were nominal; the contrast in the degree of government control was enormous. Where the NRA effectively handed over to business leaders the responsibility for the details of organization, the estate system was one in which the regime bossed Germany's greatest tycoons. By decree, for example, Schacht limited corporate dividends to no more than eight percent of earnings and required managers to turn over the rest of their free cash for investment in government securities. Marxists then and since have charged that the Nazi revolution was controlled by the forces of monopoly capitalism. Actually, it exploited those forces for its own interests.[43]

The primary purpose of preparation for war coexisted awkwardly with a general economic recovery through 1936. Those industries that prospered most were autos, aircraft, chemicals, steel, and, inevitably, armaments. Those that displayed smaller increases in output and profitability produced consumer goods such as clothing, shoes, furniture, and household items. Weak and marginal enterprises of all sorts suffered severely; approximately 300,000 such businesses went under during the 1930s. Although small tradesmen had been among the core supporters of the Nazis before 1933, Hitler's social Darwinism functioned ruthlessly to their disadvantage.[44] At the same time, however, government policy created new and large, but also inefficient and heavily subsidized, players in such areas as synthetic rubber and steel.

Superficially impressive, the German business recovery was heavily dependent on questionable state management and never achieved a self-sustaining momentum of its own. Top-down control was pervasive and often economically irrational. Official, oft-stated government policy was to achieve an impractical autarkic self-sufficiency, bolstered with the complementary goal of a special (i.e., hegemonic) economic relationship with smaller central European states. This dictated a host of subsidies for agriculture and numerous industries. The government especially put a high premium on energy independence, boasting of the achievement of forty-six percent domestic production of motor fuels as a breakthrough at the beginning of 1936. To avoid costly imports of nonstrategic raw materials, consumer goods such as clothing were made with cheap and shoddy synthetics.

Such policies made a normal foreign trade impossible. The mark was theoretically convertible and backed by gold at a ratio of four to the dollar; in reality, German foreign exchange was so tightly managed, transaction by transaction, that German bonds sold at deep discounts in foreign markets. "Trade" often meant "barter," with foreign nations accepting equivalent amounts of German goods in order to sell their wares to the Reich. Bilateral arrangements of this sort gave Germany the benefits of currency depreciation without the stigma of a formal devaluation, but businessmen in search of the best deal frequently found themselves subjected to the whims of the state. The government subsidized many exports, especially to nations that were frequent trading partners, but the subsidized businesses were rarely happy. A porcelain manufacturer, for example, required a 30,000 mark subsidy to undercut Czechoslovakian competition and make a sale in India. When the government told him he could have only 25,000, he protested, "Why should I go to all this trouble and take a loss?" The answer was blunt: "We need the foreign exchange. If you refuse to carry the deal through you will get no more government contracts, or you may be replaced by a more patriotic manager."[45]

Recovery there was, then, but profits were a different story for all but the most favored businesses. The leader who attracted the resentment was not Hitler, who was covering himself with glory as the restorer of German sovereignty and self-respect, but Dr. Schacht, who ironically possessed increasing misgivings about the durability of the recovery he had engineered.

The acid test of the Nazi program was reemployment. Enjoying the benefit of at least a tepid economic upswing that was already in progress when it took power in 1933, the Nazis, much like the New Dealers, quickly initiated a series of showy public works projects that combined a maximum public relations impression with a modest number of actual jobs created. Enlarging on plans already begun by Papen and Schleicher, Hitler emphasized road-building and development of the auto industry. He spoke to work gangs who listened to him bearing picks and shovels on their shoulders as if they were rifles. The theme of roads and autos for all appealed to the popular imagination. It also had obvious military implications.[46]

Most of the public employment projects were generated not from Berlin, but by regional Nazi leaders, who received general orders to cut joblessness by whatever means possible. They did so with varying degrees of effectiveness and much ruthlessness. Sometimes they paid subsidies to employers adding to their workforces. More typically, Germans without work were virtually impressed into projects by the threat of losing their unemployment benefits or, in extreme cases, being sent to a concentration camp. In contrast to the United States, where relief workers usually received good wages, Germans got a pittance. Although such jobs were temporary, Nazi statisticians counted these workers as employed. Another means of reducing official unemployment was a drive to exclude women from the workforce. A by-product of the Nazi ethic that the destiny of all women was childbearing and homemaking, it was more successful in keeping young women at home than in displacing those with jobs. As late as 1939 one-third of all German workers were female.[47] Young men in the youth labor camps or in military service were, by definition, employed. Still, there can be little doubt that the Nazi regime was able to effect significant gains in conventionally defined employment by early 1935.

The cost was substantial, despite the low-wage nature of most work programs, but it gave Hitler the near-term victory he needed. The Führer and his immediate circle took the credit for what good their local subordinates had done and began to shift the economic emphasis to rearmament. Schacht and other economic officials, believing the work programs placed an unsustainable burden on the state's finances and contributed to inflationary price increases, seconded the phaseout. In April 1935, Berlin ordered an end to all work programs in localities that were running budget deficits. The termination led to an unexpected rise in year-end seasonal unemployment and a temporary crisis of confidence, but spending on the military and heavy industrial development quickly overcame it.

During Hitler's first four years in power, the government spent freely, more than doubling the cumulative national debt and enlarging the money supply by about thirty percent. Yet the Nazi budget deficits were never as imbalanced as the New Deal's over the same period. The Nazis worked with considerable success to maintain price levels against increasingly severe inflationary pressures. Hitler, fully as much as Göring, attributed his success in preventing an economic blowoff to the fear of totalitarian retribution. "Inflation does not arise when money enters circulation, but only when the individual demands more money for the same service," he told some companions several years later. "Here we must intervene. That is what I had to explain to Schacht, that the first cause of the stability of our currency is the concentration camp." The explanation was a bit facile, but it had an element of truth. Never as important as rearmament, public works spending may have accounted for as much as twenty-five percent of the recovery that was in full bloom by mid-1936.[48]

Even in recovery, however, the life of the ordinary German was drab and marked by scarcity. From workers one might have expected especially bitter resentment. With swift ruthlessness, the Nazis had crushed their unions, either imprisoning their leaders or forcing them into exile. After unemployment was largely vanquished, the working class still made do with subpar wages and a mediocre standard of living. Sporadic food shortages plagued Germany from late 1934 into early 1936. They stemmed from a bad harvest, poor state management of agricultural policy, and government refusal to free up enough foreign exchange for ample imports of such staple commodities as butter and meat. In the summer of 1935, a prominent Nazi publication floated the possibility of eliminating lemons, a wholly-foreign-grown commodity, from the national diet and substituting home-produced rhubarb. German blood, it declared, was linked to German soil. Only through the products of the soil could "delicate spiritual aspirations be communicated to the blood and through it to the body and the soul." In early 1936, the journalist Josephine Herbst reported that even loyal Nazis complained about high prices. The average working-class family in 1937 lived on a less rich (albeit nutritionally adequate) diet than in 1927.[49]

The British Marxist historian Tim Mason appears to make a self-evident point when he declares that a primary problem of Nazi rule was "the containment of the working class." But workers, as much as any segment of the population, acquiesced in Nazi rule. Comprising perhaps a quarter of the party's support, the Nazi working-class voter had been motivated by disgust at the failure of Weimar democracy, by the lure of a union of nationalism and socialism, and by the broad cross-class appeal of Nazism. The new order secured at least the passive acceptance of other workers by providing jobs and bread and by deft carrot-and-stick tactics.[50]

That some "containment" was necessary is undeniable. Workers experienced the same authoritarian prodding as did all Germans. Conspicuous "grumblers" had a way of disappearing from shop floors and turning up in concentration camps. On average, Mason believes, the Gestapo arrested a thousand "working-class activists" per month. Many of these were probably Communists, but there can be no doubt that the police state was as salient in the lives of the workers as in those of any other class. A government body, the Trustees of Labor, set wages, kept them at as low a rate as possible, and constantly trumpeted the necessity of sacrifice for the common good. Still, abolition of labor unions did not mean a total abolition of representation. The government-controlled German Labor Front assumed many of the old union functions. Operating always within the boundaries of government policies, it did not sanction negotiations for higher wages or strikes, but it did frequently achieve improvements in working conditions.

The Labor Front initiated the "Strength through Joy" (*Kraft durch Freude*) program, designed to enrich (and control) the leisure time of workers. Strength through Joy offered workers lectures, concerts, organized recreation of all sorts, cheap vacation excursions, even inexpensive ocean cruises. One-week ski outings in the Bavarian Alps were available for an all-inclusive rate of forty-four marks ($11), an ocean cruise to Madeira for a hundred marks ($25). Between low wages and pressures on food prices, most workers surely found it difficult to pay for the cheapest cruises, but thrift and accumulated savings made it possible for many to take advantage of less expensive opportunities. Most probably felt that the Nazi party was narrowing the gap between themselves and the middle class. Observing the German scene from Prague, the exiled social democratic organization Sopade commented ruefully that Strength through Joy "cleverly appeals to the *petit bourgeois* inclination of the unpolitical workers who want to participate in the pleasures of the 'top people.'"[51]

The most storied of the Nazi initiatives for the workers was the *Volkswagen*. Perhaps no American influenced Hitler more than Henry Ford, who was also a vocal anti-Semite. Ford had made cheap auto transportation available to every American laborer and in consequence transformed the American landscape. Speaking at the Berlin International Auto Show on February 11, 1933, just twelve days after becoming chancellor, Hitler praised the automobile as a German invention that would bring freedom of mobility to every individual, proclaimed his commitment to the revival of the nation's auto industry, and pledged an extensive program of road-building. Nazi propagandists filled out the picture by promising a "people's car" that could be purchased for no more than a thousand marks. The Nazi strategy of development, however, reversed the sequence of events in the United States. The roads would be built first—a planned 14,000 kilometer system of spacious divided motorways (the *Autobahn*) that would tie the Reich together. The cheap cars would follow. The *Autobahn* became the emblematic public works project of the Third Reich. Yet its construction was among the meanest of the public relief jobs, housing its workers in shabby construction camps and requiring hard manual labor for sixty pfennigs (fifteen cents) an hour. By 1939, just over 3,000 kilometers had been constructed, tying together a number of major German cities and featuring a "Party Road" that moved northward from Hitler's birthplace in Linz, Austria, to Munich, Nuremberg, and Berlin.

The people's car, or *Volkswagen*, remained a mirage glimmering on the horizon. In 1934, Hitler commissioned the great automotive engineer Ferdinand Porsche to design it. Working from concepts he already had developed, Porsche by 1936 had built prototypes of a small auto with a rounded design; if not visionary, it was advanced for its time and destined to set a standard for combining functionality and economy. The party designated the north German city of Wolfsburg as the site for a huge factory that would build one and a half million cars a year. Posters, even a postage stamp, carried images of the vehicle that left an exaggerated impression of its size and sleekness. The Strength through Joy program set up a savings plan, whereby workers could, the slogan promised, "save five marks a week and get your own car." Construction on the Wolfsburg factory, however, did not begin until early 1938. The first autos rolled off the assembly line in mid-1939, just in time for the war and retooling of the facility for military production. It appears that no worker ever took delivery of a people's car. The effect of the plan was to divert millions of marks in wages out of the civilian economy into preparations for war. Intentional or not, the result was consistent with the Nazi emphasis on guns instead of butter.[52]

What sort of recovery had Hitler brought to Germany? One that by mid-1936 was providing jobs for all but was built on low wages, shoddy consumer goods, and declining international trade. Lacking much to buy, ordinary Germans saved unusually high percentages of their incomes, which the state then recycled into economically inefficient industries dedicated to autarkic self-sufficiency and militarization. Over the long run,

Hjalmar Schacht privately asserted with increasing vehemence in the councils of state, such a recovery carried within it the seeds of its own collapse. Hitler and Göring responded that a Germany militarily dominant among nations would be economically secure. At the Nuremberg party rally in September 1936, Hitler unveiled a Four Year Plan, to be administered by Göring. Devoting most of the nation's resources to armaments, it openly relied upon a top-down command system enforced by the coercive power of the state. Schacht's star thereafter steadily dimmed.

However much the German working class may have been swindled by the Nazis, indications are that its attitudes toward them roughly paralleled that of other segments of the population. The assumption that workers should feel a primary sense of identification with their class instead of their nation is a common fallacy of intellectuals. It had been proven untrue by the World War, and it remained so in the 1930s. Germans, whether workers or not, had been reared in an authoritarian political culture that (like most European national cultures) defined national identity in terms of blood ties. The Nazis may have transformed Völkisch pride into murderous racism and traditional authoritarianism into totalitarianism. It made no difference. Workers, like Germans of all classes, either accepted these changes enthusiastically, acquiesced out of a sense of self-preservation, or suffered terribly.

By 1936 a majority of Germans, by the accounts of the most hostile observers, apparently supported the new order with varying degrees of enthusiasm. Hitler—unlike the Weimar chancellors, unlike even Hindenburg—had transformed a chaotic society into an orderly one. However unsatisfactory the living standards, he had put people back to work and had avoided repeating the catastrophic inflation of the early 1920s. Most of all, he had given Germans a sense of collective pride. He had repudiated the Versailles treaty, reasserted German sovereignty, made the country equal among nations, and seemed poised to make it dominant. Triumph was at hand.

For two weeks in August 1936, Berlin enjoyed the attention of the world as host to the Olympic games. The new Germany impressed even those who wished to see otherwise. The spectacle highlighted not just a good host and an impressive city, but the strength and power of a resurgent nation. It reflected a new German confidence with roots in the Nazi achievements of economic recovery and national restoration.

Over a three-and-a-half-year period, the Nazis had defied every expectation of failure. In 1933, many observers had envisioned a worldwide backlash against their persecution of the Jews, but the international community had neither the will nor the mechanism for such an action. Others assumed that the regime would collapse from resistance within. In mid-1934, eighteen months after Hitler had taken power, Senator William E. Borah of Idaho expressed amazement that the German people had "tolerated" the Nazis for so long and assured Americans, "Hitler cannot last much longer." Germany's aggressive and repeated displays of contempt for international institutions and accepted norms of behavior led numerous analysts to assume she would be isolated and encircled by powerful enemies. However, her major antagonists—Britain, France, Italy, and the Soviet Union—shared little common ground. The first three were as hostile toward the USSR as toward Germany. Italy, at first opposed to Germany's ambitions in Austria, found only the Nazis supportive of Mussolini's subjugation of Ethiopia, made common cause with them in Spain, and was by mid-1936 on the verge of becoming a formal ally. Even Britain and France could never agree on the best ways of confronting Germany, or indeed whether to do so at all. The USSR, consumed by its own bloody totalitarianism, was no threat.[53]

In the face of such irresolution, the Germans moved decisively. In October 1933, the Nazi government withdrew from the League of Nations and the continuing Geneva disarmament talks, signaling an intention to build its armed forces well beyond the limits of the Versailles treaty. In June 1934, the regime suspended payments on all foreign debts. Hitler's only serious setback came the following month, when Austrian Nazis botched a coup attempt against the Vienna government of Engelbert Dolfuss and nearly precipitated an Italian intervention. The embarrassment was great but temporary. The German-speaking Saar region, a coal and iron producer of great strategic and economic importance that had been under a fifteen-year French occupation, voted freely in January 1935, by a margin of more than 9–1, to return to Germany.

Two months later, Germany officially announced plans to increase its army at least fivefold, institute conscription, and establish an air force. The declaration formally renounced the Treaty of Versailles. The other European powers responded only with hopes that Germany might forego further military expansion. Britain, fearing a rerun of the pre–World War naval expansion race, swiftly negotiated a naval treaty. In March 1936, Hitler ordered his still-weak armed forces to march into the demilitarized

Rhineland; prepared to retreat if met by French resistance, they instead moved unopposed fifty kilometers to the Rhine bridges, then crossed them to near-hysterical celebrations from Dusseldorf to Frankfurt. Those everywhere who followed international affairs understood that a mighty new force was emerging in the heart of Europe.

Berlin in the late summer of 1936 was a city seething with power and energy. Cleaned up to greet the horde of visitors, it was devoid of the highly visible anti-Semitic slogans that customarily could have been found on the windows of hundreds of storefronts, but it was unmistakably a Nazi city with swastikas everywhere. For the government, the purpose of the games (which had been awarded to Berlin before Hitler's rise to power) was self-legitimation. Hitler ordered the construction of a new stadium, larger than any ever used for the Olympics. He commissioned Leni Riefenstahl to film a comprehensive documentary. Utilizing the newest of broadcast technologies, television cameras brought much of the competition live to Berliners, who watched in viewing rooms scattered around the city. Plays, pageants, concerts, operas, art exhibitions, and non-Olympic athletic competitions supplemented the festivities. Designed to eclipse the Los Angeles event of 1932, this was to be the Nazi Olympiad.[54]

From a ragtag beginning the modern Olympics had grown in size and spectacle during the 1920s. Pageantry was rapidly becoming as important as the actual sporting competition. Here the Nazis excelled. The torch relay from Olympia, Greece, had never been done before; it was an inspiration of Goebbels. Three thousand runners traversed a 3,000 kilometer route and built anticipation well in advance of the competition. The opening day was a display of German nationalism and Nazi self-assertion. As Hitler entered the stadium filled with 110,000 people, the composer Richard Strauss conducted a choir of 3,000 singing "Deutschland Über Alles" and the Nazi anthem, "The Horst Wessel Lied," in advance of his "Olympic Hymn." Over 5,000 athletes paraded past the reviewing stand, many of them recognizing their host with a stiff-armed fascist salute. Overhead, the great airship *Hindenburg* hovered, trailing behind it a huge Olympic banner.

In the following days, Göring, Goebbels, and other Nazi leaders entertained crowds of foreign notables at lavish receptions that called to mind Versailles in the days of Louis XIV. The Strength through Joy program brought 20,000 workers a day into Berlin and put them up in a village specially constructed to house them. Radio, by now a staple of information and popular entertainment throughout the developed world, broadcast all over the globe descriptions of not simply the athletic events but the magnificence of the setting. Foreigners, many of them in Germany for the first time, were typically impressed by the unity of the German people and the devotion they displayed for their Führer and his government.[55]

The sporting competition, if somewhat overshadowed by all the pomp, was equally a triumph for Germany and for a Nazi program of athletic development that would set a standard for future totalitarian regimes. By an impressive margin, it was true, Americans prevailed in the events that mattered to them—men's swimming, track, and field—but even here Germany managed three gold medals. Jesse Owens, the black American who won four gold medals, impressed much of the world, but the Germans only scoffed at the U.S. deployment of Negroes who were second-class citizens at home. They also displayed an array of talent, both male and female, remarkable in its depth and achievement. If largely shut out in sports that Americans took seriously, they were good in almost everything else. They won more gold medals and more medals of any kind than any other country. By the unofficial scoring system of the *New York Times* they took the games by a margin of 628 ¾ to 451 ⅓ over the United States. The Olympiad had been the biggest and best ever, superbly organized and played out in the finest facilities ever constructed for the quadrennial occasion. The standard set by Los Angeles four years earlier had been eclipsed.

Nazi Germany had scored a major propaganda victory. It also had impressed itself. In the heady afterglow of triumph, all things seemed possible, self-respect became hubris, and the man who had willed it all basked in the adulation of his people. As the closing ceremonies came to an end, the predominantly German crowd in the vast Olympic Stadium rose to its feet in a mood an American newsman described as one of "patriotic frenzy," shouting time and again, "Sieg heil! Our Führer, Adolf Hitler, sieg heil!"[56]

HEADLINES AND MOVIE NEWSREELS

{1933}

JULY 28   "Sterling Bloc" Voted by British Empire

{1934}

OCTOBER 2   British "New Deal" Had 20-Year Start; Social Policies Well-established

{1935}

JANUARY 13   Virus of New Deal Attacking Britain; Lloyd George to Open Campaign for Public Works Policy Like That of United States

JANUARY 16   British Welcome Outcome in Saar; Hitler Expected to Be More Amenable

JULY 7   Ethiopian War Cloud Darkens All Europe; Existence of the League of Nations, Future of Italy, and Friendship of France and Britain Threatened

{1936}

JANUARY 26   A New King—A New Era—For England; Accession of Edward VIII

MARCH 8   Germany's Rhineland Action Assailed by Eden; Attitude of Cabinet Is Milder

DECEMBER 12   Edward Broadcasts Farewell to Empire; Parliament Votes the Accession of George VI

{1937}

JANUARY 2   *"More Employment in Britain"* (The Economist)

SPRING   *War Minister Alfred Duff Cooper appealing for recruits. Half the volunteers, mostly from the long-depressed North, are rejected as unfit. A newspaper headline declares "50% Starving." The army promises enlistees four square meals a day (March of Time [reenactment documentary]: "Britain's Food Defenses")*

MAY 29   Baldwin Retires; Steered Safely in Crises; Achieved Recognition of Greatness

{ 7 }

MUDDLING TOWARD RECOVERY

BRITAIN, JUNE 1933–JUNE 1937

Personalities: Spurned Saviors

Among active British politicians in the 1930s, none had a more formidable record as an engineer of reform and social change than David Lloyd George. Among politically engaged economists, none was more impressive, whether as theoretician or policy intellectual, than John Maynard Keynes. Both were dynamic forces; both were rejected as subversive viruses by the immune system of British politics. No one can say whether Lloyd George's political agenda and Keynes's economics would have brought their country more quickly out of the economic slump from which it fitfully recovered in the mid-1930s. What is certain is that, in contrast to many other countries, Britain preferred the sure, the steady, even the plodding to the quick, the imaginative, the risky. The nation's most charismatic politician and its greatest economist were relegated to the sidelines, the first to remain a continuing irritant, the second waiting for the war that would allow him at last to be an invaluable public servant.

Mr. Lloyd George: The Lion in Winter

After David Lloyd George came to Buckingham Palace to present his resignation as prime minister in 1922, King George V remarked to an aide that he would be back. The monarch's prediction seemed probable at the time. Yet the man who had been the driving personality in British politics for nearly two decades was through as a dominant figure, undone by his own political and personal excesses.

Born in 1863, to a Welsh schoolmaster and farmer who died before his son reached the age of two, young David George was effectively fathered by his mother's brother, Richard Lloyd. A master shoemaker, a fierce Protestant dissenter, a Welsh cultural nationalist, and a political "radical" hostile to the local Tory landowning establishment, Richard Lloyd instilled in his foster son broad-ranging resentments—of the Anglican Church, of English landowners, of an English cultural hegemony that threatened the language and traditions of Wales, of oppressions visited on his country by forces of "privilege" predominantly rooted in England. It was a tribute to his influence that the boy reformulated his surname to "Lloyd George."

A brilliant student who made the most of a rudimentary education in hated Anglican schools, he passed his law examination at the age of twenty-one and soon established a successful practice. A fiery speaker, he became a political activist, adopting causes associated with Welsh nationalism and identifying himself with the majority's dissenting Protestantism. In 1890, running as a Liberal, he won a narrow victory in a by-election for Parliament in Caernarvon. Only twenty-seven when he took his seat, he would represent the district for fifty-five years. Quickly established as the leader of Welsh dissent, he fused the religious and social complaints of his people with multiple attacks on the established church, state support for its schools, and the structure of privilege which it represented. Still, he never advocated full independence for Wales, simply more autonomy within a continuing framework of union.

When in 1905 the Liberal party formed a government under Sir Henry Campbell-Bannerman (succeeded in 1908 by Herbert Asquith), Lloyd George became a leading figure in it. Forced for the first time to establish a national vision and identity, he did so powerfully and irresistibly, shaking an apparently immutable social order and making himself the father of the British social welfare state. No longer simply a spokesman for downtrodden Welshmen, he transformed himself into a tribune of workers and farmers. Chancellor of the Exchequer under Asquith, he pushed through redistributive taxation, secured path-breaking social welfare programs, and spearheaded the successful drive to subordinate the House of Lords to the will of the Commons. He showed devastating power as a debater in Parliament. Quite unlike any Liberal leader before him, he rallied popular support with nobility-bashing speeches to working-class audiences. His tactics made his party a plausible alternative to Labour for workers; they also alienated much of the Liberal upper-middle class.

In the World War, he headed, first, the Ministry of Munitions, where he was instrumental in greatly increasing war production, then the War Office itself. Frustrated with military reverses, feeling hamstrung by a cautious cabinet, he intrigued against Asquith. In December 1916, he forced the prime minister's resignation and succeeded him as the chief of a national coalition. Vast talent and unquenchable ambition had triumphed—at the cost of a split from which the Liberal party would never recover. Now fifty-four, half his life spent in Parliament, the new prime minister was, as Thomas Jones has written, "the most widely known, the most dynamic, and the most eloquent figure in British politics."[1]

Lloyd George saw the war through to a successful conclusion, then defied all the norms of British party politics by standing for reelection as the leader of the wartime coalition. He won an enormous victory, but one in which Conservatives outnumbered his Liberal loyalists by two and a half to one. The government endured through four years of economic turmoil and Irish rebellion, but it carried the seeds of its own destruction, less in differences of opinion and party than in the person of its prime minister, who was, to put it delicately, morally careless. As chancellor of the Exchequer in 1913, he had barely avoided parliamentary censure for unethical investments. As prime minister, he was accused of flagrantly bartering peerages and other official honors for cash contributions. Those on the inside knew that he was a prodigious womanizer. Such traits especially repelled Tory back-benchers who saw him as an impediment to their advancement. With Stanley Baldwin playing a pivotal role, the Conservatives threw him off in 1922.

Functioning as a one-man policy generator and retaining control over a large political fund he had raised as prime minister, Lloyd George regained leadership of the Liberal party. Under the tutelage of John Maynard Keynes, he advocated large programs of public works, agrarian land reform, an actively managed economy, and planned national development. But in the wake of the General Strike of 1926, it was the hour of Labour, which took what it liked from his platform and successfully mobilized the working classes. In the election of 1929, Labour won 287 seats to the Conservatives' 261 and the Liberals' pathetic 59. With the Welsh wizard's sufferance, but not his participation, Ramsay MacDonald formed the government that would collapse in 1931. The crisis that led to the National government further pushed Lloyd George to the periphery. He was not asked to join, and most of the Liberals rejected his vehement opposition to its formation. The 1931 election left his party divided between Herbert Samuel (free trade) and Sir John Simon (protectionist). Lloyd George led only a small personal faction—himself, his son, his daughter, and his son's brother-in-law—in the House of Commons.

Seventy-two years old in 1935, readily identifiable at a distance by his imposing mane of white hair and matching mustache, he still possessed energy and magnetism. He argued for a New Deal for Britain and came close to pushing his way into the cabinet. In the end, the difficulties were as much personal as programmatic. Neville Chamberlain might have compromised on spending details, but not on the individual. He refused, he told his colleagues, to serve in the same cabinet with that man. Most of them understood. Rebuffed for once and for all, the old statesman visited Hitler in 1936 shortly after the end of the Berlin Olympics. He contemplated attendance at the annual Nuremberg rally as an honored guest, but contented himself with a statement praising the German dictator's achievements. In the minds of men like Baldwin and Chamberlain, the declaration revealed not simply an erratic nature, but the way in which the dynamic politician's fascination with power could override liberal democratic values. The firebrand statesman who had shaken the foundations of the Edwardian order had become a magnificent, irrelevant gadfly.

Maynard Keynes: Economic Theory, Policy Wonkery, and the Middle Way

"The decadent international but individualistic capitalism, in the hands of which we found ourselves after the War, is not a success. It is not intelligent, it is not beautiful, it is not just, it is not virtuous—and it doesn't deliver the goods. In short, we dislike it and we are beginning to despise it. But when we wonder what to put in its place, we are extremely perplexed."[2] So wrote John Maynard Keynes in his pamphlet *The Means to Prosperity* (1933). The passage concisely expressed his quest for a viable "middle way" between the extremes of left and right to combat the Great Depression.

No academic economist before or since has possessed Keynes's charismatic appeal to a trans-Atlantic policy intelligentsia. Probably none has ever had so revolutionary an impact upon his profession. Only a handful have possessed equivalent skills as an advocate and polemicist. How then does one explain his near-total failure to influence the economic policies of the English-speaking world in the 1930s?

Keynes's family was of the long-established middle class; his father, John Neville Keynes, was a noted economist. As a student, he ran with the brightest of the bright at Eton and Cambridge. By heritage and education, he qualified for a place in Britain's ruling establishment. His talent as student, thinker, writer, and debater all but guaranteed him one. His above-average height, well-kept mustache, tailored suits, and demeanor of self-assured superiority told the world he was a man of importance. By the age of thirty, he had put in two years at the India Office, accepted an appointment at Cambridge, written a major treatise on Indian finance, and taken up the editorship of an important scholarly journal of economics. By the age of thirty-five, he was a key official at the Treasury and influential adviser to the British peace delegation at Versailles. A seat in the House of Commons and a prospective cabinet post could have been his. It was by choice that he sought to influence politicians as a writer and critic.

For all his surface establishmentarianism, he was a profoundly unconventional man, unsettling to those who believed in virtues of slowness and steadiness, exhilarating to cultural rebels who detested the stuffy old order represented by men in power during the 1920s and 1930s. For the first thirty or so years of his life, he was a confirmed homosexual, who spent much of his early manhood in a passionate relationship with the artist Duncan Grant. After Grant broke off the physical (but not the affectionate) relationship, he began a crossover that eventually resulted in his marriage at the age of forty-two to a divorced Russian ballerina and aspiring actress, Lydia Lopokova. He lived his day-to-day life, not among fellow senior civil servants and academic economists, but with avant-garde intellectuals. Making his London home in Bloomsbury, he was a leading figure in a social set that included Lytton Strachey, Vanessa Bell, his former male lover Grant, and Virginia Woolf. He delighted in their common rejection of convention, and their affirmation of a morality dictated by reason and individual needs.

He was also a practical, swashbuckling financier, able to live beyond the means normally available to scholars because he speculated daringly in currency futures and other risky instruments. He seems to have found the experience, however personally rewarding, unsettling. Perhaps as a sort of penance, he supplied most of the financing for a new Arts Theater at Cambridge University. "He was both fascinated and disgusted by the psychology of capitalism," writes Robert Skidelsky, "and concerned about the social and ethical implications of a system which, as he was to put it in 1930, exalted and rewarded 'some of the most distasteful human qualities.'"[3] In this attitude he epitomized the outlook and the inner contradictions of the Atlantic liberal mind in the twenties and thirties. Rejecting the bland acceptance of an existing moral and economic order, he was equally put off by a class-based advocacy of state socialism. By temperament, philosophy, and economic conviction, Keynes was irresistibly drawn to the post-Victorian Liberal party of Lloyd George and Asquith, which he saw as representing the best hope for a middle way between Tory reaction and socialist revolution, as a vehicle that could synthesize the virtues of an open capitalist economy with the cushioning security of a democratic welfare state. The allegiance made him increasingly irrelevant.

It did not help that, by British standards of party regularity, he was a loose cannon. In 1919, at the peak of his meteoric rise within the government, he resigned from the British delegation at the Versailles peace conference. A series of magazine articles in Britain and the United States culminated in his book *The Economic Consequences of the Peace,* a bitter attack on the punitive reparations provisions of the postwar settlement. While he focused his rhetoric on the failure of the American president, Woodrow Wilson, enough deflected on Lloyd George to leave them estranged until 1926, when he effectively became the old Welshman's chief brains truster. It was too late. Hope of a Liberal resurgence was dashed by a disappointing showing in the 1929 election and the fragmentation of the party after the formation of the National coalition.

In Britain and the United States after 1931, Keynes, as much as Lloyd George, was a magnificent gadfly, capable of attracting attention by the formidable mind and sharply honed literary skills that made him one of the foremost intellectuals of the English-speaking world. But in neither country was he a member of a policy-making network with access to those in power. In fact, his efforts at influence displayed a clumsiness that leaves one suspecting he preferred the role of rejected prophet to that of the policy maker who would inevitably have to compromise ideals in the give and take of democratic politics. Chamberlain received him with civility in 1933, but quickly dismissed his proposals. Roosevelt had a pleasant audience with him the following year, may have been more impressed than he admitted, but gave no sign of interest in his policy advice.

Keynes's mightiest intellectual blow, *The General Theory of Employment, Interest, and Money* (1936), would in the course of time acquire hegemonic status among liberal economists. Its central assertions were that capitalism did not necessarily trend toward a normal equilibrium of maximum production and full employment, and hence that government intervention in the form of large-scale stimulus might be necessary in major slumps. They would seem commonplace within a generation, but in the short run, their policy impact was negligible. *The General Theory* veered between lucid prose and algebraic proofs in a fashion that baffled the ordinary reader. Its policy recommendations were not new—Keynes had been advocating them for years—but the book more frontally than ever challenged still-reigning paradigms of classical economic theory. It generated a last-ditch effort at refutation from much of the academic establishment but had a seductively subversive appeal to younger economists.

The Keynesian middle way, which became so attractive to Western policy liberals, stressed enormous public spending directed toward jobs and socially useful projects. Keynes also advocated limited public ownership of, say, utilities or railroads. However, there were other middle ways in the 1930s. The British National government and the American New Deal pursued numerous public works and socially conscious enterprises. It was not evident then—nor is it now—that a Keynesian formula of massive public investment would have achieved full employment on either side of the Atlantic in the late 1930s. It is at least possible that such a program would have undermined confidence in both countries and in Britain would have done severe damage to a currency whose strength seemed vital to the nation's position in the world.

In May 1937, Keynes suffered a severe heart attack. He spent much of the year convalescing and never fully regained his old vigor. In February 1938, in the midst of the American recession, he made a last, ineffectual attempt to influence Roosevelt. By then war clouds were gathering on the horizon. A final and more productive call to duty was at hand.

The Muddle Way

After the failure of the World Economic Conference, Britain faced the Depression alone, attempting to marshal the support and resources of the Empire and Commonwealth, establishing a "sterling bloc" that included a few other nations, making the occasional trade agreement, and attempting to develop its own economy behind the tariff barrier of 1932. The National government, in so many ways an expression of the country's dominant middle class, continued to pursue policies that combined fiscal conservatism and cheap money with generous social provision for the unemployed and the poor. Beyond the conviction that Britain was one democratic nation, the government possessed neither ideology nor coherent program. From time to time, it excelled at the manipulation of traditional national symbols and beliefs, providing a sense of continuity with a long and proud past. It demonstrated that purposeful leadership did not require charisma. The muddle of doctrine and the ordinariness of the cabinet ministers may have expressed a core English sensibility.

Somehow the formula seemed to work. By late 1935, the Depression was over, and the government returned to power with a handsome victory. When Prime Minister Baldwin retired in May 1937, most of Britain was prosperous and the cabinet was beginning to address the problem of chronically depressed areas. The outside world was far less cheerful, presenting challenges to British interests around the globe and mocking the nation's increasingly surreal faith in the League of Nations. As Baldwin stood down, rearmament was beginning in earnest, but optimists were not yet compelled to face the looming catastrophe that lay over the horizon.

<hr/>

The National government had a Labour prime minister, Ramsay MacDonald; a Liberal foreign secretary, Sir John Simon; a Conservative chancellor of the exchequer, Neville Chamberlain; and a Conservative lord president of the council, Stanley Baldwin. None of them could be accused of dynamism. The struggle against Britain's most urgent problem, the Depression, was captained by Chamberlain, who slogged on through six budgets (1932–37), raising enough money to balance the national accounts while meeting social needs and directing the British economy back toward recovery. Dutiful and conscientious, possessing a genuine concern for the working class, instinctively orthodox in his economics, Chamberlain saw fiscal conservatism as a policy that would sustain the value of a pound sterling no longer anchored to gold, create confidence in the business and financial communities, hold interest rates to a low level, and thus create the environment for a steady economic uptrend. Wanting to keep taxes as low as possible, he sought to hold government spending to a minimum, whether in funding the dole, rescinding the government pay cuts of 1931, or dealing with the defense establishment.

Chamberlain's backers called him wise and prudent. Most of the opposition believed him small-minded and heartless. The midstream Liberal *Economist* magazine caustically referred to the "comfortless courage of his own lack of constructive convictions" and promoted public works. By the spring of 1933, much of the British left had come around to large-scale loan-financed public spending of the type promoted by Keynes and Lloyd George, either as a method of rehabilitating English capitalism or as a stopover on the way to state socialism. As late as January 1936, the left-wing *New Statesman* declared, "the recuperative powers of world capitalism are not, under the conditions which now exist, capable of creating a level of economic activity high enough to employ the available working population or bring the available resources of production into use without the aid of the State."[4]

Yet recuperate the economy did, slowly, fitfully, and on a jagged upward trend line. At the beginning of 1933, the number of insured unemployed peaked at just under 3,000,000, a rate of about twenty-three percent.* By January 1934, it was down to 2.4 million (18.6 percent), by the end of 1935 under 1.9 million (14.1 percent). When Neville Chamberlain became prime minister on May 28, 1937, the figure had fallen below 1.4 million, less than half the number the National government had inherited when it came to power in August 1931. By then, moreover, owing to an expansion in their total number, more insured workers were employed than ever before. Other classic gauges of an economic depression displayed a similar trend. By the end of 1935, total industrial output already well exceeded that of 1929; so did Gross Domestic Product (GDP), the total of all goods and services produced within the United Kingdom. Britain was at last back to pre-Depression levels and more prosperous than at any time since the World War.[5]

Expressed so compactly and in bare statistical terms, the National government's struggle against the Depression may seem an outstanding success. In fact, it was a long, hard fight that often seemed to falter. If the unemployment problem was never as great as in the United States or Germany, it blighted the lives of over three million people (both workers

---

* The insured unemployed amounted to a little more than half the total workforce. In general, the noninsured had more stable employment. Thus, the insured unemployment rate overstated total workforce unemployment by approximately 50 percent. Total workforce unemployment in January 1933, for example, would have been approximately 16 percent. Peter Dewey, *War and Progress: Britain, 1914–1945* (London and New York: Longman, 1997), 254.

and their families) as late as 1937. Each year from 1932 through 1936 more than one-third of insured workers experienced a period of unemployment. If industrial production and GDP recovered more quickly than in the U.S. or Germany, they did so unevenly and amidst large, visible, and seemingly hopeless patches of derelict industries and despairing towns and cities in the depressed mining, manufacturing, and shipbuilding areas of Wales and the North.[6]

In April 1934, journalist Ferdinand Kuhn, Jr., provided prototypical examples of the "heroes" who had sacrificed to achieve Chamberlain's balanced budgets and right the national economy. One was "Mr. Thimble," a bookkeeper squarely in the middle of the middle class with a £10 per week salary, carrying a mortgage on a modest house in Wembley, barely making ends meet before the crisis of 1931. He suffered both a ten percent pay cut and a ten percent tax increase. Still, he was more fortunate than his neighbor, another white-collar worker who had lost his job, was ineligible for unemployment insurance, and could anticipate only downward mobility.

Kuhn also imagined an unnamed coal miner, living well to the north in Durham. He had worked only intermittently since 1921, never bringing home more than £2 per week but had managed to support a wife and small child; over the years, he had managed to accumulate £30 in a savings account. In 1931, his mine closed, leaving him dependent on a dole of £1, 7s, 9d (approximately £1.38)* Government budget cuts reduced the dole to £1, 5s (£1.25). The means test required him to draw down every penny of his accumulated savings. Pieces of furniture had to be sold. Charity provided shoes for the child. Bread, margarine, and fried potatoes were the staples of the family diet, with meat on the table only at Sunday dinner.

Mr. Thimble, living in a London suburb, probably brought himself and his family through two and a half straitened years; with returning prosperity he could anticipate a restoration of his salary and an easing of the tax burden. His neighbor had a good chance of finding new employment befitting his class and training. The Durham miner, like tens of thousands of others in mining areas of Wales and the North, textile mill towns of Lancashire, and coastal shipyards, had experienced worse and could look

---

* The British pound sterling of the time was divided into twenty shillings, each further divisible into 12 pence; a penny was customarily abbreviated as "d"—for *denarius*, the Roman penny mentioned in the New Testament. After the decimalization of British currency a generation later, the penny was abbreviated as "p."

forward to little more than a modest restoration of the dole. Effectively a pauper on state subsidy, he might never work regularly again.[7]

From the beginning in Britain, the Depression had been a regional phenomenon; what was striking was the way in which the contrast between North and South increased during the 1930s. Unable to compete in many foreign markets, the big export industries became unattractive candidates for capital investment. A young American visitor to Stoke-on-Trent was overwhelmed by the soot and slag, the black smoke and cinders belching from the chimneys of the one-third of the ancient factory buildings still at work, the sight of unemployed men picking up cigarette butts in the streets. It was a region, wrote Victor Reuther many years later, where "the Industrial Revolution seems to have had its beginnings—and to have undergone no improvement."[8]

By contrast, newer industries—electrical equipment, automobiles, chemicals among them—thrived as soon as the initial shock passed. They tended to locate farther south. Morris Motors took the lead in transforming the university town of Oxford into a manufacturing center. Traditionalists, then and later, decried the noise and smokestacks and bustle, but Oxford in 1934 had only a five percent unemployment rate. The auto worker making perhaps £4 a week and able to afford a house in nearby Cowley might have quite a different perspective than the custom-bound don.[9] Such a worker, positioning himself on the threshold of middle-class status, might have a sense that the paternal capitalist values of the National government were more attractive than the socialism still professed by the Labour party.

In 1931, the National government had fought to preserve the gold standard because it feared a surge of inflation akin to the immediate post–World War I experience. Instead, tight government budgets, high taxes, and economic stagnation kept prices down. The 1931 cost of living, already ten percent below 1929, was not exceeded until 1937. It is a shock to the twenty-first-century eye that the prices of most everyday items were customarily quoted in shillings and pence. "Mr. Thimble," the fictional Wembley bookkeeper, for example, could have a hearty lunch of mock turtle soup, roast ribs of beef, Yorkshire pudding, potatoes and spring greens, topped off with custard and tea in an ABC Tea Room for 1/8 (1 shilling, 8 pence), service included. He could buy a good suit at Burton ("the tailor of taste") for fifty-five shillings. His wife could purchase all manner of small items for home or person at Woolworth's ("nothing over sixpence") for pocket change. The thrifty middle class (or the skilled worker with a regular job) could live in comfort.[10]

Housing of the type the Oxford auto worker could have purchased was a primary driver of the British recovery. Without a gold standard to protect and with prices trending downwards, the Bank of England could let interest rates fall to market levels. Moreover, Britain had experienced none of the banking panics that had devastated Germany before the Nazis and the United States before the New Deal. A substantial hoard of savings at declining rates in a time of mild deflation fueled a remarkable boom in modest middle-class housing. By 1935, a three-bedroom "non-parlour" workingman's house could be purchased in much of Britain for £300–350, ninety percent of the cost financed by a 4.5 percent, twenty-five-year mortgage. The monthly payment on a £300 loan would be just 33/9. The upper crust of the working class and the lower half of the middle class leaped at such opportunities. In the United States, private home building stagnated; in Britain it grew remarkably. From 1934 through 1937, private enterprise built new houses at rates in excess of 250,000 per year, providing work for suppliers of construction materials, the building trades, furniture makers, and appliance manufacturers. A fair number of these were shoddily built but preferable to what they replaced. By the summer of 1939, experts estimated that Britain since the end of the World War had constructed four million privately built and publicly subsidized houses, effectively rehousing half the population.[11]

The National government's approach to the Depression may have featured fiscal conservatism, but it was neither frugal (in the sense of minimal expenditures) nor socially callous. Insisting on balanced budgets, it was nonetheless activist in its support of benefits for the dispossessed and its sense that the state had a large role to play in managing the economy. It practiced a style of socially aware conservatism that some observers called "Tory Socialism."[12]

Publicly-owned "council housing" aimed primarily at the working class proceeded at an impressive rate. Local authorities, working with substantial parliamentary subsidies, built most such worker housing. From the end of the World War, there had been bipartisan agreement that the British housing stock was in dire need of upgrading. Conservatives were scarcely less enthusiastic than Labour or Liberals on the point, whether it involved replacing rural shacks with neat white two-chimney farmhouses on the Isle of Skye or tearing down filthy and decrepit slums in Birmingham for new row housing. Adding to previous legislation, the National government passed a new slum clearance act in 1933 and an Overcrowding Act in 1935. Under these and previous programs, it subsidized the building of about a half-million council houses.[13]

In the United States, New Deal agencies such as the Public Works Administration (PWA) or the Resettlement Administration (RA) or the Tennessee Valley Authority (TVA) directly managed the construction of new housing for clients, sometimes planned whole communities, and served as administrator or landlord of the finished product. But it was not until 1937 that the Wagner Housing Act specifically targeted urban slum dwellings for replacement and established a U.S. Housing Authority. In Britain, civil servants in the Ministry of Health administered housing grants with little publicity and made no effort at national coordination or the establishment of priorities. In both countries, progress was uneven and depended on the activism of local officials. Critics at the time and since have rightly observed that at best the British program left hundreds of thousands still living in unfit quarters by the fall of 1939, but few can doubt that it also improved the lot of other hundreds of thousands. The National government increased housing expenditures every year of its existence and, with a population a third that of the United States, subsidized ten times as much public housing as the various New Deal programs.

In the spring of 1937, the *Economist* nevertheless complained that the government's definition of the slum problem was too limited. "Courageous measures" such as the development of self-contained suburban cities were nowhere to be seen. The government needed to impose central planning on industrial development and the housing that accompanied it. Such a conclusion was strong testimony to the grip that ideals of top-down planning and impersonal direction of the lives of the masses achieved on social reformers in the 1930s, but Britain's broader political culture long had preferred step-at-a-time change and individual freedom to sweeping rationalist reconstructions of existing arrangements.[14]

The government pursued other forms of public works also. Britain's communications and transportation infrastructure, like that of the United States and Germany, needed enormous investment in the 1930s. Responding to Lloyd George's (and by extension Keynes's) call for massive spending on such projects, Chamberlain reminded them that, in addition to already-accomplished housing legislation, the government had spent £34 million on a national telephone system. In 1933 it had effectively nationalized the London transport system (tubes, buses, and trams) and improved it to the tune of £35 million in loan guarantees. Run by a state-appointed board, the new system was effectively a socialist institution. It had been established by a predominantly Conservative administration motivated by the practical need to move ten million people around an enormous metropolitan era.[15] London Transport was not an exercise in Keynesian stimulus; but neither was it inconsequential in providing employment.

There is considerable merit in considering the United States during the first two years of the New Deal as a country with an enormous emergency employment relief policy and no long-term social policy. There is equal merit to the generalization that the situation in Britain was the reverse. But generalizations always need qualification. If public works in Britain never achieved an American scale, there were nonetheless many more such projects than generally understood—in part because they often were offshoots of ongoing public policy, in part because they were generally small in individual scale, in part because the government executed them with a lack of fanfare that would have been unimaginable in American politics.

American conservatives (mostly in the Republican party) vehemently rejected state interference in the economy. In Britain, a conservative government engaged in economic management of a type the country had not seen for a century, save for the World War. It fostered state-underwritten marketing cooperatives (first authorized by the Labour government in 1931) to support commodity prices. In 1932, an act of Parliament subsidized wheat production, the first in a series of enactments that underwrote livestock farming, milk production, and sugar beets among other commodities. In sharp contrast to the U.S. New Deal, however, the program sought to increase production rather than reduce it. The agricultural policies of Britain, the United States and (for a time) Nazi Germany all had the common objective of keeping farmers on the land away from glutted urban job markets. All tapped into national traditions by romanticizing farm life. All talked about (but never achieved) large-scale rural resettlement.

Britain acted with an eye toward greater self-sufficiency, albeit in the knowledge that it could never produce enough to feed itself. The imperial preference system established at Ottawa facilitated agricultural imports from within the Empire/Commonwealth, but special arrangements also had to be made for other trading partners within the sterling bloc, especially Denmark and Argentina. The task of encouraging increased domestic production, while juggling import quotas for preferred foreign nations, was both difficult and inefficient. The agricultural budget rocketed. Free market thinkers ridiculed the enterprise as a massive tax on the British population. Food prices moved up slightly despite the deflationary bias of the larger economy. The cost of agricultural support in terms of outright subsidies, tax breaks, and increased costs to consumers, about £45 million in 1934, reached approximately £100 million by 1939.[16]

It never occurred to the National government to organize the entire economy, NRA style. What it was willing to do (rather like the United States after the NRA was ruled unconstitutional) was to support in various ways industries in distress. The Import Duties Advisory Committee, a rough counterpart of the U.S. Tariff Commission, godfathered a steel cartel that established domestic production quotas and bargained with continental steel cartels on imports to Britain and exports to the European countries. The result was a contraction in British steel production until 1937, when defense production began in earnest. A similar managed decline took place in shipbuilding along with loan subsidies for new merchant shipping to keep surviving yards alive. The Cotton Spinning Act of 1936 codified a government-business agreement to cut capacity in cotton textiles; in 1939 further legislation established minimum prices and output quotas. District quotas for coal production perhaps distributed misery more fairly than otherwise would have been the case, but mine owners resisted reduction of capacity. In an important symbolic act in 1938, the government nationalized coal royalty payments (providing for restitution to the owners of the royalty rights) with the understanding that the proceeds would be used to help reshape the industry and provide for the welfare of the workers. All this amounted less to a grand plan than piece-by-piece short-run interest group politics. Consolidation of weak industries may have contributed to efficiency, but subsidies institutionalized inefficiency and consumed resources that might have been better deployed. It is doubtful that government policy created many new jobs or put money into workers' pockets. As was the case with the NRA, it may have gotten in the way of a healthy recovery.[17]

Although the government had cut the pound loose from gold, it did not ignore the currency. Sterling briefly had fallen as low as $3.40, giving

British industry some foreign trade benefit. Roosevelt's dollar devaluation of 1933 swiftly reversed that development, sending the pound back into a range of around $5.00. Chamberlain was content to keep it there, and he clearly saw resumption of the gold standard as a briar patch to be avoided. Government policy was to let the pound "float" within a narrow band against other currencies—and to guarantee it would stay there with a substantial stabilization fund that could be used to support the national currency if the money markets became too volatile. Perhaps the most important result was to maintain sterling as a strong basis for the international trading and financial bloc attuned to London. Imperial preference and the sterling bloc provided some stability for commonwealth members, colonies, and client nations, thereby contributing to British geopolitical interests in areas ranging from Norway to Portugal, New Zealand to South Africa, but the home results were not necessarily positive. Britain was a net importer within the bloc because the dominions found ways of protecting their industries against competition from the "mother country." Moreover, a strong pound, although probably less consequential than worldwide tariff barriers, depressed British exports outside the sterling bloc.[18]

The British recovery, then, was a home market recovery, driven by domestic consumption, most noticeable in newer industries that enjoyed a measure of tariff protection. The older sectors that had needed foreign sales to flourish—coal, steel, shipbuilding, textiles—limped along, fighting against their counterparts in other nations, demanding (and generally receiving) protection, subsidies, or government-sanctioned cartel arrangements. These kept the best-managed companies alive, but could not solve a more general problem that required a revival of an open international trading system. Democratic statesmen on both sides of the Atlantic routinely gave lip service to the ideal while ignoring it in practice. Astoundingly, it was not until 1938 that the United States and Britain finally got around to negotiating a trade agreement under the American reciprocal trade program. Neither side had been much interested in doing so until the probability of war in Europe forced a recognition of larger mutual interests.

Even after an economic recovery that brought Britain back close to where the country had been in 1930, the depressed areas ("special areas") harbored a million and a half workers trapped in states of perpetual joblessness. The government thrashed around in search of solutions, even floating back-to-the-land schemes that never got past the talking stages.

In truth there was no simple answer for economic obsolescence and the devastation left in its wake, whether in Yorkshire or in West Virginia. At the beginning of 1937, President Roosevelt would declare a third of his nation ill-housed, ill-clad, ill-nourished. Britain was no worse off. And the German recovery, so superficially impressive, rested on a level of deprivation and unfreedom that no democratic society would ever accept. As late as 1937, definitions of "recovery" in each of the world's three largest economies were necessarily modest and would remain so in the absence of an open international trading system.

The National government presents an obvious challenge to any interpreter thinking in sharp, easily defined ideological terms. From an American perspective, it might be said to have combined a Hooverian fiscal policy with Rooseveltian social welfarism but without New Deal–style public works. Speaking to an assembly of London bankers in October 1934, a time at which the American New Deal seemed to be running out of steam and German unemployment remained as severe as England's, Neville Chamberlain scoffed at his critics, observing that their "favorite instrument of chastisement, namely, a comparison between the wretched conditions prevailing here and the glowing prosperity elsewhere, has not been very easy to discover." And even if an unfavorable comparison could be made with another nation, "it may well be what is right and proper for an old, highly developed country like ours is quite unsuitable for a newer community whose people are less experienced and perhaps less patient." Admitting with more than a trace of pride that the government's policies had lacked drama, he declared they had "delivered the goods." The implicit contrast with Roosevelt—or Hitler—was all the more obvious for being left unstated. In the House of Commons four months later, Chamberlain delivered a blunt rebuff to Lloyd George's call for large-scale public works: "I would tell those of you who call on the government to be bold and courageous and to start out on new adventures, that you are playing with fire. . . . This policy of providing public work always fails."[19]

The steady-as-you-go, balance-the-books attitude was quintessential Chamberlain in its Establishment arrogance and smug superiority, but it was also very British. Where Hoover, expressing the classical nineteenth-century liberal side of his brain, had recoiled from direct relief, Chamberlain and the entire Conservative leadership accepted as given that the government had to provide at least minimal relief for the jobless, recognized public housing for the poor as a national necessity, and actively sought support from the working class. British workers, for their part, generally accepted the dole, despite episodes of discontent with its administration, as insurance payments preferable to public works projects. England's national history played a role in their perception. "Work offered them by public authority, which they would not have been able to refuse and retain their eligibility," Bentley Gilbert has written, "would have been unpleasantly similar to the ancient labour test required by the Poor Law."[20] In that context, Chamberlain's budgets and National social policy could seem at once conservative and caring.

Stanley Baldwin, the government's other major face, seemed the personification of John Bull to many Americans—an Englishman's Englishman who talked endlessly of the glories of his nation and the beauty of its landscape. But Baldwin also cast himself as a spokesman for freedom, democracy, and liberal values. More pervasive in Britain than in any major continental country, these concepts gave the United Kingdom and the United States a common ground far more important than differences of custom and geography. In his domestic political rhetoric, Baldwin depicted the National government as the authentic voice of a middle way between "a dictatorship of the Left and an autocracy of the Right." A product of consensual cabinet government, he was apprehensive not only of Hitler, Mussolini, and Stalin but from time to time of what appeared to him to be the strong-armed leadership of Franklin Roosevelt. England, he declared in 1935, had become "the torchbearer of ordered freedom in Europe." In his rhetoric and public image, he personified the way in which the bedrock values of classical conservatism and classical liberalism were all mixed together in British politics. If the result was a muddle, it was a natural one, inherent in English history. Baldwin's eloquent expression of his personal values and success in tying them to a parliamentary program gave his government a strong claim to a political center midway between the reactionaries of his own Conservative party and the socialist Labourites of the left. The muddle of conservatism and liberalism which he and Chamberlain formulated established itself as a viable alternative to a more radical middle way promoted by Keynes and Lloyd George.[21]

Franklin Roosevelt admitted as much in a fireside chat on "government and modern capitalism," September 30, 1934. Responding to American critics who contrasted Britain's gathering recovery with the American economic stall, he declared: "England has her peculiarities and we have ours, but I do not believe any intelligent observer can accuse

England of undue orthodoxy in the present emergency." The British government had made a virtue of being forced off the gold standard and had refunded its debt at a lower interest rate with the cooperation of the banking community. It had been in the vanguard of social reform. "Is it not a fact that ever since the year 1909, Great Britain in many ways has advanced further along lines of social security than the United States? Is it not a fact that relations between capital and labor on the basis of collective bargaining are much further advanced in Great Britain than in the United States?" It was not strange that the British conservative press had characterized the New Deal as "only an attempt to catch up with English reforms that go back ten years or more." Roosevelt made these points primarily to fend off charges of radicalism and to help prepare the country for his developing social security program; he also appears to have meant them sincerely.[22]

<hr />

Britain had no Tennessee Valley Authority, no huge dams or enormous bridges in its public works portfolio. But it did have the *Queen Mary,* a monumental project that demonstrated both the government's interest in managing industrial consolidation and its adeptness at exploiting nationalistic sentiments. In 1930, Cunard lines had begun work on a new flagship passenger liner, but in December 1931, the company, its finances reeling from the Depression, suspended construction. For two years, with Cunard unable to raise capital in the private financial markets, the keel lay untouched in the largely shut-down John Brown shipyards near Glasgow. Cunard, in the meantime, attempted to deal with the problem of North Atlantic overcapacity by acquiring its great rival White Star. In late 1933, with the new Cunard keel threatening to become a rusted shipyard hulk and negotiations with White Star at an impasse, the government intervened. Without a merger, both large companies faced possible ruin, an event that would intensify still widespread economic misery and damage national morale.

Cries for work in economically battered Scotland dovetailed perfectly with national economic imperatives. With some government encouragement and an offer not to be refused of a £9.5 million loan for ship construction, the two lines assented to a merger. The shipbuilding machinery at John Brown, well-oiled by the Treasury, went back to work in April 1934. At the government's behest Cunard No. 524 acquired the name of King George V's consort, *Queen Mary.* Chamberlain, in the words of

Keith Feiling, defended the subsidy as part of a policy "to concentrate assistance on revenue-producing schemes or purposes of public import."[23]

The work at John Brown provided direct employment for 4,000 men, the majority of them skilled and semiskilled craftsmen. The project, moreover, drew on components manufactured elsewhere through the efforts of many hundreds of workers, perhaps as many as two thousand.[24] A Keynesian analyst could justly have invoked the multiplier effect of public works spending and argued that one additional job was indirectly created by every instance of direct employment. Even so, a possible 12,000 jobs for 24 months at the cost of £9,500,000 averaged out to approximately £395 per job per year, thus providing vindication to Chamberlain and others who argued that the cost of providing publicly financed employment for 1.5 to 2 million jobless was beyond the capabilities of the government.

The decision to subsidize the *Queen Mary* had a strong symbolic justification. Celebrating the British monarchy, the great ship quickly became a source of national pride. When she set off from Southampton on her maiden voyage, May 27, 1936 (one day after the birthday of her namesake), 250,000 spectators lined the shore. Widely praised for her grace and speed at home and abroad, she broke the transatlantic speed record at the end of her first summer. She had, the *Economist* mused, paralleled tumultuous and difficult years in British history. "In 1929–30 she was born at a time of national optimism. In 1931 she was abandoned in a mood of despair. In 1934 came the day of re-awakening, and in 1936 of triumph. What will the next chapter bring?"[25]

What indeed? The year 1935 raised the question in another way. It was George V's Silver Jubilee year, a happenstance that the government exploited to the utmost. The King had ascended to the throne in 1910 with Britain still at the high noon of its world ascendancy, led the country through the Great War, presided over the coming of mass democracy in the 1920s, and weathered the Depression from which the country was emerging. His father, Edward VII, had favored the Continent to England and spent abundant time there as the most famous of privileged playboys during his long tenure as Prince of Wales; George V lived in bourgeois connubiality with his Queen. In the war, he had changed the name of the British ruling dynasty from Saxe-Coburg and Gotha to Windsor.* He had

---

* "Saxe-Coburg and Gotha" was the Germanic dynasty of his grandfather and consort of Queen Victoria, Prince Albert.

made more frequent public appearances than any other monarch, had demonstrated distaste for the resorts of the Continent and preference for the hunting lodges of the English and Scottish countryside, had spoken on the radio in the rich, well-modulated voice of a king, who nonetheless, the *Economist* would put it several months later, "was a friendly person talking in homely language from his fireside to his people." In many ways, he had shown himself to be a quintessential Englishman, a hardworking exemplar of middle-class morality.

Most Britons respected him. With economic recovery mounting in the spring of 1935, most were ready for pageantry and celebration. Done up with royal pomp and featuring celebrations that ranged from grand balls to street dances, the Jubilee was observed in every British town and throughout the Empire. The effect was rather as if Noel Coward's *Cavalcade* had been revived for a roving engagement in the streets of one city after another. On May 6, the twenty-fifth anniversary of his accession, the King with his Queen, riding in a grand procession from Buckingham Palace to St. Paul's Cathedral, received the cheers of perhaps a million spectators who lined the streets. He appeared later at the balcony of the palace to acknowledge a crowd of 50,000, then broadcast his thanks to the Empire and Commonwealth. More than a good party, the Jubilee was a national catharsis, expressing the sense that Britain was one nation, united behind a king who had embraced the democratic spirit.[26]

Eight and a half months after the procession to St. Paul's, the King died. The event seemed to many all the more portentous because it came just three days after the death of Rudyard Kipling. The royal funeral brought forth yet another outpouring of patriotism, common memories, and tributes. Even more clearly than the Jubilee, the eulogies of the old monarch made it clear that his people imagined him as very much like a typical successful middling Englishman who, rather than standing apart from his countrymen, was a living representation of all their best values. Perhaps the most eloquent—surely the most widely heard—such eulogy came from Stanley Baldwin, who had succeeded MacDonald as prime minister six months earlier. In a worldwide radio broadcast, he was at once sincere and maudlin as he spoke of the king's happy marriage, his attachment to his family, his incessant toil at his job, his success at winning the hearts of a democratic people. His closing words, more meaningful in retrospect than they seemed at the time, summarized the legacy of the old king to his son, now Edward VIII: "He earned the loyalty and respect of all parties. . . . He hands down to his son the throne . . . with its foundations strengthened, its moral authority, its honour, and its dignity enhanced. It is an incomparable and awe-inspiring inheritance. The young King knows the confidence we all repose in him." Before the year was out, Edward must have wondered if these sentences were a warning shot.[27]

King George died two months after the National government had consolidated an electoral revolution. Few would have predicted its sweeping return to power in early 1935. During its first years in office, the government was at best tolerated and respected by the people, loved by very few. It was utterly devoid of the democratic charisma that one could find in the New Deal. Most Britons found Franklin Roosevelt exciting almost from the day he took office. Opposition leaders from the Labour party or Lloyd George (representing mainly himself) clamored for a "New Deal" for Britain, whether that meant the establishment of an NRA or a huge public works program.[28] Instead, the National government provided a long difficult trek—two steps forward, one back—from 1931 to mid-1935, providing a wearying experience for a British population that could have no assurance of future prosperity.

The government labored under the handicap of having to provide leadership without charisma. Baldwin was capable of producing oratory that might temporarily lift the national spirit, but no one accused him of consistent dynamism. Much of Britain had a deep affection for him; the House of Commons listened to his speeches with unusual respect; the Conservative caucus mostly accepted him as a respected leader. But for most of the government's first four years he was not a visible leader at the helm. The non-Conservative leaders—MacDonald and Simon—were burned-out mediocrities in the minds of many. Chamberlain was as drab as he was capable, which is to say "very."

The government was at least fortunate in its critics. The Conservative party's most exciting personality, Winston Churchill, behaved more as a member of the opposition, leading the struggle against dominion status for India and often criticizing other government policies from positions that defied prediction. Lloyd George roared impressively but futilely, failing in the end to convince the Conservative leaders that he was the British answer to Roosevelt. Both he and Churchill had by this time established reputations as erratic, opportunistic, and altogether self-serving in their complaints. Impressive perhaps to a certain kind of voter, they seemed to most unsound, unprincipled, and in the end unpersuasive as alternatives to the gray steadiness of the incumbents. The Labour party, under Arthur Henderson and George Lansbury, remained saddled with the failures of 1931, the label of "socialism," and a dogmatic pacifism that put off even a peace-minded British citizenry. The Liberals, half in the government, half in opposition, had long since ceased to be a viable alternative.

The appearance on the far right of Sir Oswald Mosley's British Union of Fascists (BUF) was probably good for the government also. Mosley was a dynamic figure, no doubt about that. He and his black-shirted followers attracted a lot of attention and precipitated even more disorder, whether searching for Jews and Communists to brutalize or attempting to fend off the attacks of angry leftists themselves. Mosley was too charismatic to be ignored, but his career path from the Conservative party to Labour to his evanescent New party to his Fascist organization was hard to take seriously. Few believed his claim that the BUF had 500,000 members.

Interviewing Mosley in 1934, Clair Price concluded that he had been in the presence of a spoiled egocentric, who had traveled to the fringes of British politics. "He is showy, spectacular, perhaps a bit unstable. He has everything—everything but dogged patience and selfless humility." Surrounded by acolytes in his imposing Chelsea headquarters, the Fascist leader seemed impressive—until one got a few blocks away and back in touch with reality. The Mother of Parliaments, Price concluded, had little to fear from him. In fact, the government was already laying plans to ban paramilitary uniforms. In the fall of 1935, the Fascists admitted their insignificance by declining to put up any candidates for Parliament. Mosley's major function in politics was to establish a menace on the right that gave credibility to Baldwin's claim that the National government was the middle way. He also confirmed an underlying prejudice of British life—that the brilliant and flashy political leaders were erratic and authoritarian.[29]

All the same, at the beginning of 1935, the recovery appeared to be stalling and the government largely composed of uninspiring men. MacDonald had become a shadow of his former self, frequently unable to respond coherently to questions in Parliament. The bureaucracy was maladministering new rules of eligibility for the dole. It seemed that Lloyd George might be needed simply to give some appearance of direction to a rudderless administration. In March, Neville Chamberlain wrote in his diary: "I am more and more carrying this government on my back. The P.M. [MacDonald] is ill and tired, S.B. [Stanley Baldwin] is tired and won't apply his mind to problems. It is certainly time there was a change."

Chamberlain, of course, thought he should be at the head of that change, but his description of the situation was not inaccurate.[30]

What a difference a few months of improving employment figures made! What a change in mood with spring and the celebration of the King's Jubilee! At the beginning of June, Baldwin took over as prime minister, relegated MacDonald to the symbolic post of lord president, and engineered a cabinet reshuffle that injected some relatively youthful energy into the government, primarily in the persons of Sir Samuel Hoar at the Foreign Office and Anthony Eden as minister for League of Nations Affairs. Chamberlain remained as the indispensable man at the Exchequer. The meaning of Baldwin's decision to assume power was unmistakable. An election loomed in the fall, one year before it was legally required.[31]

Most observers expected that the campaign would see a return to traditional politics, but Baldwin insisted on maintaining the National coalition, understanding that, however nominal it might be, it would still appeal to independent voters. Chamberlain agreed. Every serious prognosticator knew the government would win. The Liberal party was shattered beyond repair. Lloyd George raged ineffectually against the government. The Labour party seemed a bigger threat, but internal divisions on whether to support sanctions against Italy's invasion of Abyssinia erupted into public display at its convention in early October, just a week before Baldwin set a November 14 election date. When the convention decided in favor of sanctions, the party's pacifist leader, George Lansbury, resigned. His replacement, Clement Attlee, struck most watchers as an unimposing little man likely to be displaced after the election by the trade union leader Ernest Bevin or the head of the London County Council, Herbert Morrison.[32]

Labour, supplemented by the fiery speeches of Lloyd George, attacked the government as stingy, uncaring, and failing to achieve complete economic recovery. The National response was summed up by Baldwin, who declared that Britain was "the happiest, the most prosperous, and the most envied of all nations" and that a victory for the Labour party, "committed to the most extreme forms of Socialism, would spell nothing but economic chaos and disaster."[33]

The results were another landslide, only slightly less impressive than that of 1931. The National coalition won 53.3 percent of the vote and elected 429 members of parliament, 387 of whom were Conservatives, quite a few of them elected in working class districts. Labour trailed far

CHAMPION CAMPAIGNER, 1932

Wheeling, West Virginia, October 19, 1932. CORBIS

Near Warm Springs, Georgia, October 23, 1932. FRANKLIN D. ROOSEVELT LIBRARY

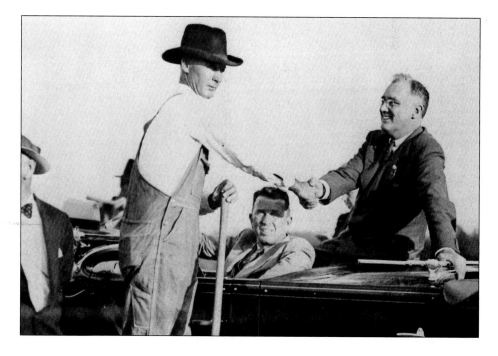

Panic! Run on a bank, early 1933. FRANKLIN D. ROOSEVELT LIBRARY

President and First Lady, the White House, 1933. FRANKLIN D. ROOSEVELT LIBRARY

Washington, D.C. soup kitchen, 1935. FRANKLIN D. ROOSEVELT LIBRARY

Down and out in America, 1935. FRANKLIN D. ROOSEVELT LIBRARY/DOROTHEA LANGE

PWA project: New York's Triborough Bridge. FRANKLIN D. ROOSEVELT LIBRARY

Eleanor Roosevelt visits a WPA Negro nursery school, Des Moines, Iowa, June 8, 1936. FRANKLIN D. ROOSEVELT LIBRARY

First Fan, April 24, 1934. FRANKLIN D. ROOSEVELT LIBRARY

Fireside Chat, April 28, 1935. FRANKLIN D. ROOSEVELT LIBRARY

(above) FDR visits a CCC camp in Virginia's Shenandoah Valley, August 12, 1933. Seated, left to right: Maj. Gen. Paul B. Malone, Louis McHenry Howe, Harold Ickes, Robert Fechner (Emergency Conservation Work director), FDR, Henry Wallace, Rexford Tugwell. FRANKLIN D. ROOSEVELT LIBRARY

Family business, Blue Eagle. FRANKLIN D. ROOSEVELT LIBRARY

(facing, bottom) CCC workers clear burned-over land. FRANKLIN D. ROOSEVELT LIBRARY

Strike! Minneapolis teamsters clash with police, 1934. FRANKLIN D. ROOSEVELT LIBRARY

Media politics, British style. National government leaders Stanley Baldwin, Ramsay MacDonald, and Sir John Simon stand next to one of 11 "cinema vans" set to tour the country with a film highlighting the government's achievements, June 22, 1934. The poster claims 742,000 new jobs. CORBIS

Dissenting from center-left, John Maynard Keynes. HULTON ARCHIVE/GETTY IMAGES

Aspirant to power. Chancellor Adolf Hitler greets President Paul von Hindenburg at the Garrison Church, March 21, 1933. HULTON ARCHIVE/GETTY IMAGES

Absolute ruler. Reichsführer Hitler, Buckeberg, October 1934. HULTON ARCHIVE/GETTY IMAGES

Hitler in a typical pose, taken while he was chancellor of Germany, February 1933 to August 1934. CORBIS

Leading henchmen: Hermann Göring, Julius Streicher, and Joseph Goebbels, Nuremberg, September 1937. HULTON ARCHIVE/GETTY IMAGES

The Nazi Olympiad, Berlin, August 1, 1936.

The people's car. Hitler speaks at the foundation-laying of a Volkswagen factory, Fallersleben, May 27, 1938.

On the campaign trail again, Charlotte, North Carolina, September 10, 1936.

"More Security for the American Family."

Rural electrification.

HARNESSING THE WATERS

TVA project: Norris Dam, January 1937. FRANKLIN D. ROOSEVELT LIBRARY

PWA project: Bonneville Dam under construction, October 1936.
FRANKLIN D. ROOSEVELT LIBRARY

PERSISTENT POVERTY

Eighteen-year-old migrant worker and child in a California camp.

Rural Alabama school. Note picture of FDR at upper right.

FDR AND FRIENDS (CLOCKWISE, FROM TOP)

George Cardinal Mundelein, November 18, 1932. FRANKLIN D. ROOSEVELT LIBRARY

Henry Morgenthau, Jr., February 9, 1934. FRANKLIN D. ROOSEVELT LIBRARY

Fiorello La Guardia, August 27, 1938. FRANKLIN D. ROOSEVELT LIBRARY

(above) "Peace in our time." Neville Chamberlain, just back from Munich, displays his agreement with Hitler, September 30, 1938. HULTON ARCHIVE/GETTY IMAGES

(below, left) Alliance in the making. Queen Elizabeth, King George VI, and FDR, June 1939. HULTON ARCHIVE/GETTY IMAGES

(below, right) Winston Churchill and Anthony Eden walking to the House of Commons, August 29, 1939, three days before the start of World War II. HULTON ARCHIVE/GETTY IMAGES

behind with 38 percent and 154 MPs. The Liberals followed with 6.7 percent and 21 MPs. In 1931, Baldwin had managed the greatest triumph in twentieth-century British political history; four years later, he led his party and the coalition he had formed around it to the second greatest such victory, both of them highly personal.

The 1935 election occurred at a time of disquieting threats to peace. Britain faced an aggressive and hostile Japan in the Far East, a resurgent Germany in the heart of Europe, and an Italy bent on imperial greatness. The nation responded with slender resources, inconstant allies, and a growing national mood of denial. By late 1935, foreign policy and national defense were at least as important politically as the economy. Yet they competed for attention and funds with such domestic needs as better housing and redevelopment of the "special areas." The memory of 1914–18 hung over every discussion of the country's place in European politics. Weak and acutely aware of it, Britain responded to external threat by invoking old tradition and recent ideal.

The old tradition was based on the nation's insular isolation from the Continent, the sense of cultural difference that went with it, and the doctrine that the prime British interest in mainland Europe was to preserve the balance of power there while avoiding a mass military presence or binding alliances. The recent ideal, which would become the constant refuge of the weak in the twentieth century, was the concept of collective security embodied in an international organization enforcing international law and morality. The flaws in hindsight are obvious. Collective security required a widely shared sense of purpose and common interest which would have made an international body unnecessary. International bodies by their nature produced legalistic quibbling and worked against unequivocal moral judgment. In practice, "collective security" fostered the hope that someone else would provide the security the collective needed.

The crisis of 1931 and its aftermath had established certain Depression-driven imperatives. To preserve a gold-free pound and keep interest rates low, the national budget had to be balanced. The exercise required painful cuts everywhere, including the military. As recovery slowly set in, social decency, mass democratic opinion, and political calculation all coalesced to require tax decreases, improved social benefits, restoration of full pay for public employees, and subsidies for economic interest groups of all sorts. The military got scarcely a nod.

Behind all this was an intense longing for peace—at almost any price. On February 9, 1933, ten days after Hitler had come to power in Germany, the Oxford Union concluded a spirited debate by voting 275–153 to accept the resolution that "this House will in no circumstance fight for its King and Country." The Union was simply a debating society, its membership composed of immature young people. It had no official standing as a voice of Oxford University, as a policy advocate, or as a political organization. All the same, the resolution had a wide impact. Oxford was a bastion of a privileged establishment, its students future leaders of the country. This was no socialist working class manifesto to be greeted with scorn and horror. Rather it represented, if a bit extremely, an antiwar sentiment widespread among the middle and upper classes. When Winston Churchill's son, Randolph, and other alumni members attempted to secure a reversal, they were defeated by a much larger vote of 750–138; thereupon a gang of young "pacifists" bent on divesting young Churchill of his trousers sent him scurrying for refuge. Many Britons and probably most foreign observers took the Union resolution as a telling indicator of the nerve of the ruling elites.[34]*

A few months later, another event seemed to confirm the existence of a rising tide of pacifism. A parliamentary by-election in the East Fulham district of London produced a superficially astonishing 5,000-vote Labour victory. Although the district had been inclined toward Labour in the 1920s, the Conservatives had carried it by 14,000 votes in the October 1931 general election. Dispassionate observers might persuasively find numerous explanations for the result. No one could gainsay, however, that the Conservative had been a vociferous advocate of increased military spending and that the Labour challenger had skirted the edges of pacifism. The *Times* of London commented dourly that in the absence of more credible issues, "the Labour Party will use every effort to further the idea that parties can be divided into 'peace men' on the one hand and

---

* The commentary of two historians who lived through the period perhaps merits special interest. A. J. P. Taylor remarks, there may be "no documentary evidence that foreign governments noticed it or drew from it the moral that Great Britain had ceased to count in the world." But Charles Loch Mowat seems to have the better case in his judgment that it "received world-wide notice . . . as a sign of Britain's pacifism and decadence which was an encouragement to dictators abroad." Charles Loch Mowat, *Britain between the Wars, 1918–1940* (Chicago: University of Chicago Press, 1955), 422, 537, and A. J. P. Taylor, *English History, 1914–1945* (New York and London: Oxford University Press, 1965), 362.

'war mongers' on the other." It was easy to attribute great importance to the antiwar component of the outcome. The message, as Stanley Baldwin would later admit, went directly to the top.[35]

The widespread sentiment for peace translated into a national consensus in favor of disarmament and wide hopes for the long-running arms reduction talks at Geneva until Nazi Germany effectively scuttled the Geneva conference in the fall. Thereafter, dominant opinion in the country transferred its hopes to the League of Nations. The League provided an effective umbrella for numerous shades of sentiment ranging from outright pacifism to inward-looking social reformism, all in rough accord on the need to hold down military spending. Collective security and lower military spending were articles of faith among the Labour party and the Liberal opposition.

The National government did little to fight the sentiment. Prime Minister MacDonald was an ardent proponent of any mechanism that held out hope of international conciliation. Foreign secretary Sir John Simon, a jurist uncomfortable with the realities of power, was a strong League supporter and advocate of disarmament.[36] Chamberlain, as chancellor of the exchequer, was locked into a position in which it was natural for him to view the military as simply one of many claimants whose requests for increased budget lines had to be denied in the name of fiscal responsibility. He seemed more practical than his idealistic colleagues, but in his heart, as events would demonstrate, he shared their desperate hopes. Stanley Baldwin as Conservative party leader was probably the most clear-eyed of the lot, but also acutely cognizant of the need for coalition unity, doubtless convinced that the government would do better for the defense of the realm than a more pacifist opposition, and inclined to tack cautiously against prevailing winds.

In mid-1934, after the aborted Nazi putsch in Austria, Baldwin spoke solemnly to a hushed House of Commons. Advocating already budgeted increases for the Royal Air Force, he declared: "Since the day of the air the old frontiers are gone, and when you think of the defense of England you no longer think of the white cliffs of Dover, but you think of the Rhine. That is where today our frontier lies." Baldwin's speech, and the enlarged air budget, seemed to indicate that Britain was alive to a rising menace and that it would be an active participant in continental politics. In fact, Baldwin's rhetorical flourish was no indication of actual policy.[37]

In the months after his dramatic speech, a coalition of peace and pro-League groups carried out a remarkable door-to-door opinion survey.

Called the "Peace Ballot," it asked 11.627 million persons for a yes or no answer to a series of loaded questions. Should Britain remain in the League of Nations? Should there be arms reductions, even the abolition of military aircraft, by international agreement? Should the arms producers be put out of business by international agreement? Should nations confront aggressors by collective means, non-military if possible?

Not surprisingly, the answers were overwhelmingly in the affirmative. The formal announcement of the results to a packed meeting at Albert Hall in London generated extensive press coverage and discussion. Never mind that the sample had no scientific basis; that was inconsequential in an age just beginning to fathom modern polling techniques. Never mind that the questions were flagrantly leading and abstract in the extreme. Nearly twelve million people had spoken. As the *Economist* put it: "No political leader dare ignore such a decisive demonstration. Nor need any leader who is sincere in his profession of zeal for the collective system be afraid of being left without popular support if he attempts to turn that zeal into action."[38]

The League of Nations and the concept of collective security had become a warm and fuzzy mode of denial. For the most part, British political leaders assumed that economic sanctions, presumably enforced by all peace-loving nations in the form of a blockade, would bring down an aggressor. Thus it was unnecessary to worry about a buildup of military power. "Facade became reality," A. J. P. Taylor recalled a generation later. "Men believed the phrases which they heard and themselves used."[39]

From afar, in September 1935, a generally approving *New York Times* editorial mused over the incongruity of a government statement declaring that "the Admiralty ordered four more battleships to the Mediterranean today in pursuance of the plan urged in the Peace Ballot."[40] But problems of aggression and collective security had already tested both the League and British resolve. In the Far East, the Japanese rampage had moved beyond Manchuria. Nazi Germany was two and a half years into its emergence as an outlaw state. Given Italy's ambitions in Abyssinia and East Africa, the Mediterranean loomed as a trouble spot that might well demand the dispatch of battleships. In each case, the responses of the League and of Great Britain displayed both the limitations of liberal sentimentalism and the inadequacies of British power.

Relations with Japan served as an early case study that should have been instructive. Britain had many territorial and economic interests in China and the Western Pacific. Virtually every one of them faced challenges from a rising Japan. Proud and aggressive, technologically advanced, motivated by a sense of destiny, the Japanese Empire had built a strong military, spearheaded by a superb navy. Britain simply did not have the military resources to challenge Japan. The League of Nations responded to the Japanese subjugation of Manchuria by creating a special commission headed by the English statesman Lord Lytton. In late 1932, following a lengthy investigation, it issued a mild, after-the-fact repri-mand that effectively validated the conquest. Japan nonetheless gave notice of its intention to leave the League. It also by that time had under-taken an bloody occupation of Shanghai. In early 1933, its troops crossed the Manchurian border to begin operations in the northern Chinese province of Jehol.

All the same, British foreign policy continued not simply to pay lip ser-vice to the ideals of the League but to hope that these might actually achieve some realization. In the meantime, military weakness dictated a course summarized in a mid-1934 defense review: "our [Far Eastern] Empire security depends on the avoidance of hostilities with Japan." Efforts to improve relations seemed the only practical course. In the cir-cumstances of the early thirties, the reaction was understandable; unfor-tunately, it established a pattern instead of sounding an alarm.[41]

The rise of Nazi Germany made it absolutely necessary to relegate ten-sion with Japan to a secondary priority. But the British response to Ger-many also exhibited impulses that inhibited a strong policy. On the one hand, most Britons clearly loathed Nazism; it was perhaps the primary negative example implicit in Baldwin's assertion that Britain was carrying the torch of freedom. On the other, harsh nationalistic dictatorships were hardly uncommon in central and eastern Europe; even the Nazi regime could seem from afar to be simply an extreme example of a common type. Most Britons felt an affinity for German cousins who were ethnically closer to them than the French. Indeed, for most of the modern era, Eng-land's most frequent enemy had been France. During the Depression, relations between the two countries were prickly on a range of economic and financial issues, making a common foreign policy difficult. Many Britons believed that Germany had been treated with vengeful harshness by the Treaty of Versailles and Germany's chief oppressor for a decade and a half had been France. From there, it was but a step to the conclu-sion that to recognize Germany as an equal and make reasonable conces-sions to its legitimate demands was both a more moral and wiser course than perpetual suppression. Britain's role in Europe thus was not to side unequivocally with the French, but to serve as a balancing force between Germany and France, just as it might have done during the reign of Queen Victoria.

━━━━━

Government spokesmen made it clear that no formal alliance with France was contemplated. Most fundamentally, there was no way in the long run that democratic Britain could outspend totalitarian Germany on weaponry. In Britain, any government would still have to deal with trade-offs between rearmament and social programs, between the need to raise more money and the wrath of the taxpayers. Even after recovery had manifestly taken hold by late 1935, military spending still had to compete with such social needs as the continuing problem of the desolate industrial North and the demand for better council housing—issues pressed not simply by the Labour opposition but also by such pillars of the establishment as the Archbishops of York and Canterbury.[42] Germany, as its leaders made increasingly obvious, solved all such problems through the control mechanism of a fiercely coercive state.

Just weeks after the Nazis had taken control of Germany, Winston Churchill had begun criticizing the government's foreign policy. The main themes of his many eloquent speeches were the following: Nazism was a reversion to barbarism and a danger to the peace of Europe; rather than push France in the direction of arms reduction, England should thank God for the French army and move toward a closer relationship with Paris; and Britain needed to increase military expenditures drastically, giving first priority to its air power, second to the navy. Why did it require hindsight to recognize the message as prophetic?

Churchill's consignment to the fringe resulted from more than his willingness to fight a tide of wishful thinking. He had a long, erratic history. He had twice changed parties. He had abandoned a Conservative leadership position to make himself the primary spokesman against the National government's most enlightened international move, its determination to enact self-government for India. He was loosely associated with, but not the leader of, a band of about sixty maverick Tory "diehards" who refused to accept the party whip and were mostly too solidly entrenched to be deposed. They ranged from the senior member of Commons, Colonel John Gretton, a wealthy brewer who in appearance and demeanor might have been mistaken for Colonel Blimp, to Leo Amery, a Birmingham colleague of Chamberlain with a quick mind, no romantic illusions, and a thought-through conservative grasp of human nature. In terms of eloquence and talent, Churchill had no peer in the House; but even many of the diehards thought him unpredictable and perhaps motivated by ambition. His lack of the steadiness and consistency so valued in British political leadership cost him dearly in credibility.[43]

British military spending in the mid-1930s did increase substantially. The defense budget, £103.3 million in 1932, ballooned to £256.3 million in 1937, an increase of 148 percent. But over the same period German arms spending exploded from RM 720 million to RM 10,960 million, an increase in the range of 1,400 percent. Translated into pounds sterling at prevailing exchange rates, this was about twice the British expenditure. The British effort was far from piddling, but it was irrelevant as a deterrence to a Nazi regime bent on war and conquest.[44]

Wariness of Germany was combined with hope that the Nazis could be tamed and brought into a normal international system by a policy of concessions and relative tolerance. In 1935, the government had welcomed the huge Nazi victory in the Saar referendum, then had unilaterally concluded a naval treaty that conceded the German right to develop a navy thirty-five percent the size of Britain's. In March 1936, the cabinet decided against a strong protest of Germany's remilitarization of the Rhineland. All of these policies would have made sense in dealing with a traditional, civilized power. They displayed a fundamental misunderstanding of the Nazis. Moreover, each decision angered and demoralized the French, who possessed the only ground forces capable of resisting Germany. (It remained British military doctrine that the army would be relatively small, utilized for home and empire defense only, and would not be committed to a continental war.)[45]

Surprisingly, when the first crisis came, it was not in the heart of central Europe but in the Mediterranean and the horn of Africa. And it forced Britain to respond to aggression, not by Hitler, but by Benito Mussolini. The episode graphically displayed the tug between self-interest and realism on the one hand and moralism on the other. It also showed that the moralists still dominated the discussion.

Mussolini's Fascist regime in Italy presented European democracies with hard choices. On the one hand, it was thuggish and repugnant. On the other, it did not seem to constitute a major threat, had established itself as the major guarantor of Austrian independence after the assassination of Dolfuss in 1934, and was still a credible counterpoise to Germany in central Europe. France, concerned with Germany, had cultivated good relations with Italy and was anxious to preserve them. Meeting at Stresa, Italy, in April 1935, Prime Minister MacDonald, French Premier Pierre Laval, and Mussolini issued a joint declaration of support for the existing borders in Europe. The so-called "Stresa Front" thus emerged as a significant factor in British foreign policy.

As it became clear in mid-1935 that Italy was determined to conquer Abyssinia and make it a colony, Britain faced a choice between moralistic opposition or realistic accommodation. Abyssinia had a long history of independence and was a member of the League of Nations; it also was a despotism ruled by an emperor who had seized power in a coup d'etat, a state in which slavery was still openly practiced, and in reality more a collection of quasi-independent fiefdoms than a unified country. Britain had actually opposed its admission to the League in 1932. Geographically, Abyssinia was landlocked, cut off from the sea by Italian Eritrea to the north, the small colonies of French and British Somaliland to the east, and Italian Somaliland to the south. The Italians, who had suffered a humiliating defeat at Adowa forty years earlier, saw an opportunity for revenge and the consolidation of a sizable East African empire. At most, this could be a nuisance for the British position in the area, but no one thought it a danger. The British and French national interests in an independent Abyssinia were minimal.[46]

Hoping to avoid war and preserve some semblance of Abyssinian independence while acting in concert with France, London dispatched League of Nations minister Anthony Eden to Rome to offer Mussolini a deal that would countenance Italian occupation of part of Abyssinia and cede to Italy a corridor through British Somaliland to the port of Zeila. The Italians not only rejected the settlement but seemed encouraged in their aggressive spirit by the proffered appeasement. In Britain, the attentive public reacted negatively, preferring to see the Abyssinian nation as the helpless target of a rampaging bully. With an election coming in the fall, the government backtracked rapidly. Foreign Secretary Hoare and other leaders promised unconditionally to support the League, and by implication sanctions, if aggression developed. Such pronouncements, made as the Labour party went through a divisive debate on the sanctions issue, did much to consolidate the government's support in the weeks before the election.[47]

With the end of the rainy season, Italy began its invasion in early

October. What followed did the government little credit, but should also have put to rest faith in the League and collective security. With Britain unwilling to lead, France acting as a drag on any action, and neither the government nor the British public showing an appetite for military action, the League moved slowly, initiating numerous sanctions but holding off on an oil embargo. Neither Britain nor France ever contemplated denying Italy transit through the Suez Canal. Nor did either country provide any assistance to Abyssinia. Finally in December, with the Italians advancing steadily against their ill-armed opponents, the League voted in favor of an oil embargo. At almost the same point, it became known that Hoare and French Foreign Minister Pierre Laval had tendered a new and enlarged version of the previous summer's offer to Italy, basically offering to recognize Italian control of two-thirds of Abyssinia. Italy, assured of victory despite heavier than expected resistance, was not impressed. The British and French publics were outraged, and their governments shaken. Baldwin attempted to justify the proposal with a weak and rambling speech in the House of Commons. In the end, the government survived the storm with little damage. Hoare, the obvious designated scapegoat, resigned, to be replaced by Anthony Eden.

Historians for the next two generations would write that the Hoare-Laval plan doomed the League of Nations. In fact, it was more a symptom than a cause and never would have surfaced if the faith in the League had possessed a basis beyond wishful thinking. A stronger line against Italy would have carried the very real risk of a naval war with Italy in the Mediterranean and the certain rupture of the already fragile relationship with France. (Winston Churchill, who realistically saw Mussolini as a minor nuisance compared to Hitler, declared that Britain should simply back whatever the League decided, no more.[48]) That Italy had behaved as a bully was indisputable; that Abyssinians were worse off under Italian rule was much less certain.

British public faith in the League and in sanctions had never been accompanied by a fervor to employ military force. That was perhaps the major reason that the uproar passed so quickly. How long could the government be faulted for acting out a charade that public opinion had mandated? At least it was now increasingly understood that the League was ineffective, that Britain had to protect itself with whatever allies it could muster on a basis of common interest, and that greater military spending could not be avoided. In the messy process of getting there, however, Mussolini had been driven into the embrace of Hitler.

Could the government have acted earlier and more decisively? In a parliamentary exchange with Churchill on November 12, 1936, Baldwin tendered a reply that seemed devastating:

> I would remind the House that not once but on many occasions . . . when I have been speaking and advocating . . . the democratic principle, I have stated that a democracy is always two years behind the dictator. I believe that to be true. It has been true in this case.
>
> I put before the whole House my own views with an appalling frankness. From 1933, I and my friends were all very worried about what was happening in Europe. You will remember at that time the Disarmament Conference was sitting in Geneva. You will remember at that time there was probably a stronger pacifist feeling running through the country than at any time since the War. . . . You will remember the election at Fulham in the autumn of 1933, when a seat which the National Government held was lost by about 7,000 votes on no issue but the pacifist. . . .
>
> . . . I asked myself what chance was there . . . within the next year or two of that feeling being so changed that the country would give a mandate for rearmament. . . . does anyone think that this pacific democracy would have rallied to that cry at that moment! I cannot think of anything that would have made the loss of the election from my point of view more certain.[49]

From the perspective of World War II, the explanation was indeed appalling, a confession of opportunistic, unprincipled leadership to be contrasted with the stentorian exhortations of Churchill. But as an explanation of the situation in which Baldwin had to function as a leader, rather than a lone-wolf insurgent, it possessed considerably more merit than liberal-minded scholars, hesitant to criticize democracy, like to admit. Baldwin, like Franklin D. Roosevelt in the United States, felt little room for dramatic leadership when confronted with enormous popular revulsion against preparations for another war. Both men found it prudent for their careers and their parties to choose social spending over armaments and to defer to strong antiwar sentiments. Baldwin's increases in the defense budget during the period 1933–36 were, if insufficient, at least substantial. Roosevelt accomplished much less. Neither leader covered himself with glory, but perhaps it is understandable that both chose not to hand over the "peace issue" to parties likely to pursue even weaker military preparations. Both amply understood the reasons that Churchill was a voice in the wilderness during the 1930s.

In late May 1936, the *New York Times* carried a brief report that Colonel and Mrs. Charles Lindbergh had been guests at a small, glittering dinner party hosted by King Edward VIII at St. James's Palace. The only guests not to possess a great name were Mr. and Mrs. Ernest Simpson. The story noted briefly that the Simpsons, listed for the first time in the official Court Circular, "have long been known as intimate personal friends of the King before and after his accession." With no further attention to Mr. Simpson, it continued that Mrs. Simpson "has long been celebrated in London society for her charm and beauty and the distinguished friend-ships she has made here." The article said enough to allow those who read between the lines to understand that the intimate relationship was mainly between the King and Mrs. Simpson. A relatively closed coterie in Britain realized that the King had decided to make public an affair with an American woman, once divorced and encumbered with a second hus-band. Worse yet, it soon became clear that he intended to marry her.[50]

For all the sincere mourning at the death of George V, Britain had wel-comed Edward VIII. As Prince of Wales, he had been an idol throughout the Empire, combining the aura of royalty with a common touch that allowed him to relate to ordinary persons. In March 1936, he toured the slums of Glasgow, telling tenement dwellers that their homes were too small or they were paying too much rent; responding to a five-year-old waif who asked him if he were really the new king, he patted the boy on the head and responded, "Yes, little man, I am." He disarmed "red" anti-monarchist city council members by having tea with them. Workers putting the finishing touches on the *Queen Mary* at the John Brown ship-yard hailed him as "Good old Teddy." In November, he went to Wales, met with unemployed workers and their families in the same spirit of informality, displayed shock at their miserable conditions and declared "something must be done." Stung, Neville Chamberlain responded with a hasty speech detailing plans to provide help to depressed areas. Edward's sincere concern and good spirit were not in question, but did the King understand his role as a constitutional monarch?[51]

By then, Edward's relationship with Mrs. Simpson was open, her hus-band had receded into invisibility, and she was seeking an uncontested divorce. Gossip journalism all over Europe and America followed her every move and speculated about the prospect of her becoming Queen. But in Britain self-censorship and fear of the sedition laws produced a conspiracy of silence from the BBC and the press. Mrs. Simpson's divorce granted at Ipswich on October 27, to take effect in six months, made marriage a live possibility. On November 16, the King raised the eventuality with Baldwin. The prime minister attempted to demonstrate the impossibility of the project. He found Edward unshakably determined to wed the woman he loved, unwilling to heed contrary advice from cabinet ministers, his siblings, or his mother. Discussions between the King and politicians, among cabinet members, between Baldwin and church leaders, went on for the next two weeks. Somehow within Britain, the journalistic embargo stuck, although gossip disseminated over much of London. Finally, on December 3, the Bishop of Bradford criticized the King. The story could no longer be held back.[52]

The early twenty-first century mind, living in an altogether different moral universe and crammed with images of a dysfunctional, divorce-ridden royal family, naturally asks, what was the crisis? The English, whether they supported Edward or not, knew at once.

The crisis was moral. While it is a caricature to depict events as a struggle between romantic free spirits (the King and his vivacious lady) on the one hand and blue-nosed Victorians (Baldwin, church leaders, and assorted hypocrites) on the other, the moral issue was a salient, mainstream consideration. The idea of the King having a mistress was apparently not a problem for Baldwin or most of the other upper-crust establishment; the idea of him marrying her was an enormous issue. The Church of England, of which the king was ex officio head, did not recognize divorce; British law made it difficult and embarrassing. The nonconformist Protestant sects, especially important for their deep roots not simply in the middle class but in the culture of the working classes, were genuinely shocked at the idea of Britain's national symbol forging a union with a disreputable woman.[53]

The crisis was constitutional. The incongruity of the wife of the Defender of the Faith being twice-divorced was the least of it. Edward in numerous ways was challenging the British constitutional order. It seemed doubtful that every Commonwealth nation would accept him as monarch—Canada was especially unlikely. Yet allegiance to the Crown was the tie that held the Commonwealth together. At home, moreover, the King had acted like a monarch determined to be a policy activist rather than a constitutional figurehead. Even those who approved of his behavior in Wales doubted the legitimacy of his lecturing to the govern-ment. Unspoken but of concern to insiders was his tolerance of Nazi Ger-many and the fear that in various ways he could make a democratic foreign policy difficult. In a tumultuous week of open discussion, as citi-zens and politicians began to take sides, the marriage debate opened the possibility of a nightmare realignment in British politics—a King's party versus a parliamentary party. The Labour leadership signaled unmistak-ably that if the government resigned, it would refuse to attempt to form or participate in a new cabinet. Winston Churchill at his most erratic met with the King, counseled delay, and struck most observers as making an opportunistic bid to bring down Baldwin and Chamberlain while estab-lishing himself as the monarch's champion. Worse yet, in the streets of London, Oswald Mosley's Black Shirts demonstrated in support of Edward.[54]

Briefly, the outcome seemed uncertain. Edward had great crowd appeal. Large numbers of Britons, especially in cosmopolitan London, sympathized with his romantic story. But the establishment held firm—Baldwin at the head of it, Attlee backing him from the left, the important newspapers nearly solid. Pressured for a law to permit a "morganatic mar-riage" in which Mrs. Simpson would be simply the King's wife, with their offspring not eligible for the succession, the prime minister refused to budge. Wavering members of Parliament who scattered to their con-stituencies for the weekend of December 5–6 mostly discovered strong grassroots antipathy to Mrs. Simpson. When Baldwin entered the House of Commons on December 7, he received what the New York Times described as an ovation that "rolled and reverberated from all parts of the House long after he had taken his seat on the front bench." Churchill attempted a question that actually was a declaration in behalf of the King. The same members shouted him down.[55]

Edward's emotional support was scattered, inchoate, and surely no more than a vocal minority. The reorganization of British politics around his plight was never a real possibility. The prospect of establishing him as a king with a strong political voice was even less likely. After a week of debate and demonstration, his only recourse, should he remain devoted to Mrs. Simpson, was to leave office as if he were a defeated prime minis-ter. On December 10, he informed the Cabinet that he would go, and signed the instrument of abdication, ratified that evening by act of Parlia-ment. On December 11, he made his last radio address to the British peo-ple. Announcing his departure in favor of his brother, Albert, Duke of

York (who proclaimed himself George VI), he denied that he had ever meant to damage the empire or challenge Parliament. His final words underscored the fragile position of any monarch who overstepped his constitutional limits: "And now we all have a new King. I wish him and you, his people, happiness and prosperity with all my heart. God bless you all! God save the King!"[56]

On the afternoon of December 10, abdication already an accomplished fact, Baldwin spoke for an hour to a rapt House of Commons, professing an attitude of fatherly solicitude for the former king, detailing his actions in the crisis, and quietly explaining the inexorable necessity of an outcome all of them would have found inconceivable a month earlier. Many who had heard him at his best on other occasions thought it was his finest effort. Attlee seconded him, as did Liberal leader Sir Archibald Sinclair. Churchill rose to respond, gracefully retrieving at least a few of the tatters to which his reputation had been reduced: "What has been done, or left undone, belongs to history, and to history, as far as I am concerned, it shall be left. . . . We must obey the exhortation of our Prime Minister to look forward." The House responded with loud cheers. Six months later, as the coronation of George VI neared, *The Economist* magazine commented that throughout the British Commonwealth "seldom, if ever before, has the feeling for constitutional monarchy and for democracy been so strong, so unanimous."[57]

Baldwin was four months past his sixty-ninth birthday on the day that Edward renounced the throne. It was only a few weeks earlier that he, in response to Churchill, had embarrassingly admitted to trimming in the face of antiwar sentiment. Now all was forgotten or forgiven. Once again, he was the most admired politician in the Empire. He stayed on only for a few more months, appointing himself friend and counselor to the new king. On May 28, 16 days after the coronation of George VI, he announced his retirement in favor of Neville Chamberlain. Widely loved and admired, he took leave of office to a multitude of tributes, delivered in the glow of a still-growing economic recovery and a sense that Britain remained safe in the world.

In terms of political achievement, he had been the most successful Conservative leader since his idol Disraeli. Three times prime minister and the animating force behind MacDonald's National regime, he had been the dominant figure in British political life for two decades. No other British politician had possessed so astute a grasp of the requirements of mass democratic politics. Baldwin's use of radio as a medium of communication as early as 1924 had set a standard for democratic leaders everywhere. His rhetoric established the concept of a middle way as surely as did that of Roosevelt in the United States. His handling of the abdication crisis displayed a deft grasp of the subtleties of British constitutional politics and the mood of the people over whom his government presided. It preserved a monarchy that British democracy badly wanted and needed. Unlike Roosevelt, he had brought back considerable prosperity to his nation; unlike Hitler, he had preserved and strengthened its democracy. Unlike them both, he had won the affection of the electorate by pretending to be an ordinary, not especially quick, person. The tactic was a dangerous one, tenable so long as accompanied by success but carrying the risk of popular scorn if accompanied by a record of mistakes and failures. In 1937, the success was evident and the popular veneration widespread.

HEADLINES AND MOVIE NEWSREELS

{1935}

MAY 28   New Deal Is Dazed; Three Smashing Supreme Court Blows

JUNE 17   Hoover Assails New Deal Economy of Scarcity and Bureaucracy; Constitutional Government With a Division of
Authority "Only Successful Protection"

JUNE 18   Jobs Ready Soon; Work Relief Program Under Way Next
Month

JUNE 20   Social Aid Wins; Senate Follows House in Approving the
Administration's Security Bill; Old-Age Assistance of $18 a
Month Is to Be Available Soon

JULY   *Senator Huey Long welcomes newsreel cameras to his suite
at a New York hotel to introduce the anthem of his Share
Our Wealth movement, "Every Man a King." Tin Pan Alley
veteran Harry Link, seated at a grand piano, plays and
sings with the Kingfish moving his upraised hands as if
conducting: "Ev'ry man a king . . . there's enough for all
people to share . . . peace without end . . . every neighbor
a friend."* (Newsreel)

NOVEMBER 12   Olson Sees a Party of Radicals in 1940; Production for Use
Must Replace Profit; Assails Supreme Court

CHALLENGES

THE ORIGINS OF THE SECOND NEW DEAL,

JANUARY–MAY 1935

Personalities: Drivers of Relief and Reform

By early 1935, the New Deal was developing a shift in emphasis. Organization and state management gave way to a populist-progressive attack on big business, the empowerment of organized labor, a vast expansion of work relief, and new welfare programs. The practical effect was that the tone of the New Deal was increasingly set by the people who managed its most widespread and attention-getting products of relief and reform.

Harry Hopkins: Minister of Relief

When Franklin Roosevelt appointed Harry Hopkins to head the newly created Works Progress Administration (WPA) in the spring of 1935, Americans already knew him as the man who had spent $2 billion in public money as administrator of the Federal Emergency Relief Administration (FERA) and the Civil Works Administration (CWA). He was now charged with deploying a big part of another $4.8 billion, a sum that just two years earlier would have exceeded the annual spending of the United States government. To the task he brought a long-cultivated sympathy for the underdog, twenty years of experience with the dispossessed, and a restless energy that focused on the deed rather than the concept.

Born in Grinnell, Iowa, in 1890, Hopkins was a product of the small shopkeeper class. His family was respectable, but lived frugally. His father ran a small harness store; his mother was a devout Methodist who taught him a Christian conscience. He went to public schools, then to Grinnell College, where he won honors as a student and campus leader. There he developed values of work and compassion he had been taught from an early age. In 1912, just after commencement at Grinnell, he left Iowa for New York to work in a summer camp for deprived youth. He never returned. An outstanding representative of the way in which social work was transformed from an avocation of benevolent ladies with good intentions to a profession rooted in private and public bureaucracies, he became a Red Cross administrator and director of public health agencies. Mastering the skills of nonprofit and public administration, he never abandoned a personal concern for clients who suffered from inadequate diets, lung diseases, and the manifold afflictions of poverty. A visit to England in 1928 gave him a chance to observe the poverty of London's East End and admire Britain's far more developed public programs for its poor. Back in New York in 1931, he accepted appointment as director of Governor Franklin Roosevelt's Temporary Emergency Relief Administration and created the most important model of a state response to the Depression. It was natural enough that he would follow FDR to Washington.

Hopkins's impact was quick. A major relief administrator from the beginning, he distributed funds with abandon. Unlike Harold Ickes, he was more concerned with getting money into the hands of the needy as quickly as possible than with accounting for every dollar. He responded to charges of inefficiency, boondoggling, and graft with a curt dismissal. Of course, huge sums had been filtered through forty-eight state organizations to millions of beneficiaries. Some of it would stick to fingers, some would be poorly spent, some would go to people who did not really need it. That was the way the world worked. The greater good was served nonetheless. He might add bluntly, "Some people just can't stand seeing others make a decent living."[1] He had no need to justify to himself or others the job he was doing. Given the crisis he faced, that was a strength, not a weakness.

Forty-two years old when he assumed command of the FERA in 1933, lean and shabbily dressed, he chain-smoked, drank coffee by the gallon, and worked his will with nervous energy. In his public and personal life, he went out of his way to avoid being typed as a Methodist do-gooder. He had given up church attendance, divorced his first wife, and learned to enjoy a good whiskey with his cigarettes; he frequented New York night-clubs, and took occasional days betting on the horses at the racetrack. In the style of Depression America, he seemed hard-boiled, but just beneath his tough exterior, bleeding-heart idealism ruled.

Hopkins approached his duties in Washington with three core convictions: the needy had to be helped; the jobless had to be given work relief in order to preserve their skills and their dignity; the New Deal's leader had to be tendered absolute loyalty. Roosevelt liked Hopkins, praised his activism, and never considered him a threat. "Someday you may well be sitting here where I am now as President of the United States," he told Wendell Willkie in 1941. "You'll learn what a lonely job this is, and you'll discover the need for somebody like Harry Hopkins who asks for nothing except to serve you."[2]

Frances Perkins: Social Welfarist

It is the fate of most secondary historical figures to be tagged with one line in the nation's collective memory. In the case of Frances Perkins, it is "secretary of labor, 1933–1945; first woman to be a member of a presidential cabinet." Actually, that was among the lesser of her accomplishments. Where Harry Hopkins focused on short-term relief, primarily for victims of the Depression, Perkins focused on the establishment of long-term help for classes that would be unable to support themselves in times of prosperity—the elderly, the handicapped, widows, orphans. More than anyone else in the New Deal, she midwifed the beginnings of the American welfare state.

Born in 1880, Fanny Perkins had grown up in Worcester, Massachusetts, in a comfortable middle-class environment dominated by family and the Congregational Church. It taught her traditional values of work, duty, and education, all of which were transformed as her generation faced the challenge of industrial capitalism. She went off to Mount Holyoke College in 1898. A demanding institution, it taught Darwinian evolution, the new reform-oriented social sciences, and a robust Christian missionary spirit. She enrolled in an American history course taught by a professor who took her students on field trips to local factories and required them to survey the miserable conditions of the working class. Florence Kelley, America's greatest female social reformer, delivered a memorable lecture to the college's National Consumer League chapter. Perkins graduated as class president and a coming figure among a new cadre of educated women determined to be agents of change.

Five years of teaching at exclusive girls schools did not deter Fanny, who by now was signing her name "Frances," from her deepest ambition, social work. By 1907, she was in Philadelphia as director of a small group formed to protect exploited immigrant and Negro women. On the side, she took graduate courses at the University of Pennsylvania, including one with Rexford Tugwell's influential teacher Simon Patten. In 1910, she moved to New York to work with the Consumer League and Florence Kelley, grappling with issues that included malnutrition, sanitation, and safe working conditions. She made speeches for women's suffrage in her spare time. Soon a seasoned legislative lobbyist, she worked successfully for a fifty-four-hour-workweek bill, then served on a commission with Robert F. Wagner and Alfred E. Smith to investigate the infamous Triangle Shirtwaist Fire of 1911. Major factory legislation resulted from the body's report. When Smith was elected governor in 1918, he appointed her to a place on the state Industrial Board, which she subsequently chaired. Succeeding Smith as governor in 1929, Franklin Roosevelt made her state industrial commissioner. Determined to be a model of independent womanhood, she refused, despite substantial inconvenience, to adopt her husband's name. By and large, however, her feminism was low-key, reflecting her understanding that displays of aggression were generally counterproductive, but the hardest-bitten politicians might accommodate an idealistic lady.

By early 1933, Frances Perkins was a noted social worker, state official, and consistent advocate of legislative solutions to meet the legitimate needs of the working class and the dependent groups in society. Never a foe of trade unions, she recognized that they could achieve justice and benefits only for their members, frequently discriminated against women and minorities, and divided communities. Looking back late in her life, she remarked, "I'd much rather get a law than organize a union." Roosevelt named her secretary of labor just days before the inauguration. (She was not the first woman in the English-speaking world to hold such a post. Margaret Bondfield had served as minister of labour in Ramsay MacDonald's last Labour cabinet, 1929–31.) She accepted the appointment only after the president agreed to support her in developing a comprehensive system of social security. Labor, she told a journalist in May 1933, was first and foremost a group of citizens with vital interests in economic stability and social justice. William Green, president of the AFL, denounced her appointment. Most labor leaders never approved. They had to deal with her nonetheless for the next twelve years.[3]

Crisis

By the spring of 1935, the New Deal was in a shambles with recovery stalled, unemployment hovering just below twenty percent, and uncertainty about the future emanating from the White House throughout Washington to the rest of the country. The president himself was under increasingly vehement attack from an angry right, assorted extremists who did not yield to ready classification, and independent radicals hoping for a new party that would change American politics forever. His response and that of his loyalists was as much a matter of instinct as of calculation. It was to mobilize the underprivileged and to support labor unions. It also was to co-opt his critics on the left by opening an offensive against the wealthy, the bankers, and the big corporations. To the extent these decisions were tactical, they were nonetheless sincere, reflecting Roosevelt's deepest feelings.

<hr />

The fundamental challenge that the Roosevelt administration faced was summed up in the title of a *Fortune* magazine article published in October 1934: "On the Dole: 17,000,000"—and, the piece added, another ten million somehow subsisting without receiving public assistance. The figure assumed 10.8 million jobless workers and added 1.5 dependents for each of them. No one questioned the statistics. The New Deal had succeeded only in bringing the country back from a catastrophic condition to a desperate one. At enormous expense, the Public Works Administration (PWA) and the Civilian Conservation Corps (CCC) would provide employment for a fortunate minority; the rest would subsist on a Federal Emergency Relief Administration (FERA) "dole." The article concluded that "a group of from 17,000,000 to 20,000,000 people on the dole is a political, social, and economic menace to the nation"; ways would have to be found to put them to work, ways that might involve "state socialism" and would surely "change the pattern of life for everyone." A New Deal at best semisuccessful had to fend off loud, growing, and diverse manifestations of political dissent.[4]

The most irritating example to the New Dealers—and the one from which Roosevelt assuredly benefited—was the American Liberty League. Formed in 1934, it was the work of conservative Democrats, alarmed by their party's departure from Jeffersonian values of small government and harried by undertones of class warfare. The League's organizers, benefactors, and supporters included the du Ponts (whose associations with Jeffersonianism went back to Jefferson himself), William Randolph Hearst, and the last two Democratic nominees for president, John W. Davis and Al Smith. Spending twice as much money as the national Republican party in 1934, it issued pamphlet after pamphlet blasting the New Deal as incipient totalitarianism. It is too easy to dismiss the League as the instrument of fat cats who resented regulation, hated labor unions, and wanted to protect their personal wealth. Many of its leaders were clearly sincere in their conviction that Roosevelt was laying the groundwork for either a fascist or a communist state. The changes being wrought by the New Deal seemed immense, even to men who had backed the progressivism of Wilson two decades earlier. By 1936, after Roosevelt had aligned himself with militant labor, bashers of business, and soakers of the rich, while engaging in unprecedented deficit spending, the departure from the past would appear even greater. Smith displayed the difficulty that many old Democratic progressives had adjusting to the new order. Doubtless influenced by resentment of the way in which the once lightly regarded Roosevelt had eclipsed him, he also was true to his past as a state-level reformer who balanced his budget and avoided raw class politics. He became the Liberty League's most prominent speaker.

Realists understood all along that the League was little more than a noisemaker. Herbert Hoover, although persuaded that the United States was in the early stages of fascism, curtly rejected an invitation to join, noting that its founders had "financed the Democratic smearing campaign" against him in 1932. "The League set up a great clatter," the old president wrote years later, accurately concluding that "it boomeranged to aid Roosevelt."[5]

Senator Huey Long of Louisiana was a far more formidable commotion-generator.[6] A force of one in his state's politics, he was at the peak of a political career guided by a confusing amalgam of populist ideology, boundless lust for power, and a remarkable talent for self-promotion. Governor of Louisiana, 1928–32, he pursued a program of taxing big business and providing the poor charity hospitals, free schoolbooks, and better rural roads. He made Louisiana State University a first-line state school. By and large, his programs did not discriminate against the state's blacks, and he avoided race-baiting. Whatever his faults, he substituted the realism of class politics for the shabby romanticism of racial oppression.

He was intelligent, avaricious, and cynical. William Howard Taft called him one of the most impressive attorneys to appear before the U.S. Supreme Court during his term as chief justice. He took bribes freely; sometimes he kept his word to the bribers. State agencies facilitated lucrative oil and gas leases for a small corporation from which he profited mightily. He was a notorious woman-chaser. After surviving an impeachment trial in 1929, he ruled the state with an iron hand, making the highway patrol his personal gestapo, surrounding himself with a retinue of armed bodyguards, and establishing a de facto dictatorship. Some of his opposition came from special interests. His most vehement opponents simply believed in good government and democratic norms. One of them, nearly quivering as a newsreel camera captured his words, declared: "Huey Pierce Long, Jr., represents the extreme development of all the evil and corruption that has cursed the government of Louisiana within our memory. He typifies personally all that we would not want our children to be."[7]

Unfortunately, the reformers could offer nothing but virtue, which traded at a steep discount in Louisiana. Long, on the other hand, not only did something for ordinary people, he also entertained them. He took to calling himself the Kingfish, after a buffoonish character on the "Amos 'n' Andy" radio show. He appeared regularly at LSU football games, personally chose the band director, and frequently joined the halftime show. A grateful state elected him to the U.S. Senate in 1930, but he remained governor for nearly two years until he had overseen the election of his faithful associate O.K. Allen as his successor. In January 1932, he was finally sworn in as a U.S. senator and was determined to make a national impression.

Long held key Southern delegations in line for Roosevelt at the 1932 Democratic convention, but from the beginning the two leaders disliked each other. The new administration denied him patronage and, after some hesitation, authorized an intensive Treasury department investigation of him and his associates for income tax evasion. The senator in turn became a strident critic of the New Deal, attacking from a position on the populistic left, going after the NRA and blasting away at the crop reduction efforts of the agricultural program. In February 1934, he announced the establishment of a new organization, the Share Our Wealth Society, and proclaimed a new slogan, "Every Man a King." His program would confiscate all the excess assets of the great families of America (leaving them still with riches beyond the dreams of the average citizen) and would redistribute it to ordinary people in the form of "homestead grants," modest guaranteed incomes, old-age pensions, college scholarships, and veterans bonuses. He would continue the New Deal agricultural program, would give industrial workers a thirty-hour week with one month of vacation a year. Arms flailing, he outlined his plan to friendly audiences. God had given America unheard-of abundance. He had called a barbecue, but the super-rich had "walked up and took eighty-five percent of the vittles off the table."[8] Take money from the Rockefellers and Morgans, the Mellons and the Baruchs; leave them enough for their yachts and palaces, for a Reno divorce and another wife if they wanted one.

The mathematics of Share Our Wealth were comically inaccurate, as Long himself almost certainly realized; even the super-rich were not rich enough to provide more than a fraction of what he promised. Nevertheless, the plan got a lot of attention and evident enthusiasm. Long's Senate office processed tens of thousands of letters. The senator's devoted lieutenant, the Rev. Gerald L. K. Smith, spearheaded grassroots organization throughout the country. (A charismatic orator who spoke the language of the alienated poor and lower-middle classes, Smith was, according to H. L. Mencken, "the champion boob-bumper of all epochs."[9]) By 1935, the movement extravagantly claimed 4.7 million members. Although concentrated heavily in Louisiana, Mississippi, and Arkansas, it *seemed* national; about every state had at least a few chapters. It was easy to think that Long had unleashed a widespread sentiment for income redistribution that was more emotional than conventional politicians had gauged. He began work on a book to be called *My First Days in the White House*. He actually seemed to have a chance of spoiling Roosevelt's bid for a second term, especially if he could consummate a developing rapprochement with two other dissenters of national prominence—Dr. Francis Townsend and Father Charles Coughlin.

Townsend was among the most sympathetic characters who came to prominence during the Depression. He possessed no lust for power, displayed little talent as a speaker, and looked like the stock political cartoon image of John Q. Public. A physician who had moved to California after a long and financially unrewarding career in rural South Dakota, he pursued a public clinic practice that consisted heavily of indigent oldsters. He was moved to public action after seeing elderly women rummaging through garbage cans for food. A letter to the local paper followed, then development of an old-age pension plan, a petition drive, and, with the help of a real estate developer named Robert Clements, an organized movement, Old Age Revolving Pensions, Ltd.

The Depression had laid bare the festering national problem of a vast and growing population of impoverished and forgotten old folks. At age sixty-six, Townsend became their unlikely messiah; his movement, quasi-religious in its style, spread like wildfire across the country. His plan, like Long's, was simple and wildly impractical. It would provide a pension of $200 a month to every retired person over the age of 60, subject to the provision that the recipient would forego all gainful employment and spend every cent every month. This would stimulate the economy and provide jobs for younger people. It would be financed by a "transactions tax" (similar to present-day European value-added taxes) that the Townsend organization claimed would raise $1.6 billion a month. The economics were sheer hokum. The tax would be a prohibitive drag on the economy and mercilessly regressive to boot. (As Norman Thomas put it, speaking to a Townsend convention, "There are a lot of transactions that go into making the coat on my back, and by the time they are taken out of it, I won't have much coat left.") It would soak up half the national income and distribute it to about nine percent of the population. Sub-stantially underestimating the number of eligible pensioners, it would require even more revenue than Townsend understood. The doctor brushed off such details; the movement grew rapidly.[10]

Townsend's critics looked hard for evidence of fraud and illicit skim-ming of funds. They found very little. Townsend was boringly honest and sincere, convinced that the principle of aid to the elderly was more important than details of implementation, conducting his personal life with modesty and frugality. A congressional investigation of him and his movement in 1936 resulted in a backlash against the investigators. Whether the old people would be mollified by the New Deal's social security plan remained uncertain as the Townsend movement enrolled new members by the tens of thousands in the first half of 1935.

Long and Townsend promised income redistribution. Father Charles Coughlin matched them and upped the ante with generalized promises of social justice.

Soon after appointment in 1926 to a tiny parish in the Detroit suburb of Royal Oak, Coughlin had begun to broadcast Sunday homilies over Detroit's powerful clear channel radio station WJR. His mellow, well-modulated voice, his gift for developing simple messages, his priestly instinct for speaking to and converting individuals—all won him a devoted audience. Until the Depression achieved the proportions of a national catastrophe, he kept his messages focused on religion, Catholic morality, and the virtues of toleration (the Klan had burned a cross on his church's lawn). Stations in Chicago and Cincinnati picked up his broadcasts. In 1930 the fledgling Columbia Broadcasting System began to carry him on its growing national network. No American public figure had mastered the new medium so effectively.

As the Depression deepened, Coughlin turned increasingly to things secular. Catholicism in Europe and America had long since responded to the social problems of modern industrial capitalism by developing a version of what Protestants had called the Social Gospel. Pope Leo XIII had committed the church to social justice in his encyclical *Rerum Novarum* (1891). Pius XI underscored the commitment in *Quadragesimo Anno* (1931). In Germany, social Catholicism was a strong force, contesting with both socialists and Nazis for the allegiance of the labor movement. In the United States, it was more muted but still an influential presence, personified by the redoubtable Msgr. John Ryan. It seemed therefore not unusual that the "Radio Priest" would begin to talk about the travails of farmers and workers, that he would condemn bankers and big business, that he would be openly critical of the Hoover administration. The shift was popular. When CBS refused to renew the program for the 1932–33 season, Coughlin was able to put together his own national network and pay the costs of transmission via telephone from contributions that flowed to him from all over the country.

His enormous radio talents and the atmosphere of national crisis obscured the muddled nature of his message, which reflected more the limitations than the merits of Catholic social thinking. Demonstrating an outlook rooted in medieval corporatist assumptions, he launched into a sustained critique of the elites of modern capitalism that had little to do with the causes of the Depression but meshed nicely with a prevalent hostility toward bankers and big business. A European might recognize much of what he said as a plea for a corporatist state, akin to that of Salazar in Portugal or Mussolini in Italy, but without a dictatorship. In the American context, however, it was in many ways similar to the populist critique of industrial capitalism that had surfaced in the late nineteenth century. As Alan Brinkley has argued, Coughlin, like Long, could seem to be speaking to the individualist aspirations of downtrodden Americans, not inviting them to participate in an alien experiment.[11] He attacked the big guys, defended workers and labor unions, advocated income support for farmers. He talked nationalization of the banks and large areas of the American economy. He argued for inflation—free coinage of silver, huge increases in greenbacks—in ways that would have reconciled William Jennings Bryan to the Catholic Church. Harshly critical of Herbert Hoover, he stopped just short of an outright endorsement of Roosevelt in the 1932 election.

For the first year or so of the New Deal, he seemed to be one of the president's most ardent supporters. "Roosevelt or ruin," he declared. But as the New Deal appeared to bog down, he was increasingly critical. Roosevelt was not sufficiently enlarging the money supply, had refused to nationalize the banks, had allowed big business to control the NRA. By mid-1934, he was oscillating between criticism and praise of the administration, groping for an independent position. Roosevelt in turn wavered between buttering him up and attempting to discredit him, between inviting him for personal visits and allowing the Treasury department to reveal that his private secretary was speculating heavily in silver futures.[12]

Visiting Coughlin at his Royal Oak headquarters in the spring of 1934, Marquis Childs found the tiny parish church displaced by an enormous Shrine of the Little Flower, an office force of 145 stenographers struggling to acknowledge the small mountains of mail that arrived every day, bookkeepers dealing with donations that ran as high as $20,000 a week. Father Coughlin, he ruefully acknowledged, was "a success story of the depression." He had preached to more people than Jesus and all his disciples combined. His radio talks had reduced complex social and economic issues to questions of individual villainy. He had become a celebrity, had every intention of continuing to be one, and would employ the rhetoric necessary to keep his audience and its contributions. The nation would hear more of him.[13]

That November, Coughlin founded the National Union for Social Justice on a platform that included such contradictory specifics as an inflationary expansion of the money supply and price stability; widespread nationalization of big business and protection of private property; broader taxation and alleviation of taxation; conscription of wealth and sanctity of property rights. To these he more forthrightly added fair profits for farmers and the right to organize for workers. Brilliantly gauging Roosevelt's weaknesses, he launched a last-minute campaign in January 1935 to prevent the Senate from ratifying an administration-backed treaty for U.S. adherence to the World Court. More than a dozen senators, intimidated by a deluge of letters and telegrams, abandoned pledges to support the pact, thereby depriving it of the two-thirds majority it needed. The episode provided a reminder that the Radio Priest was under no circumstances to be discounted as a political power. That June, he addressed a packed audience in New York's Madison Square Garden. The crowd, wrote Hamilton Basso, was sober and serious, "a composite, living portrait of the American people." It applauded and cheered him hysterically and booed lustily at every mention of President Roosevelt.[14]

In the heated atmosphere of early 1935, politically engaged intellectuals cast wary glances in the direction of Europe. It seemed natural to speculate whether Long and Coughlin with Townsend in tow and possibly with the collaboration of a charismatic general (read "Douglas MacArthur") might be harbingers of a coming American fascism. Sinclair Lewis—at that point the only American ever to have been awarded the Nobel prize for literature—supplied a full scenario with his novel *It Can't Happen Here*. It depicted the coming of authoritarianism to the United States under the auspices of characters clearly based on Long, Coughlin, MacArthur, and lesser lights. Lewis's novel, more notable for its timeliness than its artistic achievement, built on well-established fears. A. B. Magil called Coughlin "the Paul Joseph Goebbels of Royal Oak." In March 1935, a *Christian Century* editorial asserted "the Long-Coughlin type of politics may be roughly but not inaccurately described as the threat of fascism." Raymond Gram Swing, a serious journalist who had witnessed the collapse of democracies in Europe, published *Forerunners of American Fascism* in the same year, arguing that Huey Long was a potential, indeed probable, dictator. Fascist movements in their first stage appeared radical and nationalist, then made their peace with Big Money and seized power.[15]

Such commentary had surface plausibility. Neither Long nor Coughlin would have refused a dictatorship, if offered, although their egos would not have allowed them to work in concert. But, even by the loose standards of fascism, neither had a developed political doctrine. Long allegedly once remarked, "When the United States gets fascism it will call it anti-fascism."[16] Whether he actually said it, the quotation was in line with his indifference to programmatic ideology. He, Coughlin, and Townsend had specific proposals, but no larger doctrine. Hitler and Mussolini by comparison were political philosophers of the first rank.

There were, of course, genuine fascists and protofascists in America. A few were intellectuals of some substance—*American Review* editor Seward Collins, the architect Philip Johnson, the poet Ezra Pound, the writer Lawrence Dennis. They had doctrine but no followers. There were paramilitary movements—Khaki Shirts, Silver Shirts, and the like, all led by would-be dictators ("General" Art Smith, William Dudley Pelley, Rev. Gerald Winrod); they made noise, attracted attention beyond their importance, and evaporated into the mists. The combined effect of all their efforts was to make Sir Oswald Mosley look like Napoleon.[17]

By early 1935, however, it seemed that another force was emerging in American politics. It was a style of independent left-liberalism that spilled over into American socialism while stopping well short of affiliation with the Communist Party of the United States. For doctrine it drew on renowned intellectuals. For experience and organization, it could look to several politicians around the country who had actually won elections, reigned supreme in their bailiwicks, and increasingly seemed to discern a common cause. The 1934 elections, they believed, had signaled a surge of reform sentiment in the United States. The New Deal, they were certain, was an incoherent mishmash on the verge of collapse. They would pick up the pieces.

John Dewey, the great philosopher of American liberalism, vigorously summarized the indictment in *Liberalism and Social Action*, a tract widely read on the democratic left. Liberalism, he declared, sought the liberation of the individual by collective means rather than through freedom from government. The crisis of the Depression could not be solved "by piecemeal policies undertaken *ad hoc*." Social welfare legislation was worthwhile, "but the cause of liberalism will be lost for a considerable period if it is not prepared to go further and socialize the forces of production." Individual liberty thereby would "be supported by the very structure of economic organization." How could so drastic a change happen? Not by violent revolution but through "socially organized intelligence"—presumably by a regime of benign technocratic elites chosen by democratic means, imposing "regimentation of material and mechanical forces."[18]

How odd that the leading philosopher of democracy was so fuzzy! Dewey was clear on one thing, however—the New Deal was a dead end. In an article, he curtly dismissed the argument that Franklin Roosevelt was presiding over a promising exercise in political experimentation. "Experimental method is not just messing around nor doing a little of this and a little of that, in the hope that things will improve." In the fifth year of the American Great Depression, Dewey spoke the mind of many important politically engaged intellectuals. He also demonstrated that the intellectual path to a new society was at best indeterminate. The political path was equally so, for it had to involve a new mass-based democratic socialist party.[19]

In 1935, that new party seemed to many within reach. In New York City two years earlier, the people had elected the dynamic Fiorello La Guardia mayor on a "fusion" ticket. La Guardia had national ambitions. As an insurgent congressman in the 1920s, he had sought alliances with hinterland progressives. Two of the most famous, Philip and Robert La Follette, Jr., of Wisconsin, had bolted the Republican party to establish a state Progressive party. Bob, Jr., had coasted to reelection as a U.S. senator, Phil had been elected governor. Both reveled in the tradition of their father, "Fighting Bob." Next door in Minnesota, Floyd B. Olson was reelected governor on the Farmer-Labor ticket. No leader of the non-Communist left was more exciting. A working-class Swede turned smooth politician, a spellbinding orator, he gloried in being called a radical, but rejected talk of the violent overthrow of capitalism and ostentatiously disowned Marxism. ("Marx? He was some German writer, wasn't he?") In California, the old socialist Upton Sinclair had lost the governorship but transformed the Democratic party. His EPIC (End Poverty in California) program lived on as a political force, producing up and coming politicos of the liberal left such as Sheridan Downey (elected U.S. senator, 1938) and Culbert Olson (elected governor, 1938). Up the coast an assortment of left-wing forces joined together in the Washington Commonwealth Federation, exerted considerable leverage within the Democratic party, and helped elect Lewis Schwellenbach to the U.S. Senate.[20]

Independent and quasi-independent men of the left were scattered around the country in large numbers and possessed a lot of visibility. Many could be found in Congress—perhaps a dozen in the Senate, 35–40 in the House. The two major leaders in the upper chamber were La Follette, Jr., and the venerable Independent George Norris of Nebraska. The two most noted House leaders were Democrat Maury Maverick of San Antonio, a loud, brilliant, plain-talking Texan who defined liberalism as "freedom plus groceries," and Wisconsin Progressive Tom Amlie, a political intellectual convinced that the end was near for capitalism and engaged in an earnest search for an American style of democratic collectivism.[21]

In May 1935, La Guardia aligned himself with Phil La Follette in support of a farmer-labor party. That November, Floyd Olson spoke to a meeting of the recently formed Commonwealth Federation of New York, affirming his belief that America had to develop an economic system in which need came first and profit second. But generalizations were no substitute for a clear program. The independent radicals were independent operators by nature. It was easier for them to talk about a new party than to start one. The closest thing they had to an organization was the League for Independent Political Action, founded in 1929 by Dewey, Amlie, and the University of Chicago economist Paul H. Douglas. The League was more a collection of political intellectuals than of practical politicians.[22]

The biggest barrier to a new party remained Roosevelt and the New Deal. The independents agreed that circumstances would have to remove both from the scene. It would require the implosion of FDR's program and his subsequent defeat in 1936 to clear the way for the reconstruction of American politics no earlier than 1940. And that strangely distant scenario was complicated by a fact of political life. Many of the independent politicians were in one way or another either outright dependent on the success of the New Deal (none more so than La Guardia) or stood to gain in one fashion or another from benefits only FDR's Washington could bestow. If the New Deal did indeed collapse, they might be able to launch a successor movement that would either take over the Democratic party or displace it altogether. Until then, they were more prisoners of FDR's program than definers of America's political destiny.[23]

At the beginning of 1935, Roosevelt and his advisers had arrived at a strategy of response for the next two years. It was primarily one of continuity. Where the radicals saw the 1934 election results as an opportunity, the administration could see them as a validation. Steady as she goes with some midcourse correction was a logical direction.

The agricultural program was functioning well. The industrial recovery program, which required congressional reauthorization no later than mid-June, clearly needed a significant overhaul. It would have to concentrate on the regulation of fewer and less fragmented industries. It was especially important to establish clear and enforceable rules for labor-management relations. Sentiment in Congress was decidedly hostile to NRA extension, but Roosevelt remained drawn to the idea of economic management. And why not? To varying degrees this was the common denominator of economic policy throughout the developed world. The president probably believed that he was strong enough to get what he wanted from the legislative branch. The Public Works Administration (PWA), just beginning to hit its stride, would continue on as planned, primarily building needed infrastructure across the country. So would the Tennessee Valley Authority (TVA), bringing badly needed jobs to a long-suffering region and eventually providing a model of planned development. To all this, the president would add a comprehensive social security program, contemplated from the beginning but requiring a long period of gestation.

⟶

That left the nagging problem of unemployment. Roosevelt might be a political warrior without peer, but if he had an Achilles heel, this was it. With prosperity nowhere in sight by the end of 1934, he was ready to accept a drumbeat of advice that came to him primarily from Harry Hopkins but also from newly appointed Federal Reserve chairman Marriner Eccles and numerous congressional progressives. All wanted a massive jobs program akin to the CWA. This would be accompanied by devolution of direct relief (or dole) to the states with matching federal subsidies (as provided by the social security plan) and would result in the termination of the FERA. The administration would continue the Civilian Conservation Corps (CCC) and increasingly ambitious rural relief efforts. As with the original plans of early 1933, this program in overview possessed far more coherence than its critics conceded.

The larger issue was whether the country could afford it. The president's budget message for fiscal year 1936 (July 1, 1935–June 30, 1936), a document likely to err on the side of understatement, estimated a deficit of $4.5 billion with total expenditures of $8 billion.[24] The administration recycled the government line that the "regular" budget was in balance and that the deficit was wholly to finance "emergency" (presumably temporary) programs. Conservative and not-so-conservative critics retorted that a roughly balanced budget was necessary for the fiscal survival of the government. Key administration officials privately agreed. Director of the Budget Lewis Douglas, a former congressman of some political standing, had already resigned in quiet protest the previous summer. Secretary of the Treasury Henry Morgenthau, possessing a loyalty bred of long friendship, suppressed his own doubts. As for Roosevelt, he almost certainly believed that his outsized budgets were a temporary expedient to get the nation's needy through the Depression, jump-start the economy—and get through the next election.

So long as deficit-generated New Deal programs brought paychecks to millions of people, budgetary issues could not cut deeply in American politics. Nevertheless, widely-read political pundits such as Frank Kent, David Lawrence, and Mark Sullivan hammered away at reckless spending in articles that reached a majority of the nation's newspaper readers. The issue of the deficit resonated with an opposition that radiated out from Wall Street citadels of financial orthodoxy to small-town bankers and struggling businessmen.[25]

The president's first priority was his new social security program. Although it possessed the political merit of responding to the Townsend Plan, it had been in the works well before Townsend had become a national figure—and the benefits it promised were inconsequential by comparison. The proposal that Roosevelt sent to Congress on January 17, 1935, had been worked out by a special committee chaired by Frances Perkins. Passed without major alterations seven months later, it provided for: (1) a system of old age and survivor's annuities funded by compulsory payroll deductions, one-half of one percent paid by employee and one-half of one percent paid by employer on the first $3,000 of earnings, providing retirees over the age of 65 payments of $10 to $85 a month, that, after the accumulation of a substantial reserve fund, would begin in 1942; (2) state unemployment insurance systems funded primarily by another federal tax on payrolls, reaching three percent by 1938; (3) substantial federal subsidies to a series of state welfare programs for the indigent elderly, the blind, and dependent children; (4) federal grants to states for social services such as public health, vocational rehabilitation, and maternity assistance. Largely because of opposition from the American Medical Association and financing difficulties, the committee decided not to include a medical insurance plan.

To some observers, the British social security system seemed the committee's model. In fact, it served more as a reference point, general inspiration, and legitimizing example. The framers of the Social Security Act were familiar with many European programs. Roosevelt himself, as Daniel Rodgers has observed, had devoted considerable thought to social insurance issues and may have seen himself as equaling or surpassing the accomplishments of Bismarck and Lloyd George. In the summer of 1934, he dispatched Harry Hopkins on a seven-week trip to Europe with instructions to "look over the housing and social insurance schemes in England, Germany, Austria, and Italy." Upon his return, Hopkins held a long off-the-record press conference in which he expressed admiration for British housing and social security programs, but also a general sense that he had seen little that was readily transferable. Americans, including Roosevelt and Hopkins, recoiled from "the dole," had to grapple with the implications of federal-state jurisdictions, and possessed a different ethic of cross-class obligation.*

Roosevelt called the Social Security Act "a cornerstone in a structure that is being built but is by no means complete. . . . a law that will take care of human needs and at the same time provide for the United States an economic structure of vastly greater soundness." But why "social insurance" at that point, and what did it have to do with fighting the Depression? The president understood that social security taxes would be a drag on the economy, that they were regressive, and that over several decades the reserve fund would face a deficit. Advisers ranging from Rexford Tugwell to Morgenthau told him so. He also probably realized that the British and German social insurance systems had long since ceased to bear any resemblance to an actuarially sound plan and drew heavily on general revenues.

Knowledgeable critics outside the administration told the larger public in irrefutable detail the same things. The public, focused on near-term benefits, did not much care. The use of the word "insurance" and the reliance on worker contributions gave political protection to a system the president and a host of New Dealers desperately wanted to institutionalize as a permanent aspect of American life, even if it got in the way of economic recovery. As Roosevelt told Luther Gulick years later, "With those taxes in there, no damn politician can ever scrap my social security program." Before becoming New Dealers, he and his lieutenants had been early-twentieth-century progressives concerned with institutional reform, not economic cycles. The Depression had given them an oppor-

---

* I have profited greatly from Daniel Rodgers's chapter on the New Deal in his admirable work *Atlantic Crossings* (Cambridge: Harvard University Press, 1998). It does seem to me, however, that his stress on European examples is somewhat less than half the story. The American social security system surely profited from European experiences, but it was put together in an entirely different spirit with its own emphases. On the idea that Britain was a model, see, e.g., *New York Times*, Jan. 6, 1935. On differences, e.g., Raymond Gram Swing, "Social Security in Great Britain," *Nation* (Feb. 13, 1935), 179–81. For the Hopkins trip, Searle F. Charles, *Minister of Relief: Harry Hopkins and the Depression* (Syracuse: Syracuse University Press, 1963), 91–92; Robert E. Sherwood, *Roosevelt and Hopkins*, rev. ed. (New York: Grosset & Dunlap, 1950), 63–64; and Hopkins, Press Conference, Aug. 24, 1934, WPA Papers, National Archives, as reproduced at *http://newdeal.feri.org*.

tunity they would not let pass—and besides, social security might actually provide some cushioning in future economic dips. Social welfare ideas the New Dealers possessed in abundance; economic recovery strategy was by comparison a mirage on the horizon.[26]

The one anti-depression measure that had worked politically and that might stimulate recovery was work relief. In the winter of 1933–34, the Civil Works Administration had provided millions of jobs and given a brief jolt to the economy. Nonetheless, it had been terminated in the belief that it was too expensive and that too many of its programs were sham make-work improvisations. By early 1935, after a difficult winter without it, there were demands to bring it back. Roosevelt and those around him all saw work relief as morally preferable to the dole, especially if the projects left something solid behind them. They were also sufficiently experienced in public life to understand that jobs and contracts could be leveraged into political power far more effectively than anonymous checks handed out indiscriminately. Members of Congress, primarily Democrats, generally agreed with one or more of these motivations. The social security bill crept slowly through the legislative process. A $4.88 billion Emergency Relief Appropriation Act moved on a fast track—$4 billion for works projects, $880 million for the phaseout of the dole. Roosevelt signed it on April 8, 1935, less than a hundred days after the new Congress had convened.

Ten months earlier, John Maynard Keynes's article "Agenda for the President," copied to the White House a week after Keynes's meeting with Roosevelt, had declared that $400 million a month of deficit spending would create "a strong business revival." Perhaps by sheer coincidence, perhaps because Keynes had a greater impact than he realized, the $4.88 billion relief appropriation provided precisely that amount for twelve months.[27] In a very real sense, the new work relief program would test the promise and limitations of the Keynesian formula.

The two major claimants for the greatest bundle of legislative funds ever voted in peacetime were Harold Ickes and Harry Hopkins. As secretary of the interior and PWA administrator, Ickes had established an imposing record. After a slow start, the PWA had assumed a prominent presence as the one continuing builder of public projects. Although its name was most conspicuously attached to such huge endeavors as New York's Triborough Bridge, a new Chicago sewer system, huge hydroelectric dams in the Pacific Northwest, and the aircraft carriers *Yorktown* and *Enterprise*, the agency also had done many minor local improvements. Matching state funds frequently had to be raised through packages that promised something to almost every locality. In Missouri, for example, the PWA built structures such as the massive Kansas City Municipal Auditorium, but also modest two-story brick school buildings like the one that housed the entire educational effort of the little town of Humansville.* In Montana, it would build the Fort Peck Dam but also construct a variant of its basic schoolhouse plan to replace a shack that had been the city hall of Libby.[28] The agency did its work with remarkably little waste and few irregularities. Ickes, a man of boundless territorial aspirations, could naturally see himself as the major beneficiary of the new relief bill.

Hopkins had a relationship with Roosevelt that stretched back to the New York Temporary Emergency Relief Administration. He enjoyed the president's affection to a far greater degree than did the prickly, grasping Ickes. Most importantly, as administrator of the CWA, he had demonstrated a knack for finding and quickly implementing small-scale, labor-intensive projects that could employ lots of workers. In a fireside chat on April 28, 1935, Roosevelt stated his goals for the new program: putting to work 3.5 million persons, employing them on useful projects, spending "a considerable portion of the money" on labor, deploying the funds promptly. His words were a description of the way in which CWA had functioned. A CWA-type job had cost about $1,000 a year per employee, a PWA job four times as much. In Germany, the Nazis had put the unemployed to work with state coercion and bare-survival wages. In England, Chamberlain had decided that large work relief programs were financially impossible. It would be up to Hopkins to demonstrate there was an American middle way.[29]

The Emergency Relief Act appropriation was sliced up among several agencies. The Resettlement Administration (RA), the Rural Electrification Administration (REA), the Civilian Conservation Corps, the National Youth Administration (NYA), and some lesser beneficiaries divided up about $750 million. Around $1.25 billion eventually had to be diverted to FERA dole payments. A half-billion went to roads and highways, mostly funded through the Department of Agriculture's Bureau of Roads. A half-billion went to non-emergency agencies for various purposes. Most of the rest was split between Ickes and Hopkins, who

---

*In which the author received his primary and secondary education.

engaged in a bitter turf battle within a Rube Goldberg–style administrative structure. The PWA got about $445 million, most of the rest (less than $1.2 billion) went to Hopkins for the new Works Progress Administration (WPA). Even after that, however, the organizational lines of control remained fuzzy. The feud between Ickes and Hopkins simmered on without end. Roosevelt may have feared that Ickes, a much-respected old progressive, would resign if formally made subordinate to Hopkins. As in other cases, he may have hoped to maintain ultimate control by dividing authority and fomenting rivalries. The tactic, more suited to a dictator fearing overthrow by a lieutenant than to a democratic leader, simply created friction and inefficiency.[30]

For the moment the focus was on the unprecedented task of creating 3.5 million jobs. The WPA, although not the only agency in the effort, was front and center. Expenses had to be held to $1,100–1,200 per employee, including materials and overhead as well as salaries. The projects had to be useful. The president made it clear that he did not want to be accused of funding "invented work." What could be done under such limitations? *Time* magazine predicted "an abundance of wooden bridges, sidewalk and sewer repair, touring theatrical companies and a census-taking on practically everything from retail liquor stores to the number of unemployed." Hopkins and Ickes soon worked out an agreement that in general any project costing more than $25,000 would be done by the PWA, any project costing less by WPA. There were plenty of modest but useful endeavors left for Hopkins's operation—malaria control, clearing woodland, rechanneling small rivers, repairing public buildings, constructing small bridges, improving roads, among other things. Inevitably there were also the censuses, including one of dogs in Kansas City (justified as a rabies-control measure). Eventually, Hopkins and his aides discovered ways of breaking up larger projects into small packages that were within the $25,000 limit.[31]

The public expected jobs immediately, but it was impossible to generate and approve applications that would employ millions in a matter of months. The need to keep projects cheap inevitably produced embarrassments. The schoolhouse at Palermo, North Dakota (205 residents), burned down, generating a request for a new one, the building of which could provide work for many of the hundred or so citizens on the relief rolls. WPA officials rejected the request as too expensive, offering instead to develop a golf course and a bird sanctuary. By mid-September, the WPA had less than 400,000 workers on its payroll, 125,000 fewer than the CCC.[32]

Critics from the right attacked the WPA's disorganization, bureaucratic limitations, and political favoritism. Critics from the left agreed on all these counts, but they saw the new works program as just one more case of what the *New Republic* called "sudden whims and vagaries at the top . . . lack of planning and the attempt to rush through impossible jobs overnight" that had long characterized the administration. What the country needed, the magazine editorialized in the aftermath of the British general election that had returned Stanley Baldwin's National government to power, was a thoughtful, comprehensive European approach that saw the needy—employables and unemployables—as a single problem. The New Deal should plan big public works, say "a real housing program, and . . . such things as a modern transcontinental highway." It should spend whatever it took to meet human needs and bring back prosperity. "Conservative England" had already built a million and a quarter houses with public money, imposed taxes fifty percent higher than in the U.S., taken on a per capita debt three times as large. Reflecting the spirit of John Dewey, it declared, "Perhaps most important of all, England has taken one line and stuck to it, instead of starting a new plan about every Monday and abandoning it ten days later." The results of these policies, the magazine concluded, were "written large for all the world to see."[33]

The *New Republic*'s admonitions had some merit, but Hopkins had just begun to fight. By February 1936, WPA employment was at just over 3 million plus another 300,000 NYA workers. Costs exceeded the budget, but with an election looming, Congress was generous with extra funds. In October 1936, all the work relief agencies combined had about 4.2 million on their rolls; another 2.66 million people were receiving some form of non-work federal public assistance. None of this was as systematic or as imbedded in American political culture as in a European social service state, but neither was it a niggling effort.

If the problem of numbers was mainly a matter of time, the problem of politics was present from the beginning. Roosevelt admonished the WPA to follow the principle of non-discrimination in religion, race, and political affiliation. From the perspective of Washington, this made perfect sense. To the extent politics was a motivation, relief recipients, whether Republican or Democrat, Protestant or Catholic, white or black, were unlikely to resent the administration that helped them in time of need and likely to vote for it overwhelmingly. At the state and local level, however, considerations were different. Politicians instinctively saw the WPA and related agencies as giant patronage opportunities. Jobs for the unemployed and contracts for public projects were the loaves and fishes that attracted political loyalists and built organizations. The Depression amplified their importance.

The organization of the WPA was of necessity decentralized. So great an operation, involving so many small projects, could not be run on a top-down basis. Washington exercised loose overall supervision, intervening in extreme cases. In early 1935, Hopkins had taken control of the Ohio FERA operations away from Governor Martin Davey, after he had shaken down contractors for campaign and inaugural expenses.[34] But it was difficult to establish sufficient grounds for the takeover of a state relief operation, and logistically hard to effect a comprehensive shift in management at the grass roots. And who could profit but the Republicans?

The key players in the politics of WPA were the state administrators, who were at the center of a web of contacts that went into every county and town within their jurisdictions. Approved by the dominant Democratic organization, the state director appointed politically amenable subordinates at the grassroots level, giving due deference to independent local factions, but usually freezing out irreconcilables. In the little town of Dixon, Illinois, for example, men seeking WPA employment went to Jack Reagan, an affable Irish-Catholic foot soldier in the state Democratic machine headed by Chicago mayor Ed Kelly. (In later years, his son, Ronald, could never quite bring himself to condemn New Deal work relief.) Successful candidates were understandably likely to be not just probable Democratic voters but also grateful party workers. In many places, they also were seen as sources of campaign funds and badgered for kickbacks in the way that patronage recipients always had been. However Roosevelt and Hopkins felt about this, they could do little about it.

Democratic congressional delegations saw all this as normal politics. Senator Harry S. Truman responded to a correspondent who asked for help in obtaining a WPA job, "If you will send me indorsements from the Kansas City Democratic organization, I will be glad to see what I can do for you." Democrats from the same state might squabble uninhibitedly for WPA control. The young newly elected West Virginia senator Rush Holt, unable to take the oath of office until he reached the constitutional age of thirty in late 1935, had to watch in dismay as his fellow Democrat Matt Neely staffed every significant WPA office in their state. Congressional Democrats, fearful that Hopkins would be relatively nonpartisan if permitted, required Senate confirmation for any WPA employee paid more than $5,000 a year. After that, there was little for Hopkins to do but play along with any political request that was not patently illegal.[35]

For many conservatives, the WPA highlighted an administration strategy of maintaining power through "votes by subsidy," as *Kansas City Star* Washington correspondent Theodore Alford put it. "Those who pay the taxes to support the government are far outnumbered by those who receive the direct benefits. . . . jobs and government gratuities are the most effective vote makers." As if to confirm such predictions, the WPA and related programs had a way of getting larger in the months before elections. The WPA gave many Democratic machines an important source of patronage and must have produced votes for them. It is much less clear how many reliefers bothered to vote and did so with a sense of gratitude. Among those—always a small minority—touched for campaign funds, how many took revenge in the privacy of the voting booth? And how did unsuccessful applicants for WPA jobs react? Conversely, was there anything wrong in a jobless person voting for a government that had provided work? Did not governments engage in a social good by giving employment to those who needed it?

The WPA would endure until 1943, doing far more good than harm. It would never at any one time provide jobs for 3.5 million people, much less a majority of the unemployed. Still, over its lifetime it employed perhaps ten million individuals. For those critics who valued hard, tangible public works, it left behind monuments galore. A list of new construction (as opposed to repairs or renovations) through December 1941 included more than 500,000 miles of "low-type surface roads," another 50,000 miles of "high-type surface" streets and highways, 75,000 bridges and viaducts, a million culverts, nearly 23,000 miles of storm and sanitary sewers, 880 sewage treatment plants, 3.6 million linear feet of airport runways, nearly 6,000 athletic fields and playgrounds, 770 swimming pools, 8,333 recreational buildings, and 5,584 educational buildings. Among the more ephemeral accomplishments were nearly 900 million school lunches. Many of its softer projects, such as the much-criticized Federal Theater, state and city guides, and oral histories with former slaves, possessed value. The professionals they hired, in common with manual laborers, had to eat. Politics, waste, and boondoggling were always there to some extent. So were millions of lives made a little bit better by a helter-skelter, imperfect endeavor. After mid-1935, the WPA, more than any other program, was the face of the New Deal.[36]

Other offshoots of the Emergency Relief Appropriation worked at improving the lives of the underprivileged. The Rural Electrification Administration (REA) was perhaps its most popular product. It is nearly impossible at the dawn of the twenty-first century to imagine the lives of farmers, still about twenty-two percent of the total population, during the Depression. Nine out of ten, from one end of the country to the other, had no electricity, and lived lives of grim drudgery with no refrigeration, running water, washing machines, reliable radios, indoor toilets, or other modern conveniences. By and large, the utility companies had not ventured into areas in which the population was too scattered and sparse to constitute a profitable market. The REA was established as a lending agency charged with financing rural electric cooperatives or publicly owned entities. Its first administrator, Morris L. Cooke, was capable and energetic. Arriving at a time when price supports had put money in the pockets of farm families, his agency had a ready clientele. The private utilities now frequently found themselves barred from areas that had begun to seem feasible for expansion and were undercut by their subsidized, nonprofit competition.[37]

Wherever the lines went, most farm families signed up. Few could aspire to the fully electrified model farm the REA set up in Fairfax County, Virginia. The house had every conceivable comfort, including "air-cooling" and a dishwasher. The shop was filled with electrically powered tools. The dairy barn had electric milking machines, refrigeration, and screens that zapped flies trying to get at the livestock. In 1936, Congress passed a bill sponsored by George Norris and Sam Rayburn establishing REA as a permanent agency. By 1937, it had electrified half a million farms, by 1941 another million. To the New Dealers, the agency demonstrated the superiority of public enterprise and the cooperative principle. To the electric utilities, it was socialism incarnate. Most of its customers probably just saw it as a good deal and made little distinction between it and other utility companies.[38]

Another beneficiary of the Emergency Relief appropriation was the Resettlement Administration (RA), which Roosevelt established by executive order on May 1. He named Undersecretary of Agriculture Rexford Tugwell to head it. Pulling together a group of overlapping divisions from the Department of the Interior, the FERA, and the AAA, the RA signaled a new focus on agriculture's neglected constituency, the rural poor. For Tugwell, his standing severely damaged by the purge of the lib-erals from the AAA, the new position was an opportunity to run an agency of his own freed from the inexorable constraints of the agricul-tural interest groups. He hoped to deliver sorely needed help to some of America's most underprivileged individuals and gain a niche within the New Deal for social rehabilitation through collectivist planning.

RA inherited numerous planned community projects. These were new towns built by the government with modest but up-to-date housing, a community center, health plans, credit unions, retail co-ops, collective ownership of the land, and locally developed regulations for orderly living. To one degree or another, they were projects conceived by policy intellec-tuals influenced by European examples.[39] Most were either agricultural vil-lages organized around collective farming enterprises or small towns with collectively owned light manufacturing. The three most successful were suburban developments, populated by working- and lower-middle-class families: Greenbelt, Maryland (near Washington); Greendale, Wisconsin (near Milwaukee); and Greenhills, Ohio (near Cincinnati). In these places, it was not necessary to invent the means of economic sustenance and far easier to take advantage of an industrial recovery.

The most famous of the small-town communities was Arthurdale, West Virginia, just south of Morgantown. Its godmother was Eleanor Roosevelt, who in the mid-1920s had attempted a similar, if less ambi-tious and ultimately unsuccessful, project for poor farmers around Hyde Park, New York. Arthurdale, underwritten by a reluctant Harold Ickes, was conceived as an inspirational showpiece; it would house about 150 families, mostly headed by unemployed and homeless coal miners, on 1,200 acres purchased by the government. Each family would own its own little house ($2,000 with a 30-year mortgage) on a two to five acre plot—large enough for a good-sized garden and a few head of livestock. (The First Lady had wanted a community garden and herd.) A subsidized factory manufacturing equipment for the post office department would provide regular employment. In addition to the usual social services, the community would have a school practicing the progressive education of John Dewey and headed by a Dewey protégé. There would be a handi-craft center engaged in furniture making, basket weaving, and the like. The community would stage theatrical performances, folk music, singing, and dancing.[40]

To describe the vision is perhaps sufficient to demonstrate its impracti-cality. The West Virginians of Arthurdale were hard-working people who were victims of bad times, and probably at least as good as any random sample of Americans. They were not happy peasants to be uplifted by an enlightened intelligentsia. They lived in a segregated state and had deeply imbedded prejudices about race. To Mrs. Roosevelt's special distress, they refused to accept Negro residents, telling her "we feel we should not risk the loss of the respect we have gained." The project suffered one cost overrun after another. Congress forbade any subsidized manufacturing, in part because of the efforts of a congressman from an Indiana district with a factory that supplied the post office. The state of West Virginia refused to accredit the school until Dewey's disciple was thrown out and it accepted the jurisdiction of the county school board. Some critics of the New Deal picked up on Arthurdale's multiple problems and wrote scathing articles decrying waste, regimentation, and the debt burden foisted on its mortgaged citizens. Others were outraged that its housing was better than that of most working West Virginians.[41] Arthurdale was an extreme example because it enjoyed the special patronage of Eleanor Roosevelt, but it exemplified wider problems.

The farm cooperatives, easily caricatured as Stalinist collectives, bred even worse public relations. While they provided comfort and a degree of security to their clients, they also ran against the basic impulses of most of the people they served. As a grizzled old Arkansas farmer put it to Tugwell's chief aide, Will Alexander: "I believe a man could stick around here for five or six years and save enough money to go off and buy himself a little hill farm of his own." Arthurdale had been scandalously expensive, mainly because no one—the president least of all—wanted to cross the First Lady. But all the community projects were far more costly than conventional forms of relief for the poor. Roosevelt himself finally laid down the law on expense. Tugwell, the most radical senior member of the administration and from the beginning a whipping boy of its opponents, resigned shortly after the 1936 election. The RA would give way to the Farm Security Administration, a different sort of attempt to rehabilitate impoverished farmers.[42]

＞＜

On Capitol Hill, in the meantime, the New Deal veered sharply to the left of its original game plan. In May 1935, a revolutionary labor bill was making its way through the legislative process. Attempts at union organization had mostly failed to this point, but in the wake of the November elections labor strength in Congress was greater than ever. All union leaders agreed that the NRA labor provisions (section 7a) had been ineffective. They advocated tough legislation to facilitate union organization.

That February, Senator Robert F. Wagner of New York introduced a bill to institutionalize section 7a by enacting it into law outside the structure of a collapsing NRA and setting up an independent quasi-judicial agency to enforce it. The Wagner bill specifically established the right of workers to organize and bargain collectively, specified as illegal a series of antiunion "unfair management practices," and authorized a freestanding National Labor Relations Board to enforce the law. In effect, this was labor's alternative to Roosevelt's request for another two years of the NRA. FDR watched silently as Wagner's bill moved steadily through the Senate. NRA renewal languished, and the administration waited with increasing anxiety for the Supreme Court to rule on the agency's constitutionality. On May 16, the Wagner bill passed the Senate by a whopping 63–12 vote. It seemed likely to sail through the House also. Eight days later, Roosevelt cautiously announced that he supported the principles of the legislation.

Very early on in the new Congress, the administration had established yet another priority. It decided to attack the large electrical utility combines that had been put together in the 1920s and flourished until the Depression had brought them down. Electricity in the early twentieth century had been a growth industry without visible limits, expanding rapidly to meet what seemed an insatiable demand, stimulating consumer purchases of household appliances, regularly cutting rates as it achieved economies of scale, generating ever greater cash flows. Financiers and entrepreneurs saw opportunities in consolidation. They acquired local and regional electric companies through "leveraged buyouts" made possible by "junk bonds," sold to the investing public. Such transactions were premised on the assumption that the constantly increasing revenues of the acquired utilities would pay for the purchase. The utility consolidators united their acquisitions by creating extraordinarily complex holding company structures with substantial debt loads. The greatest of them was Samuel Insull, who built an enormous, if scattered, empire that included Commonwealth Edison in Chicago and was controlled by seven holding companies.

These techniques were all legal and well-established; they had been employed in other industries with varying degrees of success, most notably by J. P. Morgan in his creation of U.S. Steel, International Harvester, and other great "trusts" of the early twentieth century. All the same, the big utility combines outraged traditional progressives who hated and feared them in the same spirit they had attacked Morgan's creations. The Depression provided an opening; reduced demand and declining revenues sent the big utilities crashing to the ground with huge losses to investors. Insull, pilloried as a robber baron, was subjected to three separate trials on charges of mail fraud, embezzlement, and violating bankruptcy laws. He was acquitted each time.

From the early 1920s progressives had argued that the generation and sale of electricity should be a public function. Senator Norris had blocked the sale of the federal hydroelectric facility at Muscle Shoals, Alabama, for a decade, saving it to be the cornerstone of the Tennessee Valley Authority. If it were infeasible—as it clearly was—to achieve a total government takeover of electrical power, then the combines had to be broken up. Fragmented private enterprise was by definition more virtuous than consolidated, monopolistic private enterprise.

The progressive critique was simplistic in its analysis of the economics of capitalism and assumptions about the superiority of state enterprise. Nevertheless, New Dealers of all types embraced it passionately, not just old-time trust-busters like Norris, but younger, sophisticated intellectuals trained in law and economics. Most importantly, so did Franklin D. Roosevelt. In early February 1935, Senator Burton K. Wheeler of Montana and Representative Sam Rayburn of Texas introduced a White House–drafted bill that called for the elimination of *all* public utility holding companies by January 1, 1940. In March, the president sent a message to Congress underscoring his commitment to the legislation. "I am against private socialism of concentrated private power as thoroughly as I am against governmental socialism," he declared. "Destruction of private socialism is utterly essential to avoid governmental socialism."[43]

Utility company executives interpreted Roosevelt's policy as disingenuous and fought back forcefully. Leaders in other lines of business were aware that Roosevelt's declaration could as easily be applied to any unit of big capitalism. The Wheeler-Rayburn bill, whatever Roosevelt's intentions, was a challenge to big business in general. Senator Hugo Black of Alabama, the most radical Southerner in the upper house, conducted a withering investigation of the intensive lobbying activity undertaken against it. Finding little or nothing that was illegal, he exposed a massive effort to influence congressional opinion, uncovered tens of thousands of telegrams that obviously had fraudulent signatures, badgered hostile witnesses mercilessly, and continued the probe long after the bill had achieved final passage. Raymond Clapper, a respected liberal columnist, called the tactics "Nazi methods." Walter Lippmann, increasingly pulling back from the New Deal, wrote "when lawlessness is used for supposedly good ends, it will be used even more viciously for bad ones."[44]

The Black investigation galvanized a lot of indignation against the utilities. At the same time, it redoubled the commitment of all of American business against the direction in which the administration was moving, and it produced an attractive new spokesman for the utilities. Wendell Willkie, president of Commonwealth and Southern Corporation, was young (forty-three), aggressive, and an active Democrat with a record of moderate progressivism. The outright abolition of the holding company, he asserted, would wreck the industry. If bad or incompetent men had misused it in the past, then the remedy was regulation.

Willkie's argument had considerable merit. The apparent administration vision of a private electrical utility industry composed of relatively small local and regional companies made little sense in the world of twentieth-century corporate capitalism, especially when contrasted with federal plans for large-scale power production in the Tennessee Valley and the Pacific Northwest, or with the establishment of the Rural Electrification Administration. It was not unreasonable for the utilities and their stockholders to perceive a hidden agenda of the total socialization of electricity behind the Holding Company bill and these other activities.[45] What should have been a compromisible argument about the scope of regulation necessary to prevent future financial excesses had become a matter of principle that fed growing resentment of the New Deal within the business community, on Main Street as well as on Wall Street.

There was a lot of moderate opinion on Capitol Hill for legislation that would block convoluted corporate structures while preserving the right of utility corporations to use the holding company. Yet the congressional progressives and the White House were spoiling for a fight against the utilities, which responded in kind. By late May, it was clear that it would be an uphill fight to preserve an unconditional "death penalty." The White House, having drawn the line, was determined to fight to the finish.

At the same time, the administration was pushing through an important but less emotional bill that transformed American banking and finance. The legislation was largely the work of Marriner Eccles, the new chairman of the Federal Reserve Board. The oldest son of a devout and fertile Utah Mormon businessman who fathered 21 children by two wives, Eccles had inherited a third of his father's $7 million fortune to manage for his mother and eight maternal siblings in 1912. Over the next twenty years, he built a family empire in banking, construction, dairy products, and lumber. Only forty-four when he came to Washington, he brought with him the outlook of a regional banker sensitive to the way in which the New York Federal Reserve Bank had dominated the system. Determined to be a consequential Fed chairman, Eccles sought to concentrate power in the board rather than in the twelve quasi-independent and privately controlled Federal Reserve district banks. The existing decentralized system had reflected the underlying Jeffersonianism of Woodrow Wilson's New Freedom; the new bill reflected a fundamental centralizing tendency of the New Deal.[46]

To most of the banking world (and not a few non-banker commentators) the bill raised the specter of political control of the banking system, rampant inflation, and the eventual collapse of the dollar. There was wide support for decentralization, not least from Senator Carter Glass of Virginia, one of the key authors of the original Federal Reserve Act. The noted economist Irving Fisher declared that the bill would come near to making the president (through his control of the Fed chairman) "an economic dictator." In one of the first of many editorials against the bill the *New York Times* pointed out that the erratic credit policy of the Federal Reserve Board had contributed greatly to the crash of 1929 and suggested the possibility that greater wisdom might emanate from district banks not under the thumb of Washington politicians. Disagreements between Eccles and Glass on points of principle spilled over into a bitter personality conflict that stalled the bill. Much of the nation's financial establishment was convinced that New Dealers could not be counted on to preserve the integrity of a currency they already had devalued.[47]

By early 1935, then, empowered by the lurch to the left in the 1934 elections, Roosevelt had decided not simply on a big relief program and social security reform, but was also backing a number of measures that amounted to a declaration of war against the business community. By the last week in May, with traditional congressional adjournment time just weeks away, the Wagner, Wheeler-Rayburn, and banking bills were still up in the air, with the administration leaning distinctly toward the first and determined to get the last two.

In his 1934 article "Agenda for the President," Keynes had sought to advise Roosevelt on the importance and sources of weak business confidence. Corporate and financial leaders, he declared, were affected by "the perplexity and discomfort which the business world feels from being driven so far from its accustomed moorings into unknown and uncharted waters."[48] The administration had created a climate of uncertainty about the future; it also contributed to a self-perpetuating cycle of mutual loathing between business and government that was bad for the country. Perhaps the most inept example of this phenomenon was the administration's effort to prosecute former Secretary of the Treasury Andrew Mellon for income tax evasion.

Emotionally backed by Roosevelt and Morgenthau, personally handled by Assistant Attorney General Robert H. Jackson, the action was an effort to discredit a hated partisan figure and, in effect, criminalize the porous tax code he had done so much to shape in the 1920s. The main government contention was that Mellon had established an illegal trust to develop his huge and immensely valuable art collection. *Fortune* commented fairly that "The plain fact of the matter was that Mr. Mellon had made out his tax return in one economic era and was being prosecuted for it in another." A federal grand jury rejected Jackson's case for an indictment. Government claims wound up in federal tax court, which dismissed most of them in 1937. It pointedly observed that the law gave every man the "presumption of good faith in his business dealings." By then, Mellon was dead, but at the end of 1936, the old tycoon had scored an embarrassing public relations coup by giving his art collection to the nation and endowing the National Gallery of Art, leaving Roosevelt no alternative but to praise his "very wonderful offer to the people of the United States."[49]

On the morning of Monday, May 27, the New Deal seemed to be moving along purposefully, if with some hitches and midcourse corrections. At the end of the day, the Supreme Court had thrown its future into profound doubt.[50]

The Court that Roosevelt inherited and that sat unaltered through his first term had always been problematic. Seven of the nine members were Republican appointees. Observers saw it as roughly divided into three factions: the conservatives (Willis Van Devanter, James McReynolds, George Sutherland, Pierce Butler), who could be counted on to oppose almost any New Deal measure; the "liberals" (Louis Brandeis, Harlan Fiske Stone, Benjamin Cardozo), usually willing to give the benefit of a doubt to elected legislatures; the swing judges (Chief Justice Charles Evans Hughes and Owen Roberts), moderate Republicans who possessed no sharply etched outlook of their own. As a group, the justices were jurists of distinction. The conservatives would be too peremptorily dismissed in later years because they ended up on the wrong side of history. The swing judges would look confused because they zigged and zagged from case to case. The three liberals inclined toward the idea that law was based on experience rather than abstract principle, that the Constitution was malleable; but even they had a sense of limits. Inherently the most conservative branch of government, composed of unelected judges, prone to think in terms of abstract principles, the judiciary suddenly found itself facing legislation and administrative action that centralized government as never before and thereby thrust it into areas where it never had been. The results were bound to be a muddle.[51]

In 1934, a 5–4 majority composed of the liberals and the swing judges had appeared willing to give state legislatures near-total authority to deal with the Depression. One key decision upheld a Minnesota law suspending mortgage foreclosures and thereby impairing the obligations of contracts (*Minnesota Mortgage Moratorium Case*). Another (*Nebbia v. New York*) sustained a New York state law designed to protect dairy farmers by setting a minimum price for milk.

But in January 1935, by an 8–1 vote, the Court struck down the NRA petroleum code, specifically those provisions that imposed state-by-state production quotas (*Hot Oil Case*) as an improper congressional delegation of power to the executive branch. The remedy was easy enough. The administration got Congress to enact the petroleum code, which had wide support among oil drillers and refiners, as a freestanding law.

A few weeks later, February 18, 1935, the Court rejected a challenge to the devaluation of the dollar and suspension of gold payments. Its 5–4 decision, agreed on by the liberals and swing judges and written by Hughes, declared that the government's power to coin money overrode private contracts. The decision also said that the government was not required to keep its own promise to redeem U.S. bonds in gold, because the plaintiffs could not demonstrate a loss of value. The latter argument declared in effect that the administration's monetary policy had been saved by deflation rather than by its inherent authority.

The next big case came on May 6. By a 5–4 decision—Roberts writing the majority opinion, Hughes voting with the liberals—the Court struck down one of the relatively minor acts of the early New Deal, the Railroad

Retirement Act of 1934, which required the railroads to establish pension plans for retirement-age employees. Roberts held that certain of the
law's regulations violated the "due process" clause of the Fifth Amendment *and* that the primary justification for the law—the congressional
power to regulate interstate commerce—could not be used to establish a
mandatory pension plan. The very narrow definition of the interstate
commerce power was ominous.[52]

This set the stage for May 27—Black Monday to New Dealers.

That Monday, the Court issued three stunning 9–0 decisions. One
rejected Roosevelt's dubious attempt to remove a Republican member of
the Federal Trade Commission (*Humphrey's Executor v. United States*).[53]
The second (*Louisville Bank v. Radford*) invalidated the rather extreme
Frazier-Lemke antiforeclosure act of 1934, a bill that Roosevelt had
signed with some reluctance. Neither of these decisions represented a
threat to the New Deal; neither amounted to a severe rebuke to the president; both likely would have been rendered by a quite different Court
fifty years later. The third (*Schechter v. United States*) seemed aimed at the
heart of the New Deal.

The plaintiffs, the Schechter brothers, had been convicted of violating
several provisions of the NRA poultry code, most grievously by selling
diseased chickens. They perhaps were better defendants for the government than Fred Perkins, but the code itself, involving a fragmented
industry of small family businesses, was a case study of NRA overreaching. The decision, written by Hughes, repeated and somewhat clarified
the *Hot Oil* doctrine on excessive delegation of legislative power to the
executive. (So far, so good; codes with sufficient support could be enacted
directly by Congress.) But Hughes went on to declare that the codes were
also invalid because they regulated businesses that were primarily
intrastate in their operations.

The interstate commerce power had been a primary tool for the extension of federal authority since the early days of the republic. It also had
been perhaps the most controversial clause in the Constitution, periodically expanded or contracted by successive Supreme Courts. Hughes
employed an extremely narrow definition that dismissed the fact that the
Schecters purchased much of their poultry from out of state before selling
it within the state. His conclusion was that the power to regulate interstate commerce applied only to transactions that in one way or another
actually crossed state lines. How much of the New Deal could survive
constitutional scrutiny of this sort? What would happen to social secu-

rity? The Wagner labor bill? The agricultural program? Any sort of economic regulation? Any new federal activity?

Roosevelt, like most presidents, usually made a show of responding to setbacks with detached serenity. This time he made no effort to conceal his anger. His entire life had been one in which he usually got his way. His revered cousin Theodore had given him an example of a strong and vociferous presidency. He was convinced that a national revival depended upon a reorganization of American economic life that could be directed only by an executive branch given extraordinary powers. Personal experience, political example, and ideology all merged to produce a sense of unfettered outrage. On May 31, he held his regular press conference, delivering an angry and masterful monologue that lasted more than an hour.

First, he read from letters and telegrams—a dozen of the two or three thousand that already had landed in the mail room of the White House—all them from small businessmen decrying the Court's action on the NRA and asking for help. "Nobody resents a Supreme Court decision," he said. "You can deplore a Supreme Court decision, and you can point out the effect of it." Deplore and point out, he did, displaying abundant resentment as he proceeded. Comparing *Schechter* to the *Dred Scott Case* and invoking the emergency legislation of the World War as a rightful analogue for the emergency of the Depression, he launched into an extended disquisition on the importance of the interstate commerce clause. The Supreme Court's doctrine, he declared, had stripped the federal government of most of its regulatory powers. "We have been relegated to the horse-and-buggy definition of interstate commerce."[54]

If the Supreme Court had meant to convey a message to end social experimentation, the president was returning it to sender.

HEADLINES AND MOVIE NEWSREELS

{1935}

JUNE 20   Huge Taxes for Rich; Roosevelt Calls for Great Increases in Levies on Big Inheritances and Incomes; To Share Wealth; Large Corporations Also Would Pay More

JUNE 20   Pass Wagner Bill; End to Company Unions; Permanent Tribunal Created

JUNE 26   Utilities Test Near; House Battle Over "Death Sentence" for Holding Companies

SEPTEMBER 11   Senator Long Dies; Succumbs to Assassin's Bullet

{1936}

JANUARY 7   Farm Program Unconstitutional; Supreme Court 6–3 Ruling

JUNE   *Panning in tightly on the president at the speaker's podium of the Democratic convention, the camera captures an aggressive, confident president reading the last lines of his speech: "We are fighting to save a great and precious form of government for ourselves and for the world. I accept the commission you have tendered me. I join with you. I am enlisted for the duration of the war." (Newsreel, "Democrats Nominate Roosevelt")*

OCTOBER 26   Landon Rips at New Deal; "America Must Be Free"

NOVEMBER 4   Avalanche of Faith; Greatest Vote of Confidence Given Any President

NOVEMBER 8   Air Priest Quits; Coughlin Withdraws From Radio

HIGH TIDE

SECOND HUNDRED DAYS,

SECOND NEW DEAL, SECOND TERM,

JUNE 1935–NOVEMBER 1936

Personalities: Idealist and Realist

It took all kinds to make a New Deal—dreamers, academic intellectuals, bureaucratic planners, calculating politicians, a charismatic electoral natural, and hard-edged men of power. Eleanor Roosevelt was a dreamer who kept the administration's conscience. John L. Lewis, little concerned with the finer aspirations of social reformers, but willing to pin his career on a drive to organize a hitherto unrepresented industrial workforce, supplied much of the money and muscle that kept it in power.

Eleanor Roosevelt: First Lady of Reform

The most admired woman of the mid-twentieth century began life as an ugly duckling, became an orphan, struggled with self-doubt the first thirty-five years of her life, cultivated an affinity with the underdogs of society, and became the greatest female politician of her time. Anna Eleanor Roosevelt was born in 1884 to wealth and power. Her father's older brother was Theodore Roosevelt; her mother, Anna Hall, was descended from the Livingstons, one of New York's first families. Father was a charming, indolent alcoholic, mother an uncaring parent quick to scorn her daughter's plain appearance. Both died when she was eight, leaving her to the care of a stern grandmother. Her brightest years of a bleak childhood and adolescence were the three she spent away from her family. Sent at the age of fifteen to Allenswood, an English finishing school, she developed both self-confidence and a social conscience under the tutelage of the institution's French headmistress.

In the summer of 1902, she came back to the United States to stay. Her Uncle Theodore was president, establishing an example of energy, social concern, and moral leadership that inspired her and excited much of the country. Out of a sense of duty and perhaps as a refuge from the dreary and demoralizing rounds of high society, she became involved in the types of social work and charitable activities associated with early-twentieth-century progressivism. She met and fell in love with her distant cousin, Franklin, then a charming twenty-year-old Harvard junior who shared her interest in reform causes and idolized TR. When they were married in March 1905, the president gave the bride away.

However much delight the young couple took in each other, the marriage stifled her personal aspirations. Her domineering mother-in-law was a constant, hostile presence. Six pregnancies in ten years left her with five children to care for (one died in infancy). The social obligations of the wife of an increasingly prominent politician kept her from the social service enterprises that once had engaged her. The marriage began to go flat. At the end of 1918, she discovered that her husband had been engaged in an affair with her social secretary, Lucy Mercer. The resolution, arrived at with the participation of her mother-in-law, was very Victorian. For the sake of the children—and Franklin's career—they would stay together without a sexual relationship. Franklin promised never to see Lucy again. After he was stricken with polio in 1921, Eleanor became his working partner—his legs, his ears, his eyes. Yet their personal lives were increasingly distant. Writing to her close friend Lorena Hickok in the fall of 1936, she was brutally frank: "I realize more & more that F.D.R. is a great man, & he is nice to me but as a person, I'm a stranger & I don't want to be anything else!"[1]

As her husband struggled to regain his mobility and reconstruct his political career, Eleanor served in many ways as his public proxy, affiliating with social welfarist organizations, developing ties to settlement house leaders and the Women's Trade Union League, joining the Women's Division of the New York Democratic State Committee, delivering speeches, making new contacts for Franklin. Never a suffragette nor a conspicuous feminist, she nevertheless was a tireless promoter of female engagement with politics, authoring magazine articles with titles such as "Women Must Learn to Play the Game as Men Do."[2] After FDR was elected governor of New York in 1928, her activism continued. She traveled around the state, making speeches and inspection trips, cultivating an ever-growing political network.

She came to the White House in 1933 a significant public figure, sure to be different from any First Lady before her. Uncertain how to present her to the public, press advisers arranged for newsreel cameramen to film her on horseback—in formal riding habit and accompanied by her friend Elinor Morgenthau—cantering through Washington's Rock Creek Park. Her own instincts were far surer. She held formal press conferences, for women journalists only. In 1936, she began a daily newspaper column. Possessing in many respects the same social worker's conscience as Frances Perkins (although the two were not particularly close), she saw herself as an advocate for the voiceless victims in American society—the poor, the unemployed, blacks. She had a special interest in the plight of underprivileged youth and women. She assiduously promoted work relief and more diverse opportunities for them. FDR, a calculating politician in the day-to-day business of constructing fragile coalitions, felt the need to be cautious. Eleanor could be more daring. From the beginning, it was she who supported the drive for an antilynching bill, worked in various ways to improve the lives of black Americans, and criticized racial segregation. A quiet feminist, she was at the head of an informal network of women reformers who held significant New Deal positions.[3]

A self-made public person, she possessed none of her husband's natural attributes, inbred security, or sense of entitlement to leadership. Her high-pitched speaking voice and patrician tone might have been the product of a talented comedienne. Her physical presence was unimposing, her sense of style non-existent. Those Americans most hostile to the New Deal by 1936 hated her even more vehemently than they hated the president. A greater number loved her for the causes she had adopted and brought to the forefront of American politics.[4]

John L. Lewis: Labor Baron

Americans became generally aware of him in the mid-1930s, an old coal miner in his fifties with a great, booming voice, a big head of dark red hair, and large, bushy eyebrows. John L. Lewis had begun the decade as the embattled head of a dwindling union; by its end, he was the voice of American labor. Born in Iowa to Welsh immigrants, Lewis had followed his father into the mines at an early age; attempts at other endeavors failed and brought him back to the underground occupation he came to represent. To be a coal miner was to enter a hard, dangerous profession in exchange for a somewhat higher wage than other types of semiskilled manual labor paid. Those who stayed the course tended to be proud, tough men with streaks of stubbornness and an easily aroused militance. Lewis fit the type perfectly. An amateur actor in his youth, he reveled in Shakespearean rhetoric. Far more articulate than the average worker, he was also a natural leader. A union activist from the beginning, he was by 1910 president of one of the largest United Mine Workers (UMW) locals in the southern Illinois coalfields.[5]

In 1920, Lewis became president of the union. It had grown to 400,000 men during the World War because of heavy demand for coal and supportive federal policy, but during the twenties, American coal was caught up in the same decline that gripped the rest of the world. American miners could not escape the wage cuts and layoffs that afflicted their counterparts in Wales, Yorkshire, or the Ruhr. Attempting to hold the line, Lewis sanctioned numerous strikes that mostly failed and left the UMW in a steep decline. As early as the mid-twenties, he faced a strong opposition, composed primarily of socialists and militants. He won a no-holds-barred struggle in which neither side was squeamish about violent intimidation. Perhaps no more ruthless than the opposition, he had greater resources. Accusing his opponents of Communist party affiliations, rigging union elections, and not hesitant to display armed force, he beat back repeated challenges. In the process, he made himself absolute dictator of what had been a relatively decentralized organization. What he could not do was stem the UMW's sharp decline. The Depression made things much worse. By the early thirties, UMW membership was down to about 80,000.

Although a registered Republican who had supported Herbert Hoover for president in 1928 and may have voted for him again in 1932, Lewis quickly adapted to the Roosevelt presidency. Using section 7a of the National Industrial Recovery Act as a basis for action, he initiated a highly successful campaign to reorganize the coal areas, telling the miners that President Roosevelt wanted them to join the union. By early 1936, the UMW claimed 540,000 members and a treasury of $2.3 million that would provide a basis for wider labor activism and political action.[6] He targeted the big non-union mining operations owned by the steel companies, a goal that pointed naturally also toward the organization of all steel company employees. From there, it was but a step to press the AFL to take advantage of the passage of the Wagner Act in July 1935 and engage in a serious attempt to organize the nation's big mass-production industries. Suddenly, the once-conservative Lewis found himself at the radical vanguard of the labor movement. He was joined by two unlikely partners, Sidney Hillman and David Dubinsky, New York Jewish socialists who headed the two major garment workers unions.

The craft unionists who still dominated the AFL resisted the concept of "one big union" for entire industries. A bitter debate at the AFL convention in October forecast defeat for the industrial organizers. Lewis terminated it characteristically. After a stiff exchange with William "Big Bill" Hutcheson of the Carpenters Union, he walked over to his adversary, felled him with one hard punch and left the hall. He and his New York partners proceeded to establish the Committee on Industrial Organization (CIO; later Congress of Industrial Organizations) to organize steel, autos, and other big targets. Through 1936, the CIO would work on two objectives—laying the groundwork for the union campaigns to follow and ensuring the reelection of Roosevelt, along with like-minded New Dealers at the state and local levels. Toward the first goal, Lewis understood that the human resources of the UMW and the garment unions were insufficient. He engaged in quiet negotiations with the Communist party, which had swung toward a "Popular Front" strategy of collaboration with other "progressive forces." He promised them control of minor unions and a chance at power in bigger ones.[7] The Communists, fanatically dedicated organizers, were a cheap and valuable resource. It is reputed that when uneasy associates worried that he might be turning over the American union movement to them, he replied, "Who gets the bird? The hunter or the dog?" Toward FDR's reelection, he envisioned a labor alliance with the Democratic party, cemented by big money and thousands of organizers.

John L. Lewis frequently told a story, perhaps true, about his early days in the mines. Once he was given the job of driving a coal car pulled by a strong but dangerous mule named Spanish Pete, reputed to be a man killer. Pete was valuable because of his pulling power, more valuable perhaps than a man's life. The animal reared up to kick its handler as Lewis led it around a tunnel curve. Lewis dodged the flailing hooves and grabbed the car's sprag (a heavy plank with a sharp spike, used as a brake on descending inclines). With a mighty blow, he drove the spike into Pete's head between the eyes, killing him instantly. Using clay to cover the wound, he persuaded his foreman that Pete had simply dropped dead. A blunt instrument, possessing no illusions about human nature, Lewis obsessively sought power for himself and cared only for the men who accepted his leadership. He pursued his mission with no regard for the sensibilities of middle-class America. He understood that he could succeed only with government support and that the goal would require more labor money and activity in politics than ever before.

Class Card, Political Surge

Roosevelt and the New Deal had established a fundamental direction before the *Schechter* decision. The Supreme Court aroused his fighting instincts. So did the belligerence of his opposition from the banking and business communities. Convinced that the people were on his side, personally affronted by his critics, Roosevelt determined to fight through the summer of 1935 for a program that would tame the forces of privilege, erect a social welfare state, and build an irresistible political coalition. As usual, his skills as a tactician were unmatched. They were deployed not solely for personal vindication but in the service of a strategic goal that was in many respects admirable. The unfolding scenario nonetheless raised anew the question of whether the New Deal was primarily about recovery or about reform, about restoring prosperity or about taming capitalism and humbling capitalists.

The Supreme Court decisions had rewritten the rule book within which an administration program had to be played out. Roosevelt hinted at his May 31 press conference that he might mount a direct challenge, perhaps in the form of advocating constitutional amendments that would give clear and broad definition to federal authority. But even with solid majority support amending the Constitution would be slow, difficult, and, most likely, a lost cause. In the meantime, the energies of the New Deal had to be channeled in different directions. The president quickly realized that the NRA, for all his attachment to the ideal, was beyond resuscitation. An executive order continued it in skeleton form, largely as an information-gathering agency. Its demise liberated him from a failing program. It also required a quick reformulation of his objectives and allowed him to recast his political base in light of the changing configurations of power around him. Something had to replace the NRA's charter for labor, Section 7a. The Wagner labor bill now received the president's strong backing, and the New Deal alignment with an emerging, militant labor movement was suddenly far less equivocal than before. Roosevelt liked from time to time to compare himself to Andrew Jackson. In that spirit, he found it easy to interpret the Supreme Court majority as one more component of a coalition of reactionaries in business and banking, representing the interests of entrenched wealth. Like Jackson, he was quick to take on a fight.

Not all bankers and businesspeople had welcomed the Court's action, but even those who had reaped benefits from the NRA were wary of the potential of an all-embracing cartelism that might be more directly controlled by the government, instead of their trade associations. The big banks and brokerage firms chafed under new regulatory restrictions already imposed or in the works. The utilities were at war with the administration. Businesses of all sorts saw the New Deal as having unleashed militant labor organizers. Meeting in Washington late in April, the United States Chamber of Commerce, an organization with a heavy representation of small and medium-size enterprises, passed resolutions opposing the extension of the NRA, the social security bill, the public utility holding company bill, the banking bill, the agriculture program, and the Wagner labor bill. The speakers were close to unanimous in their vehement condemnation of the administration. Elite business leaders who had been influential in the movement to establish the NRA quietly tried to reassure the president, but from Roosevelt's perspective organized business was no longer just drifting away; it had cut its lines to the administration.

At a more personal level, Roosevelt knew that he faced the active opposition and personal hostility of many of his own privileged kind, men whom he had known as fellow students at Harvard, with whom he had practiced law, with whom he had shared club memberships. A year later, the *New Yorker* cartoonist Peter Arno would provide an unforgettable depiction of their mood with a drawing of a group of the well-born inviting a tuxedoed friend and his companions to join them for an evening at a famous Manhattan newsreel theater: "Come along. We're going to the Trans-Lux to hiss Roosevelt." The real sentiment in such circles was much nastier, if equally impotent. As Roosevelt saw it, he faced an alliance of privileged groups that were attacking him. The logical response was to play the class card with an alliance of the underprivileged.[8]

A few days after his press conference attacking the Supreme Court, he met with congressional leaders who expected to wind up the session, as was customary in those days, by the end of June, carrying over until 1936 much of the legislation that had been making its way through the legislative sausage grinder. Speaking firmly, literally banging his fist on his desk, he demanded passage of the four big bills still pending—social security, Wagner labor, banking, utility holding company. This was the beginning of a full-court press in which the president used all his powers of persuasion, all the patronage at his disposal. He established to a greater extent than ever had existed a White House legislative operation, headed by Thomas G. "Tommy the Cork" Corcoran, a smart, tough young Irishman who had been sent to the White House by Felix Frankfurter, his teacher at Harvard Law School. Corcoran was brilliant, he was capable of enormous charm, but no one ever accused him of subtlety. Speaking to senators or congressmen twice his age, with the authority of the president behind him, he was more intimidating than deferential. He became the inevitable scapegoat for the real arm-twister, the president. Even many of the New Deal supporters on the Hill learned to detest him.[9]

On June 19, without the slightest warning, Roosevelt asked Congress for a new tax bill, designed to "distribute the burden of taxes equitably." His message went on to say, "Our revenue laws have operated in many ways to the unfair advantage of the few, and they have done little to prevent an unjust concentration of wealth and economic power." The rest of his communication asked for increased rates on inheritance, income, and gift taxes for individuals and for taxing the income of corporations according to the size of the enterprise. As the clerk of the Senate read it, Huey Long swaggered up and down the aisles pointing to himself as the source of Roosevelt's inspiration. The president had boldly and unambiguously put forward a policy of redistribution of wealth, or "soaking the rich." His anger at a smug upper crust no doubt had a lot to do with his decision. He likely also had acted out of a sense that Long possessed a growing constituency. Most congressional Democrats cheered. Upper-income America, which had hardly gotten over Hoover's 1932 tax increase, mostly reacted with fury. The proposal finalized a growing rupture between Roosevelt and the nation's most influential publisher, William Randolph Hearst, who called it "essentially Communism," and suggested renaming the president "Stalin Delano Roosevelt." "SDR" added the bill to his "must" list.[10]

Many cooler observers, noting that Roosevelt had not specified a date for passage of legislation, thought the request was a charade, designed to divert attention from the continuing Depression, the slow startup of work relief, and the Supreme Court setbacks. Whatever Roosevelt's intentions, the "wealth tax bill" took on a life of its own, when independent progressives led by Robert La Follette, Jr., declared they would block adjournment until the bill passed. Practically forced to work hard for it, FDR joined in with gusto, telling a press conference that he had personally looked over the tax returns of those who in 1932 had reported taxable income of more than $1 million. "Tax avoidance," he declared was what "tax evasion" became after the ministrations of a $250,000 lawyer.

More moderate critics than Hearst asked sober questions about the bill. The economic case for it was that an excess of wealth among the upper classes in the 1920s had laid the basis for speculative capital investment that culminated in the Wall Street crash and the Depression. It was better for the government to confiscate some of that wealth and recycle it downward in the form of benefits that might give the underprivileged more purchasing power. A thesis widely held in one form or another among New Dealers, it was nevertheless conspicuous by its absence in the presidential message. The Treasury department talked about the need to close the budget deficit. Critics countered that an economic revival would need private capital that was being taxed out of existence. They also warned that taxing a small number of millionaires would not solve the government's fiscal problems; soaking the rich would be a prelude to higher taxes for the littlest of the little guys, as was already the case in England.[11]

As a frustrated and irritable Congress fought it out over the presidential must list through the scorching Washington summer, a Roosevelt victory was by no means assured. The Republicans could not stop anything, but each measure seemed to generate a different group of Democratic opponents with interested constituencies to serve. A New York Times analyst described the mood of the legislative branch as "sulky" and likened it to that of "a small schoolboy who was being detained after hours to [complete] . . . a lesson which had not been given him until the time for the 3 o'clock bell was in sight." Proclaiming "the magic fades," the Kansas City Star's Washington correspondent suggested that the country was beginning to tire of Roosevelt's "superiority complex" and arrant opportunism.[12]

In the end, the White House pressure, combined with some opportunistic flexibility, was too much. One by one, the bills, some of them modified a bit to appease congressional egos or important constituencies, came to Roosevelt's desk:

JULY 5   The Wagner Act made it federal policy that workers had a right to engage in collective bargaining. It established rules of the game to be enforced by a quasi-independent National Labor Relations Board (NLRB), which Roosevelt would pack with pro-labor appointees. The result would be to cement the alliance between the Democratic party and organized labor.

AUGUST 14   The Social Security Act emerged from a long, grinding process much as Frances Perkins had wanted it. It provided for a series of state-administered welfare programs heavily funded by federal grants and an old-age and survivors insurance system managed by the federal government. Critics pointed to problems obvious even then. The development of a huge reserve fund would drain billions of dollars out of the economy for five years before it began to be recycled in the form of payments to elderly recipients. To the horror of Townsendites and their fellow-travelers, the first payments would not come until January 1, 1942. The short-term effect would be to ease the Treasury's problem of financing the large New Deal deficits, since social security taxes by law could be invested only in government securities. Republican partisans could not help but notice that the first payroll deductions would not be made until January 1937, two months after the next election. These critiques were far more than quibbles, but they could not stop a piece of legislation that seemed certain to deliver at least minimal benefits to millions of needy people.

AUGUST 23   Somewhat altered, but not fundamentally changed, the Banking Act provided that all members ("governors") of the Federal Reserve Board were to be presidential appointees and eliminated ex officio members from the regional, privately controlled Fed banks. Its most significant step was to give statutory definition to the Open Market Committee, the seven board members plus five rotating representatives of the regional banks. The Open Market Committee would control the supply of money and establish interest rates by determining the discount rate for loans between banks and buying or selling the increasingly enormous supply of government bonds that the New Deal's deficit spending required.

In the power-conscious world of Washington, everyone realized that the most immediate impact of the bill was to increase greatly the power of the Fed chairman, while cutting down several notches the authority of the Wall Street community that had controlled the New York Fed. For all the fear of political control, the fourteen-year terms of Fed governors made it difficult for any administration to dominate the Board. The Fed under its most consequential chairmen—Marriner Eccles, William McChesney Martin, Paul Volcker, and Alan Greenspan—would continue to be a quasi-independent institution, embodying traditional banking values but charged with a more general responsibility for management of the economy. The act, a product not only of Eccles's vision but also of Roosevelt's dislike of the banking establishment, created the modern Federal Reserve system.

AUGUST 28   The Holding Company Act brought the trend toward consolidation in gas and electric utilities to a sudden halt. It increased the regulatory power of several federal agencies over the utilities and backed away only slightly from the holding company "death penalty." Utility combines could be consolidated in *one* holding company after 1940 *if* that company could demonstrate that its operations were localized, useful, and efficient. However technical such provisions might seem in the cold light of a later day, New Dealers and their progressive allies considered the act a signal victory for justice and democracy. The practical result for the next half-century was to make electrical utility consolidations, whether rational and reasonable or not, exceedingly difficult.

AUGUST 30   The Wealth Tax Act came through with a menacing array of increased levies on incomes, estates, gifts, and excess profits. The act, William Leuchtenburg has written, "destroyed most of the Brandeisian distinction between big and small business, did little to redistribute wealth, and did still less to raise revenue." (Its highest tax bracket—seventy-nine percent—probably affected only one taxpayer, John D. Rockefeller.) It produced perhaps $250 million to help close a deficit north of $4 billion. But its increases stung sharply enough to create fierce resentment from business interests and the well-to-do.[13]

To these, the administration also could add several lesser acts, including the Motor Carrier Act, placing trucking and passenger buses under the regulatory authority of the Interstate Commerce Commission; a new Railroad Retirement Act, attempting to restore in somewhat different form the system that the Supreme Court had struck down; the Guffey-Snyder Coal Act, an effort backed by business and labor to restore the NRA code for a desperate bituminous coal industry; and a new, more restrained Farm Mortgage Moratorium Act to replace Frazier-Lemke.

When Congress finally adjourned as the clock was striking midnight on the morning of August 27, it was three months to the day since Black Monday. Roosevelt looked like a winner who still had the magic. Employing some poetic license, his supporters would declare that he had presided over a Second Hundred Days. But to what purpose?

Scholars later on would write of the events of 1935 as establishing a Second New Deal, quite distinct from the First. They would argue that the Second New Deal's political economy renounced the corporatist aspirations of the First and substituted a generalized suspicion of big business in the tradition of Woodrow Wilson's New Freedom. The Second New Deal, they believed, identified aggressively with the victims of the Depression, lavishing more money and attention on them than before. Conversely, it attacked a smug upper crust that had too much power and wealth. The New Deal would be less about a "broker state" in which Roosevelt tried to unify the country behind him and appease all classes, and more about class politics. The Democratic party would become the party of labor and "the common man."[14]

These distinctions were roughly sensed at the time, but they were more products of events than a conscious shift in ideology or political strategy at the top. Roosevelt had never liked bankers ("money changers" driven from the temple of government in his first inaugural) and big businessmen. He gave up efforts to cartelize the economy reluctantly and only after the Supreme Court had struck down the NRA. He turned naturally to large-scale work relief after the failure to achieve recovery in the summer of 1934. He and his advisers had planned social security from the start. The policy of organizing and subsidizing agriculture never changed.

But things happened. As the business and financial groupings turned increasingly hostile, as the large newspapers became more critical, as the wealthy displayed bitter personal hostility, the president and his administration responded in kind. As organized labor grew increasingly militant and politically engaged, it became a natural, and indispensable, ally. The New Deal never made a concerted effort to break up big business and finance, but by the fall of 1935, the relationship had taken on a new and ominous bitterness.

One could see the difference in Roosevelt's shifting newspaper support, a significant gauge in a day when print was the only media that flaunted political opinions. The defection of William Randolph Hearst was emblematic; a lifelong Democrat who had styled himself a progressive reformer, Hearst had swung the Democratic nomination to Roosevelt in 1932. But he had grown increasingly restive with the president even before the tax bill. From that point on his national chain of news-papers, the largest media empire in America, was compulsively anti-Roosevelt. The flagship Pulitzer paper, the *St. Louis Post-Dispatch*, usually a standard bearer of democratic progressivism, would likewise turn against him.

The defections came not just from wealthy and egocentric barons of journalism. As late as mid-May 1935, Walter Lippmann had defended the president in a speech to the Boston business elite. The New Deal, he reminded them, had been a response to an unprecedented crisis; activism, even if sometimes mistaken, had been preferable to paralysis. The business community should meet the president halfway, swallow its insistence on a balanced budget for another year, seek compromises on the banking, utility, and social security issues, and avoid irreconcilable partisanship. It should wait until the fall of 1936 to make a final judg-ment. Just three months later, his tone had changed. Roosevelt, he still thought, had done great things in his first two years, but the emergency had passed and recovery was beginning. The president could no longer claim the right to "announce a new policy suddenly, as he did in his tax message, and then railroad it through Congress without adequate hearing or decent debate." The American people "have the right to feel sure that their government is that of a democratic republic, and that it is not a gov-ernment concentrated in the personality of one man." Privately Lipp-mann oscillated between fearing that Roosevelt had dictatorial tendencies and feeling affection for him, but his drift was steadily away from the president. In the fall of 1936, he urged his readers to vote for Landon.[15]

Roy Howard, president of the Scripps-Howard chain, raised similar concerns in a widely published (and probably prearranged) exchange of public letters with Roosevelt. In a respectful communication written as the Second Hundred Days ended, Howard expressed unease at the monolithic hostility toward the New Deal emanating from the business community. "Many business men are frightened," he said, not just the scoundrels, but leaders of the highest caliber. They sincerely believed that the tax bill aimed "at revenge rather than revenue—revenge against business." There could be no real recovery until these fears were addressed by "the granting of a breathing spell to industry, and a recess from further experimentation until the country can recover its losses." The president, he concluded, had to quell the sense that the New Deal was a "revolution in disguise."

Roosevelt responded about a week later. He understood that some of his critics were honest and sincere. The interests of business were identical with those of the general public. The New Deal had sought only "a wise balance in American economic life." The tax program affected only the wealthy (individuals with incomes of over $50,000 and estates valued at more than $40,000); its purpose was "not to destroy wealth, but to create broader range of opportunity, to restrain the growth of unwholesome and sterile accumulations and to lay the burdens of Government where they can best be carried." A national crisis had required "drastic and far-reaching action." The administration program, however, had "reached substantial completion and the 'breathing spell' of which you speak is here—very decidedly so."[16]

Perhaps Howard and other political centrists were reassured. Independent liberals feared that the president really meant his words and were dismayed. Most business conservatives saw his response as just more Rooseveltian hokum.[17] Roosevelt had little or nothing in the way of a further agenda in mind at that point. Still, there was plenty of natural uncertainty. The program of 1935 had to work itself out with consequences that remained unknown.

<hr />

Roosevelt by this time had a transformed political coalition to nurture, but first he took his own breathing spell. After a brief vacation at his Hyde Park home, he embarked upon a train trip across the country that was a triumphal tour. He proclaimed the return of prosperity everywhere. Farmers, he told a big audience at Fremont, Nebraska, "know from the contents of their own pocketbooks that their income has been increased." Two days later, he spoke at the dedication of Boulder Dam, praising the way in which the unharnessed forces of nature had been tamed for the good of humankind, perhaps understandably failing to mention that the project had been initiated by President Hoover and at first had been named for him. In Los Angeles, his motorcade traversed fifty miles of streets, lined by a million cheering spectators. There and in San Diego, he proclaimed the success of the New Deal. Boarding the cruiser *Houston,* he sailed for Panama, where the country's president greeted him in a manner befitting the potentate of an informal hemispheric empire. In Charleston, South Carolina, his last stop before returning to Washington, he declared: "Yes, we are on our way back—not just by pure chance, my friends. . . . We are coming back more soundly than ever before because we are planning it that way. Don't let anybody tell you differently."[18]

He returned to a changed political landscape. Most stunningly, on September 8, Huey Long, who had been preparing his third party candidacy, had been fatally wounded by an assassin's bullet in Louisiana. A Share Our Wealth/Union for Social Justice/Townsend Plan party could not hope to come up with an adequate replacement. During the fall, the WPA got traction. By the end of the year, it was the employer of 2.667 million workers. Other federal work and non-work programs supported another 4.6 million people. An army of voters could feel they owed something either to the president or to local politicians, usually Democratic, who had assisted them.[19]

Organized labor was emerging as a political force. John L. Lewis, Sidney Hillman, and David Dubinsky established the CIO as an insurgent force within the old American Federation of Labor. They quickly designated subcommittees to organize steel, autos, and other major nonunion industries. Lewis, Hillman, Dubinsky and their associates represented passionate commitment, big money, and bigger numbers—in politics as well as in the cause of organization. "It is the duty of labor to support Roosevelt 100% in the next election," Lewis told an interviewer late in November. The older, stodgier mainline AFL would be pulled along despite itself.[20]

No administration, not even Woodrow Wilson's, had so consistently recognized ethnic and religious minorities. Roosevelt in his first term appointed fifty-one Catholic federal judges, forty-three more than had been appointed by his Republican predecessors during their twelve years in office. He made one of the most prominent Irish-Catholics in America, Joseph P. Kennedy, chairman of the Securities Exchange Commission. Numerous leading American prelates made their support of the president clear and in the process undercut Father Coughlin. Roosevelt also constructed an administration in which Jews were remarkably prominent. All this was natural enough for a New York Democrat; still it was a departure of considerable note from any Democratic presidency before him. It came also at a critical time. The urban minorities still valued their distinct ethnic identities, but these were less primary than they had been a decade and a half earlier. The termination of open immigration in 1921 had cut off the flow of cultural reinforcements from the old world. The national media of film and radio had squeezed out distinct ethnic entertainments. The Depression underscored one's economic group identity rather than one's cultural heritage. The urban minorities were mostly working class and increasingly prone to think of themselves as such. With ethnic particularism a secondary consideration, they represented a much bigger and more inviting target for labor organizers, the Democratic party, and Franklin D. Roosevelt.[21]

Finally, FDR and especially his wife displayed solicitude for a Negro population the party had always scorned. The main New Deal recovery programs, the NRA and the AAA, delivered little to blacks; on balance, they likely were detrimental. The relief agencies, especially in the South, did not always give blacks fair and equal treatment, but they provided a lot of help. The administration also tendered symbolic recognition, if rarely from FDR, who had to deal with powerful Southern congressmen. Eleanor Roosevelt visited Howard University escorted by two Negro ROTC cadets, who posed with her for a photograph that enraged Southerners and ruffled the feelings of a fair amount of the rest of the country. Even Eleanor might temporize at times, but no one could doubt where her heart was.

Enough savvy young blacks were appointed to visible sub-cabinet positions that the administration could boast to the Negro press of having a "black cabinet." Secretary of the Interior Ickes, who had been president of the Chicago chapter of the National Association for the Advancement of Colored People, made the most notable such designation in the person of Robert Weaver. Weaver later would become Secretary of Housing and Urban Development under Lyndon Johnson; in the 1930s, he was an effective ambassador from the New Deal to the black community. In various ways, the administration spread the word that Negroes, as the country's most deprived group, received New Deal benefits in excess of their population percentage. Recognition was appreciated; work and direct relief even more. Unemployed blacks who had usually received subpar wages even in times of prosperity were especially grateful for WPA paychecks. The era in which "black politics" meant "civil rights" was still over the horizon. In the mid-1930s economic help was enough to initiate a steady shift in black voting preferences.[22]

Roosevelt, far more than he had expected in 1933, was at the head of a coalition of the dispossessed. It had a class edge, but by no means had relegated racial, ethnic, or religious identities to the wastebasket. Its short-run political promise was extraordinary, but it was fundamentally a creature of an economic catastrophe. Could it remain intact if the New Deal failed to achieve recovery?

The president's task was to cultivate its loyalty without alienating a traditional old-stock, middle-class America. Perhaps the most ill-founded conceit of the New Dealers was to envision the opposition as consisting of bankers, corporate executives, and, in general, "the rich." In reality, uneasiness about the New Deal, especially after the Second Hundred Days, extended far beyond corporate boardrooms, exclusive clubs, and yachting parties. As in Britain, the United States had a large and varied middle class. Even more than in Britain, the American middle class was a state of mind rather than a self-evident by-product of the nature of one's work. It could include the small shopkeeper who relied on his family, children, and possibly an employee or two, perhaps clearing two thousand dollars a year; owners of tiny manufacturing establishments, such as Fred Perkins, barely meeting a payroll; a small-town bank president, making four or five thousand a year, keeping a close eye on outstanding loans; in larger towns, the manager at an A & P supermarket, or a Walgreen's drugstore; a lawyer or accountant in a solo practice.

In an age of mostly independent businesses, every town had its family-owned clothing, furniture, drug, hardware, grocery, and dime stores running from one end of main street to the other, supplemented by barber and beauty shops and gas stations. Some of the proprietors could live comfortably; others scrimped. All had a business-driven ethic. All valued property rights. All lived by paying close attention to budgets. All worried about government spending and taxes, were suspicious of labor unions, wondered whether they were receiving fair value for the cost of programs like the WPA. Those who hired help might complain about the New Deal driving up the cost of labor or dislike the new social security payroll taxes.

Yet many also had relatives who had benefited from New Deal programs and might otherwise have been dependent on them. Some had been able to refinance a mortgage through the Home Owners Loan Corporation and keep their homes. Some, the banker for instance, had seen their businesses steadied by New Deal programs. The reflexive ethic of a business-oriented middle class would not necessarily determine a voting decision, but it was an initial bias Roosevelt had to deal with. Fred Perkins, whose business was barely surviving after being freed from the yoke of the NRA, had no doubts. In 1936, the Republican party engaged him to make speeches for Landon. "The New Deal tried to ruin me, and now I'm going to do my best to try to ruin the New Deal," he told *Time* magazine.[23]

Polls taken in late 1935 and early 1936 displayed widespread ambivalence about the administration. Straw votes, reflecting relatively indiscriminate sampling techniques, had long been a part of the American political scene. More scientific public opinion surveys were just beginning under the aegis of the Gallup and Roper organizations. Within the administration, the president increasingly relied on Emil Hurja, a journalist turned political operative and a self-made statistician. One of Hurja's efforts, showing widespread support for Huey Long, may have precipitated the "wealth tax" message to Congress. Hurja found a pattern of steadily declining support for the president, from 69 percent in February 1934 to just 50 percent by September 1935. Gallup confirmed the finding. Later in the year, he reported that in the 1936 election 52.6 percent of the voters would likely cast votes for FDR and 47.4 percent would back a generic Republican; he gave the president but only 250 safe electoral votes. The *Literary Digest*, already being criticized for unrepresentative sampling techniques that relied on telephone directories and auto registrations, showed 58.5 percent disapproving of the New Deal. The best interpretation anyone could put on these figures was that a second term campaign would be a hard fight.

Roosevelt could draw hope from one aspect of the various polling results. By a significant margin he was more liked than were his policies. His trend line in Hurja's monthly analyses had actually blipped upward after the *Schechter* decision had slain the NRA. As George Gallup put it, "Many people at this time do not approve of New Deal policies but vote for President Roosevelt regardless." The policies themselves had yet to be sorted out by an electorate with a large mushy middle that approved of some and did not like others. A *Fortune* poll conducted by Elmo Roper in late 1935 asked respondents to agree with only one of four propositions:

a. Roosevelt's reelection is essential for the good of the
    country.   31.5%

b. Roosevelt may have made mistakes but there is no one else
    who could do as much good.   29.3%

c. Roosevelt did many things that needed doing, but most of
    his usefulness is now over.   14.1%

d. About the worst thing that could happen to this country is
    another Roosevelt administration.   17.7%

e. Undecided   7.4%

The *Fortune* survey not only reaffirmed FDR's personal popularity; it indicated that close to 61 percent of the electorate thought he and the New

Deal on balance had been good for the country. "Steady as she goes" was his best policy for the future.[24]

The "breathing spell" the president had proclaimed in the fall by and large remained in effect through the first half of 1936. However, the first six months were eventful and not without conflict. On the first Monday in January, the Supreme Court, sticking to its narrow definition of federal authority, ruled the agricultural program unconstitutional. Writing for the majority, Justice Roberts asserted that the taxing authority of Congress could not be invoked primarily as a means of regulation and went on to declare agricultural production to be a local problem, not a matter of interstate commerce. Writing for the minority, Justice Stone declared: "Courts are not the only agencies of government that must be assumed to have the capacity to govern."[25]

The stage was set for another press conference in which the president would come out guns blazing, but Roosevelt was more interested in buying time than in throwing down another gauntlet. He talked soberly with reporters about the need for an agricultural policy that would be affordable and would limit production in order to conserve the nation's farmland. This time, the authorized quotation was not about horse-and-buggy interpretations of the Constitution. It was: "We must avoid any national agricultural policy that will result in shipping our soil fertility to foreign Nations." The decision had not been unexpected. The administration quickly rushed the Soil Conservation and Domestic Allotment Act through Congress. The bill had behind it not simply the assertion of a national interest in conservation but also the fact of the dust storms that were destroying the drought-ridden Great Plains. In practice, all the same, the act fundamentally restored the AAA under a different name. How could the Court possibly approve it?[26]

A few weeks later, the Court in an 8–1 decision upheld the right of the Tennessee Valley Authority to generate and sell electricity from the original Muscle Shoals site, the Wilson Dam. But that May, in a thoroughly predictable action, it overturned the Guffey-Snyder Coal Act—the attempt to salvage the NRA code for bituminous coal. Shortly afterwards, it declared a New York state minimum wage law unconstitutional, creating a constitutional "no man's land" in which neither the state or national governments could regulate private enterprise. Few doubted that most of the legislative products of 1935 would soon be dead if the Court hewed to the line its majority had laid down.

By the time the Court adjourned for the summer, the nation was embroiled in a fierce debate about the Court. Its defenders invoked the majesty of the law. The critics, increasingly numerous and vocal, popularized in one way or another the view of legal pragmatists that law, over the centuries, had evolved with the necessities of the time and had to continue doing so. A number of them were prominent members of the administration, including Secretary of Agriculture Wallace and Assistant Attorney General Robert Jackson. The independent progressive bloc in Congress joined in stridently. Roosevelt himself made only a couple of brief comments and contented himself with an angry private memorandum for his files. It was not good politics to go after the Court. The constitutional crisis could wait.[27]

In the meantime, the president had taken a defeat from Congress. As setbacks go, it was a minor one, but it had significant implications for the economy and the federal budget. Roosevelt had stood firm every bit as much as Hoover against early payment of the veterans bonus. In 1935, Congress had sent the bonus to him, and he had responded with a stinging veto, delivered personally before a joint session of Congress and nationally broadcast by the major radio networks. The House had overridden him, but the Senate had sustained him. By January 1936, election year pressures made a repeat passage of the bonus inevitable and a veto futile. FDR went through the motions with a brief message that both houses swiftly overrode by huge majorities.

The act conferred a significant benefit on a group that mostly could not claim deprivation; as in 1932, some veterans were poor, a very few rich, and the rest somewhere in between. It also pumped about $2 billion into an economy that in 1935 had produced a Gross National Product of just over $72 billion; this was a big economic stimulus that would be added to the more than $4 billion in emergency relief spending anticipated for the calendar year. It was also a gaping hole in the federal budget. Worse yet, the Supreme Court had not only invalidated the agricultural processing tax, it had ordered a refund. The administration saw it as imperative to reduce a deficit of awesome proportions.[28]

The primary result was a tax on undistributed corporate profits. In the end, it was less notable for the revenues it raised than for what it said about the New Deal. The primary argument for a tax on profits not distributed to shareholders as dividends recalled the debate of 1935 on the Wealth Tax. Corporations paid a much lower income tax rate on their earnings than did the high-bracket wealthy on their income. Therefore, the New Dealers believed, retained corporate earnings were a form of tax avoidance; the rich increased the value of their assets by leaving them in corporate treasuries rather than taking them in dividends, from which a higher tax could be extracted. The way to deal with this horror was to impose a surtax on retained earnings that brought the total rate to that paid by the rich.[29]

The whole concept assumed that enterprises did not need to build reserves against bad times, or for the financing of capital expenditures, or for research and development. Raymond Moley, still active on the fringes of the New Deal as an occasional adviser and speechwriter, wrote: "Surpluses are the life insurance policies of business firms." Testifying before Congress, George O. May, a distinguished accountant and tax authority, cited, of all people, John Maynard Keynes* in support of the proposition that corporate profits were most efficiently reinvested by management rather than the government.[30] In early 1937, one lonely voice within the administration, Interstate Commerce Commissioner Joseph Eastman, America's greatest authority on the railroads, warned that the tax would do serious damage to rail corporations, which required large amounts of capital and were too sensitive to the fluctuations of the business cycle to produce year-after-year profits. The same could be said for most of what constituted American industry in the smokestack thirties—steel, coal, rubber, automobiles, and similar enterprises.[31]

More than any other issue of the congressional session, the undistributed profits tax revived the class card that Roosevelt had promised to put down. Behind the incomprehension of the way in which businesses operated there seemed to lie the assumption that the government knew better than corporate managers how to use its profits. The final result, signed into law by Roosevelt on June 22, was a tepid compromise that deprived the tax of any lethal bite, produced far less revenue than predicted, and exacerbated the ill-will between the administration and big business.

The rest of the congressional session was calmer. A supplemental appropriations bill threw another $1.5 billion at the WPA. The Robinson-Patman Act, a "fair trade" law designed to protect small retailers from "predatory price" discrimination by wholesalers and large chain operations, made its way through Congress without active administration sup-

---

* Arthur Schlesinger, Jr. (*Politics of Upheaval*, 506), claims that Keynes had given "powerful support" to the case for an undistributed profits tax in *The General Theory* (p. 100). Kenneth Davis (*FDR: The New Deal Years, 1933–37*, 619) follows Schlesinger right down to the use of the phrase "powerful support." *The General Theory*, published in early 1936, actually has little to say about taxation and nowhere specifically advocates taxing undistributed profits.

port, was signed by the president, and ultimately did little for the constituency it was supposed to assist. The Walsh-Healey Act attempted to resurrect the labor standards provisions in section 7a of the National Industrial Recovery Act by requiring that any contractor doing more than $10,000 in business annually with the U.S. government had to observe an eight-hour day and forty-hour week, extra pay for overtime, federally established safety and health standards, and a minimum wage scale that would mirror "prevailing minimum wages" in the contractor's industry and part of the country. Politically, the act underscored Roosevelt's commitment to both organized labor and the unorganized working class.[32]

With the adjournment of Congress, the presidential campaign was underway. As expected, there was no third-party challenge from the assorted lot of independent progressives and radicals who had banded together in the League for Independent Political Action. Labor, the one force that might have funded a new party and provided it with foot soldiers, was forming a solid phalanx of support for Roosevelt. None of the independent leaders could match the president's popular appeal. Some of them, as Roosevelt had planned, had become instruments with which he could pull his own party farther left.[33]

Floyd Olson had long cultivated a relationship with FDR, who had refused to support Democratic challenges to him in Minnesota's 1934 gubernatorial election. They apparently envisaged a fusion of the state Democratic and Farmer-Labor parties. The project collapsed after Olson was diagnosed as suffering from inoperable stomach cancer. Before his death in August 1936, he sent a public telegram to Robert La Follette, rejecting a third party and endorsing Roosevelt for reelection. The president provided an epitaph: "The nation has lost a personality of singular force and courage."[34]

Fiorello La Guardia talked independent radicalism, but all the practical imperatives of his position as mayor of the nation's largest metropolis drew him toward an alliance with the New Deal. On July 11, 1936, President Roosevelt presided over the dedication of the great Triborough Bridge, built by the PWA. It was only the most visible of an enormous range of New Deal projects throughout the city. During the first year of its existence, the WPA allocated more than one of every six dollars it spent to New York, which, in the words of Thomas Kessner, had become New Deal City. In his political dealings, Roosevelt bypassed Manhattan's

Tammany organization, worked through Bronx boss Ed Flynn, and dealt with La Guardia as if he were the Democratic mayor of New York.[35]

The other source of radical dissent—the Long-Coughlin-Townsend axis of 1935—gave birth to a new Union party. It faced a harder road than could have been imagined in June 1935. Long was ten months in his grave. His Louisiana associates happily transferred their allegiance to Roosevelt in return for patronage and the quashing of federal criminal investigations. (Cynics called the understanding the Second Louisiana Purchase.) What was left of the Share Our Wealth movement fell to Gerald L. K. Smith. Often dressing as if he were a refugee from Hitler's Brownshirts, he had a way of responding to an ovation from a worked-up crowd by launching his right arm into the beginnings of a fascist salute, then quickly drawing it back.[36] Dr. Townsend could complain with some justice that social security was doing little to meet the problems of the elderly, although he remained incapable of producing a realistic program of his own. Father Coughlin, although a golden-voiced orator with sophisticated rhetorical skills, was disqualified from a presidential run by Canadian birth and priestly vocation.

In mid-June, Representative William Lemke of North Dakota agreed to accept the party's nomination. Singlemindedly devoted to his hard-pressed wheat farming constituents, best known as co-sponsor of the Frazier-Lemke mortgage relief act, Lemke on paper was a good fit for the party. Lemke in person was a soporific speaker and a provincial far out of his depth. David Bennett has aptly described him delivering his acceptance speech as "a bald-pated, grinning figure in striped galluses and a baggy gray suit." Father Coughlin promised to swing nine million votes for the ticket or leave the airwaves. Alarmists thought he might be able to deliver. Cooler heads realized that he would need someone more credible than "Prairie Bill." The Union party would poll well under a million votes.[37]

With no serious challenges from the fringes, Roosevelt was free to concentrate on the Republicans, who on June 11 had presented him with a challenger in the person of Governor Alf Landon of Kansas. Landon had been a solid two-term governor of a small, normally Republican state. In background, style, and values, he epitomized Main Street Republicanism. The son of a mid-level oil company executive, raised in Marietta, Ohio, he had moved with his family to Kansas, attended the University of Kansas, joined Theodore Roosevelt's Progressive party in 1912 and stayed with it until its return to the GOP in 1916. A successful independent oilman, who had gone into politics, he had combined traditional Republican virtues of budgetary frugality and sound management with social concern. In style, appearance, and experience, he resembled a Missourian who had grown up less than a hundred miles from the Kansas state capitol and once had dabbled in oil himself—Senator Harry S. Truman.

One of a dwindling band of Republican politicians with sterling electoral credentials, Landon accepted New Deal relief measures as emergency necessities. He could market himself as a sound, but cautious, progressive. It was, however, emblematic of the difficulties of his party that his backers thought it best to describe him as a "Kansas Coolidge." Ultimately, he won the nomination because he was a fresh face with experience at governing, had no ties to Herbert Hoover or to Washington, and yet seemed an orthodox Republican. The vice-presidential nod went to Frank Knox, publisher of the *Chicago Daily News*. Like Landon, Knox was a 1912 Bull Mooser, but a more astringent critic of the New Deal. As Donald McCoy has written, the delegates to the 1936 Republican convention "were not of the private club and Wall Street, but of the small-town country club and Main Street." The Landon-Knox ticket amounted to an overthrow of the Old Guard, but not an embrace of the New Deal. Landon hoped to walk a fine line as a moderate conservative sensitive to the needs of common people.[38]

Because Landon honored the tradition that presidential nominees made their acceptance speeches at notification ceremonies in their home towns weeks after the end of the convention, Roosevelt fired the first major shot in the campaign. The president accepted renomination at 10:00 p.m. on Saturday, June 27. He spoke over national radio and in front of newsreel cameras in a brilliantly staged media event before 100,000 spectators at Philadelphia's Franklin Field. The platform was set up in the middle of the huge open air stadium, the president driven right to it, helped out by his security detail, all but invisible to the crowd. The platform party surrounded him. One of the guests, the aged and beloved poet Edwin Markham, extended his hand to the president and was somehow pushed into him. One of FDR's leg braces snapped loose; he fell toward the wet turf. A Secret Service man caught him just before he hit the ground. Others scurried to pick up the scattered pages of his speech. As the guards and dignitaries surrounded the president, his leg brace was locked back into position and his suit brushed off. A moment of fury came and went. Composed again, he shook hands with his elderly admirer, and leaning on the arm of his son James, walked to the platform. Few, if any, in the cheering crowd realized what had transpired.[39]

The performance that followed was Roosevelt's greatest political speech, delivered without a misstep, combining all the authority of his patrician upbringing with the democratic appeal of his concern for ordinary Americans. If at times it verged on the demagogic, its power and effectiveness were undeniable. Evoking the Philadelphia of the American Revolution and the spirit of the Declaration of Independence, it pictured the America of the 1930s as engaged in a struggle not against the long-vanquished political tyranny of George III, but oppression by "economic royalists." "Privileged princes" had made subjects of "small businessmen and merchants . . . the worker . . . the farmer . . . even honest and progressive-minded men of wealth." (Was the last an autobiographical reflection?) Opportunity had been limited by monopoly. Private enterprise had become privileged enterprise. Political equality had become meaningless in the face of economic inequality. Americans in 1932 had given their government "a people's mandate" to end economic tyranny. "If the average citizen is guaranteed equal opportunity in the polling place, he must have equal opportunity in the market place." Economic royalists complained that the administration sought to overthrow American institutions. "What they really complain of is that we seek to take away their power." They had hidden behind the flag and the Constitution, but these stood for democracy, not tyranny; for freedom, not subjugation. The palace of privilege would be replaced by a temple built out of faith, hope, and charity.

Then his most memorable lines:

> Governments can err, Presidents do make mistakes, but the immortal Dante tells us that divine justice weighs the sins of the cold-blooded and the sins of the warm-hearted in different scales.
>
> Better the occasional faults of a Government that lives in a spirit of charity than the consistent omissions of a Government frozen in the ice of its own indifference.
>
> There is a mysterious cycle in human events. To some generations much is given. Of other generations much is expected. This generation of Americans has a rendezvous with destiny.

In other lands, he explained, people had yielded their democracy for the illusion of a living. America was waging a great and successful war—not just a war against want and destitution. "It is a war for the survival of democracy." The nation was fighting to save a great and precious form of government, for itself and for the world.

"I accept the commission you have tendered me. I join with you. I am enlisted for the duration of the war."

The cheers were thunderous and incessant. After a time, the president and his party returned to his car. It made one circle around the field and exited into the night.[40]

Landon could not match theater of this sort when he accepted the nomination in Topeka on the steps of the Kansas statehouse a month later. Still the event drew uncommon interest because his views remained largely unknown. He spoke in generalizations, but they were those of a middle-of-the-roader, who gave signs of being influenced by a small group of Republican moderates, among whom the most prominent were Roy Roberts, publisher and managing editor of the *Kansas City Star*, and Charles P. Taft of Cincinnati, the relatively liberal son of William Howard Taft.

The country's primary need, Landon declared, was work for the unemployed. Jobs could be created by a business community—especially a small-business community—"freed from incessant governmental intimidation and hostility. . . . from excessive expenditures and crippling taxation. . . . from the effects of an arbitrary and uncertain monetary policy." He attacked monopoly. He would continue relief for those who needed it. Government economies would come "out of the hides of the political exploiters." He would amend the Social Security Act "to make it workable." Decrying deficit spending and increasing taxes, he declared "nothing to be of more importance than putting our financial house in order." He endorsed a continued soil conservation program, a national land-use policy, flood prevention efforts, and continuing cash subsidies for those dependent on foreign markets. He affirmed the right of workers "to join any type of union they prefer." Finally, and by implication foremost, he stood for liberty, which could not long survive with continued executive usurpation. Neither political nor civil liberty could long survive the loss of economic liberty. If he were elected, he would "restore our Government to an efficient as well as constitutional basis."[41]

The hometown crowd loved the speech and the candidate. Thoughtful conservatives could take heart from it. But it was vague and left Landon open to incursions from the right wing of his party. And it demonstrated that he was at best a journeyman facing a virtuoso in the game of rhetorical politics.

Roosevelt in the main followed the direction in which he had started at Philadelphia. He campaigned extensively across the country, tacking back toward moderation from time to time, describing himself as "a little bit left of center" but also playing a class card that placed him squarely on the side of hard-working, oppressed masses and describing his opposition as an uncaring elite. No upper-class interests had a passkey to the White House, he said, nor employers who underpaid their workers and put anti–social security leaflets in their pay envelopes, nor anyone indifferent to improving the welfare of working people. In his final address at Madison Square Garden in New York, he laid it on hard:

> Government by organized money is just as dangerous as Government by organized mob.
>
> Never before in all our history have these forces been so united against one candidate as they stand today. They are unanimous in their hate for me—and I welcome their hatred.
>
> I should like to have it said of my first Administration that in it the forces of selfishness and of lust for power met their match. I should like to have it said of my second Administration that in it these forces met their master.[42]

Such language cost him some support. Raymond Moley was taken aback, not simply by "the violence, the bombast, the naked demagoguery" but by the angry "cadences of the voice that uttered them." He had begun to wonder, he later recalled, if the president felt that the merit of a program could be measured by the extent to which it offended the business community. Steel executive Ernest T. Weir, one of the nation's most prominent industrialists, penned an attack in *Fortune* that demonstrated the vast gulf between the president and the business community. Roosevelt, Weir charged, was a politician who never had faced the competitive battle, "never experienced the anxiety of the man who must find work for a large group of employees and must meet a payroll week after week." He was opposed not just by a "small minority," as he claimed, but "almost unanimously by the business and professional men of the country."[43]

Weir's critique was harsh, but not unjust in assessing Roosevelt's incomprehension of the mentality of American business. Other opponents spewed out venomous anger with no pretension to reason or balance. The Hearst newspapers and the *Chicago Tribune* (which enjoyed the second largest circulation in the United States) worked overtime to link the New Deal with Soviet Communism, among many other lapses. (Two memorable *Tribune* headlines were: MOSCOW ORDERS REDS IN U.S. TO

BACK ROOSEVELT and ROOSEVELT AREA IN WISCONSIN IS HOTBED OF VICE.) Attacking along the same front, William Randolph Hearst declared that Roosevelt "willingly receives the support of the Karl Marx Socialists and the Frankfurter Radicals and the Tugwell Bolshevists and the Richberg Revolutionists, and all the malcontents and disturbers in this country." A few Democratic newspapers responded in kind. A *New York Post* headline read: PRO-HITLER STAFF AT HEADQUARTERS OF REPUBLICANS. The by now faintly ridiculous Liberty League poured on the invective and trotted out Al Smith for a series of denunciations.[44]

Such enemies were assets. They doubtless played a role in the decision of one independent progressive after another to endorse FDR. Robert and Philip La Follette; George W. Norris and liberal Republican Senator James Couzens of Michigan were the most famous. They solidified the support of union labor, with its ample cash and thousands of dedicated workers. Most of these people would have rallied behind the president anyway, but his right-wing enemies, all of whom he in turn subjected to exaggerated demonization, inadvertently underscored the urgency of supporting him and precipitated breaks from old habits of political business.

Newspaper endorsements meant more then than they would in a later age. Most publications were more measured than the *Chicago Tribune*, the Hearst chain, or the *New York Post*. Across the country, Landon had a 4–1 edge, but Roosevelt received some substantial backing: the *New York Times*, the Scripps-Howard papers, the *Cleveland Plain Dealer*, among others. It is noteworthy, all the same, that many of his backers expressed the hope that, as the *Times* put it, he would practice conservatism "in the sense that conservatism means consolidating ground already gained and perfecting measures hastily enacted."[45]

Ultimately, in order to have a polarizing election, both candidates have to appear to be polar opposites. Whatever his shortcomings—and he was not a very good presidential candidate—Landon had started out as a mushy middle-of-the-roader, conceding many of the New Deal's goals while arguing they were badly done and asserting he would do them better. He was on the mark when he asserted that the NRA had retarded recovery for two years. He could at least speak to popular intuition and count on roars of approval from a partisan audience when he condemned the administration's deficit spending. He argued, perhaps accurately, that Roosevelt was consciously following the "amazing" advice of John Maynard Keynes to spend at the rate of $400 million a month and then asserted (with some exaggeration) than nonetheless 11 million remained unemployed. He legitimately denounced numerous examples of political manipulation of the WPA.

It was fair, moreover, for him to remind Americans that beginning on January 1, 1937, many of them would start to be taxed for the social security fund. The tax could be increased from one to three percent in periodic steps. None of them would get a penny back until 1942 *if* Congress appropriated the funds. The employer's share of the benefits really amounted to money employees would have received without the tax. After this accurate dissection, it was little more than standard partisan rhetoric to refer to the system as a "cruel hoax." Where many Americans saw the campaign as a struggle between right and left, foreign observers, such as the Washington correspondent of the London *Times*, were more likely to see the two major party candidates as contesting for a center that lay between the nineteenth-century individualistic liberalism of the capitalist right and the socialist alternative of Norman Thomas.[46]

Landon's outline for a Republican program was another matter. It was thin and unconvincing. He wanted to balance the budget without explaining how. He advocated handling the farm problem, social security, and work relief through the states without addressing some obvious impracticalities. He promised to get rid of the agricultural domestic allotment program and develop foreign markets for farm surpluses. One did not have to be a policy wonk to understand that something was missing here, that it was one thing to profess concern for groups truly afflicted by the Depression and assure them continued support, another to offer them fuzzy alternatives that by all appearances were out of touch with reality.

Landon's effectiveness as a candidate waned the more people saw of him and heard from him. His persona lacked the power and authority that Roosevelt projected so easily. The Republican core constituency, easily reduced to incoherent rage by the president, wanted their man to be, not a quasi-Roosevelt, but an anti-Roosevelt. On this score, his running mate Knox, a master of vituperative denunciation, was well ahead of him from the beginning. The more rabid Republican press provided a steady drumbeat of Roosevelt-bashing that they ate up. To some extent, the Republican campaign may have been taken over by "extremists"; advisers like Roberts and Taft were not as visible at the end as they were at the beginning. Toward the end of the campaign, Landon, surely understanding that he was behind, did what most trailing candidates do. He began to talk tougher, emphasizing the possibilities for regimentation provided by issuance of social security cards to every worker and questioning whether free government could survive another term under Roosevelt. His partisans loved this development. A huge swing vote was repelled by it.[47]

Landon's deficiencies as a campaigner were not nearly as important as his increasing loss of the one issue that really mattered. He was correct in asserting that the country was not out of the Depression and that unemployment remained very high, but this was overshadowed by one obvious and omnipresent fact—the economy was surging. Landon's estimate of 11 million unemployed would have been very close to the mark at the beginning of the year; by November, the ranks of the unemployed totaled 8.3 million. In a matter of eleven months, the American economy had created about 2.7 million jobs! The New York Times business index had been on an upward trend line since July 1935, moving from 80 to 101 by election day 1936. One industrial corporation after another, including such behemoths as General Motors and U.S. Steel, reported its best results since 1929. Farm prices were strong also, in part because of especially determined government support efforts. (In January 1936, after cotton had fallen sharply, the president told Secretary of Agriculture Wallace, "I want cotton to sell at twelve cents. I do not care how you do it.") It was hard to doubt that the economy was in the first stage of a full recovery and moving at high speed toward the end of a long tunnel. Of the remaining unemployed—still more than fifteen percent of the workforce—about half had work relief jobs, thereby reducing the percentage of those wholly without work to under eight percent.[48]

The strong economy made the larger ideological debate irrelevant and surely submerged much of the uneasiness about Roosevelt's inflammatory rhetoric. It may well have made Landon, with his talk of fundamental change in policy, seem downright dangerous to many voters. In the summer, polls had demonstrated considerable tentative support for a Republican candidate who was an attractive new face and apparent moderate. In the closing weeks of the campaign, the challenger encountered indifferent-to-hostile crowds. The president, by contrast, seemed to be mobbed by enthusiastic throngs everywhere he went. By late October, Roosevelt's charisma, experience, and—above all—apparent economic success had produced a clear lead in every poll except the already widely disregarded Literary Digest straw vote.[49]

A few days before the election, James A. Farley—postmaster general, chairman of the Democratic National Committee, and Roosevelt's campaign manager—declared: "In my humble judgment President Roosevelt will carry every State in the nation except Maine and Vermont."[50] Maine, which still paid deference to its frigid winters by holding its elections in September, was already lost. Vermont came through for Landon. Roosevelt carried the other forty-six states. Landon got about 17 million votes, Roosevelt about 28 million. Very much in line with the *Fortune* poll at the beginning of the year, he won approximately 60 percent of the popular vote.

The majority was so huge that at first glance it seemed hard to break down in terms of discernible groups. After all, FDR carried over 2,600 of the nation's 3,000 counties. The most important and lasting aspect of his victory, however, was his overwhelming majority in the cities. Of the 104 cities with populations of over 50,000, he carried 102. In 1928, Al Smith had been the first Democrat to carry the twelve largest cities. His margin had been 210,000. Roosevelt had done more than a million and a half better in 1932; in 1936, his margin was 3.5 million. Several big cities—Chicago, Philadelphia, and St. Louis among them—had been Republican in the 1920s, had broken loose from the GOP before Roosevelt became president, and now had their political transformation confirmed. FDR and the New Deal had created what would prove to be an enduring political loyalty. The keys to this change were class, ethnicity, religion, and race.

If a sense of class was never as deeply rooted in American life as in Europe, it always had existed to some degree and had been a basis for political allegiance. In very general ways, the Democratic party always had been the party of "the people, " the Republicans the party of the middle and upper groupings. The Depression sharpened differences between haves and have-nots, giving class differences a cutting-edge presence in American life. The surge of labor organization that had begun in 1934 reinforced this tendency. The CIO took the lead in establishing Labor's Non-Partisan League (which had token AFL participation), to support Roosevelt and labor-friendly (mostly Democratic) candidates. The league and its backers gave the Democratic party in excess of $500,000, an enormous sum by the campaign standards of those days. Heretofore, organized labor had wielded some influence at local levels. Almost overnight, it had become a national political power.[51]

In the 1920s, politics had been about cultural divisions. Al Smith in 1928 had run poorly in cities where the working class was heavily old stock and Protestant; he had swept cities where it was of immigrant stock and heavily Catholic. The Depression reversed these priorities.

Nonetheless, ethnic and religious identities were far from insignificant in determining the way people voted. To be Catholic or Jewish and southern or eastern European in national origin was more often than not to be working-class. Republican discrimination against these groups in the immigration legislation of the 1920s had reinforced an already-strong propensity to vote Democratic. The Smith candidacy had provided a catalyst. Roosevelt conspicuously recognized and appointed Catholics and Jews to his administration. He enjoyed warm and supportive relationships with their leaders. Such displays from a president manifestly of the old Protestant ruling class won not just votes but an emotional loyalty.[52]

Race constituted the final dramatic aspect of the electoral upheaval. Southern blacks, where they could vote at all, continued to mark their ballots for the Republicans. Northern cities, where Democratic organizations were already aggressively courting the Negro vote, were a far different environment. George Gallup estimated that 76 percent of northern black voters went for Roosevelt. As with the white minorities, economic assistance and empathetic concern were a potent combination.[53]

Although the outlines of what would come to be called the "Roosevelt coalition" were clear, no one in the aftermath of the election blew a trumpet to proclaim that the Democratic party had remade itself and replaced the Republicans as the nation's natural majority. It was easy enough to take the results as a national vote of gratitude from all those who needed and received help in a time of economic catastrophe. The election was only Roosevelt's first affirmative victory; 1932 had been a vote against Hoover.

The Roosevelt vote possessed profound inner contradictions. The farm vote was notoriously independent and least likely to stay firmly aligned with the Democrats. On the other hand, labor, short of a new party, had nowhere else to go. Southern Democrats—white, Protestant, antiunion, intensely race-conscious—would soon realize that they were being displaced as the core constituency of their party. The jumble of northern white ethnic and religious minorities that was replacing them had multiple inner tensions of its own—and in general a common distaste for Negroes.

What Roosevelt would make of his triumph was unclear. He had in effect requested a referendum on what he had done, not on any new programs he might want to try. Yet the future of the New Deal was precarious. The Supreme Court and the constitutional doctrine it had established hung over the whole campaign, as if it were a poltergeist making occasional thumps in the attic, not talked about in the hope that it would go away.

On November 4, 1936, one thing was certain. Franklin D. Roosevelt had been reelected with an enormous national vote of confidence. He already had shown himself a president who relished power and knew how to use it. Few could doubt that he would make the most of his mandate.

HEADLINES

{1937}

JANUARY 17   Reorganization Plans Leave Congress Dazed

JANUARY 21   Throngs See Inauguration; President Promises to Continue His Battle for the Rights of the Common People of America; No Details of Program

FEBRUARY 5   To "Purge" Court; President Asks Permission to Pack Nation's Highest Tribunal

JULY 14   Robinson Dies; Senate Leader Worn Out in Court Fight; Legislation in Doubt

SEPTEMBER 12   Wall St. Gloomy; Worst Break in More than Four Years

{1938}

JANUARY 2   New Deal Opens Fight Against Big Business Front

NOVEMBER 10   Coalition in Congress to Halt the New Deal Urged as the Republicans Appraise Victory; Gain 80 in House, 8 in Senate, 11 Governors; Taxpayers Revolt

{1939}

MARCH 19   WPA Knit Into Nation's Life; Biggest Industry, Employing 3,000,000

STALLING OUT

THE UNITED STATES, 1937–1939

Personalities

By early 1937, the New Deal faced the question of legacy. With President Roosevelt beginning his second and presumably last term, with economic recovery apparently underway, one sensed that the final meaning of the Roosevelt presidency was being shaped—in terms both of institutions and the men who would take its heritage into the future.

Walter Reuther: Worker, Union Man, Social Democrat

Franklin D. Roosevelt's second term effectively began, not on Inauguration Day, January 20, 1937, but on December 30, 1936, when militant members of the CIO United Auto Workers (UAW) union seized a General Motors Fisher Body plant in Flint, Michigan, and began a sit-down strike. Over the next two weeks, union activists got control of six other Flint GM facilities and crippled the huge corporation's national operations. Michigan's new Democratic governor, Frank Murphy, sent the National Guard allegedly to maintain order, but actually to protect the strikers from local authorities who would have evicted them. On February 11, 1937, GM, which had been losing an estimated $1 million a day, capitulated, agreed to recognize the union, and began bargaining over wages and working conditions. The outcome validated John L. Lewis's advocacy of organizing industrial workers. It set the stage for a similar action and victory against the Chrysler Corporation. In the meantime, mammoth U.S. Steel recognized the United Steel Workers.

The Flint sit-downs demonstrated what a small group of determined activists could do, given political backing. The Wagner Act legitimated unions but did not require their recognition without a majority vote. Most workers remained apathetic. A strike with traditional picket lines could not have closed down GM or Chrysler. A sit-down could, so long as the strikers could avoid eviction. The 1937 sit-downs spread from Flint to Detroit and thence around the country, producing mixed results. The losers included unions striking against employers who could wait them out or throw them out, and many pro-labor Democrats ousted in the 1938 elections. The winners included the triumphant new unions, John L. Lewis, and the 29-year-old head of the Flint UAW local, Walter P. Reuther.

Reuther had been born just seven years before the outbreak of the World War in Wheeling, West Virginia, into a working-class family of democratic socialists. Walter's father, Valentine, was a unionized brewery worker. The family was stable and relatively prosperous, save for a bad stretch when Valentine was thrown out of work by prohibition. It was indicative of the household's bourgeois norms that Valentine remade himself as a successful insurance salesman and real estate agent, but without renouncing his socialism. At the age of eleven, Walter and his younger brother Victor accompanied their father to visit Eugene V. Debs, the revered socialist leader who had been arrested for opposing the war. By then, Walter knew well three of the elements most essential to his identity. He was a worker, a union man, and a democratic socialist—all at a time when socialism was collapsing in America and unionism of any sort was moving into decline.

Quitting high school after his sophomore year, he quickly found employment as a tool-and-die worker with a Wheeling company. After four years, he was off to Detroit, a bright, accomplished young craftsman with an overweening desire to get ahead. Soon he was a valued, highly paid employee at the Ford Motor Company, earning his high school diploma on the side, then taking college courses. Sober, frugal, and earnest, he was, as Nelson Lichtenstein has put it, "a young man full of lofty but undirected idealism."[1]

The Depression confirmed Reuther's radical upbringing. In Detroit, as the auto industry ground toward a halt, the miseries of unemployment were pervasive, the apparent crisis of capitalism self-evident. Reuther, joined by his brothers Victor and Roy, became increasingly involved in radical politics, photographing Hoovervilles, contrasting them with the mansions and lifestyles of Detroit's elite, convinced that revolution was at hand. In 1932, the brothers participated in hunger marches and campaigned for the Socialist Norman Thomas. Walter joined the Communist-dominated Auto Workers Union (AWU) and became friends with a local Communist who helped him get employment in a new auto factory in the Soviet Union. By then he already was a prominent young figure on the left wing of the American socialist movement. In late 1932, Walter and Victor Reuther left Ford and Detroit for Europe. They toured England, making connections with the Labour party left, visited relatives in Germany just after the Nazi seizure of power, and finally made their way to the Soviet Union.

For about a year and a half, the Reuthers were part of a valued and privileged cadre of foreign workers at a vast new auto plant in Gorky, brought there to transmit their knowledge of American technology and industrial organization to peasants being transformed into mass production operatives. The experience of being elite tutors assisting in the making of a new society was exhilarating. Women workers found them attractive and intriguing; Walter lived with one for several months. Letters from the USSR left no doubt of their admiration for the Soviet experience and their feeling that it ultimately was the best hope of humankind. In the spring of 1935, just as the virulent Stalinist purges were beginning, they left Gorky to return to America by way of China and Japan. They disembarked in Los Angeles, cosmopolitan revolutionaries determined to empower the American working class.

In Detroit, they found that the old Auto Workers Union, in line with the new international Communist Popular Front policy, had effectively folded into the new CIO United Auto Workers Union. Walter quickly found an influential place in the new enterprise. He orchestrated the sit-downs and was constantly at or near the plants as they went on, frequently exhorting the strikers from a sound truck. Soon he was on the UAW executive committee. But, while the sit-downs had been a revolutionary tactic, they had not wrought a revolution. Recognition at GM and Chrysler were only tentative victories. The young union, severely riven by personal rivalries and divergent political agendas, was frequently dysfunctional at the local level. Only top-level CIO intervention held it together and maintained its status as a bargaining agent.

When Reuther and a fellow UAW leader, Richard Frankensteen,

attempted to hand out organizing leaflets on an overpass leading to Ford's River Rouge plant, a gang of Ford operatives mercilessly beat them. (Both sides could be rough. A Pulitzer Prize news photo taken four years later caught UAW organizational pickets attacking an anti-union Ford worker with a gusto that Ford's goons would have admired.) Under intense government pressure, Ford finally recognized the union in 1941. Reuther in the meantime worked closely with a heterogenous mixture of Communists, socialists, and unionist activists to consolidate his own position in the UAW. He emerged as head of its GM division in 1939, widely considered the labor movement's brightest young star.

Over the next three decades, Walter Reuther, always assisted by brothers Victor and Roy, fulfilled his personal potential, but he would do so by a constant process of jettisoning utopian visions and accommodating to American realities. First to go was his allegiance to the Socialist party, which the world crisis had shown to be irrelevant. Like many of his comrades, he took his ideals into the Democratic party and did what he could to pull the New Deal farther to the left. What faith he had left in the Soviet Union crumbled after the Nazi-Soviet Pact of 1939. By 1940, he was a militant antifascist who had repudiated both Norman Thomas's pacifism and Stalin's totalitarian opportunism. Appointed to the National Defense Advisory Commission, he hectored the auto companies to begin tooling immediately for production of 500 planes a day. When war came, he was among the most influential labor leaders in defense planning.

For more than a decade after that, he seemed to be the one American labor leader capable of linking the traditional union demand of "more" with a large and generous social vision. From the beginning, the UAW had been big labor's strongest advocate of racial integration. Reuther himself expressed bold challenges: companies declaring they could not afford generous wage increases should throw open their books to the public, workers should be participants in management, the time had come for regularized cost-of-living wage increases and a guaranteed annual wage. Some of this was public relations posturing, but most was a genuine legacy of Reuther's socialism. In 1947, he was elected president of the UAW. Succeeding Philip Murray as president of the CIO in 1952, he became the leading voice of America's industrial workforce.

Until Reuther's death in a plane crash, May 1970, the UAW remained a prominent crusader for social democracy on the left wing of the Democratic party, but it could not avoid the necessity of attentiveness to its own constituency, first and foremost. Inevitably, its revolutionary dynamic gave way to bureaucratic routine. Its repeated insistence that ever-higher wages for low-skilled assembly workers served a larger social purpose rang increasingly hollow. Reuther secured his position with a well-oiled machine that easily beat back dissent and suppressed unauthorized work stoppages. Like many survivors of the 1930s who had once considered themselves part of a left vanguard, he found it difficult to comprehend the racial politics and New Left radicalism of the 1960s. Young leftists for their part muttered that the UAW was just another bourgeois labor union. Yet the UAW had brought a working class that lived on the edge to membership in the American bourgeoisie. The accomplishment had been made possible by the New Deal, and the organizational tactics were frequently ugly, but building the union also had required courage, daring, and vision. Big Labor a generation later would seem notably lacking in these qualities.

David E. Lilienthal: Democrat

From the beginning, no single New Deal project drew as much attention as the Tennessee Valley Authority. None was so ambitious. It proposed the electrification and thorough modernization of a vast river valley that ran for approximately 860 miles through the hill country of seven states. Few American regions were so beautiful, few so impoverished. The TVA's design was unprecedented in its ambition. It would include a multistate regional authority, a series of dams for flood control and electrical power, production of fertilizer for farmers, a comprehensive redesign of the valley's economic basis. Appointed to the TVA's three-person board of directors in June 1933, just weeks before his thirty-fourth birthday, David Lilienthal seemed at first glance destined to be a junior partner in an enormous undertaking. When he left thirteen years later, his name was synonymous with the TVA. No person had done more to determine the nature of the agency, define its principles, and formulate the argument that it embodied the future of democracy.

Born in 1899 to a modest family of immigrant Jewish merchants, Lilienthal had spent his childhood and adolescence in several small Illinois and Indiana towns. A brilliant student at DePauw University in Greencastle, Indiana, he went on to Harvard Law School, where he won the attention and respect of Felix Frankfurter. Joining the Chicago law firm of Donald Richberg, Lilienthal was soon a noted expert in utility law, famed as the successful lead attorney in cases that challenged rates charged by several large companies. He was also earnest, idealistic, and hungry for public service. In 1931, he gave up his comfortable job and income to accept an appointment from Governor Phil La Follette to the Wisconsin State Utility Commission. A militant critic of rate increases, he attracted national attention; one of his local admirers was the daughter of Justice Louis Brandeis. In 1933, Roosevelt, mindful of powerful endorsements from Frankfurter, Brandeis, and the La Follettes, appointed him an associate director of the TVA.

His two colleagues on the board were men of considerable repute in their own spheres. The other associate director was sixty-six-year-old Harcourt A. Morgan, president of the University of Tennessee, former dean of its College of Agriculture, and loved throughout the state. Shrewd, pragmatic, and tactful, Harcourt Morgan ("H. A.") had strong ties to the regional establishment. He wanted to develop a better life for the valley's residents, within the existing social order. The chairman of the board, Arthur E. Morgan ("A. E."; no relation), was an altogether different type. Imposing in height, intensely committed to his goals, he impressed all who met him. A renowned civil engineer and former president of Antioch College, he was at heart a messianic socialist determined to remake the Tennessee Valley.[2]

During the first two or three years of the New Deal, the board members coexisted in surface harmony, A. E. in charge of dam building, H. A. selling the project to local interests and promoting assistance to farmers, Lilienthal planning a huge public electrical program. Dam construction brought thousands of jobs to the valley. It required the resettlement of more than ten thousand farm families and the building of new towns. By 1936, with the initial system of dams completed or nearing completion, with the Supreme Court having affirmed TVA's right to produce and market electrical power, a fundamental conflict was unavoidable.

A. E. already had riled a number of people by suggesting that farm families should not have free title to their land and should be required to observe detailed mandates on management and conservation. He even had floated the possibility of TVA issuing its own scrip in lieu of U.S. currency. To the extent possible, he excluded his board colleagues from decision-making and denied them information. Above all, he saw TVA as an agent of revolutionary social change. Its one function that did not interest him was energy production, which he considered incompatible with the environmental purposes of watershed management.

For Lilienthal, whose entire career had been based on the progressive critique of the "power trust," TVA's main mission was the generation and marketing of electricity. Moreover, on this point the agency had a direct mandate from Roosevelt himself. For most New Dealers, TVA, the Rural Electrification Administration, and the huge hydroelectric projects of the Pacific Northwest were of a piece with the Public Utility Holding Company Act in the larger struggle against greedy private interests that needed to be supplanted with beneficent public agencies. H. A. was less zealous in his hatred for the power companies, but convinced that the economic development of his region required abundant and inexpensive electricity. Moreover, he and Lilienthal were comfortable in working with established institutions. Rather than a complete remake of society, they wanted TVA to foster a mixed economy in which public and private enterprise could raise living standards.

On these points, Roosevelt was in clear agreement. In 1936, he reappointed Lilienthal despite A. E.'s open opposition. In 1938, he terminated what had become a long and embarrassing feud by dismissing A. E. By then, Lilienthal was the TVA's dynamic force, pushing ahead with plans to electrify the entire region with TVA power and expel the private utilities. In early 1939, the major opposition, Commonwealth and Southern, a large utility holding company headed by Wendell Willkie, agreed to a buyout. Soon, TVA was a major electrical utility, providing power not only to the Tennessee Valley watershed but to adjoining areas, including much of northern Mississippi, and charging rock-bottom rates. World War II magnified its achievements. Oak Ridge, Tennessee, became one of the centers of the atomic bomb project, which created an enormous demand for electricity. By 1944, TVA was the largest producer of electric power in the United States.

The narrowing of TVA's originally expansive mission distressed Rexford Tugwell, who wrote in 1950 that a promising experiment had been reduced to "the Tennessee Valley Power Production and Flood Control Corporation."[3] In fact, this in itself would have been a major achievement, but the TVA did far more through its promotion of fertilizer cooperatives, soil conservation, scientific farming, and economic development. Moreover, its regional focus belied assertions that the New Deal stood for top-down social engineering. The TVA's headquarters were in Knoxville, not Washington; it reported directly to the president, not to any cabinet department. Its directors worked on a daily basis with regional influentials who shared its objectives. The TVA itself was politically invincible throughout its area. It attracted international attention as a model for social and economic development. Many liberals saw the TVA as the New Deal's most important accomplishment. Lilienthal, reinterpreting a Jeffersonian tradition long important in the South, hailed his agency as an example of "grass-roots democracy." By then, he was one of the New Deal's most attractive heroes.[4]

Yet the TVA had critics from both left and right who could not be summarily dismissed. The agency's displacement of tens of thousands of people, however equitably done, was disquieting. Civil rights leaders complained to no effect about the pervasive exclusion of Negroes, especially skilled workers, from its construction projects. They observed that its "model town" of Norris was as lily white as Arthurdale.[5] Nor did the TVA provide much help for the agricultural poor, who had no representation at its policy-making levels. As early as 1949 in a trenchant work of political sociology, Philip Selznick argued that "grassroots democracy" was more a myth that masked co-optation by local elites than a working reality.[6] The private utilities were surely correct in arguing that TVA's heavily subsidized electrical business could not provide anything approaching a national "yardstick" with which to measure the actual cost of producing electricity. Other critics questioned whether cheap power had really given the region good, diversified economic development or simply attracted low-skill, non-union manufacturing in search of cheap labor. Praise for "grassroots democracy" gave way to scorn toward "grassroots bureaucracy."[7]

Styles of liberalism change. By the late 1960s a new environmental movement asserted that TVA had defiled nature on a large scale, fought to stop dam construction forever, and wrote it off as just another big, polluting electrical utility. Bad management decisions and environmental policies that made electrical generation more expensive turned the TVA into a high-cost provider. Yet whatever it had become and whatever its shortcomings, it was hard to avoid the conclusion that TVA did more good than harm. In this, its history paralleled that of the New Deal.

Hubris

Roosevelt's astonishing reelection and the huge party majorities that accompanied it appeared formidably empowering. The president had not only won another term, he had achieved wide recognition as the world's most imposing democratic leader. He was presiding over an apparently powerful economic recovery that was still gathering steam. Anything seemed possible. The president began 1937 with a formidable agenda. He wanted to consolidate the New Deal through a vast administrative reordering that would greatly magnify the power of the presidency, focus social policy away from the temporarily unemployed to the chronically impoverished, tame the big interests that had opposed him, and, most portentously, gain control of the Supreme Court. The ambitions were understandable and the drive behind them neither as dictatorial nor as sinister as critics asserted. Still, they represented a profound challenge to the way in which American democratic politics had functioned for a century and a half and called forth a determined resistance that revealed the limitations of an electoral victory that had been more personal than programmatic.

As a reelected incumbent, Roosevelt did not have to wait until his inauguration to lay out an agenda. Two messages to Congress at the beginning of January 1937 defined most of his objectives for his second and presumably final term. The first was the annual report on the state of the Union. Delivered on the afternoon of January 6 to an audience ready to cheer almost every sentence, it successfully negotiated a path somewhere between a humdrum legislative laundry list and an inspirational oration. Its message was that the Depression was over or at the least rapidly coming to an end, but much work remained to be done toward the establishment of a free and equitable society. FDR called for the modernization and improvement of the executive branch of the government; attention to widespread poor housing and to the plight of impoverished tenant farmers; the further development of the social security system. Still hopeful of strong business regulatory authority, he advocated mechanisms reminiscent of the National Recovery Administration that would allow the government to deal with excessive speculation and with "reckless overproduction and monopolistic underproduction of natural and manufactured commodities." Rejecting the argument that the federal government lacked the constitutional authority to do these things, Roosevelt declared that the framers of the Constitution had sought to establish a strong government, able to respond to the necessities of changing times. The people expected the judicial branch to do its part in making democracy successful.[8]

The budget message came the next day. Its central theme, carefully hedged but still front and center, was that the era of big deficit spending was over. The administration was clearly serious in its belief that economic recovery would allow for the phaseout of the WPA and other relief programs over the next year or two. For fiscal year 1938 (beginning July 1, 1937), the president submitted a budget that made no clear provision for relief spending and would bring the budget close to balance. The New Deal would stand ready to help the unemployed in the event of an unexpected economic turndown, but it also sought to hold the line on spending and thereby implicitly meet what had become the biggest concern of the business and financial communities.[9]

Roosevelt's inauguration—the first to be held on January 20—took place in a bone-chilling rain. Determined to demonstrate strength and vigor, he stood hatless as he took the oath of office, right hand raised, left hand on a seventeenth-century family bible. His speech, heard on radio by perhaps 100 million Americans and Europeans, resonated an authority and confidence that the world had come to expect. Self-congratulatory about the achievements of his first term, outlining big tasks for the second, it was the self-conscious manifesto of a leader with a vision.

First, an admonition to the Supreme Court: "The essential democracy of our Nation and the safety of our people depend not upon the absence of power, but upon lodging it with those whom the people can change or continue at specified intervals. . . . The Constitution of 1787 did not make our democracy impotent." Next, a swipe at big capitalism: "We have always known that heedless self-interest was bad morals; we know now that it is bad economics." Then, the vision. The last four years had made the United States a more moral and confident nation. The next four had to bring the bounty of American life to the least favored of its citizens: "I see one-third of a nation ill-housed, ill-clad, ill-nourished. . . . The test of our progress is not whether we add more to the abundance of those who have much; it is whether we provide enough for those who have too little." It was necessary to achieve "a nation uncorrupted by cancers of injustice," to understand that "we all go up, or else we all go down, as one people." He would "assume the solemn obligation of leading the American people forward along the road over which they have chosen to advance."[10]

There was little dissent from the laudable generalizations, little inclination to criticize an address so exemplary in its delivery. Democrats predictably loved it. Republicans understood this was no time to be churlish. Signaling the way in which Roosevelt had established himself as a world champion of the middle way, Britain's *Economist* asserted, "The world can be grateful that it has at least one leader who speaks in accents of true

Liberalism."[11] Yet, all the inspirational oratory notwithstanding, most of the details and all of the struggles were yet to come. As the president returned to the White House on the evening of January 20, he must have known the next four years would likely be tumultuous.

For weeks, Roosevelt had been discussing with his advisers ways to control the Supreme Court. The nine robed men ensconced in their new temple behind the Capitol constituted the most likely viable opposition to FDR's plans. Anticipating a relatively close election, he had refused to confront the Court in 1936. There were as yet no big constituencies that had been financially damaged or mortally offended by its key decisions. Most Americans had said good riddance to the NRA. Farmers had enjoyed the benefit of price supports by other means after the AAA had been overturned. The TVA's right to sell electricity had been affirmed. Yet the power to destroy much of the New Deal remained inherent in the narrow concept of interstate commerce the Court had laid down. (The power to demolish state and local regulation of business was equally manifest in its *Morehead* decision of 1936.) The Wagner Act and the Social Security Act, perhaps also the Holding Company Act, faced grave danger. Constitutional scholars and policy intellectuals understood this. The larger public paid little attention. Those who gave any thought to executive-legislative-judicial relationships probably thought the Court would take notice of the election returns and accommodate a popular president. Above all, however, Americans valued an independent judiciary. Even many who had voted for Roosevelt likely saw it as a salutary check on his tendencies toward radical experimentation.

The stakes were high. The Wagner Act and social security, once undone, could not as easily be reconstituted as farm price supports. Roosevelt's hopes for general minimum wage/maximum hours legislation would likely be doomed. On these matters the president knew he could count on only three votes: Brandeis, Cardozo, and Stone. He would have realized that four were automatically against him—McReynolds, Butler, Sutherland, and Van Devanter. That left Chief Justice Hughes, a man of vast experience and wisdom but little apparent love for the New Deal, and Roberts, best described as well-intentioned but unpredictable. It was possible, maybe probable, that Hughes would respect the election results. It was not possible to be confident that he could consistently bring Roberts along with him. Add to this the president's deep frustration that in his first four years, he had been unable to appoint a single justice. Political calculation and emotion led inexorably to the conclusion that, however prudent it had been to follow a policy of postponement in 1936, it was now necessary to face the Supreme Court head on and to do it before the electoral mandate was forgotten.

Through the month of January, the White House put out assurances that it contemplated no offensive against the Court. The tribunal's first round of decisions since the election upheld several lesser pieces of New Deal legislation. By the beginning of February, observers generally assumed that Roosevelt was willing to wait at least for the major decisions on the Wagner Act or social security, perhaps for the inevitable retirements sure to come over the next couple of years.[12] Then, on February 5, the president fired a wholly unexpected "bombshell."

At a press conference, he presented to assembled reporters a message to Congress that would accompany a bill designed to achieve "the same kind of reorganization of the Judiciary as has been recommended to this Congress for the Executive branch of the Government." The performance that followed, *Time* magazine believed, was reminiscent of his "horse and buggy" criticism of the Supreme Court nearly two years earlier, but far superior. "He fairly smacked his lips over his adroit phrasing, revealing to the Press by intonation and ironic interjection his exhilaration over the most daring stroke he had yet attempted." The presentation entertained the press and boosted Roosevelt's morale. It was the first shot in his hardest political fight yet.[13]

The judicial reform bill had several important provisions, including restrictions on the power of federal district judges to stay the execution of laws they found unconstitutional and expedition of appeals to the Supreme Court. Formally, the president presented the legislation as a companion to his executive reorganization plan, claiming that it would bring younger blood, new efficiency, and greater capacity to the judicial branch. However, the direct and immediate impact of the bill would be to allow him to dominate the courts. Its key clause provided for the enlargement of the federal judiciary at all levels by presidential appointment, subject to numerical maximums, of one new federal judge for each one over the age of seventy. Specifically, it allowed for the appointment of up to six new members of the Supreme Court, a number matching that of the "old men" already on it. Roosevelt's request for judicial reform did not simply complete his legislative agenda. To a degree he had not anticipated, it would become his agenda, crowding most other things out. For the next six months, court-packing was the face of the New Deal on Capitol Hill.

JUNE 1937

A horde of picketers, men and women armed with two-by-fours, block the entrance to the Monroe Republic Steel plant. They turn back a motorcade of several hundred local workers who have voted not to honor the Steel Workers Organizing Committee (SWOC) strike for recognition. Monroe police, backed by a brigade of armed vigilantes, fire gas grenades into the mass picket line, break it up, pursue its members through a nearby field, burn their tents, and destroy automobiles they have left behind. The SWOC vows to return. Governor Frank Murphy sends a battalion of National Guardsmen to maintain order. Ten thousand unionists from all over the region stream into Monroe. Union official Van Bittner, fist clenched, tells the crowd: "We're going to make these hoodlums in Monroe just as decent as any other citizens in America. We're going to bring our union into Monroe." The scene shifts to Mayor Daniel Knaggs, flanked by armed bodyguards, reaffirming his determination to defend the right of Monroe citizens to work without union control. (*Newsreel,* "Labor Violence at Monroe, Michigan")

The turbulent politics of the first half of 1937 played out in an environment that appeared to confirm the administration's claim of economic recovery. Despite numerous high-profile labor strikes, unemployment dropped steadily while major manufacturing jobs inched toward 1929 highs. By June, according to the AFL's reckoning, the number of jobless had fallen to less than 8 million from the nearly 11 million of January 1936. This was still somewhere in the neighborhood of fourteen percent. (By 1937, the workforce was about four million larger than in 1929.) But the direction was well established and the momentum strong. In line with administration policy, federal relief rolls likewise declined. The WPA had begun to cut its enrollees almost as soon as the election was over—from 2.55 million in the fall of 1936 to less than 1.50 million a year later.[14]

By the spring of 1937, increasing numbers of Americans were concerned less about jobs than about labor turmoil. CIO organizing strikes rippled through the economy for much of the year. From March through July, at least 350,000 workers were out; in June, the number approached a half-million.[15] The new CIO unions gained recognition from General Motors, Chrysler, and numerous lesser auto makers, but Ford resisted successfully. U.S. Steel gave in quickly, but the "Little Steel" companies, led by Republic, fought back tenaciously and successfully. Expansive in its ambitions, the CIO established organizing committees in one industry after another with vastly mixed results, but bringing almost everywhere they went an unsettling tumult and putting a drag on the economy.

Sit-downs spread willy-nilly through much of the country. To John L. Lewis and many other labor leaders they were simply an effective tactic. To much of the American middle class, workers who took over a plant were appropriating the possessions of others and attacking the idea of private property. Critics accurately noted that radical French unionists had employed the tactic and that Communists and Socialists were prominent among the American sit-downers. In practice, CIO organizers were a self-authorized vanguard for a workforce consisting largely of non-union members who gave little active support to their efforts.[16]

Conventional strikes were only slightly less objectionable to a wide spectrum of the public. Occurring in a society not yet accustomed to the concept of industrial unions, accompanied by an atmosphere of menace and potential violence common to most labor actions, they easily could be taken for revolutionary activity. Local elites in most industrial towns opposed them; local law enforcement usually sided with management. Violent episodes were common. The most infamous such incident in 1937 was the "Memorial Day Massacre." In South Chicago, Illinois, local police fired on a large crowd of picketers marching on a Republic Steel plant, killing ten and wounding thirty. In Ohio, picketers blockaded all rail and highway routes to Republic plants at Warren and Niles and shot at light airplanes delivering food to workers. Most Americans did not view such events as a morality play in which oppressed workers were fighting for dignity against predatory capitalists. The CIO strikes drew strong negative reaction from a political center Roosevelt could not afford to lose.[17]

The president intermittently tried to distance himself from militant labor. When John L. Lewis visited the White House in late January to request outright support of the GM sit-downs as repayment for labor's political support in the recent campaign, Roosevelt rebuffed him, winning wide praise.[18] With public uneasiness growing into the summer, labor outraged by the Memorial Day Massacre, and Little Steel holding firm, he was under increasing pressure to take sides. Asked for comment at a press conference on June 29, he declared, "The American people are saying just one thing: 'A plague on both your houses.'" Perhaps calculatingly, perhaps impulsively, he authorized direct quotation. Lewis was enraged. Two months later, in a Labor Day radio address, he responded with characteristic oratory:

Labor, like Israel, has many sorrows. Its women weep for their fallen, and they lament for the future of the children of the race. It ill behooves one who has supped at labor's table and who has been sheltered in labor's house to curse with equal fervor and fine impartiality both labor and its adversaries when they become locked in deadly embrace.[19]

The Roosevelt-Lewis alliance had ended. The Roosevelt-labor alliance was scarcely nicked. Most other labor leaders understood that the president of the United States could not be a cheerleader for the CIO. Most workers understood that Roosevelt was on their side; most managers thought likewise. In fact almost everything the president did and said with regard to the labor turmoil of 1937 leaned toward the union cause. During the sit-down strikes at GM, he went out of his way to criticize GM chairman Alfred Sloan. At the height of the Little Steel troubles in June, as strikes threatened to collapse at Republic and Youngstown Sheet & Tube steel plants in Ohio, he made private and public pleas to management for a settlement with the union. Tom Girdler of Republic Steel, a business executive whose hatred for unions was matched only by his defective sense of public relations, rebuffed him at every point. It was only after the strike collapsed that he made his "plague on both your houses" remark.[20]

The administration backed labor in other and more important ways. After the Supreme Court upheld the Wagner Act in April 1937, the National Labor Relations Board consistently acted as an advocate for unions, especially the CIO industrial unions. In May, the administration asked Congress for a fair labor standards act, specifying minimum wages and maximum hours and prohibiting child labor. In most of the nation's industrial belt, from Pennsylvania and New York west through Illinois and Wisconsin, governors and local Democratic officials openly sided with labor. As many relatively neutral and moderate observers complained, the Wagner Act as administered placed no responsibilities on unions and put employers and non-union workers in an untenable position. Pro–New Deal progressive Robert La Follette, Jr., chaired a Senate subcommittee on civil liberties which ignored union strong-arm tactics, publicized the brutality of the Memorial Day Massacre and undertook a sustained critique of anti-union management practices as inconsistent with the Bill of Rights.[21]

Roosevelt and New Deal Democrats like him were irretrievably linked to the labor movement, the big industrial strikes, and the sit-downs. Poised to reap the political benefits, they could not dodge the anger among Democrats from the South and other parts of the country in which organized labor was distrusted. On April 1, Senator James F. Byrnes of South Carolina, a shrewd pragmatist who enjoyed friendly relations with the White House, offered an amendment to the Guffey coal bill condemning the sit-downs. Roosevelt and Vice President Garner got into a shouting match over it at a White House meeting. The administration defeated the Byrnes amendment only after a hard weekend of rounding up votes. The incident, overlapping with differences over the court-packing bill, revealed an emerging split within the Democratic party.[22]

By the fall, the big strikes were over, the battles either won or lost. The CIO unions claimed three or four million members, but this was a gross exaggeration based on a generous estimate of the workforces for which they had been recognized as bargaining agents, not on actual membership. Initial collective bargaining agreements generally included pay increases and somewhat better working conditions, but did not buy mass loyalty. Established in many places by relatively small cadres of dedicated activists, the industrial unions fought indifference on the part of most of the workers they represented. Their contracts generally did not provide for a dues checkoff, making collection so great a problem that in extreme cases "dues picketers" armed with clubs and baseball bats extracted cash from their union brothers at factory gates. Leadership crises and factional infighting left some important CIO unions in fragile condition. A force that was now a main prop of New Deal Democracy was unpopular, erratically led, and dependent upon an administration that needed its money and votes more than ever.[23]

The struggle over the court-packing plan and the labor turmoil were the two great national attention-getters of 1937, but Roosevelt had another urgent objective. The executive reorganization proposal FDR had dropped on Congress at the beginning of January has often been treated as an academic technical exercise prepared in the cause of administrative efficiency. It was that, but also much more. Developed by a committee of three experts in public administration—Louis Brownlow, Charles E. Merriam, and Luther Gulick—it sought efficiency in ways that would strengthen the presidency and institutionalize New Deal liberalism. It was designed to impose order on a federal executive branch that was a tangle of conflicting jurisdictions with no effective locus of control—the logical outcome of an older American liberalism that distrusted big, top-down government.

The committee had looked to Europe for examples, especially to Great Britain with its strong and effective professional civil service, led by an elite that ran cabinet departments for one government after another and inevitably imposed its view of things on everyday management, whatever the partisan tides. Brownlow had been impressed by a discussion with Tom Jones—deputy secretary to the British cabinet from 1916 to 1930. Jones, who had worked equally closely with David Lloyd George, Ramsay MacDonald, and Stanley Baldwin, was the consummate insider of British politics. He had explained the importance of the cabinet secretariat, an executive staff that provided the British prime minister with resources of supervision and control that an American president lacked. It needed to be headed, he told Brownlow, by an individual of "high competence, great physical vigor, and a passion for anonymity." The last phrase captured Brownlow's imagination and appeared in his report as a prerequisite for the new presidential administrative assistants that it recommended.[24]

The reorganization program had five major points:

1. A cadre of administrative assistants to the president, providing continuous contact with and information about the activities and plans of the executive departments and agencies
2. Stronger managerial and budgetary agencies, directly under the control of the president
3. Reorganization and strengthening of the civil service, establishing in effect a permanent coterie of career managers similar to the British model
4. Expansion of the cabinet to twelve departments and the assignment of all previously independent agencies administrations, authorities, boards, and commissions to these departments
5. Abolition of the post of Controller General, a congressional unit, and establishment of an Auditor General to review for the Congress all executive fiscal transactions, thus providing accountability to Congress for management of its appropriations; otherwise full responsibility for fiscal management would go to the more centralized executive branch[25]

Full implementation would have created an executive-centered administrative state, common enough in Europe but hitherto outside the American experience. The president would gain direct jurisdiction over every component of a formerly ramshackle, untidy executive branch. Professionalization of the civil service would provide lifetime tenure for thousands of high-level New Deal appointees and therefore do much to ensure the long-term continuance of the New Deal itself. The plan would bring power and energy to the executive at the expense of Congress. It would disrupt many tight relationships between powerful congressmen and the agencies or departments for which their committees authorized funds. Minimizing the impact of future partisan or ideological change, it would empower bureaucrats at the expense of politicians and political parties.[26]

The executive reorganization plan seemed sensible to British observers. In the United States an opposition began to develop quickly, spearheaded in the beginning by Senator Harry Byrd of Virginia, a vocal proponent of strict economy and Jeffersonian decentralization. But the bill generated a visceral emotion that had other sources—its threat to congressional prerogatives, its ideological implications, and, most critically, the sense that FDR was making yet another power grab in tandem with his effort to control the Supreme Court. Ultimately, his increasingly vocal opponents asserted, his goal was to become a de facto dictator.

Those critics included Walter Lippmann. In the fall of 1937, Lippmann published *The Good Society*, his attempt at finding a middle way between an obsolete laissez-faire liberalism and the statist totalitarianism that threatened to engulf all of Europe. He openly stated his distrust of Roosevelt's motives and judgment, making it clear that he feared the president was veering in the direction of a statist economic control that endangered liberal democracy. Lippmann's main purpose was to declare large principles, not to attack the New Deal, but his critique seemed especially timely. Few read beyond the immediate political context.[27]

Roosevelt and his supporters responded that centralized power was essential to the survival of American freedom. A strong executive could be a vital expression of liberal democracy, not a threat to it. To function effectively, in the modern world, government required rationalization, professionalization, and maximum efficiency. The president all the same would have to wait a long time for a congressional decision. Executive reorganization languished, pending resolution of the Court controversy. Just before adjournment in the summer of 1937, the House passed it 260–88. It would not come to a vote in the Senate until 1938.[28]

Through the spring of 1937, the administration continued to reflect a spirit of conflict and reform. The president requested a major new pro-

gram to make impoverished tenant farmers self-sustaining small operators; a fair labor standards act; and the establishment of seven new
regional development authorities, inevitably (and somewhat inaccurately) dubbed "little TVAs." Seemingly unable to stay away from 100-
proof soak-the-rich politics, he demanded revision of the internal
revenue code to prohibit tax shelters that amounted to "tax evasion."[29]

Roosevelt also acquired an unplanned agenda item that he could neither affirm nor disown. Having aggressively wooed the black vote, he
could not oppose antilynching legislation, but neither could he embrace
any sort of civil rights action without alienating the entire Southern contingent of the Democratic party. Civil rights organizations, spearheaded
by the National Association of the Advancement of Colored People
(NAACP), had worked for an antilynching bill, sponsored by Robert F.
Wagner of New York and Edward Costigan of Colorado, since 1935. The
House passed the Wagner-Costigan bill in April 1937, 282–108; the vote
laid bare a yawning gap in racial sensibility between the Northern and
Southern wings of the Democratic party. The legislation ran into a stone
wall in the Senate, where the Southerners were supported by a few older
progressives convinced that so great an expansion of federal police functions was unconstitutional. Wagner agreed to withdraw it, subject to an
agreement that it would have a preferred position on the Senate docket
in early 1938. But nothing could move Southerners determined to maintain white supremacy in all its manifestations and convinced that antilynching legislation was simply an opening move in a comprehensive
attack on racial discrimination. The NAACP, for its part, struggling to
maintain its position as the leading civil rights advocacy group, would
bring back antilynching for one try after another.[30]

Roosevelt's own position on all this was a difficult straddle. Meeting
with civil rights leaders, he stressed his opposition to lynching, but suggested means other than legislation, perhaps a congressional investigation. He knew that even at the height of his prestige he could do little to
win over the Southern senators on racial matters. He clearly sympathized
with the civil rights advocates and wanted to mollify a valuable new constituency, but he had other priorities that might be lost if the Senate were
tied up by weeks of heated debate and accumulated ill feelings. He never
delivered an outright endorsement of antilynching or other civil rights
bills. Instead, he combined symbolic gestures with wide economic benefits for Negroes. The approach worked with those Northern blacks who
could vote, even as it frustrated their leadership.

The strategy played less well with Southern Democrats. Not just obsessed with race, they tended to be traditional states rights conservatives on all issues. Old-stock white Anglo-Saxon Protestants, they were reflexively hostile toward newer immigrant groups, Jews, and Catholics. Sharing a wide consensus that the economic modernization of the South depended on low wages, they abhorred unions. In the most placid of times, their relationship with their Democratic brethren from Northern big cities was at arm's length. The New Deal minus civil rights had put a considerable strain on Democratic unity; the New Deal plus civil rights brought it to the breaking point. The moderate-minded South Carolinian James Byrnes would declare that the people of the South had "been deserted by the Democrats of the North." Tom Connally of Texas and Richard Russell of Georgia, both of whom enjoyed wide respect on Capitol Hill, linked the antilynching drive with Communist influences in the New Deal. Unable either to obtain or block consideration of civil rights legislation, Roosevelt watched helplessly as it became a wedge being driven ever deeper into the structure of his party.[31]

As all these issues festered in early 1937, the administration devoted most of its time and attention to the court-packing bill. Roosevelt believed it was the essential first step in protecting his program. Moreover, he surely sensed that if he were beaten in the first big legislative battle of his second term, most of the rest of his program would be in serious trouble. He dug in for a fight that revealed the limitations of his leadership and left him seriously wounded.

It did not help that the debate took place in the midst of a strong economic surge that made court reform seem less urgent. Playing down the recovery, the president invoked the cause of the underprivileged third of a nation. Delivering one of his longest fireside chats in March 1937, he recalled the national emergencies the New Deal had faced and overcome, then asserted the need for a cooperative judicial system. All branches of the government had to work together. A farmer behind a plow pulled by three horses could not succeed if one horse continually bolted in another direction. The president had a way with homey analogies, but this failed to take.[32]

Public support for the court plan seemed to peak in March, but the polls never got convincingly beyond fifty percent. Much of the reaction, public and private, ranged from dismay to outrage. Normally friendly newspapers, including the *New York Times* and the *Cleveland Plain Dealer,* opposed it as disingenuous in presentation and dangerous in its disregard of constitutional checks and balances. Adversarial columnists and editorialists charged that Roosevelt wanted to institute a purge, conjuring up visions of the terror Stalin had orchestrated in the Soviet Union. The three liberals on the Court—Brandeis at age eighty most of all—were against it. Some of FDR's closest aides thought he had made a terrible mistake.[33]

At the beginning most observers made the same mistake as Roosevelt. They assumed the country had written him a blank check in the last election, that his mandate was too big to be opposed. This fit the tone of a decade in which rule by strong men, legitimated by large margins in popular plebiscites, had become common. Actually, the context of authoritarianism backed by popular mandate was a major problem for the president. Critics ignored the British example, which demonstrated that unitary government could be compatible with liberal values and democratic rule. (Indeed, the British, puzzled by the idea that courts could invalidate legislative acts, tended to sympathize with FDR's judicial plan.) New Dealers and radicals saw the federal judiciary as the last surviving protector of a predatory plutocracy. As a whole, the nation distrusted concentrated power, worried less about social equality than about equality of opportunity, and saw the Court as the last independent guardian of individual rights.[34]

Court packing—at least on the scale Roosevelt requested—never had a chance, in part because of the president's tactical missteps but more fundamentally because it ran against the grain of American political culture. The bill was destined to fail for the following reasons:

1. *It clashed with the principles of a classical liberalism dating back to the American Revolution and deeply embedded in the American mind.* However inarticulately, most Americans who thought about politics believed in the principle of separation of powers and harbored a particular distrust of a powerful executive. Moreover, few Americans questioned the proposition that they possessed as a matter of course individual rights that could be protected only in the courts. "Only a fearless and independent court, not subject to being overpowered, awed, or influenced by either the Executive or Legislature, can protect the citizen against the exercise of power beyond that which the people through their Constitution have placed in the hands of the President,"

declared Democratic Senator Edward Burke of Nebraska. A *New York Times* editorial concluded ominously that the court-packing argument was made in the name of democracy, "But it is an argument which, in other hands, has been used to destroy democracy."[35]

2. *The Court had read the election returns.* The bill's one chance of passage rested on the assumption that the Supreme Court would continue down a relentlessly anti–New Deal road. Instead, the "swing men"— Chief Justice Hughes and Justice Roberts—swung, giving the liberals a 5–4 majority. On March 29, the Court upheld a Washington State minimum wage statute, effectively reversing its decision of the previous year that had created a "no-man's land" for social legislation. Just two weeks later, April 12, by another 5–4 vote, it affirmed the Wagner Act, chapter and verse. Hughes wrote both majority opinions. The Social Security Act passed constitutional muster on May 24, 5–4 once again. In the meantime, on March 22, the Senate Judiciary Committee made public a letter from Chief Justice Hughes. It systematically refuted the assertion that an aging court could not keep up with its workload. On May 18, Justice Van Devanter announced he would retire at the end of the court's session. Roosevelt at last would have a chance to appoint a New Deal justice. By the time the Supreme Court went into recess for the summer, the fight for an accommodative judiciary had been won.

3. *The Roosevelt coalition was all-powerful at the polls, but not on Capitol Hill.* Many members of Congress, especially in the House with its two-year terms, might be awed and intimidated by Roosevelt's popular support, but many others had their own electoral base, their own ideas about governance, and their own resentments of an overreaching chief executive. This was especially true in the Senate, where members faced the electorate only every six years and generally possessed expansive views of their importance. It was one of Roosevelt's many miscalculations that instead of starting the court-packing bill in the House, where at the beginning he might have rammed it through despite the quiet opposition of House Judiciary Committee Chair Hatton Summers, he agreed to have it introduced in the Senate.

Republicans—all sixteen of them—opposed the bill, but they knew it would be a tactical mistake to make it a partisan issue. The GOP leadership remained quiet, leaving only the independent progressives among them to speak against it. That left the Democrats and the independent bloc—eighty senators in all. To the astonishment of the president and many others, they split nearly down the middle. Southern and moderate Democrats broke against the administration. Most of this group had delivered votes for more of Roosevelt's programs than they had opposed; a few had been loyal supporters. Most remarkably, the leader of the opposition Democrats, Burton K. Wheeler of Montana, was a progressive of impeccable credentials who brought most of the older progressives behind him. By May, Roosevelt faced a restless, angry Congress; he could count on several more than half the seventy-six Democratic senators, probably only two of the independents (Norris and La Follette), and none of the Republicans. Whether the total would be a majority was anybody's guess. Confirming the sense of a sinking ship, Vice President Garner ostentatiously decamped for Texas in mid-June.[36]

4. *Roosevelt himself consistently miscalculated and displayed poor tactical judgment.* Time and again during the first three months of debate, the president rejected compromise. The people were with him, he told aides and journalists, referring to the 1936 election or to warm receptions from crowds at public appearances or to supportive letters and telegrams received at the White House. Realists on the Hill knew early on that he would have to settle for half a loaf, but could not negotiate without authorization from him. He did not give it until after Van Devanter's retirement announcement. He then further hurt his cause by refusing to make at least a semi-public commitment to appoint Senate Democratic leader Joe Robinson of Arkansas to one of the new vacancies.[37]

Robinson had a special position in Washington. He was a much-admired unifier within the Democratic party. He had agreed to a hopeless run as Al Smith's vice-presidential candidate in 1928, although he represented a state in which Smith, Catholicism, Northern minorities, and prohibition-flouting were all decidedly unloved. A strong and effective Senate leader, he was liked by Republicans almost as much as by his fellow partisans. Sixty-five years old, in questionable health, and at heart conservative, he was not Roosevelt's ideal Supreme Court justice. Yet everyone knew that he wanted to end his career on the Court. FDR pointedly held off on selecting a nominee to replace Van Devanter. Making no commitment to his Senate leader, he asked Robinson to work for a bill that would give him one new justice a year over four years.

The court-packing debate continued as the main feature of business into the hot Washington summer. The odds seemed at best even that the Majority Leader could call in enough debts of politics and friendship to achieve the legislation. As the Senate debated in semi-filibuster conditions into July, Robinson began to show the strain. Chest pains forced him to take a day off. At eight o'clock the following morning, his maid called him to breakfast, entered his bedroom when there was no response, and found him dead on the floor, a copy of the *Congressional Record* at his side.

Court packing died with Robinson. It probably would have gone under even if he had gotten it through the Senate. The day before Robinson's heart gave out, House Judiciary Committee chairman Hatton Summers had broken a long silence and publicly pledged that no court-packing bill would ever emerge from his committee. Many senators believed their deceased colleague was a martyr to Roosevelt's ambition. As a funeral train filled with grieving legislators and politicians, many of them bitter, carried Robinson's remains back to Arkansas, a struggle to succeed him was already underway and had to be decided before any further significant Senate business could be transacted.[38]

The two contenders were Assistant Majority Leader Alben Barkley of Kentucky and Pat Harrison of Mississippi. Barkley, sixty years old, had served fourteen years in the House before being elected to the Senate in 1926. A connoisseur of good bourbon and teller of good stories, a stem-winding old-time orator, about as liberal as it was safe for a Kentuckian to be, he was liked by his colleagues but not greatly admired. Harrison, fifty-six, had been in the Senate eight years longer than Barkley, was equally well liked, and was far more respected. A masterful parliamentarian and negotiator, he was the dominant figure in the Southern establishment. A loyal supporter of the New Deal right down to the court-packing bill, he was nonetheless widely understood to be a conservative at heart, especially uneasy with Roosevelt's redistributionist tax policies.[39]

Roosevelt publicly professed neutrality, but the White House applied scarcely concealed pressure for Barkley on every senator and political boss who might be responsive. Most of the reliable New Dealers supported Barkley; Southerners and more independent Democrats backed Harrison. When the ballots were counted, Barkley prevailed 38–37. It was widely known that Senator William Dieterich of Illinois had reversed a commitment to Harrison at the behest of Chicago's Boss Kelly, following a call from the president. (Ironically, Kelly would drop him from the ticket in 1938 anyway.) Barkley's victory was a hollow one; he faced the impossible task of unifying a party more angrily divided than at any time since the Smith presidential candidacy of 1928.

A much-diluted judicial reform bill finally passed. It contained useful procedural changes and expedited appeals to the Supreme Court. An unhappy White House released a presidential memorandum listing of what the bill did not do. The Supreme Court had lost not a whit of independence.[40]

What Roosevelt still had was the ability to replace Van Devanter. On August 13, he nominated Senator Hugo Black of Alabama. A militant populist who was among the Senate's most radical members, Black was also among its least-liked figures. But in the world of 1937, most senators were willing to tender a quick confirmation. Someone brought up the issue of whether Black, who like all Southern senators opposed the anti-lynching bill, was associated with the Ku Klux Klan and received assurance that he was not a member. Without formal hearings, he was quickly approved, 63–16. Scarcely a month later, investigative journalist Ray Sprigle of the *Pittsburgh Post Gazette* published a story proving that Black had been a prominent member of the KKK from 1923 to 1926 and had tendered only a pro forma resignation in order to facilitate a run for higher office. Black resisted demands to quit the Supreme Court (some of them from former Senate colleagues), insisted that he had long since left the Klan, and undertook a long judicial career as not simply a New Dealer but also a fervent supporter of civil rights and civil liberties. In the short run, however, the episode was an enormous embarrassment.[41]

Black's appointment was a turning point in American constitutional law, giving supporters of the New Deal a solid majority. Sutherland retired in January 1938, to be replaced by Solicitor General Stanley Reed. Cardozo's death and Brandeis's retirement brought Felix Frankfurter and William O. Douglas to the Court. By mid-1939, the Four Horsemen had been reduced to two inconsequential old men whose time had passed.* A "Roosevelt Court" had materialized.

Roosevelt liked to say that he had lost the battle but had won the war. And so he had, but was the court-packing proposal the means of victory or a debilitating side campaign? Scholars would later determine that the Washington minimum wage ruling had been decided before the adminis-

---

*Butler would die in late 1939, to be replaced by Frank Murphy. McReynolds retired in 1940 and was succeeded by James F. Byrnes.

tration announced its judicial reform proposal. It is not certain, but likely, that Hughes and Roberts were prepared to expand the powers of the national government also. At best, it is speculative that the threat of court packing was required to turn them around.

Roosevelt, and the New Deal, lost a lot. A radical proposal put out as good times seemed to be returning, court packing never won truly enthusiastic mass support.[42] It led millions of Americans who had voted for FDR in 1936 to reconsider him and pay attention to assertions that he harbored dictatorial ambitions. Congressmen sensed the public's doubts. The struggle deeply divided the Democratic party, definitively alienating the most conservative Democrats and stoking the independent impulses of numerous moderates. It badly split a progressive bloc of insurgent Republicans, Western Democrats, and independents that had previously been solid for the New Deal; a number found themselves propelled into an adversarial stance they never dropped. The debate, in short, created an effective long-term opposition.

It also consumed an entire session of Congress, crowding out numerous issues of importance. In the interest of avoiding an emotional distraction, Roosevelt acquiesced in sweeping neutrality legislation that he never believed in. The wages and hours bill stalled. So did a needed overhaul of the agricultural program. Executive reorganization was stopped in its tracks. The administration did get a tax act that eliminated many of the loopholes the president had characterized as means of "evasion." The Guffey-Vinson Coal Act effectively reinstated most of the NRA bituminous coal code. The Wagner Housing Act appeared to establish a basis for a major national public housing program, although it would produce little in its first two years. Perhaps the most notable accomplishment was the Bankhead-Jones Farm Tenancy Act, which established the Farm Security Administration (FSA) in a well-meaning but misguided effort to attack the problem of rural poverty. In the fall, Roosevelt called a special session of Congress and presented it with the unfinished portions of his agenda. After five weeks in which the anti-court-packing coalition blocked one request after another, it adjourned, having accomplished nothing.

What of the "one third of a nation" to whom the second term was supposedly dedicated? It was still mired in deprivation. Government statisticians were not as fully into poverty studies as they would be twenty-five years later, but they had done more than enough to demonstrate that at least a third of the nation indeed lived in hard circumstances. A large marginal urban working class constituency in one big city after another subsisted on a family income of less than $1,000 a year, considered the baseline minimum for a decent living. In rural and small town areas, want was more pervasive. A government study of rural populations in North Carolina, South Carolina, Georgia, and Mississippi found that fifty-five percent of the white farmers and eighty-five percent of their black counterparts made less than $1,000 a year. More than two-thirds of the sharecroppers, white and black, lived on less than $500 a year.[43]

It was in the South, predominantly rural, that poverty was a way of life, with economic development blocked by an inadequately educated workforce and a primitive infrastructure. The South's ruling establishment—and almost all its white population, down to the most wretched white manual laborers and sharecroppers—was committed to a racial caste system that generated a fear of any change. To say simply that the South was the American equivalent of England's Wales and North Country would be to understate the case. The social pathology, derived as it was from a virulent racism not present in homogeneous England, was far deeper. In late 1936, Henry Wallace, accompanied by *New York Times* reporter Felix Belair and a couple of aides, traveled incognito along the back roads of the region, stopping at shacks and shanties to talk with the poorest of the poor. Shocked by the chronic disease, malnutrition, filth, and shabbiness for which he had been intellectually but not emotionally prepared, Wallace rightly declared it far worse than the misery that existed among European peasants. In the summer of 1938, the president's National Emergency Council would release a report that typed the South as, in Roosevelt's own words, "the nation's No. 1 economic problem." The characterization was accurate, but it generated vocal outrage from many regional defenders of the status quo.[44]

It seemed logical enough then that the New Deal's most conspicuous and ultimately most controversial attempt to deal with the chronically poor was an attack on farm tenancy. The Farm Security Administration (FSA), established by the Bankhead-Jones Farm Tenancy Act of 1937, took over the operations of Rexford Tugwell's Resettlement Administration. The RA had stressed community collectivism; the FSA soft-pedaled these, and undertook an effort to deal with tenant farmers one at a time. It gave them loans to buy 160-acre parcels of their own, provided start-up assistance, and proclaimed the virtues of individual proprietorship. Its first director, Dr. Will Alexander, was a much-admired idealistic but pragmatic reformer who had devoted much of his life to the cause of racial conciliation in the South.

Even in the flush of a new beginning the FSA was vulnerable. Its model of resettlement was more expensive and riskier than Tugwell's. Worse yet, although not fully evident in 1937, the 160-acre farms it financed were on the verge of technological obsolescence; few would survive more than a decade or so. While the FSA's constituency was biracial, many of its clients were black, thus politically powerless and scorned in their home region. Property-owning blacks, even property-owning poor whites, could threaten established patterns of society. The Farm Bureau Federation saw the FSA as an irrelevant drain on federal funds that might better go to support farm prices. In the rest of the country, it became one more target for the growing uneasiness with the large amounts of money devoted to one form or another of "relief."[45]

In the end, the New Dealers largely agreed that the best antipoverty program would be a full economic recovery that would provide the jobs and incomes to allow almost everyone to enjoy a decent standard of living. By late 1937, however, the economy was in the grip of a sudden and severe dip that further weakened the president and cast doubt on not simply his leadership but the future of the New Deal itself.

Into the fall of 1937, Roosevelt and those around him had assumed that economic recovery was yesterday's problem. The administration generally accepted the conventional wisdom that relief programs aimed at the normally employable had to be cut back and eventually eliminated. In an emergency, significant deficit spending for economic stabilization and aid to the jobless had perhaps been unavoidable (although quite a few analysts noted that Britain had achieved its recovery without deficits). That emergency, most believed, was now over. To the extent that the United States had an independent economic policy establishment, it was the Brookings Institution. At the beginning of the year, it issued a 709-page analysis of "the recovery problem" that featured an unequivocal call for a balanced budget.[46]

Numerous economists worried about sharp increases in commodity prices. Gold, still flowing into the United States Treasury (since 1933 the only legal holder of the metal) at $35 an ounce, and "monetized" by the issue of new currency to pay for it, was another problem. Federal Reserve officials worried that a rapidly increasing money supply would set off a rampant inflation. The Treasury responded by "sterilizing" much of the new gold; rather than pay for the bullion by issuing new paper money, it borrowed in the open market to finance the purchases. Thereby it preempted money that might have gone into a reviving private economy. Secretary Morgenthau justified the policy as a means of maintaining a substantial unencumbered gold reserve and steadying the bond market. During the last half of 1936 and first half of 1937, moreover, the Federal Reserve sharply increased reserve requirements for its member banks, thereby significantly reducing the nation's supply of credit and money. Underlying these moves, which were strongly deflationary, was the way in which years of depression had altered economic perspectives. Prices remained well below their 1929 levels, but the rising cost of living loomed as an issue. Eight million workers were still unemployed. Yet policy makers, tending to see 1929 as an unnatural boom year, were less concerned with ending the widespread distress of economic collapse than with preventing a powerful inflationary surge and a possible bust![47]

The most obvious route to cooling off an apparently overheating economy was government retrenchment. It seemed all the more necessary in April 1937, when the administration admitted that revenues were running well below expectations. Given the assumption of continuing economic recovery, the relief programs were an obvious target, especially the WPA with its multitude of small, short-term projects and enormous roll of employees. WPA cuts had begun shortly after the election. Harry Hopkins managed to beat off draconian economizers but found himself with a strict mandate to stay within a $1.5 billion budget in the fiscal year beginning on July 1. By September, WPA employment was down to 1.45 million, a million below its peak of the previous fall.[48]

By then also, the economy was in a free fall. One could choose an indicator at random; all suddenly broke straight down. By the beginning of December, the *New York Times* Index of Business Activity had fallen twenty-three percent from its August peak. For a New Dealer, the most damaging development was the rapid calamitous increase in unemployment. In October, unemployment began a rapidly escalating increase that demonstrated a severe collapse of the country's manufacturing economy. During the last three months of the year, all the progress that had been made since January was wiped out. By the end of the winter of 1937–38, joblessness was back to the nineteen percent levels of three years earlier.[49]

By the end of the year, relief crises reminiscent of those that occurred in 1932 began to appear in one city after another. Northeastern Ohio, for example, had seemed ready to settle into good times after the violent and disruptive steel strikes of the first half of the year. Instead the region appeared to have gone through a time warp back to the days of Herbert Hoover. In January 1938, the city of Cleveland had to suspend relief payments for six days, prompting *Der Angriff* (Berlin) to tell its readers with considerable exaggeration and great *schadenfreude* that 65,000 persons were starving and freezing in the streets of one of America's largest cities. The municipal treasury ran dry again in May. *Time* reported the plight of a mother of seven, pregnant with her eighth child, keeping herself and her family alive with the aid of neighbors: bread and tea for breakfast, bread and spaghetti for lunch, bread and salmon for dinner. Mayor Harold H. Burton issued a statement that attempted to balance hopelessness with encouragement: "Although there are no funds available, no one will starve."[50]

The consequences went well beyond laid-off workers, their families, and the chronically dependent. Businesses, large and small, just beginning to rebuild their balance sheets and plan expansion, were forced back into retrenchment. Corporations that had accepted unionism in the flush of recovery were now saddled with high wages and falling revenues. Many workers who avoided layoffs had to settle for reduced hours. Farm commodity prices began to drop sharply as production grew more rapidly than the ability of the government to control it. So did the prices of other basic commodities. Bankers, seeing few opportunities for sound lending, let their cash reserves accumulate beyond the already high Federal Reserve limits, almost as if they were anticipating another round of runs by depositors.[51]

The swiftness of the setback left Roosevelt and his policy makers reeling from the political implications and looking for someone to blame. By the end of the year, they had hit on an explanation straight from the early twentieth-century progressive heritage they shared. The recession was the result of monopolistic, or quasi-monopolistic, pricing practices by huge corporations able to set high prices for their products and thereby block the natural forces of recovery. The banking community was engaging in a politically motivated "strike of capital"; so were corporations that continued to defer plans for new plants and equipment. But what about organized labor, the strikes, and the settlements that had led to higher wages? U.S. Steel declared that wage increases required a substantial price increase. Labor, Roosevelt and others responded, was entitled to good wages, but companies should be able to pay them without higher prices.

In angry speeches at the end of the year, Secretary of the Interior Ickes and Robert H. Jackson, antitrust chief in the Justice Department, asserted that the administration was locked in combat with an inter-locked elite of "sixty families" that controlled big business and finance in the country. In the meantime, the TVA and the utility companies remained at each other's throats, with Roosevelt at one point telling a press conference that he was committed to the elimination of every single holding company in the utility industry—and for that matter in every other line of business. On Capitol Hill, Burton K. Wheeler and Harry S. Truman were winding up a neopopulistic investigation of the railroad industry built around the thesis that the railroads were on the verge of collapse, not because of the depression, the rapidly expanding trucking companies, and the automobile, but because they had been looted by Wall Street manipulators.[52]

All this was, not to put too fine a point on it, poppycock. It exhilarated the older progressives and many younger liberals, but failed to convince most of the undecided. *New York Times* columnist Arthur Krock dis-missed it as "hate oratory" that reflected administration "pride, prejudice, and politics." Toward the end of March, David Lawrence, a distinguished columnist devoted to the memory of Woodrow Wilson, declared that Roosevelt "has aroused in the financial and business communities a fear amounting almost to terror and a distrust which has broken down the morale of the whole economic machinery." The antibusiness rhetoric was all the same sincerely believed by most of its advocates. The president once again semiprivately compared himself to old Andy Jackson in his fight to the death against Nicholas Biddle and the banking establishment of a century earlier.

Roosevelt, Ickes, Jackson, and others had naturally and honestly tapped into the most basic tenet of progressive theology—antitrustism. The more modernist views of the original Brains Trust about regulation and state management were long forgotten. A revised New Deal pro-fessed its harshest antibusiness tone yet. At the end of April, Roosevelt sent a message to Congress lambasting a growing concentration of wealth, industry, and finance that, he asserted, threatened to become "stronger than the democratic state itself." Such a condition "in its essence, is Fascism." He asked Congress to undertake "a comprehensive study of the concentration of economic power in American industry and the effect of that concentration upon the decline of competition." The result was a joint Temporary National Economic Committee, charged with investigating the problem of monopoly in America. Chaired by Democratic senator Joseph O'Mahoney of Wyoming, it would hold hearings for two and a half years, eventually print thirty-seven volumes of reports, and produce no significant legislation.[53]

The administration of this new direction would fall to Thurman Arnold, who took over the antitrust division of Justice in early 1938. Formerly dean of the Yale Law School, Arnold came to Washington well-established as an exemplar of the skeptical realism that long had dominated legal studies at Yale. The intelligentsia knew him as the author of two books, *The Symbols of Government* and *The Folklore of Capitalism*, which debunked the conventional wisdom of American politics. One of his targets had been the antitrust myth. The large corporation in America, he declared, routinely attacked as evil, was nonetheless a necessity that met pressing social needs; thus, it was roughly equivalent to the institution of prostitution, socially and legally condemned but tolerated and covertly regulated.

Like O'Mahoney a native of Wyoming, Arnold knew the rhetoric of populism; when it was convenient he could lash into big business with a fervor William Jennings Bryan would have admired. But as a practical matter, he understood that it made little sense to talk about busting trusts in the middle of a depression. Bigness, he realized, usually was accompanied by economies of scale that could contribute to a wider distribution of the nation's prosperity. During his five years in office, he filed more antitrust suits than any of his predecessors, but invariably aimed them at practices that made goods more expensive for consumers. Unlike most of the old progressives in Washington, he believed the purpose of antitrust was to discipline big business rather than to destroy it. In attacking U.S. Steel, for example, he went after its pricing practices rather than making an issue of its enormous size. His policies were in line with the administration charges against business, but they inadvertently demonstrated the hollowness of assertions that corporate greed was responsible for the country's economic problems. His legal actions ended numerous abuses that were real, but also relatively small. Big businesses did indeed enjoy some marginal above-market pricing advantage, but possessed neither the power to wreck an economy nor an interest in doing so. Antitrust offered no way out of the Depression.[54]

Another possibility was a return to large-scale deficit spending. It was impossible to escape notice that the recession coincided with the budget-balancing drive and the big cuts in the WPA rolls. Was not therefore deficit spending the way back to prosperity? And was there not anyway an obligation to provide help to the millions suddenly thrown out of work just as they were getting back on their feet? Such questions were not as self-answering as they might sound. The national debt, approaching $40 billion, was at an unprecedented high and gave every appearance of becoming increasingly difficult to finance. Large temporary deficits as short-run measures were perhaps justifiable, but no one believed they could go on forever without destroying the nation's credit.

It was natural enough for Secretary of the Treasury Morgenthau, the government's chief financial officer, concerned with a problematic bond market, to take the lead in arguing that the time had come to cut spending and stay the course. As the winter of 1938 ended, however, he was outnumbered by a large group most prominently and persistently led by Harry Hopkins and Marriner Eccles. By the end of March 1938, Hopkins had added nearly 900,000 to the WPA rolls but was still providing for less than a third of the newly unemployed and rapidly running out of money. Eccles argued simply that deficit spending was the only feasible alternative to massive state regimentation of the economy, thereby drawing the backing of not only liberals, but moderate to conservative types such as Jesse Jones and James Farley.[55]

In early February, John Maynard Keynes entered the argument with a letter to the president, written from Cambridge. The communication was remarkable, less for its predictable promotion of more spending and public works (here Keynes especially cited working-class housing) than for its admonition against business bashing. "What is the use of chasing the utilities around the lot every other week?" Keynes asked. The real criminals among their managers were long since gone; holding companies, properly and equitably organized, were not ipso facto evil. Buy them out in those areas where such a policy was possible, but otherwise guarantee them fair earnings on their investments. Nor was there any point in beating up the railroads. "Nationalise them if the time is ripe. If not, take pity on the overwhelming problems of the present managements. And here too let the dead bury their dead. (To an Englishman, you Americans, like the Irish, are so terribly historically minded!)" In general, handle businessmen more gently. Treat them not as wolves and tigers, but as badly brought up and trained domestic animals. "It is a mistake to think that they are more *immoral* than politicians. If you work them into the surly, obstinate, terrified mood, of which domestic animals, wrongly handled, are so capable, the nation's burdens will not get carried to market; and in the end public opinion will veer their way." He remained an enthusiastic supporter, he assured the president, but "I am terrified lest progressive causes in all the democratic countries should suffer injury, because you have taken too lightly the risk to their prestige which would result from a failure measured in terms of immediate prosperity."[56]

Roosevelt's reply, drafted by Morgenthau, was bland and noncommittal. Still one cannot casually dismiss Keynes's contribution to the argument over spending, if for no other reason than two months later, Roosevelt gave up on the economy drive. Likely, however, he did so for a more direct reason, bluntly stated by Eccles: "The New Deal and all it stands for is in danger of being discredited." The discussion was never theoretical. It involved distressed constituencies and real issues of political power. By the end of March, pressure for vigorous government spending was coming from all parts of the New Deal coalition. Ultimately it was easier for the president to reverse himself on the deficit than on his deeply felt hostility toward big business and finance. In early April, he asked Congress for an additional $2 billion in spending and nearly another billion in federal loan authorizations, then followed up with a speech to the nation.

> Roosevelt, seated in front of a microphone, delivers the twelfth fireside chat of his presidency. Speaking carefully and persuasively he makes the case for a big new spending program to fight the renewed Depression. "Democracy has disappeared in several other great nations—disappeared not because the people of those nations disliked democracy, but because they had grown tired of unemployment and insecurity, of seeing their children hungry while they sat helpless in the face of government confusion, government weakness. . . . we need to act together, to meet the problems of the nation boldly, and to prove that the practical operation of democratic government is equal to the task of protecting the security of the people."[57] (Newsreel, "President Speaks to Nation")

Given the atmosphere of emergency, Congress responded with relative speed, sending the president what he wanted on June 21. WPA employment expanded rapidly in the fall, peaking at around 3.2 million in the election months of October and November. Unemployment declined apace, dropping from June's high of 11.4 million to 10.3 million in December—still around eighteen percent. It would take another six million jobs to get that rate into single digits. They were nowhere in sight.[58]

The dreary end to a hard economic year had its match in an equally unhappy end to the political year. On paper, the administration scored some signal victories in Congress. A new Agricultural Adjustment Administration was created with strong powers to control production and thereby raise agricultural prices. A Fair Labor Standards Act, in effect a restoration of equivalent provisions in the old NRA codes, established minimum wages and maximum hours for industrial workers; it also outlawed child labor. Considerably watered down from its first draft, the Fair Labor Standards Act nevertheless drew strong opposition from Southern legislators who believed that their impoverished, underdeveloped region could attract investment only with the lure of cheap labor. (In view of the South's deficiencies in education and its lack of a large experienced industrial workforce, there was much to be said for this argument. Condemning the bill's failure to provide regional wage differentials, Walter Lippmann called the legislation a "sectional bill disguised as a humanitarian reform.")

Most of the rest of the president's agenda, however, was left in shreds. Congress infuriated Roosevelt by effectively eliminating the undistributed profits tax. The so-called little TVA proposal never stirred. Most mortifying of all, the executive reorganization bill, reduced to a shadow of its original content, failed of passage once again, despite a full-court press by Roosevelt. (In a public letter refuting charges that he sought absolute power, he declared "I have no inclination to be a dictator." The episode only confirmed that when such denials seem necessary, they are invariably futile.) The president felt the defeat keenly. It was one of the primary motivations for an unprecedented effort to change a Democratic congressional party that he felt had let him down.[59]

As the New Deal became harder-edged and more class-defined, Roosevelt faced opposition from increasing numbers of Democrats on Capitol Hill, not all of them Southerners. (Representative John J. O'Connor of New York, Chairman of the House Rules Committee, had led the fight to stop executive reorganization.) Dissatisfaction was clearly strongest within the Southern faction, defined especially by hostility to black civil rights and organized labor, but also by an ideological commitment to states rights. The Southerners were a special problem because they had the position and power that came with long seniority. Roosevelt regarded his Democratic opponents just as he had the Supreme Court. He had won reelection with an overwhelming popular mandate; they were flouting the will of the people. As if he had learned nothing from the experience of a year earlier, he decided to sweep them out of his way.

Sometime in the spring of 1938 he and close political advisers drew up what became a semipublic hit list of non-supporters they hoped might be defeated. Senators who had apparently strong primary opponents and would be openly fought by the president were Walter George (Georgia), Millard Tydings (Maryland), Ellison D. "Cotton Ed" Smith (South Carolina), and Guy Gillette (Iowa). The president hoped, but eventually failed, to find suitable opponents for a half-dozen others from outside the deep South. In truth, none were dead-end opponents of the New Deal, but all had fought court packing and at least one or two other measures close to FDR's heart. The list consisted of about one-third of the Democrats up for election; the ratio roughly reflected conservative strength in the party's entire Senate delegation. Its geography indicated the breadth of anti–New Deal sentiment among Senate Democrats, the enormity of Roosevelt's task, and just perhaps a strong whiff of arrogance in the belief he could pull it off.[60]

Two early results had given him encouragement. In January, Lister Hill, an unapologetic New Dealer, handily defeated Tom Heflin for Hugo Black's Alabama Senate seat. In May, another strong New Dealer, Florida's Claude Pepper, who had won a special election to the Senate in 1936, triumphed with equal ease over strongly conservative opposition. Then the tide turned. In early June, Gillette prevailed in Iowa's Democratic primary despite the open opposition of Harry Hopkins. Gillette's victory probably convinced the president that he would have to be more direct. In a fireside chat on June 24, Roosevelt openly committed himself to a purge. The Democratic party had to stand for principles of New Deal liberalism. "As the head of the Democratic party . . . charged with the responsibility of carrying out the definitely liberal declaration of principles set forth in the 1936 Democratic platform, I feel that I have every right to speak in those few instances where there may be a clear-cut issue between candidates."[61]

Concentrating on the three New Deal skeptics who had credible liberal competition, Roosevelt intervened personally and openly. In August, he criticized Senator George when the two of them shared a Georgia platform, then less directly he threw a shaft at Senator Smith in South Carolina. Just days later, he attacked Tydings as a legislator who had "betrayed the New Deal in the past and will again." George, Smith, and

Tydings cruised to victory that summer with margins of 20, 11, and 20 percent. As for the rest, the president, realistically understanding that he could not beat them, hardly uttered a whisper against them. The only person on his covert hit list to lose was George Berry of Tennessee, an interim appointee who fell to Tom Stewart, mistaken by no one for a New Dealer.[62]

There were some consolations. Roosevelt targeted one member of the House, John O'Connor (New York), whose obstructionism on the Rules Committee he took especially personally because O'Connor's brother, Basil, was a close friend. Roosevelt knew his home state's politics intimately, his clout was enormous, his local contacts legion. O'Connor was a goner. And at least no New Deal Democrat was unseated in the primaries. The political scientist J. B. Shannon, analyzing the results in the South, determined that 53.4 percent of the voters there who faced a clear choice marked their ballots for a New Deal candidate. As for Roosevelt himself, no one doubted that he remained personally popular. *Time* magazine described an extended Western trip he made in July: "Starting as a statesmanlike sortie into certain critical primary elections, it ended as a march of personal triumph."[63]

Yet the president was also politically wounded, facing a Senate in which around twenty Democrats were seething with resentment against him and another ten or so would frequently vote with them. He had demonstrated that he still failed to grasp the limitations of his 1936 mandate. Nor did he understand the nature of American political parties, which functioned from the grass roots up, not from the top down. Even in Britain—a country whose politics Roosevelt fancied he knew better than he actually did—prime ministers at the apex of a centralized party organization could not sack dissenters who had strong personal followings. In the United States, local voters normally decided on Democratic and Republican candidates without interference from above. Entrenched officeholders had their own state or district organizations and networks that rejected outside pressures like a healthy immune system. Americans in general did not think in terms of party responsibility as most British habitually did. The mystery is how a politician of Roosevelt's skill and intelligence could fail to understand this. Hubris had led to blindness.

Under the best of circumstances, the Democrats had to anticipate losses in the general elections; their 1936 congressional margins were unsustainable. The turmoil of the past twenty-one months—the court controversy, labor upheaval, economic slump, the administration's class-based rhetoric, the purge—made their prospects worse. Roosevelt still attracted intense loyalty from most of those who had palpably benefited from the New Deal, but his base was considerably narrower than in 1936 and the level of skepticism far higher.

The most wobbly constituency of the 1936 coalition, the farmers, grumbled about declining prices, a result of bumper crops that had overwhelmed the acreage allotments of the 1936 Soil Conservation Act. The administration had responded with large-scale Commodity Credit Corporation subsidies that left government warehouses bulging with surpluses. Secretary of Agriculture Wallace, attempting to make a virtue of necessity, had preached the virtues of an "ever-normal granary," but the real-world task was to cut production. The second Agricultural Adjustment Administration had been established too late to impact prices significantly and was considerably more bureaucratic and coercive than its predecessor. The nation's agrarian heartland was no longer filled with grateful tillers of the soil.

Wallace and his advisers found themselves inexorably pushed toward the conclusion that only the return of industrial prosperity could provide a satisfactory market for agricultural production, but this stance propelled them in the direction of an urban liberalism that had little attraction for the countryside and positively repelled most leaders of the agrarian establishment. By 1938, the major farm pressure group, the Farm Bureau Federation, had distanced itself from the administration, in part because the agricultural policy makers had cozied up to the far less consequential, but much more ideologically congenial National Farmers Union. Nonetheless, writing off the Farm Bureau was the practical political equivalent of a self-administered gunshot to the foot. With more than a fifth of the population still living on farms, agricultural disenchantment was important.[64]

The political dynamics of 1938 ran against the administration in numerous other ways. Unhappiness with labor disorders still ran high. The return to hard times and crushing unemployment delegitimized the New Deal among vast swaths of the populace. The vocal hostility toward big business and finance not only got in the way of economic recovery, it also resonated down through the ranks of small enterprisers, many of whom feared the CIO and detested government regulation more than their larger counterparts. Charges that state WPA administrators were squeezing reliefers for campaign contributions began in the primaries and continued through the fall. Roosevelt's attempts at an activist foreign policy—increased military spending, talk of quarantining aggressors, reacting strongly against the Japanese sinking of the American gunboat *Panay*—worked against him. Not simply Republicans, but many independent progressives (and a few Democrats) muttered that the president was turning to foreign relations in an attempt to hide his domestic failures.[65]

The voters spoke on November 8, delivering to Roosevelt and the New Dealers a strong and decidedly uncongenial message. The raw statistical losses were unlovely but on the surface sustainable; viewed in specific detail, the outcome was devastating. The Republicans gained eighty-one seats in the House of Representatives, nearly doubling their delegation but still coming up forty-nine short of a majority; in the Senate, they picked up eight, bringing their number to a paltry twenty-three. A net gain of thirteen governors left them with only eighteen out of forty-eight. Yet every serious analyst realized the GOP had scored an important victory.

The Republicans ran very well in important industrial states with strong labor movements. Democratic governors who had been close to unions suddenly seemed an endangered species: Republicans came to power in Pennsylvania, Ohio, and Michigan. In those three states alone, the Republicans gained twenty-eight of their new House seats. In Wisconsin, Governor Phil La Follette, who just six months earlier had launched with great fanfare the long-deferred National Progressive party, was defeated for reelection. He was gone for good, and so was his new party. Next door in Minnesota, Farmer-Labor Governor Elmer Benson lost to young Republican star Harold Stassen. In those two states, strongholds of independent progressivism, the Republicans picked up another dozen House seats. George Gallup, declaring "America is essentially a middle-class country," cited a continuing reaction against the court-packing plan and the sit-down strikes among the fifty percent or so of the electorate that was neither rich nor poor, owned property, and longed for social stability. They had no interest, he believed, in returning to the 1920s, but had voted out of a conviction that Roosevelt had lurched too far to the left.[66]

The implications for Washington politics were great. The new Republican strength in the House made it all but impossible for Democrats to ram legislation through by suspending the rules, a maneuver that required a two-thirds margin. It also practically ended the possibility of bringing legislation to the floor with a discharge petition, if, as *Time* put it, "bills unwanted by a conservative coalition are locked up in committee." O'Connor's defeat notwithstanding, the possibility of such a lockup in the powerful Rules Committee was more likely than ever because of the defeat of three of its loyal New Deal members and the increased Republican strength on it.

Time's mention of a conservative coalition was prescient. Forty-six House Democrats, joining with a solid Republican delegation, could form a majority in the House. In the Senate, Vice President Garner, Pat Harrison, and Jimmy Byrnes quietly indicated their intention to establish a frugal, small-government Democratic economy bloc at arm's length from the White House. Tradition and institutional attachments precluded a formal alliance with the Republicans, but the conservative Democrats shared many values with them, were no longer amenable to dictation from the president, and willing to be participants in an informal alliance.[67]

The New Deal was effectively dead.

During the first eight months of 1939, the debates over recovery and reform at home increasingly became overshadowed by the threat of war in Europe. The economy improved fitfully but relatively steadily, assisted by defense orders from Britain and France, but unemployment remained sticky. In August, it was still at about eighteen percent. The WPA rolls, under pressure from the new bipartisan "economy bloc" in Congress, nevertheless dropped from just under 3 million in January to a little less than 2 million in August. Although under fire from conservatives as a beehive of waste, corruption, and political patronage, the WPA seemed likely to continue as a more or less permanent national fixture. After Harry Hopkins was made secretary of commerce in December 1938, it was routinized by the appointment of a career army officer, Colonel F. C. Harrington, as its administrator. The argument between the administration and the economy bloc was not about its continuance but about how much money should be spent on it. America in mid-1929, whatever its shortcomings, had been a dynamic, expanding, optimistic nation. America in mid-1939 was stagnant, shabby, and wary of the future.[68]

The president himself remained popular, but the stalemated condition of Washington politics provided little room for dramatic new initiatives and less tolerance for a continuation of militant New Dealism. He played a difficult game of pressing for high relief appropriations while attempting to throw out lines of conciliation to the business community. Insiders began to speculate about his successor in 1940; the names bruited about were uninspiring at best: Vice President Garner, Secretary of State Hull,

Postmaster General Farley, Phillippines High Commissioner Paul McNutt, Missouri Senator Bennett Champ Clark, and Secretary of Commerce Hopkins. None seemed good bets when contrasted to the Republican front-runners, New York racket-buster Thomas E. Dewey and Michigan Senator Arthur Vandenberg. Already, news analysts wondered aloud if FDR were contemplating a third term—and questioning whether the public would buy it.[69]

Roosevelt did achieve one important victory in March, when Congress finally passed an executive reorganization bill after an excruciatingly narrow vote. The Executive Reorganization Act of 1939 appeared to be hardly more than a skeleton of the president's original proposal. Nevertheless, it was a milestone in the institutionalization of a modern presidency that Roosevelt had created with personal charisma and an instinctive understanding of the exercise of power. The act gave the president limited authority to rearrange the executive agencies, subject to a congressional veto. Roosevelt quickly used it to create an Executive Office of the President, the most important component of which would be the Bureau of the Budget, relocated from the Department of the Treasury. Budget, with its director and his large staff under the chief executive's direct control, would allow for presidential management of a coordinated legislative program and a rapidly expanding executive branch as never before. The bill also provided the president with six new administrative assistants, each with his own staff.

Roosevelt also moved ahead with his plans to expand the civil service, effectively giving protection to New Deal bureaucrats. He had taken some initial steps in 1938 by executive order, providing shelter to 71,000 federal employees, who had been classified as emergency temporary hires. Congress responded with the Hatch Act of 1939, which forbade federal civil servants from engaging in political activity. After some hesitation, Roosevelt signed the bill rather than risk a veto fight. This decision paved the way for the Ramspeck Act of 1940, which would transform another 200,000 New Deal functionaries into career civil servants. In that year, Roosevelt also would sign a second Hatch Act, which applied to state and local workers supported by federal funding. As Sidney Milkis has observed, Roosevelt, by disavowing any intent of building a civil-service-based political machine, had perhaps done the Democratic party a disservice, but had achieved an ideological goal that he valued above party—the development of a New Deal liberal bureaucracy.[70]

Other bitter domestic issues sputtered their way to resolution.

On August 11 Roosevelt signed a bill, based on the recommendations of a board he had appointed, liberalizing the social security system in several ways. The most important provision moved the date for the first retirement insurance payments up two years to January 1, 1940, from January 1, 1942. The course of the legislation through Congress had been accompanied by numerous controversies on matters of detail, but its final passage with wide support indicated that the campaign debate about social security in 1936 was "history," dead and long forgotten.[71]

The administration and the utility companies were reaching a modus vivendi, based on the understanding that the TVA, REA, and other federal power programs would not go away, but that Congress would not allow the establishment of new ones. On August 15, 1939, in a ceremony covered by the national press, David Lilienthal handed Commonwealth and Southern Chairman Wendell Willkie a check for $44.7 million, TVA's share of a $78.4 million buyout of Commonwealth and Southern's properties in the Tennessee Valley. The much-reduced private utility for its part agreed to buy power from the TVA. The goodwill that suffused the event was forced, but it also reflected the relief of each man that the battle was done and he was still standing. "After all the crises and the worries and the uncertainties and the thin ice and the long, long chance," Lilienthal wrote in his diary later that day, "it is over and beyond recall."[72]

So was much that had occurred over the previous six and a half years. Alan Brinkley has referred to Roosevelt's second term as initiating "the end of reform." It assuredly did put an end to the First New Deal objective of close government management of the industrial economy along the lines of an American corporatist state. The effort had run too much against the American grain. The Second New Deal had provided reform aplenty also, but many Americans had been queasy about or downright hostile to its tone of class warfare, encouragement of CIO militance, and its leader's widely perceived lust for power. Above all, it had not ended the Depression. By mid-1939, that failure was not only pervasively apparent, it was beginning to tell politically.

In early August, Henry Wallace sent the president a bleak but informed analysis. Millions of farmers, small-town residents, and small businessmen—decent people whose votes the administration needed—had supported the president in 1932 and 1936, but were turning away from him. "On a straight division of the electorate on a basis of the broadly liberal and the generally conservative, the definite majority is conservative," Wallace concluded. "We have to have some means of getting basic, general support, and then covering that foundation with a liberal superstructure."[73] Wallace, whose own presidential ambitions were probably beginning to stir, wrote from the still widespread assumption that Roosevelt would not run for a third term.

The future even more than usual was shrouded by a thick and impenetrable fog; the past was a clear vista, marred by stark imperfections. It must have seemed to those who thought about such things that history would remember Franklin D. Roosevelt as an interesting and attractive president who could claim substantial achievements but had failed at his fundamental task.

On August 24, Germany and the Soviet Union proclaimed their infamous nonaggression pact. On September 1, Germany invaded Poland.

The future, still enveloped by that fog, was suddenly open in a way it had not been before.

HEADLINES AND MOVIE NEWSREELS

{1937}

MARCH 6 — British Military Outlay 40% Higher Than U.S. Bill; Increase in the Income Tax

APRIL 28 — Historic Basque Town Wiped Out; Rebel Fliers Machine-Gun Civilians; German-type Planes Fling Thousands of Bombs and Incendiary Projectiles on Guernica

MAY 1 — Washington Will Try Wartime Neutrality; Cash-and-Carry Plan Included

AUGUST — *Billowing clouds of smoke rise over the old city of Shanghai. The Japanese bombardment illuminates night skies. Retreating Chinese soldiers blow bridges behind them. Accompanied by hundreds of thousands of refugees carrying meager possessions, sometimes driving livestock, they stream into the French zone of the city.* (Newsreel, "Japan Attacks Shanghai")

OCTOBER 6 — Roosevelt Arraigns War Makers; Would Try "Quarantine"

DECEMBER 13 — U.S. Gunboat Sunk by Japanese Bombs; British Warship Hit; Nanking Encircled

{1938}

FEBRUARY 21 — Eden Resigns Over Issue of Seeking Deals with Dictators

MARCH 12 — Nazis Seize Austria After Hitler Ultimatum

OCTOBER 1 — Britain and Germany Make Anti-War Pact; Germans Begin Czech Occupation; "Peace with Honor," Says Chamberlain

NOVEMBER 11 — Nazis Smash, Loot and Burn Jewish Shops and Temples

{1939}

MARCH 15 — Hitler Dissolves Czecho-Slovak Republic

MARCH 29 — Madrid Yields, Ending War; Republican Leaders Flee

APRIL 1 — Hushed Commons Hears Chamberlain's Decision to Fight If Poles Attacked

AUGUST 22 — Germany and Russia Agree on Non-Aggression; Ribbentrop Going to Moscow

IRREPRESSIBLE CONFLICT,
1937–1939

Personality

In mid-1937, there were few indications time was running out for the men at the top of Britain's National Government. Its new leader, Neville Chamberlain, was by common consent Stanley Baldwin's natural successor. His steadiness, diligence, and lack of color implicitly affirmed the regime's rejection of "dynamic forces." It would be his misfortune, however, to have to come to grips with challenges from abroad that no longer could be ignored and that revitalized the aimless figure who in crisis times was Britain's most dynamic force.

Mr. Churchill

Nearly sixty years later Lady Violet Bonham Carter recalled her first meeting with Winston Churchill. They had been seated next to each other at a dinner party in 1906, both still unmarried, he thirty-one and already world famous, she the lovely and brilliant nineteen-year-old daughter of Liberal party notable Herbert Asquith. For a long time her companion was silent, as if in some sort of reverie. Then he took notice of her and "burst forth into an eloquent diatribe" about the human condition, speaking "in a torrent of magnificent language which appeared to be both effortless and inexhaustible." She remembered his concluding sentence as if it had been spoken yesterday: "We are all worms. But I do believe that I am a glow-worm."

The performance was typical of Churchill—the casual appropriation of a grand theme, the masterful deployment of the English language, the memorable rhetorical flourish, the flaunting of a massive ego. Violet

Asquith later told her father, "for the first time in my life, I have seen genius." Herbert Asquith replied that Winston would surely agree with her but that others who had more experience with him might not.[1]

Churchill had been born November 30, 1874, at Blenheim Palace, the enormous manor Queen Anne had built for his distant ancestor, John Churchill, first Duke of Marlborough. A child of privilege, he nonetheless had to struggle for identity, position, and livelihood. His father, Lord Randolph Churchill, was the younger brother of the eighth duke, his mother, Jennie Jerome, the sublimely attractive daughter of a wealthy American. Both parents were of the beautiful people of their time, endowed with prodigious appetites, self-indulgent, financially pinched by an income that would have supported three dozen middle-class families, and ultimately self-destructive. Neither had much time for Winston or his younger brother, Jack.

Lord Randolph made his way in the world of politics with spectacular success. Elected to the House of Commons at 25, he was chancellor of the exchequer in Lord Salisbury's Conservative government at the age of thirty-seven. He possessed star quality. He was also opportunistic, erratic, and widely disliked. He and Winston's mother had lost interest in each other; both immersed themselves in multiple extramarital relationships. In the midst of an intraparty dispute, Lord Randolph tendered a pro forma resignation in 1886. To his astonishment, Salisbury instantly accepted it. For the next eight years, he was a back bencher, occasionally attracting attention but in progressively bad health. He died in January 1895, three weeks short of his forty-sixth birthday, after years of a degenerative illness believed to be syphilis. Winston's mother, forty years old at the time of Lord Randolph's death but still ravishing, took a series of lovers and two much younger husbands, the last of whom lived until 1964. She died in 1921.

The dysfunctional Churchills followed the upper-class custom of sending sons to boarding school at as early an age as possible—eight in Winston's case. Despite a prodigious memory and flashes of brilliance, he was a mediocre student. Lord Randolph, convinced Winston was too dull to earn a living in some civilian profession, pushed him toward a military career. On his third attempt, he passed the entrance examination for Sandhurst. Four weeks after his father's death, twenty years old, he graduated with a commission as a second lieutenant of the King's cavalry.

His military career was brief and eventful. In the Sudan, he led his company of lancers in the last great cavalry action of the British Army.

He served in India on the northwest frontier at the zenith of the British Raj. On the side, he wrote dispatches for the *Daily Telegraph, The Times,* and other publications, which paid him handsomely. On furlough in England, he was in demand as a speaker. He authored a novel that was serialized in the popular press. By then he realized his future was as a writer and politician. Given a place on the Conservative ticket for a by-election in the difficult constituency of Oldham, he lost his first race for the House of Commons. Then came the Boer War, service as a uniformed correspondent on active duty with British forces, ambush, capture, imprisonment, escape, "Churchill: Wanted, Dead or Alive" posters, and his triumphal reemergence in Portugese East Africa. Amplified by his talent for self-promotion, the adventure made him a popular hero. On the ticket at Oldham again in the general election of 1900, he narrowly won election to Parliament.

Churchill quickly confirmed the fears of older and more stable leaders that he would be as erratic and unreliable as his father. Disenchanted with his party's turn toward trade protectionism and resistance to the current of social reformism coming to a head in Edwardian England, he dramatically crossed the aisle in mid-1904 to join the Liberal party. Less than two years later, the Liberals were in power, and Churchill, just thirty-one, was undersecretary of state for colonial affairs; after Herbert Asquith became prime minister in 1908, he was successively president of the Board of Trade, home secretary, and first lord of the admiralty. No man in the government, save David Lloyd George, attracted more attention. His failed plan to seize the Dardanelles and take Turkey out of the World War in 1915 temporarily derailed his rapid ascent. Asquith packed him off to the Western Front as a battalion commander.

By 1917, however, he was back in London, serving in the new government of Lloyd George as minister of munitions, then after the armistice as secretary of state for war and colonial secretary. With the breakup of the wartime national coalition in 1922, he was temporarily out of office. Recruited by Stanley Baldwin, he returned to the Conservative party and, after it won the election of 1924, was made chancellor of the exchequer. He served in the post for five years, overseeing with misgivings the pound's return to gold, while attempting to develop budgets that would balance military and social demands. Along the way, he produced a steady stream of books and articles, and lectured widely, especially in the United States, where he enjoyed great fame.

Out of power after the Conservative defeat in 1929, he was increasingly at loggerheads with Baldwin on the general issue of maintaining the

British Empire and the specific matter of self-governing dominion status for India. In February 1931, after the two of them openly disagreed on the floor of the House of Commons, he resigned from the shadow cabinet. An act of principle, the resignation was also a grievous political miscalculation. It left him on the outside when, just months later, Baldwin engineered the National government and the enormous election victory of 1931. It also demonstrated a certain distance from the spirit of the times.

Churchill assuredly had a romantic devotion to the British Empire, but there was also realism in his belief that the lifting of British rule in a divided India would lead to chaos. Yet he failed to assess another reality: a predominantly liberal Britain lacked both the will and the means to maintain colonial rule over a subcontinent of three hundred million people who wanted to be independent. The more he pressed a hopeless cause, the more he marginalized himself—and the more he took up other unwise causes. His behavior during the abdication crisis, the nadir of his career, confirmed a widespread sense that he was dangerously unsteady. Most of the House found him both impressive and consumed by a self-serving ambition. Like a rogue elephant, he was at once awesome and scary. The dangers of being at his side outweighed any benefit.

By early 1937, Churchill had for four years consistently pursued another unpopular cause—warning of the menace of Nazi Germany and calling for vigorous rearmament. If he understood nothing else, he understood Hitler clearly and terribly. He did so in the spirit of a realist willing to make compromises with less-threatening dictators—notably Mussolini—if it served the interests of Britain. He was motivated not by an amoral assessment of power, however, but by his sense that Britain, along with the United States, embodied liberal values that had to be defended and preserved against truly menacing dangers. Utilizing sources inside the government, he hammered away in Commons, in public addresses, and in newspaper articles at the German air threat and called for huge increases in the capabilities of the Royal Air Force. At times he clearly exaggerated German strength; his descriptions of the horrors of bombing may even have ramped up British peace sentiment by making war unthinkable. Yet he grasped a trend that a government committed to disarmament negotiations until 1937 failed to understand—Germany was rearming at full-tilt while Britain contented itself with half-measures.

The journalist Vincent Sheehan recalled him talking informally with a small group of fellow vacationers in the summer of 1935 about the way in which the whole post–World War international structure was collapsing:

"Who is to say what will come of it in a year, or two, or three? With Germany arming at breakneck speed, England lost in a pacifist dream, France corrupt and torn by dissension, America remote and indifferent." Addressing a Frenchwoman in the group, he said: "Madame, my dear lady, do you not tremble for your children?"[2]

Baldwin and Chamberlain found him increasingly obnoxious and excluded him from the government, but they reluctantly committed themselves to increased military spending. Most Conservative members of Parliament in mid-1937 dismissed Churchill as too mercurial to lead them. There would have been merit to this assessment in ordinary times, but those already had ended. After Churchill had been forced to leave the Admiralty in 1915, Conservative leader Andrew Bonar Law had remarked, "He has the defects of his qualities, and as his qualities are large, the shadow which they throw is fairly large also; but I say deliberately, in my judgment, in mental power and vital force he is one of the foremost men in our country."[3] The deepening crises of the late thirties would provide an opening for a vital, dynamic, force.

Global Crackup

When Franklin Roosevelt began his second term as president, the United States seemed to be rapidly emerging from the Depression. Adolf Hitler was just days away from the fourth anniversary of his own rise to power in what had become a resurgent Germany. Britain was enjoying a steady and understated economic revival under its own National leadership, returned to office fourteen months earlier. It was possible to believe that the two great democracies could check the Nazi juggernaut. Yet a year later, the United States was again mired in Depression and Roosevelt on the defensive. Britain, experiencing a milder economic hiccup and still distant from an America whose partnership it badly needed, was overextended around the globe and irresolutely led in world affairs. Germany, dynamic and aggressive, malign beyond the imagination of Western liberalism, seemed unstoppable. Around the globe, the old order was crashing at every turn. The new order was appallingly grim and menacing.

In 1930, the Versailles settlement, amplified by multinational agreements of the 1920s, still constituted a governing force. Progressive disarmament seemed a distinct likelihood. It was possible to believe the League of Nations was a viable instrument for collective security. By 1937, those illusions were gone.

The economic obligations of Versailles had been universally abandoned. The territorial arrangements were increasingly shaky. Disarmament negotiations were dead and prior treaties denounced. Germany, Italy, and Japan were farthest along in developing military might, all flaunting their power and asserting the right of expansion by conquest. The Soviet Union, building a totalitarian variety of socialism in isolation, possessed a huge land and air military capability. Britain, France, and the United States were beginning to realize that postponement of rearmament was no longer an option. After the Italian conquest of Abyssinia, the League of Nations was irrelevant. Germany and Japan had both left it; Italy would withdraw at the end of the year. Japan already had seized Manchuria and conducted punitive military actions against China; in mid-1937, it began a full-scale invasion. Civil war raged in Spain, Germany and Italy openly assisting General Francisco Franco's Falangist rebels, the Soviet Union funneling aid to the Socialist Republican government. The international environment, without a dominant nation or group of nations to enforce order, had reverted to a Hobbesian state of nature. This reality was enthusiastically accepted by the four authoritarian nations among the seven major powers. The three democracies tended toward denial and policy paralysis.

Among the seven, Germany was Europe's most dynamic nation.[4] The manufacturing powerhouse of continental Europe, it was running at full capacity. In 1938, German steel production exceeded that of Britain, France, and Italy combined. With the occupation of the Rhineland, the German state had reasserted full control over its territory and extended its defensible borders. Hitler had admirers around the world, many of them in democratic nations. German military power appeared awesome, especially in the production of new aircraft. In fact, German strength measured on the basis of hardware was routinely overestimated; but even the few skeptics correctly respected the professionalism and discipline of the *Wehrmacht*. No one could doubt that Germany's expansionist drive was just beginning. It seemed unlikely that the democracies could block it.

Italy, the other dynamic expansionist among the European powers, had consistently projected strength throughout the decade, preventing a German absorption of Austria in 1934, positioning itself as a central European power, undertaking a naval program that caused some concern in London, apparently succeeding in organizing a productive corporatist economy. Mussolini drew attention and respect for uniting and modernizing a divided society, then projecting its power in the international arena. But actually Italy was overextended. Its state-managed economy had more weaknesses than strengths. Not until 1937 did its industrial production finally surpass that of 1929. Unable to feed itself, heavily dependent on imports of vital raw materials, all branches of its military poorly equipped and hampered by mediocre leadership, Italy had advanced in the esteem of the world through showy public works projects and by taking on easy-to-beat opposition (Libya, Abyssinia, the Spanish Republicans). Mussolini sorely lacked Hitler's focus, risk-taking traits, and decisiveness, but he still appeared formidable. Italy also seemed to be a natural ally for Germany—a fact Mussolini acknowledged toward the end of 1936 when he declared the line from Berlin to Rome to be "an axis round which all those European States which are animated by a desire for collaboration and peace can revolve."[5]

France was the democratic anchor of continental Europe, but its congenital weakness and instability displayed the fragility of liberal democratic institutions during the Great Depression. From mid-1932 to mid-1940, France was governed by seventeen cabinets, eleven different premiers, and ten distinct foreign ministers; the faces were usually familiar, but the perpetual reshuffling of their places hampered predictable leadership.[6] The nation's politics were turbulent, roiled by the presence of a large and vocal, if fragmented, fascist movement and a militant, class-conscious left. It was by no means certain that the center would hold. The industrial economy, which in the twenties had recovered more smartly than that of Great Britain, stagnated during the thirties, at least partly because of the country's tenacious and deflationary defense of the gold standard. At the beginning of 1937, manufacturing was still at eighty-one percent of its 1929 output. Unemployment appeared low only because many workers returned to their rural villages. The 1936 devaluation of the franc provided a needed boost to the economy but also initiated a steady outflow of gold from the central bank's enormous reserves.

Militarily, France appeared formidable. Its standing army was the largest in Europe west of the Soviet border. Its navy was at least a match for Italy's. Slow to develop a modern air force, it was never hopelessly behind Germany. France's real military problem lay in doctrine and leadership, both forged by the experience of the World War. The trauma of six million casualties, 1.7 million of them dead and another 700,000 permanently disabled, hung over the entire country. War planners worked from vivid memories of a conflict that had been dominated by defensive trench combat and the machine gun. The few visionaries who conceived of warfare as a dynamic, moving process driven by mobile armor and tactical aircraft attracted little attention.

In 1929 France began building the Maginot Line—an expensive and complex series of fortifications running along the border with Germany from Switzerland to Belgium. At its strong points, the Maginot Line bristled with artillery and machine guns emplaced in hardened pillboxes atop layers of bunkers several stories deep into the ground. It ended at the Belgian border. Water table problems made construction to the sea impossible and would in any event have alienated Belgium, which understandably expected French assistance in the event of war. The Maginot Line made a lot of sense for a country facing a stronger power, but its semifinished nature left France dependent on a Belgian resistance to a future German invasion.

It was all the more ironic then that in 1936, Belgium, intimidated by German troops again in the Rhineland, renounced its treaty with France and proclaimed its neutrality, leaving the French with a strategic problem they never resolved. Just as the occupation of the Rhineland had neutralized Belgium, it also severely damaged the other pillar of French security policy—its system of alliances with Eastern European nations, who came to realize that France, behind the Maginot fortifications and facing strong German defenses in the Rhineland, likely would do nothing to assist them against a German attack.[7]

Bereft of strong civilian and military leadership, hampered by a stagnant economy, unstable in its politics, France lacked will and direction. Its main hope for becoming a reliable prop of democracy in Europe lay in an alliance with Great Britain, but that relationship had been historically hostile until the rise of a unified Germany forced an entente before the World War. After the peace settlement, both nations were again at arm's length, with the British far less inclined to believe that the Germans were a menace to be kept down at all costs. The Depression had brought French protectionism and a refusal to support the pound. By 1937, it was imperative for the two countries to rebuild their relationship, but the task was by no means easy or natural.

Britain's assets complemented those of France rather well. Although its naval construction after the World War had been insignificant until 1936, it was still the world's number one sea power and arguably ahead of the German curve in aircraft development, if lagging in production. Its army in contrast to France's was small, but its empire and control of the sea lanes would give an alliance access to critical natural resources. Britain seemed to be riding a wave of economic recovery, but its coal mines, steel manufacturing, shipyards, and armament industries all still had excess capacity that could be swiftly utilized for military purposes. Its political leadership was about as well entrenched and widely supported as could be expected in any democratic polity.

The obstacles to an alliance were nonetheless great. Traditional British antipathy to France was but one aspect of a historical antipathy to involvement in continental politics. The World War, which traumatized the British fully as much as the French, had encouraged both these attitudes. The Empire/Commonwealth, moreover, may have provided Britain with assets far beyond those of the United Kingdom, but it also imposed substantial limits on the conduct of a foreign policy. The self-governing dominions, no longer subject to the will of a mother country, had to be consulted on major issues. All had endured great sacrifice during the last war; even more than London, all were wary of commitments to Europe. The colonies, moreover, drained scarce military resources. An always restive Middle East was on the brink of open revolt, in part because of increased Jewish settlement in Palestine. The failure to achieve satisfactory self-government for India meant that disorder would continue to be an intermittent fact of life there. Most pressingly, Japan posed a militant threat to British interests in China and Southeast Asia. Obligations of empire alone absorbed most of Britain's military capability and tasked even the world's strongest navy to the limit.

France and Britain together at the beginning of 1937 were indisputably stronger than Germany and Italy in terms of men under arms and military hardware. It was questionable, however, whether either nation had the will to fight and the military doctrine that would carry a war to a successful conclusion. Both faced a powerful challenge to their colonial positions in East Asia from Japan.

Japan brought to the world scene a strength and ruthless dynamism that made it a far larger force in global affairs than it had been in the World War. An isolated preindustrial society in the mid-nineteenth century, it had become the great imperialist power of East Asia by the second third of the twentieth. Its manufacturing economy had grown more than 500 percent since 1900 and had rebounded from the Depression more quickly than that of any other major nation. Only the United States,

Germany, and Britain surpassed it in heavy industrial capability; in the British case, the margin was rapidly narrowing. No nation, not even Germany, had so militarized its economy. The Japanese navy was the world's third largest, trailing only Britain and the United States; it possessed a higher percentage of recently built first-line vessels; its men were superbly trained. It was ahead of every other navy in its understanding of the potential of the aircraft carrier. Its air capabilities, naval- and ground-based, rivaled the best the Western powers could offer. Its army, with a million men on active duty, was the most formidable fighting force in East Asia, save possibly the big Soviet Siberian defense establishment. Its victories, utilizing mediocre weaponry against ill-trained and -equipped Chinese formations, encouraged hubris. But no one could deny the tenacious fanaticism with which it fought.

Japan's plans for dominance of East Asia and the Western Pacific were no secret. And they meshed well with the German and Italian challenges to the world order. In late 1936, Japan joined Germany in a loose Anti-Comintern agreement. It signaled not only that they were opposed to the spread of international communism (and Soviet influence) but also that they recognized the legitimacy of each other's ambitions. Mussolini kept Italy aloof from it for the time being, but few could doubt the direction of his diplomacy. Japan was especially feared and loathed by European colonial powers with Asian interests. United States popular opinion and policy-making calculation—both too smug in the much larger size of the U.S., too prone to assume the inferiority of a colored race, and naively inclined to judge the Japanese by the cheap consumer goods they exported—tended to relegate them to the level of a disorderly nuisance.

Alone among the seven major powers, the Soviet Union, ruled autocratically since 1925 by Josef Stalin, occupied vast areas of both Europe and Asia. Gigantic in size, population, and natural resources, it possessed all the features customarily associated with great power status. Its development of the heavy industry needed to undergird a war machine was remarkable. During the Depression, its manufacturing output had increased by an astonishing 300 percent. By the end of the decade its industrial capacity was likely behind only that of Germany and the United States. Much of this development, however, was at the price of policies that consumed half the nation's product and inflicted enormous hardship on the Russian masses. The peasants the Reuther brothers trained at Gorky were there because of policies that forced them off the land. The collectivization of agriculture, the killing of many independent proprietors, the appropriation of grain harvests for export induced not simply sporadic shortages of certain foods, as in Nazi Germany, but widespread famine in the Ukraine and high prices for a minimal diet elsewhere. Stalin's far-reaching purges, beginning in 1935, made Soviet life even more chaotic and terror-ridden. The industrial behemoth that emerged from this near-genocidal process was impressive, but also exhibited many of the weaknesses of a socialist command economy and a totalitarian state—a disregard of civilian consumer needs, inflexibility, statistical reports fudged to satisfy Moscow, an unproductive agricultural system, and a lack of incentive at almost every turn.

The Soviet military exhibited the same strengths and weaknesses. The Red Army matched Germany's in size and possessed the greatest array of tanks in the world. The Soviet air force was the largest in Europe. But much of the equipment was shoddy and outdated, the product of a system that made it difficult to bring new designs into production. Worse yet, Stalin's purges all but destroyed the senior officer corps, depriving his military of the experienced and creative leadership that would have equipped it better and been prepared to direct it in war. With some hesitation and after extracting exorbitant payment, Stalin sent tanks, fighter planes, and a couple of thousand advisers to aid the Spanish Republic in the Civil War. He also sanctioned the formation of Communist International Brigades. Initially effective in staving off a quick Falangist victory, the equipment proved to be no match for German aircraft and armor. The Soviet military of 1937 was less capable than it had been five years earlier and still in decline. The purges lasted into early 1938. At their end, Stalin, having killed off every rival and potential rival, having in addition sanctioned the murder of millions of others, finally realized that an enfeebled Soviet state faced real danger from Japan in the east and Germany in the west.

The Soviet call for a Popular, or United, Front to confront an aggressive fascism in 1935 captured the imagination of many Western liberals and socialists, who tended to see the USSR as the indispensable ally in the struggle for a progressive society. Franklin Roosevelt himself and many of the New Dealers regarded it at the least as a society moving in a considerably more positive direction than Germany. This yearning, of course, demonstrated woefully unrealistic thinking about a regime that had only contempt for core liberal values of human rights and dignity. It equally demonstrated wishful thinking about what the Soviet Union could bring to the defense of Western democracy.

The United States, although potentially the world's most powerful country by a wide margin, was scarcely a player in international politics. Roosevelt's withdrawal from the World Economic Conference in mid-1933 set a tone of economic and political aloofness that endured through his first term. The policy was clearly in line with the wishes of a substantial majority of the American people and even more in tune with the preferences of the progressive coalition FDR so effectively put together. The nation looked inward, sought reform, and attempted to beat the Depression—with little sense that isolation might be counterproductive, both as a matter of economics and as a matter of national security. The Johnson Debt Default Act of 1934 forbade loans to nations in arrears on their World War debt payments. A Senate committee chaired by Senator Gerald Nye of isolationist North Dakota wrote off American intervention in that war as the work of profit-seeking munitions makers ("merchants of death") and international bankers who had made big loans to France and England. Important "public intellectuals" such as Charles A. Beard and Walter Millis applauded its work and repeated its message in their own writings.

As Italy and Abyssinia (Ethiopia to most Americans) lurched toward war in mid-1935, the administration proposed a neutrality act that would give the president discretionary power to bar arms shipments to either side. Congress instead adopted legislation that required an embargo on weapons sales to all belligerents. However, it did not forbid the sale of important commodities, most significantly oil, thereby putting the United States in conflict with the more ambitious sanctions that the League of Nations ultimately imposed on Italy. The White House might have been able to block the sale of American oil to Italy but chose not to try. Domestic priorities trumped international concerns. The United States supplied Mussolini with much of the petroleum he needed for his war. The Neutrality Act of 1935 was renewed the following year to avoid entanglement in the Spanish Civil War.[8]

Even laid low by the Depression, the United States was a formidable military presence. Its army was no larger than Britain's, but its navy—an object of special interest to Roosevelt—was first-rank and qualitatively on a par with the British. In 1937, it possessed six aircraft carriers—two of which had been built with PWA funds—and a substantial cadre of senior officers who had staked their careers on the possibilities of naval aviation. American aircraft production lagged behind that of the other major powers, but the nation's decentralized system of a dozen or so private aeronautical companies gave free rein to competitive innovation and provided more sources of production than did that of any other country. The United States had easy access to most of the raw materials it needed. Its industrial capacity was unparalleled. In 1937, it accounted for 35 percent of the world's manufacturing. Germany, after an enormous expansion of its steel industry in the mid-1930s, still possessed no more than half the capacity of the U.S. (In the recession year of 1938, with perhaps two-thirds of its steel capacity idle, the U.S. outproduced Germany, which ran its mills at full tilt, by a margin of approximately 5–4.) With a population estimated at 130 million, the United States could muster more manpower than any of the other major powers save the Soviet Union. As Franklin Roosevelt began his second term, however, it remained a sleeping giant, looking inward, coping with its own troubles, and little interested in those of the wider world. America and the other Western democracies, to a far greater degree than they realized, were on a slippery slope. The slide downward was about to begin.

<hr />

Berlin, T. S. Matthews reported at the end of 1936, remained in many ways a more pleasant city than a foreigner might expect. But the traces of the old Berlin existed uneasily alongside the frightening Nazi architecture, incessant marches by paramilitary groups, ubiquitous pictures of Hitler frowning down on his subjects, and a wildly applauded cabaret act proclaiming Germany's determination to recover its colonies. The army's goose-step march, pounding the ground with a force not evident in newsreels, "a perfect picture of controlled violence," made the biggest impression on him. The guns were still silent, but Germany was at war.[9]

Germany in fact was living under the constraints of a war economy. Four-Year Plan director Hermann Göring adopted the slogan "Guns, Not Butter," the purchase of which required a ration coupon after January 1, 1937. Shortages of eggs and other staples were a routine fact of life. So were ersatz fabrics in clothing, including something called "vistra," a wood-based synthetic that tended to rot after a few wearings. Businessmen were squeezed by the government, workers regimented and not allowed to strike. Western liberals were more convinced than ever that a regime that provided so meanly for its people had to implode. But, however shabby civil life, Hitler had provided jobs for almost everyone, no matter how bare their subsistence. The Strength through Joy program provided recreational diversions for cooperative workers; the totalitarian state silenced dissenters. Businesspeople kept quiet and retained what profits they could. Above all, the Nazi regime satisfied nonmaterial yearnings. It had restored Germany's national self-respect; that alone won it wide sufferance.[10]

After the unopposed reoccupation of the Rhineland, the Reich's international prestige and freedom of action had risen sharply; so had Hitler's adventurism. The world knew that Germany was steadily increasing military production, building up its army and establishing a formidable air force. The great American aviator Charles A. Lindbergh provided confirmation when he visited the Reich in 1936 and 1937 as an informal representative of the U.S. government. The stream of aircraft coming off the assembly lines of numerous factories and the many air bases made a strong impression. Here, he believed, was an awakening power that would dominate the skies in a matter of years if its adversaries continued to dally. Here also, he frankly declared in personal communications and public addresses, was a nation proud of its achievements, destined to be a greater force in the world, and perhaps even surpass the United States. The evils of Nazism seemed to him—and his wife Anne Morrow—to be of small consequence by comparison.

Lindbergh did not realize that only about twenty percent of German military aircraft production before 1938 consisted of first-line fighters and bombers; trainers made up more than half. Correct in his estimate of design and construction quality, he underestimated British and American progress. (The British Hurricane and Spitfire fighters were well along in development by the time of his second visit.) He presented his impressions not as a clarion call for the Western democracies to catch up, but as a revelation of the inevitable reordering of the world balance of power.[11]

Hitler reinforced those impressions with a bold and surprising decision to intervene in the Spanish Civil War. General Francisco Franco's Falangist rebellion against the Popular Front Republican government of Spain was not, strictly speaking, a fascist movement, but it was close enough, and from a standpoint of *Realpolitik*, intervention made sense. A Republican victory might mean a Spanish-Soviet alliance; a Falange victory would at the least make Spain a friendly neutral on the Iberian peninsula. Most of all, however, Spain gave Germany an opportunity to display its new air power with ruthless brutality, thus providing enormous satisfaction to a regime that elevated nihilistic savagery to a first principle. Germany committed 10,000 men—eight air squadrons organized as the Condor Legion, and ground support forces for them. On April 26,

1937, operating in tandem with Italian air power, the Condor Legion bombed the small Republican town of Guernica, inflicting 2,500 casualties in three hours of continuous attack and displaying to the world the most ghastly example yet of terror from above.[12]

Italy's cooperation with Germany demonstrated the way in which Mussolini, once considered the strongman of Europe, had given in to the gravitational pull of a more powerful state. Mussolini contributed 40,000–50,000 troops to Franco's cause; their generally ineffective performance, however, contrasted starkly with the killing efficiency of German air power. Italy would not join the Anti-Comintern treaty until near the end of 1937 and would remain unbound by a formal military alliance with the Nazis until 1939, but Mussolini effectively had become a junior ally of Hitler. Once hoping to become the dominant force in south-central Europe, he now settled for a German-supported attempt at hegemony in Mediterranean Europe and North Africa. The Western European democracies nonetheless still sought an alliance with him.

No country was more directly impacted by the Italian change of course than Austria. As early as the first half of 1936, Italy had signaled the small German state that it could no longer count on Italian protection. That July, Germany and Austria announced a treaty that, in the words of Ian Kershaw, "turned the Reich's eastern neighbour into an economic and foreign-policy dependency."[13] Thereafter, its nominal independence existed on borrowed time.

Hitler's main obstacle to an outright *Anschluss* was a reluctant, cautious German army that he did not yet fully control. The Führer's opportunity came unexpectedly, almost capriciously, in early 1938, when his war minister, Field Marshall Werner von Blomberg, created a scandal by marrying a much younger woman of humble birth and a suspect past. Hitler dumped him at the insistence of senior generals, but then went on to find excuses to jettison a dozen more and advance many pro-Nazi officers. The purge transformed the German high command. One of the winners, General Alfred Jodl, wrote in his diary that Austrian Chancellor Kurt von Schuschnigg should be "trembling."[14]

Once his new military leadership was in place, Hitler put intense pressure on Austria for measures that inevitably would lead to unification with Germany—a currency union, the lifting of all restrictions on the Austrian Nazi party, the appointment of its leader Arthur Seyss-Inquart as minister of the interior. When Schuschnigg countered by scheduling a referendum that would ask the Austrian people to affirm their independence, the

Führer acted. Once again he had shrewdly measured the reaction of the democracies. France would do nothing about Austria. Britain could do little on its own. On March 10, Schuschnigg, having received an ultimatum from Germany and realizing he could expect no help from any quarter, resigned. Wanting to avoid needless loss of lives, he ordered the Austrian army not to resist, and recommended the appointment of Seyss-Inquart as his successor. On March 12, German troops, hailed by Nazi mobs and paramilitaries, entered Austria and took possession of the country without a fight. One detachment made straight for the Brenner Pass and a friendly rendezvous with Mussolini's Alpine troops. On March 14, Hitler entered Vienna, standing in an open car, arm extended in fascist salute; a wild crowd, estimated at a half-million, cheered deliriously. Political and economic assimilation into the Reich, the establishment of a one-party Nazi despotism, and an ugly persecution of the Jews all followed rapidly.[15]

Hitler's further ambitions were no mystery. A glance at a map of Europe showed Czechoslovakia, with its large German minority, now bordered on three sides by Germany. German threats against the smaller state began almost immediately, but the Czechs mobilized to fight, and the Reich backed off for the time being.[16] Beyond Czechoslovakia, as anyone who had bothered to read *Mein Kampf* or listen to Hitler's speeches knew, Germany sought dominance in or outright control of the Baltic states: Poland, Hungary, Romania, Yugoslavia, Bulgaria, and the Soviet Ukraine. "The Church may have the mandate of God, but we have the mandate of the people" declared Joseph Goebbels in a response to Vatican indications of unhappiness with the Anschluss. "THIS WORLD IS OURS!" The Nazi agenda reflected boundless ambition, but few could doubt Hitler's determination, Germany's euphoria, and the democracies' lack of will.[17]

When Neville Chamberlain became prime minister of Great Britain at the end of May 1937, his personal strengths and deficiencies were well established. Few of his party colleagues had a deeper concern for social services directed at the working class. As the chief operating officer of the government, under Baldwin, he had displayed a sharp eye for detail and a boundless capacity for hard work. (Declining an invitation to dinner from a close family friend, he wrote: "Dinner doesn't suit me very well, as I always have so much work to do in the evening, but I should be delighted to come to lunch.")[18]

A man of will and intelligence, he enjoyed the unreserved admiration of nearly all the Conservative members of the House of Commons, but the love of practically none. He was notoriously "unclubbable." (The word appears in almost every description of him.) Stiff and formal, he seemed cold and uncaring to most of those with whom he came in contact. His efforts at mass communication suffered grievously in comparison to Baldwin's intimate fireside radio manner. After watching himself in a newsreel, he remarked, "if I had not previously seen the person who addressed us from the screen, I should call him pompous, insufferably slow in diction and unspeakably repellent in person!" Having bluntly judged himself, however, he decided that, at 68, he was too old to learn new tricks and might as well cultivate the talents he already possessed. "I can't do all the things that S. B. did, as well as all the things he didn't do, and I consider that at present at any rate the latter are more important."[19]

If Chamberlain had some insecurity about his ability to inspire the public, he had no doubt whatever about his capacity for controlling the work of every cabinet minister. Where Baldwin had been a loose coordinator, he was a micromanager. Sensing that foreign policy was the most important issue confronting the country, he was prepared to act as his own foreign minister, although diplomacy was an area in which his training was nil and his experience mostly secondhand. All the same, he formulated a coherent view of Britain's strategic position in the world, a reasonable ordering of its priorities, and a rearmament program far more defensible than would be generally remembered later. But he also saw himself as a leader who might bring peace to Europe through a policy of conciliation with and reasonable concession to Germany and Italy. His failures lay in an inability to grasp the character of the enemies with whom he sought to come to terms and to cultivate friends his nation needed.

Sharp increases in British defense spending had already begun and would continue through Chamberlain's tenure at No. 10 Downing Street. In calendar year 1937 British shipyards began construction on five new battleships and four new aircraft carriers—an initiation of major ship construction that far dwarfed that of any other country in the world. The Royal Air Force began to take delivery of Hawker Hurricanes in the fall of 1937 and Supermarine Spitfires in mid-1938. An impressive early warning radar system for the south of England would be largely finished by the end of 1939. Churchill might correctly complain that German aircraft production still doubled that of Britain's, although, as Richard

Overy has observed, had Churchill's advice on air spending been followed from 1935 through 1937, the RAF would have been equipped with huge numbers of instantly obsolescent biplanes. Instead, Britain would move into World War II with a first-class air force capable, if just barely, of fighting a successful defensive battle.[20]

The army got little of the increase. Traditional British doctrine saw it largely as an instrument for policing the Empire and rejected the idea that Britain was a continental land power. The view from London looked primarily toward a worldwide Empire/Commonwealth that had to be protected, developed, and encouraged to look back toward London for leadership. Western Europe was a secondary concern with three pressing interests: friendly nations just across the English Channel, a cooperative strategic relationship with France, unimpeded access through the Mediterranean to the Suez Canal. If this view possessed the odor of *Realpolitik* in its indifference to the morality of issues, it seemed a rational, hardheaded way to conduct the nation's affairs in a difficult world and suited Chamberlain's practical, no-nonsense manner.

He found France, which would have to provide the troops for any assertion of democratic power in Europe, to be unstable, uncertain of its interests, and at key crunch points unwilling to act. "She can never keep a secret for more than half an hour, nor a government for more than nine months," he wrote privately. "In the absence of any powerful ally, and until our armaments are completed, we must adjust our foreign policy to our circumstances, and even bear with patience and good humour actions which we should like to treat in very different fashion."[21]

Italy, whose growing naval power seemed the one possible obstacle to British dominance in the Mediterranean, was still unencumbered by any alliance. Strong enough to demand respect but not a deadly threat, it was in the eyes of both the French and the British a country with which one could strike an accommodation on a basis of mutual interests. Prodded by the French, Britain had periodically talked deals with the Italians, but British opinion leaned in the more idealistic direction of collective security through the League of Nations. The Abyssinian crisis thus had produced the Hoare-Laval proposal to appease Mussolini, then its abandonment under public protest and Hoare's resignation as foreign secretary. His successor, Anthony Eden, although fundamentally League-minded, pursued negotiations with Italy after its African conquest had been consolidated beyond recall. In early 1937, a "gentlemen's agreement" appeared to signal mutual recognition of the status quo in the

Mediterranean, but soon sank beneath the surface—along with merchant ships trading with Republican Spain and torpedoed by Italian submarines.[22]

By early 1938 Eden had given up on a deal with Mussolini. Moreover, he was increasingly resentful of Chamberlain's interference; in November, the prime minister had badly undercut him by sending Deputy Foreign Secretary Lord Halifax to Berlin for informal talks with Hitler. In January 1938, FDR, increasingly concerned with the trend toward war, secretly suggested to Britain cosponsorship of a large international conference focused on economic issues between the big powers. Eden, by now convinced that the great fault line in international relations was between dictatorships and democracies, supported the proposal, carried a cabinet debate, then watched his victory evaporate as the American president began to waffle on details and postpone a date. Chamberlain, who had thought the idea "preposterous" from the beginning, renewed his push for an understanding with Italy. On February 20, Eden resigned in what was generally understood as a protest against appeasing dictators. His successor, Halifax, was close to Chamberlain, and, as a peer, unable to speak in the House of Commons. Thereafter Chamberlain himself took all foreign policy questions.

Eden's resignation sent shock waves through Europe, touching off celebrations in Rome and Berlin, despair in Paris. Momentarily the government seemed in danger, but the Conservatives held firm behind their leader. Eden, young and handsome, seen by many as Chamberlain's probable successor, conducted himself in too gentlemanly a way. Handicapped by the still-secret nature of Roosevelt's project, he was unable fully to spell out the differences between himself and his prime minister. Churchill would have made the most of the occasion with an eloquent denunciation. Ambitious for the premiership, Eden kept his distance from Churchill. In the short term, he seemed more attractive. He spoke to a middle-class idealism strong in England, but, as Chamberlain rightly understood, not always practical. What the prime minister missed in his pursuit of the feasible and the specific, however, was Eden's vision. The sense that democratic America and Britain needed to forge a common purpose against a dynamic totalitarian bloc had far more validity than Chamberlain's belief that a policy of concession ("appeasement") might achieve a grand settlement in Europe.[23]

Roosevelt, probably miffed at being put off, was privately skeptical. In early March, he wrote to a friend: "As someone remarked to me—'If a

Chief of Police makes a deal with the leading gangsters and the deal results in no more hold-ups, that Chief of Police will be called a great man—but if the gangsters do not live up to their word the Chief of Police will go to jail.' Some people are, I think, taking very long chances."[24] Still, the president's vaporous proposal had given Chamberlain little reason to believe that America would ever be of practical help. Without a strong, reliable ally in Europe, he considered it impossible to dictate to Mussolini. And if Mussolini was free to misbehave, Hitler was inevitably at large. So long as the Mediterranean lifeline was intact, so long as Britain did not face a bitter enemy across the Channel, Chamberlain was willing to let other dominoes fall in Europe. In hindsight, the policy might appear ostrich-like. In context, it made some sense and had the support of a majority of the British people.

The British left deplored the government's lack of support for Republican Spain at least as much as the American left criticized Roosevelt's neutrality. Where the president's policy was heavily determined by political calculation, Chamberlain's policy was a clear-eyed power move. A Republican victory, he reckoned, would mean a quantum leap in Soviet influence, perhaps a Communist-dominated government. Portugal, in many respects a client state of Britain, was already an orderly, authoritarian, right-wing dictatorship. Its dictator, Antonio Salazar, vouched for Franco. The war itself was, in the way of most civil wars, characterized by atrocities on both sides. Any semblance of a center was so squeezed out by extremists, Republican as well as Falangist, that it is hard today to understand the passion of foreign observers who saw a conflict as between total good and absolute evil. Chamberlain and his aides were reasonable in assuming that a Communist dictatorship on the Iberian peninsula would not be in Britain's interest and prescient in believing that Franco would keep Germany and Italy at arm's length.[25]

As for Austria, it was already a right-wing dictatorship, German-speaking, and heavily in favor of union with the Reich. Above all, it was beyond the reach of British power unless France was willing to move against Germany. Chamberlain was initially unsettled by the German *putsch*, which he sharply condemned in Commons. But he also thought that if Halifax had been in office earlier to deal with Mussolini, Italy might have been mobilized to confront Hitler as it had in 1934. If anything, it reinforced his belief that a deal with Italian Fascism was still the best bet for stopping German Nazism. He knew that Czechoslovakia was almost certainly Hitler's next target. But, personal pique aside, he and

Halifax cared little about the loss of Austria and already felt they could do little about the plight of the Czechs.[26]

Chamberlain confidentially stated his belief that force was the only argument Germany understood and that a policy of collective security was useless without "overwhelming strength, backed by determination to use it." Perhaps he would be driven to alliances, "which don't require meetings at Geneva, and resolutions by dozens of small nations who have no responsibilities." With whom might Britain ally, if not Italy? Not the Soviet Union, which the prime minister viscerally distrusted and which had devoured its own officer corps in the purges. Not the Americans, who were only episodically engaged with Europe and still led by the president who had ruined the 1933 World Economic Conference. The Americans would provide only talk. Chamberlain reluctantly undertook negotiations for a trade agreement with the United States in 1938, but his impatience with Roosevelt never slackened. On two occasions, the American president invited him to visit Washington; each time he put off the request, and thus backed away from an opportunity to develop good atmospherics between the two English-speaking powers. The two men never met, but the clash of temperament was nonetheless palpable across 3,000 miles of ocean. It was similar to the conflict of mood and philosophy between FDR and Hoover.

So Britain pressed on in pursuit of a deal with Mussolini. In April, Lord Halifax negotiated an agreement in which Britain pledged to tender de jure recognition of an Italian Abyssinia when the League agreed to it; Italy promised to work for "a settlement of the Spanish question." Chamberlain and Halifax thought this was progress; less hopeful realists knew it was fluff. All the same, however flawed his hopes for tea with Mussolini, Chamberlain's evaluations of the Soviet Union and the United States in the spring of 1938 could not be lightly dismissed.[27]

Was Chamberlain pro-fascist? Many on the left in Britain and the United States made that charge. In addition to pointing to his wooing of Italy and his refusal to back the Spanish Republicans, he and his party delegation in Parliament were predominantly drawn from an upper crust that produced well-publicized notables enamored of Hitler ("the Clive-den Set"). The most important Conservative newspaper, *The Times*, was at best squishy on Nazi Germany and perhaps on occasion its partisan. But such charges amounted to little more than vulgar Marxist agitprop. Chamberlain abhorred fascism, Nazism, and bolshevism, although he probably hated bolshevism most. The real political problem of British diplomacy was that the Conservative base was a middle class that desperately wanted to avoid war, and that the Labour base was a working class that wanted to do the same. On top of that, the British long ago had reached a pre-Nazi consensus that the Versailles settlement was unfair to Germany and was in need of revision.

As some historians have contended, Chamberlain in the end saw himself as a practical businessman willing to deal with the world as it was, engage in hardheaded negotiations with others, and strike a mutually beneficial bargain on the assumption that all parties would honor their parts of the deal. Like the vast majority of his countrymen, he had vivid and terrible memories of the World War and felt revulsion at the thought of a new generation dying on the killing fields of Western Europe. In both instances, he was a liberal—a man of humane sentiments and reasoned intellect. The *Realpolitik* he tried to practice was itself largely a creation of the eighteenth-century Enlightenment in reaction to previous catastrophic wars of religion; it thought of states and their leaders as rational actors seeking to maximize advantage but pursuing limited aims. Chamberlain expressed the most important weakness of his superficially tough-minded realism when he declared his determination to deal with the grievances of adversaries through the application of "our common sense, our common humanity" in seeking the solution to outstanding problems.[28] *Realpolitik* in the age of Hitler and Stalin required an understanding of the darker angels of human nature. Businessman in background, Unitarian in religious training, liberal politician in vocation, Chamberlain had scant conception of the phenomenon of evil.

Few, if any, American presidents had begun a second term with as much international prestige as did Franklin Roosevelt. His standing rested on the widespread sense that he was far and away the strongest and most impressive leader of the few major democracies left in the world. Jules Sauerwein, editor of *Le Paris-Soir*, respected in the United States for his clear-eyed, liberal, and realistic analyses of European politics, had declared in the aftermath of FDR's reelection, "Henceforth democracy has its Chief!" It would be Roosevelt's role, he predicted, to lead the defense of the liberal democratic West against the challenges of left and right that already were prominent on the European continent.[29]

Sauerwein's sentiments were by no means unusual. Roosevelt himself often talked about being at the head of a fight for democracy. Usually, he identified the struggle with that for the New Deal and left the implication that his opposition was in some fashion anti-democratic. But he also embraced the idea that he had become a symbol of something that transcended American politics. In late 1936, he had traveled to South America for an Inter-American conference, visiting Brazil, Argentina, and Uruguay. The crowds that cheered his motorcades in Rio de Janeiro and Buenos Aires, he told Anne O'Hare McCormick, shouted "Viva Roosevelt!" as his car passed, but more loudly and more often, they cried "Viva democracia!" He accepted the symbolic role with pride, but also with the traditional sense that America was leading by example, not by active participation in the politics of the wider world. On Inauguration Day 1937, it was uncertain that he would be able to maintain that distinction much longer.[30]

By virtue of training and background, Roosevelt was better prepared to conduct a foreign policy than most presidents who had preceded him. He had traveled widely in Europe from the time he was a small child. His mother's family had made its money in the China trade. His parents had given him a copy of Alfred Thayer Mahan's *The Influence of Sea Power Upon History* for his sixteenth birthday; he became a devotee of the great naval theorist. His boyhood hero and third cousin was Theodore Roosevelt. He had served as assistant secretary of the navy (chief operating officer) under Woodrow Wilson. His conceptualization of foreign policy contained the synthesis of moralism and power politics that one could find in TR; to this he added the vision of collective security and world organization that Wilson had expressed. At times overly confident about his knowledge of history and his competence in diplomacy, he was too prone to believe he could conduct his own foreign policy without the interference of Secretary of State Cordell Hull. His greatest assets were his large vision that democracy around the world was imperiled and his increasing sense that he had been given the mission of defending it.

Roosevelt pretty clearly never sympathized with the isolationist currents that ran so strong during the thirties, but he found it hard to swim against them. If mistaken in rejecting a possible international economic agreement in 1933, he was correct in sensing that his priorities were domestic. Hitler had just come to power, Mussolini was unthreatening, and Japan, consolidating its new regime in Manchuria, was still formally adhering to naval limitations agreements. By FDR's third year in office, chaos loomed, and his concern, generally expressed in private, was increasingly urgent. "These are without doubt the most hair-trigger times the world has gone through in your lifetime or mine," he wrote to his ambassador to Italy in March 1935. "I do not even exclude June and July, 1914, because at that time there was economic and social stability."[31]

Important Democratic constituencies discouraged his attention to the international scene. Independent and quasi-independent progressives were predominantly isolationist and already muttering about the president's widely perceived concerns over German, Italian, and Japanese aggressiveness. Roosevelt needed them in his coalition in order to pull the Democratic party away from the Southern conservatives. Italian-Americans, a key ethnic group, tended to admire Mussolini. The Spanish Civil War threatened to rip the Democratic party apart. Liberals and progressives reflexively sided with the socialist Republican government, but many American Catholics regarded Franco as the savior of Christianity. (Roosevelt told Harold Ickes in May 1938, much to Ickes's disgust, that aid to Spain would cost the Democratic party "every Catholic vote.")[32] Pacifist groups, composed predominantly of political liberals, pressed hard for a White House declaration against war.

In August 1936, Roosevelt appeased the doubters with a notable speech at Chautauqua, New York. Yes, he told his audience, he worried about nations that violated their agreements and bred "new-born fanaticisms," and he wanted the United States to be involved with the rest of the world. But his main concern was to remain at peace. "We are not isolationists except in so far as we seek to isolate ourselves completely from war." He then went into an attack on monopolists and bankers that stopped just short of explicitly embracing the argument of progressives like Beard and Millis. His most memorable passage referred to a World War trip to France:

> I have seen war. I have seen war on land and sea. I have seen blood running from the wounded. I have seen men coughing out their gassed lungs. I have seen the dead in the mud. I have seen cities destroyed. I have seen two hundred limping, exhausted men come out of line—the survivors of a regiment of one thousand that went forward forty-eight hours before. I have seen children starving. I have seen the agony of mothers and wives. I hate war.
>
> I have passed unnumbered hours, I shall pass unnumbered hours, thinking and planning how war may be kept from this Nation.[33]

At the beginning of 1937, FDR made a tactical decision to ask Congress for sweeping neutrality legislation in order to be able to concentrate on court reform, executive reorganization, and other items on his domestic agenda. Replacing similar temporary legislation passed in 1935 and 1936 to deal with the Ethiopian crisis and the Spanish Civil War, the Neutrality Act of 1937 forbade the sale of weaponry and the extension of loans to belligerents. It did permit the export of other commodities, but only on a cash-and-carry basis—the purchasing nation had to pay cash on delivery and arrange for shipment in non–American flag vessels. And just to be certain of avoiding any controversy over submarine warfare, it prohibited American citizens from traveling on any vessel flying the flag of a belligerent. Roosevelt had asked for presidential discretion in applying it, so as to be able to distinguish between aggressor nations and their targets, but, embroiled in the court-packing controversy, he was unable to press hard. He surely would have been unsuccessful anyway.

Roosevelt signed the Neutrality Act on May 1, 1937. By then Mussolini had completed his conquest of Ethiopia, putting an end to the illusion that any nation could base its foreign policy on collective security through the League of Nations. Germany's military production was taking off at an alarming rate. The Reich was demanding colonies and other concessions from the European democracies. The savage Spanish Civil War was in high gear, the Falange relentlessly making gains with assistance from their fascist allies. In July, Japan began its full-scale war against China, attacking Shanghai, then Nanking. Roosevelt clearly feared things were spinning out of control, wanted to do something, but was boxed in by politics and public apathy.

On October 5, he delivered a nationally broadcast speech in Chicago, the informal capital of American isolationism. "A greed for power and supremacy which is devoid of all sense of justice and humane considerations," he said, had reversed the progress of civilization toward law and order. Aggressors terrorizing others knew no limits. An "epidemic of world lawlessness" was spreading. An epidemic of a physical disease would lead to a quarantine of the patients. "War is a contagion, whether it be declared or undeclared. . . . we cannot have complete protection in a world of disorder in which confidence and security have broken down."[34]

The speech had come out of the blue with no warning. It sounded an alarm of peril, but it provided no plan of action. It suggested a "quarantine" without quite calling for one, much less explaining what that would mean. At a press conference the next day, Roosevelt dodged all attempts at obtaining an elaboration. Was the address a repudiation of existing neutrality policy? "Not for a minute. It may be an expansion." Was it a euphemism for economic sanctions? "Look, 'sanctions' is a terrible word to use. They are out of the window." Would there be a conference of the peace-loving nations? "No. . . . You never get anywhere with a conference." Was it, as the London *Times* had said, an attitude without a program? "It is an attitude, and it does not outline a program; but it says we are looking for a program." This was Roosevelt's frankest statement—off the record, as was the entire colloquy.[35]

Even the attitude began to evaporate as public opinion surveys failed to disclose strong sentiment for a more active foreign policy. The *New York Times* summarized its own soundings as follows: "(1) There is sentiment for moral cooperation with other nations, but opposition to any step that might lead to the brink of war. (2) There is sentiment for going slow." The president's core liberal support was especially opposed to anything that might lead to war. Roosevelt later told Sam Rosenman, "It is a terrible thing to look over your shoulder when you are trying to lead—and to find no one there." Perhaps he was realistic. Perhaps he retreated too quickly. What he had hoped would serve as a fire bell in the night had scarcely disturbed a still-sleeping nation. Abroad, it had an even more transitory impact. "I read Roosevelt's speech with mixed feelings," Neville Chamberlain privately remarked with wry sarcasm, "seeing that patients suffering from epidemic diseases do not usually go about fully armed."[36]

Most observers at the time thought that the quarantine speech was directed primarily at Japan, at that point the world's most conspicuous aggressor nation. The Japanese war against China was not aimed simply at gaining control of the world's largest nation; it was also designed to expel Western imperialism from East Asia. China was riddled with formal territorial concessions that amounted to small pockets of colonialism, mostly in the trading areas along the coast. Moreover, foreign investment created interests throughout the country. The United States, Britain, France, and other European countries maintained small military presences to protect those interests. On December 12, 1937, the day Nanking fell to Japan, the Japanese army shelled two nearby British gunboats, *Lady Bird* and *Bee*, in the Yangtze River. Some twenty-seven miles upstream, Japanese naval aircraft repeatedly attacked and sank an American gunboat, the *Panay*, then went after three nearby Standard Oil tankers and destroyed two of them. The Yangtze River attacks were early episodes in the rape of Nanking, where for weeks an out-of-control Japanese army engaged in an orgy of indiscriminate rape, murder, and pillage that horrified the world.

The *Panay* had been clearly marked; it was crowded with civilian diplomats and newsmen who had sought its protection. Three men were killed, another eleven seriously wounded. There could be no doubt that the Japanese military had gone after it and the Standard Oil vessels in full knowledge they were American. The administration at first gave signs of a strong reaction, dispatching a naval attaché to London to discuss joint operations with the British Navy, possibly in the form of a limited naval blockade. Momentarily, it seemed that a de facto U.S.-British alliance might be taking shape. In Britain, Neville Chamberlain privately allowed himself some wary hope: "It is always best & safest to count on *nothing* from the Americans except words, but at this moment they are nearer to 'doing something' than I have ever known them." But Japan quickly defused the crisis by claiming (probably accurately) that the attack had not been authorized by Tokyo, apologizing profusely, and paying an indemnity for the ship and loss of life. Nor did an angry public outcry follow the incident, which was an outrage but not enough of one to generate a war. Instead, several progressive congressmen called for an end to the American military presence in China. The prospect of American-British cooperation quickly evaporated, a victim of both British doubts about U.S. seriousness and the unsupportive political climate in America.[37]

Representative Louis Ludlow, an isolationist Democrat from Indianapolis, utilized the incident to gather signatures on a discharge petition that brought a proposed constitutional amendment to a vote on the floor of the House of Representatives. The "Ludlow Amendment," long bottled up in committee, took the power to declare war away from Congress and required a national referendum, unless the United States had actually been invaded. Briefly, it appeared that the resolution might get a simple majority (although not the two-thirds needed to send it to the Senate). Roosevelt was alarmed enough to make a public attack on the proposal in the form of a letter to Speaker William Bankhead. On January 10, 1938, the House voted down Ludlow's amendment, 209–188; so narrow a margin confirmed that the isolationist impulse remained at high tide. There was, it seemed, still not much of a crowd when Roosevelt looked over his shoulder.[38]

Yet it was at this point that Roosevelt went ahead with his proposal to Neville Chamberlain for an international initiative. If the British agreed, he would make a general announcement to the Washington diplomatic corps, then would mobilize unaligned nations to draft agreements on arms limitations, equal access to raw materials, and rules on the rights and obligations of neutrals and belligerents in time of war. The plan envisioned nothing less than a general international settlement. It did not specifically propose an international conference, but likely would have led to one, with Roosevelt presiding. The idea, which had been developed by Roosevelt's friend Undersecretary of State Sumner Welles without any clearance from Hull, dated back to October and may have been originally conceived as a follow-up to the quarantine speech.

One can hardly blame Chamberlain for dismissing what appeared to be a utopian proposition. What could Roosevelt bring to the project? What sort of diplomatic or economic commitments? How much disposable power? In Washington, Hull moved strongly behind the scenes to quash the proposal. Yet the long-experienced British ambassador in Washington, Sir Ronald Lindsay, advised acceptance. Anthony Eden fought for it in London. Neither anticipated world peace. Both understood that the real potential of the president's initiative was to bring the U.S. and Britain closer and possibly establish an international democratic front. Eden, and perhaps Lindsay, also believed that Chamberlain's hopes for a meaningful understanding with Italy, perhaps even Germany, were equally fantastic. Chamberlain's initial frosty reaction, Hull's opposition, and Roosevelt's subsequent equivocation killed the idea. In the end, each side could blame the other for the fact that they remained at arm's length.[39]

Americans in the late 1930s generally loathed the Japanese, whom they more and more saw as brutally aggressive, anti-American, and a future enemy in the Pacific. On the other hand, they mostly romanticized the Chinese, for generations a primary target of American Christian missionary efforts, as oppressed and hard-working underdogs. There were many sources of this attitude, but in the thirties probably the most influential was the work of the novelist Pearl Buck, a daughter of American missionaries who had spent most of her first forty years in China. Buck's *The Good Earth* (1931), a story of the struggles of Chinese peasants, had won the Pulitzer Prize for literature in 1932, had been made into a hit motion picture (1936), and had been the major consideration in awarding her the Nobel Prize for literature in 1938. Buck depicted the typical Chinese as a peasant who represented the universal virtues of a life tilling the soil. A reviewer in the *Christian Century* wrote that the spiritual nature of its central character "would not have differed greatly had he toiled on the

Nebraska prairie rather than in China." *The Good Earth* sold 1.5 million hardcover copies; perhaps 23 million Americans viewed the film.[40]

Popular anger toward a militarily superior Japan attacking a still-backward China with deliberate savagery found an apparently peaceful outlet. Shortly after Roosevelt's quarantine speech, Herbert Hoover's former secretary of state, the widely admired Henry L. Stimson, initiated a drive for an economic boycott of Japan. For the seventy-year-old statesman, it was the continuation of an effort that had begun with the Stimson Doctrine of 1931 in protest against Japan's takeover of Manchuria. The boycott movement effectively pointed out that the Japanese war against China was fueled by American petroleum, that huge shipments of American scrap iron and steel to Japan rained down on the Chinese as shrapnel from hostile artillery shells and bombs. But there was no basis either in international law or congressional legislation to impose an embargo. Roosevelt and most of his diplomats had sympathy for the sentiment behind the movement, but also were wary of embittering relations with the Japanese. Since war had never been formally declared by either Japan or China, the administration did not even invoke the Neutrality Act, a decision that redounded to the benefit of Japan.

The United States and Britain possessed easily perceived joint interests in East Asia. Separately, neither nation had the disposable naval power to intimidate the Japanese. Together they could dominate the Pacific. Yet cooperation never materialized. Chamberlain concluded, correctly, that the United States was not ready to get tough with Japan and that Britain would have to put up with Japanese depredations. What Roosevelt could do was work for a strong navy. In January 1938, he asked Congress for a large naval appropriation to begin a building program that would take the United States twenty percent beyond the limitations that had been imposed by the now-defunct treaties of the 1920s. Many of his progressive allies in Congress were stunned. Maury Maverick expressed their dismay in a vocal critique that accused Roosevelt of trying to change the subject of national discussion from the devastating economic recession: "We Democrats have got to admit we are floundering. The reason for all this battleship and war frenzy is coming out: we have pulled all the rabbits out of the hat and there are no more rabbits." Congressional conservatives, Southern Democrats especially, were supportive. With Britain, Japan, Germany, and Italy all adding to their naval capacity, the argument that the navy was a first line of defense prevailed. In May, Roosevelt signed the Naval Expansion Act, sponsored by Representative Carl

Vinson of Georgia. It gave him substantially what he had asked for, and was the first step in building a true two-ocean navy.[41]

Still disengaged from the other democracies, beginning to rearm later than any other major power, the United States waited for the next shoes to drop in Europe and Asia.

———

The first Czechoslovakian crisis began only a couple of months after Hitler had digested Austria. The Führer's stated complaint involved alleged discriminatory treatment of the German-speaking minority. Czechoslovakia was a fragile entity that had emerged out of the old Austro-Hungarian empire from the World War peace process. Like other such nations, it was a triumph of national self-determination, compromised by the need to build a viable country. Numbering 6.75 million, the Czechs were the dominant force in a country that also included two million Slovaks, 3.25 million Germans, a million or so Magyars, a half-million Ruthenians, and perhaps a quarter-million Poles. All were restless under Czech political and cultural domination; all lived mostly within their own territorial clusters. The Germans, concentrated in the mountainous western border area (the Sudetenland), had been incorporated into the new state in order to give it defensible frontier terrain. The small nation had made the most of the gift, establishing a strong system of fortifications as its main line of defense against an attack from Germany.

For all its internal divisions, Czechoslovakia was no pushover. It was the most industrialized of the small Eastern European nations, especially noted for its arms industry. The Skoda works supplied its professionally led standing army with high-quality weaponry and was the main provisioner for much of the rest of the region. Possessing a large ready reserve, the Czech military could quickly mobilize a million-strong force. Czechoslovakia was in addition Central Europe's one true liberal democracy. It had avoided instant disintegration by treating minorities with respect and tendering them full rights of citizenship. But grievances of varying seriousness were inevitable; none was too small to be worth a fight. The Sudeten Germans felt them most keenly. By 1938, the large majority of the Sudetens had been organized into their own Nazi party, which was controlled directly from Berlin. That May, using an incident in which a Czech border guard shot two Germans attempting an illegal crossing, Hitler ordered his army to mobilize for an invasion. The Czechs responded with a partial mobilization of their own; the Soviet Union indicated that it would support the smaller country; France stood by its treaty obligation; British foreign secretary Lord Halifax personally told the German ambassador to London that Britain likely would fight if France did. Reluctantly and bitterly, Hitler, under pressure from his military, backed off.

The European breathing spell lasted only through the summer. Demanding action, literally screaming at his officers, Hitler brought the Czech crisis back to a boil in September. Essentially, nothing had changed. In terms of numbers, the correlation of forces was against Germany. The Third Reich could muster a million-strong army; the western defenses it had begun to construct after occupying the Rhineland were still flimsy. Although the British and the French feared an enormous bombing campaign, German air capability, still far less than what Lindbergh (and Churchill) believed, was actually unable to cause extensive damage to London or Paris. The Czechs could bring their own million-man army to defend well-fortified high ground. France could send another million troops into Western Germany. Britain could control the seas and make short work of the small German surface fleet if it were unwise enough to attempt an engagement. The Soviet Union stood by its earlier pledge, although it had no assured transportation route into the country. The German people clearly had no enthusiasm for another war. At the peak of the crisis, September 27, Hitler stood at the window of the Reich Chancellery to review an army division as it paraded past. The crowds along the street were sparse and sullen, demonstrating that "ordinary Germans," as opposed to committed Nazis, neither shared Hitler's faith in the virtues of war nor felt an obligation to their supposedly persecuted Sudeten cousins. A clique of German generals began serious planning to remove their Führer from power if he ordered an attack.[42]

Yet just days later, Hitler won an enormous victory that changed the balance of power in Europe. The triumph decisively demonstrated that his instincts of May had been sound and the hesitation of his subordinates wrong. It thereby delegitimized the opposition, made his rule more absolute than ever, and left Europe at the mercy of his unlimited hubris.

Sentiment in France and Great Britain always had been heavily in favor of peace. Hitler was especially shrewd in his understanding that the two large democracies lacked a will to fight and his sense that their leaders embodied this irresolution. The French premier, Edouard Daladier, headed a rickety coalition government committed to a Maginot Line military doctrine that neutralized the power of its army; he was receptive to finding a way of avoiding its treaty commitment. Chamberlain reflected in his own behavior the global overstretch of the Empire and a sense that his personal destiny was that of a peacemaker.

Chamberlain is rightly remembered as the pivotal figure in the fevered negotiations of September 1938. Persuaded that collective security was a delusion, perceiving Eastern Europe as an area of minimal importance to Britain, determined to be a practical statesman who brought peace to the continent, he decided that Czechoslovakia was not worth a war. It was Chamberlain who took the lead in developing a "solution," conveniently floated in a London *Times* editorial on September 7—allow the Sudeten German districts to return to Germany. Coming from a publication widely considered the government's unofficial voice, the proposal raised eyebrows and touched off knowing nods all over Europe. Next came the telegram to Hitler, offering to meet with him to discuss a settlement.[43]

Before dawn on September 15, Chamberlain, leaving Lord Halifax in London, departed by plane to meet with Hitler at Berchtesgaden. At the age of sixty-nine, he made his first flight, seven hours to Munich, then three hours by train, then a lengthy auto ride to meet the Führer at his mountain retreat. They plunged directly into discussions and soon agreed in principle on plebiscitary self-determination for the Sudetens, subject to the approval of the British cabinet. Chamberlain obtained that approval back in London the next day and two days later had no trouble persuading Daladier also. On September 22, he traveled again to Germany for a second meeting at Godesberg, in which after having made every concession and beaten the Czechs into submission, he encountered an angry, raving German dictator declaring his intention to invade Czechoslovakia and take what he wanted.

Chamberlain thereupon redoubled his determination to give Hitler what he probably could not have taken by force. In a radio address to the British people on September 27, as defense preparations were underway, he said: "How horrible, fantastic, incredible it is that we should be digging trenches and trying on gas-masks here because of a quarrel in a far away country between people of whom we know nothing." The tone of defeat and surrender was unmistakable.[44]

For the third time in two weeks, the prime minister undertook the long trip to Germany. At Munich, September 30, a meeting formally brokered by Mussolini, Chamberlain and Daladier agreed to the immediate German occupation and absorption of the Sudetenland. Britain and France, moreover, also assented to Polish and Hungarian acquisition of smaller portions of Czechoslovakia. What was left was a small, indefensible, barely functional nation. The agreement, prepared without Czech participation, sported hardly a fig leaf to cover Hitler's aggressive assertion of power. The closest semblance was a document Chamberlain had drawn up and asked Hitler to sign with him; it committed the two governments to negotiate future disagreements and never go to war with each other. It was this that Chamberlain would display on his return, asserting that he had achieved "peace for our time."*[45]

It is impossible in retrospect to think of Munich as anything other than a thoroughly dishonorable proceeding unworthy of a liberal democratic power, but Chamberlain and Daladier returned to their countries as heroes. Parisians expressed elation. In London, King George called his prime minister to the balcony of Buckingham Palace to receive an ovation from a packed mass of humanity. The *Economist* magazine, an intelligent and representative voice of realistic liberalism, went to press the day the agreement was announced with a last-minute editorial:

> All of us have looked over the precipice and seen a vision of the hell of totalitarian war, which would have been waged with all the devilry and ruthlessness of modern science. We are to-day reprieved; and in every country men and women will utter a prayer of thanksgiving.
>
> . . . the world owes to Mr Neville Chamberlain a tribute of unstinted and unqualified gratitude for the magnificent perseverance and tenacity with which he has refused to abandon the search for peace.[46]

What might have happened if Chamberlain had opted for war? He then and sympathetic historians later would argue that Britain and France were militarily and psychologically unprepared; they would add that key dominions—Canada, South Africa, and Australia—would not have joined in the fight. Others would respond that the democracies had the means to overwhelm Germany, that the French and British people (and the dominions) would have responded to leadership. The French and British governments made no effort to counter fears that Paris and London lay naked before German bombers and that the German air force had 10,000 frontline planes. Yet sober analysts the world over knew these were wild exaggerations. The fairest assessment seems to be that the democracies had the means to win a war, but they lacked the will. Hitler had will aplenty. The

*On most other occasions, Chamberlain spoke of "peace in our time."

acquisition of the Sudetenland greatly enhanced Germany's geostrategic-position, giving it control of important coal-, iron-, and zinc-producing areas, adding significantly to its industrial strength. Politically, Munich was a victory of incalculable significance for totalitarianism. "Germany last week became the strongest nation in Europe," declared *New York Times* analyst Hanson Baldwin, "and Adolf Hitler a more powerful and absolute ruler than Kaiser Wilhelm II ever was."[47]

"You have everything in your own hands now,—for a time—and you can do anything you like," Stanley Baldwin had written Chamberlain on September 30. "Use that time well, for it won't last." Time was indeed a wasting asset for the prime minister. The first indication of opposition appeared when Alfred Duff Cooper promptly resigned as first lord of the Admiralty. During the House of Commons debate on the Munich agreement, he declared that Chamberlain had dealt with his German counterpart "in the language of sweet reasonableness whereas the mailed fist is the only language Hitler understands." Eden delivered another of his hedged, gentlemanly critiques. Churchill emerged as the most eloquent and vocal critic of the government.

> We have sustained a total and unmitigated defeat. . . . Silent, mournful, abandoned, broken, Czechoslovakia recedes into the darkness. . . . we have passed an awful milestone in our history, when the whole equilibrium of Europe has been deranged. . . . And do not suppose that this is the end. This is only the beginning of the reckoning. This is only the first sip, the first foretaste of a bitter cup which will be proffered to us year by year unless, by a supreme recovery of moral health and martial vigour, we arise again and take our stand for freedom as in the olden time.[48]

Dissenters outside Parliament laid down their markers. "Germany enters on the new era strengthened both materially and morally," declared the *Economist*, its editors disillusioned after a careful reading of the Munich agreement. "The price we have paid for peace is clear enough. But how much peace have we got in return?" From the beginning, the Conservative *Daily Telegraph* bucked a broad newspaper consensus: "It was Mr. Disraeli who said that England's two great assets in the world were her fleet and her good name. Today we must console ourselves that we still have our fleet." American observers were more skeptical than not. *New York Times* correspondent Edwin L. James called the settlement "a peace-at-any-price respite of a few months or a few years."

His Pulitzer Prize–winner colleague Frederick T. Birchall agreed. "What the world seems to face . . . is a continuous series of surrenders until the point is reached when surrender becomes no longer possible," he wrote, adding "with each surrender and each new month of warlike preparation Germany grows stronger." Chamberlain nonetheless easily survived a vote of confidence in which less than three dozen Conservatives abstained. Too much emotion was invested in Munich for opinion to change overnight. Instead, the sense of triumph and relief drained, drop by drop, for the next several months as Hitler ignored one procedural provision after another of the agreement. As 1938 ended, it appeared likely that appeasement would continue indefinitely as the cornerstone of British foreign policy.[49]

Had Munich at least bought time for Britain? Certainly eleven months of shipbuilding, aircraft production, and radar construction were useful. But Germany, fundamentally unprepared for a major war in the fall of 1938, profited also. Its air resources were still thin in late 1938 and incapable of the massive bombing campaigns so feared in Paris and London. By 1939, however, its aircraft industry was turning out first-line fighters and bombers at twice the rate of Britain. Its shipyards were putting the finishing touches on the *Bismarck* (commissioned August 1940) and the *Tirpitz* (commissioned February 1941), battleships more powerful than those the British were building. German technicians were aware of the British development of radar and swiftly catching up. Germany's control of the Czech arms industry and expropriation of the Czech Army's weaponry in early 1939 hugely expanded its military capacity and sealed its domination of Central Europe. Chamberlain likely gave time and advantage to Hitler. As Williamson Murray and Allan Millett have put it, he and those around him shared in the two major misjudgments of Western democratic statesmen up through 1938—a great exaggeration of Nazi Germany's actual military power and an equally great underestimation of its ambitions.[50]

Where had Roosevelt been during the events of September 1938? The simplest, and fundamentally accurate, answer is that he was still intimidated by the strength of American isolationism and preoccupied by the exigencies of the difficult off-year election campaign. The tone of American relations with Britain remained good; the substance was still one of cautious non-commitment. The undercurrent of mutual suspicion that long had existed between him and Chamberlain endured. Roosevelt, we now know, was outraged by Hitler's actions, hoped Britain and France would face him down, but felt he could offer no tangible support. Britain and France, he told a cabinet meeting the day Chamberlain returned from Berchtesgaden, would sacrifice Czechoslovakia and then "wash the blood from their Judas Iscariot hands." A few days later, he met with British Ambassador Sir Ronald Lindsay, floated the idea of a large international conference, and suggested that if Hitler invaded Czechoslovakia, the United States would recognize a retaliatory British naval blockade of Germany. But to his discredit, Roosevelt's public role in the Munich agreement consisted simply of two messages asking all parties to arrive at a peaceful settlement. When the prime minister announced he would fly to Munich on September 28, FDR sent him a two-word telegram: "Good man." Words, all words, no substance—yet another confirmation of Chamberlain's assessment of the Americans.[51]

Munich, of course, brought neither peace nor order in Europe. A British accord with Italy continued to be a mirage in the diplomatic desert. The weakness of Chamberlain and Daladier simply made Hitler a more valuable ally for Il Duce. More than ever, Italy's ambitions lay in the Mediterranean and North Africa, thus creating demands to be made on Britain and France. Mussolini began to assert claims to the French possessions of Tunisia and Corsica as well as the city of Nice. It also became apparent that the Third Reich harbored yet more territorial ambitions, most obvious among them the port cities of Danzig and Memel, which were predominantly Germanic, and beyond that less well-defined objectives to the east. Even more ominously, Germany behaved in ways less civilized than ever.[52]

Most shocking and terrible was its reaction to the assassination of a minor German official in Paris by an angry young Jew. On the night of November 9, 1938, the Nazi party unleashed a reign of terror against Jews throughout the Reich that came to be known as *Kristallnacht*, for the broken glass from the windows of homes, shops, and synagogues that littered the streets everywhere. But broken glass was the least of it, nor did the officially sanctioned pogrom end after one horrible night. Widespread looting and destruction, the random killing of dozens and the brutalization of thousands, indiscriminate mass arrests, the razing of at least a hundred synagogues—all done openly and widely reported around the world—stunned millions of Europeans and Americans who somehow had managed to convince themselves that German anti-Semitism was short of barbaric. The Nazi government followed up the violence against the Jews by announcing that the Jewish community would be fined for all the property damage that it had caused, that Jewish shops would be closed, and that all Jewish assets would be confiscated.

Roosevelt read an on-the-record statement to a press conference, announcing that he had recalled the American ambassador to Germany and declaring "I myself could scarcely believe that such things could occur in a twentieth century civilization." No such declarations came from British and French governments still committed to the hope of a normal relationship with Germany, although Stanley Baldwin, now the Earl of Bewdley, lent his name to a Jewish refugee fund that within eight months raised £500,000. Churchill asked the House of Commons, "Is not this the moment when all should hear the deep, repeated strokes of the alarm bell, and when all should resolve that it shall be a call to action, and not the knell of our race and fame?" It was now an act of unlimited faith to believe that Germany was simply a traditional state with limited objectives rather than a dynamic force of irrational savagery.[53]

In mid-March 1939, Hitler overnight sent his army into what was left of Czechoslovakia, incorporating Bohemia and Moravia into the Reich and establishing Slovakia as a nominally independent puppet state. One wonders how much genuine surprise the move occasioned, but the deed was stunning and significant because it confirmed that Germany was not just a racial state, but also an imperialist one, pursuing, if not world domination, then at least the subjugation of large foreign territories and populations. The Reich quickly followed up the absorption of Czechoslovakia with demands on Poland for Danzig and a portion of the "Polish Corridor" between German territory and the city. It also forced Lithuania to hand over the city of Memel.

By then, the revulsion against Munich was widespread. Almost all of Britain understood that preparations for war had to be redoubled. Chamberlain formally, if reluctantly, gave up on appeasement.[54] On March 30, the government issued a formal guarantee of the Polish boundaries and France reaffirmed its already existing treaty with the Poles. By then, Franco had achieved full power in Spain. A week later, Mussolini took possession of Albania. Fascism, it seemed, was on the march. Could the democracies stop it?

Certainly an alliance with Poland, a nation that was authoritarian and essentially indefensible, was a poor swap for one with Czechoslovakia, which had been democratic and highly defensible. As Lloyd George put it bluntly in the House of Commons, Britain had no way to put a single battalion into Poland. Chamberlain hoped, foolishly, that a solemn commitment by Britain would deter Hitler. He failed to understand that the Führer, in the aftermath of Munich, likely did not expect him to keep it and in any case welcomed the prospect of war if it came. The government began discussions with the Soviet Union on an anti-Nazi alliance, but they dragged inconclusively into the summer. It also attempted to underscore its determination by instituting military conscription, but the act called only for six months of basic training and assignment to the reserves. In mid-1939, the government established a Ministry of Supply—an agency to coordinate defense production—but limited its functions and appointed a minor figure to head it. The prime minister, moreover, refused to establish a genuinely national government that would include Churchill and other Tory critics. Nor would he bring in leaders from the Labour party, which under Clement Attlee had swung hard in favor of a strong antifascist foreign policy and defense budgets it would have excoriated just a few years earlier. Nevertheless, the February defense estimate of £580 million, a fifty percent increase over the previous year's already large sum, was enormous. By mid-1939, Britain was wearily bracing for war.[55]

Since Munich, the British also had paid more attention to President Roosevelt's words and deeds on the international scene. Roosevelt himself was convinced that Chamberlain and Daladier had left a vacuum that only he could fill. The setbacks in the November 1938 midterm elections, moreover, effectively ended opportunities for strong leadership and new departures domestically. The president was determined to push ahead. By the end of 1938, American "static isolationism," journalist Turner Catledge wrote, was beginning to be displaced by a "dynamic isolationism" that could quickly become something else. Roosevelt set the tone with his annual message to Congress at the beginning of January 1939: "There comes a time in the affairs of men when they must prepare to defend, not their homes alone, but the tenets of faith and humanity on which their churches, their governments and their very civilization are founded." It was at last time to don the mantle of international leadership.[56]

At the end of his first term, the president had been inspired by the crowds that had greeted him in Latin America. It was natural enough to begin by establishing a position as leader of the Western Hemisphere, where from the beginning of his presidency he had pursued a "Good Neighbor" policy of non-intervention and liberal trade agreements. As early as the late 1936 conference that had taken him to Rio de Janeiro, Montevideo, and Buenos Aires, the Good Neighbor policy had broadened into a quest for "hemispheric solidarity." In his speeches on that trip, Roosevelt had referred to the darkening situation in Europe and the need, as he put it in Buenos Aires, to "stand shoulder to shoulder in our final determination that others who, driven by war madness or land hunger, might seek to commit acts of aggression against us."[57]

Within a space of ten weeks in early 1939, he requested large supplemental appropriations, primarily to build up American air power and add to the large naval building program already underway. In late 1938, U.S. military aircraft production was about 2,600 a year. In talks with army generals, the president pushed for an increase to 20,000, with the idea that much of the production would be made available for purchase by Britain and France. The actual military budget was more balanced after the generals protested that large numbers of planes required big investments in new air bases and training facilities, that moreover the ground army needed modernization desperately.[58]

Foreign sales continued to be pursued. The most important customer was France, which possessed a far less developed aircraft industry; the British were also in the market. There was nothing illegal about selling weaponry to a country still at peace, but the politics were delicate. The military, after having secured a reduction in production goals, attempted to block transfers of new first-line fighters and light bombers. Roosevelt overrode them. Then he faced down a brief storm of criticism about compromised military secrecy when a test version of the new Douglas DB-7 attack bomber crashed in California on January 23, 1939, with a French observer on board. Despite a congressional investigation, the order went through. Roosevelt defended it as good business, conducted under the cash-and-carry rule, and a means of building up the American military aviation industry. By September, 200 DB-7s had reached France.*[59]

"The two great European democracies," Edwin L. James wrote at the time, "have found important help here in their drive to match the air strength of the Rome-Berlin axis." That, of course, was Roosevelt's purpose, but he knew he had to pursue it with great care. After the DB-7 crash, he met secretly with the Senate Military Affairs Committee and laid out the strategic importance of Western Europe to the United States.

---

*The DB-7 was indeed an advanced aircraft for its time. It saw service through World War II in the U.S. Air Force as the A-20, P-70, and F-3, depending on the function for which it was employed. In the British RAF, it was called the Boston or the Havoc. Enzo Angelucci, *The Rand McNally Encyclopedia of Military Aircraft, 1914–1980* (New York: The Military Press, 1983), 289.

One of the legislators leaked to the press that the president said that America's frontier was on the Rhine. Roosevelt seems not to have used that phrase, but it was not far from the import of what he said. It also was politically toxic.

A newsman asked whether the report was true.

PRESIDENT: "Shall I be polite or call it by the right name?"
QUESTIONER: "Call it by the right name."
PRESIDENT: "Deliberate lie."[60]

Maybe so, but many Europeans wanted to think otherwise. No other Western statesman, wrote Harold Callender from London in March, not even Anthony Eden during his tenure at the Foreign Office, had drawn the contrast between dictatorship and democracy so starkly. Roosevelt appealed to the instincts of millions of Europeans, not a few of them German and Italian. He had made himself and his country "bearers of hope to an imperiled world."[61]

It was in the spirit of that role that the United States responded to the partition of Czechoslovakia with a statement, "edited and approved by the president," from Acting Secretary of State Sumner Welles. "It is manifest that acts of wanton lawlessness and of arbitrary force are threatening world peace and the very structure of modern civilization," the key sentence declared. A month later, Roosevelt sent an open message to Hitler and Mussolini, asking each to pledge he would not attack any of thirty European and Middle Eastern nations. Neither would reply formally, but Hitler in a remarkable display of satirical talent and ethical amorality scornfully responded in a 140 minute speech to the Reichstag. Germany had made inquiries. Each country had assured him it did not feel threatened. It was the cleverest effort of the Führer's career. His audience cheered and laughed convulsively. About a month later, Germany and Italy finally announced a full-fledged military alliance, "the Pact of Steel." The British outreach to Mussolini was definitively at a dead end. Hitler was driving events. Europe waited for his next move.[62]

In the aftermath of the Pact of Steel, Americans read daily newspaper reports covering the plight of some 907 Jews on the German passenger liner St. Louis. They had arrived in Cuba with visas purchased from a corrupt Cuban consul, been denied admission there, then rejected by the United States and Canada. Championed by the ship's German captain, who did all he could to publicize their fate and even threatened at one point to scuttle his own ship, they finally were divided between Britain,

Belgium, Holland, and France. The *St. Louis* passengers were only the most noticed among thousands of stranded refugee Jews, some attempting to get into other Latin American countries, others trying to make their way to Palestine. The democracies abstractly sympathized with them but did not want to take them in. Roosevelt refused to reply to an appeal sent directly to him. In such cases, principle and politics clashed. Principle lost.[63]

Britain by 1939 was facing an angry Arab revolt against increasing Jewish settlement in Palestine, undergoing constant Japanese harassment in China, and still concerned with Italy's challenge in the Mediterranean. Chamberlain's skepticism notwithstanding, the American connection was more vital than ever, and London's policy moved in that direction. At last, the Atlantic divide was closing.

That June, millions of Americans hailed the most famous of all English celebrities—King George VI and Queen Elizabeth. The first visit ever of a British sovereign to the United States was an enormous success, stage-managed on both sides for maximum goodwill and demonstration of a common commitment to democracy. The King impressed American officials as an alert and responsible monarch; Roosevelt took an instant liking to him. The Queen demonstrated the vivaciousness and common touch that would make her a beloved figure for the next sixty-three years. Millions cheered them in Washington and New York, where they visited the World's Fair. On their last day in the United States, they stayed with the Roosevelts at Hyde Park. FDR symbolized their commonality by serving hot dogs. In a serious confidential conversation, the King and the president discussed the situation in Europe. Roosevelt gave assurances that within the limits of his constitutional authority he would give as much assistance as possible in the event of war. When the royal couple boarded their train for Canada the next day, the crowd at the Hyde Park station bade them good-bye with a hearty "Auld Lang Syne."[64]

Roosevelt and the American nation looked at once east across the Atlantic and west across the Pacific. As Japan moved ever closer to Germany the problems of both areas began to merge. The Japanese repeatedly displayed contempt for all Westerners—American, British, and French—in China. At the end of November 1938, they openly proclaimed their intent to build a new order in East Asia that would give them economic self-sufficiency, based on the raw materials and cheap labor of their conquests. The unstated but obvious logic was that Western possessions in the region were among their targets. The administration responded with a $25 million loan to the Chinese government of Chiang Kai-shek. The cash infusion had little effect on a conflict in which the Chinese forces were too poorly trained, equipped, and led to do much more than fight delaying actions. That summer, Japanese forces in the city of Tientsin blockaded the British compound and forced London to sign an embarrassing agreement recognizing Japanese authority. By then American public opinion favored strong steps to express displeasure not simply with the humiliation of Westerners, but with the military terrorism that Japan used against the Chinese. Republican senator Arthur Vandenberg introduced a resolution to abrogate a 1911 trade treaty with Japan; without waiting for a Senate vote, Roosevelt junked the agreement on July 26. Although popular, the move was no answer to Japan's xenophobic crusade.[65]

Whether in Asia or Europe, the world crisis came down to one central objective for Roosevelt that summer—amend the Neutrality Act to extend cash and carry to weapons and allow the president to discriminate against aggressors. He had worked throughout the congressional session for the measure, only to see it tied up in the Senate Foreign Relations Committee by a coalition of progressive and conservative isolationists. On the evening of July 18, he met with the vice president, the secretary of state, and a half-dozen Senate leaders in one final attempt to get revision to the floor. Secretary Hull and the president told their audience that war was imminent, but might be deterred by neutrality revision. Senator Borah, the dean of Capitol Hill isolationism, erupted in anger and denounced manufactured war hysteria. Hull responded that the cables from Europe told a different story. The senator shot back that his sources were more reliable than the State Department's. Around midnight, Vice President Garner polled the legislators and delivered the bad news: "Well, Captain, we might as well face the facts. You haven't got the votes, and that's all there is to it." The group agreed that the senators would issue a statement to that effect, and the president would restate his position that neutrality revision was an urgent necessity. Roosevelt had tried hard. He had delivered only words.[66]

Meanwhile, British-Soviet talks limped along, hampered by a lack of trust on both sides and by doubts that either party could provide much of value to the other. On August 21, all hopes for an agreement crashed when Germany announced that Foreign Minister Joachim von Ribbentrop was flying to Moscow to conclude a nonaggression treaty with the Soviet Union. On August 23, Ribbentrop and his Soviet counterpart,

Vyacheslav Molotov, affixed their signatures to the pact. By then Germany was protesting one invented grievance after another against Poland and preparing an invasion. Hitler overrode his still-reluctant but now compliant generals and took no notice of the qualms of his apathetic population. He appears to have believed that Britain, deprived of its prospective Soviet ally, would back off. Instead, it went ahead with a formal signing of the defense agreement it had made with the Poles in April. Angry, perhaps a bit apprehensive, the German dictator would not be deterred. At last he would have his war.[67]

At dawn, on September 1, 1939, the German Army attacked Poland.

Neville Chamberlain would have gotten the news with the first rays of light in London. To the end he had persisted in believing that war could be averted. Now at seventy years of age he would have to manage one. He surely realized that he would have to call for Churchill that very day and offer him an important cabinet post. And the emotions, if not the exact words, he would vent to the House of Commons two days later had to be welling up within him: "everything that I have worked for, everything that I have hoped for, everything that I have believed in during my public life, has crashed into ruins."[68]

Franklin Roosevelt was awakened at 2:50 a.m. in Washington with a telephone call from Ambassador William Bullitt in Paris, relaying information from the American ambassador in Warsaw. FDR probably recalled his July 18 meeting with the senators, rued his lack of success in aligning the United States more firmly with the democracies, and began to weigh the political problems of assisting the allies without getting too far in front of an isolationist nation. To Bullitt, he simply said: "Well, Bill, it's come at last. God help us all."[69]

HEADLINES AND MOVIE NEWSREELS

{1939}

MAY 1   President Opens Fair as a Symbol of Peace; Vast Spectacle of Color and World Progress Thrills Crowds; Mayor, Governor Voice Welcome to the "World of Tomorrow"

JULY   *Columbia Lou, the Iron Horse, the greatest first baseman ever, is honored at Yankee Stadium on July 4. A native New Yorker, born to immigrant parents who lived on the margin of poverty, Gehrig had lived the American dream. Steady and quiet, he exemplified ideals of duty and team spirit. Years later, a historian would call his short response baseball's Gettysburg Address. Less articulately and more intuitively, many of its listeners perceived the spirit of an indomitable countryman, a common man who had done great things. Knowing that he faced a struggle with a deadly disease, he spoke in a clipped accent that might have typed him as a New York cop or fireman or longshoreman. His voice echoed through the enormous ballpark: "You have been reading about a bad break I got. Yet today I consider myself the luckiest man on the face of the earth. . . ."* (Newsreel, "Lou Gehrig Says Farewell")

SEPTEMBER 1   German Army Attacks Poland; Cities Bombed, Port Blockaded; British Mobilize

SEPTEMBER 25   362,522 Pack Fair on its 2nd-Best Day; Surpassed only by Labor Day Sunday

SEPTEMBER 28   Warsaw, a Shambles, Surrenders; Blazing Capital Faced Famine and Pestilence

EPILOGUE

Where Does the Future Lie:
Flushing Meadows or Warsaw?

By September 1939, Franklin Roosevelt had been president of the United States for six and one-half years. Few chief executives had made so powerful an imprint. Through all the ups and downs, he had retained a devoted mass following. He had touched the lives of virtually all Americans through his mastery of the new tools of mass communications that had suddenly become available in the second quarter of the twentieth century. He also had made contact with them in direct, tangible ways. A WPA job, a relief check, a federally subsidized pension, a mortgage refinancing, commodity price supports, minimum wages, maximum hours, a new bridge, school building, swimming pool, or city hall—traces of the New Deal could be found almost everywhere. In the minds of most Americans, Roosevelt *was* the New Deal.

No single story can fully convey the impression left by both the man and the program. One may provide an indication. Some forty years later, William E. Leuchtenburg recalled his success in raising the money he desperately needed for the balance of his tuition at Cornell University by selling Good Humor ice cream bars on the outer fringes of a huge crowd at an outdoor Roosevelt speech in Queens. Next came his good fortune in getting the spending money he needed to live on at Cornell by landing a National Youth Administration job. "I never did get to see President Roosevelt," he writes. "But in September 1939, like millions of other Americans who never saw him, I was powerfully aware of his influence on us."[1]

Leuchtenburg went on to become a leading historian of the New Deal, writing of it eloquently and engagingly in a small masterpiece that defined the period for a generation of history students. In another work, he argued with equal grace and conviction that Roosevelt in many ways had defined the office of the presidency for the next half-century.[2] Needless to say, he

approved of both the movement and the man. So would most other historians, whether so directly affected or not. Intellectuals who grew up with
the New Deal and those of the succeeding generation generally found
Roosevelt a charismatic figure and mostly approved of what he had done.
They especially delighted in his recognition of a university intelligentsia as
a source of policy ideas and his continuing combat with the world of commerce and finance. Identifying vicariously with the working class, they
hailed his support of the industrial union movement, which they tended to
depict as a struggle of unalloyed virtue against callous, exploitative business forces. They of course approved of the relief programs, if often wish-
ing these had been larger, and of social security, if usually lamenting that it
fell short of full social democratic welfarism. In general, they cheered the
growth of government ("the state") as a positive development that provided for the public interest, empowered farmers and workers, displayed
concern for the poor, and reduced the overblown power of big capital. FDR
and the New Deal, they agreed, had transformed America.

Or had it? To a person looking backward in September 1939, the
answer was less clear.

Monuments to the New Deal could be found almost everywhere. So
could grateful beneficiaries. Otter Tail County (population, 51,000) in
rural Minnesota provides a random example. By 1939, federally subsidized state old age pensions were putting a quarter of million dollars a
year into the county's economy. Other subsidies, and federal surplus commodities, helped provide for the indigent. The FERA, CWA, and PWA
pursued numerous projects, including road work, repair of public buildings, sewer construction, the laying of water mains, a water treatment
plant, and three new school buildings. From 1935 on, the WPA was a
major presence, providing employment at any given time for 500 to 2,200
workers. The CCC provided work for hundreds of the county's young
men. Acreage allotments and farm credit programs kept the farmers
afloat. Rural electrification brought power to 800 farms. "Electricity was
so wonderful to the people," one REA member recalled, "it was almost
like getting God there!"[3]

The New Deal probably did more to improve the quality of life in rural
counties like Otter Tail than in the big cities that provided its greatest
support. Otter Tail, like the rest of the country, had given up on Hoover
by 1932 and had voted for Roosevelt by a solid majority. But it was normally Republican. In 1936, it narrowly went for Landon. In 1940, it
would give Wendell Willkie a 2–1 margin over FDR. Looking back on

that phenomenon in 1985, an elderly resident remarked that the New Deal programs had done a great deal for the county. "They gave us more security, but they didn't change our way of looking at things. We're still conservative."[4] Voting judgments of the New Deal ultimately depended on more than simple economic calculus. Often they stemmed from long-held assumptions about the functions of government and the nature of society. Higher taxes, relief policies that seemed overly generous, encouragement of labor unions, interference with business—none of these things went down well in counties like Otter Tail. Religious and ethnic hostilities probably played a part also. By 1939, the great divide between the people and cultures of big city America and those of the small towns and the countryside was reappearing, taking rather different forms than in the 1920s, but reflecting the same impulses.

For those who thought and acted in terms of economic calculus, moreover, the New Deal was equally problematic. The mining town of Johnston City, Illinois, struck by the decline of the coal industry in the 1920s and then by the Depression, had been the grateful beneficiary of a lot of street work, a city park, and a new grade school. Men with union jobs in the mines made good money, but on nice days many unemployed miners still loitered on the main street sidewalks. A federal labor survey estimated that sixty percent of the city's workforce was still unemployed, two-thirds of them staying afloat on federal work programs.[5]

Local conditions varied greatly, of course, as they always do, but small towns generally were hardest hit by the Depression and least likely to bounce back. Johnston City, built around a depressed industry, was an extreme representation of a reality that existed more than halfway into Roosevelt's second term. In August 1939, the AFL estimated that just under 10 million Americans were unemployed nationally—a bit more than eighteen percent of the workforce. Measurements of business activity all agreed that the economy was functioning far below its potential. Whatever else the administration had done, however many benefits it had delivered to Americans, it had not ended the Depression. Yet as the world's largest economy, the United States was uniquely positioned to pull itself out of the morass.

What had gone wrong? Some answers lay in the nature of the Depression itself. Almost no one in the general public or the political classes fully understood it or readily comprehended the various nostrums offered by professional economists. For many Americans it was more like a phenomenon of nature than a mechanical problem subject to quick repair—

say, a smallpox epidemic rather than a blown automobile engine. As the New Deal busied itself addressing the symptoms with displays of concern and activity that exceeded those of the Hoover administration, the people responded with support. Others imagined that the Depression had been caused by the actions of bad people—unfeeling Republican politicians, wicked speculators, crooked businessmen, predatory bankers and financiers. The national scene presented many scapegoats, some of whom deserved prosecution, others of whom had been guilty of little more than poor business judgment. Roosevelt and the New Deal prosecuted some and denounced others with gusto—and generally it seems with sincerity rather than cynicism.[6]

The New Deal was at least as much social vision as economic recovery program. Frequently, the social vision got in the way of recovery. Early on, a narrow economic nationalism failed to develop enough economic stimulus to charge economic growth, and tied the industrial economy in knots with the National Recovery Administration. The turn to a de facto Keynesian strategy with the establishment of the Works Progress Administration seemed to bring a roaring recovery in 1936, but this was aborted in 1937 by premature spending cuts and questionable monetary policy. At the same time, attacks on business, finance, and wealth injected into political discussion unsettling themes of class warfare that discouraged entrepreneurial activity and seemed outside the mainstream American political tradition. Labor turmoil, often accompanied by violence, further destabilized the economy. The sharp recession that took hold in the fall of 1937 deprived Roosevelt of much of his authority and began what looked to be a period of stagnation with no discernible end in sight. Through it all, the president retained a devoted following and profited from the small-bore character of much of his opposition. All the same, in the summer of 1939 he was clearly diminished and by no means a sure bet for the third term some observers thought he already had in mind.

Increasingly, the relief programs, which had been the source of much of his support, were as much a liability as an asset. Once widely applauded emergency measures, they had taken on all the attributes of permanence. In August 1939, the WPA—by far the largest employer in the nation—had a payroll of 1.9 million. Other federal work programs provided jobs for another million. The WPA took the brunt of criticism because it was the most political of the relief agencies—a "vote army"—and because it was the most visible. Charges of political favoritism in WPA hiring often had merit; so did accusations of coerced campaign contributions. The conservative "economy bloc" in Congress went after it on matters of cost. But even more fundamental was the sense that in many places with little economic opportunity, it was becoming a career choice for its workers rather than a temporary helping hand. The prospect of a permanent class of federal relief employees was one that long had troubled many moderate observers. "Most of the 85% of U.S. citizens who still earn their livings in private industry wonder whether the remaining 15% will forever remain dependent on the Government for daily bread," *Time* observed in July 1938.[7]

In mid-1939, many of the achievements of the New Deal were neither evident nor perceived as permanent. The first federal social security check was still to be issued, after two and a half years of payroll contributions. Far from having established a constructive balance between capital and labor, the new CIO unions were unstable and ill-established; large segments of the American population viewed them as violent, illegitimate interlopers. American farmers were more and more critical of an increasingly coercive agricultural program that was having trouble supporting prices. The business and financial communities, large and small operators alike, were mostly alienated from a government that had hampered them with too many ill-conceived regulations and was prone to utilize them as political punching bags. It seemed reasonable to expect untold years of double-digit unemployment ahead.

Reduced to paper, the Roosevelt record was hardly impressive, even if one assumed that most New Deal beneficiaries expressed their gratitude in votes. But Roosevelt *was* impressive. His charisma, rhetorical talents, and dynamism made the New Deal more than the sum of its parts. American democracy differed perhaps most fundamentally from its British counterpart in demanding a strong leader at the top during times of crisis. Roosevelt, for all the inconsistencies of his agenda, emanated a sense of purposeful forward direction. However unsound his judgments may have been at critical times, however mixed his record, he had emerged as democracy's most dynamic force in a menacing decade. As Bonar Law had remarked of Churchill some two dozen years earlier, Roosevelt had the defects of his qualities, but the qualities were large and cast an enormous shadow.

In *Since Yesterday,* a vivid and useful instant history of the 1930s, Frederick Lewis Allen imagined two New York cocktail parties a decade apart, each attended by intellectuals—writers, critics, artists, musicians, political journalists, activist scholars, "men and women interested in the newest ideas and the newest tendencies in the arts." The first, in 1925, would have featured guests affirming to each other as they sipped their bootleg booze that America needed more personal freedom, especially in the realms of sexual behavior and alcohol consumption; that old-style progressive reform was hogwash; that the American business classes consisted of Babbitts and boobs; that ordinary Americans were nitwits; that the heroes of American history had been over-mythologized and needed to be taken down several pegs; that Europe was the planet's one refuge for thinking people who dared to challenge the stultifying conventions of American culture. The second, in 1935, attended by the same types (and many of the same people) stood every one of these propositions on its head, save the general assessment of businessmen. With near-unanimity, the party-goers were New Dealers or farther left. They agreed that "the masses of the citizenry were the people who really mattered, the most fitting subjects for writer and artist, the people on whose behalf reform must be undertaken." One might even hear a literary critic of the most effete appearance proclaiming his identification with the proletariat. One would discern general agreement that America, not Europe, was the hope of civilization, worth studying in all its aspects, good and ill, and on balance worth affirming more than ever.[8]

The people—the poorer and harder-working the better—themselves had to be revealed and explained to the world of the middle class and above. Archibald MacLeish, a once apolitical poet, had spent most of the 1920s living in Paris, hobnobbing with other American expatriates of the "lost generation." Returning to the United States just as the Depression hit, MacLeish wrote articles on contemporary society for *Fortune* and sharply reoriented his work as poet and playwright. In 1938, he published *Land of the Free*, a collection of eighty-eight photographs designed to illustrate every social pathology the American nation faced: the plight of sharecroppers and migrant workers, the violent suppression of union organizers, the despoliation of forests and farmlands. A *New Republic* reviewer wrote: "a copy of it ought to be got at once into the hands of every man, woman and child in the United States." It led inevitably, he concluded, to the conviction that a liberty once achieved by owning land could now be attained only by a people acting together.[9]

Most of the popular culture of the 1930s, whether in music, literature, film, or the theater, was, as always, simply mass entertainment. Some distinguished works, such as the novels of Thomas Wolfe and William Faulkner, spoke to concerns other than social commentary. Still, the social edge was unmistakable. A tide of democratic liberalism in some ways inspired and encouraged by the New Deal largely defined the cultural and intellectual life of the 1930s. Not an officially imposed ideology, it was more the spontaneous response of an intelligentsia attempting to find new bearings amidst domestic turmoil and global upheaval. It became stronger in the last half of the 1930s, as the Depression persisted, fascism increased its grip on Europe, and Japan ran wild in China. Its two most salient and persistent themes were the recovery of the American past for the cause of democracy and the celebration of the common man.

The 1930s were important years for the rediscovery of the American democratic tradition, which achieved its greatest impact through biography. The three most important subjects were Andrew Jackson, Thomas Jefferson, and Abraham Lincoln.

Jackson, since the mid-nineteenth century dismissed as a frontier ignoramus by patrician historians and progressive intellectuals alike, seemed to take on a new salience in the midst of the Depression. That he was a tribune of the common man had never been disputed and now became an asset in an age when common people were no longer considered dolts by intellectuals. That he had been an enemy of big bankers and a foe of corporations likewise made him attractive. That he had been a Democrat—the first president to apply that one-word term to himself and his party—made him both a partisan and an ideological symbol of importance. Roosevelt's talks at Democratic party Jackson Day events, along with his semiprivate claims that he also was fighting antidemocratic bankers, resuscitated the old president's tattered image. Speaking in Little Rock at the beginning of the 1936 presidential campaign season, FDR made the comparison explicit:

> I need not describe the dismay that the election of Jackson excited . . . in the hearts of the hitherto elect, or the widespread apprehension that it aroused among the so-called guardian groups of the Republic.
>
> . . . it will never be possible for any length of time for any group of the American people, either by reason of wealth or learning or inheritance or economic power, to retain any mandate, any permanent authority to arrogate to itself the political control of American public life.[10]

Marquis James's fast-paced and uncritical biography of Jackson sealed the deal. Awarded a Pulitzer Prize in 1938, it was a best-seller that presented Jackson as a rough-hewn but valiant leader of ordinary people. A young graduate of Harvard, Arthur Schlesinger, Jr., was just beginning to embark on a project that would make the parallel without equivocation. Published in 1946 as *The Age of Jackson*, it also would be a Pulitzer book. An intellectual class that had come to see democracy as the most fundamental of all social-political institutions placed Old Hickory in the presidential pantheon.[11]

Thomas Jefferson long had presented quite a different problem. No one questioned his cosmopolitan intellect. He long had been a patron saint of the Democratic party. But "Jeffersonianism" before the 1930s had universally been interpreted as coupling democracy and individual freedom with ideals of small, frugal government and states' rights. Republican progressives such as Theodore Roosevelt had characteristically debunked him. The progressive thinker Herbert Croly in his influential book *The Promise of American Life* (1912) had written of the need to combine Jeffersonian ends (democracy and liberty) with Hamiltonian means (strong, active, centralized government), but this formula seemed more liberal Hamiltonianism than nationalistic Jeffersonianism. A reinterpretation had begun in the 1920s with Claude Bowers's popular *Jefferson and Hamilton* (1925); a biography-centered account of the party wars of the 1790s, it depicted Jefferson as a champion of democracy fighting the authoritarian impulses of Hamiltonian Federalism. Franklin Roosevelt had reviewed the book enthusiastically for the *New York Evening World*, the flagship Democratic paper that Bowers edited. Even then, as an out-of-work politician fighting polio, FDR had no doubt that the struggles of Jefferson's time replicated the contemporary fight of the people against a business-financial elite.[12]

Bowers was among the most partisan of journalist-historians; he had intentionally written a Democratic manifesto, which he followed in the election year of 1936 with another volume, *Jefferson the President*. Roosevelt, the New Dealers, and almost anyone thinking of himself as a liberal eagerly adopted his vision. The New Deal put Jefferson on the five-cent coin and the standard first-class postage stamp; it authorized the Jefferson Memorial. Jeffersonianism, Roosevelt and others argued, was in essence a pragmatic faith in democracy that adapted itself to the needs of an era, not a rigid doctrinal program. If one accepted that assumption, then all things were possible—certainly a Jefferson who would have tolerated national planning, big government, and deficit spending. Roosevelt, probably more convinced than ever that history was repeating itself, stated his own formulation when, two and a half months into World War II, he spoke at the laying of the cornerstone to the Jefferson Memorial on November 15, 1939:

> He lived, as we live, in the midst of a struggle between rule by the self-chosen individual or the self-appointed few and rule by the franchise and approval of the many. He believed, as we do, that the average opinion of mankind is in the long run superior to the dictates of the self-chosen.[13]

The Lincoln revival owed less to the New Deal than to a more spontaneous sense that Lincoln's personal history, especially his origins among the commonest of the common people, had special relevance to the 1930s. The godfathers of this realization were the poet and biographer Carl Sandburg and the playwright Robert E. Sherwood. An offspring of working-class immigrants, Sandburg, fifty-five years old at the start of the New Deal, was a senior figure in American letters. As a poet, he already had positioned himself as a champion of "the Poor, millions of the Poor, patient and toiling." He renewed this stance in 1936 with an epic, book-length ode to the masses, *The People, Yes*. He was by then even better known as the author of *Abraham Lincoln: The Prairie Years* (1926), a sprawling, lyrical, and at times semifictional, two-volume account of its subject's prepresidential years. Through the thirties, he worked on his four-volume *Abraham Lincoln: The War Years*, published to great acclaim in 1939.[14]

Sandburg's work on Lincoln's early years had captured the imagination of Sherwood, who used it as the basis for his *Abe Lincoln in Illinois*, first performed on Broadway in 1938. Perhaps America's finest active playwright, Sherwood, just forty-two, had been strongly attracted to the New Deal and soon would find himself working with FDR as a speechwriter. The tall, gaunt, powerful Canadian actor Raymond Massey performed memorably as the title character, giving the part, as Jeffrey Richards has observed, "dignity, humanity, and a Christlike sense of destiny." Massey remarked of his interpretation that Lincoln "was definitely a New Dealer." Near the end of the play, Lincoln declares in an important speech, "Thank God we live under a system by which men have the *right* to strike!" Sherwood and Massey would bring their joint product to millions in a film version released in 1940. A year earlier, the director John Ford and Henry Fonda gave the public their own interpretation in *Young*

Mr. Lincoln. Both films were critical and box-office successes. By then, even the Communist party had given Lincoln's name to the volunteer military unit it raised to fight in Spain. What historical character could provide more inspiration to a democratic nation facing its own fight for freedom?[15]

In the climate of the 1930s, Jefferson, Jackson, and Lincoln were important not simply for themselves but because in one way or another they represented the strengths and aspirations of the common people. But acclamation by proxy was not enough.

Some intellectuals, in the tradition of Frederick Lewis Allen's effete literary critic, took up the cause of the workers, advocating their cause as writers or occasionally as amateur labor activists. But, even more than the workers, who at least had unions to fight for them, sharecroppers and tenant farmers drew attention and sympathy. The New Deal's Farm Security Administration (FSA) was a key player in publicizing what amounted to an agrarian *lumpenproletariat.* Its photography program depicted sharecroppers sitting at bare wooden tables, standing in front of shacks scarcely sealed against the weather, at the wheel of decrepit autos—always posed to send the message that even the poorest of the poor, while urgent objects of social concern, also had an enduring dignity. What the New Deal had done so much to start, John Steinbeck carried forward in *The Grapes of Wrath* (1939), his best-selling epic of dispossessed sharecroppers making a trek to California in search of a new life and being exploited along the way by almost everyone they encountered, except the management of an FSA migrant worker camp. The movie followed a year later, featuring Henry Fonda in his most memorable role. A people the intellectuals of the 1920s scorned as ignorant, degraded poor white trash had become emblematic Americans.

Other previously neglected groups acquired a new visibility and a greater measure of influence also. When Franklin Roosevelt became president in 1933, the term "American" in the symbolic (rather than legal) sense of full, legitimate citizenship still referred to people mostly like himself—white, Northern European, Protestant. By 1939, other groups had moved up the ladder of public consciousness, and citizenship expanded proportionately.

April 1939

Beautiful and talented, possessing one of the greatest contralto voices of her time, but also black, Marian Anderson was barred from giving a concert

*in Washington at Constitution Hall, which was owned by the Daughters of
the American Revolution. Eleanor Roosevelt and Harold Ickes floated the
idea of a concert on the Mall at the Lincoln Memorial; the President acquiesced. The New Deal thereby symbolically recognized the full citizenship of
Negro Americans. Wrapped in a fur coat on a cold Easter Sunday, she
appears in front of the great statue of Lincoln before an integrated crowd of
75,000, beginning with a medley of patriotic songs in a clear, chilling voice:
"My country 'tis of Thee, sweet land of liberty. . . ."* (Newsreel, "Marian
Anderson Sings at the Lincoln Memorial")

Negroes emerged from the 1930s as a political bloc of some importance with significant political power inside the Northern Democratic
party. They also produced talented figures who won admiration in the
white world. Jesse Owens and Joe Louis were hailed as national champions when they defeated Nazi foes. Hattie McDaniel became the first
black film performer to win an Oscar, for of all things *Gone with the Wind.*
Marian Anderson's concert at the Lincoln Memorial demonstrated a rare
talent to the rest of the nation. Two months later, she sang at the White
House for King George and Queen Elizabeth. Even in the most liberal
areas of the North, Americans remained confused and contradictory in
their racial attitudes. Yet Owens, Louis, McDaniel, and Anderson were
more than tokens; their recognition was a first step for all blacks.

The "new immigrant" ethnics likewise emerged during the decade,
partly simply on the basis of maturation and adaption to America, partly
because their aspirations were also recognized and encouraged by the
president and his administration. Irish-Catholic multiethnic political
machines had for a generation been powerful in numerous large cities
and had occasionally controlled statehouses. Never before, however, had
the immigrant bloc been so central in electing a president. By 1939, it
was the hard, unwavering core of FDR's support and its leaders were
more politically prominent than ever. Still predominantly low-income
and working class, the new ethnic groups had received a lot of economic
aid from the New Deal. They also had gotten intangible, but valuable,
recognition and respect. And political power. Before the New Deal, their
success stories had been likely to be athletes—Lou Gehrig or Joe DiMag-
gio or the basketball star Hank Luisetti. Now they were walking the corri-
dors of power. Jews, foremost among them the secretary of the treasury,
had a greater presence in Washington than ever before. New York state
had a governor (Herbert Lehman) who was Jewish and a lieutenant-

governor (Charles Poletti) who was Italian. The mayor of New York City (Fiorello La Guardia) was both.

Roosevelt deftly established the theme of inclusiveness in a talk to the Daughters of the American Revolution just a year before Eleanor would resign from the organization in protest against its refusal to schedule Marian Anderson in Constitution Hall. With open impish delight, he told the 3,000 upper-crust delegates to its annual Continental Congress: "Remember, remember always that all of us, and you and I especially, are descended from immigrants and revolutionists."[16] The Republican party remained predominantly old-stock and not particularly welcoming to more recent immigrants, much less revolutionists.

The idea that the United States was a nation of immigrants took on special importance in a world of turmoil and expanding dictatorship. (Roosevelt himself in his talk to the DAR had asserted, with considerable poetic license, that the American revolutionaries of 1776 had fought "to throw off a fascist yoke."[17]) The classic affirmation of the country's distinctiveness and importance was produced by a child of the new immigration who was also its greatest songwriter, Irving Berlin. On Armistice Day, November 11, 1938, just six weeks after the Munich agreement, Kate Smith introduced Berlin's "God Bless America." Miss Smith, a stout woman devoid of conventional glamour, possessed a big voice; in the pre-television age, she was the country's most popular singer. Introduced by a solemn spoken prelude that referred to storm clouds across the sea and reminded its visitors that America was a land of the free, the song, performed with Smith's customary bravura, struck a nerve in the national psyche. Whether Berlin had meant to depict America as a place of refuge or the redeemer of the world is unclear. He reminded all Americans, from the just-naturalized to the oldest of the old stock, that they were citizens of a free nation that deserved God's blessing.

Ten years after the Wall Street crash, Americans were still optimistic enough about the future to stage two world fairs—the Golden Gate International Exposition in San Francisco and the New York World's Fair. Both sported large amusement midways; both celebrated science and technology; both assumed that, whatever the current headlines, progress was the central theme of history. Both, in short, reflected a congenital optimism too deeply ingrained in the American character to be overwhelmed by a decade of bad times and an impending world war. "The eyes of the United States are fixed on the future," declared President Roosevelt in the address that opened the New York fair. "Yes, our wagon is still hitched to a star."[18]

The New York event was larger than its West Coast counterpart, located in America's communications capital, and more sharply focused on its theme, "The World of Tomorrow." It drew more attention and became a defining cultural event. Opening on April 30, 1939, it extended over 1,216 acres in the large and undeveloped Flushing Meadows area of Queens. Its exhibits and amusements were connected by sixty-five miles of paved streets. Its two central structures—a 610-foot high "Trylon" (a three-sided pylon) and a "Perisphere" (globe) 180 feet in diameter—established an architectural theme of clean, streamlined modernity. Visitors to the Perisphere paid twenty-five cents to be taken up 120 feet on escalators, step on a revolving platform, and look down at Democracity, the thriving city of tomorrow, organized on a radial plan, with spacious homes on large tree-studded lots and broad streets heading outwards from the hub to a rim of clean industries and government offices.[19]

From there, they might have gone to the corporate industrial exhibits, usually free, instructive, often entertaining, invariably celebratory. More than two dozen companies—all household names—had their own pavilions; a dozen or so other industries operated cooperative ventures. The bigger attractions included the railway industry's Railroads on Parade, a drama of historical growth and development complete with real moving locomotives; Eastman Kodak's Cavalcade of Color, a remarkable array of photography projected onto huge panels; American Telephone and Telegraph's enormous illuminated network map of the United States, accompanied by a lottery that allowed winners to make free long distance calls; the General Electric "House of Magic" with its ten-million-volt thunder and lightning show, an enormous mural tracing the progress of mankind, and displays of the company's latest products; Ford and Goodrich exhibits that demonstrated the production process. The biggest attraction was General Motors' Futurama, a vast panorama of the United States that featured the metropolis of the year 1960—a gleaming city of tall buildings, fourteen-lane elevated highways, and sleek tear-shaped cars.[20]

International pavilions were clustered over to the east, across the Lagoon of Nations. Two were spectacular. The Soviet exhibition employed giant maps, films, and a full-sized replica of a Moscow subway station to celebrate Communism's social and industrial progress. A statue of a Stakhanovite worker holding aloft a red star stood atop a 269-foot tower. The Italian pavilion was equally imposing—a depiction of "Roma" as female warrior seated above a multistory waterfall; a monument to Marconi at the base of a statue of an amazonian nude; the prominently displayed Fascist motto: *Credere! Obbedire! Combattere!* (Believe! Obey! Fight!). The democratic national exhibits were mundane by comparison. Nazi Germany, rightly understanding that its presence was unwelcome, was not represented.[21]

Two pavilions drew great sentimental interest. The Czechoslovakian building, unfinished when the Nazis occupied the country in March 1939, was completed and operated through a fund-raising drive chaired by Mayor La Guardia. Although it was not officially open the first day of the fair, crowds flocked to it. An official fair publication said that it symbolized the spirit of freedom. After the opening, the nation's former president, Eduard Benes, declared "Czechoslovakia is still alive. It will continue to live. And here is the evidence of that fact." There was also a Jewish Palestine pavilion, opened on May 28 with a speech by Albert Einstein, a week and a half after the British had sought to stop the Arab rebellion by suspending Jewish immigration to the mandate. The real world did not, after all, stop at the fair's gates.[22]

The crowds came throughout the feverish summer of 1939, increasingly large but never quite as big as expected—it was not a cheap day out, and the Depression, after all, was still with the country. Sunday, September 3, the day before Labor Day and two days after the German invasion of Poland, nearly half a million people paid to pass through the gates. It was the largest one-day attendance. They kept coming through the month as the war rolled on, almost as if to affirm the fair's vision of the future against the reality taking place in Poland.

Germany was Europe's leader in science and technology, but these skills were directed toward military conquest and continental domination, not a contented consumer democracy. Poland had a small, ill-equipped army. The campaign was quick, ugly, and tragic. The German Luftwaffe quickly destroyed what little air power Poland could array against it, then bombed and strafed at will. A multipronged German offensive slashed through Polish defenses with overpowering might. By the second week of the war the main Polish forces were cut off from each other, surrounded, and being reduced systematically. Their one hope of survival—a French offensive that would require Germany to send major units to the Western front—never materialized. France remained behind the Maginot Line. At the beginning of the third week, the Soviet Union invaded from the east. Warsaw held out until, exhausted and in flames from bombs and artillery, it surrendered on September 27. The Nazis and Soviets exterminated what resistance remained elsewhere in the next week or two. In one month, Poland had suffered 100,000 soldiers killed. A million survivors were marched off to prison camps. "The whole country," Gerhard Weinberg has written, "was once again occupied by foreign troops who would install new systems of terror—one animated by racial and the other by class ideology."[23]

The Nazis and Soviets, whatever their different motivations, proceeded along parallel tracks—expropriation of food supplies, forced labor, arrests and extermination of the Polish leadership classes. The Nazis were perhaps more systematic about it, but the aims were similar. An entire nation was to be decapitated, its remaining citizens turned into vassals of a new order. The barbarism sweeping over Poland was there for all to see, yet so horrible that the Western liberal mind found it nearly impossible to comprehend.

The crowds at the World's Fair thinned out in the chill of October. At the end of the month, the great exposition closed. It would reopen for a second season on May 11, 1940, one day after the beginning of the Nazi offensive against France and the low countries, and would proclaim a new slogan: "For Peace and Freedom."

By then humankind faced two competing prospects for the future: science, progress, peace, freedom—the vision at Flushing Meadows. Science, conquest, militarism, totalitarianism—the reality of Warsaw.

For Europe, Warsaw seemed most probable. Americans continued to hope for the world of Flushing Meadows.

HISTORIOGRAPHICAL NOTE

This book has been primarily an account of American life and politics during the Great Depression, but it is also a foray into comparative history. Believing that ultimately people, not abstract forces, make history, it emphasizes personalities, foremost among them Franklin Roosevelt, but also many other Americans and not a few Europeans. This essay briefly discusses some of the issues and problems with which I was compelled to grapple.

Roosevelt and the New Deal

The "founding fathers" of serious New Deal historiography in the 1950s and early 1960s—James MacGregor Burns, Arthur Schlesinger, Jr., and William E. Leuchtenburg—established a tone that still dominates the study of American politics in the 1930s: a near-adulatory perspective, occasionally nagged by a sense that FDR was too "conservative" to lead us entirely into the promised land of equalitarian social democracy. In the 1960s and 1970s, a few "New Left" historians attempted to challenge the consensus with more strident critiques, but these quickly fizzled. Conservative scholars have had scant impact, in part because their numbers are so few, in part because the climate of opinion within the historical profession and the larger intellectual community is nearly bulletproof against revisionism from the right. By and large, most professional historians, up through David Kennedy's recent splendid narrative, still work from within the viewpoint of the founding fathers, or somewhere to the left of it. They have produced books that elaborate, sometimes brilliantly, on established insights, but do not challenge established higher wisdom about the beneficence of the New Deal or the greatness of the president who led it. All concede that Roosevelt and the movement he headed failed to end the Depression, most find other missteps to criticize; but they operate from the assumption that the lapses were minor in comparison to the New Deal's social legislation, attacks on big business, empowerment of organized labor, and general transformation of America's social structure.

The professional historians have too cavalierly dismissed the conservative critics of Roosevelt as an economic policy maker. Books by Gary Dean Best and, more recently, Gene Smiley may in some ways act as a mirror image of the liberal viewpoint by focusing almost exclusively on the problem of economic recovery and ignoring much else that was happening in the 1930s. Nevertheless, they deserve far more attention than they have received. The New Deal did in numerous ways hinder the struggle against the Depression. It left the United States saddled with mass unemployment and a sluggish economy after the other developed countries had achieved recovery by one means or another. Moreover, the American economic malaise surely deepened and prolonged the worldwide Depression. These conclusions raise two important issues, which this work attempts to address: Why, despite failure at what should have been considered his central task, did Roosevelt achieve so much political success? Why do historians overwhelmingly consider him a great president?

Comparative Political Cultures, Political Leadership, and the Issue of "American Exceptionalism"

Since the first settlements at Jamestown and Plymouth Rock, Americans have tended to insist on their differences from Europe. Europeans, with mixed amounts of wariness and condescension, by and large have agreed. Alexis de Tocqueville, writing in the 1830s, saw the major distinction in the uncritical American acceptance of democracy (equality and majority rule). He fretted about whether this would be compatible with order and individual liberty but hoped for the best. In the early twentieth century, writing in the wake of the industrial revolution, the German sociologist Werner Sombart drew a far different line: "Why is there no socialism in America?" The strong American hostility to socialism, indeed the failure of a significant socialist movement ever to emerge, became a haunting question for Marxists and others trying to explain the problem of "American exceptionalism." The political scientist Louis Hartz provided the most influential response in his landmark book *The Liberal Tradition in*

America (1955), arguing that from its inception, America, a new country unencumbered by the repressive institutions of the old world, had been a "liberal society," monolithically dominated by values of individual freedom and blessed by an environment that offered large opportunities for social mobility.

So sweeping an argument was bound to have weak spots, but after fifty years and many attacks on it, the Hartz thesis stands up pretty well as a description of American attitudes. Its weakest point is its implicit assumption that "Europe," indeed the rest of the world, was (and implicitly remains) a monolithic Non-America. The large generalization, which was roughly accurate, obscured crucial differences among the non-Americans. The Europe of the interwar years was a complex jumble of nations that possessed distinct national characters, histories, and political cultures. These distinctions reflected differing internal social structures, degrees of class conflict and cross-class mobility, political institutions, and expectations of leadership. In general, one could find a fair amount of "liberalism" in much of Western Europe and a steadily diminishing supply as one traveled east. Moreover, liberal values, as important as they were, did not constitute the only denominator of politics and society. It seems more meaningful in a book of this sort to talk about "national differences," rather than "American exceptionalism."

Who can deny, for example, that for all the genuine contrasts between them Britain and the United States shared a far larger core of common values than either nation shared with Germany, before or after the Nazis came to power? Mass democracy was more recent in Britain and its electorate far more deferential to a ruling establishment than was the case in the United States, but both countries concurred on a bedrock commitment to majority rule, individual freedom, and a civil society. These overrode differences that were substantial and widely acknowledged. The United States had a written constitution (as did Germany); Britain did not. Britain was comfortable with collective party leadership and possessed a sense of unity that gravitated naturally to the idea of a national coalition government in times of crisis. The United States (and Germany) favored strong men in uncertain times.

The essential characteristics of political cultures tend to be imbedded deep in the distinctive experiences of nations, but traumatic contemporary developments can impact them hard. Germany was the product of a long history of militarism and authoritarianism. Its highly structured society produced a politics based on class identities. The experience of defeat in war and postwar hyperinflation increased its political fragmentation and encouraged extremism. The Weimar constitution, a product of reason rather than experience, established governmental machinery that facilitated the rise of a political malaise. The Great Depression was one blow too many to a shaky state with little popular legitimacy.

The Depression brought fundamental issues of individual freedom and democratic rule to the forefront of politics everywhere. It also called forth large personalities to meet them. Among the democratic statesmen, Franklin Roosevelt remains the most admired of an extraordinary group of world historical figures from that decade, Stanley Baldwin the most underrated. However repugnant Mussolini, Hitler, and Stalin may have been, their achievements seemed enormous to many of their contemporaries. They enjoyed a wide admiration that is hard to grasp from the perspective of the twenty-first century. Their threat to decent civilization was real.

The history of the world crisis of the 1930s is about more than a few national leaders. It was nonetheless up to these statesmen to manage the unmanageable, strengthen their nations, and weather the storm. It is to their personal stories as well as to the distinctive characters of their nations that we must look if we are to understand the most critical decade of the twentieth century. Each was a distinctive product of his political culture, possessing attributes and skills that were not readily transferrable. Americans and Britons would have written Hitler off as a raving lunatic; even after he was doing terrible things in Germany, it suited their popular cultures to satirize him as a clown. Germans, whether in the bitterly polarized Weimar era or the totalitarian Nazi order, would have found both Roosevelt and Baldwin alien in their democratic values and revulsion to class conflict. FDR possessed a charm and charisma that appealed to the British population, but it is hard to imagine him rising through the mill of legislative politics that was the path to the British premiership. Baldwin, a patrician House of Commons man, would likely have seemed to most Americans a quaint literary fuddy-duddy lacking a common touch.

That said, the dictators and democrats did possess certain similar skills and attributes. Most noticeably at the time, they superbly utilized new skills of mass communication—radio broadcasts, movie newsreels, and press management. All possessed formidable oratorical skills, which they employed to mobilize large followings. All had instincts for power. They thought it natural to use government to one degree or another to organize the economy. For the most part, they remained detached from the messy and detailed work of policy implementation. They probably understood that authority and popular appeal were best maintained by remaining above most frays and concentrating on inspirational exhortation. Both Roosevelt and Hitler, moreover, seem to have consciously played off subordinates against one another as a means of preserving their ultimate power.

In the end, individual leadership made a difference. Baldwin and Roosevelt, exposed to a free press and democratic criticism, experienced a mixture of failure and success and functioned under constant opposition. But each also possessed an ethical inner compass that helped keep their societies free, relatively united, and resolute in their values through a harrowing decade. Hitler unfortunately made the biggest difference. Imposing his will and nihilistic values on a great nation that might otherwise have simply experienced a run-of-the-mill right-wing dictatorship, he led it into history's greatest inferno. What leader before him so changed the world?

Essential Resources

For Roosevelt and the New Deal: The works of the historiographical "founding fathers" are James MacGregor Burns, *Roosevelt: The Lion and the Fox* (New York: Harcourt Brace and World, 1956); Arthur M. Schlesinger, Jr., *The Crisis of the Old Order, 1919–1933* (Boston: Houghton Mifflin, 1957), *The Coming of the New Deal* (Boston: Houghton Mifflin, 1959), and *The Politics of Upheaval* (Boston: Houghton Mifflin, 1960); William E. Leuchtenburg, *Franklin D. Roosevelt and the New Deal* (New York: Harper and Row, 1963). The early critics include Barton J. Bernstein, "The New Deal: The Conservative Achievements of Liberal Reform," in Bernstein, ed., *Towards a New Past: Dissenting Essays in American History* (New York: Pantheon, 1967); Ronald Radosh, "The Myth of the New Deal," in Ronald Radosh and Murray Rothbard, eds., *A New History of Leviathan: Essays on the Rise of the American Corporate State* (New York: E. P. Dutton, 1972); and Gabriel Kolko, *Main Currents in Modern American History* (New York: Harper and Row, 1976), ch. 4. All gloried (or once did) in the label "New Left." Paul K. Conkin, *The New Deal*, 1st ed. (New York: Thomas Crowell, 1967), the most influential of the doubters, went at the New Deal from a position far closer to that of John Dewey than Karl Marx.

Two recent works that have focused on the New Deal failure to deal with the Depression are Gary Dean Best, *Pride, Prejudice, and Politics: Roosevelt versus Recovery, 1933–1938* (Westport, CN: Praeger, 1991), and Gene Smiley, *Rethinking the Great Depression* (Chicago: Ivan Dee, 2002). The first is perhaps too relentless in its attack, the second too brief. Both deserve attention and respect. Robert Dallek, *Franklin D. Roosevelt and American Foreign Relations* (New York: Oxford University Press, 1979), is still the standard account. Charles C. Alexander, *Nationalism in American Thought, 1930–1945* (Chicago: Rand McNally, 1969), remains the most useful starting point for its subject. Richard H. Pells, *Radical Visions and American Dreams: Culture and Social Thought in the Depression Years* (New York: Harper and Row, 1973), is likewise still a standard. Among more general works from the past fifteen years or so, see especially Anthony Badger, *The New Deal* (New York: Hill and Wang, 1989); Jordan Schwarz, *The New Dealers: Power Politics in the Age of Roosevelt* (New York: Alfred A. Knopf, 1993); Alan Brinkley, *The End of Reform: New Deal Liberalism in Depression and War* (New York: Alfred A. Knopf, 1995). Kenneth S. Davis, *FDR: The New Deal Years, 1933–1937* (New York: Random House, 1986), and *FDR: Into the Storm, 1937–1940* (New York: Random House, 1993), are the two New Deal volumes in Davis's thoughtful and essential five-volume biography of Roosevelt. David Kennedy, *Freedom from Fear: The American People in Depression and War, 1929–1945* (New York: Oxford University Press, 1999), is the new standard narrative of its subject.

On political cultures and American exceptionalism, the starting point is Alexis de Tocqueville, *Democracy in America*, 2 vols. (1835, 1840), since republished in many editions. The two English standards are the translations by Henry Reeve and Francis Bowen, updated by Phillips Bradley (New York: Alfred A. Knopf, 1963); and by Harvey C. Mansfield, Jr., and Delba Winthrop (Chicago: University of Chicago Press, 2000). On the question of socialism in America, see Seymour Martin Lipset and Gary Marks, *It Didn't Happen Here: Why Socialism Failed in the United States* (New York: W. W. Norton, 2000). On the Hartz thesis, Louis Hartz, *The Liberal Tradition in America* (New York: Harcourt Brace and World, 1955); James T. Kloppenberg, "In Retrospect: Louis Hartz's *The Liberal Tradition in America*," *Reviews in American History* (2001), 460–78; Leonard Krieger, "A View of the Farther Shore," *Comparative Studies in History and Society* (1963–64), 269–73. The two major attempts at comparative histories of the Depression are Charles P. Kindleberger, *The*

World in Depression, 1929–1939 (Berkeley: University of California Press, 1973), and John A. Garraty, *The Great Depression* (New York: Harcourt Brace Jovanovich, 1980).

For Britain in the 1930s, the best single book is probably Charles Loch Mowat, *Britain between the Wars* (Chicago: University of Chicago Press, 1958), a full and useful account by a superb historian who wrote with the passion of a participant. A. J. P. Taylor, *English History, 1914–1945* (London and New York: Oxford University Press, 1965), will not disappoint those in search of sharp opinions. Among more recent books, I found Peter Dewey, *War and Progress: Britain, 1914–1945* (London and New York: Longman, 1997), especially useful for its treatment of economic and social trends. For personalities, see Philip Williamson, *Stanley Baldwin: Conservative Leadership and National Values* (Cambridge: Cambridge University Press, 1999); Keith Feiling, *The Life of Neville Chamberlain* (London: Macmillan, 1946); David Dutton, *Neville Chamberlain* (London: Arnold, 2001); Robert Skidelsky, *John Maynard Keynes: The Economist as Savior, 1920–1937* (New York: Penguin Books, 1994); Graham Stewart, *Burying Caesar: The Churchill-Chamberlain Rivalry* (Woodstock and New York: The Overlook Press, 2001); Martin Gilbert, *Churchill: A Life* (New York: Henry Holt, 1991), the one-volume condensation of Gilbert's massive biographical project, and Roy Jenkins, *Churchill* (New York: Farrar, Strauss and Giroux, 2001). William Rock, *Chamberlain and Roosevelt: British Foreign Policy and the United States, 1937–1940* (Columbus: Ohio State University Press, 1988), deserves mention for its thorough coverage of Anglo-American diplomacy in the two years before the war.

For the Third Reich, one might best begin with three books by Ian Kershaw that in combination provide an intellectually enriching mixture of narrative biography and historical interpretation: *The Nazi Dictatorship: Problems and Perspectives of Interpretation*, 4th ed. (London: Arnold, 2000); *Hitler, 1889–1936: Hubris* (New York: W. W. Norton, 1999); and *Hitler, 1936–1945: Nemesis* (New York: W. W. Norton, 2000). Alan Bullock, *Hitler and Stalin: Parallel Lives* (New York: Alfred A. Knopf, 1992), is a rewarding exercise in the comparative psychology of totalitarianism. Eberhard Kolb, *The Weimar Republic*, trans. P. S. Falla (London: Unwin Hyman, 1988), is an excellent brief introduction; Hans Mommsen, *The Rise and Fall of Weimar Democracy*, trans. Elborg Forster and Larry Eugene Jones (Chapel Hill: University of North Carolina Press, 1996), is fuller and near-definitive. Joachim E. Fest, *The Face of the Third Reich*, trans. Michael Bullock (New York: Da Capo, 1999), sketches Hitler, many other Nazi leaders, and archetypical followers. William L. Shirer, *The Rise and Fall of the Third Reich* (New York: Simon and Schuster, 1960), has survived countless efforts by professional historians to drive a stake through its heart because, for all its interpretive deficiencies, it is good, comprehensive journalism, especially for those years of the 1930s when Shirer was resident in Berlin. Richard Overy, *The Penguin Historical Atlas of the Third Reich* (London: Penguin, 1996), is a valuable compact reference. Harold James, *The German Slump: Politics and Economics, 1924–1936* (Oxford: Clarendon Press, 1986), is the standard interpretation. Other useful works include David Schoenbaum, *Hitler's Social Revolution: Class and Status in Nazi Germany* (New York: Oxford University Press, 1966); David Welch, *The Third Reich: Politics and Propaganda* (London and New York: Routledge, 1993); and Michael Burleigh and Wolfgang Wippermann, *The Racial State: Germany, 1933–1945* (Cambridge: Cambridge University Press, 1991).

NOTES

Author's note: *New York Times* has been abbreviated *NYT.*

Prologue

1. *NYT,* March 5, 1929.

2. Samuel I. Rosenman, ed., *The Public Papers and Addresses of Franklin D. Roosevelt, Volume Two, The Year of Crisis, 1933* (New York: Random House, 1938), 11–16.

3. For the economic causes and consequences of the Great Depression, see Charles Kindleberger, *The World in Depression, 1929–1939* (Berkeley: University of California Press, 1979); John A. Garraty, *The Great Depression* (New York: Harcourt Brace Jovanovich, 1980); Michael Bernstein, *The Great Depression: Delayed Recovery and Economic Change in America, 1929–1939* (New York: Cambridge University Press, 1987); Barry Eichengreen, *Golden Fetters: The Gold Standard and the Great Depression, 1919–1939* (New York: Oxford University Press, 1965).

1. World Crisis

1. Charles Loch Mowat, *Britain between the Wars, 1918–1940* (Chicago: University of Chicago Press, 1955), 148–49.

2. Hajo Holborn, *A History of Modern Germany, 1840–1945* (New York: Alfred A. Knopf, 1969), 666.

3. Zweig, as quoted in Gerald Feldman, *The Great Inflation* (New York: Oxford University Press, 1993), 858.

4. *Ibid.,* 856.

5. *NYT,* Jan. 25, 1931.

6. Kenneth Moure, *Managing the Franc Poincare* (New York: Cambridge University Press, 1991), chs. 1–2.

7. Peter Dewey, *War and Progress: Britain, 1914–1945* (New York: Longman, 1997), esp. chs. 3–7.

8. R. J. Overy, *The Nazi Economic Recovery, 1932–1938,* 2nd ed. (Cambridge: Cambridge University Press, 1996), chs. 1–2; William C. McNeil, *American Money and the Weimar Republic* (New York: Columbia University Press, 1986).

9. Alfred E. Eckes, Jr., *Opening America's Market: U.S. Foreign Trade Policy since 1776* (Chapel Hill: University of North Carolina Press, 1995), 89, 113.

10. George Soule, *Prosperity Decade: From War to Depression, 1917–1929*, Harper Torchbook ed. (New York: Harper & Row, 1968), 249–51.

11. John Kenneth Galbraith, *The Great Crash: 1929*, Sentry ed. (Boston: Houghton Mifflin Co., 1961), 197.

12. Eckes, *Opening America's Market*, ch. 4, makes the case for Hawley-Smoot. Charles Kindleberger, *The World in Depression, 1929–1939* (Berkeley: University of California Press, 1973), 131–34, makes a measured case against it. For some contemporary reaction, see *NYT*, June 18, 1930.

13. *NYT*, Oct. 18, 1930.

14. Richard K. Vedder and Lowell E. Gallaway, *Out of Work: Unemployment and Government in Twentieth-Century America* (New York: Holmes and Meier, 1993), 77; *NYT*, Nov. 5, 9, 1930.

15. *NYT*, Sept. 14, 1930.

16. *NYT*, Oct. 14, 1930.

17. Peter Dewey, *War and Progress: Britain, 1914–1945* (London and New York: Longman, 1997), 205, 255.

18. Mowat, *Britain between the Wars*, 403–06.

19. This paragraph draws with thanks on the separate work of two Ohio University graduate students, Meredith Heinz and Bradley Merritt.

20. Richard Lowitt, *George W. Norris: The Persistence of a Progressive, 1913–1933* (Urbana: University of Illinois Press, 1971), 457–65.

21. Martin L. Fausold, *The Presidency of Herbert C. Hoover* (Lawrence: University Press of Kansas, 1985),142.

22. Kenneth S. Davis, *FDR: The New York Years* (New York: Random House, 1944), ch. 8.

2. Plumbing the Depths

1. Mary Lee, "Hitler in Action: The Voice of the Mob," *NYT Magazine* (Sept. 11, 1932), 4, 17.

2. On Brüning's economic policy, see Hans Mommsen, *The Rise and Fall of Weimar Democracy*, trans., Elborg Forster and Larry Eugene Jones (Chapel Hill: University of North Carolina Press, 1996), ch. 10; Michael Farber, "The Twilight of German Capitalism," *New Republic* (Feb. 10, 1932), 338–40; *NYT*, Dec. 13, 1931 (Carl Pueckler).

3. Alois Pfaller and Wolfgang Teubert in *The Nazis: A Warning from History* (British Broadcasting Company, 1997).

4. See, e.g., Harold Callender, "Hindenburg Links the Two Germanys," *NYT Magazine* (Feb. 21, 1932), 13, 20, and Emil Lengyel, "Three Men of Destiny, Iron Rulers All," *ibid.* (Jan. 29, 1933), 8–9.

5. Hitler quoted in Alan Bullock, *Hitler and Stalin: Parallel Lives* (New York: Alfred A. Knopf, 1992), 255.

6. On the Berlin rally, see *NYT*, Feb. 28, 1932; for the campaign more generally,

Bullock, *Hitler and Stalin*, 240–42. On early journalistic impressions of Hitler, William C. White, "Adolf Hitler, the Man and His Program," *NYT Book Review* (March 6, 1932), 5, 21.

7. Mommsen, *Rise and Fall of Weimar Democracy*, 411–14; *NYT*, May 1, 1932 (John MacCormac).

8. Harold Callender, "German Contrasts: Order and Disorder," *NYT Magazine* (April 10, 1932), 6, 20; *NYT*, March 6 ("Reich Carries On"), April 24 (Hugh Jedell), May 15 (Jedell), 1932.

9. For a convenient graphic representation of the ups and downs of employment, see Richard J. Overy, *The Penguin Historical Atlas of the Third Reich* (London: Penguin Books, 1996), 17.

10. These and subsequent paragraphs are heavily based on Mommsen, *Rise and Fall of Weimar Democracy*, chs. 11–12, and Eberhard Kolb, *The Weimar Republic*, trans. P. S. Falla (London: Unwin Hyman, 1988), 96–126, 179–96.

11. *NYT*, July 3 (Jedell), 10 (Edwin James), 17, 1932.

12. *NYT*, July 10 (Emil Lengyel), 31 (Birchall, James, Jedell, Guido Enderis, and other stories), 1932; Mary Lee, "Hitler in Action: The Voice of the Mob," *NYT Magazine* (Sept. 11, 1932), 4,17.

13. Kolb, *Weimar Republic*, 194–95.

14. Mommsen, *Rise and Fall of Weimar Democracy*, 458–70, Bullock, *Hitler and Stalin*, 246–48. See also *NYT*, Aug. 7 (James, Jedell, Augur), 14 (Birchall), 1932.

15. Mommsen, *Rise and Fall of Weimar Democracy*, 471–75; *NYT*, Aug. 14 (Augur), 21 (Ferdinand Kuhn), 28, (Birchall; Hans Luther), 1932.

16. *NYT*, Aug. 28 (Birchall and "Hindenburg Urges . . ."), Sept. 18 (Birchall), 1932; Mommsen, *Rise and Fall of Weimar Democracy*, 467–71.

17. *NYT*, Sept. 25, 1932 (Callender).

18. *NYT*, Oct. 16 (Enderis), 23 (Enderis), Nov. 6, 1932 (Birchall), 1932; Overy, *Penguin Historical Atlas of the Third Reich*, 16–17.

19. Kolb, *The Weimar Republic*, 194–95.

20. Mommsen, *Rise and Fall of Weimar Democracy*, 484–89.

21. *NYT*, Dec. 18 (editorial), Dec. 25 ("Germany Enjoys Strifeless Yule"), 1932, Jan. 1, 1932 (Enderis). See also Frederick T. Birchall, "Hindenburg and Hitler: An Epic Duel," *NYT Magazine*, Dec. 18, 1932, 3, 17, and Joseph Shaplen, "Germany Struggles in the Grip of Reactionary Forces," *NYT Book Review* (Jan. 8, 1933), 3 [rev. of Edgar Ansell Mowrer, *Germany Puts the Clock Back*].

22. Mommsen, *Rise and Fall of Weimar Democracy*, 490–531.

23. Henry Ashby Turner, Jr., *Hitler's Thirty Days to Power* (Reading, MA: Addison Wesley, 1996), ch. 7.

24. Philip Williamson, *Stanley Baldwin: Conservative Leadership and National Values* (Cambridge: Cambridge University Press, 1999), 83–85. This is by far the most impressive and perceptive interpretation of Baldwin, but for a thorough narrative, the standard remains Keith Middlemas and John Barnes, *Baldwin: A Biography* (New York: The Macmillan Co., 1970). See also the insightful biographical article by Thomas Jones in L. G. Wickham Legg and E. T. Williams, eds., *Dictionary of National Biography* (London: Oxford University Press, 1959), 43–51, and Clair Price, "A Statesman Who Personifies John Bull," *NYT Magazine* (March 12, 1933), 6, 17.

25. Wickham Steed, "The Dearth of British Leadership," *Current History* (Nov. 1933), 137–42.

26. David Dutton, *Neville Chamberlain* (London: Arnold, 2001), 31.

27. Keith Feiling, *The Life of Neville Chamberlain* (London: Macmillan, 1946), 1; see also Ian Macleod, *Neville Chamberlain* (New York: Atheneum, 1962).

28. Charles Loch Mowat, *Britain between the Wars, 1918–1940* (Chicago: University of Chicago Press, 1955), 415–17.

29. *NYT*, Jan. 3 (Augur), 17 (Callender), Feb. 7 (Kuhn), March 13 (Augur), 1932.

30. Philip Hoare, *Noel Coward: A Biography* (New York: Simon & Schuster, 1996), 228–29, 231–36; *NYT*, Sept. 11, 1932, Jan. 6, 12, 15, March 5, 1933.

31. Harold Callender, "Britain Fights on the Economic Front," *NYT Magazine*, April 24, 1932, 3, 20; *NYT*, Jan. 17 (*Punch* cartoon), Feb. 28 ("British Duke Sells His Coronet . . ."), March 20 ("Travel by Britons . . ."; Selden feature article).

32. *NYT*, March 20, 1932 (Selden feature article); Feiling, *Neville Chamberlain*, ch. 14.

33. H. M. Brailsford, "The Myth of England's Recovery," *New Republic* (July 20, 1932), 251–53, is probably too condemnatory of the National program, but clearly accurate in its debunking of the claim of recovery and perceptive in the contrasts it makes with the American situation. The classic exposition of the straitened conditions of life in the British North is George Orwell, *The Road to Wigan Pier* (London: Victor Gollancz, 1937; U.S. ed., San Diego: Harcourt Brace & Company, 1958).

34. Charles Loch Mowat, *Britain between the Wars, 1918–1940* (Chicago: University of Chicago Press, 1955), 480–86.

35. *NYT*, Aug. 28, 30, Sept. 4, 1932; "Lancashire Cotton Weavers' Strike and Terms of Settlement," *Monthly Labor Review* (Nov. 1932), 1113–18. See *NYT*, Nov. 6, 1932, for subsequent labor unrest. On the plight of the cotton industry generally, see Mowat, *Britain between the Wars*, 271–74, 281–83.

36. *NYT*, Nov. 6, 1932 (esp. Selden art.); Keith Laybourne, *Britain on the Breadline* (Wolfeboro Falls, NH: Alan Sutton, 1990), ch. 9, for a brief account of British fascism.

37. *NYT*, Sept. 14 (Joad), Nov. 6 (Lansbury), 1932.

38. Walter Runcilman ("Quotation Marks" columns), *NYT*, May 1, 1932.

39. *NYT*, July 17, 1932 (Augur; Sect. 8, "The Empire and the Issues at Ottawa"); on de Valera's intentions, see esp. *NYT*, March 27 (Kuhn), April 3 ("Augur"), June 19 ("De Valera's Note Irritates Britain"), and Claire Price, "Ireland Revives Her Old Dream," *NYT Magazine* (May 1, 1932), 1–2, 22.

40. See, e.g., numerous articles in *NYT*, July 24 (Selden, James), 31 (Selden; editorial), Aug. 7 (Shaplen), 14 (editorial), 21 (Selden, Shaplen, related non-byline items, editorial), 1932; "While Ottawa Achieved Little, It May Have Started Something," *Business Week* (Aug. 24, 1932), 20–21; "We Lose More British Trade Than Canadian by New Tariffs," *ibid.* (Oct. 26, 1932), 24–25; Mowat, *Britain between the Wars*, 417–19; Feiling, *Neville Chamberlain*, 211–16.

41. On MacDonald and Simon, see *NYT*, Oct. 16, 1932 (Charles Selden), and Feiling, *Neville Chamberlain*, 249, as well as the Kenworthy article, below. On the French-British relationship, see e.g., *NYT*, April 3 (Edwin L. James, P. J. Philip), June 12 (P. J. Philip), July 31 ("Augur"), 1932, Andre Siegfried, "England and France: A Vivid Contrast," *NYT Magazine*, July 24, 1932, 2–3, 14–15, and P. J. Philip, "A

Changed France Stresses Friendship," *ibid.*, Aug. 7, 1932, 2–3, 14. On Japan, see e.g., *NYT*, Jan. 3 ("Augur"), 1932; J. M. Kenworthy, "Where Britain and America Disagree," *Current History* (Dec. 1932), 266–72; and Martin L. Fausold, *The Presidency of Herbert Hoover* (Lawrence: University Press of Kansas, 1985), 184–85.

42. This controversy can be followed conveniently through *NYT.* See especially *NYT*, Dec. 4 (Edwin James, Charles Selden), 11 (James, "Augur"), 25 (James), 1932, Jan. 1 ("Augur," Selden). Harold Callender, "Again John Bull Eyes Uncle Sam," *NYT Magazine*, Dec. 18, 1932, 1–2, intelligently explores British-American relations.

43. John Maynard Keynes in *The Times* (London), March 13–16, 1933; Robert Skidelsky, *John Maynard Keynes: The Economist as Savior, 1920–1937* (New York: Allen Lane/The Penguin Press, 1994), ch. 13, esp. 459–75.

44. Macleod, *Neville Chamberlain,* 167.

3. Power Shift

1. William N. Macfarlane, *The Magic City of Egypt* (El Paso: Complete Printing, 1991), ch. 9. This is a useful, if somewhat unsystematic, history of Johnston City, Illinois, written by a town native and former professor of business.

2. Macfarlane, *Magic City of Egypt,* 130–32.

3. *Ibid.,* v, 141–43.

4. Jerold Simmons, "Dawson County Responds to the New Deal," in Bernard Sternsher, ed., *Hope Restored: How the New Deal Worked in Town and Country* (Chicago: Ivan R. Dee, 1999), 221–42 [originally published in *Nebraska History,* (Spring, 1981), 47–72].

5. David L. Davies, "Impoverished Politics: The New Deal's Impact on City Government in Providence, Rhode Island," in Sternsher, ed., *Hope Restored,* 57–73, quote on p. 60 [originally published in *Rhode Island History,* 42 (Aug. 1983), 86–100].

6. Davies, "Impoverished Politics," esp. 60–64.

7. Lyle W. Dorsett, "Kansas City and the New Deal," in John Braeman, Robert Bremner, and David Brody, eds., *The New Deal: The State and Local Levels* (Columbus: Ohio State University Press, 1975), 407–19; Roger Biles, "The Persistence of the Past: Memphis in the Great Depression," in Sternsher, ed., *Hope Restored,* 131–60 [originally published in the *Journal of Southern History* (May 1986), 183–212].

8. Harvard Stikoff, *A New Deal for Blacks* (New York: Oxford University Press, 1978), 39; Rita Werner Gordon, "The Change in Political Alignment of Chicago's Negroes During the New Deal," *Journal of American History,* 56 (Dec. 1969), 584–603, 591; Randy J. Sparks, "'Heavenly Houston' or 'Hellish Houston'? Black Unemployment and Relief Efforts, 1929–1936," in Sternsher, ed., *Hope Restored,* 182–95.

9. *NYT*, Dec. 23, 1932.

10. Alonzo L. Hamby, *Man of the People: A Life of Harry S. Truman* (New York: Oxford University Press, 1995), 162–67.

11. *NYT*, Oct. 28, 1932, for AFL estimate; Richard K. Vedder and Lowell Gallaway, *Out of Work: Unemployment and Government in Twentieth-Century America* (New York: Holmes & Meier, 1933), 77, for retrospective estimates.

12. Herbert Hoover, *The Memoirs of Herbert Hoover: [vol. 3] The Great Depression, 1929–1941* (New York: The Macmillan Co., 1952), 334–35 (hereafter, Hoover, *Memoirs*, III); Martin L. Fausold, *The Presidency of Herbert C. Hoover* (Lawrence: University Press of Kansas, 1985), 116–18; Arthur Schlesinger, Jr., *The Crisis of the Old Order, 1919–1933* (Boston: Houghton Mifflin, 1957), 181–83; *NYT*, Aug. 14, 1932, for details of Harriman plan.

13. Fausold, *Presidency of Herbert C. Hoover*, ch. 6, incisively surveys Hoover's thinking; quote on 154.

14. David E. Finley, Assistant to the Secretary of the Treasury, makes the case for the Hoover program as a coherent plan of attack in *NYT*, Feb. 21, 1932.

15. Albert U. Romasco, *The Poverty of Abundance: Hoover, the Nation, the Depression* (New York: Oxford University Press, 1965), 191; Thomas Kessner, *Fiorello La Guardia and the Making of Modern New York* (New York: McGraw-Hill, 1989), 183; *NYT*, July 23, 1932; Richard Lowitt, *George W. Norris: The Persistence of a Progressive, 1913–1933* (Urbana: University of Illinois Press, 1971), 497–98.

16. Romasco, *Poverty of Abundance*, ch. 6; Eliot A. Rosen, *Hoover, Roosevelt, and the Brains Trust: From Depression to New Deal* (New York: Columbia University Press, 1977), 55–57.

17. David Kennedy, *Freedom from Fear: The American People in Depression and War, 1929–1945* (New York: Oxford University Press, 1999), 57–58.

18. Hoover message quoted in *NYT*, Dec. 9, 1931; "So This Is a Social Triumph!" *Christian Century* (April 20, 1932), 500.

19. Fausold, *Presidency of Herbert C. Hoover*, 140, 158–61.

20. Rosen, *Hoover, Roosevelt, and the Brains Trust*, 289–92.

21. *NYT*, July 2, 1932.

22. *NYT*, June 28, 29, Aug. 18 (ed.), Sept. 16, 1932; Fausold, *Presidency of Herbert C. Hoover*, 162–63; Arthur M. Schlesinger, Jr., *Crisis of the Old Order*, 236–39.

23. For the origins of the relief act, see Patrick J. Maney, *"Young Bob" La Follette: A Biography of Robert M. La Follette, 1895–1953* (Columbia: University of Missouri Press, 1978), 93–101; J. Joseph Huthmacher, *Senator Robert F. Wagner and the Rise of Urban Liberalism* (New York: Atheneum, 1968), 92–101. The act's provisions are summarized somewhat confusingly in *NYT*, July 22, 1932; *NYT*, July 28, 1932; Romasco, *Poverty of Abundance*, 223–27; Schlesinger, *Crisis of the Old Order*, 241.

24. Fausold, *Presidency of Herbert Hoover*, 125–29, 195, 207–08; Hoover, *Memoirs*, III, 318–22.

25. Ernest Angell, "The Veterans versus the Country," *Harper's* (August 1932), 257–66; "All Uproarious on the Bonus Front," *Literary Digest* (April 23, 1932), 5–6; Walter Davenport, "But the Dead Don't Vote," *Collier's* (June 11, 1932), 10–11, 46–48; "The Veterans and the Federal Treasury," *Christian Century* (April 20, 1932), 500; "The Soldier Racket," *ibid.* (May 11, 1932), 598–99; *NYT*, June 5, 1932.

26. *NYT*, May 30, 31, 1932; "'On to Washington' With the Bonus Hikers," *Literary Digest* (June 11, 1932), 8.

27. "The 'Ghost Parade' of the Bonus Seekers," *Literary Digest* (June 18, 1932), 6–7; *NYT*, May 31, 1932.

28. *NYT*, June 15, 16, 1932; "Approval of the Bonus Bill Defeat," *Literary Digest* (July 2, 1932), 9.

29. *NYT,* July 3, 13, 17, 21, 26, 1932; Schlesinger, *Crisis of the Old Order,* 260–62.

30. D. Clayton James, *The Years of MacArthur: Volume I, 1880–1941* (Boston: Houghton Mifflin, 1970), 382–95.

31. James, *ibid.,* 395–405; *NYT,* July 29, 31, 1932. Donald J. Lisio, *The President and Protest: Hoover, MacArthur, and the Bonus Riot,* 2nd ed. (New York: Fordham University Press, 1994), 210–15, convincingly makes the case that MacArthur deliberately ignored Hoover's explicit, written orders. It is less successful in explaining Hoover's after-the-fact acquiescence.

32. *NYT,* Aug. 5, 14, Sept. 18, Dec. 25, 1932, for Olympics.

33. *NYT,* May 2, Oct. 23, 1931.

34. *NYT,* Aug. 29, Nov. 3, 1931.

35. Walter Lippmann, *Interpretations, 1931–1932* (New York: The Macmillan Co., 1932), 260–62.

36. For a good, and vigorously argued, interpretation of the three top Brains Trusters, see Rosen, *Hoover, Roosevelt, and the Brains Trust,* chs. 6–8. See also Joseph P. Lash, *Dreamers and Dealers* (New York: Doubleday, 1988), esp. ch. 8; Bernard Sternsher, *Rexford Tugwell and the New Deal* (New Brunswick: Rutgers University Press, 1964); Michael V. Namorato, *Rexford G. Tugwell: A Biography* (New York: Praeger, 1988); Jordan A. Schwarz, *Liberal: Adolf A. Berle and the Vision of an American Era* (New York: Free Press, 1987); and Raymond Moley (with the assistance of Eliot A. Rosen), *The First New Deal* (New York: Harcourt Brace and World, 1966).

37. Samuel I. Rosenman, ed., *The Public Papers and Addresses of Franklin D. Roosevelt, Volume One, The Genesis of the New Deal, 1928–1932* (New York: Random House, 1938), 624–27, 639–47.

38. *Ibid.,* 624–47, for key Roosevelt pronouncements. For Smith quote, Matthew and Hannah Josephson, *Al Smith: Hero of the Cities* (Boston: Houghton Mifflin, 1969), 438.

39. James MacGregor Burns, *Roosevelt: The Lion and the Fox* (New York: Harcourt Brace and Company, 1956), 138; Schlesinger, *Crisis of the Old Order,* ch. 28; convention ballot totals from Rexford G. Tugwell, *The Brains Trust* (New York: The Viking Press, 1968), 253n.

40. Krock in *NYT,* July 3, 1932.

41. Rosenman, *FDR, Public Papers, 1928–32,* 647–59.

42. *Ibid.,* 659–69.

43. For a quick summary of the contrasting positions, see *NYT,* Oct. 30, 1932. For Roosevelt's position, *ibid.,* Oct. 23, 1932 (text of Louisville speech), and *FDR, Public Papers, 1928–32,* 669–80 (Columbus, Ohio, speech, Aug. 20, 1932). For Hoover, see, e.g., *NYT,* Aug. 27, 1932, and Hoover's speech at Des Moines, Oct. 4, 1932, in *Public Papers of the Presidents of the United States: Herbert Hoover, 1932–33* (Washington: U.S. Government Printing Office, 1977), esp. 464–66.

44. *FDR, Public Papers, 1928–32,* 669–84, 723–42, 756–71, 795–812.

45. *Ibid.,* 693–723, 742–56.

46. *Ibid.,* 771–80, 786–95, 812–19; *NYT,* Sept. 29, 1932; Tugwell, *The Brains Trust,* chs. 37, 41; Rosen, *Hoover, Roosevelt, and the Brains Trust,* 352–56.

47. Tugwell, *The Brains Trust,* 504–05.

48. For employment figures, *NYT,* Oct. 28, 1932. For a sampling of the spectrum

of U.S.-French difficulties, see *NYT*, Oct. 11, 13, 15, 18, 19, 1931, Jan. 17, April 17, 24, June 19, 1932. On the tariff, *NYT*, Aug. 12, Oct. 25, 1932; Hoover speech in *Hoover, Public Papers, 1932–33*, 656–80, quote at 659.

49. *NYT*, Oct. 23, 1932.

50. U.S. unemployment estimate in Vedder and Gallaway, *Out of Work*, 77; British and German statistics in Charles Loch Mowat, *Britain Between the Wars, 1918–1940* (Chicago: University of Chicago Press, 1955), 433, and Richard Overy, *The Penguin Historical Atlas of the Third Reich* (London: Penguin Books, 1996), 126.

51. Keith Feiling, *The Life of Neville Chamberlain* (London: Macmillan & Co. Ltd, 1946), 219; FDR, *Public Papers, 1928–32*, 873–84.

52. Kennedy, *Freedom from Fear*, 65–69, 77; Susan Estabrook Kennedy, *The Banking Crisis of 1933* (Lexington: University Press of Kentucky, 1973), ch.1.

53. Kennedy, *Freedom from Fear*, 66; Frank Freidel, *FDR: Launching the New Deal* (Boston: Little, Brown, 1973), 181.

54. Kenneth Davis, *FDR: The New York Years, 1928–1933* (New York: Random House, 1985), 441.

55. Freidel, *FDR: Launching the New Deal*, ch. 8; Schlesinger, *Crisis of the Old Order*, 475–76.

56. William Starr Myers and Walter H. Newton, *The Hoover Administration: A Documented Narrative* (New York: Charles Scribner's Sons, 1936), 338–41, 360; Freidel, *FDR: Launching the New Deal*, 183–89.

57. Davis, *FDR: The New York Years*, 428–37.

58. Schlesinger, *Crisis of the Old Order*, 1. Whether Hoover said "rope" or "string" (as quoted later in *ibid.*, 481) is, mercifully, beyond the scope of this inquiry.

4. The New Deal

1. On this point, see Richard S. Kirkendall, "Franklin D. Roosevelt and the Service Intellectual," *Mississippi Valley Historical Review*, 49 (Dec. 1962), 459–63, and Patrick D. Reagan, *Designing a New America: The Origins of New Deal Planning, 1890–1943* (Amherst: University of Massachusetts Press, 1999).

2. On Moley, see especially Raymond Moley, with the assistance of Elliot A. Rosen, *The First New Deal* (New York: Harcourt, Brace & World, Inc., 1966); Elliot A. Rosen's biographical sketch in Otis L. Graham, Jr., and Meghan Robinson Wander, eds., *Franklin D. Roosevelt: His Life and Times* (Boston: G. K. Hall, 1985), 259–61; and the perhaps overly acerbic treatment by Arthur M. Schlesinger, Jr., in *The Coming of the New Deal* (Boston: Houghton Mifflin, 1959), esp. 181–82.

3. For Berle, see especially Jordan Schwarz, *Liberal: Adolf A. Berle and the Vision of an American Era* (New York: Free Press, 1987), as well as Schwarz's sketch of Berle in Graham and Wander, *Franklin D. Roosevelt*, 24–25; and Beatrice Bishop Berle and Travis Beale Jacobs, eds., *Navigating the Rapids, 1918–1971* (New York: Harcourt, Brace & World, 1973).

4. Bernard Sternsher, *Rexford Tugwell and the New Deal* (New Brunswick: Rutgers University Press, 1964), 5; in addition to Sternsher's pioneering study, see also

Michael V. Namorato, *Rexford G. Tugwell: A Biography* (New York: Praeger, 1988); and Otis Graham's brief sketch in Graham and Wander, *Franklin D. Roosevelt*, 428–30.

5. Kenneth Davis, *FDR: The New York Years, 1928–1933* (New York: Random House, 1994), 270–71.

6. Samuel I. Rosenman, ed., *The Public Papers and Addresses of Franklin D. Roosevelt, Volume Two, The Year of Crisis, 1933* (New York: Random House, 1938), 11–16, for the formal, prepared text of the inaugural address. For description of the event *and* for the text as actually delivered, *NYT*, March 5, 1933.

7. Eleanor Roosevelt quoted in Arthur M. Schlesinger, Jr., *The Coming of the New Deal* (Boston: Houghton Mifflin Co., 1959), 1; Lippmann in Ronald Steel, *Walter Lippmann and the American Century* (Boston: Little, Brown and Co., 1980), 300.

8. Editorial reaction summarized in *NYT*, March 5, 1933.

9. Kenneth S. Davis, *FDR: The New Deal Years*, 43–45; FDR, *Public Papers, 1933*, 30–38, for an abridged transcript; *ibid.*, 38–45, for appended comments by Roosevelt and an article by Theodore Joslin.

10. FDR, *Public Papers, 1933*, 45–47.

11. FDR, *Public Papers, 1933*, 49–54.

12. Russell Buhite and David W. Levy, eds., *FDR's Fireside Chats* (Norman: University of Oklahoma Press, 1992), ix–xx (introd.), 11–17.

13. See, e.g., Schlesinger, *Coming of the New Deal*, 5, and Raymond Moley, with the assistance of Elliot A. Rosen, *The First New Deal* (New York: Harcourt, Brace & World, 1966), 177–80.

14. Anne O'Hare McCormick, "'Let's Try It!' Says Roosevelt," *NYT Magazine* (March 26, 1933), 19; Jules Sauerwein in *NYT*, March 26, 1933.

15. Patricia Clavin, *The Failure of Economic Diplomacy: Britain, Germany, France and the United States, 1931–36* (New York: St. Martin's Press, 1996), 43, and chs. 3–4 generally, delivers a deft treatment of the international context of the conference; Barry Eichengreen, *Golden Fetters: The Gold Standard and the Great Depression, 1919–1939* (New York: Oxford University Press, 1995), ch. 11, authoritatively covers monetary issues. For quotes, see FDR, *Public Papers, 1933*, 14; Davis, *FDR: The New Deal Years*, 122–23, 193–94; Buhite and Levy, *FDR's Fireside Chats*, 26.

16. These and the following paragraphs draw on Moley, *The First New Deal*, chs. 34–38; Davis, *FDR: The New Deal Years*, 130–31, 153–98; Schlesinger, *Coming of the New Deal*, chs. 12–13. See also Herbert Feis, *1933: Characters in Crisis* (Boston: Little, Brown, 1966).

17. Fairly full documentation of the Moley mission and the conference crackup can be found in Edgar B. Nixon, ed., *Franklin D. Roosevelt and Foreign Affairs, Vol. I: January 1933–February 1934* (Cambridge: Harvard University Press, 1969), 248–54, 263–80. The text of the bombshell message is also in FDR, *Public Papers, 1933*, 264–66.

18. Donald Moggridge, ed., *The Collected Writings of John Maynard Keynes, Vol 21: Activities, 1931–1939* (New York: Cambridge University Press, 1982), ch. 3, esp. pp. 251–84, contains Keynes's *Daily Mail* articles, June 20, 27, July 4, 14, 27, 1933, as well as other significant writings, including a radio dialogue with Walter Lippmann, June 14, 1933. See also the too brief treatment in Robert Skidelsky, *John Maynard Keynes: The Economist as Saviour, 1920–1937* (New York: Penguin Books, 1992), 480–82.

19. *The Secret Diary of Harold L. Ickes: The First Thousand Days, 1933–1936* (New York: Simon & Schuster, 1953), 58–59.

20. Ian MacLeod, *Neville Chamberlain* (New York: Atheneum, 1962), 174; Keith Feiling, *The Life of Neville Chamberlain* (London: Macmillan, 1946), 325, 371.

21. *NYT,* May 28, 1933, May 27, 1934.

22. *Official Guide Book of the Fair* (Chicago: A Century of Progress, 1933), 20; R. L. Duffus, "The Fair: A World of Tomorrow," *New York Times Magazine* (May 28, 1933), 1–3.

23. *Official Guide Book,* 123; Duffus, *ibid.;* John E. Findling and Kimberly D. Pelle, eds., *Historical Dictionary of World's Fairs and Expositions, 1851–1988* (Westport, CT: Greenwood Press, 1990), 266–74, 379 (attendance figures include both paid and gratis admissions).

24. *Official Guide Book,* 92.

25. *NYT,* May 21, 1933 (news story); Steel, *Walter Lippmann and the American Century,* ch. 24.

5. Recovery in One Country?

1. This and the subsequent paragraphs draw heavily on Jordan Schwarz, *The New Dealers: Power Politics in the Age of Roosevelt* (New York: Alfred A. Knopf, 1993), ch. 3, and James S. Olson's sketch in Otis L. Graham, Jr., and Meghan Robinson Wander, eds., *Franklin D. Roosevelt: His Life and Times* (Boston: G. K. Hall, 1985), 220–22.

2. John C. Culver and John Hyde, *American Dreamer: The Life and Times of Henry A. Wallace* (New York: W. W. Norton, 2000), is the fullest and most useful, albeit uncritical, biography of its subject.

3. *Ibid.,* ch. 7.

4. Frances Perkins, *The Roosevelt I Knew* (New York: Viking, 1946), 206.

5. Raymond Moley, with Elliot A. Rosen, *The First New Deal* (New York: Harcourt, Brace & World, 1966), 283, 353–55. See also Ellis W. Hawley's biographical article in Graham and Wander, *Franklin D. Roosevelt,* 218–19, and Schwarz, *The New Dealers,* ch. 4.

6. On the comparisons to war, see especially William E. Leuchtenburg, "The New Deal and the Analogue of War," in *The FDR Years: On Roosevelt and His Legacy* (New York: Columbia University Press, 1995), 35–75, Roosevelt quotes at 46, 50.

7. Norman Thomas article, *NYT,* June 18, 1933.

8. Arthur M. Schlesinger, Jr., *The Coming of the New Deal* (Boston: Houghton Mifflin, 1959), chs. 16–17, vigorously and effectively, if rather uncritically, summarizes the early relief programs.

9. Ickes article in *NYT,* Jan. 1, 1935 (year in review section).

10. Schlesinger, *Coming of the New Deal,* ch. 14; Russell Buhite and David Levy, *FDR's Fireside Chats* (Norman: University of Oklahoma Press, 1992), 43–44 (paragraph formatting altered in my quotation).

11. Keynes's letter appeared in *NYT,* Dec. 31, 1933, and is reprinted in Donald Moggridge, *The Collected Writings of John Maynard Keynes, Vol. 21* (London: Macmil-

lan, 1982), 289–97. For an acute examination of the shortcomings of the gold-buying policy, see Barry Eichengreen, *Golden Fetters: The Gold Standard and the Great Depression* (New York: Oxford University Press, 1995), 342–47.

12. See, e.g., W. Elliot Brownlee's useful summary of "Monetary Policy" in Graham and Wander, *Franklin D. Roosevelt,* 261–65, and the more broadly based analysis in Eichengreen, *Golden Fetters,* chs. 11–12. On the consequences of silver buying, see Charles P. Kindleberger, *The World in Depression, 1929–1939* (Berkeley: University of California Press, 1973), 234–35, and John M. Blum, *From the Morgenthau Diaries; Years of Crisis, 1928–1938* (Boston: Houghton Mifflin Co. 1959), ch. 5.

13. Douglas A. Irwin, "From Smoot-Hawley to Reciprocal Trade Agreements: Changing the Course of U.S. Trade Policy in the 1930s," in Michael D. Bordo, Claudia Goldin, and Eugene N. White, eds., *The Defining Moment: The Great Depression and the American Economy in the Twentieth Century* (Chicago: University of Chicago Press, 1998), 325–52, esp. 337–44; Kindleberger, *World in Depression,* 236–38.

14. For the origins of the AAA, Schlesinger, *Coming of the New Deal,* ch. 2, and Kenneth Davis, *FDR: The New Deal Years, 1933–37* (New York: Random House, 1986), 69–76 [hereafter Davis, *FDR,* III].

15. William E. Leuchtenburg, *Franklin D. Roosevelt and the New Deal, 1932–1940* (New York: Harper and Row, 1963), 74; Schlesinger, *Coming of the New Deal,* 64–67; Davis, *FDR,* III, 288–90.

16. Culver and Hyde, *American Dreamer,* 148–50, 250–51, 432.

17. Davis, *FDR,* III, 281–83.

18. On these points, see Theda Skocpol and Kenneth Finegold, "State Capacity and Economic Intervention in the Early New Deal," *Political Science Quarterly,* 97 (Summer 1982), 255–78, and Richard S. Kirkendall, *Social Scientists and Farm Politics in the Age of Roosevelt* (Columbia: University of Missouri Press, 1966), esp. introd. and chs. 1–4.

19. Gilbert C. Fite, *George N. Peek and the Fight for Farm Parity* (Norman: University of Oklahoma Press, 1954), sympathetically and definitively surveys Peek's life.

20. Kirkendall, *Social Scientists and Farm Politics,* ch. 6; Schlesinger, *Coming of the New Deal,* 49–59; Davis, *FDR,* III, 275–76, 279–80.

21. On the "purge," see in addition to works cited above Culver and Hyde, *American Dreamer,* 152–57.

22. *The Public Papers and Addresses of Franklin D. Roosevelt: Vol. 2, The Year of Crisis, 1933* (New York: Random House, 1938), 246.

23. Harold Ickes in *NYT,* Jan. 1, 1935 (year in review section).

24. On the cotton code, *NYT,* June 20, July 2, 10, 18, 1933; on slowness of other major codes, *NYT,* Aug. 14, 1933. For a summary impression at the end of 1933, Louis Stark feature article, *NYT,* Dec. 31, 1933.

25. See, e.g., *NYT,* Aug. 11, 19, 23, 30, Sept. 10, 13, 30, 1933, for articles re Johnson, Mrs. Wilson, speakers, slogans, and radio campaigns.

26. *NYT,* Sept. 13, 1933.

27. *NYT,* Sept. 13, 14, 1933; Schlesinger, *Coming of the New Deal,* 118.

28. *The Secret Diary of Harold L. Ickes: The First Thousand Days, 1933–1936* (New York: Simon & Schuster, 1953), 108–09; *NYT,* Oct. 1, 1933 (A. Krock column; roundup of editorial opinion on currency inflation).

29. Leuchtenburg, *Franklin D. Roosevelt and the New Deal*, 68. On the NRA generally, Ellis W. Hawley, *The New Deal and the Problem of Monopoly* (Princeton: Princeton University Press, 1966), introd., chs. 1–7, remains a fine overview.

30. *NYT*, July 30, 1933, for motor car code.

31. Walter Lippmann to John Maynard Keynes, April 17, 1934, in Moggridge, ed., *Writings of John Maynard Keynes, Vol. 21*, 305.

32. Irving Bernstein, *Turbulent Years: A History of the American Worker, 1933–1941* (Boston: Houghton Mifflin, 1969), 217–98.

33. Bernstein, *Turbulent Years*, 298–315; Bernard Bellush, *The Failure of the NRA*, 126–131; Martha Gellhorn to Harry Hopkins, Nov. 11, 1934, Hopkins Papers, Franklin D. Roosevelt Library, online at http://newdeal.feri.org.

34. Martha Gellhorn to Harry Hopkins, Nov. 11, 1934, *ibid.*

35. For Long and Coughlin declarations, view *Perspectives on Greatness: Dreamers and Dissenters* (Hearst Metrotone film documentary, 1963); more generally, see Alan Brinkley, *Voices of Protest: Huey Long, Father Coughlin, and the Great Depression* (New York: Alfred A. Knopf, 1982).

36. Richard Lowitt, *George W. Norris: The Triumph of a Progressive* (Urbana: University of Illinois Press, 1978), 34; Schlesinger, *Coming of the New Deal*, ch. 8; Otis L. Graham, Jr., *An Encore for Reform: The Old Progressives and the New Deal* (New York: Oxford University Press, 1967), 29, 66; Bellush, *Failure of the NRA*, 136–150.

37. Henry W. Francis to Harry Hopkins, Dec. 1, 1934, Harry Hopkins Papers, Franklin D. Roosevelt Library (FDRL), as reproduced at http://newdeal.feri.org.

38. *NYT*, April 21, 22, 23, 24, 27, 1934.

39. *NYT*, June 28, 29, July 16, Dec. 2, 5, 6, 7, 8, 10, 14, 1934, Jan. 27, April 18, May 22, 1935.

40. Bellush, *Failure of the NRA*, 161.

41. Theda Skocpol and Kenneth Finegold, "State Capacity and Economic Intervention in the Early New Deal," *Political Science Quarterly*, 97 (Summer 1982), 255–78, quote at 257.

42. Frances Perkins, *The Roosevelt I Knew* (New York: Viking, 1946), 225–26.

43. Moggridge, ed., *Writings of John Maynard Keynes, Vol. 21*, 322–29.

6. Triumph

1. William L. Shirer, *The Nightmare Years: 1930–1940* (Boston: Little, Brown & Co., 1984), 195; *NYT*, March 19, 1933 (Guido Enderis).

2. *NYT*, March 19, 1933 (Enderis).

3. Emil Lengyel, "Schacht Challenges the Nazi Hotheads," *NYT Magazine* (Sept. 1, 1935), 7, 12.

4. Thomas S. Baker in *NYT*, Feb. 5, 1933.

5. Hugenberg quoted in *NYT*, Feb. 12, 1933 (Guido Enderis).

6. Alan Bullock, *Hitler and Stalin: Parallel Lives* (New York: Alfred A. Knopf, 1992), 306–11; Ian Kershaw, *Hitler, 1889–1936: Hubris* (New York: W. W. Norton, 1999), 452–61; *NYT*, Feb. 19 (Frederick T. Birchall), 26 (news dispatch), March 5 (Birchall news and feature articles), 1933. On Hugenberg, Emil Lengyel, "Hugenberg:

Giant Shadow Over Hitler," *NYT Magazine* (Feb. 26, 1933), 7, 19. For an example of the underestimation of Hitler and his movement by observers who should have known better, *NYT*, Feb. 26, 1933 (editorial).

7. *NYT*, Feb. 26, Mar. 5, 1933; Bullock, *Hitler and Stalin*, 311.

8. Eberhard Kolb, *The Weimar Republic*, trans. P. S. Falla (London: Unwin Hyman, 1988), 194–95. Jedell, *NYT*, March 12, 1933. Bullock, *Hitler and Stalin*, 984–85, usefully sorts out the significant major and minor parties of interwar Germany.

9. On the flag, *NYT*, March 26, 1933 (Jedell).

10. On early Nazi anti-Semitic terror, as reported to the United States, see, e.g., *NYT*, March 12 (editorial)and Lion Feuchtwanger, *Kansas City Star*, March 20, 1933.

11. This event is well described in Bullock, *Hitler and Stalin*, 315, and Kershaw, *Hitler, 1889–1936*, 464–65. See also *NYT*, March 19, 1933 (Guido Enderis) on the Nazi use of the theme of national unity.

12. Kershaw, *Hitler, 1889–1936*, 467.

13. *NYT*, July 9, 1933 (news art. by Arnoldo Cortesi; editorial section art. by Guido Enderis), provides solid contemporary comment. For retrospective criticism, John Cornwell, *Hitler's Pope* (New York: Viking, 2000), and Daniel Jonah Goldhagen, *A Moral Reckoning: The Role of the Catholic Church in the Holocaust and Its Unfulfilled Duty of Repair* (New York: Alfred A. Knopf, 2002).

14. Kershaw, *Hitler, 1889–1936*, 495 for ballot language and evaluation; *NYT*, Nov. 11, 12, 13, 1933; Hitler and Hindenburg quoted in William L. Shirer, *The Rise and Fall of the Third Reich* (New York: Simon & Schuster, 1960), 211–12.

15. Kershaw, *Hitler, 1889–1936*, 495.

16. The story of the Night of the Long Knives and the events leading up to it is well told in numerous standard sources. On Röhm, see Joachim E. Fest, *The Face of the Third Reich* (New York: Pantheon, 1970; Da Capo Press ed., 1999), 136–48 ("Night of the Long Knives" quote, 146). The quotation from the Reichstag speech is in Bullock, *Hitler and Stalin*, 343.

17. Abbott Gleason, *Totalitarianism: The Inner History of the Cold War* (New York: Oxford University Press, 1995), chs. 1–2.

18. *NYT*, June 18, 1933 (Enderis).

19. *NYT*, June 19, 1933, for Hitler quote; Shirer, *The Rise and Fall of the Third Reich*, 256.

20. Shirer, *Rise and Fall of the Third Reich*, 249–52; Bullock, *Hitler and Stalin*, 325.

21. Shirer, *Rise and Fall of the Third Reich*, 234–40, deftly surveys the Nazi subjugation of the Protestant churches, albeit with perhaps too much emphasis on the enduring influence of Martin Luther's anti-Semitism.

22. In addition to Shirer, *Rise and Fall of the Third Reich*, 234–40, see Bullock, *Hitler and Stalin*, 324, and Ian Kershaw, *Hitler, 1936–1945: Nemesis* (New York: W. W. Norton, 2000), 39–41. For contemporary reporting on Protestant dissent and repression, *NYT*, Jan. 8, 11, Oct. 12, 1934, March 10, 17, April 27, July 1, 1935; Feb. 19, 1936.

23. In addition to the sources cited above, see contemporary reports in *NYT*, June 12, 1933; July 17, 24, Sept. 2, 1935 (pastoral letter), Feb. 12, 19, May 26, Aug. 24, 1936, March 15, 1937 (papal encyclical).

24. Kershaw, *Hitler, 1889–1936*, 479.

25. Shirer, *Rise and Fall of the Third Reich*, 244–48; David Welch, *The Third Reich: Politics and Propaganda* (London: Routledge, 1993), 30–34.

26. *NYT*, Nov. 4, 1932.

27. Stephanie Barron, et al., *"Degenerate Art": The Fate of the Avant-Garde in Nazi Germany* (New York: Harry N. Abrams, 1991), is an indispensable source on the Munich contrast. Hitler's words are from Shirer, *Rise and Fall of the Third Reich*, 244.

28. Arthur M. Schlesinger, Jr., *A Life in the Twentieth Century: Innocent Beginnings, 1917–1950* (Boston and New York: Houghton Mifflin Company, 2000), 105–06; H. J. Haskell, *Kansas City Star*, Aug. 11, 12, 1935 [followed by six other articles running through Aug. 18, 1934]; *NYT*, April 6, 1936, for retaliation against non-voters.

29. On the Nuremberg laws and the motives behind them, see Kershaw, *Hitler, 1889–1936*, 559–573.

30. On these issues, see the side-by-side articles by Hugh Jedell and Arnoldo Cortesi, *NYT*, Feb. 19, 1933.

31. See, e.g., Peter Gay's memories of his adolescence in Nazi Germany in Peter Gay, "My German Question," *American Scholar* 67 (Autumn 1998), 25–49.

32. Michael Burleigh, *The Third Reich: A New History* (New York: Hill & Wang, 2000), ch. 5; Kershaw, *Hitler, 1889–1936*, 486–87.

33. H. J. Haskell, *Kansas City Star*, Aug. 17, 1935.

34. Welch, *The Third Reich*, 30–34.

35. Kershaw, *Hitler, 1889–1936*, 529–30.

36. See, e.g., *NYT*, May 8, 1933 (F. T. Birchall).

37. On these points, and many others involving comparisons and contrasts between the Nazi program for Germany and the New Deal, see the path-breaking article by John A. Garraty, "The New Deal, National Socialism, and the Great Depression," *American Historical Review* 78 (Oct. 1973), 907–44.

38. H. J. Haskell, *Kansas City Star*, Aug. 14, 1935.

39. Bullock, *Hitler and Stalin*, 447.

40. David Schoenbaum, *Hitler's Social Revolution: Class and Status in Nazi Germany* (New York: Oxford University Press, 1966). On the "one-pot" meals, see David Welch, *The Third Reich: Politics and Propaganda*, 38, and illustrations 5–6; *NYT*, Oct. 14, 1933, is a contemporary notice.

41. H. J. Haskell, *Kansas City Star*, Aug. 15, 1935. An interesting and frequently revealing contemporary exposition of Nazi economic policy is Arnold Bergstrasser, "The Economic Policy of the German Government," *International Affairs* 13 (1934), 26–46. My thanks to Steven Remy for bringing this article to my attention.

42. Harold James, *The German Slump: Politics and Economics, 1924–1936* (Oxford: Clarendon Press, 1986), 355–57, quote on 357; Garraty, "The New Deal, National Socialism, and the Great Depression," 918–21, 926–27 (illustrations).

43. R. J. Overy, *The Nazi Economic Recovery, 1932–1938*, 2nd ed. (Cambridge: Cambridge University Press, 1996), 56; Sidney B. Fay, "The German Recovery Program," *Current History* 47 (Jan. 1935), 486–91.

44. See, e.g., Ludwig Lore, "The Little Man's Fate in Germany," *Current History* 46 (Nov. 1933), 143–50.

45. H. J. Haskell in the *Kansas City Star*, Aug. 14, 1935. See also stories in *NYT*,

April 26, 1933 (F. T. Birchall), April 1, 1934 (O. D. Tolischus), Sept. 13, 1935 ("U.S. to Raise Tariffs Against Reich . . ."), Jan. 2, 1936 ("In Germany 1935 Was Unsatisfactory Year"), Feb. 23, 1936 (O. D. Tolischus; "Hungarians Hurt by Reich"; "Reich Produces 46% of Its Own Motor Fuels"); and James, *The German Slump*, 387–97.

46. This and the following paragraphs on work relief draw heavily on Dan P. Silverman, *Hitler's Economy: Nazi Work Creation Programs, 1933–1936* (Cambridge, MA: Harvard University Press, 1998).

47. R. J. Overy, *The Penguin Historical Atlas of the Third Reich* (London: Penguin Books, 1996), 31; Claudia Koonz, *Mothers in the Fatherland* (New York: St. Martin's Press, 1988); *NYT*, July 7, 1935 ("German Women Accept New Role").

48. *NYT*, March 21, 22, 1934, for early Hitler declarations about work programs; James, *The German Slump*, 353 (Hitler quote); Silverman, *Hitler's Economy*, 245.

49. "Good-by to Lemons," *Time* (Aug. 5, 1935), 14; Josephine Herbst, "The German Underground War," *Nation* (Jan. 8, 1936), 41–43, as reproduced at http://newdeal.feri.org; Overy, *The Nazi Economic Recovery*, 60 (Table XV).

50. Tim Mason, *Nazism, Fascism and the Working Class*, ed. Jane Caplan (New York: Cambridge University Press, 1995), esp. ch. 7; Kershaw, *Hitler, 1889–1936*, 334–35, for early working class support of the Nazis.

51. Mason, *Nazism, Fascism, and the Working Class*, 269; Welch, *The Third Reich*, 56–59; Shirer, *Rise and Fall of the Third Reich*, 265–66, recounts the author's own observations of Strength through Joy as a foreign correspondent in Germany during the 1930s. For a generally approving comment on the program, see H. J. Haskell in the *Kansas City Star*, Aug. 15, 1935.

52. *NYT*, Feb. 12, 1933 (Guido Enderis) for auto show speech; Kershaw, *Hitler, 1889–1936*, 450–52; R. J. Overy, *The Penguin Historical Atlas of the Third Reich*, 44–45; Welch, *The Third Reich*, 57.

53. Borah quoted in *NYT*, July 9, 1934. Perhaps no journalist of note was so consistent in emphasizing the problems of the Third Reich than Edwin L. James, the influential managing editor and chief foreign affairs interpreter of the *New York Times*. See, e.g., columns by James in *NYT*, April 2, 16, May 14, June 11, July 30, 1933; June 17, 1934; March 22, 1936. James strikes one as fairly representative of an American sensibility that found the Nazi regime so unimaginable that its survival and acceptance by a majority of the German people seemed impossible. On the prospect of encirclement of the Nazi state, see also the article by Nicholas Roosevelt, *NYT*, July 9, 1933.

54. On preparations for the Olympics, see, e.g., *NYT*, Aug. 7 ("Nazis' Dread of Losing Olympics . . ."), Nov. 27, 1935 (Diana Rice), July 26, 1936 (separate articles by Arthur T. Daley Albion Ross), and John Kieran, "On Your Mark for the Olympic Games," *NYT Magazine*, July 26, 1936, 10–11, 16. The Riefenstahl documentary, *Olympia*, appeared in 1938. Frequently described as a propaganda film, it probably will seem to most modern viewers a remarkably straightforward depiction of athletic competition.

55. This description is taken primarily from Kershaw, *Hitler, 1936–1945*, 6–9. For the impressions of visiting Americans, see Shirer, *The Nightmare Years*, 231–38.

56. *NYT*, Aug. 16 (Frederick T. Birchall), 17 (separate stories by Birchall and Albion Ross), Dec. 29 (Arthur T. Daley), 1936.

7. Muddling Toward Recovery

1. Thomas Jones, "Lloyd George, David," in L. G. Wickham Legg and E. T. Williams, eds., *Dictionary of National Biography, 1941–1950* (London: Oxford University Press, 1959), 515–29, quote at 520.

2. Donald Moggridge, ed., *The Collected Writings of John Maynard Keynes, vol. 21, World Crises and Policies in Britain and America* (London: Macmillan, 1982), 239.

3. Robert Skidelsky, *John Maynard Keynes: The Economist as Savior, 1920–1937* (New York: Penguin Books, 1994), 26, 528–30.

4. "Small Beer," *New Statesman and Nation* [hereafter *New Statesman*] (Apr. 29, 1933), 524–25; "A Half-and-Half Budget," *Economist* (Apr. 29, 1933), 891–93; "The Economic Outlook," *New Statesman* (Jan. 4, 1936), 4–5.

5. Bentley B. Gilbert, *British Social Policy, 1914–1939* (Ithaca: Cornell University Press, 1970), 314–16; Charles H. Feinstein, Peter Temin, and Gianni Toniolo, *The European Economy Between the Wars* (New York: Oxford University Press, 1997), 172; Peter Dewey, *War and Progress: Britain, 1914–1945* (New York and London: Longman, 1997), 338.

6. Dewey, *War and Progress*, 256, 258.

7. *NYT*, April 29, 1934 (F. T. Kuhn, Jr.).

8. Victor G. Reuther, *The Brothers Reuther* (Boston: Houghton Mifflin Co., 1979), 83; "More Employment in Britain," *Economist* (Jan. 2, 1937), 5–6, for a detailed contemporary view of the contrast between the old and new economies.

9. Peter Clarke, *Hope and Glory: Britain, 1900–1990* (London: Allen Lane/The Penguin Press, 1996), 178; Reuther, *The Brothers Reuther*, 81–83.

10. Price examples from L. C. B. Seaman, *Life in Britain Between the Wars* (New York: G. P. Putnam's Sons, 1970), 48–50; cost-of-living information from Charles Loch Mowat, *Britain between the Wars* (Chicago: University of Chicago Press, 1955), 452.

11. Mowat, *Britain between the Wars*, 458–61; "Housing and Building," *Economist* (Jan. 2, 1937), 7; *NYT*, June 11, 1939 ("Half of Britain Rehoused").

12. *NYT*, May 2, 1937 (F. Kuhn, Jr.).

13. Dianne Diacon, *Deterioration of Public Sector Housing Stock* (Aldershot: Avebury, 1991), 9–12 (numbers from table on p. 12).

14. Mowat, *Britain between the Wars*, 506–10; Gilbert, *British Social Policy*, 197–203, 310. For a useful quick summary of the diverse New Deal housing efforts, see Joseph L. Arnold, "Housing and Resettlement," in Otis L. Graham, Jr., and Meghan Robinson Wander, eds., *Franklin D. Roosevelt: His Life and Times* (Boston: G. K. Hall, 1985), 187–89; "Housing in Britain," *Economist* (April 24, 1937), 192.

15. Keith Feiling, *The Life of Neville Chamberlain* (London: Macmillan & Co., Ltd., 1946), 242; Mowat, *Britain between the Wars*, 450–51; "London's Transport Problems," *Economist* (May 8, 1937), 23–25 [supplement].

16. Mowat, *Britain between the Wars*, 437–40.

17. Mowat, *Britain between the Wars*, 441–48; Alan Booth, "Britain in the 1930s: A Managed Economy?" *Economic History Review*, 2nd series, 40 (1987), 499–522.

18. For a contemporary view of policies re the pound and the sterling bloc, see

NYT, Oct. 3 (article re Chamberlain speech), 4 (editorial), 7 (H. Callender), 1934, March 17, 1935 (Callender). R. F. Holland, *Britain and the Commonwealth Alliance, 1918–1939* (London: Macmillan, 1981), ch. 8, is a useful survey of trading and financial issues. For an interesting case study, see also Holland, "Imperial Collaboration and Great Depression: Britain, Canada and the World Wheat Crisis, 1929–35," *Journal of Imperial and Commonwealth History* 16 (1988), 107–27. Thanks to James Waite for calling these works to my attention.

19. *NYT,* Oct. 3, 1934 (F. T. Birchall), Feb. 15, 1935 (C. Selden).

20. Gilbert, *British Social Policy,* 193. On widespread acceptance of the dole among the working class, see, e.g., F. T. Kuhn in *NYT,* Feb. 25, 1934.

21. For contemporary impressions see, e.g., C.P., "British Liberalism Shows Signs of Life," *NYT Magazine* (July 9, 1933), 13; *NYT,* Oct. 28, 1934 (Evelyn G. Kessel); P. W. Wilson, "Baldwin Is Called to the Helm Again," *NYT Magazine* (June 9, 1935), 6–7; "Mr. Baldwin Was Wrong" (editorial), *Kansas City Star,* June 19, 1935. For Baldwin's own words and ideals, Stanley Baldwin, *This Torch of Freedom* (London: Hodder & Stoughton, 1935).

22. Russell D. Buhite and David W. Levy, eds., *FDR's Fireside Chats* (Norman and London: University of Oklahoma Press, 1992), 61.

23. Feiling, *The Life of Neville Chamberlain,* 242. See also Mowat, *Britain between the Wars,* 448. Useful background material on the *Queen Mary* exists in numerous reference works. A good web-based resource is www.ocean-liners.com.

24. *NYT,* Nov. 26, 1934 ("Work on Super-Liner . . ."); *The Times* (London), Nov. 8, 1935 ("The Queen Mary").

25. *NYT,* Jan. 19 (Clair Price), May 28 (F. T. Birchall), 31 (Russell Owen), 1936; "The 'Queen Mary,'" *Economist* (Sept. 5, 1936), 425–26.

26. On the Jubilee and its meaning, see, e.g., Clair Price, "London Burnishes for a Jubilee Season," *NYT Magazine* (Apr. 14, 1935), 7, 21; Philip Gibbs, "To the King! The Empire Drinks a Toast" and Harold Callender, "Amid Turmoil, Britain Still Stands Firm," both in *NYT Magazine* (May 5, 1935), 2, 20, and 3, 21; *NYT,* May 5 ("London Is Joyous . . ." and editorial), 7 (F. T. Birchall); "George The Fifth: King-Emperor: 1910–1936," *Economist* (Jan. 25, 1936), 169; Mowat, *Britain between the Wars,* 532–33.

27. Baldwin speech in *The Times* (London), Jan. 28, 1936. See also Baldwin's similar but more incisive tribute in the House of Commons, *The Times,* Jan. 24, 1936.

28. On Roosevelt and calls for a British New Deal, see, e.g., *NYT,* June 24 ("M.P.'s Prefer Roosevelt"), Sept. 6 ("British NRA Plan Is Asked"), Nov. 26 (Augur), 1933, Mar 4 (C. Selden), March 21 ("Roosevelt Hailed by Lloyd George"), 1934, Jan. 13 (C. Selden), 20 (F. T. Kuhn), March 15 (MacDonald Receives Text of Lloyd George 'New Deal'"), 1935.

29. Clair Price, "In London, Too, the Blackshirts Clamor," *NYT Magazine* (Feb. 25, 1934), 6, 18; on uniforms, *NYT,* Feb. 25, 1934 (C. Selden); on the decision not to run candidates in 1935, *NYT,* Oct. 28, 1935. See also Harold Callender, "Mosley's Creed: A Revealing Interview," *NYT Magazine* (June 24, 1934), 3, 16.

30. *NYT,* Feb. 13 (editorial), March 10 (H. Callender); Feiling, *The Life of Neville Chamberlain,* 242 (Diary entry, March 8, 1935).

31. *NYT,* June 8 (C. Selden; editorial).

32. *NYT,* Nov. 13, 14, 1935 (both by C. Selden).

33. Baldwin quoted in *The Times* (London), Nov. 4, 1935; for other examples of election rhetoric, see *The Times,* Nov. 1–13, 1935.

34. *NYT,* March 17, 1933 (F. Kuhn, Jr.), provides an American interpretation. In addition to sources cited in the textual footnote, see Martin Gilbert, *Churchill: A Life* (New York: Henry Holt and Co., 1991), 513, and Graham Stewart, *Burying Caesar: The Churchill-Chamberlain Rivalry* (Woodstock and New York: The Overlook Press, 2001), 200–01.

35. A. J. P. Taylor, *English History, 1914–1945* (London and New York: Oxford University Press, 1965), 367; Mowat, *Britain between the Wars,* 422. Any election result is the outcome of numerous factors, but contemporary mainstream British comment clearly underscores the salience of the peace issue. Historians ignore such impressions at their peril. See, e.g., *The Times* (London), Oct. 24, 25, 27, 1933 (quote from Oct. 27 editorial), and "The Fulham Landslide," *Economist* (Oct. 28, 1933), 807.

36. On Simon as Foreign Secretary, see David Dutton, *Simon: A Political Biography of Sir John Simon* (London: Arum Press, 1992), chs. 6–8.

37. For Baldwin's speech and the reception to it, *NYT,* July 31 (C. Selden), Aug. 1 (Herbert Matthews, C. Selden, and numerous unsigned articles), 5 (H. Matthews), 1934.

38. "The Peace Ballot," *Economist* (June 29, 1935), 1476. See also news item and editorial in *The Times* (London), June 28, 1935.

39. Taylor, *English History, 1914–1945,* 319, 369.

40. *NYT,* Sept. 20, 1935 (editorial).

41. Peter Bell, *Chamberlain, Germany, and Japan, 1933–4* (New York: St. Martin's Press, 1996), 199; Taylor, *English History,* 370–73, for a prescient overview.

42. On the push for social spending and the equivocal attitude toward military increases, see, e.g., articles in *Economist* (Feb. 2, 1935) relating to housing and depressed areas and in *ibid.* (March 16, 1935) on defense spending v. collective security. On the radical clerics, *NYT,* March 9 ("Assails York Archbishop"), 25 (F. Kuhn), 1934.

43. Stewart, *Burying Caesar,* superbly surveys both Churchill's political career in the 1930s and the parliamentary politics of the time. I have drawn on it for his descriptions of Gretton (165) and Amery (34).

44. Richard Overy, with Andrew Wheatcroft, *The Road to War,* rev. and updated ed. (New York: Penguin Books, 1999), 367–69.

45. On the budgets and defense, see, e.g., *NYT,* March 4 (C. Selden), 11 (Selden; Augur), 13 ("Treaty Navy Bill"), 23 ("New Arms Outlay"), Apr. 22 ("Britain Has Funds"), 1934; May 2 (F. Kuhn), Sept. 1 (Kuhn), 1935; Feb. 28 (Selden), March 1(Selden), 8 (Selden), 1936. On attitudes re Germany and France, *NYT,* Jan. 16 (Selden; P. J. Philip), July 2 (Selden), 1935; March 8 (Augur), 1936. See in addition numerous articles on budget choices in the *Economist,* mostly during the second quarters of 1934–36.

46. The crisis is nicely summarized from beginning to end with the passion of a historian who lived through it in Mowat, *Britain between the Wars,* 542–46, 550–53, 556–63.

47. See, e.g., *NYT,* July 2 (Selden), 3 (Arnoldo Cortesi, Selden, Anne O'Hare

McCormick), 7 (F. Birchall, Selden); Anne O'Hare McCormick, "The Empire Spirit Stirs Britain," *NYT Magazine* (Sept. 15, 1935), 1–2, 8. The pieces cited above are two of the earliest with which McCormick launched a distinguished career as the *Times* chief foreign affairs analyst.

48. For Churchill's remark, *NYT,* Oct. 9, 1935.

49. Keith Middlemas and John Barnes, *Baldwin: A Biography* (New York: Macmillan, 1970), 970.

50. *NYT,* May 28, 1936; Middlemas and Barnes, *Baldwin,* 980–81.

51. *NYT,* March 8, Nov. 19, 20, 1936.

52. This account follows Middlemas and Barnes, *Baldwin,* 981–1005.

53. For the importance of nonconformist sentiment, see, e.g., *NYT,* Dec. 3 ("Topics" comment), 7 ("Workers Divided"), 9 ("Stamp Lays Crisis to Divorce"), 1936.

54. Coverage of the abdication crisis was intense in both the United States and Great Britain. The *New York Times* probably delivered a fuller and more analytical perspective than the English papers, but for authoritative and detailed, if formalistic and opaque, coverage of the words of notables and the proceedings of Parliament, *The Times* (London) remains definitive. For the themes outlined in this paragraph, a blanket reference to both these papers for the period Dec. 3–12 must suffice. Especially useful items are the summary feature "Crown or Cabinet?" and the more interpretive piece by F. T. Kuhn, *NYT,* Dec. 6, 1936, and the article on the Labour party attitude by Harold Laski, *NYT,* Dec. 7, 1936. On the undiscussed concern about Edward's solicitude for Germany, Middlemas and Barnes, *Baldwin,* 979–80.

55. For the importance of the weekend return to parliamentary constituencies, Middlemas and Barnes, *Baldwin,* 1012.

56. *NYT,* Dec. 12, 1936.

57. *NYT,* Dec. 11, 1936, for text of Baldwin speech and partial text of responses. Churchill quote from Gilbert, *Churchill: A Life,* 570; "Sceptre and Crown," *Economist* (May 8, 1937), 321–22.

8. Challenges

1. "Harry Hopkins," *Fortune* (July, 1935), 59–64, 126, 129, quote at 59; this is an excellent piece of contemporary interpretive journalism. On Hopkins, see also George McJimsey, *Harry Hopkins* (Cambridge: Harvard University Press, 1987), a work that primarily covers its subject's World War II years; Searle F. Charles, *Minister of Relief: Harry Hopkins and the Depression* (Syracuse: Syracuse University Press, 1963), after all these years still the best account of its subject; and June Hopkins, *Harry Hopkins: Sudden Hero, Brash Reformer* (New York: St. Martin's Press, 1999).

2. Robert E. Sherwood, *Roosevelt and Hopkins: An Intimate History,* rev. ed. (New York: Grosset & Dunlap, 1950), ch. 1, quote on p. 2.

3. George Martin, *Madam Secretary: Frances Perkins* (Boston: Houghton Mifflin, 1976), 121; Alice Rogers Hager, "Miss Perkins Talks of the Tasks Ahead," *New York Times Magazine* (May 7, 1935), 3, 17. For Perkins's own account of her life and career, Frances Perkins, *The Roosevelt I Knew* (New York: Viking Press, 1946).

4. "On the Dole: 17,000,000," *Fortune* (Oct., 1934), 55–60, 146–58, 182.

5. Arthur Schlesinger, Jr., *The Politics of Upheaval* (Boston: Houghton Mifflin, 1960), 517–20; Christopher M. Finan, *Alfred E. Smith: The Happy Warrior* (New York: Hill & Wang, 2002), 308–17; Herbert Hoover, *The Memoirs of Herbert Hoover: The Great Depression, 1929–1941* (New York: Macmillan, 1952), 454–55; George Wolf-skill, *The Revolt of the Conservatives* (Boston: Houghton Mifflin, 1952).

6. T. Harry Williams, *Huey Long: A Biography* (New York: Alfred A. Knopf, 1970), remains the authoritative account of its subject and the major source for the following paragraphs. For contemporary impressions, see, e.g., "Huey Long's Forty-four Laws," *New Republic* (Nov. 28, 1934), 63; "Huey Long," *ibid.* (Sept. 18, 1935), 146–47; Hamil-ton Basso, "The Death and Legacy of Huey Long," *ibid.* (Jan. 1, 1936), 215–18; Paul Hutchinson, "Concerning Huey Long," *Christian Century* (April 3, 1935), 791–94.

7. From *Perspectives on Greatness: Dreamers and Dissenters* (Hearst Metrotone film documentary, 1963).

8. Quotation from *ibid.*

9. Alan Brinkley, *Voices of Protest: Huey Long, Father Coughlin, and the Great Depression* (New York: Alfred A. Knopf, 1982), 173.

10. For some typical contemporary discussion of the Townsend Plan, see "Con-cerning the Townsend Plan," *New Republic* (Jan. 23, 1935), 305–06; "The Townsend Plan," *Christian Century* (Feb. 12, 1936), 254–56; "After the Townsend Plan," *ibid.* (April 15, 1936), 560–61; "Townsend Investigation Viciously Unfair," *ibid.* (June 3, 1936), 788. The Norman Thomas remark is from *Dreamers and Dissenters.*

11. Brinkley, *Voices of Protest*, ch. 7. See also Charles J. Tull, *Father Coughlin and the New Deal* (Syracuse: Syracuse University Press, 1965), and Sheldon Marcus, *Father Coughlin: The Tumultuous Life of the Priest of the Little Flower* (Boston: Little Brown, 1973).

12. Quotation from Schlesinger's brief but perceptive treatment in *Politics of Upheaval*, 23.

13. Marquis Childs, "Father Coughlin: A Success Story of the Depression," *New Republic* (May 2, 1934), 326–27.

14. "Father Coughlin's Program," *New Republic* (April 24, 1935), 299–300; Paul Hutchinson, "Heretics of the Air: I. Father Coughlin," *Christian Century* (March 20, 1935), 365–68; Hamilton Basso, "Radio Priest—In Person," *New Republic* (June 5, 1935), 96–98.

15. On Long, see e.g., Rose Lee, "Senator Long at Home," *New Republic* (March 30, 1934), 66–68; "Huey Proposes," *ibid.* (March 20, 1935), 146–47; Hamilton Basso, "The Kingfish: In Memoriam," *ibid.* (Dec. 18, 1935), 177. On Coughlin and Long, "The Churches and American Fascism," *Christian Century* (March 13, 1935), 327–29. A. B. Magil's characterization is in Magil, "Can Father Coughlin Come Back?" *New Republic* (June 24, 1936), 196–98. For Lewis and Swing, Schlesinger, *Poli-tics of Upheaval*, 88–91.

16. Williams, *Huey Long*, 760–61.

17. Schlesinger, *Politics of Upheaval*, ch. 5, treats the Fascist phenomena with intelligent balance.

18. John Dewey, *Liberalism and Social Action* (New York: Capricorn Books, 1963; reprint of 1935 original), ch. 3, quotes on pp. 62, 87–88, 90. R. Alan Lawson, *The Fail-ure of Independent Liberalism, 1930–1941* (New York: G. P. Putnam's Sons, 1971), ch. 2.

19. John Dewey, "The Future of Liberalism," *Journal of Philosophy*, 22 (1935), 225–30, quoted in Kenneth S. Davis, *FDR: The New Deal Years, 1933–1937, A History* (New York: Random House, 1986), 233. Schlesinger, *Politics of Upheaval*, ch. 10, remains an acute discussion of the intellectuals' dilemmas of the democratic left in the 1930s.

20. Schlesinger, *Politics of Upheaval*, chs. 6–8, is a masterful summary. Olson quoted in Robert Whitcomb, "Floyd B. of Minnesota," *Common Sense* (Feb. 1936), 18–22. See also Selden Rodman, "Floyd Olson: A Tribute," *ibid.* (Oct. 1936), 25–27, and "Revolt in the Northwest," *Fortune* (April 1936), 113–19, 178–90.

21. Schlesinger, *Politics of Upheaval*, ch. 9; Maverick quotation on p. 143.

22. Thomas Kessner, *Fiorello H. La Guardia and the Making of Modern New York* (New York: McGraw-Hill, 1989), 406; *NYT*, Nov. 16, 1935, for Olson talk. On the League for Independent Political Action, see Lawson, *The Failure of Independent Liberalism*, esp. ch. 1. Paul H. Douglas, "Public Ownership of Monopolies: What the Progressives' Demand Means," *Common Sense* (Nov. 1936), 15–18, discusses a common aspect of the various independent liberal platforms.

23. *NYT*, July 1 (J. Shaplen), 7, 1935.

24. *Public Papers and Addresses of Franklin D. Roosevelt: Volume Four: The Court Disapproves, 1935* (New York: Random House, 1938), 26–40. [Hereafter *Public Papers FDR, 1935*].

25. "No-Men," *Time* (May 4, 1936), 45–46. On Kent, see "Relief: 'I Don't Know,'" *ibid.* (Oct. 28, 1935), 12–13, and Kent columns ("The Great Game of Politics") in *Kansas City Times*, June 20, 22, 1935.

26. *Public Papers FDR, 1935*, 324–26; "Social Security by Any Other Name," *Fortune* (March, 1935), 82–87, 116, 118; Arthur M. Schlesinger, Jr., *The Coming of the New Deal* (Boston: Houghton Mifflin, 1959), 301–09, FDR quote at 308–09.

27. Keynes, "Agenda for the President," in *NYT*, June 10, 1934, and *The Times* (London), June 11, 1934, and letter to the editor, *ibid.*, June 23, 1934, in Donald Moggridge, *The Collected Writings of John Maynard Keynes: Activities 1931–1939* (London: Macmillan, 1982), 322–29.

28. For Humansville, author's experience; for Libby, William E. Leuchtenburg, *Franklin D. Roosevelt and the New Deal* (New York: Harper & Row, 1963), photos 15 and 16.

29. Russell D. Buhite and David W. Levy, eds., *FDR's Fireside Chats* (Norman: University of Oklahoma Press, 1992), 67–69.

30. Harold Ickes, *The Secret Diary of Harold L. Ickes: The First Thousand Days, 1933–1936* (New York: Simon & Schuster, 1953), 310–610 (March 5, 1935–May 25, 1936), sporadically documents the long-running feud. For a brief summary, Schlesinger, *Politics of Upheaval*, 343–51. My figures on the allocation of funds are from Arthur W. Macmahon, John D. Millett, and Gladys Ogden, *The Administration of Federal Work Relief* (Chicago: Public Administration Service, 1941), 2, 122.

31. *Public Papers, FDR, 1935*, 260–63; "The Presidency: Personal Problem," *Time* (July 1, 1935), 9; "Relief: Headlines and Deadlines," *ibid.* (July 15, 1935), 19–20.

32. *Kansas City Times*, June 18, 1935; "Relief: Schools v. Golf Links," *Time* (Sept. 23, 1935), 13–14; "Boondoggling," *New Republic* (Oct. 2, 1935), 1231–33. WPA statistics in this and subsequent notes from Donald S. Howard, *The WPA and Federal*

Relief Policy (New York: Russell Sage Foundation, 1943), Appendix Table 1 (pp. 854–57).

33. "Liquidate the W.P.A.!" *New Republic* (Jan. 1, 1936), 211–13.

34. *NYT,* March 17, 1935; Frank P. Vazzano, "Harry Hopkins and Martin Davey: Federal Relief and Ohio Politics During the Great Depression," *Ohio History,* 96 (1987), 124–39.

35. Alonzo L. Hamby, *Man of the People: A Life of Harry S. Truman* (New York: Oxford University Press, 1995), 206; "Relief: Fraud v. Fraud," *Time* (March 23, 1936), 21; Charles, *Minister of Relief,* 187–90; Schlesinger, *Politics of Upheaval,* 355.

36. Howard, *The WPA,* 127, for list of accomplishments.

37. For an eloquent survey of farm life without electricity and the impact of the REA, Robert Caro, *The Years of Lyndon Johnson: The Path to Power* (New York: Alfred A. Knopf, 1982), chs. 27–28.

38. "Electrical Elysium," *Time* (Aug. 3, 1936), 12–13; Schlesinger, *Politics of Upheaval,* 379–84.

39. Daniel Rodgers, *Atlantic Crossings,* 449–56.

40. Davis, *FDR: The New Deal Years, 1933–1937,* 352.

41. *Ibid.,* 352–54, 373–75; Blanche Wiesen Cook, *Eleanor Roosevelt: Volume 2, 1933–38* (New York: Viking, 1999), 139–44; Blair Bolles article, *Kansas City Star,* Nov. 2, 1936. For useful information and photos, http://www.arthurdaleheritage.org.

42. Schlesinger, *Politics of Upheaval,* 371–73; John M. Collins article, *Kansas City Star* (weekly farm ed.), Aug. 14, 1935.

43. *Public Papers, FDR, 1935,* 98–103, quote at 101. See also Schlesinger, *Politics of Upheaval,* ch. 17, and Jordan A. Schwarz, *The New Dealers: Power Politics in the Age of Roosevelt* (New York: Alfred A. Knopf, 1993), esp. chs. 7, 8, 10.

44. "The Congress: Black Booty," *Time* (March 16, 1936), 17–18; Lippmann quoted in Schlesinger, *Politics of Upheaval,* 322.

45. On this point, see Paul H. Douglas, "Public Ownership of Monopolies," *Common Sense* (Nov. 1936), 15–18.

46. "Marriner Stoddard Eccles," *Fortune* (Feb., 1935), 63–65, and Francis Brown, "The Storm Centre of the Banking Bill," *NYT Magazine* (May 5, 1935), 5, 15 are perceptive contemporary articles. Alan Brinkley, *The End of Reform: New Deal Liberalism in Recession and War* (New York: Alfred A. Knopf), 78–81, is a splendid brief sketch. For Eccles's own account of his life and the Banking Act, see Eccles, *Beckoning Frontiers* (New York: Alfred A. Knopf, 1951), esp. pt. 4.

47. The progress of the bill can be followed in *NYT,* Feb. 6 (ed.), 10, 11, 13, 14 (ed.), March 11 (ed.), 23, 24, April 17 (ed.), May 5 (H. Hinton), 19 (C. Merz), 26 (Eccles speech), 29 (O. Mills speech), 30 (O. Young testimony and ed.), June 2 (ed.), July 2 (ed.), 4 (ed.), 27 (A. Krock), July 29 (ed.), 1935.

48. Moggridge, *Collected Writings of John Maynard Keynes, 1931–1939,* 324.

49. Blum, *From the Morgenthau Diaries,* 324–26; Schlesinger, *Politics of Upheaval,* 569–70; *Public Papers FDR, 1936,* 630–34; Robert L. Gale, "Mellon, Andrew William," *American National Biography Online,* http://www.anb.org.

50. Schlesinger, *Politics of Upheaval,* 252–62, 274–90, incisively covers constitutional issues through *Schechter,* but should be supplemented with a good constitu-

tional history with wider perspective, such as Alfred Kelly and Winfred A. Harbison, *The American Constitution: Its Origins and Development,* 4th ed. (New York: W. W. Norton, 1970), ch. 27.

51. Barry Cushman, *Rethinking the New Deal Court: The Structure of a Constitutional Revolution* (New York: Oxford University Press, 1998), and G. Edward White, *The Constitution and the New Deal* (Cambridge: Harvard University Press, 2000), both underscore the complexity of New Deal constitutional issues within the context of the time.

52. In addition to sources listed above, see William E. Leuchtenburg, *The Supreme Court Reborn: The Constitutional Revolution in the Age of Roosevelt* (New York: Oxford University Press, 1995), ch. 2, for the railroad retirement case.

53. *Ibid.,* ch. 3, for *Humphrey's Executor.*

54. FDR Press Conference, May 31, 1935, FDRL, as reproduced at http://newdeal.feri.org.

9. High Tide

1. Quoted in Kenneth S. Davis, *FDR: Into the Storm, 1937–1940, A History* (New York: Random House, 1993), 5n.

2. Eleanor Roosevelt, "Women Must Learn to Play the Game as Men Do," *Red Book* (April 1928), 78–79, 141–42, and "What Ten Million Women Want," *Home* (March 1932), 19–21, 86, both reproduced at http://newdeal.feri.org.

3. Susan Ware, *Beyond Suffrage: Women in the New Deal* (Cambridge: Harvard University Press, 1981), esp. ch. 1.

4. Tamara Hareven's long essay on Eleanor Roosevelt in Otis L. Graham and Meghan Robinson Wander, eds., *Franklin D. Roosevelt: His Life and Times* (Boston: G. K. Hall, 1985), 360–67, remains a good introduction. Among the many works written on its topic, see especially Joseph P. Lash, *Eleanor and Franklin* (New York: W. W. Norton, 1971), and Blanche Wiesen Cook, *Eleanor Roosevelt,* 2 vols. in progress (New York: Viking, 1992–).

5. On Lewis in general, see Melvyn Dubofsky and Warren Van Tyne, *John L. Lewis: A Biography* (New York: Quadrangle, 1977), the big standard biography, and Robert Zieger, *John L. Lewis: Labor Leader* (Boston: G. K. Hall, 1988), an excellent brief synthesis. For a fine quick overview, see Zieger, "Lewis, John L.," *American National Biography Online* (Feb. 2000), http://www.anb.org.

6. "Miners Meet," *Time* (Feb. 10, 1936), 12–13, for this and the Spanish Pete story below.

7. Harvey Klehr, John Earl Haynes, and Kyrill M. Anderson, *The Soviet World of American Communism* (New Haven: Yale University Press, 1998), 48–68.

8. Arthur M. Schlesinger, Jr., *The Politics of Upheaval* (Boston: Houghton Mifflin, 1960), 270–74. The much-reproduced Arno cartoon can be found, among many others from the 1936 campaign, in "Campaign Cartoons," *Time* (Oct. 26, 1936), 14–15.

9. Kenneth S. Davis, *FDR: The New Deal Years, 1933–37, A History* (New York: Random House, 1986), 522–23; Schlesinger, *Politics of Upheaval,* 225–29, depicts

Corcoran as a rather more benign figure than many congressmen saw him. See, e.g., Joseph P. Lash, *Dealers and Dreamers: A New Look at the New Deal* (New York: Doubleday, 1988), 168–69, 213, 306–08.

10. *Public Papers and Addresses of Franklin D. Roosevelt: Volume Four: The Court Disapproves, 1935* (New York: Random House, 1938), 270–77; Schlesinger, *Politics of Upheaval*, 326–31.

11. Frank Kent in *Kansas City Times*, June 26, 1935; editorials in *ibid.*, June 25, 26, 1935; "New Rabbit," *Time* (July 1, 1935), 13; "Thrift, Hope & Charity," *ibid.* (Aug. 12, 1935), 12–13; Arthur Krock columns in *NYT*, June 23, 30, July 7, 14, 1935. For an unemotional defense of the bill in terms of the need for more federal revenue, see Roswell Magill, "The Too Well Remembered Man," *Fortune* (April 1935), 100–03, 204.

12. *NYT*, July 7, 1935 (T. Catledge); *Kansas City Star*, July 14, 1935 (T. Alford).

13. William E. Leuchtenburg, *Franklin D. Roosevelt and the New Deal, 1932–1940* (New York: Harper & Row, 1963), 154: David Kennedy, *Freedom from Fear* (New York: Oxford University Press, 1999), 276.

14. This distinction appeared as early as Basil Rauch's pioneering *The History of the New Deal* (New York: Creative Age Press, 1944), but has been most influentially stated in James MacGregor Burns, *Roosevelt: The Lion and the Fox* (New York: Harcourt, Brace, 1956) and Arthur M. Schlesinger, Jr.'s magisterial volumes on the Roosevelt presidency, *The Coming of the New Deal* (Boston: Houghton Mifflin, 1959) and *The Politics of Upheaval*.

15. Walter Lippmann, "The President's Responsibilities to Industry," *Vital Speeches of the Day* (June 3, 1935), 568–70, and "Genuine Recovery—And the Future?" *ibid.* (Aug. 26, 1935), 746–47; Ronald Steel, *Walter Lippmann and the American Century* (Boston: Little, Brown and Co., 1980), ch. 25.

16. Roy Howard to FDR, Aug. 26, 1935, and FDR to Howard, Sept. 2, 1935, in *Public Papers: FDR, 1935*, 352–57; "'Breathing Spell,'" *Time* (Sept. 16, 1935), 11–12.

17. Schlesinger, *Politics of Upheaval*, 500.

18. *Public Papers, FDR, 1935*, 379–86, 397–411, 424–25.

19. For WPA and relief numbers, Howard, *The WPA*, 854.

20. Schlesinger, *Politics of Upheaval*, 424–25; Robert Zieger, *The CIO, 1935–1955* (Chapel Hill: University of North Carolina Press, 1995), ch. 2; "Five Rounds," *Time* (Oct. 28, 1935), 12; "'Dear Sir & Brother,'" *ibid.* (Dec. 2, 1935), 14; "Miners Meet," *ibid.* (Feb. 10, 1936), 12–14; "Plunge for Roosevelt," *ibid.* (May 11, 1936), 17. Lewis quote in Selden Rodman, "Labor Leader No. 1," *Common Sense* (Jan. 1938), 8–12, 10.

21. Schlesinger, *Politics of Upheaval*, 425; George Q. Flynn, *American Catholics and the Roosevelt Presidency, 1932–1936* (Lexington: University of Kentucky Press, 1968), 208–14. Lizabeth Cohen, *Making a New Deal* (New York: Cambridge University Press, 1992), discusses the Americanization process and its political consequences with detail and nuance.

22. Raymond Wolters, *Negroes and the Great Depression: The Problem of Economic Recovery* (Westport, CT: Greenwood Publishing Corp., 1970), highlights the inadequacies of the New Deal recovery programs. Harvard Sitkoff, *A New Deal for Blacks: The Emergence of Civil Rights as a National Issue* (New York: Oxford University Press, 1978), provides wider coverage. Rita Werner Gordon, "The Change in the Political Alignment of Chicago's Negroes During the New Deal," *Journal of American History*

(Dec. 1969), 584–603, remains a useful case study. On Weaver as New Deal spokesman, Robert Weaver, "The New Deal and the Negro: A Look at the Facts," *Opportunity* (July 1935), 200–01. On Eleanor Roosevelt, e.g., Eleanor Roosevelt, "The Negro and Social Change" [address to the National Urban League], *ibid.* (Jan. 1936), 22–23, and Cook, *Eleanor Roosevelt*, II, esp. chs. 5–6, but also 138–40, 243–47, 254–57, 278–80, 291–93. For contemporary commentary, see, e.g., "Black on Blacks," *Time* (April 27, 1935), 10–11, and "Black Game," *ibid.* (Aug. 17, 1936), 10–11.

23. "Little Martyrs," *Time* (Sept. 28, 1936), 13.

24. Melvin G. Holi, *The Wizard of Washington: Emil Hurja, Franklin Roosevelt, and the Birth of Public Opinion Polling* (New York: Palgrave, 2002), 62–68; "Now and November," *Time* (Jan. 6, 1936), 12; "The Fortune Quarterly Survey: III," *Fortune* (Jan. 1936), 46–47, 141–157, esp. 47, 141–44.

25. Mason, *Harlan Fiske Stone*, 410.

26. *Public Papers and Addresses of Franklin D. Roosevelt, Volume Five: The People Approve, 1936* (New York: Random House, 1938), 45–50 [hereafter *Public Papers FDR, 1936*].

27. Schlesinger, *Politics of Upheaval*, chs. 25–26; *Public Papers FDR, 1936*, 191–92, 280–81.

28. Davis, *FDR: The New Deal Years*, 513–14, 617, 663; John M. Blum, *From the Morgenthau Diaries: Years of Crisis, 1928–1938* (Boston: Houghton Mifflin, 1959), 249–59.

29. FDR, Supplemental Budget Message, March 3, 1936, in *Public Papers FDR, 1936*, 102–07.

30. "Cushions Provided," *Time* (March 23, 1936), 23–24; "May Over Morgenthau," *ibid.* (May 18, 1936), 13–14; Blum, *Morgenthau Diaries, 1928–1938*, 321.

31. Marriner Eccles, *Beckoning Frontiers* (New York: Alfred A. Knopf, 1951), 259; Blum, *Morgenthau Diaries, 1928–1938*, 321–22.

32. For Robinson-Patman, Ellis W. Hawley, *The New Deal and the Problem of Monopoly* (Princeton: Princeton University Press, 1966), 251–54, 266–68. For Walsh-Healey, Martin, *Madam Secretary*, 379, and Perkins, *Roosevelt I Knew*, 253–54.

33. "Roosevelt: Radicals' Nemesis," *Common Sense* (June, 1936), 3–4

34. Schlesinger, *Politics of Upheaval*, 103–04, 595; "Death of Olson," *Time* (Aug. 31, 1936), 13–14.

35. Lyle W. Dorsett, *Franklin D. Roosevelt and the City Bosses* (Port Washington, NY: Kennikat Press, 1977), 49–60; Thomas Kessner, *Fiorello H. La Guardia and the Making of Modern New York* (New York: McGraw–Hill, 1989), ch. 9; John D. Millett, *The Works Progress Administration in New York City* (Chicago: Public Administration Service, 1938), 197 (Table 15) itemizes WPA expenditures for FY 1935–36 of $210.2 million. Total WPA spending for that period was somewhat less than $1.2 billion.

36. William E. Leuchtenburg, *Franklin D. Roosevelt and the New Deal*, 180; Smith film footage in *Dreamers and Dissenters*.

37. David H. Bennett, *Demagogues in the Depression: American Radicals and the Union Party* (New Brunswick: Rutgers University Press, 1969), 20; Leuchtenburg, *Franklin D. Roosevelt and the New Deal*, 182.

38. Donald McCoy, *Landon of Kansas* (Lincoln: University of Nebraska Press, 1966), chs. 1–10; *NYT*, June 7 (C. Michael), 14 (A. O'Hare McCormick), 1936.

39. Schlesinger, *Politics of Upheaval*, 583–84, for a magnificent description of this incident.

40. *Public Papers FDR, 1936*, 230–36; "I Accept," *Time* (July 6, 1936), 9–10.

41. "I Accept," *Time* (Aug. 3, 1936), 9–10.

42. *Public Papers FDR, 1936*, 566–73.

43. David Kennedy, *Freedom from Fear* (New York: Oxford, 1999), 282; Schlesinger, *Politics of Upheaval*, 637–38.

44. "Red Issue," *Time* (Sept. 28, 1936), 12–13; "Red Issue (Cont'd.)," *ibid.* (Oct. 12, 1936), 16–17; "Political Press," *ibid.* (Nov. 9, 1936), 12–14.

45. *NYT*, Oct. 1, 1936. *Ibid.*, Nov. 4, 1936, for survey of editorial comment on outcome.

46. McCoy, *Landon of Kansas*, chs. 11–13, quotes at 306, 314–15; Schlesinger, *Politics of Upheaval*, ch. 33, for emphasis on the overheated Republican rhetoric. *The Times* (London), Nov. 3, 1936.

47. *The Times* (London), Nov. 2, 3, 1936. *Time* magazine (Sept.–Nov. 1936) provides brisk and reasonably balanced coverage of the 1936 campaign.

48. Unemployment figures are the widely accepted AFL estimates; others vary, but not significantly, and show the same trend. For these and for relief jobs, which were generally not counted as employment, Donald Howard, *WPA and Federal Relief Policy* (New York: Russell Sage Foundation, 1943), 854–56. For workforce estimates and issues in counting the unemployed, Michael R. Darby, "Three-and-a-Half Million U.S. Employees Have Been Mislaid: Or, an Explanation of Unemployment, 1934–1941," *Journal of Political Economy* (Feb. 1976), 1–16, and Robert A. Margo, "Employment and Unemployment in the 1930s," *Journal of Economic Perspectives* (Spring 1993), 41–59. On the general economic climate, "Recovery and the Election" and "Industries Working at 'Capacity,'" *Economist* (Oct. 31, 1936), 207–08. For *New York Times* Business Index, *NYT*, Dec. 6, 1936. For cotton support, John C. Culver and John Hyde, *American Dreamer: A Life of Henry A. Wallace* (New York: Norton, 2000), 161.

49. "Polls," *Time* (Nov. 2, 1936), 14; "Last Guesses," *ibid.* (Nov. 9, 1936), 14; for dismissal of the *Literary Digest*, see, e.g., report by Washington correspondent, *The Times* (London), Nov. 2, 1936.

50. "Last Guesses," *Time* (Nov. 9, 1936), 14.

51. Zieger, *The CIO*, 39–40.

52. Samuel Lubell, *The Future of American Politics*, 3rd ed., rev. (New York: Harper & Row, 1965), 62.

53. Sitkoff, *A New Deal for Blacks*, 95.

10. Stalling Out

1. Nelson Lichtenstein, *The Most Dangerous Man in Detroit: Walter Reuther and the Fate of American Labor* (New York: Basic Books, 1995), 23.

2. Kenneth S. Davis, *FDR: Into the Storm, 1937–1940, A History* (New York: Random House, 1993), 165–66.

3. Davis, *ibid.*, 181.

4. David E. Lilienthal, "The TVA and Decentralization," *Survey Graphic* (June

1, 1940), 335–37, 363, 365–67, and *TVA: Democracy on the March* (New York: Harper & Brothers,1944).

5. Harvard Sitkoff, *A New Deal for Blacks: The Emergence of Civil Rights as a National Issue* (New York: Oxford University Press, 1978), 50–51.

6. Philip Selznick, *TVA and the Grass Roots: A Study in the Sociology of Formal Organization* (Berkeley: University of California Press, 1949).

7. Erwin Hargrove and Paul K. Conkin, eds., *Fifty Years of Grass Roots Bureaucracy* (Urbana: University of Illinois Press, 1984).

8. *The Public Papers and Addresses of Franklin D. Roosevelt, vol. 5, The People Approve, 1936* (New York: Random House, 1938), 634–42. [Roosevelt's pre-inaugural January 1937 papers are included in this volume.]

9. *Ibid.*, 642–57.

10. *The Public Papers and Addresses of Franklin D. Roosevelt. 1937 Volume: The Constitution Prevails* (New York: Macmillan, 1941), 1–6. For press coverage, *NYT*, Jan. 17 (O. E. Dunlap on radio coverage), 21 (A. Krock, F. R. Daniell, T. Catledge), 1937.

11. *NYT*, Jan. 21 (T. Catledge), 1937; "Mr. Roosevelt's Inauguration," *Economist* (Jan. 23, 1937), 165. See also the sympathetic editorial in *The Times* (London), Jan. 22, 1937.

12. See, e.g., *NYT*, Jan. 15, 1937 (editorial); *Kansas City Star*, Jan. 19, 1937 ("No Club on Court").

13. "Judiciary," *Time* (Feb. 15, 1937), 16–19.

14. For unemployment estimates and relief employment, Donald S. Howard, *The WPA and Federal Relief Policy* (New York: Russell Sage Foundation, 1943), Appendix I (854–57). On plans to decrease WPA enrollment, "Relief," *Time* (Feb. 8, 1937), 17.

15. Strike statistics in *Public Papers, FDR, 1937*, 273.

16. *NYT*, March 21 (H. Feldman), 28 (editorial), 1937.

17. See, e.g., the coverage in *Time* (Jan. 18, 1937), 17–19; (Feb. 8, 1937), 14–15; (Feb. 15, 1937), 19–21; (June 14, 1937), 13–15; (June 21, 1937), 18–20; (June 28, 1937), 11–14; (July 5, 1937), 9–11; (July 12, 1937), 17–19, and *NYT*, June 13, 1937 (F. R. Daniell). Robert H. Zieger, *The CIO, 1935–1955* (Chapel Hill: University of North Carolina Press, 1995), chs. 3–4, is a sound, if sympathetic, account.

18. *NYT*, Jan. 23 (editorial), 24 (press survey; A. Krock), 1937.

19. David Kennedy, *Freedom from Fear: The American People in Depression and War, 1929–1945* (New York: Oxford University Press, 1999), 319.

20. *Public Papers, FDR, 1937*, 20–21; Irving Bernstein, *Turbulent Years: A History of the American Worker, 1933–1941* (Boston: Houghton Mifflin, 1969), 494–96.

21. On the La Follette committee, see "Frightful Film," *Time* (June 28, 1937), 13–14; "Cops," *ibid.* (July 12, 1937), 17–18; and Jerold S. Auerbach, *Labor and Liberty: The La Follette Committee and the New Deal* (Indianapolis: Bobbs-Merrill, 1966), a model monograph. On dissatisfaction with the Wagner Act and Democratic law enforcement *NYT*, March 21, (A. Krock), March 28 (L. Stark), April 4 (A. Krock), 18 (H. Dorris, F. Belair, Jr., editorial), May 2 (F. Belair, Jr.), June 27 ("Right vs. Right"), July 4 (A. Krock), 1937.

22. David Robertson, *Sly and Able: A Political Biography of James F. Byrnes* (New York: W. W. Norton, 1994), 258–59.

23. Melvyn Dubofsky, "Not So 'Turbulent Years': Another Look at the American

1930's," *The New Deal: Conflicting Interpretations and Shifting Perspectives* (New York: Garland Publishing, 1992), 123–45.

24. Sidney Milkis, *The President and the Parties: The Transformation of the American Party System since the New Deal* (New York: Oxford University Press, 1993), esp. ch. 6; Davis, *FDR: Into the Storm, 1937–1940,* 20–28.

25. Milkis, *President and the Parties,* 114–15.

26. *Ibid.* 115–22.

27. Ronald Steel, *Walter Lippmann and the American Century* (Boston: Little Brown, 1980), 323–26; "Elucidator," *Time* (Sept. 27, 1937), 45–48.

28. *NYT,* Jan. 13 ("Plan's Opponents Rally in Congress"; editorial), 14 (editorial), 15 (editorial; A. Krock; "Defends Roosevelt Plan"), 17 (T. Catledge), 23 (editorial), March 9 (A. Krock), 1937; "New Tools for Uncle Sam," *New Republic* (Jan. 27, 1937), 371–72; "Second Objective," *Time* (January 25, 1937), 15–17; "'Pure, Plain Cussedness,'" *ibid.* (Aug. 9, 1937), 9.

29. *Public Papers, FDR, 1937,* 80–85, 209–18, 238–50, 252–58.

30. This and the following paragraphs draw primarily on Sitkoff, *A New Deal for Blacks,* 281–93.

31. Sitkoff, *A New Deal for Blacks,* 292–93.

32. *Public Papers, FDR, 1937,* 111–21 (Dem dinner), 122–33 (chat).

33. James MacGregor Burns, *Roosevelt: The Lion and the Fox* (New York: Harcourt Brace & Company, 1956), 299–300; *NYT,* Feb. 6 (lead story; surveys of editoral opinion and congressional reaction; editorial), 14, March 6, 7, 11, (editorials), 1937; *Kansas City Star,* Feb. 5, 1937 (use of "purge"). For the liberal viewpoint, "Curbing the Supreme Court," *New Republic* (Feb. 17, 1937), 31–32. Davis, *FDR: Into the Storm, 1937–1940,* chs. 2–3, covers the court-packing controversy clearly and in detail. For an authoritative analytical account based on many years of thought and research, see William E. Leuchtenburg, *The Supreme Court Reborn* (New York: Oxford University Press, 1995), chs. 4–5.

34. For British reaction, *NYT,* Feb. 6 (F. Kuhn, Jr.), 9 ("British Approval Grows"), 1937; for concern with rights, *Kansas City Star,* Feb. 28, 1937 (editorial).

35. *NYT,* March 7, 1937 ("Foes of Court Bill" and editorial).

36. James T. Patterson, *Congressional Conservatism and the New Deal* (Lexington: University of Kentucky Press, 1967), chs. 2–3, is especially useful for the congressional divisions on court packing.

37. *NYT,* May 23, July 11, 1937 (A. Krock columns).

38. "The Congress," *Time* (July 10, 1937), 10–11; *ibid.* (July 26, 1937), 10–13.

39. For quick sketches of Barkley and Harrison, Alonzo L. Hamby, "Barkley, Alben William," *Dictionary of American Biography, Supp.* 6, *1956–1960,* ed., John A. Garraty (New York: Charles Scribner's Sons, 1980), 34–36, and Martha H. Swain, "Harrison, Pat," *American National Biography Online* (Feb. 2000).

40. *Public Papers, FDR, 1937,* 338–42.

41. See, e.g., front-page stories in *Kansas City Star,* Sept. 17, 1937; Davis, *FDR: Into the Storm, 1937–1940,* 108–112.

42. *NYT,* July 25, 1937 (T. Catledge).

43. *NYT,* June 20, 1937 (R. Duffus).

44. John Culver and John Hyde, *American Dreamer: A Life of Henry A. Wallace* (New York: Norton, 2000), 169–70; *The Public Papers and Addresses of Franklin D. Roosevelt, 1938*, comp. Samuel I. Rosenman (New York: Macmillan, 1941), 421–26.

45. The fullest history of the FSA is Sidney Baldwin, *Poverty and Politics* (Chapel Hill: University of North Carolina Press, 1968).

46. *The Recovery Problem in the United States* (Washington: Brookings Institution, 1937). For discussion of the above, see *Kansas City Star* (editorial), Feb. 7, 1937, and George Soule review, *New Republic* (March 10, 1937), 143.

47. *NYT*, March 7 (editorial), 21 ("Another 1929?"; F. Belair), 28 (E. Bell), April 4 (editorial), 11 (A. Krock), May 2 (editorial), June 13 (E. Bell), Oct. 3 (H. Hinton), 1937; John M. Blum, *From the Morgenthau Diaries: Years of Crisis, 1928–1938* (Boston: Houghton Mifflin, 1959), 358–79; Barry Eichengreen, *Golden Fetters* (New York: Oxford University Press, 1995), 345–47, 386–87; Gene Smiley, *Rethinking the Great Depression* (Chicago: Ivan Dee, 2002), 118–20.

48. *NYT*, March 28 ("Curtailing PWA"), April 11 (L. Stark), 18 ("The Nation: Ways and Means"), 25 ("The Economy Drive"; A. Krock; T. Catledge; F. Belair), May 23 (F. Belair), June 27 (R. Post), 1937; "Relief: 600,000 Drop?" *Time* (Feb. 8, 1937), 17. WPA employment figures from Donald S. Howard, *The WPA*, 854–55; these figures do not include National Youth Administration clients.

49. Howard, *The WPA*, 855; Richard K. Vedder and Lowell E. Gallaway, *Out of Work* (New York: Holmes & Meier, 1993), 77.

50. "May in Cleveland," *Time* (May 16, 1938), 16–17.

51. Smiley, *Rethinking the Great Depression*, 188–123; *NYT*, Jan. 21, 1938 (W. Case).

52. On the Wheeler-Truman investigation, see Alonzo L. Hamby, "Vultures at the Death of an Elephant: Harry S. Truman, the Great Train Robbery, and the Transportation Act of 1940," *Railroad History* (Autumn 1991), 6–36.

53. Krock in *NYT*, Jan. 2, 1938; Lawrence quoted in Frederick Lewis Allen, *Since Yesterday: The 1930s in America* (New York: Harper & Brothers, 1939), 247; *Public Papers and Addresses of Franklin D. Roosevelt, 1938, vol. 7, The Continuing Struggle for Liberalism* (New York: Macmillan, 1941), 305–33 (message to Congress and FDR's retrospective remarks).

54. For Arnold, the antitrust program, and issues of larger context, see Brinkley, *End of Reform*, esp. ch. 6; Ellis Hawley, *The New Deal and the Problem of Monopoly* (Princeton: Princeton University Press, 1966), chs. 21–23; Richard Hofstadter, "What Happened to the Antitrust Movement?" in Hofstadter, *The Paranoid Style in American Politics* (New York: Alfred A. Knopf, 1965), ch. 6. For contemporary comment, see, e.g., *NYT*, June 19, 1938 (F. Barkley); "The Attack on Monopoly," *New Republic* (May 11, 1938), 5; Fred Rodell, "Arnold: Myth and Trust Buster," *ibid.* (June 22, 1938), 177–78; and Charles A. Beard, "The Anti-Trust Racket," *ibid.* (Sept. 21, 1938), 182–84.

55. Alan Brinkley, *The End of Reform* (New York: Alfred A. Knopf, 1995), 82–85, neatly summarizes the liberal argument. For Morgenthau's view, Blum, *Morgenthau Diaries, 1928–38*, ch. 9. For WPA levels and budget constraints, Howard, *The WPA*, 855, and *NYT*, Jan. 30, 1938 (R. Duffus).

56. John Maynard Keynes to FDR, Feb. 1, 1938, and FDR to Keynes, March 3, 1938, in Donald Moggridge, ed., *The Collected Writings of John Maynard Keynes*, vol. 21 (New York: Cambridge University Press, 1982), 434–39.

57. Russell D. Buhite and David W. Levy, *FDR's Fireside Chats* (Norman: University of Oklahoma Press, 1992), 111–23, 119 (quote); Brinkley, *End of Reform*, 82, 94–101.

58. Statistics from Howard, *The WPA*, 855.

59. *Public Papers, FDR, 1938*, 179–92; Milkis, *President and the Parties*, 122–24; James T. Patterson, *Congressional Conservatism and the New Deal* (Lexington: University of Kentucky Press, 1967), ch. 7, for an excellent summary of the congressional session; Lippmann quote, *ibid.*, 243.

60. "Primaries," *Time* (Sept. 26, 1938), 13.

61. Buhite and Levy, *FDR's Fireside Chats*, 124–35, 134 (quote).

62. J. B. Shannon, "Presidential Politics in the South—1938, II," *Journal of Politics* (Aug. 1939), 278–300, 288 (quote); Patterson, *Congressional Conservatism*, ch. 8.

63. Shannon, "Presidential Politics in the South—1938, II," 296–97; "The Presidency," *Time* (July 25, 1938), 7–8.

64. Culver and Hyde, *American Dreamer*, 176–79; Christiana McFadyen Campbell, *The Farm Bureau and the New Deal* (Urbana: University of Illinois Press, 1962), ch. 10; Richard S. Kirkendall, *Social Scientists and Farm Politics in the Age of Roosevelt* (Columbia: University of Missouri Press, 1966), chs. 12–13. For contemporary impressions, see the periodic articles by Felix Belair, Jr., in *NYT*, April 11, Aug. 15, Nov. 28, Dec. 5, 1937; agricultural opinion surveys in *ibid.*, May 15, Sept. 4, 1938, and *ibid.*, June 5 (J. H. Crider), Oct. 9 (L. Huston), 1938; "Second AAA," *Time* (Feb. 21, 1938), 19–20, and "White & Red," *ibid.* (July 18, 1938), 11–12; "Ache, Agony, Anguish," *ibid.* (Oct. 10, 1938), 10–11.

65. See, e.g., *NYT*, Oct. 23 (T. Catledge), Oct. 30 ("Campaign Finale"; A. Krock), Nov. 6 (L. Huston), 1938; "Campaigns," *Time* (Nov. 7, 1938), 9–10.

66. *NYT*, Nov. 13, 1936 ("GOP Groundswell"; G. Gallup); "The Congress" and "Elections," *Time* (Nov. 21, 1938), 12–15.

67. "The Congress," *Time* (Nov. 21, 1938), 12–13; *NYT*, Nov. 13, Dec. 25, 1938 (Krock); Patterson, *Congressional Conservatism*, chs. 9–10.

68. Howard, *The WPA*, 855–56; *NYT*, March 19 (T. Catledge), April 9 (F. Barkley), 23 (D. Clark), 30 (L. Stark), May 14 (D. Clark), June 18 (F. Barkley), Aug. 13 (H. Dorris), 1939, for the WPA. On business and the economy at midyear, *NYT*, June 18 (W. Case), July 23 (D. Clark), 1939.

69. See, e.g., *NYT* feature articles by Turner Catledge, March 19, April 30, May 7, May 21, July 30, 1939, and by Arthur Krock, May 28, June 4, 1939.

70. Milkis, *President and the Parties*, ch. 6.

71. *The Public Papers and Addresses of Franklin D. Roosevelt, 1939, War and Neutrality* (New York: Macmillan, 1941), 439–41; Arthur J. Altmeyer, *The Formative Years of Social Security* (Madison: University of Wisconsin Press, 1968), chs. 3–4.

72. David E. Lilienthal, *The Journals of David E. Lilienthal, vol. 1, The TVA Years, 1939–1945* (New York: Harper & Row, 1964), 119; *NYT*, June 25 (F. Barkley), Aug. 20 (T. Swift, A. Krock).

73. Culver and Hyde, *American Dreamer*, 198–99.

11. Irrepressible Conflict, 1937–1939

1. Violet Bonham Carter, *Winston Churchill: An Intimate Portrait* (New York: Harcourt, Brace & World, 1965), 15. There are many good biographies of Churchill. Two that well repay the reading are Martin Gilbert, *Churchill: A Life* (New York: Henry Holt, 1991), and Roy Jenkins, *Churchill: A Biography* (New York: Farrar, Strauss & Giroux, 2001). They are the main sources for the following paragraphs.

2. Gilbert, *Churchill*, 545.

3. *Ibid.*, 329.

4. The following survey of the seven Great Powers draws heavily on Paul Kennedy, *The Rise and Fall of the Great Powers* (New York: Random House, 1987), 291–333.

5. Ian Kershaw, *Hitler, 1936–45: Nemesis* (New York: W. W. Norton, 2000), 26.

6. Eugen Weber, *The Hollow Years: France in the 1930s* (New York: W. W. Norton, 1994), 111.

7. Richard Overy with Andrew Wheatcroft, *The Road to War*, rev. and updated ed. (London: Penguin Books, 1999), 128–140.

8. Robert Dallek, *Franklin D. Roosevelt and American Foreign Policy, 1932–1945* (New York: Oxford University Press, 1979), chs. 1–5, remains a splendid overview of FDR's foreign policy during his first term.

9. T. S. Matthews, "Walled Cities," *New Republic* (Dec. 23, 1936), 239–41.

10. "Nazi Morale Begins to Crack," *New Republic* (Dec. 30, 1936), 257–58; Guenter Reimann, Five Years of Hitler Capitalism," *ibid.* (Feb. 9, 1938), 12–15; "Butter v. Might," *Time* (Jan. 25, 1937), 15; "Labor Shortage," *ibid.* (Aug. 23, 1937), 17; "Nazi Economics," *Economist* (April 1, 1939), 4.

11. A. Scott Berg, *Lindbergh* (New York: G. P. Putnam's Sons, 1998), 355–70; Overy and Wheatcroft, *The Road to War*, 367–69.

12. Alan Bullock, *Hitler and Stalin: Parallel Lives* (New York: Alfred A. Knopf, 1992), 537–38; Kershaw, *Hitler, 1936–45*, 24–25.

13. Kershaw, *Hitler, 1936–45*, 24. See also Frederick Birchall in *NYT*, May 2, 1937.

14. *Ibid.*, 48–60.

15. *Ibid.*, 67–83; "Hitler Comes Home," *Time* (March 21, 1938), 18–19.

16. For contemporary accounts see "Public Enlightenment," *Time* (April 11, 1938), 19–20; "Wandering Jews," and "Czechoslovakia," *ibid.* (May 2, 1938), 16–17; "'Land of Justice,'" *ibid.* (May 9, 1938), 16–17; *NYT*, May 29, 1938 (Otto Tolischus); "Hitler's Bluff Is Called," *New Republic* (June 1, 1938), 88–89.

17. See, e.g., *NYT*, March 27, 1938 (Shepard Stone; accompanying map); Goebbels in "Public Enlightenment," *Time* (April 11, 1938), 19–20.

18. R. A. C. Parker, *Chamberlain and Appeasement: British Policy and the Coming of the Second World War* (New York: St. Martin's Press, 1993), 5.

19. Ian Macleod, *Neville Chamberlain* (New York: Atheneum, 1962), 202; Keith Feiling, *The Life of Neville Chamberlain* (London: Macmillan, 1946), 306.

20. Overy and Wheatcroft, *Road to War*, 96. For naval construction, *Conway's All the World's Fighting Ships, 1922–1946* (Annapolis: Naval Institute Press, n.d.), 15, 19–20; for aircraft, Enzo Angelucci, *The Rand McNally Encyclopedia of Military Air-*

craft, 1914–1980 (New York: The Military Press, 1983), 217–19. For contemporary comment, see, e.g., "Britain's Navy—and Ours," *New Republic* (March 3, 1937), 97–98.

21. Macleod, *Neville Chamberlain*, 207.

22. Parker, *Chamberlain and Appeasement*, 107–26; *NYT,* May 8 (Harold Callender), Sept. 5 (Eugene Young), 12 (Arnoldo Cortesi), 1937.

23. For the Chamberlain-Eden relationship in detail, Parker, *Chamberlain and Appeasement,* ch. 6, and William R. Rock, *Chamberlain and Roosevelt: British Foreign Policy and the United States, 1937–1940* (Columbus: Ohio State University Press, 1988), 78–83. For the impact of Eden's resignation, *NYT,* Feb. 21, 1938.

24. Roosevelt to John Cudahy, March 9, 1938, quoted in David Reynolds, *The Creation of the Anglo-American Alliance* (Chapel Hill: University of North Carolina Press, 1982), 32.

25. Parker, *Chamberlain and Appeasement,* ch. 5; Feiling, *Life of Neville Chamberlain,* 315. For an excellent overview of the public debate, Charles Loch Mowat, *Britain between the Wars, 1918–1940* (Chicago: University of Chicago Press, 1955), 572–82.

26. Parker, *Chamberlain and Appeasement,* 129–35; Feiling, *Life of Neville Chamberlain,* 341–42, 347–48.

27. Feiling, *Life of Neville Chamberlain,* 341–42; Parker, *Chamberlain and Appeasement,* 125–26; "Mussolini Wins," *New Republic* (April 27, 1938), 346–47. For Roosevelt's invitations to Chamberlain, Rock, *Chamberlain and Roosevelt,* 28–32, 127–28.

28. Overy and Wheatcroft, *Road to War,* 94.

29. "World Pleased," *Time* (Nov. 16, 1936), 30.

30. Anne O'Hare McCormick, "As Mr. Roosevelt Sees His Role," *NYT Magazine* (Jan. 17, 1937), 1–2, 27. See also *NYT,* Feb. 28, 1937 (A. Krock).

31. Franklin Roosevelt to Breckinridge Long, March 9, 1935, in Edgar B. Nixon, ed., *Franklin D. Roosevelt and Foreign Affairs, Vol. II, March 1934–August 1935* (Cambridge: Belknap Press of Harvard University Press, 1969), 437–38.

32. Kenneth S. Davis, *FDR: Into the Storm, 1937–1940* (New York: Random House, 1993), 250–51.

33. *The Public Papers and Addresses of Franklin D. Roosevelt: Vol. 5, The People Approve, 1936* (New York: Random House, 1938), 285–92, quote at 289.

34. *The Public Papers and Addresses of Franklin D. Roosevelt, 1937, The Constitution Prevails* (New York: Macmillan, 1941), 406–11.

35. *Ibid.,* 422–24.

36. *NYT,* Oct. 10 (H. Hinton; H. Callender), 17 (regional survey); James MacGregor Burns, *Roosevelt: The Lion and the Fox* (New York: Harcourt, Brace, 1956), 318–19; Feiling, *Life of Neville Chamberlain,* 325. On the liberals, see, e.g., "Forcible-Feeble Diplomacy," *New Republic* (Oct. 20, 1937), 283–85.

37. Davis, *FDR: Into the Storm,* 154–58; Rock, *Chamberlain and Roosevelt,* 48.

38. *The Public Papers and Addresses of Franklin D. Roosevelt, 1938, The Continuing Struggle for Liberalism* (New York: Macmillan, 1941), 36–37.

39. Dallek, *Roosevelt and American Foreign Policy,* 130, 138–39, 145, 149, 155–57; Rock, *Chamberlain and Roosevelt,* ch.3; David Dutton, *Anthony Eden: A Life and Reputation* (London: Arnold, 1997), 99–101.

40. Michael H. Hunt, "Pearl Buck—Popular Expert on China, 1931–1949," *Modern China* (Jan. 1977), 33–64.

41. *Public Papers, FDR, 1938,* 68–71; *NYT,* Dec. 19 (E. James), 26 (H. Baldwin), 1937, Feb. 8 (H. Hinton), 20 (H. Baldwin),1938; "Army & Navy," *Time* (Feb. 7, 1938), 9–10; "Peace & Preparedness," *ibid.* (Feb. 14, 1938), 9–10; "Behind the Big Navy," *New Republic* (Feb. 9, 1938), 5–6; Charles A. Beard, "Rough Seas for the Super Navy," *ibid.* (March 30, 1938), 210; Maverick quote in William E. Leuchtenburg, *Franklin D. Roosevelt and the New Deal* (New York: Harper & Row, 1963), 284.

42. Overy and Wheatcroft, *Road to War,* 104–05; Kershaw, *Hitler, 1936–45,* 118.

43. "Sawed-Off Sudetens?" *Time* (Sept. 19, 1938), 17–18.

44. Feiling, *Life of Neville Chamberlain,* 372.

45. Narratives of Munich are legion. William L. Shirer, *The Rise and Fall of the Third Reich* (New York: Simon & Schuster, 1960), chs. 11–12, is solid, opinionated reporting, which should be supplemented by Kershaw, *Hitler, 1936–1945,* 95–125, and Bullock, *Hitler and Stalin,* 578–90; Mowat, *Britain between the Wars,* 604–19, excellently summarizes the episode from the British perspective.

46. "Eleventh-Hour Reprieve," *Economist* (Oct. 1, 1938), 1–3.

47. "German Air Power," *New Republic* (Oct. 5, 1938), 226; Baldwin in *NYT,* Oct. 2, 1938.

48. Feiling, *Life of Neville Chamberlain,* 382; "Millions for Czechoslovakia," *Time* (Oct. 10, 1938), 19; Winston S. Churchill, *The Gathering Storm* (Boston: Houghton Mifflin, 1948), 326–28.

49. "The Price of Peace," *Economist* (Oct. 8, 1938), 53–54; David Dutton, *Neville Chamberlain* (London: Arnold, 2001), 54; *NYT,* Oct. 9 (James; Birchall), Dec. 18 (F. Kuhn),1938.

50. Williamson Murray and Allan R. Millett, *A War to Be Won: Fighting the Second World War* (Cambridge: Belknap Press of Harvard University Press, 2000), 10–17.

51. Rock, *Chamberlain and Roosevelt,* 112–25, quotes at 116, 125.

52. *NYT,* Dec. 25, 1938 (E. James), Jan. 29 (A. McCormick), Feb. 26 (H. Callender), 1939.

53. *Public Papers, FDR, 1938,* 597; Keith Middlemas and John Barnes, *Baldwin: A Biography* (New York: Macmillan, 1970), 1048; Gilbert, *Churchill,* 604. See also the analysis by Otto Tolischus, *NYT,* Nov. 20, 1938.

54. "England Awakes," *Economist* (March 25, 1939), 601–02.

55. For contemporary discussion of these issues, see, e.g., *The Times* (London), Oct. 19 ("Mr. Churchill . . ."), 29 ("Labour's Call . . ."), Dec. 31 ("Labour and National Defense"), 1938; Feb. 16 ("Price of Defence"), March 22 ("Democracy and Defence"), April 3 ("Defence Against Aggression"), April 15 ("After the Debate"), 1939; and H. N. Brailsford, "Does Chamberlain Mean Business?" *New Republic* (May 24, 1939), 66–68.

56. *NYT,* Dec. 25, 1938 (T. Catledge); *The Public Papers and Addresses of Franklin D. Roosevelt, 1939: War—and Neutrality* (New York: Macmillan, 1941), 1–2.

57. *Public Papers, FDR, 1936,* 606.

58. *Public Papers, FDR, 1939,*103–04,146–47; Dallek, *Roosevelt and American Foreign Policy,* 172–74; *NYT,* Jan. 8 (H. Baldwin), 15 (A. Krock), 1939.

59. Dallek, *Roosevelt and American Foreign Policy*, 174–75.

60. *NYT*, Feb. 19, 1939 (E. L. James); *Public Papers, FDR, 1939*, 112–13.

61. Harold Callender, "Roosevelt's Words Re-echo in Europe," *NYT Magazine* (March 12, 1939), 4–5, 18.

62. *Public Papers, FDR, 1939*, 165–66, 201–05; Kershaw, *Hitler: 1936–1945*, 189; *NYT*, March 19 (A. Krock), April 16 (A. Krock, E. L. James), 30 (Krock, James), 1939; Parker, *Chamberlain and Appeasement*, 246–48.

63. The *St. Louis* incident is summarized in Davis, *FDR: Into the Storm*, 370–71. See also "In Search of a Country," *New Republic* (June 14, 1939), 143, and "And Pilate Washed His Hands," *ibid.* (June 28, 1939), 197.

64. Burns, *Roosevelt: The Lion and the Fox*, 393; Rock, *Chamberlain and Roosevelt*, 188–92.

65. Dallek, *Roosevelt and American Foreign Policy*, 192–96.

66. Davis, *FDR: Into the Storm*, 449–58, quote at 458.

67. For the British-Soviet negotiations, Parker, *Chamberlain and Appeasement*, 223–45; for Hitler and Germany, Kershaw, *Hitler, 1936–1945*, ch. 5.

68. Feiling, *Life of Neville Chamberlain*, 416.

69. Burns, *Roosevelt: The Lion and the Fox*, 394.

Epilogue

1. William E. Leuchtenburg, *In the Shadow of FDR: From Harry Truman to Ronald Reagan*, rev. ed. (Ithaca: Cornell University Press, 1985), viii.

2. William E. Leuchtenburg, *Franklin D. Roosevelt and the New Deal* (New York: Harper & Row, 1963), and Leuchtenburg, *In the Shadow of FDR*.

3. D. Jerome Tweeton, *The New Deal at the Grass Roots: Programs for the People in Otter Tail County, Minnesota* (St. Paul: Minnesota Historical Society Press, 1988), 83, 145–46, for statistical estimates and quotation.

4. *Ibid.*, 168.

5. W. N. MacFarlane, *The Magic City of Egypt* (El Paso: Complete Printing, 1991), 144–47.

6. On the epidemic analogy, see John A. Garraty, *The Great Depression* (New York: Harcourt Brace Jovanovich, 1980), 3–4.

7. "Men at Work," *Time* (July 18, 1938), 9–10; see also "Relief," *ibid.* (Sept. 6, 1937), 15; Dorothy Thompson column, *St. Louis Post-Dispatch*, Oct. 22, 1936; Raymond Clapper column, *Kansas City Star*, June 13, 1939.

8. Frederick Lewis Allen, *Since Yesterday: The 1930s in America* (New York: Harper & Brothers, 1939), 201–02.

9. T. K. Whipple, "Freedom's Land," *New Republic* (April 13, 1938), 311–12.

10. *The Public Papers and Addresses of Franklin D. Roosevelt*, vol. 5, *The People Approve, 1936* (New York: Random House, 1938), 198.

11. Arthur M. Schlesinger, Jr., *A Life in the Twentieth Century: Innocent Beginnings, 1917–1950* (Boston: Houghton Mifflin, 2000), 227–28, 251, 359–74.

12. This and the following paragraph draw heavily on Merrill D. Peterson, *The Jefferson Image in the American Mind* (New York: Oxford University Press, 1960), ch. 7.

13. *The Public Papers and Addresses of Franklin D. Roosevelt, 1939, War—and Neutrality* (New York: Macmillan, 1941), 579.

14. Penelope Niven, "Sandburg, Carl," *American National Biography Online,* Feb., 2000.

15. Stark Young, "Lincoln and Huston," *New Republic* (Nov. 9, 1938), 18; Max Lerner, "The Lincoln Image," *ibid.* (March 8, 1939), 134–36; Otis Ferguson, "The Caravan (II) and Abe," *ibid.* (June 21, 1939), 189; Jeffrey Richards, "Massey, Raymond," *American National Biography Online,* Feb. 2000; Herbert Mitgang on "Abe Lincoln in Illinois," *NYT,* Nov. 28, 1993.

16. *Public Papers, FDR, 1938,* 259; "Continental Congress," *Time* (May 2, 1938), 13.

17. *Ibid.,* 259.

18. *Public Papers, FDR, 1939,* 300.

19. *NYT,* May 1, 1939; David Gelernter, *1939: The Lost World of the Fair* (New York: Free Press, 1995), ch. 1.

20. "Specialties in Flushing," *Time* (June 12, 1939), 11–12; "Life Goes to the World's Fair" (July 3, 1939), 54–69; General Electric advertisement, *Survey Graphic* (May 1939), http://newdeal.feri.org/ads/lge539.gif.

21. See *Time* and *Life* articles, cited above.

22. Gelernter, *Lost World of the Fair,* 43–44, 293.

23. Gerhard L. Weinberg, *A World at Arms: A Global History of World War II* (New York: Cambridge University Press, 1994), 57.

INDEX

Abyssinia, 213; Labour's reaction, 240, 248; failure of international community, 249; British reaction, 244, 248, 391; and League, 376; U.S. neutrality, 382, 395

Acheson, Dean, 133, 151

Agricultural Adjustment Act, 127, 153–54

Agricultural Adjustment Administration (AAA): enacted, 127; Peek and Johnson, 144; 153–55; and Peek, 156; purge, 157–59; Skocpol and Finegold on, 172–73; and Resettlement Administration (RA), 281–82; and blacks, 308; second AAA, 361, 364

Agricultural Extension Service, 156

Agriculture, Department of, 156, 276

Albania, invaded by Italy, 407

Alexander, Will, 283, 353–54

Allen, O. K., 283

Amalgamated Clothing Workers, 166

American Farm Bureau Federation, 154

American Federation of Labor (AFL): unemployment estimates, 83–84, 107, 339, 417; industrial organization, 166–67; on Perkins, 260; birth of CIO, 297; and CIO, 303; and Labor's Non-Partisan League, 323

American Liberty League, 261–62, 320

American Medical Association, 273

American Workers Party, 167

Amery, Leo, 246–47

Amlie, Tom, 270–71

Anschluss, 385–86

Anti-Comintern Pact, 380, 385

Archbishop of Canterbury, 246

Archbishop of York, 246

Arno, Peter, 299

Arnold, Thurman, 358

Arthurdale (West Virginia), 282–83, 334

Asquith, Herbert: and Lloyd George, 218–19; and Keynes, 222; and Churchill, 371–73

Atlantic Crossings (Rodgers), 274n

Attlee, Clement, 240, 254; foreign policy, 408

Austria: customs agreement with Germany and collapse of Creditanstalt, 32–33; Nazi movement in, 51; coup attempt, 213, 243; and Italy, 247, 376, 385; visited by Hopkins, 273; absorbed by Germany, 385–86; British-French acquiescence to German takeover, 390–91

Baker, Newton D., 100, 103

Baker, James, Sr., 140

Baldwin, Stanley: profile, 61–63; leadership of, 16, 64, 124, 200, 371, 434–35; Lord President in National government, 35–36, 43, 65, 239, 243, 245, 278; and "middle way," 234; on George V and Edward VIII, 237–38; and Neville Chamberlain, 239, 386–87; and 1935 election, 240–41; prime minister, 240–55; foreign policy leadership, 243, 250; and abdication crisis, 252–54; retirement and accomplishments, 254; and Churchill, 373–75; advises Chamberlain, 404; supports Jewish refugee fund, 407

Bank of England, 33, 180, 228
Banking Act (1933), 123–25
Banking Act (1935), 286–87, 299,
    302–03
Barbarossa, Frederick, 191
Barth, Karl, 192
Baruch, Bernard, 133, 144, 156
Basso, Hamilton: on Coughlin, 268
Bavarian People's party, 186
Beard, Charles, 116, 382, 394
Beckmann, Max, 195
Beer and Wine Revenue Act, 125–26
B.E.F. News, 95
Belgium, 180, 191–92, 378
Bell, Vanessa, 221
Bennett, David: on Lemke, 315
Berle, Adolf A., Jr.: profile, 117–18;
    Brains Trust, 101, 105, 115
Berlin International Auto Show, 210–11
Bevin, Ernest, 240
Bishop of Bradford, 252
Bismarck, Otto von, 17, 185
Black, Hugo, 285–86, 351
Blomberg, Werner von, 182, 189, 385
Bondfield, Margaret, 260
Bonus Army (Bonus Expeditionary
    Force), 93–98
Borah, William, 169, 213, 412
Boulder Dam, 105, 306
Brandeis, Louis: ideas of, 105; influence
    on Berle, 117–18; on Supreme
    Court, 289, 337; retirement, 351
"Brains Trust": formation, 101; and
    FDR's ideology, 105; member pro-
    files, 115–20; and trusts, 357
Braun, Eva, 201
Braun, Otto, 53
Bridges, Harry, 167
Brinkley, Alan: on Coughlin and Long,
    266; on the end of the New Deal,
    368
British Broadcasting Corporation
    (BBC), 252
British Union of Fascists, 34, 70, 239
Brüning, Heinrich: profile, 11–12;
    Chancellor of Germany, 30–33,

45–53; Center party leader, 54;
    escapes Nazi assassins, 189
Bryan, William Jennings, 86, 104: and
    Moley, 116; supported by Jesse
    Jones, 140
Buhite, Russell, 124n
Bureau of Roads, 276
Burlingham, Charles, 108
Burton, Harold, 358
Butler, Pierce, 290, 339, 353

Callender, Harold: on German elections,
    51; on dictatorship and democracy,
    410
Campbell-Bannerman, Sir Henry, 218
Canada, 71–72, 152, 403, 410
Cardozo, Benjamin, 288–89, 337
Catholic Action (Germany), 193
Catholic War Veterans (Germany), 193
Catholic Youth League (Germany), 193
Cavalcade (Noel Coward), 66–67
Center party (Germany), 11, 54–56,
    185–86
Cermak, Anton, 113
Chagall, Marc, 195
Chamberlain, Austen, 63–64
Chamberlain, Neville
    profile, 63–64
    Chancellor of Exchequer: defends
        principle of balanced budget, 68,
        74–75, 224–25; and World Eco-
        nomic Conference, 131, 133, 135;
        and Lloyd George, 220; and J. M.
        Keynes, 222; accepts social spending
        and limited public works, 229–30,
        236, 276; manages the pound, 232;
        defends undramatic recovery pro-
        gram, 233–34; drab image, 238; pri-
        vate criticism of Baldwin, 239–40;
        speech re depressed areas, 251
    Prime Minister: succeeds Baldwin,
        254; dislike of Churchill, 375; per-
        sonal style 386–87; increases
        defense spending, 387–88; diplo-
        macy of, 388–92; conflict with
        Eden re relations with U.S., 389,

397–98; on Roosevelt and U.S., 389–91, 396–97, 411; on Japan, 399; Munich agreement, 402–6; guarantees Polish boundaries, 407; rejects coalition government, 408; reacts to beginning of war, 413

Charles, Searle, 274n

Chicago Daily News, 316

Chicago Tribune: on FDR's first inauguration, 122; opposition to New Deal, 319–20

Chicago World's Fair (1933–34), 135–37

Childs, Marquis, 267

China: 1931–32 Japanese attacks, 72–73, 131; silver trade, 152; British interests, 244–45; 1937 Japanese invasion, 376, 379–80; and Delano family, 393; U.S. views, 398–99; U.S. support for Chiang, 411–12

Christian Century: on relief, 89; on Long and Coughlin, 268; and *Good Earth,* 398–99

Church of England, 218, 252

Churchill, Randolph, 242

Churchill, Winston: profile, 371–75; erratic nature, 16, 62, 238, 246–47; denounces Nazi Germany, 246–47, 249–50; in abdication crisis, 253–54; demands more military production, 387–88; and Eden, 389; overestimation of German air power, 401; on Munich agreement, 404; possible cabinet position, 408, 413

Cincinnati Plan, 37

Civil Works Administration (CWA), 148, 257, 272, 275–76, 416

Civilian Conservation Corps (CCC): established, 127; analogue of war, 146; as relief program, 147–48; 276–77, 416

Clapper, Raymond, 286

Clements, Robert, 264–65

Collins, Seward, 268–69

Columbia Broadcasting System, 266

Committee on Industrial Organization

(CIO): creation, 297, 307. *See also* Congress of Industrial Organizations

Committee on Public Information, 146

Commodity Credit Corporation (farm CCC), 155, 364

"commodity dollar," 150

Commonwealth Club speech (FDR), 105–6, 118

Commonwealth Edison, 284

Commonwealth Federation of New York, 269–70

Commonwealth and Southern Corporation, 286; and TVA, 333, 368

Communist Party of the United States: and Bonus Army, 94–95, 97; hunger demonstrations, 113; and labor, 167–68, 296–97, 329, 340; use of Abraham Lincoln's name, 424

"Confessing Church," 192–93

Congress of Industrial Organizations (CIO): political activities, 323; and UAW, 327; and Reuther, 329–30; resentment of, 364, 368; evaluation, 419

conservatism
  in Britain (primarily Conservative party): anchors National government, 10–11, 35–36; backs Indian independence and trade protectionism, 15; narrow differences with Liberal party, 16; and 1931 election, 36; early anti-Depression policy, 40, 64–68; and Stanley Baldwin, 61–63, 219; and Neville Chamberlain, 63–64, 387, 391–92; Ottawa agreements and trade policy, 70–72; rejection of deficit spending, 74; social and economic policies, 223–26; 1935 election, 240–41; foreign policy, 241–51; 387–92; abdication crisis, 251–55; and Winston Churchill, 371–75; and fascism, 391–92; reaction to Munich, 404–5

conservatism (*cont.*)
  in Germany: exemplified by Brüning
    and Hindenburg, 30–31, 45–47;
    and *Stahlhelm*, 45; Papen-Schle-
    icher cabinets, 52–61; and Schacht,
    180–81; and early Nazi regime,
    182–90
  in the United States: exemplified by
    Hoover, 7–8, 24–25, 85, 87–93,
    106–7; in Ohio, 37; and Jesse Jones,
    141, 359; and labor militance,
    167–68; opposition to National
    Recovery Administration, 171–72;
    American Liberty League, 261–62,
    320; demands balanced budget,
    272–73; criticizes Works Progress
    Administration, 280, 418–19; and
    Supreme Court, 288–90; reaction to
    Second New Deal, 304–6; Landon
    campaign, 316, 318–22; *New York
    Times re* FDR, 320; in Democratic
    party, 346; and Joseph Robinson,
    349; and Pat Harrison, 350; and
    court-packing debate, 352; and gov-
    ernment spending debate, 352; and
    1938 "purge," 362–63; emerging
    "conservative coalition," 366; grow-
    ing strength in electorate (Wallace),
    368–69; and foreign policy, 399,
    412; FDR as conservative, 431; and
    New Deal scholarship, 431–32
Consolidation Coal Company, 170
Cooke, Morris L., 281
Coolidge, Calvin: policies, 7–8, 22–23;
    compared with Hoover, 24
Cooper, Myers, 37
Corcoran, Thomas ("Tommy the Cork"),
    300
The Corporate State (Viglione), 144
Costigan, Edward, 86–87, 345
Cotton Spinning Act, 231
Coughlin, Father Charles: on NRA,
    169; popularity, 265–67; on social
    issues, 266–67; and FDR, 267;
    National Union for Social Justice,
    267–68; undercut by prelates, 307;

Union party, 315
council housing (Britain), 228–29, 246
Couzens, James, 320
Coward, Noel, 66–67
Cristgau, Victor, 159
Croly, Herbert, 116, 422
Cunard Line, 235
Curtis, Charles, 29
Cutting, Bronson, 38
Czechoslovakia, 3; German grievances
    against, 19; and German socialists,
    186; German expansionism, 386,
    390–91; first crisis, 400–401; second
    crisis and Munich, 401–4; interna-
    tional reaction to Munich, 404–5;
    evaluation of Munich, 405–6,
    407–8; absorbed by Germany, 407;
    U.S. reaction to German move, 410

Daily Mail (London): Keynes on FDR,
    134
Danzig: as German objective, 406–7
Darrow, Clarence: investigation of
    NRA, 169
Davey, Governor Martin, 279
Davis, Chester, 157–59
Davis, John W., 171, 261–62
Davis, Kenneth: on banking, 111; on
    FDR and press, 123, 313n
Dawes, Charles, 19, 91
Democratic National Committee, 322–23
Dennis, Lawrence, 268–69
Dewey, John: criticizes New Deal, 269–71;
    and Arthurdale school, 282–83
Dewey, Peter, 225n
Disraeli, Benjamin: and Baldwin, 62,
    254; on England's assets, 404
Dolfuss, Engelbert (Chancellor of Aus-
    tria), 213, 247–48
Doughton, Robert ("Muley"), 90
Douglas, Lewis, 272
Douglas, Paul, 271
Downey, Sheridan, 270
Dred Scott Case, 291
Du Ponts: and American Liberty
    League, 261–62

Dubinsky, David: and AFL, 166–67; and J. L. Lewis, 297; CIO political involvement, 307

Duesterberg, Theodor, 49–50

Duffus, R. L., 136

Early, Steve: FDR press secretary, 122–23

Eastman, Joseph, 128, 313

Eccles, Marriner (Federal Reserve chair): profile, 286–87; and deficit spending, 272, 359; importance, 303; on New Deal, 360

Economic Consequences of the Peace, (Keynes), 222

Economist, The: attacks Chamberlain, 225; on slum clearance, 229; on *Queen Mary,* 236; on George V, 237; on Peace Ballot, 244; on George VI, 254; praises FDR, 336; on Munich agreement, 403, 404

Eden, Anthony: negotiations with Italy, 388–89; supports Anglo-American cooperation in Asia, 398; critical of government, 404; compared with Baldwin, 410

Edward VII, 236

Edward VIII, 251–54

Einstein, Albert, 197, 428

Emergency Railroad Transportation Act, 128

Emergency Relief Appropriations Act, 275

Emergency Relief and Construction Act, 91–92

Emergency Unemployment Committee, 82

Enabling Act, 185–86

End Poverty in California (EPIC), 270

Enterprise (aircraft carrier), 275–76

Ethiopia. *See* Abyssinia

Falange party (Spain), 376, 381, 384, 390, 395

Farley, James, 135, 359, 366–67

Farm Credit Act, 128

Farm Credit Administration, 128, 133

Farm Mortgage Moratorium Act, 303

Farm Security Administration, 283, 352–54, 424

Farmers Holiday Association, 113

fascism: 4, 381, 421; and Nazism, 57–58, 191, and Italy, 137, 144, 191, 196, 407; and New Deal, 144, 146, 262; in U.S., 268–69, 357; and Neville Chamberlain, 391–92

FDR: The New Deal Years (Davis), 313n

Federal Coordinator of Transportation, 128

Federal Deposit Insurance Corporation (FDIC), 128

Federal Emergency Relief Act, 127

Federal Emergency Relief Administration (FERA), 127, 148, 155, 261, 276; Hopkins and, 257–58; in Ohio, 279; and Resettlement Administration (RA), 281–82; effects, 416

Federal Farm Board, 24–25, 37, 88–89

Federal Reserve Act, 87, 287

Federal Reserve system: and Depression, 25–26, 39, 287; and Glass-Steagall Act, 88; weaknesses of, 110; and First Hundred Days, 123, 125, 128; and "commodity dollar," 150; Eccles and, 272, 286–87; Banking Act, 302–3; and Roosevelt recession, 354–55

Federal Securities Act, 127–28

Federal Theater, 280

Federal Trade Commission, 290

Feininger, Lyonel, 195

Feldman, Gerald, 19

Finegold, Kenneth, 172–73

First Hundred Days: the planners (Moley, Berle, Tugwell), 115–20; FDR establishes national leadership, 119–25; banking crisis, 124–25; Beer and Wine Revenue Act, 125–26; list of New Deal measures, 127–29

First National Bank of Detroit, 111–12

Fisher, Irving, 287
Flint (Michigan) sit-down strike, 327–29
Flynn, Ed, 314–15
Ford, Henry, 111–12, 210, 339
Ford Motor Company, 24, 329–30
Fordney-McCumber Act, 22
Forerunners of American Fascism (Swing), 268
Fortune: on welfare, 261; on Mellon tax case, 288; FDR reelection poll, 310, 323; attacks FDR, 319; and MacLeish, 420
Frank, Jerome, 158–59
Frankfurter, Felix, 101, 134, 300, 320, 331–32
Frazier-Lemke Act, 290, 303, 315
Freidel, Frank, 99
Führerprinzip, 202

Gallup, George (and Gallup Poll), 310, 312, 324, 326, 365
Garner, John Nance: profile, 86, 90; 1932 campaign, 100, 102–3; and Jesse Jones, 140–41; conflict with FDR, 342, 349, 366, 412
Gastonia textile strike, 168
Gellhorn, Martha, 168–69
General Electric, 84, 427
General Strike of 1926, 62, 219
General Theory of Employment, Interest, and Money (Keynes), 223, 313n
George V, 10, 35, 67, 217, 236–38
George VI, 253–54, 411
George, Henry, 116
George Washington Bridge, 99
German Labor Front, 210
Gibbons, Floyd, 94
Gilbert, Bentley, 234
Gladstone, Margaret, 9
Glass, Carter, 86, 88, 151, 287
Glass-Steagall Act, 88, 125, 128
Glassford, Pelham, 95–96
Goebbels, [Paul] Joseph: profile, 179–80; Nazi publicist, 48–49; propaganda minister, 183–85, 188–89, 191, 194–99, 214, 268, 386

Gold Clause Repeal Resolution, 128
Gold Reserve Act (1934), 153–54
Göring, Hermann: profile, 177–78; Hitler's lieutenant, 48, 56, 60, 182–83, 188–89; German economic czar, 181, 204, 208–9, 212, 383; Berlin Olympics, 214
Grant, Duncan, 221
Green, T. H., 168
Greenspan, Alan, 303
Gretton, John, 246–47
Groener, Wilhelm, 52
Grosz, George, 195
Guffey-Snyder Coal Act, 303, 311
Guffey-Vinson Coal Act, 352
Gulick, Luther, 274, 342

Harding, Warren, 8, 142
Harriman, Henry, 84–85, 119
Harrison, George, 132–33
Harrison, Pat, 86, 350, 366
Harvard Law School, 101, 117, 300, 331
Haskell, H. J.: on Germany, 195–96, 199, 202–3
Hawley-Smoot Tariff, 28, 80, 93, 102, 105, 107, 130–31
Hearst, William Randolph: pressure on FDR, 100; and Democratic convention, 103; and Liberty League, 261–62; attacks FDR, 300, 320; leaves Democratic party, 304–5
Heidegger, Martin, 192
Heidelberg, University of, 179
Henderson, Arthur, 238–39
Herbst, Josephine, 209
Herrin Daily Journal, 81
Hess, Rudolf, 48, 195
Hickok, Lorena, 294
Hillman, Sidney, 166–67, 297, 307
Himmler, Heinrich, 184, 189
Hindenburg, 214
Hindenburg, Oskar, 190
Hindenburg, Paul von: and Brüning, 30–31, 52; and Nazis, 44, 52, 55, 188; presidency, 47; political sup-

port, 49; 1932 election, 49–50; and
liberalism, 51; and Papen, 53–55,
59; on politics, 56; on dictatorship,
57; presidential government, 60;
and Hitler, 182, 185, 187; and
army, 184; and *Sturmabteilung*
(SA), 189; death, 190
Hitler, Adolf: profile, 44–45; Weimar
politics, 42, 47–60; Chancellor
(1933–34), 75, 121, 131, 182–90,
242; leadership style, 79, 103,
199–202, 207, 220, 434–35;
Führer (domestic), 176–81,
190–91, 194–99, 204–8, 210–15,
383; and Baldwin, 234, 255;
Churchill on, 249, 374; foreign
and military policies, 376–77,
383–86, 389–92, 400–410, 413,
435; and British Conservatives,
391; Roosevelt on, 393; impact
of, 434–35; mentioned, 2, 19, 43,
107, 108, 135, 233, 247
Hitler Youth, 191
Hoare, Sir Samuel, 248–49
Hoare-Laval plan, 249, 388
Holborn, Hajo, 11
Holding Company Act. *See* Public Utility Holding Company Act
Holt, Rush, 279
Home Loan Bank Act, 88
Home Owners Loan Corporation, 128,
309
Home Owners Refinancing Act, 128
Home Relief Bureau, 83
Hoover, Herbert: profile, 7–8; presidency (to mid-1932), 2, 10, 25–29,
33, 36–40, 72–73, 84–99, 102, 140;
Secretary of Commerce (1921–29),
22–24; 1932 campaign, 105–8;
"interregnum" (Nov. 1932–March
1933), 108–13; post-presidency,
115, 262
Hopkins, Harry: profile, 257–59;
receives report from Martha Gellhorn, 168; urges jobs program, 272;
Europe trip, 273–74; heads Works

Progress Administration, 275–80,
355; urges big spending, 359; 1938
"purge," 362; Secretary of Com-
merce, 366–67
Hot Oil Case, 289
Houston Chronicle, 140
Howard, Roy, 305
Howe, Frederic, 158–59
Howe, Louis McHenry, 133
Hugenberg, Alfred, 55, 183, 186
Hughes, Charles Evans: on limited gov-
ernment, 171; New Deal cases,
288–90, 337, 348, 352
Hull, Cordell: and Moley, 117; and Lon-
don Conference, 131–33; and for-
eign trade, 152, 157; and FDR,
366–67, 393
Humansville (Missouri), 276
Humphrey's Executor v. *United States*,
292
Hungary, 43, 386
Hurja, Emil, 310
Hurley, Patrick, 95–96
Hutcheson, William ("Big Bill"), 297

Ickes, Harold: and London Conference,
134; and PWA, 148, 161–62; and
Hopkins, 258, 275–76
Import Duties Act, 65
Import Duties Advisory Committee,
65–66, 231
India: self-government, 15, 17, 62, 71,
379; and Churchill, 238, 246,
372–73
Industrial Association (San Francisco),
167
Industrial Board, 260
Insull, Samuel, 286
International Harvester, 284–85
International Ladies Garment Workers
Union (ILGWU), 166
International Longshoreman's Associa-
tion, 167
Interstate Commerce Commission, 303,
313
Invergordon "mutiny," 35

Irish Free State, 17, 72
It Can't Happen Here (Lewis), 268
Italy: example of fascist corporatism, 8,
    84, 115–16, 131, 266; Mussolini
    dictatorship, 14; makes war debt
    payment to U.S., 73; and World
    Economic Conference, 132; pavil-
    ions at World's Fairs, 137
    (Chicago), 427–28 (New York);
    and Nazism, 191; relations with
    Germany, 213, 385, 410; and
    Abyssinia, 240, 244, 247; relations
    with Britain and France, 240–49,
    387–91, 398, 406; Hopkins visit,
    274; and League of Nations, 376;
    as regional power, 376–77, 379,
    388, 399, 406, 411; relations with
    U.S., 382, 394; and Spanish Civil
    War, 385

Jackson, Andrew, 3, 86, 164–65
Jackson, Gardner, 158
Jackson, Robert H., 288, 312, 357
Japan: militarism and aggression in East
    Asia, 12, 72–73, 131, 241, 244,
    370, 376, 395–99, 421; and world
    textile industry, 69, 168; and Stim-
    son doctrine, 72–73, 399; and
    League of Nations, 108, 245; rela-
    tions with Britain, 244–45, 379,
    396–97, 399, 411–12; and *Panay*
    sinking, 365, 396–97; as regional
    power, 379–81; Anti-Comintern
    Pact and growing alliance with Ger-
    many, 380, 411; FDR's attitude
    toward, 393–96, 412; rape of
    Nanking, 396; resentment against
    in U.S., 398–99
Jedell, Hugh, 184
Joad, C.E.M., 70
John Brown Shipyards, 235–36, 251
Johnson Debt Default Act, 382
Johnson, Hugh S.: profile, 144–45;
    heads NRA, 161–64, 167, 169–70
Johnson, Lyndon, 308
Johnson, Philip, 268–69

Johnson, Tom, 116
Johnston City (Illinois), 81, 417
Jones, Jesse H. (director, Reconstruction
    Finance Corp., 1930–45): profile,
    139–42; heads RFC, 150, 359
Jones, Thomas (Tom), 219, 343

Kandinsky, Wassily, 195
Kansas City Star: reports on Nazi Ger-
    many, 195–96, 199, 202–3; critical
    of FDR and New Deal, 280, 301
Kelley, Florence, 259–60
Kennedy, Joseph P., 307
Kent, Frank, 273
Kershaw, Ian, 193–94, 201, 385
Kessner, Thomas, 314
Keynes, John Maynard
    profile, 220–23
    British activism: writes *Means to Pros-
        perity*, 73–74, 220; advises Lloyd
        George, 219; and British left, 225;
        and National government, 229–30,
        234, 236
    U.S. activism: praises FDR, 134; and
        First New Deal, 149, 151–52;
        receives Lippmann's impressions of
        NRA, 166; meets with FDR,
        173–74; advises $400 million per
        month expenditure, 275; on busi-
        ness confidence, 287–88; and
        undistributed profits tax, 313,
        313n; Landon cites as influence on
        FDR, 320; 1938 letter to FDR,
        359–60; administration turn
        toward, 418
Kipling, Rudyard, 62, 237
Klee, Paul, 195
Knox, Frank, 321
Kraft durch Freude ("Strength through
    Joy") program, 210
Krock, Arthur, 103, 357
Kuhn, Ferdinand, Jr., 226
Ku Klux Klan, 266, 351

Labour party (Britain): character of,
    8–10, 16, 32, 219, 227, 260; reac-

tion to Depression, 34, 36, 41, 230; opposition to National government, 70, 238–43, 246, 248; abdication crisis, 253–54; and coming of World War II, 392–408

La Follette, Philip, 29, 95, 177, 272, 322, 334, 367

La Follette, Robert, Jr., 39, 95, 177, 272, 302, 316, 322, 343, 351

La Guardia, Fiorello, 39, 89, 91, 119, 177, 272–73, 316, 428, 430

Landon, Alfred, 294, 307, 311, 317–18, 320, 322, 324–25

Lansbury, George, 71, 240, 242

Lausanne Accord, 53

Laval, Pierre, 249–51

Law, Andrew Bonar, 62, 421, 377

Lawrence, David, 274–75, 359

League for Independent Political Action, 271, 314

League of Nations: British support for, 10–11, 224, 243–44, 388; on Polish Germans, 19–20; and 1931–32 Japanese aggression, 72–73, 245; FDR's views, 100; Japan quits, 108; Germany quits, 213; Abyssinian crisis, 248–49, 282; collapse of, 375–76

Lee, Mary, 45

Lehman, Herbert, 163, 425–26

Lemke, William, 315

Lengyel, Emil, 47

Leo XIII: *Rerum Novarum*, 266

Leuchtenburg, William, 303, 415

Levy, David, 124n

Lewis, J. Hamilton, 94

Lewis, John L.: profile, 295–98; United Mine Workers (UMW) president, 81, 166; and Congress of Industrial Organizations (CIO), 167, 307, 327–28, 340; and FDR, 307, 340–41

Lewis, Sinclair, 268

liberalism (worldview, ideology)
General: endangered by Depression, 4, 134–35; in France, 377; and Soviet Union, 381

in Britain: MacDonald and, 9; in political culture, 15–16, 36, 40, 347, 374, 433–35; and National government, 69, 72, 225, 233–35; and Lloyd George, 217–20; and Keynes, 220–23; and foreign policy, 241–44, 374, 392, 403

in Germany: Weimar Republic, 18–19, 40, 60; Hitler's critique of, 48; skepticism about, 51; Brüning's failure, 52; in Prussia, 53–54; conservative attacks, 54; Schacht abandons, 180; Nazi suppression, 183, 194; pre-Nazi attitude toward Jews, 196; alien to German political culture, 433–35

in United States: in political culture, 12, 432–33; Communist challenge, 14; progressives and urban liberals, 38, 157–59; and FDR, 40, 103, 129, 202, 336–37; 392; and Hoover, 88–90; and New Deal, 84, 145, 157–59, 160–61, 169, 172, 173, 286, 306, 334, 357, 359, 364, 367–69; third-party movements, 269–71; 1936 election, 320–21; Supreme Court, 289–90, 347–48; "purge" of 1938, 362; Spanish Civil War, 394; coming of World War II, 396; American intellectuals, 419–24; New Deal scholarship, 431–32

Liberalism and Social Action (Dewey), 269

Liberal party (Britain): alliance with Labour, 9–10, 16, 34; and National government, 35–36, 63, 65, 224; World War coalition with Conservatives, 61; decline, 72, 239–41; and David Lloyd-George, 217–20; and John Maynard Keynes, 220–23; foreign policy, 243; and abdication crisis, 254; and Churchill, 373

Libya, 377

Lilienthal, David E.: profile, 331–34; Commonwealth & Southern buyout, 368

Lindbergh, Charles, 251, 384, 401

Link, Harry, 256

Lippmann, Walter: critical of FDR as candidate, 99–100; urges dictatorial power, 121–22; and Keynes, 134; praises FDR, 137; on NRA, 166; on Black investigation, 286; turns against FDR, 305; *Good Society*, 344; on Fair Labor Standards Act, 361

Literary Digest, 310, 322

Lithuania, 407

Lloyd George, David: profile, 217–20; and Baldwin, 16, 61; advocates public works, 34, 229, 238–39; opposes National government, 63, 240; rebuffed by Chamberlain, 220, 233, 234; and Hitler, 220; and Keynes, 222, 225; and FDR, 273; on Polish commitment, 407

London Transport, 229–30

Long, Huey: profile, 262–63; criticizes NRA, 169; opposes New Deal, 263–64; and dictatorship, 268; and wealth tax bill, 300; assassination, 307; support for, 310; successors, 315

Lopokova, Lydia (Mrs. J. M. Keynes), 221

Louisville Bank v. Radford, 290

Lubbe, Marinus van der, 183

Luftwaffe, 178, 213, 374, 384, 403, 428

Lytton, Lord, 245

MacArthur, Douglas, 95–97, 144, 268

MacDonald, James Ramsey: profile, 8–11; Labour prime minister, 34–35, 219, 260; 1931 election, 35, 145; National prime minister, 35–36, 40, 63, 65, 72, 133, 145, 224, 238–39, 243, 248; retires, 237, 240; supports League, 243; Stresa front, 248

Maged, Jacob, 170

Magil, A. B., 268

Manchuria: Japanese invasion, 72, 376; and Britain, 244–45; and U.S., 393, 399

March of Time, 171, 216

Markham, Edward, 316

Martin, William McChesney, 303

Mason, Tim, 209

Maverick, Maury, 270, 399

May, George, 313

McAdoo, William Gibbs, 102–3

McCormick, Anne O'Hare, 129, 393

McCoy, Donald, 316

McNary-Haugen plan, 23, 142, 144, 154, 156

McReynolds, James, 288–89, 351n

Means, Gardiner, 117–18

Mellon, Andrew, 23, 26, 288

Memorial Day Massacre, 340

Mencken, H. L., 264

Mendelssohn, Felix, 194

Mercer, Lucy, 294

"Middle Way." *See* Keynes, John Maynard; liberalism; "Muddle Way"

Mills, Ogden, 90, 95, 123

Minister of Relief (Charles), 274n

Ministry of Health (Britain), 229

Minneapolis Teamsters, 141–42, 167

Minnesota Mortgage Moratorium Case, 289

Mit Brennender Sorge (Pius XI), 193

Mitchell, Charles, 26

Mitchell, William, 85, 95

The Modern Corporation and Private Property (Berle), 117–18

Moley, Raymond: profile, 116–17; "Brains Trust," 101, 115, 118; World Economic Conference, 132–33; on Hugh Johnson, 145; on undistributed profits tax, 313; critic of FDR (1936), 319

Monroe (Michigan) steel strike, 339

Moravia, 407

Morgan, J. P., 26, 284

Morgenthau, Henry, Jr.: advises FDR during London Conference, 133; relationship with Jones, 141; and "commodity dollar," 150; on spending, 272, 359; on Social Security, 274; and Mellon prosecution, 288; and gold sterilization, 355

Morris Motors, 227

Morrison, Herbert, 240

Mosley, Oswald, 34, 70, 239, 269
Motor Carrier Act, 303
Mowat, Charles Loch, 9, 242n
"Muddle Way" (National government
    social policy), 223–36
Muller, Ludwig, 192
Munich agreement, 135, 400–408
Mussolini, Benito: U.S. opinions *re*, 14,
    394; compared with Hitler, 45,
    201–2; and London Conference,
    131; compared with FDR, 146; fas-
    cism, 191; Baldwin's view of, 234;
    and Abyssinia, 247–49, 382, 395;
    and corporatism, 266, 377; Anti-
    Comintern Pact, 380; and Hitler,
    385; Britain, 388–91; at Munich,
    401–2, 406; and FDR message, 410
My First Days in the White House (Long),
    264

Nanking, rape of, 395, 396
Nation, 274n
National Association for the Advance-
    ment of Colored People (NAACP),
    308, 345
National Bank of Commerce, 140
National City Bank, 26
National Consumer League, 259–60
National Credit Corporation, 87
National Employment System Act, 128
National Farmers Union, 153–54, 364
National Gallery of Art, 288
National Guard, 167–68, 327
National Industrial Conference Board, 83
National Industrial Recovery Act, 130,
    162–63, 167–68, 298, 315–16
National Labor Relations Board
    (NLRB), 284, 302, 341. *See also*
    Wagner Act
National Recovery Administration
    (NRA): established, 129; requires
    trade protection, 130; and Hugh
    Johnson, 144–45; attempt to man-
    age industrial economy, 161–74;
    compared with German counter-
    part, 206; no counterpart in
    Britain, 231, 238; attacked by Huey

Long and Father Coughlin, 263,
    267; and Congress, 271; and Wag-
    ner bill, 284; and Supreme Court,
    289–90; FDR reacts, 291; new
    departures, 298–99, 304; Guffey-
    Snyder Coal Act, 303; and
    Negroes, 308; Fred Perkins on, 309;
    and public, 310, 337; Guffey-Sny-
    der Coal Act ruled unconstitu-
    tional, 311; criticized by Landon,
    320; Guffey-Vinson Coal Act, 352;
    Fair Labor Standards Act, 361
National Youth Administration (NYA),
    276, 278, 415
Nazism and Nazi party (National Social-
    ist Workers party): in Weimar Ger-
    many, 19, 30–33, 41, 45, 47–60; in
    power, ch. 6 (*passim*), 383–86,
    400–401; N. Chamberlain's attitude
    re, 390–92
Nearing, Scott, 119
Nebbia v. *New York*, 289
Neely, Matt, 279
New Deal. *See* Roosevelt, Franklin D.
    (First 125 Days, First New Deal,
    Second New Deal); First Hundred
    Days; Second Hundred Days; *and
    individual acts and agencies*, espe-
    cially Agricultural Adjustment Act,
    Agricultural Adjustment Adminis-
    tration, Banking Act (1933), Bank-
    ing Act (1935), Civilian
    Conservation Corps, Civil Works
    Administration, Farm Security
    Administration, Federal Emergency
    Relief Administration, National
    Labor Relations Act and Board,
    National Recovery Administration,
    National Youth Administration,
    Public Utility Holding Company
    Act, Public Works Administration,
    Resettlement Administration,
    Reconstruction Finance Corp.,
    Social Security Act, Tennessee Val-
    ley Authority, Wealth Tax Act,
    Works Progress Administration
New Era (Hoover), 25

New Freedom (Wilson), 287, 304

New Republic, 278, 430

New Statesman, 225

New York Post, 320

New York Times: on Weimar planning, 46; on British protests, 69–70; on bonus, 93, 94, 96; business index, 150, 164, 322, 355; on NRA, 166; Keynes's "Agenda for the President," 173–74; on Goebbels, 179; and Schacht, 180; on Berlin Olympics, 215; on British foreign policy, 244; on Edward VIII, 251, 253; on banking bill, 287; on gridlock, 301; endorses FDR, 320; on court packing, 348; critical of FDR's antibusiness tone, 357; isolation survey, 396; on Munich, 404

New Yorker, 299

New Zealand, 71, 232

Nice (France), 406

Niemöller, Martin, 192

Night of the Long Knives, 188–90

Norris, George: Muscle Shoals plan, 38, 127, 285; and bonus, 94–95; and FDR, 106, 320; and NRA, 169; and independent left, 270; and REA, 281; and court packing, 349

Norway, 232

Nuremberg rallies, 194–95, 197, 200, 212, 220

Nye, Gerald, 169, 382

Olson, Culbert, 270

Olson, Floyd, 167, 214, 270

Olympic games: (1932, Los Angeles), 98; (1936, Berlin), 214–15

O'Neal, Edward, 154

Open Market Committee (Federal Reserve), 302

Ottawa trade conference, 65–66, 71, 107, 230–31

Otter Tail County (Minnesota), 416

Pacelli, Eugenio (later Pius XII), 186–87

Palestine, 381, 411, 428

Papen, Franz von: appointed chancellor, 52–53; authoritarianism of, 53, 56–57, 59; and Prussia, 54; and economy, 54, 56, 58, 207–8; and Hitler, 59–60, 182, 188; and foreign policy, 72; and concordat with Catholic Church, 186; criticizes Sturmabteilung (SA), 189

Patten, Simon, 118, 260

Peace Ballot, 243–44

Pecora, Ferdinand, 111

Peek, George, 144, 156–57

Pelley, William Dudley, 268–69

Perkins, Frances: profile, 259–60; and Hugh Johnson, 144; and J. M. Keynes, 173–74; Social Security Act, 273, 302; and Eleanor Roosevelt, 295

Perkins, Fred, 171, 290, 309

Philippines, 144

Pinchot, Gifford, 29

Pioneer Hi-Bred Company, 142, 155

Pius XI, 193, 266

Pius XII, 186–87

Poland: as dictatorship, 14; German minority in, 19–20; invaded by Germany and Soviet Union, 369, 413, 428–29; object of Hitler's expansionism, 386, 407, 413; alliance with Britain, 407–8

Politics of Upheaval (Schlesinger), 313n

Pomerene, Atlee, 91

Porsche, Ferdinand, 211

Portugal, 43, 232, 266, 390

Pound, Ezra, 268–69

Pressman, Lee, 158

Price, Clair, 239

Primo de Rivera, Jose Antonio, 14

Prince Albert, 236n

Promise of American Life (Croly), 116, 422

Prussia: German unification, 17, 53–54; agriculture, 51; and Hindenburg, 51; and Brüning, 52; and Göring, 60, 178, 188

Public Utility Holding Company Act: in Congress, 284–86, 299; and FDR,

300, 357; enacted, 303; and New
Deal public power objectives, 333,
357; and Supreme Court, 337
Public Works Administration (PWA):
established, 129; and Ickes, 148,
161–62; projects of, 162, 229, 261,
272, 275–77, 314, 382, 416; Hop-
kins-Ickes conflict, 275–77
Pulitzer newspapers, 305

Quadragesimo Anno (Pius XI), 266
Queen Mary (ocean liner), 235–36, 251

Railroad Retirement Act, 289–90, 303
Rand, Sally, 136
Rayburn, Sam, 86, 281, 285
Reagan, Jack, 279
Reciprocal Trade Act, 152
Reconstruction Finance Corp. (RFC):
under Hoover, 87–88, 90–91, 111;
under FDR, 125, 128, 140–41, 147,
150
Reed, David, 112
Reich Chamber of Culture, 194
Reichsbank, 180–81
Reichsbanner, 52, 186
Reichsnährstand (RNS), 205–6
Rerum Novarum (Leo XIII), 266
Reserve Officers Training Corps
(ROTC), 308
Resettlement Administration (RA),
159–60, 229, 276, 281–82, 282–83,
353
Reuther, Victor, 227, 329, 330
Reuther, Walter P.: profile and United
Auto Workers career, 327–31
Revenue Act of 1932, 90
Rhineland: Allies withdraw, 30; and
Goebbels, 179; German occupa-
tion, 213–14, 376, 384, 401; British
reaction, 247; Belgian reaction, 378
Richberg, Donald, 169, 320, 331
Riefenstahl, Leni, 200–201, 214
Roberts, Owen, 288–89, 311, 337,
351–52
Roberts, Roy, 318, 321

Robinson, Joseph, 86, 349–50
Robinson-Patman Act, 313–14
Rockefeller, John D., 303
Rodgers, Daniel, 274n
Roerich, Nicholas, 143
Röhm, Ernst, 48, 188–89
Romania, 386
Roosevelt and Hopkins (Sherwood),
276n
"Roosevelt Court," 351
Roosevelt, Eleanor: profile, 293–95;
marriage to FDR, 77–78; and
Arthurdale project, 282–83; con-
cern for Negroes, 308; and Marian
Anderson concert, 425
Roosevelt, Franklin D.
Pre-presidential and general: profile,
77–80; significance of, 3–5, 43,
415–19, 431–32. 434–35; governor
of New York, 29, 39–40, 62, 92, 98,
260; social policies, 65; attitudes re
Jackson and Jefferson, 421–23; on
immigrants, 426, opens New York
World's Fair (1939), 427
Presidential campaign (1931–32): for
Democratic nomination, 99–103;
general election, 103–8; postelec-
tion "interregnum," 108–13; Walter
Lippmann on, 99–100; as progressive, 100–106; Brains Trust, 101;
assassination attempt, 113
First 125 Days: inaugural, 2, 120–21;
on war debts, 73; and World Economic Conference, 74–75, 129–34;
and Brains Trust, 115–20; and
Lippmann, 121–22, 137; banking
and monetary actions, 122–25;
press relations, 122–23; fireside
chats, 124–25; repeal of prohibition, 125–26; legislative techniques, 126; "hundred days"
legislation, 127–29; leadership of,
129; praised by J. M. Keynes, 134;
opens Chicago World's Fair,
135–36; *see also* First Hundred
Days

Roosevelt, Franklin D. (*cont.*)

First New Deal (1933–35): and Jesse Jones (RFC), 141–42; and Henry A. Wallace (agriculture) 142–44; and Hugh Johnson (NRA), 144; invokes analogue of war, 145–47; relief programs, 147–49; monetary policy, 149–52, 153–54, 165; and Keynes, 149–52, 173–74; on bankers, 150, 164–65; trade policy, 152–53; recognizes Soviet Union, 152–53; agriculture policies, 153–60; replaces George Peek, 157; rejects radical tobacco plan, 158; accepts AAA "purge" of 1935, 159; industry-labor policy (NRA), 160–72; divides responsibility, 161; personal identification with New Deal, 163–64; and unions, 166; faces Democratic and progressive dissent, 169, 172; dismisses Johnson, 170; and 1934 elections, 174–75

Second New Deal: and Harry Hopkins (WPA), 257–59; and Frances Perkins (social welfare), 259–61; criticism from right and left, 261–73; compares self with Bismarck and Lloyd George, 273; spending plan resembles that of Keynes, 275; divides relief responsibility between Hopkins and Ickes, 275ff; acquiesces in political control of WPA, 278–79; establishes Resettlement Administration (RA), 281; demands economy from RA, 283; equivocates on Wagner labor bill, 284; supports Holding Company bill, 285; moves to left, 287, 298–99, 304; advised by Keynes on dealing with business leaders, 287–88; supports prosecution of Andrew Mellon, 288; reacts to "Black Monday" Supreme Court decisions, 290–91; hated by well-to-do, 299; fights for Wealth Tax Act, 300–301; loses support of William Randolph Hearst and Joseph Pulitzer, Jr., 300, 304–5; signs Wagner, Social Security, Banking, and Holding Company bills, 302–3; criticized by Lippmann, 305; exchange with Roy Howard, 305–6; highly popular, 306–7; develops political coalition, 307–8; faces middle-class ambivalence, 310; standing in opinion polls, 309–11; soft-pedals Supreme Court *Butler* decision, 311–12; secures undistributed profits tax, 312–13; signs Robinson-Patman and Walsh-Healey bills, 313–14; *see also* Second Hundred Days

Election of 1936: supported by independent left, 314–15, 320; opposed by Union party, 315; accepts nomination, 316–18; plays "class card," 318–19; trails in press endorsements, 320; benefits from personal charisma and economic surge, 321–22; nature and significance of victory, 323–25

Second term (domestic): question of heritage *re* labor (Reuther) and TVA (Lilienthal), 327–34; political and legislative agenda, 334–37, 344–45, 352, 361; court-packing plan, 337–38, 346–50, 351–52; and labor militance, 339–42; executive reorganization plan, 342–44, 367; criticized by Lippmann, 344; and civil rights, 345–46; intervenes in Senate leadership contest, 350–51; appoints Hugo Black to Supreme Court, 351; on South as economic problem, 353; and 1937–38 recession, 354–60; advised by Hopkins, Eccles, and Keynes, 359–60; advances spending program, 360; 1938 "purge" of conservatives, 361–63; narrowing political base, 363–65, 368–69; and 1938 congressional elections, 365–66; and third

term speculation, 366–67; signs
Social Security revisions, 368; and
"end of reform" (Brinkley), 368
International scene, foreign policy:
leadership techniques compared
with Hitler's, 177, 199–202; New
Deal and Nazi economic programs
compared, 203–4; New Deal and
British regimes compared, 233–35;
admired in Britain and emulated by
Lloyd George, 238; foreign policy
leadership compared with Baldwin's, 250; shares "middle way"
attitude with British leaders, 255;
in weak position vis-à-vis Hitler
(1938), 375; has greater regard for
Soviet Union than Nazi Germany,
381; works for strong navy,
382–83, 399–400; suggests international conference to Britain, 389,
397–98; hostility between self and
Chamberlain, 389–91; hailed as
leader of democracy, 392–93; foreign policy background, 393; gives
priority to domestic concerns,
393–95; "quarantine speech,"
395–96; reacts to Panay sinking,
opposes Ludlow amendment, 397;
and Munich agreement, 405–6; on
Kristallnacht, 406; abandons "static
isolationism," pushes military
buildup and arms sales, 408–10;
message to Hitler, 410; refuses
sanctuary to St. Louis passengers,
411; hosts British king and queen,
411; terminates trade agreement
with Japan, 412; backs cash-and-
carry arms sales, 412; reacts to
invasion of Poland, 413
Roosevelt, Theodore: 13, 77, 291, 93
Roper, Elmo, 310–11
Rumsey, Mary Harriman, 169
Runciman, Walter, 63
Rural Electrification Administration,
278, 282–83, 288, 335, 370, 418
Ryan, Msgr. John, 266

Saar, 213, 247
Salazar, Antonio, 266, 390
Samuel, Sir Herbert, 63, 220
Sauerwein, Jules, 129, 392
Scandinavia, 3, 196
Schacht, Hjalmar H. G.: profile, 180–81;
German central banker, 203,
206–9, 212
Schechter v. United States, 172, 291, 298,
310
Schlesinger, Arthur, Jr., 164, 195, 313n,
422
Schleicher, Kurt von, 52–60, 189
Schoenbaum, David, 204
Schwellenbach, Lewis, 270
Scripps-Howard newspapers, 305, 320
Second Hundred Days: personalities,
259–60, 293–98; background,
271–76; agencies, 277–87; leftward
move, 283, 287, 298–99; and
Court, 288–91; legislation,
300–303; evaluation, 304; reac-
tions, 304–6, 309–11
Securities Exchange Act, 128
Securities Exchange Commission, 307
Selden, Charles, 69–70
Shanghai, 72–73, 245, 395
Share Our Wealth movement, 263–64
Sherwood, Robert, 274n, 423–424
Shirer, William L., 179, 191–92
Silver Purchase Act, 152
Silver Shirts, 268–69
Simon, Sir John, 72, 220, 224, 243
Simpson, Mrs. Ernest, 251–53
Sinclair, Sir Archibald, 63, 254
Sinclair, Upton, 175, 270
Skidelsky, Robert, 220–21
Skocpol, Theda, 172–73
Smith, Alfred E.: 1932 election, 100,
102–3; criticizes FDR, 151; and
Frances Perkins, 260; American
Liberty League, 261–62, 320; 1928
election, 323–24, 349, 351
Smith, "General" Art, 268–69
Smith, Rev. Gerald L. K., 264, 315
Snowden, Philip, 35

Social Gospel, 266
socialism
  in Britain: MacDonald and Labour
    party, 8–11, 16, 34; Baldwin as
    "Tory socialist," 62; lacks revolu-
    tionary tradition, 70; rejected by
    Keynes, 222; supports public spend-
    ing, 225; coopted by National gov-
    ernment, 227–28, 230; and Labour
    party, 238–40
  in Germany: coopted by Bismarckian
    conservatism, 18; Nazi party and,
    32, 57–58, 188, 209; Social Demo-
    cratic and Communist parties, 32;
    opposed by Schacht, 180; Nazi
    rejection and repression of, 181,
    183, 186, 190–91, 210; and
    Catholic alternative, 266
  in Soviet Union: 14, 376, 381; call for
    Popular Front, 381
  in United States: weakness of, 41; in
    FDR's 1932 rhetoric, 106; and Tug-
    well, 119; and banking issue, 125;
    Norman Thomas on early New
    Deal, 146; New Deal programs and,
    147, 281; Upton Sinclair's EPIC
    program and, 175, 270; New Deal
    as alternative, 261; and Catholic
    alternative, 266; and independent
    left, 269–70; "concentrated private
    power" as (FDR), 285; and United
    Mine Workers, 296; and CIO, 297;
    and 1936 campaign, 320–21; and
    Walter Reuther, 328–30; and
    Arthur Morgan, 332; and labor mil-
    itance, 340; and "American excep-
    tionalism," 432
Social Security Act, 273–75, 302, 318,
    337, 348
Soil Conservation and Domestic Allot-
    ment Act, 311, 364
Somaliland, 248
South Africa, 71, 403
Southeast Asia, 379
Southern Tenant Farmers Union, 159
Soviet Union. See Union of Soviet
    Socialist Republics

Spain, 14, 376, 384–85, 390, 407
Speer, Albert, 201
Sprague, Oliver, 132
St. Louis Post-Dispatch, 304–5
Stahlhelm, 45–46, 49, 185–86
Stalin, Josef, 2, 14, 234, 380–81
"state capitalism" (Norman Thomas),
    146
sterling bloc, 223–24, 231–32
Steed, Wickham, 63
Stimson, Henry L., 72–73, 399
Stone, Harlan Fiske, 288–89, 311, 337
Strachey, Lytton, 221
Strasser, Gregor, 59, 189
Strauss, Richard, 214
Stresa front, 248
Stresemann, Gustav, 19
Sturmabteilung (SA), 48; proposed ban,
    52- 53; street violence, 54, 57,
    183–84; and military, 55, 187;
    fundraising, 58; rallies, 60, 200; and
    Reichstag, 185; absorbs Stahlhelm,
    186; purged, 188–90
Subsistence Homestead Division, 159–60
Sudetenland, 400–404
Suez Canal, 249, 388
Sullivan, Mark, 273
Supreme Court: kills NRA, 172, 284,
    304; personalities, 288–89; and
    New Deal programs, 289–90, 311,
    324–25, 332, 341; FDR's views on,
    291, 298, 300–301, 336; public
    reaction, 311–12; court-packing
    plan, 335, 337–38, 346–52
Sutherland, George, 288–89, 337, 351
Swing, Raymond Gram, 268, 274n
Swope, Gerard, 84, 119, 160

Taft, Charles P., 318, 321
Taft, William Howard, 263
Talmadge, Eugene, 168
Tammany organization (New York City),
    78, 100, 104, 175, 314–15
Tariff Commission, 107
Taylor, A.J.P., 242n, 244
Temporary Emergency Relief Adminis-
    tration (TERA), 39–40, 258

Tennessee Valley Authority (TVA): authorized, 127; activities, 229, 272, 331–34; electricity controversy, 337, 357, 368; "little TVAs," 345, 361

Thälmann, Ernst, 49

Thomas, Norman, 146–47, 265, 330

Thyssen, Fritz, 49

Tientsin (China), 412

Time magazine, 277, 309, 338, 356, 363, 364–65, 419

The Times (London), 73–74, 173–74, 242–43, 321, 391, 396

"Tory Socialism," 228

totalitarianism: concept, 181–82, 190–91; Nazi practice, 191–98, 204, 212; in Soviet Union, 213; New Deal accused of, 262; Lippmann connects with strong executive, 344; wins victory at Munich, 404; prospect for future, 429

Townsend, Dr. Francis, 264–65, 268, 273, 315

Treaty of Versailles, 18–19, 213, 245

Triangle Shirtwaist Fire, 260

Triborough Bridge, 275–76, 314

"Tribute Appeal" (Brüning), 33

Triumph of the Will (Riefenstahl), 200–201

Truman, Harry S., 83, 279, 315–16, 357

Tugwell, Rexford: profile, 118–20; Brains Trust, 101, 115; on Hoover, 107; as Assistant Secretary of Agriculture, 157–59; on Social Security Act, 274; heads Resettlement Administration (RA), 282–83, 353; attacked as radical, 320; on Tennessee Valley Authority, 333

Tunisia, 406

Turner, Frederick Jackson, 106

Ukraine, 380–91, 386

Union of Soviet Socialist Republics: overview, 14, 380–81; Tugwell travel to, 115–16; U.S. recognition, 152–53; foreign relations, 213; Reuthers' stay in, 329; nonaggression pact, 369, 412–13; military, 376, 381; U.S. views, 381; British foreign policy, 391, 408; Czech crisis, 400–401; World's Fair, 427–28; invades Poland, 428–29

United Mine Workers (UMW), 81, 166, 296, 297

United Textile Workers, 168

Uruguay, 393

U.S. Chamber of Commerce, 84, 299

U.S. Employment Service, 128

U.S. Housing Authority, 229

U.S. Navy, 78, 162

U.S. Steel, 284, 324, 328, 339, 356, 358

U.S. Supreme Court. *See* Supreme Court

Van Devanter, Willis, 288–89, 337, 348, 349, 351

Van Hise, Charles, 116

Veblen, Thorstein, 118–19

Victoria (Queen), 236n

Viglione, Raffaelo, 144

Volcker, Paul, 180, 303

Volkswagen ("people's car"), 210–11

Volstead Act, 92, 125–26

Wagner, Robert F.: criticizes Hoover, 38, 86–87; and veterans bonus, 94–95; housing, 229, 352; and Frances Perkins, 260; labor legislation, 284, 297, 299, 302, 328, 337, 341, 348; antilynching legislation, 345

Wagner Act (National Labor Relations Act), 283–84, 297, 302, 328, 337–38, 341, 348

Wallace, Henry ("Uncle Henry"), 142

Wallace, Henry A. (Secretary of Agriculture, 1933–40): profile, 142–44; and Rexford Tugwell, 119–20; first-term policies, 154–57, 322; personal wealth, 155; 1935 "purge," 159; on Supreme Court, 312; and rural poverty, 353; "ever-normal granary" and turn to urban liberalism, 364; on 1939 political situation, 368–69

Wallace, Henry C. (Secretary of Agriculture, 1921–25), 23, 142

Walsh, Thomas J., 38

Walsh-Healey Act, 314

War and Progress (Peter Dewey), 225n

War Finance Corporation, 88

War Industries Board (WIB), 140, 144, 160, 171

Warburg, James P., 130, 150–51

Warren, George, 150

Washington Commonwealth Federation, 270

Waters, William (BEF), 94–96

Wealth Tax Act, 303

Weaver, Robert, 308

Weimar Republic: Brüning, 11–12, 45–46; overview, 17–19, 51; effects of war, 19–20; economy, 21, 46–47; Depression, 29–31; disorder, 31–32; presidential election, 47–50; decline, 52–61, 182–87

Weir, Ernest T., 319

Wheeler, Burton K., 38, 285, 349

White Star Line, 235

Wickersham,, 92

Wilkie, Wendell, 261, 268, 333, 368

Wilson, M. L., 119

Wilson, Woodrow, 78, 86, 116, 140, 222, 357, 393

WJR (Detroit radio station), 265

Women's Trade Union League, 294

Woodin, William, 122, 135, 150

Woolf, Virginia, 221

Works Progress Administration (WPA), 257; budget, 277, 278, 313; criticism, 278; nondiscrimination policy, 278–79; as patronage, 279–80; state administration, 279–80; evaluation, 280, 416, 418; and small businesses, 309; in New York City, 314–15; phased out, 336, 339, 355; and deficit spending, 358–60, 366

World Economic Conference: favored by National government, 70; and 1932 election, 74; and Hoover, 110; U.S. involvement, 129–31; problems, 131–32; FDR's actions, 132–34; Keynes's reaction, 134; effect in U.S., 149–50; effect in Britain, 223–24; and U.S. isolationism, 382, 391

World War (World War I) impacts on: Hoover, 8; MacDonald, 9–10; U.S., 13; Britain, 16–17, 379; Germany, 17–18; Europe, 20; Papen, 53; Berle, 117; Jesse Jones, 140; Hugh Johnson, 144; views of Depression, 145–46, 291; NRA, 160, 163; Göring, 178; Goebbels, 179; Schacht, 180; German workers, 212; Lloyd George, 219; United Mine Workers, 296; Churchill, 373; French war planning, 377–78; Chamberlain, 392; FDR, 394

World War II, 412–13, 428–9

Yorktown (aircraft carrier), 275–76

Young Plan, 19, 30, 180

Yugoslavia, 386

Zangara, Giuseppe, 113

Zetkin, Clara, 56

Zweig, Stefan, 18–19

ABOUT THE AUTHOR

Alonzo L. Hamby is Distinguished Professor of History at Ohio University in Athens, Ohio, where he has taught since 1965. Among Hamby's many honors are three prizes for his first book, *Beyond the New Deal,* and two for his most recent, *Man of the People: A Life of Harry S. Truman:* the Harry S. Truman Book Award and the Herbert Hoover Book Award.